The Oboe

THE YALE MUSICAL INSTRUMENT SERIES

The Oboe

Geoffrey Burgess and Bruce Haynes

Yale University Press
New Haven and London

For information about this and other Yale University Press publications please contact:
U.S. Office: sales.press@yale.edu   yalebooks.com
Europe Office: sales@yaleup.co.uk   www.yalebooks.co.uk

ISBN 0–300–09317–9 (hbk)
ISBN 0–300–10053–1 (pbk)

Library of Congress Control Number 2003114791

A catalogue record for this book is available from the British Library
Typeset in Columbus by Northern Phototypesetting Co. Ltd., Bolton, Lancs
Printed in China through Worldprint

Music examples set by Geoffrey Burgess

Contents

Illustrations

Preface: the authors in conversation

The scene opens on a café in Newberry Street, Boston, in the summer of 2001. Seated at a table, two oboists meet between rehearsals to discuss a book they are writing.

Bruce Haynes. When did we first meet?

Geoffrey Burgess. Wasn't it in Versailles in 1984 during a recording of Charpentier's *Médée*? The next time was the following summer, when you played at the Utrecht Festival, and a couple of years later I took lessons with you in Brittany. Isolated encounters, but each time we seemed to be continuing a conversation already begun. . . . We'd jump into discussions about repertoire, you'd show me your latest article, I would be gathering information that overlapped in some way. . . . Do you remember the symposium on Early Double Reeds in Utrecht in 1994? We were just starting to think about our collaborations – articles for the *MGG* and *Grove* dictionaries, and for this book, still in embryo.

BH. Sure, that was a great event. Reports from colleagues from all over, concerts of music for hautboy, bassoon, dulcian . . . and Michel Piguet leading the oboe band playing the *Fireworks Music*.

GB. I like the provocative title that David Lasocki chose for the conference report: *A Time for Questioning*. And while we try to come up with some of the answers in this book, the questions keep coming.

BH. Those questions show how vital the field is. A lot has happened in the last fifty years, and our vantage-point on the oboe's history has certainly changed. That in itself is reason enough for a new book; Philip Bate's *The Oboe* has served us well, but perspectives have changed since the 1950s.

GB. Yes, and the last half-century has made a lot of history by itself. Think of the new players who've appeared, the changes in style and technique, and the important new music that has been written.

BH. And at the same time there has been an explosion of knowledge on where our instrument came from. I'm sure more than half the bibliography in our book has appeared since 1960. Many of the areas Bate would have liked to cover have now been studied, and a lot of new topics have opened up. Like Bate, we can talk about the oboe's physical properties, and can point out changes over time that are clearer today than they were then. But with the material we now have, we can also try to relate a whole complex of factors that acted to change the instrument gradually, all of them interconnected. The oboe mutated as makers and players responded to new demands of technique, for instance; technique changed as a result of new demands in the repertoire; repertoire changed as new pieces were written by composers; and composers were inspired by the players with whom they were in contact. There's no way to separate the 'chicken from the egg'; all these developments influenced each other.

GB. And all of it happened against a backdrop of steadily changing musical style – both performance style and style of composition. It's too much to hope to capture all of this process, of course, but I think our book will catch some of it.

BH. I think we can say this book is a product of both our enthusiasms for oboes of all different kinds. I know in my case, and I think in yours too, the 'book-learning' part came later, and was inspired by the need to know one or another practical aspect of how the early oboe was played that couldn't be found in somebody else's writing.

GB. That is an aspect of this book that especially pleases me: to watch the instrument's history unfold before our eyes as we write it, new to us all.

BH. I wanted to say that I think one of the reasons this book is interesting has been your willingness to go into the nineteenth century, the last great frontier of music history, and certainly of oboe history.

GB. It seemed a natural, indeed a vitally important period to explore. Growing up in Australia, there was no one to learn hautboy from, but I managed to teach myself a lot from articles and books, and at the same time I realized that the oboe in the nineteenth century was still uncharted territory. That's why I have made it my prime research area.

BH. For so long, we thought we already knew the nineteenth century, that it was just like now, that modern musicians are part of an unbroken tradition. But listening to recordings made before World War II gives a clear perspective on how fast things change, and how different oboe playing must have been in the Romantic period, even the early twentieth century.

GB. There is simply no way to hold on to the same performing style, even if you want to – it's like trying to hold water in your hands.

BH. There are many basic things your chapters uncover about the Romantic period, as well as the century we have just left – how the instrument developed, the lost German tradition (now completely swamped by the French). . . .

GB. The nineteenth century is also the part of the oboe's history that is most dear to today's players, because that is when the roots of the modern tradition were set.

BH. I'm also glad you suggested I add a section on the modern revival of the 'Baroque oboe' for the last chapter. It was a lot of fun to think back on the beginnings of that period, how it seemed then and how it appears now.

GB. And it's wonderful for everyone else to have your 'eyewitness' account.

BH. Those were the days, when an audience needed to know not only about the strange 'Baroque' instrument I was playing, but why I was doing it. . . . I'm not sure I always managed to convince them!

GB. What years are you talking about?

BH. That was at the end of the 1960s. I'd begun a career on the modern oboe when I played a season I'll never forget as second oboe in the San Francisco Opera in 1962, sitting between two players I greatly admired, Jim Matheson and my teacher, Ray Dusté; I was nineteen. But morale in the orchestra was low, and I couldn't imagine doing that for the rest of my life, so I went back to school and drifted over to the recorder, playing it first as a hobby and eventually going to Holland to study it. The 'cross-fingered oboe' was a logical next step, I suppose, after it became clear that the recorder's repertoire was not sufficient by itself. But since I couldn't afford an original early oboe and nobody was making historical copies yet, I ended up learning to make instruments. Then, in 1972, Frans Brüggen, with whom I'd studied recorder, asked me to stand in for him for his lessons in The Hague while he went off to teach for a year at Harvard and Berkeley, and during that year I persuaded the director of the Royal Conservatory to let me start a class in 'Baroque oboe'. After that it was a question of keeping a step or two ahead of my pupils! I was very lucky; The Hague was probably the only place in the world I could have been paid a salary to learn a new instrument.

Anyhow, it was from that time, the early 1970s, that a hands-on history of the hautboy seemed clearly needed, and that's when I began to collect historical material. . . . You got your start on the modern oboe too, didn't you?

GB. Yes, it was in the 1970s that I started to play, at first in the high-school band, and then, while a student at Sydney University, I got a lot of professional work around town. I was aiming for an orchestral career and had already played with some of the best orchestras in Sydney. But I had always been interested in the history of the oboe. Even from the beginning I was intrigued by those strange pieces by Vogt and Barret at the back of my study books. Who were those composers? Was there more music like that out there? I developed an appetite for books on the oboe – Bate, Goossens, Rothwell. At first I'd flip over the pages with those boring oboes – you know, the ones with no keys! – but then when I got interested in the hautboy it was the subtle differences between each of those two- and three-keyed ones that fascinated me.

BH. And how did you get going on hautboy? It must have been hard in Australia.

GB. When I auditioned for Sydney University, the Music Department had just taken delivery of a 'Baroque oboe' and the panel asked me if I would be interested in giving it a go. What could I say? I wanted to study there, so I said yes. The next thing I knew I was playing Bach cantatas on a two-keyed oboe in the Department's concert series, and over the course of the next years in the first performances of major Baroque works on early instruments in Australia. That music department was very progressive. Even in the 1970s all music students were required to take a class in performance practice and learn an early instrument. That 'Baroque oboe' was neither a historic copy nor well made, but it was good enough to give me the bug, and so I needed to get a better instrument. That's when I first wrote to you. I took up your recommendation and ordered a Denner copy by one of your students in The Hague, Toshi Hasegawa. Meanwhile I didn't stop playing the Conservatoire oboe, in fact I had a parallel passion for avant-garde music. I always programmed new music in my recitals, and a group of fellow-students invited me to workshop new pieces they had written.

BH. This was all when you were still in Australia?

GB. Right. In 1983 I got a grant to study in The Hague, and I devoted my energies to the hautboy. We missed each other there – you had just moved on, and my instructor was your colleague Ku Ebbinge. It was great finally to meet you in Versailles some months after I arrived.

GB. Writing a book together with someone else has been a new experience – it's sometimes tricky because even though we agree on the broad outlines, we have initiated debates on a number of topics.

BH. That's of course to be expected. The feedback we've given each other has been immensely valuable. Reactions before publication, especially from someone who works on the same subject, are a real luxury for an author. We were able to act as each other's 'devil's advocate', pointing out where ideas needed nuancing or shoring up.

GB. Our solution to co-authoring seems appropriate – we've made it clear which of us is talking, so although there's been considerable discussion on everything, the text and ultimate responsibility for each section belong to just one of us. You are chiefly responsible for the early period covered in chapters 2, 3 and 4, and I've dealt with the 'global' perspective in chapter 1 and the nineteenth century up to the present, that's chapters 5 to 9.

BH. Yes, while we've reviewed each other's sections, each has remained very much his own. What has been interesting is the area where our fields intersect: the period when the 'hautboy' turned into the 'modern' oboe. We've done a lot of interactive work on chapters 4 and 5.

GB. And the collaboration has gone beyond the two of us. I've called on specialists in different areas. Some of them have been incredibly generous with their time hunting down details and checking on information. In particular, I couldn't have done without James Brown, André Lardrot, Laila Storch, who each contributed valuable comments as they read my drafts, and Brenda Schuman-Post, Richard Abel and Robert Howe, who generously made their oboe collections available for study. Of many others who contributed in various ways I'd also like to acknowledge Sara Lambert Bloom, the late John de Lancie, Michael Finkelman, Forrests Music, Arnold Greenwich, Angela and Deborah Marx, Jeremy Montagu, Meg Owens, Nora Post, Edith Reiter of Wilhelm Heckel GmbH, Mme Roland Rigoutat, Emanuele Senici, André Lardrot, Christian Schneider, Dan Stolper, and our editors and review readers at Yale University Press.

BH. There are many people who have contributed indirectly to this book's contents. I think especially of Ton Koopman, who generously shared with me the contents of his extraordinary library, one of the best in the world on the subject of Early Music performance (in its broadest sense); what is especially useful is that he has personally indexed each book. I am also grateful to Marc Écochard for the many passionate discussions we have had over the years on the basic issues of hautboy history. And Ardal Powell kindly showed us the final draft of his flute book in this same series, which served as a confirmation and inspiration for the unapologetically 'revisionist' approach to the history of woodwind instruments that we share. We should also mention the godfather of this book, Malcolm Gerratt, who conceived it as part of the Yale Musical Instrument Series, and has patiently and capably nurtured it into existence. Finally, our appreciation to the many writers listed in our bibliography should be noted; these writers have enriched our understanding (much more than their own pockets) with their labours of love.

GB. Anyway, I hope the end-product will be rewarding to read. We've both tried to make the book as broad in its outreach as possible, and hope that, as well as being useful to oboists wanting to expand their horizons as players and serving as a reference tool for researchers and composers, it will be of interest to a general readership fascinated, like us, in how an 'instrument' can take on symbolic meaning. Still, if our book leaves a mark, it might be as much for the questions it raises as the answers it proposes.

Abbreviations and editorial note

Abbreviations in the text

The word 'bass', sometimes abbreviated as 'B', usually means 'continuo'.
The letter 'a.' before a date stands for 'ante' (before); 'p.' stands for 'post' (after).

Abbreviations in citations and in the Bibliography

AMZ	*Allgemeine musikalische Zeitung*
AMZÖK	*Allgemeine musikalische Zeitung, mit besonderer Rücksicht auf den österreichischen Kaiserstaat*
AWMZ	*Allgemeine Wiener Musik-Zeitung* (*Wiener Allgemeine Musik-Zeitung* from 1847)
BG	*J. S. Bach: Werke,* ed. Bach-Gesellschaft
BMZ	*Berliner musikalische Zeitung*
BrTC	Breitkopf Thematic Catalogue
CM	Berlioz, *Critique Musicale*
DR	*The Double Reed*
EM	*Early Music*
EO	Haynes, *The Eloquent Oboe*
EQL	Eitner, Robert, 1894–1904, *Biographisch-bibliographisches Quellen-Lexikon der Musiker und Musikgelehrten*
FoMRHI	Fellowship of Makers and Researchers of Historical Instruments
Gr1, 2, etc.	*Grove's Dictionary of Music and Musicians,* 1st ed., 2nd ed.
GrInstr	*The New Grove Dictionary of Musical Instruments*
GSJ	*Galpin Society Journal*
IP	*See* Bibliography *under* P., I. (1830)
JAMIS	*Journal of the American Musical Instrument Society*
JIDRS	*Journal of the International Double Reed Society*
MGG1, MGG2	*Die Musik in Geschichte und Gegenwart,* 1st and 2nd editions
ML	*Music & Letters*
NBA	*Neue Bach-Ausgabe*
NG1, NG2	*The New Grove Dictionary,* 1st edition (1980), 2nd edition (2001)
PRMA	*Proceedings of the Royal Musical Association*
RGMdP	*Revue et Gazette Musicale de Paris*
RM	*Revue Musicale*
SO	Symphony Orchestra
ZfürI	*Zeitschrift für Instrumentenbau*

Some of the information used in this study comes from personal communications, which are identified with an asterisk (*).

Fingerings for the two- and three-keyed hautboy are designated 123 456 78, counting from the top of the hautboy. '7' is the Small-key, '8' the Great-key (see ills 14–17, p. 43). The numbers indicate holes that are closed. 123 4 7 means, for instance, that the top four holes are closed and the Small-key is pressed. A slash through a number indicates that the hole is half closed, and an underlined number shows which finger is to be moved in a trill.

Note-names are given as C1 c0 c1 c2 c3 where c1 equals middle C on the piano. The standard range of the Conservatoire oboe is B♭0–g4.

Pitch frequencies are given in semitones from A–440. A semitone below A–440 is A − 1, for example; a whole step lower is A − 2; a semitone above is A + 1, etc.; A–440 itself is A + 0. Because it was so common and widespread, we also use A − 1½, which is A–403. By identifying pitch standards by semitones, we are assuming a tolerance half that size (that is, one-quarter tone, or 50 cents). Approximate pitch levels are therefore identified throughout this study as follows:

Pitch name	Hz value for A	Frequency range
A + 3	523 Hz	509–531
A + 2	495	480–508
A + 1	466	454–479
A + 0	440	428–453
A − 1	415	410–427
A − 1½	403	398–409
A − 2	392	381–397
A − 3	370	360–380

Instrument 'Y' numbers, such as Y2, refer to the numbering found in Young 1993. Libraries are sometimes identified by their RISM sigla; a list of these is included at the beginning of each volume of *NG*.

'Haute-contre' is a high tenor chest voice that extends upwards often as far as g1 at A–440, about a third higher than the regular tenor; this is not the falsetto (or head-register) voice usually called 'countertenor' in the twentieth century. The 'hautecontre de hautbois' is a straight alto hautboy in A.*

All translations are ours except those explicitly marked. Our general principle in making translations has been to try to communicate accurately the underlying sense of original texts in modern, unadorned language.

* See Haynes 2001, ch. 6, §C1

Introduction

My fate was to have played the oboe. If I had not played that instrument I would
have been loved. But I played the oboe, and what's more, it is so easy not to play
the oboe!

after Oscar Comettant

This book is about the oboe, which we shall define as a conical-bored treble double-
reed wind instrument used in western art music. We have started with ambitious aims,
and will probably not completely succeed in answering all the issues we raise. We
wish to consider the oboe's origins, its relationship to comparable instruments found
in other cultures, and how and why the oboe changed physically over time; what
music was written for oboe and why it was written as it was; who the instrument's
players were, which of them were successful and why; who made oboes, and what
were the motivations for their different designs. We shall try to define the physical
attributes of various forms of the oboe by drawing upon surviving examples, written
descriptions, and illustrations in works of art. We shall also examine why the oboe
had the role and reputation it had, and why it appears in certain musical contexts.
And we shall consider particular aspects of its technique by exploring the music
written for it.

The oboe has gone through a continuous process of change, and any oboe, from
any period, is like a snapshot, a unique moment in a fluid pattern. It may be
unnecessary to add that, in surveying these changes, we find value judgements
between oboe types irrelevant and even confusing, as they make it difficult to see
things as they were seen at the time. Our aim in writing this book is to rediscover the
oboe's history from the viewpoint of musicians who lived with it in any given period,
on their own terms. To do this, we have started with the assumption that the
instruments of each period are reasonably well-adapted to the needs of musicians of
the time, and that, since these needs regularly change, instruments adapt and evolve
with time, giving up some characteristics and gaining others. Each period, in other
words, possessed the 'best' instrument – for its time, of course.

This non-linear approach to history runs counter to the old Newtonian approach
that looked for things to follow one another in a coherent and causally related
narrative plan. Recent thinking in many fields of technology and biology suggests
that even natural evolution itself does not necessarily follow logical or systematic
paths, but consists of adaptation to randomly changing circumstances. In our view,

this model is closer to the oboe's journey through time, since it 'recognizes the role of chance in directing change and admits of no ultimate finished state, and so imputes no value to later placement in time. . . . evidence from many fields now indicates that evolution's direction is aimless and unpredictable, and that adaptation (and extinction or obsolescence) can occur not only gradually but also with surprising rapidity after long periods of relative stability – a concept termed "punctuated equilibrium".'[1]

In the same way, the brief stages in the oboe's history when the instrument remained in a relatively steady state, like the beginning of the eighteenth century (the Baroque hautboy), the end of the eighteenth century (the Classical hautboy), and the twentieth century (the Conservatoire oboe), can be seen as 'punctuations' within a continuum of change, the result of adaptations to historical contexts that were perhaps themselves arbitrary and random. Identifying these stages of temporary stability is still useful, as it allows us to distinguish periods in the oboe's history.

We do not mean by this discussion to suggest that there was no relation between successive states. Instrument design moves slowly because of the investment in time needed to master the technique of an instrument; if the design changes, it is most often done with the minimum possible demand on established technique. And, whatever the goal of the changes, that usually means taking over as many features of the old design as possible. The old design is of course important as providing a basis for the new, but if both models are regarded as equally valid, it is not necessary to see the first as an imperfect later design intended to do the same things as the second.

Until recently it has often been assumed that, compared with earlier instruments, the latest models embody the best of all possible designs, since they represent the end-point of a straight-line progression. The idea that instrument designs might become progressively better in some absolute sense might be justifiable if the perceived gains could be achieved without being paid for by matching losses. But the reality is that when one aspect is emphasized, others are inevitably compromised. As with a loop of string on a table that can be shaped in many ways but retains the same circumference, the only way to effect 'improvements' in instrument design is to sacrifice other playing characteristics. To put it vulgarly, when there are only a limited number of possible variables, 'there's no such thing as a free lunch', and as Harnoncourt has written of musical instruments of various periods, 'it comes down to a question of priorities'.[2] We shall encounter this equation at each stage of the oboe's history.[3]

To take an example, the new hautboy that was developed in the seventeenth century was a conscious rejection of certain qualities of the shawm. Tone-hole size was reduced relative to bore width, and this facilitated the use of cross- and half-hole fingerings (thus increasing the range of usable tonalities). By the nineteenth century the covered sound of cross-fingerings no longer suited musical tastes, and for the sake of greater tonal homogeneity across the full range of the instrument, dedicated holes were added for each semitone, covered by keys, and tone-holes again became larger. What had been gained on the hautboy by making the tone-holes smaller was more effective cross-fingerings and more resistance. What was lost was that rich, uncomplicated sound that shawms (especially several together) can lay down. What was lost in the Romantic period when many keys were added was the characteristic sounds of individual notes and scales, produced with cross-fingerings. In each case, one playing quality was gained by sacrificing another, and taste and a general sense of style determined which were the desirable attributes.

The new Romantic conception of a keyed oboe was grafted onto the late eighteenth-century 'small-bore' hautboy. The new oboes, which were similar to those still played in today's symphony orchestras (they can often use the same reed designs, for instance), represented not so much a radical invention, like the various attempts to create a logical and acoustically 'correct' oboe using Boehm's principles, as an ad hoc adaptation of pre-existent designs. And that particular form of the oboe became fixed into its present form by a fortuitous event: the solidification of the institution that nurtured it – the symphony orchestra. It is no coincidence that the Conservatoire oboe appeared and became institutionalized at approximately the same time as what is now considered the zenith of the symphony orchestra's repertoire, with compositions like the tone poems of Richard Strauss, ballet scores of Stravinsky, the symphonies of Elgar, and scores by Debussy and Ravel. Like previous oboes, the Conservatoire model is one of those snapshots from the past, but it is one that happened to survive considerably longer than any other – to date, some 125 years.

Since the last quarter of the nineteenth century, creative experimentation on the basic design of the oboe has all but ceased. This is probably because no reason for anything other than minor refinements has presented itself. The Conservatoire oboe's basic repertoire, that of the symphony orchestra, has become 'canonized'. Orchestras play in the framework of a received tradition and pedagogical lineage that extends far back into the nineteenth century. To be sure, there has for some time been a deliberate effort to open up the repertoire beyond the core 'classics'; it is common for orchestras to venture into other idioms such as jazz and popular music, and quite a lot of art music from the last twenty years or so is deliberately calculated to have broader and more popular appeal. Still, it is true today that departures from the sanctioned list of orchestra pieces risk a small house. Players themselves are also sometimes resistant to the idea of different oboe designs, not only extremes like the Boehm model, but even different makes of the traditional Conservatoire model.

It has been suggested that the history of a musical instrument ends when the physical design of the instrument ceases to change. That is not at all what we have found for the Conservatoire oboe, whose most innovative episode began after World War II. The recent history of the oboe bears out the observation that new demands on an instrument do not necessarily lead to physical changes, or as Laurence Libin put it, 'new messages need not compel a change in the medium'.[4]

This is the first book that can give a full perspective to the oboe in the twentieth century, and we have treated this century in as much detail as earlier periods. One of the most radical events in the oboe's twentieth-century history, and one that we are as yet unable fully to understand, was the rebirth in the 1950s and 60s of the so-called 'Baroque oboe' or hautboy. This instrument may originally have been a revival of historical models, but in a sense it has also become the most modern and innovative form of oboe in use. At present there is much talk about 'historically appropriate instruments' and 'anachronistic techniques'. These concepts would not be in the air if we were not so conscious of history. While we show great concern with respecting the wishes of long-dead composers, this was not important to our forefathers; 'period style' was a marginal subject a hundred years ago (and for that matter three hundred): after all, very little music by dead composers even got an airing. That historical concern, and the general rebellious spirit of the 1960s reacting against the traditional music establishment, was the soil in which the period oboe was again able to take root.

The hautboy has been such an immediate success, and is so often heard in modern performance, that the terms that have been used to denote it until now – 'Baroque' oboe, 'early' oboe, 'historical' oboe – have ceased to have the same meaning. The hautboy no longer belongs only to the past. One thinks somewhat differently of a horse if it is referred to as a 'wheel-less automobile'. We thought it would be more appropriate to give to the 'Baroque oboe' the name by which it was known when it was first used. 'Hautboy' was what the instrument was called in English until the end of the eighteenth century. The switchover to the Italian name, 'oboe', can be observed in the tutors of the time: in 1770 it was still 'the hautboy'; by 1780 it was 'the oboe or hoboy', by the 1790s 'the oboe'. Since the instrument had originated in France in the late seventeenth century, its original name was 'hautbois' (pronounced by Frenchmen up to the nineteenth century as 'o-bway' rather than, as now, 'o-bwa'). The word *hautboy* (usually pronounced 'o-boy', though the initial 'h' was sometimes pronounced by those unaware of the word's origin) was the English version of the old French 'hautbois'. The naturalized spelling *hoboy* was also common. The same kind of transliteration of 'hautbois' existed in other languages at the time: 'Hoboye' or 'Hoboe' in German,[5] 'hobooij' and 'hoboy' in Dutch, 'oboè' in Italian, and 'obué' in Spanish. It was at least a century before 'hautboy' became obsolete in English, and even in the early years of the twentieth century it had wide currency in English prose.[6]

We thus use the term 'hautboy', in a way analogous to the terms 'traverso' for the one-keyed flute and 'sackbut' for the early trombone, to refer to the oboes of the Baroque and Classical periods that have minimal keywork, and on which cross-fingering and half-holing are used to produce the pitches between the notes of the natural scale.[7] It seems to us that the hautboy, like the shawm, has enough of its own identity, and differs enough in basic principle from the Conservatoire oboe, to merit its own name. The earliest keyed oboes were basically hautboys with additional keys that at first supplemented and, over the course of the nineteenth century, gradually replaced the cross-fingering and half-hole techniques. Just like their names, hautboys and oboes (that is, keyed and unkeyed 'Oboes') coexisted. As we use it, then, 'Oboe' is a general term. The 'hautboy' is a type of 'Oboe' as defined in our first sentence; shawms are also 'Oboes' by the same token, as are Conservatoire models. (We draw the line at non-western instruments, however, as explained in chapter 1.) We also use 'Oboe' as the family name for other sizes, including (in ascending order) bass oboe, cor anglais/English horn, tenor hautboy, oboe da caccia, *hautecontre de hautbois*, hautbois d'amour, the keyed 'oboe d'amore', treble oboe in C, and *hautbois pastoral* and musette. We take the terms 'English horn' and 'cor anglais' as equivalents. Both these terms have currency outside America (where 'English horn' is the norm), although there is a growing trend to drop 'cor anglais'. This is regrettable because the literal English translation has lost the ambiguity of the French 'cor anglais – cor anglé' (angled horn) that is surely the origin of this curious name.

The ability to step back and see things in perspective with a measure of historical objectivity was not as easy in the oboe world before the 1960s. When there was a single type of oboe played in the West, it was the only reference point. The change came with the arrival of other kinds of oboe that share part of the same repertoire. Because of this, it was not always possible to evaluate its qualities independently. Now that various kinds of seventeenth- and eighteenth-century hautboys are played and heard regularly, as well as shawms and folk oboes, comparisons are possible, and insights can be gained into the natures and personalities of many types of oboes by 'triangulating', as it were, from several vantage points. This ability to make comparisons thus allows us to take each oboe on its own terms.

That luxury was not available to Philip Bate in the early 1950s when he wrote *The Oboe: An Outline of its History and Construction*, the most thorough history of the oboe published to date. We are indebted in a variety of ways to earlier historians of the oboe, and particularly to Bate, whose book is now out of print and has been in need of updating for a good twenty-five years. As its title implies, Bate's study concentrated on the technical aspects of the design and manufacture of oboes, and showed a deep admiration for its builders. Players and music took a secondary position; the biographies of famous players appeared only in an appendix, and Bate acknowledged that a substantial portion of the oboe's playing literature was not then accessible. Recent researches have shed light on these areas. Also, logically for his time, Bate started his survey with the familiar – the Conservatoire oboe – and his book therefore became an account of how that instrument developed from its antecedents. Now, at the beginning of the twenty-first century, we find ourselves in a position to observe the characteristics of all kinds of western oboes, each in its appropriate place within the instrument's chronology. This book will investigate how each of them came into being.

Chapter 1

The prehistory of the oboe

Hautbois, ta vie est pleine de mystères;
Un temps lointain a chanté ton pouvoir;
A tes accents les esprits des clairières
Autour de toi venaient errer le soir.

Oboe, your life is full of mysteries;
The distant times sang of your power;
To your sounds, the spirits of the forest clearings
Came wafting about you in the evenings.

Traditional [1]

In the 1986 British film *The Mission* the oboe plays a prominent and symbolic role –
in both the screenplay by Robert Bolt and the soundtrack by Ennio Morricone. After
scaling a torrential waterfall, the Jesuit priest Gabriel (played by Jeremy Irons) takes
from his satchel an oboe that not only has withstood the perilous journey but,
miraculously, is in perfect playing order. Indeed, attentive listeners will notice that
this eighteenth-century hautboy is in such good condition that it sounds remarkably
like a modern oboe in the hands of Joan Whiting of the London Philharmonic
Orchestra. Gabriel plays his oboe and waits. Out of the silence of the Amazonian
rainforest the snap of twig under human footstep is heard. Soon Gabriel is
surrounded by inquisitive natives transfixed by the mellifluous strains of his oboe. A
tribal elder approaches and challenges Gabriel. In an untranslated tirade he seems to
demand by what authority he trespasses on the territory of the Guaraní and charms
his people. Shaken, Gabriel nevertheless continues to play. The tribal elder, convinced
of the pipe's magic powers, grabs it and snaps it like the twig that signalled his
approach. Another, less aggressive native returns the instrument to its owner, but the
damage is irreparable and music can no longer be conjured from its violated body.
Consulting with the men of the tribe, the second Indian motions to Gabriel to join
them. As he follows them, his tune is revived on the soundtrack, clothed now with
full orchestral accompaniment: a sign that Gabriel's message will indeed penetrate the
hearts of the Guaraní.

I begin our tale of the oboe's life, not by situating it in a historical account, but
with this modern celluloid fantasy because it provides a particularly clear illustration

of the way contemporary art (re)constructs past musical traditions. With its soundtrack of modern orchestral music, the film literally dubs the sonic qualities of the modern oboe over one of the instrument's antecedents. *The Mission* also draws on a confluence of myths of the oboe's past. Treble double-reed instruments have for centuries been invested with the potential to captivate those who hear them and to still the savage spirit. Shawms were used by Muslims and Christians alike to muster forces for battle and to inflame their warriors with courage, and alongside their comrade-at-arms the trumpet, shawms and oboes have been the instruments of power, attendants to colonial conquest. In the New World, it was to the sound of bands of shawms that the conquistadors subjugated the indigenous peoples. Likewise in times of peace, treble double-reed instruments symbolized the sustained fruits of the victorious, their sound echoing across cities and towns. Bands of double-reed players served as heralds. They announced public decrees, mustered citizens for civil gatherings and sounded the hour.

While *The Mission* is largely fictitious, it is still founded on a modicum of historical fact. From the sixteenth century, Jesuit missionaries taught the shawm (*chirimía*) to the indigenous peoples of South America, and up to the dissolution of the order in 1773, when the events of the film purportedly took place, western musical training formed a part of the Christianizing process.[2] Double-reed instruments seem to have been unknown throughout the Americas in the pre-Columbian era, but the indigenous peoples took readily to the *chirimía*. Of the 4000 Indians sent to the Jesuit mission in Paraguay run in the late seventeenth century by Anthony Sepp, forty were trained as *chirimistas*. As well as using them as the Conquistadors intended in Christian ritual, the natives adopted the *chirimía* into their own music-making. They made instruments after European models, substituting whatever materials were available – leaves or grass in place of cane for reeds, and the quills of condor feathers instead of brass staples (ill. 1). Chirimías are still used to accompany dance dramas and processions in Guatemala,[3] and amongst the Purépechas in West Mexico they are still heard in Corpus Christi celebrations.[4]

Musical instruments and styles persisted in the Americas long after they had become outmoded in Europe. It is difficult to establish whether and at what time the Baroque-style hautboy depicted in *The Mission* would have been imported into South America, but as the film is set in the eighteenth century, it is plausible that a Jesuit missionary would have played such an instrument. While the hautboy was a direct descendant of the shawm, invented in Paris in the second half of the seventeenth century, it was designed as a more versatile instrument capable of participating in subdued music-making indoors (opera, chamber music, and so on) as well as in outdoor events. Hautboy bands (comprising oboes and bassoons, often supplemented with trumpets and drums) fulfilled much the same function as the shawm bands of former times, but the hautboy was neither as loud nor as vibrant as the shawm, and so developed other functions beyond its traditional function as a symbol of power. By virtue of its connection with folk pipes and bagpipes, the oboe has always had strong associations with things pastoral. It is the instrument of shepherds, the voice of a prelapsarian state of innocence, 'le cri plaintif de la nature'. Later, in the nineteenth century, the streamlining of the hautboy's physical form and mechanism

1. Two *chirimías*, modern (left) and antique.

further divested it of its martial and imperialist connections. Ultimately this resulted in the oboe standing for the very opposite qualities – delicacy, innocence and feminine charm – and more than any other instrument of the modern symphonic orchestra, the Conservatoire oboe is able 'to assert its small but inexpressibly poignant voice calling, as it seems, from the innermost secret places'.[5]

Morricone's soundtrack plays on the irony that the small, sweet voice of the oboe could also herald violence and destruction. Gabriel's oboe is at once the musical annunciation to the Guaraní, and the instrument of European colonization and dominance. At the same time as symbolizing the Guaraní's natural state before the western invasion, it also mourns its loss. These streams coalesce as the melody returns at telling moments in the film. The most significant recurrence takes place when the slave-trader Mendoza does penance for his injustices. Here the oboe is replaced by its more lugubrious brother, the cor anglais. As Mendoza's tears give way to new-found humility, the musical texture brightens and the oboe resumes the tune. Over the credits at the end of the film, the oboe is combined with native drumming patterns recalling the harmony achieved at Gabriel's mission between Europeans and natives, but lost through political intervention.

For the past two centuries composers have used the oboe to express the alluring and sensual nature of the exotic. By transforming human breath into wordless 'speech', the oboe can negotiate cultural and linguistic barriers, transcend the specific to touch both Christian and heathen. Morricone draws on this tradition by representing the annunciation to the Guaraní with an oboe in *The Mission*.[6] The opening scene of the film exposes western culture's gaze towards the exotic by reversing the frames of reference. The western viewer is presented with a non-western reaction to European culture: the Guaraní's fascination with what was to them the exotic sound of the European oboe.

Centuries before the Spanish and Portuguese conquest of the New World, the antecedents of the *chirimía* arrived in Europe from the Middle East through a similar clash of cultures. The Crusades brought Europeans into contact with the Muslim world and the Turko-Arabic *zurna*, but histories of the oboe invariably take the instrument's origins back much further: to the reed-pipes of ancient Egypt, Mesopotamia, the Greek *aulos* and the Roman *tibia*. This is usually followed by a brief account of the Dark Ages when the oboe all but disappeared in the west until the arrival of the Arabic *zurna* during the thirteenth century, European bagpipe instruments, and the invention of the French *hautbois* in the second half of the seventeenth century – the point at which the history of the *oboe* really begins.

To uncover the oboe's earliest traces, historians have not only searched classical antiquity but probed the obscurity of earlier times. 'Prehistories' of the oboe have usually been woven from a tenuous mixture of archaeological evidence and iconography, with missing threads supplied from dabblings in comparative anthropology and ethnomusicology, with a generous helping of creative extrapolation – a blend which has produced hypotheses that have proved false in the light of more concrete evidence.

What lies behind the desire of these historians to construct a genesis for the oboe? Histories, like mythologies, often serve to ground modern practices and ideologies in a venerated past. In the case of the oboe, most histories have been fashioned to affirm the state of the instrument and style of playing at the time of writing. 'Prehistory' implies discontinuity: it distinguishes a before from an after: a 'prehistory' from a 'history'. But the transition from the oboe's prehistory to history is not marked, as is the case with most historical projects, by a break in historical records, but by a discontinuity in the oboe's identity. The oboe came into existence at a particular moment in western music history – the arrival of the French hautboy – before which we can talk of precursor 'proto-oboes' or 'not-quite-oboes' which, while they may resemble the oboe, differ from it in a number of significant ways. It is the process of defining the western oboe's genealogy that is the central theme of this chapter.

Herbert Lindenberger has suggested that 'aesthetic genealogies are the reverse of family genealogies': 'Whereas the latter move forward from a few common ancestors to the diverse progeny they have spawned, the former progress backward from a single entity labeled a work of art to a multitude of earlier works that, however little their creators may have recognized their mutual affinities, come to resemble a family that the later member has retrospectively begotten, defined, legitimated.'[7] Taking Lindenberger's theme, I shall investigate some of the ways in which historians, organologists and oboists have constructed retrospectively begotten genealogies for a singular musical instrument, *the* oboe. More than simply acknowledging, like Gunther Joppig, that 'virtually every book on the history of musical instruments begins by stating that this instrument is the most ancient means of musical expression'[8] and providing yet another report of these findings, I shall endeavour to explain what draws historians of the oboe to this type of musical archaeology. While I will turn over terrain already tilled by earlier scholars, my intention is not so much to discover an inherent 'truth' in this material nor to provide a more objective account, but rather to uncover the assumptions and prejudices on which such 'prehistories' have been founded.

To write a history (and, by implication, a prehistory) of the oboe demands a definition of what an oboe *is* and what it is *not*, of its historical reality and its prehistorical fantasy, what it had been before it came into existence. Significantly, while the oboe has had a history for approximately two centuries, its prehistory has only existed that long as well. The first histories of the oboe were written by those who were either actively involved in or contemporaries of the emergence of the modern French oboe – the performer and teacher Auguste Vény, oboist and inventor Henri Brod, historian François-Joseph Fétis, composer F. A. Gevaert and others. The begetting of a genealogy for the oboe garnered these writers' claims by situating the latest developments as the pinnacle of an evolutionary chain.

The imaginary thread connecting retrospectively begotten ancestor to modern progeny continues to stimulate curiosity. We can read, for instance, in the sleeve notes to a recent recording of contemporary oboe music that 'despite all technical refinements the oboe has retained its original character to a larger extent than virtually any other musical instrument. It still produces the same ambivalent effect as its ancient predecessor the Greek *aulos*.'[9] According to the reckoning of Curt Sachs, one of the pioneers in the field of organology (that is, the study of musical instruments), double-reed instruments were relatively late on the musical evolutionary scale. Sachs cited ribbon reeds (simple reeds made from grass and not attached to any resonating pipe) as the most rudimentary and most ancient form of reed instrument, and discussed the magical properties that many cultures invested in them.[10] From an extensive etymological analysis, he placed the invention of double-reed aerophones – reed coupled with resonating pipe – in the Semitic world somewhere between Asia Minor and Arabia.[11]

Nineteenth-century excavations in Egypt and the Near East uncovered evidence of instruments presumed to be double-reed in Mesopotamia, Egypt and in Classical Greece and Rome. It was natural for nineteenth-century organologists to begin their quest for origins in what was considered to be the cradle of civilization. As Henry Fothergill Chorley put it, 'looking to the East as to the cradle of civilization, we naturally accept every relic and record coming thence as of the very highest importance'.[12] Common sense suggests that double-reed instruments in some form would have been developed independently in many cultures and that looking for a single point of origin is an overly simplistic model. There is good evidence, however, that a specific form of double-reed instrument developed in the Middle East, and the coincidences between the geographic distribution of double-reed instruments and the spread of Islam are striking. In many cases the *zurna* seems to have obliterated traces of earlier forms. Where the influence was not direct, such as in Latin America and Japan, the contact was with the Christian-European adaptation of the *zurna*.

2. The contest between Marsyas and Apollo: bas-relief from Mantineia.

The Greek *aulos* and Roman *tibia* have both been ascribed particular significance in the genesis of modern western wind instruments. While it is clear that both these terms refer to double pipes played by one musician, the method of sound generation remains a matter of considerable debate. Were they flutes, or did they have reeds, and if so, were they single or double? Because of imprecisions in both written and visual evidence, flautists, oboists and clarinettists have all appropriated the *aulos* and *tibia* as archetypes of their own instruments. These ancient Greek and Roman pipes had their own myths of origins. Mythology projected the invention of the *aulos* into the realm of the inexplicable, attributing it to either divine inspiration or foreign ingenuity. According to one tradition, the *aulos* was invented by Hyagnis the king of Lydia in Asia Minor in the fourteenth century BCE, and later taken to Greece by Hyagnis's son Marsyas, the presumptuous satyr who brashly challenged Apollo to a musical competition (ill. 2). Marsyas played his *aulos*, the god his *kithara* (lyre). The muses awarded the laurel to Apollo who, in accordance with the rules of the competition, flayed Marsyas alive.[13] This myth reinforces the reputation of the *aulos* as a rustic instrument, the crude antithesis to the model of disciplined art-music, the lyre (ill. 3; ill. 4).

A different account of the origins of the *tibia* is transmitted in both Pindar's Twelfth Pythic Ode and Ovid's *Metamorphoses*. These sources report that Minerva fashioned the instrument from the leg-bone of a young deer (hence the name *tibia*) and that its sound imitated the horrified shrieks of the Gorgons when they found their sister Medusa murdered. This analogy with the savage cries of a monstrous duo is one of the most vivid images of the sound of the ancient double pipes. Did the sound, as many modern writers have supposed, result from the high volume of air that was forced through the instrument, or perhaps from the two pipes being slightly out of tune with each other? The Marsyas and Minerva legends coalesce in other

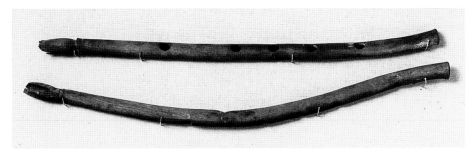

3. The Elgin *auloi*.

accounts claiming that Marsyas found the *aulos* that Minerva discarded 'on account of the distortion of her face when she played upon it'.[14]

Louis Bleuzet, professor of the oboe at the Paris Conservatoire from 1919 to 1941, disregarded these ancient speculations and substituted a myth of chance. 'We know that at that time our ancestors were attached to the pastoral life. Thus, is it not natural to think that by just blowing through a reed for amusement, a shepherd would have made a sound?'[15] The same reasoning is repeated countless times. For instance, the French-American oboist Albert Andraud wrote that 'legend represents the first

4. Female oboe player on an attic red-figure bell krater.

musical manifestation as a shepherd playing a chalumeau or Pan's pipes just as shepherds of the Pyrenées Mountains do even today'.[16] These modern explanations draw on one of the oboe's most prevalent associations – the pastoral, a theme that will feature prominently in chapter 7.

During the seventeenth and eighteenth centuries it was assumed that the *aulos* and *tibia* were types of flute.[17] This often flew in the face of the written accounts. *Peri Houpsous* (*Treatise on the Sublime*) by the third-century Greek rhetorician Longinius was to have lasting impact on European aesthetics from the seventeenth century. The influential French translation by Nicolas Boileau (1674) rendered *aulos* as *flûte*, even though passages such as the following would have made little sense to contemporary readers familiar with the dulcet tones of traverso and recorder:

> And is it not true that we see how the sound of flutes moves the soul of those who hear it, and fills them with frenzy, as if they were out of their wits [*hors d'eux-mêmes*]? That it obliges their bodies to conform to the movement of the music [*cadence*] which it impresses on the ear?[18]

Baroque composers commonly used the modern western flute as a stand-in for the *aulos* and *tibia* in operas representing antique cultures. Flutes are heard, for example, in the preparatory sacrificial rites in act III of Lully's *Bellérophon* (1679), and Gluck used them in the priestesses' chorus in act III of *Iphigénie en Tauride* (1779).

The connection between the double pipes of the ancient world and the flute continued into the nineteenth century. In his *Histoire générale de la Musique depuis les temps les plus anciens jusqu'à nos jours* (1869) Fétis observed that men were never depicted playing the double pipe in ancient Egyptian art. From this he concluded that the music of the Egyptian reed-pipe was delicate, sensual, perhaps even docile – attributes consistent not only with contemporaneous attributes of the flute but with the qualities of womankind as idealized in nineteenth-century Europe. In the late 1860s when Verdi came to compose *Aida*, set in ancient Egypt and based on a scenario by a French Egyptologist, he drew inspiration from the pipes depicted in tomb paintings recently unearthed by European archaeologists. Although he did not go as far as to use Fétis's reconstruction of ancient Egyptian scales,[19] he made extensive use of a solo flute and oboe, the latter associated particularly with the exotic, and heard in combination with the Ethiopian slave Aida.

The identification of the *aulos* and *tibia* with the delicacy and purity of the modern flute also reified the romantic myth of the aesthetic purity of ancient Greek and Roman music. Curt Sachs reported how his Classics master eulogized 'the sensitive ears of his beloved heroes, so obviously superior to the Wagner-glutted ears of modern college boys' because they could be inflamed with either ecstasy or courage for battle by the sound of 'the weakest of instruments, the flute'.[20]

However, late in the nineteenth century this idealization of antique music was challenged by new evidence. F. A. Gevaert was one of several writers to argue that the *aulos* and *tibia* were not flutes but reed instruments.[21] He translated *aulos* as 'chalumeau' and described it as a type of clarinet. Relying largely on textual evidence, and aided with a strong dose of hindsight, he reasoned that, as most *auloi* and *tibiae* were cylindrical-bored, they were undoubtedly played with single reeds, because over time double reeds had been deemed acoustically ineffective with cylindrical bores (there are, after all, no modern European instruments with this coupling).

In the early twentieth century, the double-reed theory gained greatest support, transforming *aulos* and *tibia* from dulcet flutes to strident oboes, and simultaneously revising the Romantic notion of antique purity by stressing the primitive crudity and rustic savagery of these instruments. Sachs, eager to debunk the Romantic notion, stated that 'the pipes on vases and reliefs, Greek and Roman, are not flutes, but double oboes of oriental shape, the sound of which could be as shrill and exciting as the sound of their relatives, the bagpipes of modern Scotch regiments',[22] and more than twenty years later Philip Bate affirmed that it was 'no "soft complaining flute" that excited the warlike passions of the Greek Heroes and encouraged the young men to prodigies on the athletic field'.[23]

Evidence from surviving fragments, written documentation and iconographic sources is often contradictory or ambiguous on the double- or single-reed question.[24] The 'rediscovery' of double-reed instruments also resulted in the fabrication of evidence, including restoration touch-ups that 'reveal' unmistakable double reeds.[25] Even the account by the fourth-century BCE scientist Theophrastus, who left a remarkably detailed discussion of the harvesting of cane and preparation of *aulos* reeds, is subject to multiple interpretations.

> When they have gathered the reeds, they place them in the open air for the winter, still in their skin [presumably the leaves that adhere to the cane]. In the spring they clean them down and rub them thoroughly, and then lay them in the sun. Later, during the summer, they cut them into the sections that lie between the knots, and again lay them in the sun for some time. On each such section they leave the knot nearest the growing-point [the upper end]: the length of the sections is no less than two palms' breadth.
>
> Now the best of the sections for making *zeuge* [reeds], they say, are those in the middle of the total length of the reed. The sections nearer the growing-points make very soft *zeuge*, and those nearer the root very hard ones. Tongues made from the same section sound in consonance with one another, while others do not: the one from nearer the root goes on the left, and that from nearer the growing-point on the right. When the section is divided, the mouth of each of the two tongues is made at the end towards the place where the reed was cut. If the tongues are made in any other way, they do not sound properly in consonance. That, then, is the way they are made.[26]

It is perhaps understandable that Theophrastus's elliptical explanation from book IV of the *Enquiry into Plants* has led to different, and even contradictory, conclusions on the nature of the *aulos*. Louis Bleuzet (1913–27), Leon Goossens (1977), Anthony Baines (1967) and Annie Bélis (2001) each interpret this passage as evidence for double reeds, while Heinz Becker (1966) and Kathleen Schlesinger (1939) use it to argue that it was a single-reed instrument.

Written sources give an equally confusing picture of the tonal characteristics of these ancient instruments. Both *aulos* and *tibia* are described as having a strong, resonant tone, but at other times they are described as having a soft, gracious quality. *Auloi* seem to have been used in a variety of contexts. They were used in battle but were also important in religious rites. In both of these contexts they were played by men, but at drinking parties the players were usually women.[27] Most scholars now agree that, given the wide variety of circumstances in which they were used and descriptions of their effects, both terms, *aulos* and *tibia*, must have referred to any type of musical pipe: flutes, single- and double-reed pipes.[28]

The instruments used by the professional players of Greece and Rome were not the crude rustic pipes we might imagine. They were made of wood, metal or ivory; surviving fragments show a precision workmanship, and the above passage from Theophrastus indicates the care that went into seasoning and preparing the cane for reeds. The *phorbeia* (Greek) and *capistrum* (Latin), the leather bands worn around the player's cheeks and head, have invariably entered the discussion of the *aulos* and *tibia*, and are usually taken as evidence of the high air pressure required to blow these instruments.[29] The *phorbeia* may have been an adjunct to circular breathing, which would mean that the player had to take the whole reed in the mouth. Some writers concluded from this (rather illogically) that it was not possible to vary the tone, and that they must have been constantly loud and raucous. According to Sachs, 'modification of timbre and force is not possible with this kind of blowing; the sound is emitted with unfaltering strength and shrillness',[30] and William Furlong relates the legend that 'the players' cheeks were strapped in a leather belt so that they could not burst. Even so, it is said, "they blew until they suffered abdominal haemorrhages".'[31] It is commonly held that the *phorbeia* served a cosmetic function by preventing the cheeks from becoming bloated. But if this is the case, why are there no examples of an *auletes* (female flute-player) wearing them? Becker has proposed that they may have been used only for playing the double-reed *aulos*, and that female musicians never played this instrument.[32]

Apart from the issue of their mode of sound generation, to call the *aulos* and *tibia* 'oboes' is additionally problematic because only some later Roman *tibiae* possess the oboe's characteristic conical bore. Jeremy Montagu has hypothesized that cylindrical double pipes would have sounded relatively low for their length, and that if overblowing was practised, they would have produced notes not an octave higher like conical shawms and oboes, but a twelfth like the clarinet (1988). This proposition, however, seems inconsistent with the descriptions of the 'screaming pipes of the ancients' so common in writings of the first part of the century.[33]

Those twentieth-century writers who accepted the *aulos* and *tibia* as double reeds invariably took the opportunity to contrast their purported raucous tone with the elegant and suave European instrument. There is a long-standing belief that oboes are naturally strident in tone and, unless brought under the player's mastery, can revert to their uncouth ancestors. As Jacques Lacombe wrote in 1752, 'The sound of the oboe is loud [*haut*], nasal and ungracious whenever it is not tempered [*adouci*] by the musician who plays it.'[34] More than any others, French oboists were aghast at the idea of taking the entire reed into the mouth, as this meant that its natural shrillness could not be checked by the player's lips. Louis Bleuzet was incredulous at this technique used for playing Chinese oboes, which he found piercing and unpleasant in tone.[35] Bleuzet's underlying assumption was that any sensitive musician would have accepted the superiority of modern European oboe technique. Leon Goossens, although equally proud of his delicate silvery oboe tone, was more willing to credit the *aulos* players of old with musical integrity. Instead of stressing, like many other writers, the Dionysian associations of the *aulos*, Goossens mentioned the *aulos* players' social and musical stature, concluding that 'there is no doubt that it was an instrument of high virtuosity and sensitivity'.[36]

Aulos and *tibia* were also used to translate the equally problematic Old Testament Hebrew term *halil*.[37] Although its exact identity is hard to reconstruct, the *halil* seems to have been made of bronze or copper as well as reed or bone and used in semi-religious contexts both celebratory and funereal. Evidence suggests that the translations to *aulos* and *tibia* were an apt reflection of its musical characteristics. After being rendered as *aulos* and *tibia* in the Septuagint and Vulgate, *halil* was translated more neutrally as *Pfeiffen* in the Lutheran Bible and *pipes* in the King James version.[38] Another reference to wind instruments is found in Psalm 98, verse 6. Here the word is *hatzotzerot*, probably a type of trumpet made of bronze or copper. This was translated by a variety of terms.[39] In early English translations this was rendered either as 'trumpet and cornet' or 'shawm'.[40] In other cases, the inclusion of double-reed instruments resulted from poetic licence. 'Hautbois' appears in at least one nineteenth-century French translation, for no apparent reason other than to provide a rhyme for 'voix':

> Que partout devant Dieu résonnent
> Et les instruments et les voix:
> Que partout les trompettes sonnent,
> Et les clarions, et les hautbois.[41]

If categorizing the reed-pipes of ancient Israel, Egypt, Greece and Rome as oboes is tenuous, with the Perso-Arabic *zurna* (shawm) we are on firmer ground. The theory of the Arabic origins of the shawm is founded principally on etymological evidence.[42] According to the *Oxford English Dictionary* 'shawm' entered the English language in the late fourteenth century and, after falling out of use in the eighteenth and nineteenth centuries, was resurrected in the twentieth century to provide a distinction between the oboe and its predecessor. 'Shawm' is derived from the Greek *kalamos* and Latin *calamus* meaning reed, and like the names in other languages – German *Schalmei*, Italian *ciaramella*, Spanish *chirimía*, and French *chalemie* and *chalumeau* – can be traced further back to the Arabic *zurna*. The English 'shawm' refers unequivocally to double-reed instruments, but corresponding terms in the other European languages do not distinguish between double- and single-reed forms. The French *chalumeau* and German *Schalmei* are often still used both for oboe- and clarinet-types.

It is generally held that shawms arrived in Europe in the wake of Islam. Owing to the antipathy to illustration in Islamic culture, the shawm never appears in Middle-Eastern art; the first iconographic sources are European and date from around the time of the Fifth Crusade (1217–21), but because of the dearth of written documentation, it is virtually impossible to identify the exact time of the shawm's arrival or the channels through which it passed. What seems clear is that the combination of woodwind instruments with percussion instruments characteristic of Turko-Arabic Janissary bands was then novel to Europe, and triggered great curiosity.[43]

Philip Bate remained sceptical of the Arabic origins of the European shawm, and although he acknowledged that 'through the Holy Wars of the twelfth and thirteenth centuries Europeans gained closer knowledge of Eastern arts and customs than ever before', he preferred to attribute the emergence of the invention of the European shawm to cultural inspiration rather than to direct oriental influence.[44] In an effort to defend the European oboe against non-European claimants for its invention, he argued that 'a glance at European social history suggests that in the first instance we may owe our refined and gentle oboe not so much to fresh cultural influences from the East as to the desire of Western princes to emulate the pomp and circumstance of the Orient'.[45] Bate sided with Baines, who had presented evidence that double-reed aerophones were known in Europe prior to the Crusades (possibly as survivals of the *aulos* and *tibia*) in the form of bladder pipes and bagpipe chanters, and suggested that this 'accounted for such non-oriental features as the specific material and construction of the double reed'.[46] The use of shawm bands to provide music for banquets, feasts and weddings, and to act as town watchmen, persisted in both European and Turko-Arabic cultures through the Dark Ages.

Our idea of the sound of medieval shawms is based on first-hand written accounts of non-European instruments that were deemed similar enough to represent the European shawm. Perceptions have been weighted strongly against the shawm, always with the Conservatoire oboe taken as the principal point of comparison. Karl Geiringer characterized the differences as follows: 'while the Shawm was a crudely made instrument with a wide conical bore, the Oboe is much more carefully constructed, and its bore is narrower. It has not the shrill, bleating tone of the older instrument; it is softer and more delicate.'[47] The choice of disparaging adjectives for the shawm heightens the contrast with the oboe and implicit in Geiringer's reasoning is the false reasoning that the shawm's wider bore resulted from less careful construction.[48]

Few historians failed to mention the fact that shawm reeds, like those of *tibia* and *aulos*, were taken fully in the mouth 'oriental style', with the player's lips resting against a wooden sleeve known as a pirouette. For Geiringer, this technique encapsulated the medieval *Zeitgeist*: 'The reed was inserted wholly into the mouth in the Eastern manner, so that the performer was unable to control the tone-colour with his lips. Any suggestion of personal expression was avoided, and the sound of the instrument had all the power and astringent vigour demanded by the age.'[49] In reality, medieval shawmists probably did use the lips on the reed to aid overblowing;[50] certainly by the seventeenth century lip-control was common on the shawm.[51]

Those Europeans who came into contact with shawms in their travels to the East invariably considered them as uncivilized as the musicians who played them. In 1814 Badia y Leyblich described *zurna* players as 'coarse musicians provided with even coarser pipes', and in the twentieth century Anthony Baines based his description of

Persian town bands on the recollections of a certain Binder in Kirmanshah: 'The trumpeters, with their long mediaeval trumpets, burst in intermittently with hoarse interruptions through which the shawmists unconcernedly play on.'[52] Similar ensembles found their way into European festivals. Shawms and trombones added colour to the grandiose processions held in Venice from the fifteenth to seventeenth century.

Modern oboists, proud of their privileged soloistic role in the orchestra and scornful of the cacophony of the village windband, looked down on the shawm for being (just) a 'band instrument'. Bate's comments are typical:

> With the appreciation of more subtly blended consorts of strings, cornetts, trombones and organs which marked the close of the Elizabethan Age, the shawms declined somewhat in dignity and, in general, became limited to the less refined grades of musical service – town bands and outdoor court ceremonial – and remained so for the last century of their active life.[53]

Among modern oboists Goossens was one of the few to view historical oboes sympathetically. He did not use the fact that shawms were reserved 'strictly for military and town bands' as proof of inferior musical ability. Instead, he chose a surprisingly positive image to describe the shawm's sound: 'they were a splendid sight and produced a warm, resonant sound'.[54] His description was no doubt influenced by the shawm's revival in the 1960s and 70s by groups such as David Munrow's Early Music Consort of London and the New York Pro Musica.

Whether shawm, *tibia* and *aulos* or (as we shall see shortly) the seventeenth- and eighteenth-century hautboy, the more 'primitive' oboes served as a foil onto which the deficiencies and technical blemishes the oboe could be projected as the 'refined' oboe always retained vestiges of its ancestors. Opinions were based largely on written evidence and extrapolation. A description such as Arbeau's that likened the shawm to the trumpet – 'truly, shawms [*haulbois*] bear a certain resemblance to trumpets and make quite a pleasant harmony [*une consonance assez agréable*]' – was taken as decidedly derogatory, even though originally intended to extol the shawm's tonal prowess.[55] Negative readings of this particular passage were also due to the fact that in French *hautbois* serves to designate both shawm and oboe. Ulric Daubeny, writing in 1920, was apparently unaware that the *hautbois* described by Mersenne was altogether different from the *hautboy* familiar to Mozart. Like many, he was also convinced that the wide reeds used to play the shawm and hautboy inevitably produced a coarse sound and were difficult to control.

> According to Mersenne such an instrument was shriller than all others with the exception for the trumpet and this state of affairs was little, if at all, improved even so late as Mozart's time. . . . He is said to have remarked that the 'impudence of tone' of the oboe was so great that no other instrument could contend with it in loudness. . . . The fine attenuated timbre peculiar to the modern oboe, and the delight of all musicians, is dependent far more on the adoption of the small narrow reed than on any mere mechanical improvement in manufacture and construction.[56]

Such assumptions have since been exposed as misguided. Already in 1939 Adam Carse speculated that while the tone of eighteenth-century oboes was heavier than that of the modern instrument because of their broader reeds, 'there is no reason to suppose that it was coarse or strident as is often suggested'.[57] Josef Marx confirmed Carse's suspicion from historical sources,[58] and now, some forty years since the twentieth-century revival of the hautboy, we are able to affirm that the hautboys known to Bach, Handel and Mozart are indeed capable of considerable tonal nuance and finesse.

'Wherever the Arabs went, the shawm went with them.'[59] It was not only to Europe that the Arab world brought the shawm. Bands of Islamic proselytizers left musical traces in cultures across Northern Africa, Asia and the Far East. Today modern descendants of the *zurna* are found from Morocco to Indonesia, and from Afghanistan to Niger. Just as in Europe, the Arab heritage was preserved in the names given to the *zurna*'s progeny: *sarunai* (Java and Malaysia), *shahnái* (India), *sur-na* (Kashmir), *sorna* (Iran and Afghanistan) and *sornā* (China).

Several systematic studies of musical instruments group treble double-reed instruments from around the world under the rubric of 'oboes'.[60] Thus in this system the Indian *shahnái*, Turkish *zurna* and Conservatoire oboe are all categorized as 'oboes'. While these systems were designed to be as universal as possible, they still view things from a Western perspective, and take 'oboe' not only as the familiar but the all-encompassing term. Retrospectively begotten ancestors may bear physical similarities to Western oboes, but grouping them together in this way can suppress differences and collapse practices specific to individual musical traditions into transcultural generalizations. In the attempt to make transcultural equations, such systems have often added to the polarization between Western oboe and exotic shawm and, while not as a necessary consequence, have also tended to elevate the status of Western art above that of other cultures.

Archaeologists of music such as Fétis and Curt Sachs took for granted an evolutionary model that placed European culture at its apex. In this scheme, non-Western cultures, being lower on the evolutionary scale, were thought of as being more 'primitive' – living relics of Europe's past. 'Primitive' cultures were thought of as static: if they changed at all, they did so at a much slower rate than Western culture.

With this hierarchic ordering of cultures, the chronological and spatial planes effectively collapse into each other. Just as the level of civilization is related to temporal proximity to the present moment, it is also related to geographic proximity to the perceived centre of civilization. Europeans journeyed to the East to experience their own culture of centuries past. Travel became a type of time travel: the further they travelled from their centre of civilization (Europe), the more primitive the cultures they encountered, and the further they travelled back in time. Thus one way of (re)discovering lost European traditions for nineteenth-century ethnologists was to examine contemporary practices outside Europe. The female dancers Gustave Flaubert encountered in Egypt, for example, caused him to reflect on what dancing in the ancient civilizations must have been like, and served as a

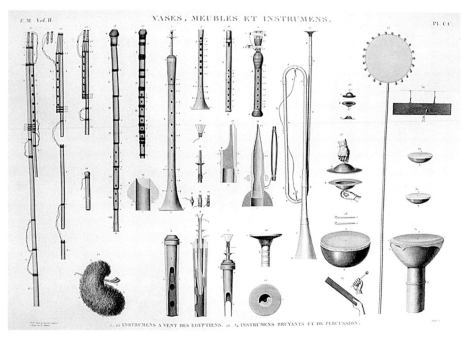

5. Egyptian wind instruments from the *Description de l'Egypte.*

reminder that the Orient was 'always young because nothing changes'.[61] It was essentially the same attitude that allowed Albert Andraud to assert that '[the oboe] has come down to us from prehistoric times without undergoing any radical changes of form',[62] and Philip Bate to declare that 'in Oriental countries today the double-reed is used with instruments that have probably not changed in form in a thousand years'.[63]

One of the earliest ethnomusicological projects to report on non-Western oboes was the *Description de l'Égypte.* This publication was the product of Napoleon's abortive 1798 Egyptian expedition. Although the campaign ended in failure, Napoleon was eager to make light of his defeat and, in addition to pillaging a significant booty, commanded the publication of a comprehensive twenty-one-volume work documenting virtually every aspect of the country. Everything was covered from geography, fauna and botany, history and archaeology to the culture of the Egyptian peoples, with additional space devoted to economics, architecture, dress, languages, customs – and music – all accompanied by copious engravings of exceptional quality. The undertaking endeavoured to claim for France the territories lost in real terms, and declared Napoleon the initiator of oriental imperialism.

Guillaume Villoteau (1759–1839), who supervised the expedition's musical researches, applied his thorough knowledge of Arab music to a detailed theoretical explanation of Egyptian music. He extracted information from players who supplied detailed information on two double-reed aerophones – the *zamr* and *zurna*. The name of each part of the instrument was carefully documented (see ill. 5; compare ill. 6); likewise the names of the notes and the fingerings are given with transcriptions into Western notation. The reed shown in the centre of the illustration is small and fan-shaped: 10 mm long, 4 mm wide at the base and 13 mm at the tip, made from straw mounted on a metal tube held in a pronged wooden fork that is inserted inside the top of the instrument.[64] Villoteau noted that the entire reed as well as the upper part of the copper tube was taken into the mouth with the lips resting on the *sadaf modaouar* (a type of pirouette). He also commented on the material used for the reed: 'This reed, too soft and fibrous, lacking totally in elasticity, would give way too easily under the pressure of the lips, and, instead of vibrating, would close entirely without letting any air pass through.'[65] While Villoteau's description of the instruments goes little beyond a straightforward physical description, he does mention some of the uses to which the instruments were put and presents transcriptions of dozens of songs and music played on a *zamr* in a wedding procession.

The presence of double-reed pipes is documented in the Indian subcontinent from around the beginning of the Christian era, but it was later at the time of the conquest of Sindh in 712 CE that the Arabic shawm arrived with the Central Asian *naubat* (military band).[66] In India as in other countries, the Arab shawm was used in bands for wedding feasts, dance and dramas, as well as in religious ceremonies at mosques and temples where it is still heard at prayer time. The *shahnái* (the North Indian version of the *zurna*) is often played with a second shawm or *sur*, a *shahnái* with its holes blocked, thus preventing it from producing more than a single drone note.

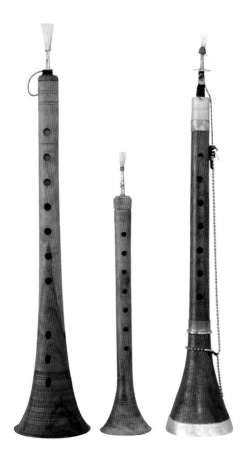

6. Modern examples of Arab double-reed aerophones; left to right: Moroccan *rheita*, Persian *sorna* (made in USA) and Iranian *zurna*.

ODEON

Bismillah Khan
RAGA TODI • MISHRA THUMRI

7. Cover photograph of Bismillah Khan from his recording of *Raga Todi* and *Mishra Thumri* (1956).

Berlioz described a player 'imported' from Calcutta for the World Fair:

> There was a double-reed wind instrument akin to our oboe, whose tube, having no holes, produces only one note. The leader of the musicians who came to Paris some years ago with the nautch-girls of Calcutta used this primitive oboe. He would make an A drone for hours, and those who love this particular note certainly got their money's worth.[67]

The modern-day use of the *shahnái* in Classical North-Indian music dates from after World War II. While in traditional contexts Indian shawm players rest their lips on a disc (similar to the pirouette of western shawms), the greater technical demands placed on the instrument in the newer virtuoso style have resulted in the abandonment of the disc. Ustad Bismillah Khan (1916–) is rightly famous for his staggering technique and versatility, combining dazzling digital dexterity with the ability to produce sounds ranging from vibrant to floating, crisp to mellifluous (ill. 7). He is able to bend pitches across astonishing intervals, and his repertoire of elaborate tonguing patterns is seemingly unlimited. Khan's reputation is based on his many recordings which have become established as the almost obligatory background music in that outpost of Indian culture in today's global village – the curry restaurant.

A few non-Western double reeds are not direct descendants of the *zurna*. The *charumera*, the double-reed instrument of the Japanese Kabuki theatre, is a special case as it was disseminated through a second wave of colonization. Like the South American *chirimía*, the *charumera* was imported not through Muslim expansion, but through Spanish and Portuguese Christian missionaries.

Each culture that adopted the *zurna* also adapted the instrument to its own practices, using whatever materials were to hand (ill. 8). Most of these instruments have seven finger-holes and often a thumb-hole at the rear of the instrument (the latter has never been a feature of European types). Apart from the details of the way the instruments themselves were formed, there is considerable variety in reed-making styles and pirouettes. Some instruments are elaborately decorated, like the Burmese *hnè*; others are much simpler in style, such as the Indian *shahnái* with its gentle, undulating turns. The body of most instruments is made of wood, less frequently bamboo (e.g., Japanese *hichiriki* and Sumatran *sarunai*) and metal; synthetic materials such as plastic are becoming increasingly common, particularly in the large numbers of instruments produced as tourist souvenirs; many are made in one piece (including the Iranian *zurna* and Moroccan *ghaita*), but detachable metal bells are also widespread (Tibetan *rgya-gling* and Japanese *charumera*, to mention but two).[68]

Arundo donax, the cane used for European reed instruments, is native to many of the areas to which the Islamic shawm was imported and its use is also quite widespread, but it is not the only material used. Several Asian cultures fashion

8. Oboes of the world; left to right: a) two ornamental Tibetan *rgya-gling*s; b) and c) two curved *soonai*; d) straight *jogi-baja* from Nepal.

reeds from dried and cured palm leaves or grasses; these materials are also used by South American *chirimía* players. Some instruments, like the Burmese *hnè* and Indonesian *selompret*, use not just a double reed, but multiple layers of the vibrating material.

Cylindrical-bored treble double-reed instruments are also found in a number of cultures, including folk traditions within Europe. In most cases the tone resulting from this acoustic coupling does not have the same loud, vibrant character as that produced on conical-bored instruments, and the names of the instruments are usually not connected to the Arab *zurna*. In Turkey it is the *mey*, in Armenia and Georgia the *duduk*, in Iran the *balāban*, in China the *guan* and in Japan the *hichiriki*. Because they are less strident than shawms, the Turkish *mey* and Caucasian *balāban* are treated as a completely separate category of instruments. The *balāban* is used in different contexts from the *zurna*, such as for accompanying poetry where the volume of the *zurna* would be impractical. A similar distinction between conical- and cylindrical-bored double-reed aerophones has existed in European medieval reed-pipes. According to Sachs, shawms had a loud, broad tone similar to that of certain folk oboes of Southern Italy (*piffero* – see ill. 79) and Spain (*caramillo*)', while the cylindrical-bored *douçaine* (or *dolzaina*) and *Rauschpfeife* were softer instruments.[69]

Reed-cap and bagpipe instruments are also closely associated with the oboe family. Here the double reed is enclosed in a cap into which air is blown from the player's mouth (such is the case with the crumhorn) or a reservoir (bagpipes). Although they are similar in construction (apart from the presence of the reed-cap) and in certain circumstances (when played without the reed-cap) become indistinguishable from oboes, these instruments are usually considered apart from oboes because of the differences in blowing technique and sound production.[70]

Amidst this diversity of forms, common themes and functions emerge. Many traditions have retained the *zurna*'s connection with conquest and power by identifying double-reed instruments with kingship or persons of power. In some cases both instrument and player enjoy elevated status. The West African *agaita* is played with drums in ensembles whose main function is to provide laudatory music at the

9. *Bombarde* (left) and bagpipe from Bretagne.

L'ALBERT MARTÍ I LA COBLA BARCELONA EL 1935

10. a) (left) *Cobla*, Barcelona, 1935; *tible* and *tenora* players in front row; b) (right) *tible* by Miquel Puigdellivol, Barcelona, late twentieth century. Note the holes on the bell section.

royal courts. The Vietnamese *kèn*, as well as being the leading instrument in the *hát bôi* theatre, is played in the *Dnai nhac* court ensemble. In other cultures, dominance reflects gender hierarchy. In the south-west of Turkey, wedding celebrations are traditionally divided into separate feasts for men and women. The *zurna* and *davul* (drum) supply the music for the men's celebrations, but are never present at the women's parties.[71] In other cultures, double-reed instruments have specific religious uses. In Morocco the *ghaita* (or *rheita*) and *nafir* (trumpet) are paired in the proclamations on Thursday of Holy Week. The *ghaita* is also credited with curative properties, and together with the *tbel* (a species of kettledrum) is prominent in the curing rituals known as *hadra*. In Sri Lanka and Armenia shawms are used in funeral music, and the Tibetan *rgya-gling* is used exclusively in Buddhist ritual. As with the conquistadors who colonized South America in the name of Christendom, it is often difficult to disentangle the religious from the political. In Agadez in Niger, pairs of *algaita* accompanied with drums herald the beginning and end of Ramadan at the palace of the Sultan, and lead him in procession through the streets. More recently certain double reeds have been adapted to popular musical contexts that are not hierarchized along royalist or aristocratic lines. The presence of the *algaita* in the

Western-influenced *Tiv* bands that accompany the *swange* dance of West Africa is an example; the folk *chirimía* of South America is another; the use of the *zurna* in much pop music produced today in the Middle East a third.

The shawm is preserved in a number of European folk traditions, notably in Spain where it is called the *dulzaina* (not to be confused with the older cylindrical-bored instrument), in northern Italy where the name is simply *piffero* (a cognate of the English 'pipe') and Bretagne where the *bombarde* is usually heard in combination with bagpipes (ill. 9).[72] But it is the Catalonian *tible* and *tenore* which have elicited greatest interest from organologists. Anthony Baines elevated the Catalan shawms with their vivid tone and phenomenal dynamic range to the status of 'art music' (1952). What is so fascinating about these shawms is the way they continued to 'evolve'. Representing a synthesis of folk traditions and modern ingenuity, they straddle high art and popular culture. These are not fossilized relics; they are shawms that have 'made it' into the modern age.

The present-day *tenora* and *tible* are products of the nineteenth century. Usually made from a single piece of jujue wood, the *tible* is approximately 60 cm in length (ill. 10b), and the *tenora* 85 cm (with a large bell usually of metal). In the 1850s the Perpignan maker André Toron added keywork not unlike the key systems adapted to oboes at the time. The vent holes below the finger-holes can be blocked with keys, thus extending the range downwards. The *tible* and *tenora* have a role in mixed bands called *coblas* that comprise *flabiol* and *tamboret* (pipe and tabor) traditionally played by the director, two *tible*, two *tenore*, two trumpets, valve trombone, two fluegel horns (*fiscorno*) and string bass (ill. 10a). These bands play outdoors and provide the music for the Sardana, the national dance of Catalonia, but as of recently this music is more often heard in concert halls. The *tible* and *tenora* often trade off parts in intricate ways that disguise the division of labour and create an uninterrupted compass of almost four octaves. The music played by the *coblas* is a hybrid of popular elements and the sentimental *kitsch* of nineteenth-century salon music, often with exaggerated contrasts between *schmaltzy* lyricism and extremely *scherzando* bravura passages.

In today's post-colonial and electronically networked world we are confronted on a daily basis with an astounding diversity of musics from many cultures, both past and present. It is to be hoped that listening will remind us all of the value of musics from other cultures not merely as precursors to the western Classical tradition, but as vital components in the lives of residents in our global village, and will teach us that our oboes, like Gabriel's, are capable of transmitting messages of peace across linguistic barriers and amidst cultural tension.

This chapter has investigated some of the ways in which modern historians and musicians retrospectively constructed the oboe's prehistory and have drawn on historical and exotic instruments in an attempt to define the modern Western oboe. In the chapters that follow we turn to a more detailed account of the oboe's gestation and birth from its immediate parent, the shawm, and the diversity of forms and functions it has taken in western culture over the past three centuries.

Chapter 2

From consort oboe to 'eloquent' oboe, 1610–1680

> A brief, and sufficiently accurate, description of the intellectual life of the
> European races during the succeeding two centuries and a quarter up to our own
> times is that they have been living upon the accumulated capital of ideas provided
> for them by the genius of the seventeenth century.[1]

The modern notion of what the oboe is, and what it is expected to do, was born in
the seventeenth century. In fact, the seventeenth century can be seen as the most
experimental period in the history of the instrument. In the first decades of that
century, the standard treble double-reed instrument was still the shawm, and by its
last decades, it had been replaced by the definitive form of the hautboy. The changes
the shawm underwent in the process of being transformed into the hautboy were
quite basic, as the instrument was swept along on the tide of a profound shift in the
conception of what music was about. While the instrument's physical form changed,
an even more fundamental mutation took place in the idea of the instrument's
character and role. The hautboy's new function was that of a soloist and orchestral
collaborator, and this job description has remained valid up to the present day.

We think of the shawm as different from the oboe because it has a separate name,
but nothing in its physical design sets it apart from later forms of oboe. It easily meets
our definition of the oboe as the normal soprano double-reed instrument of its time,
used in sophisticated art music.[2] The terminology in France, where the new hautboy
was developed, made no distinction between the shawm and the hautboy; both were
called 'Hautbois'. Naturally there were differences of detail, just as there were
between subsequent forms of the oboe. And yet in another sense, the division is valid;
not for physical reasons, but for the differences in the way the two instruments were
used. The shawm was boisterous, festive, and impressive, an 'Haut-bois' or 'loud-
woodwind', and it was heard in consorts of different sizes. The kind of music it
played emphasized equality between the voices within the group, and most of the
shawm's music was not conceived specifically for it (the same piece might be played
alternatively by consorts of different types of instruments, like recorders, cornetts or
strings). By contrast, the hautboy was created to play solos, and its own particular
character was often a part of the 'message' of the piece it was playing. The hautboy's
first solo medium, the obbligato in solo vocal arias, was quite instrument-specific. This
is why the hautboy that appeared in the seventeenth century is the direct ancestor of
the various forms of oboe that have been in vogue up until the present. Despite

changes of physical form, the oboe's musical role has remained more or less constant
since then.

One of the few contemporary descriptions of the development of the new models
of winds comes from the hand of Michel de La Barre, an important French court
composer and woodwind player from the generation that immediately followed that
event; La Barre knew personally many of the musicians who had developed and 'test-
flown' the new models. He wrote:

> [Lully's] promotion meant the downfall of all the old instruments [the musette, the
> *hauboïs*, the bagpipe, the cornett, the cromorne, and the sackbut[3]], except the
> *hauboïs*, thanks to the Filidors and Hautteterres, who spoiled so much wood and
> [?played so much music] that they finally succeeded in rendering it usable in
> ensembles. From that time on, musettes were left to shepherds, and violins,
> recorders, theorbos, and viols took their place, for the traverso did not arrive until
> later.[4]

It was La Barre's opinion that the breakthrough to 'perfection' in music had been
achieved by 'Le Camus, Boësset, D'Ambruys, and Lambert[5] [, who] were the first to
write airs that expressed their texts, and above all the famous Lully'. . . . By
'expressing texts', La Barre is probably referring to the new aesthetic of 'speaking
music' that appeared in the seventeenth century. The new hautboy did indeed appear
at just the same period as the works of these composers.[6] La Barre evidently saw these
developments as related.

It was no accident that vocal obbligatos were the hautboy's first solo medium,
exploring the instrument's expressive potential. This was what the hautboy did best,
and the reason it had been created: to convey the emotional force of words, and to
move its listeners. The hautboy was modelled on the new singer of monodic music,
a singer who performed *le nuove musiche*, developed by composers like Caccini and
Monteverdi with great success in the generation that preceded the shawm's
transformation. Monody rejected the older four- and five-part style, replacing it with
a polarized bass with a solo vocal line, and the music was used – even abused – for
the sake of the text. In a different way, the French composers of chamber airs of the
next generations, whose approach directly influenced Lully, also reflected this new
idea of expressing personal emotions in dramatic ways.[7] The new 'speaking'
instrument, the hautboy, was (as Mattheson put it) an *eloquent* oboe,[8] in a period when
speech was the operative metaphor for music making. Shawms had been better at
something else: the prototypical consort instruments, shawms could lay down a broad
expanse of sound rather than a single filigree line. From this point of view, it made
sense that, by the end of the century, the hautboy was being called an 'improved'
shawm. Talbot wrote in c.1692–5: 'The present Hautbois not 40 years old & an
improvement of the great French hautbois [= the *grand Haut-bois*, or shawm of
Mersenne's time] which is like our Weights [= shawm].'

In addition to 'speaking' texts, the hautboy had another important function as a
member of the new instrumental complex that came to be known as the 'orchestra'.
The orchestra can be said to have come into existence when consorts of strings and

winds, which had normally played separately from each other, were merged into a larger ensemble. This involved accommodating shawms and violins to each other – redesigning the former and tuning down the latter. As a wind parallel to the violin, the modified shawm had to be able to balance the other instruments, have an extended range of two octaves that matched the important notes of the violin, play easily in C and D major, and produce the standard accidentals in various keys. While the traditional shawm had been able to do all these things when necessary, certain basic modifications could facilitate things.

Besides rejecting the pirouette at the top and adding a bit of ornamental turnery, the makers who developed this new hautboy gave it a shorter bell, changed the position of the tone-holes, narrowed the side-walls, and altered the reed.[9] They also divided the instrument by adding a joint between the hands, and twinned hole 4 (and experimented with twinning hole 6 as well, as on the recorder). It has often been suggested that the hautboy's bore was narrower than that of the shawm; this is a question that needs further exploration, as at least some surviving instruments of the period show quite similar bore diameters.[10] This new instrument, the protomorphic hautboy, combined elements of the shawm with features that would eventually become part of the definitive hautboy. So far, the only evidence we have of the physical form of the protomorphic hautboy (and for that matter its very existence) are several Gobelins tapestries based on designs by Charles Le Brun, painter to Louis XIV and director of the royal Academy of Painting and Sculpture. The clearest representations are the borders of two tapestries designed by Le Brun in 1664, 'L'Air' from a series called *Les Elémens,* and 'Le Printemps ou Versailles' from the series *Les saisons*.[11] 'L'Air', appropriately, depicts many kinds of wind instruments of the time, and includes nine hautboys of the new design.

Apparently, Lully started using this protomorphic hautboy in the 1650s. At that point he was still conducting his own orchestra, the Petite Bande, and had not yet consolidated his power at court. He did not take control of the Grande Bande (also known as the Vingt-Quatre Violons) and begin producing his *ballets* and *comédie-ballets* until 1664. In the meantime, he mounted a number of *ballets* using the forces at his command, and it is thought that he introduced the new protomorphic hautboy in one of these productions staged in 1657. The work was called *L'Amour malade*.[12] The libretto gives the names of the woodwind players who played in the last *entrée* as François Descoteaux, Joseph or Antoine Pièche, Jean or Michel Destouches, and Jean [1] Hotteterre and his sons Jean [2], and Martin (called 'Obterre le pere, Obterre fils aisné, Obterre le cadet' – we shall return to these three musicians in a moment).

When Lully began working with the Vingt-Quatre Violons in 1664, he was able to mount larger productions that amalgamated the King's two orchestras. It was in this same year that another new phase in the hautboy's mutation began. Since singers took the spotlight, instruments were needed that sounded at the low pitch that singers preferred, and on which their voice categories depended (the high natural tenors known as 'hautecontres' – not the modern so-called 'countertenors' – were especially vulnerable to higher pitches). The Grande Bande was already at this low pitch, but Lully's smaller group had been playing at the old Renaissance standard a minor third higher. To lower their pitch the strings had either to be replaced or set up differently, and the protomorphic hautboys needed major modification.

At this point in the mid-1660s, as far as we can tell, Lully stopped using hautboys completely, and this during an extremely active period; between 1664 and 1670 he produced fourteen large works, not one of which seems to have involved the hautboy (though some of them called for 'flûtes' that would have employed the same musicians). Lully did not ask for hautboys again until 1670, with the performance of Molière's *Le Bourgeois gentilhomme* at Chambord Palace. It seems that from 1664, wind players were preoccupied with developing the new low-pitched hautbois, and probably learning to play it. It was also in 1664 that Jean Hotteterre 'père'[13] was appointed to the Douze Grands Hautbois at court. The association of the Hotteterre family with the development of the new hautboy is probably due mainly to this musician, who was the senior craftsman of the family at the time. Jean Hotteterre (c.1605–90/92) had set up his own instrument workshop in about 1635 and was a member of the court ensemble known as the Hautbois et musettes de Poitou from 1651. By the 1670s he was well known. Borjon (1672:38) wrote that he was 'unique as a maker of all kinds of wooden, ivory, and ebony instruments, such as musettes, flutes, flageolets, hautboys, and cromornes.[14] He is also known for making such instruments perfectly in tune. . . . His sons are in no way inferior to him in the practice of this art.' Hotteterre's elder son Jean (2) met a sudden and unexpected end when he was murdered by a fellow hautboist in 1668.[15] The younger son, Martin (born c.1640), is known to have been living and working with his father in 1658, and later became a notable player, as well as the father of the Hotteterre best-known today, Jacques 'le Romain'.

By 1668, l'Abbé de Pure was writing that 'Les Haut-bois . . ., played as they are nowadays at the Court and in Paris, leave little to be desired'.[16] The first illustration we have of the new hautboy, the familiar model that was to remain in more or less stable form for the next half-century, is Blanchet's engraving used as a frontispiece to Borjon's *Traité de la musette* (ill. 11). Borjon's book was published two years after the performance of *Le Bourgeois gentilhomme*, which may have been the first official appearance of the new hautboy. It was evidently during this period of experiment that the remaining hautboy characteristics appeared, including more elaborate turnery, reduced tone-hole size, the rejection of the fontanelle (or barrel) surrounding the Great-key, the addition of a Small-key for E flat, and the move to a lower pitch.

In 1672 Lully became head of the Académie Royale de Musique, or Opéra, so the definitive hautboy seems to have arrived in time for the first of Lully's large-scale operas, *Les Fêtes de l'Amour et de Bacchus*, put on in that year. Lully regularly called for hautboys in subsequent productions. After 1670, when he had the definitive hautboy, Lully began to write hautboy *ritournelles* or 'trios' that emerged from the larger sound of the full orchestra. This texture became popular with later composers. When these *ritournelles* specified hautbois, they could have been for two treble hautboys and either bassoon or 'cromorne' (see below). Whether the parts were doubled was left ambiguous.[17]

Instrumentation was rarely precise, being determined by the situation, such as the acoustics of the performing space, available instruments, and so on. Often the term

11. [Thomas] Blanchet: plate opposite title page of Borjon's *Traité de la musette* (by 1672).

symphonie was all a composer would specify (*symphonie* meant an instrumental ensemble of indeterminate size). Just which music was originally played on hautboys is thus unknown. Although the names of on-stage musicians (often including hautboys) appear in printed librettos of performances, the only complete list of orchestral players that survives for a Lully performance is that of *Le Triomphe de l'Amour* (1681).[18] This was no small production; there were 21 woodwind players, of whom 10 were hautboys. The strings numbered 47, and the orchestra had a total strength of about 77. Judging from the proportions of other performances, the topmost part would probably have been played by 13–14 violins, and if the same part was also played by all the hautboys (as some modern writers have suggested), the hautboys would have seriously overbalanced the violins.[19] That would conflict with the comment by Roger North at the end of the seventeenth century on the sound of a Lullian orchestra: 'Here were many instruments, all waiters upon the violin, which was predominant, and lowdness a great ingredient, together with a strong snatching way of playing, to make the musick brisk and good.'[20] It seems more likely that the 'hautboys', like the 'violins', were divided over the five parts, giving the basic string sound the unique 'bite' and 'spice' that comes from combining in unison the hautboy sound with that of strings.

The oboe, the type-instrument we see clearly now with hindsight, was a novelty in Lully's time, and its identity was still vague, so the term 'hautbois' was very inclusive. In the same way that 'violon' was used to mean any of the instruments of the violin family, 'hautbois' could mean 'bassoon' (which was often a 'basse de hautbois'). 'Hautbois', in fact, could denote any double-reed instrument (like the cromorne and the bagpipe chanters to be described in a moment), and even in some cases (bizarre as it seems now) wind instruments in general, including the flutes and the musette de cour.[21] 'Hautbois' seems to have been a sort of generic designator for a woodwind, evoking the pastoral poetic attribute (nature in its untroubled, idyllic state); the same place marked 'hautbois' in the score might be marked 'flûtes' or 'musette' in the libretto.

The generic 'hautbois' family included several other similar instruments. At least two forms of shawm survived into the eighteenth century: the 'Baroque schalmey' (often misleadingly called the 'deutsche schalmey' nowadays) and the 'hautbois d'église' (also known as the 'Musettenbas' and 'trompette d'église'). Discussion and speculation on the former can be found in Thompson (1999 and 2002), Bouterse (1999), and Haynes (2000). For the latter, recent studies include Finkelman (2001) and Girard (2001; especially 'Les conclusions', pp. 128–9). In chapter 4 we shall discuss folk oboes (the *aubòi*, the *aboès* and the *graile*) that resemble early oboe types possibly in use at the time, and flourishing until the twentieth century. Three other contemporary instruments closely related to the hautboy were the *cromorne* and the detached bagpipe chanters (the *hautbois de Poitou* and the *chalumeau simple*).

The cromorne was not the *krummhorn*. It was similar to the hautboy and came in different sizes. It had a crook and possibly a pirouette, extension keys for holes 1, 3, 4 and 6, and a distinctive shape as a result of the wooden rings on which the keys were mounted (see the long instrument lying on the ground in ill. 11). Sources suggest that, until lower hautboys and the bassoon were developed, the cromorne in various sizes was the original partner of the treble hautboy in double-reed ensembles.[22]

The *hautbois de Poitou* was the instrument that resulted when players of the bagpipe known as the *musette de Poitou* removed the chanter and played it without the bag. This instrument was described in 1635 by Mersenne; he showed three sizes. The *hautbois de Poitou* had a windcap that tapered inward toward its base, a single Great-key, and a fontanelle that covered the key. It was bored conically like the shawm and hautboy. When the cap was not used, it strongly resembled a small hautboy.

Players also detached the chanter (known in French as the *chalumeau*) from another kind of bagpipe, the bellows-blown *musette de cour*, and played it alone. Borjon showed this detached chanter on page 22 of his musette book, calling it a 'Chalumeau simple'. The musette chanter is easy to distinguish from the *hautbois de Poitou*, because it had no fontanelle, it had a key for the left thumb that entered the cap, its cap had a distinctive 'dumbbell' turning consisting of two bulbs joined by a column, and its bore was cylindrical rather than conical.[23]

The decade of the 1680s was exceptional in producing many fine hautboy players, including John Loeillet (born 1680), Robert Valentine (c.1680), Jacob Denner (1681), Anne Philidor (1681), Pierre Philidor (1681), Caspar Gleditsch (1684), Jacob Loeillet (1685), Michael Böhm (c.1685), and Christian Richter (1689). These players will be discussed in the next chapter. There is an age-old belief that oboe playing is bad for the health, and it is true that a number of prominent players in history died prematurely, including Anne Philidor (at 47), John Loeillet (50), Pierre Philidor (50), Jacob Denner (54), Richter (55), and Valentine (c.55). But in the same period, at least three players are known to have reached their eighties: Galliard (81), André Philidor (c.83), and Penati (c.90).

As for the instrument itself, most of the components that made up the hautboy were plant products: the body was made of wood, the reed of cane (actually a species of grass called *Arundo donax*, still used for reeds today), and the bindings were of flax or hemp thread. Like other woodwinds, hautboys were normally made of boxwood, *Buxus sempervirens*; other materials included (in descending order of frequency) ebony, ivory, and fruitwoods (plum, pear and cherry). The keys and reed staple (the tube on which the cane was tied) were usually made of brass (and on fancier instruments, of silver). The Great-key produced c1 and c♯2, the Small-key gave the E flat. About a third of the surviving instruments have only these two keys, but the others have a duplicated Small-key that would have allowed right- or left-handed playing. There were sometimes ornamental mountings called 'tips' at the ends of joints, made of ivory or silver. It is surprising how many of the products used in making hautboys and reeds are golden in colour: the cane, the brass, beeswax for the thread and for tuning, and boxwood (even if it was usually stained darker).

Almost all antique hautboys have twinned third holes, since closing hole 3 halfway was the only feasible way to play G sharp/A flat in the lower register. More often than not, the fourth hole was also twinned so it could be used to get G flat (and sometimes F sharp). One of the unusual features of the new hautboy was the small size of its tone-holes. This affected the tone, making it softer and darker, thus tending to make the instrument blend with other instruments rather than standing out. Small tone-holes had another advantage: they made the notes relatively unstable between registers. This meant that register shifts could be produced on the hautboy over the range of over two octaves solely by the action of the breath and lips, without 'speakers' like the thumb-hole on the recorder, or an octave key. Smaller tone-holes also helped to produce accidentals with cross-fingerings, giving a clearer, more specific pitch.

Cross-fingerings (also called forked-fingerings) can be regarded as a defining feature of hautboys, and indeed of Baroque woodwinds in general. On any woodwind instrument, there is a natural six-hole scale that usually gives D or G major. To obtain the in-between notes that are not part of this scale, there are three different options: 1) opening holes halfway (half-holing); 2) opening close-standing keys over dedicated holes for these notes; 3) using cross-fingerings.[24] Half-holing lowered a fingered note a semitone by half-closing the next lowest hole. The note A, for example, produced by closing holes 1 and 2, was lowered to A♭ by playing A and half-closing hole 3. Half-holing was most effective on holes of relatively large diameter, which meant that it worked poorly on instruments with small tone holes like the hautboy. Cross-fingering, on the other hand, worked well on the hautboy. Cross-fingering involved lowering a simple fingering by closing one or more holes immediately below the first open hole. The B produced by closing the first hole could be lowered to a B♭, for instance, by closing holes 1 and 3, leaving hole 2 open.

In developing the hautboy from the shawm, makers had to choose between these three methods of producing notes that were not part of the natural scale. They ended up with a little of each. The half-hole was used for g♯/a♭. To produce the bottom c1 that was sounded through a tone-hole beyond the reach of the fingers, an articulated open-standing key (that came to be known as the 'Great-key') was borrowed from the shawm. As for the E♭, the corresponding note on the treble shawm had been obtained by half-closing hole 6; that had worked well because of the shawm's long bell and large tone-holes. But when the new short-belled hautboy was developed, another solution had to be found. At first, the sixth hole was twinned (as on most modern recorders), so e♭1 was obtained with a half-hole. But twinning hole 6 was not the ideal solution. Hole 6 on most Baroque woodwinds is already higher up the bore than it should be because it is otherwise too low for the fingers. But being higher, it has to be smaller than holes 4 and 5, which makes it stuffier than the other notes. Twinning made it worse. Since it couldn't be produced with a cross-fingering, the e♭ was eventually entrusted to a key like those on the musette, called the Small-key; the same solution was later applied to the traverso and sometimes the bassoon.[25]

Close-standing keys would have produced the rest of the notes that were not part of the hautboy's natural scale (f1, b♭1, c2, f2, a♭2/g♯2, b♭2 and c3), as they eventually did for nineteenth- and twentieth-century oboes. But the musicians and makers who developed the new hautboy opted instead for the third choice, cross-fingering, which had been used on the shawm. It is interesting that cross-fingering was selected instead of more keys. If, as we have speculated above, the principal designer of the new instrument was Jean Hotteterre, we know he was active in making improvements to the musette,[26] an instrument that had as many as thirteen close-standing keys by the 1670s (see ill. 37). Adopting keys was therefore a viable option for Hotteterre. It seems, then, that at the time the effects of an hautboy using cross-fingerings was preferred to one that could produce the same notes using keys. The two methods have a noticeably different sound; dedicated holes under keys produce a more open and direct sound than cross-fingerings.

That is why half-holing and cross-fingering are defining traits of the types of oboe that existed before the Romantic period. One of the earliest pictures of the hautboy is another Gobelins tapestry (1684, ill. 12) that shows a player using a fictitious

12. Gobelins tapestry: 'Danse des Nymphes, de la gauche'; fifth piece in the series *Sujets de la fable*, 1684–1795 (model by 1684), c.4 x 4 m.

fingering (12 5) obviously inspired by a cross-fingering. Cross-fingerings had long been required in shawm music, but the smaller tone holes of the hautboy made them more effective.[27] As more and more tonalities came into use, cross-fingerings were regularly called for. On the hautboy, there was more difference in timbre between natural and cross-fingered notes than on the shawm because the tone-holes were smaller and because the hautboy lacked the shawm's long bell and the acoustic advantages it afforded.[28]

Cross-fingerings were an integral feature of the hautboy's technique as well as its sound quality. They demanded complex finger combinations, and produced notes more compatible with meantone tuning than equal temperament. They added colour, variety and character to different tonalities, because cross-fingerings, which sounded different from natural fingerings, fell on different degrees of each scale.[29] Cross-fingerings thrive in a meantone environment. The tuning model that was in general use when the hautboy was developed was quarter-comma meantone. In this tuning (also known as 'true meantone' because it makes no compromise with pure thirds, as do the later 'modified meantones'), sharps are lower than their equivalent flats by about 41 cents, approaching a quarter of a tone (a quarter-tone is 50 cents). A characteristic of meantones is that flats get generally higher and sharps lower in the order they appear in a key signature. Thus the note E flat is sharper than B flat, A flat sharper still, and so on. Likewise, C sharp is lower than F sharp, G sharp lower than C sharp, and so on. The following chart shows how notes in meantone vary in cents from equal temperament (assuming that A is the tuning note):

                              C +10
                   C♯–14   D♭+27
                              D + 3
                   D♯–21   E♭+20
                              E –4
                              F +13
                   F♯–11   G♭+30
                              G +7
                   G♯–17   A♭+23
                              A o
                   A♯–25   B♭+17
                              B –7
                              C +10

Although fingering charts for the hautboy frequently distinguished flats from their corresponding sharps (especially G♯2/A♭2), separate fingerings were not available or convenient for all these notes (such as D♯/E♭1 or E♯/F1). To produce flats and sharps as far from each other as 41 cents, embouchures must have been extremely flexible.[30] Of course, the cross-fingerings on the hautboy (F and B♭) tended to be high, and the leading notes (B, D♯, F♯, G♯, C♯, E and A) were low or could easily be played low. The too-narrow tuning of the notes produced through the fifth tone-hole, F–F♯, fit the meantone model, where these two notes are 24 cents closer to each other than in equal temperament. Thus the natural tuning of the hautboy corresponded fairly well to meantone.

For most of the eighteenth century, sources suggest that the standard tuning of orchestral instruments was compatible with the keyboard tuning known as 'sixth-comma meantone'.[31] As in any meantone, sharps in this 'modified' form remained lower than their equivalent flats, but now the difference was only a comma, or about 21/22 cents, considerably less than in 'true meantone'. The notes in sixth-comma meantone vary from equal temperament like this:

                              C +5
                   C♯–8   D♭+14
                              D +1
                   D♯–11   E♭+10
                              E –2
                              F +7
                   F♯–6   G♭+16
                              G +3
                   G♯–10   A♭+12
                              A o
                   A♯–13   B♭+9
                              B –4
                              C +5

As can be seen, the enharmonic notes are separated by a comma: C♯ is 22 cents lower than D♭, D♯ 21 cents lower than E♭, and so on.

13. Nicolas Henri Tardieu (soon after 25 Oct. 1722). Detail from fifth tableau in the series 'Le Sacre de Louis XV'.

The fingerings of woodwinds (and thus their basic tuning) did not change between the seventeenth and eighteenth centuries, so it is unlikely that makers and players consciously distinguished quarter-comma and sixth-comma meantone; probably they simply adjusted as necessary to get satisfying intervals within the broad concept of 'meantone'. For instruments without a fixed tuning (that is, most non-keyboard instruments), 'temperament' is in fact an overly specific concept; intonation is influenced by technical situations, subjective perceptions, even differences in dynamics. No violinist or hautboist is capable of playing consistently in a keyboard temperament, even if they wanted to.[32] Since both quarter-comma and sixth-comma meantone had the same general tendencies, either would have served as an approximate tuning model.

All the first-generation hautboy players must have been connected in one way or another with the French court, where the new hautboy was developed. Even in other countries, the first contacts with the instrument in the 1670s and 80s were through travelling Frenchmen. The court wind players were employed by the Grande Écurie (or Royal Equerry), which consisted of a number of different ensembles that included woodwinds. The king's most active hautboy ensemble was the Fifres et Tambours. This group was responsible for the daily ceremonies at court,[33] and they are the group portrayed in the well-known etchings of Louis XV's coronation in 1722 (ill. 13). Part of the repertoire of the Fifres et Tambours is preserved in the Philidor Manuscript (*Partition de plusieurs marches*, Paris, Rés. F.671). This collection, copied under the supervision of André Philidor around 1705, is one of the largest sources of original hautboy band music that survives.[34]

It was another ensemble, the Douze Grands Hautbois, that probably had the highest status among the hautboys at court. This band had only three set duties per year, but appeared for other exceptional events.[35] The players were thus seldom present at court, unless they played in other royal ensembles. Although only twelve players held titles at any given time, there was considerable turnover; some two dozen players held positions in the period between 1640 and 1670, and sixteen others were appointed before the turn of the century. Another important court ensemble were the Mousquetaires, also called the Plaisirs du Roi. This band originally participated in battle campaigns until a royal decree in 1683 forbade the use of hautboys in military engagements. The Mousquetaires evidently had a favoured position; they had adopted the (protomorphic) hautboy extremely early (by 1663), and Lully himself wrote several marches for them.[36] Hautboy players may have been attached to the Chambre by the 1680s,[37] playing orchestral music, since in the Baroque period 'chamber music' did not normally mean smaller ensembles, as it does now, but rather instrumental music of any kind. The Chambre, for instance, included both the Petits Violons and the Grande Bande.

During this period of gestation at the French court, nothing is known of hautboy developments in other parts of Europe that might have been parallel. It is conceivable that the entire process of formulating the hautboy out of the shawm, which happened in the space of a generation, took place in Paris. In any case, events at the French court were quickly known abroad, and (as discussed in chapter 3) the intense interest in Louis XIV's court brought the instrument to the attention of other European countries almost immediately.

The hautboy quickly became an indispensable component of the music-making of the period. Whereas other instruments specialized in certain kinds of music, the hautboy found itself being used in virtually every genre; Eisel wrote in 1738 (96–7), 'it is used in the battlefield, in opera, in social gatherings, as well as in churches'. It was played in solos, in tutti with strings in orchestras, in chamber music, and in military ensembles and hautboy bands. Almost any maker who made woodwinds in the seventeenth and eighteenth centuries had a line of hautboys, and the instrument was being made before the traverso and bassoon and long after the recorder. As discussed above, the hautboy was regarded as the type-instrument for the woodwinds, just as the violin was for the strings.

Early in its career, several sources documented one of the hautboy's remarkable attributes: its lively, animated, 'sprightly' quality. Menestrier, for instance, wrote in 1681 (123) that 'if trumpets enliven the cavalry, and even the horses, experience proves that hautboys make soldiers march more happily, and that in playing at festivities and even in combat they give the effect of going off to a wedding'. Banister (who is credited with the publication of *The Sprightly Companion* for hautboy in 1695) quotes 'a great Lover of Musick' to the effect that

> MUSICK will give our hardest Labours Ease;
> The *Hautboy* charms in War, the *Flute* in Peace.
> Where Love or Honour calls, these Sounds inspire;
> *This* charms with Love, *That* Courage sets on fire.[38]

The hautboy was also seen as the personification of peace, and set symbolically in contrast to the trumpet, the instrument of glory and battle. Colasse, in his *Ballet des Saisons* (1695), used hautboys when the chorus sang

Chantons, chantons la victoire . . . au milieu des horreurs d'une guerre cruelle nous jouissons des douceurs de la paix.

Let us sing of victory . . . in the midst of the horrors of a cruel war, we can enjoy the sweetness of peace.

In Rameau's *Fêtes d'Hébé* II/7 (1739), Iphise sings

Éclatante trompette annoncez notre gloire,

Dazzling trumpet, announce our glory,

followed by

Répondez-nous tendres hautbois.

Reply, you tender hautboys.

And in the prologue to Lully's *Thésée* (1675),[39] Mars sings

Que les Hautbois, et les Musettes l'emportent sur les Trompettes, et sur les Tambours. Que rien ne trouble icy Venus et les Amours.

Let the hautboys and musettes prevail over the trumpets and drums. Let nothing here trouble Venus and the Amours.

Hautboys were also used to call to mind the pastoral sentiments, often in the idyllic form of an innocent shepherd's life. Flutes and hautboys shared this rustic association, but flutes more often had the attribute of love, while hautboys represented peace.

The hautboy was thus an instrument of contrasts; it was coupled with the extremes of pastoral peace as well as the animation and shock of war; with gentle tenderness, delicacy and charm, but also a lively and sprightly affect. Its divergent characters were summed up by John Banister in 1695 with these words:

For besides its Inimitable charming Sweetness of Sound (when well play'd upon) it is also Majestical and Stately, and not much Inferiour to the Trumpet.[40]

Chapter 3

The sprightly hautboy, 1680–1760

Indeed it looks strange at first sight: But on the other hand, if a Man considers the Excellency and Use of it, this Wonder will soon vanish. (Bannister 1695:i)

The spread of the new French hautboy

It is interesting to observe the enthusiasm with which the hautboy was taken up by courts all over Europe; it must have been something like the introduction of the personal computer today. Three years after its probable début in France in 1670, the hautboy was being played in London, and within another decade or so it had caught on in Turin, Amsterdam, The Hague, Madrid, Celle, Stuttgart and Brussels. By the end of the century (thus in the space of a generation), the hautboy was not only established but familiar everywhere in Europe.[1]

At the moment of the hautboy's development in France, both England and Germany were recovering from wars that had devastated their musical infrastructures. Thus renewal and renovation were in the air. There were also a number of inducements to French hautboists to go abroad. Many French wind players and makers were Protestants – Huguenots – and in 1685 Louis XIV revoked their charter of religious and civil liberties, the Edict of Nantes. This resulted in a mass relocation of many Huguenots; nearly half a million intellectuals, artists, craftsmen, businessmen, international traders, and musicians left France for more tolerant regimes. This exodus was amplified by the unfair monopoly of power enjoyed by Lully, which by the 1670s had forced a number of musicians to leave for other courts (in this sense, too, Lully was unintentionally the godfather of the hautboy). Even more compelling to French hautboists were the bottom-line rewards on offer by rich foreigners avid for this conspicuous symbol of French culture. That the instrument (and good players of it) were highly valued can be seen from court financial records in the course of the next century. Top of the line hautboists like François La Riche, Onofrio Penati, Michael Böhm, Christian Richter, Jacob Loeillet, Giuseppe Sammartini, Alessandro and Antonio Besozzi, and Joan Baptista Pla (to name some of them) were scouted like expensive star athletes today, and were often paid more than other members of orchestras.

The first country to which the hautboy was exported was England. The instrument arrived there almost simultaneously with its development in Paris, in fact, and under curious circumstances. Four French hautboy players were among a company of musicians who accompanied Robert Cambert when he moved to London in 1673. Cambert had produced successful theatre works in Paris at the Opéra that included the new hautboy in 1671, before Lully acquired exclusive rights from Louis XIV to mount operatic productions in France. Louis apparently had other plans for Cambert. It happened that the mistress of the English king, Charles II, was French (her name was Louise de Kéroualle), and Charles gave her the title of Duchess of Portsmouth. It is now thought that on Louis's orders, both Kéroualle and Cambert were deliberately sent to England as a means of reinforcing France's influence on the English throne.[2] Charles had a taste for French music, and Cambert worked in London for the Duchess as her Maître de musique. Thus at Louis XIV's bidding, Cambert and his band entertained King Charles and members of his court in informal soirées, playing compositions by Lully that had been on the Paris stage less than a year.[3] This meant that London was introduced to the latest, most up-to-date instruments heard at the Paris Opéra: the hautboy, recorder and bassoon. Despite the anti-French feelings at the time, the English readily adopted the new French hautboy, using it in stage works (Purcell's, for instance) and military bands. The court even engaged three French players of flute and hautboy at the Chapel Royal in the 1670s. A royal chamber band of eight players, many of them doublers on other instruments, was established in the 1690s and continued into George I's reign (starting in 1714).[4]

By the 1690s, the hautboy had arrived in all the major cities of the Italian peninsula. The court of Savoy in Turin, which had close ties to the French court, was probably the first place in Italy to establish places for the instrument when in 1677 it created a 'Scuderìa' (or Écurie) of six hautboy players, some of whom had names that look French.[5] In Italy, the hautboy's name (*oboè*, or variations on it like oboè, obbuè, and so on) suggests that it had come from France. In France until the nineteenth century, hautbois was pronounced o·bway (or [*obwe*]), rather than, as it is now, [*obwa*]. The Italian *oboè* is simply a phonetic transliteration of the Baroque French [*obwe*].

Although Louis XIV had invaded the Dutch Republic in 1672 and was only just prevented from conquering it, the Dutch too were interested in Lully's works, which were regularly performed in Holland from 1677. Lully's operas, libretti and collections of *airs* and instrumental pieces were in fact published in Amsterdam. Hautboys, we can assume, were probably known there from at least this time. And as early as 1679, French hautboy players arrived in Madrid. They were accompanying Marie-Louise d'Orléans, niece of Louis XIV, who had gone into virtual exile by marrying King Charles II of Spain.[6] At the time, however, Spain was apparently not disposed to accept foreign musicians, and the French players soon returned to France. A cold reception also awaited another group of French players who moved to Madrid in 1702; they remained only until 1705. Spain's reluctance to adopt the hautboy, a symbol of French culture, may also have had to do with the fact that the country was politically antagonistic to France. For similar reasons, Vienna was also slow to adopt the new instrument. French woodwinds are first documented in the Habsburg Empire in the mid-1690s. Although court composers included the hautboy in pieces from 1698 and 1699, hautboists did not officially join the court Capelle at Vienna until 1701. In Switzerland, especially Bern with its close relation to France, hautboys were adopted by at least 1695.[7]

In the patchwork of German states, the hautboy came into being during the period in which they were rebuilding themselves after the devastation of a terrible war. From 1680, French hautboists started to be engaged by a number of German courts. Mattheson wrote from Hamburg (1713:268): 'The eloquent *Hautbois* (*Ital.* Oboe) are to the French, and now also to us, what shawms [Schalmeyen] (which were called *Piffari* by the old musicians) used to be in Germany, although they are constructed somewhat differently.'

Most hautboy players doubled on strings, and could thus provide a chamber orchestra as well as a wind band. French influence was also important in German military circles, and officers took up the custom of sponsoring 'French' hautboy bands.

When it arrived in all these places, the hautboy was in the hands of Frenchmen, who immediately began to train local woodwind players. Resident makers also lost no time making copies of the French models. The Amsterdamer Richard Haka was making what he called 'franse Haubois' (French hautboys) by at least 1685, and in the 1690s excellent instruments were being made in Nuremberg by Christoph Denner and Johann Schell, in Leipzig by Andreas Bauer, and in London by Peter Bressan.

The form of the hautboy

Despite the clear distinctions that existed between French and Italian composition, and between harpsichords and violins in the north and south of Europe, the hautboy's form and playing style was decidedly international until at least 1730. Hautboys were small, portable, and inexpensive compared with violins and harpsichords, and were relatively easy to replace as new models appeared. Players frequently travelled or moved to other countries, taking with them new techniques of playing and instruments of the latest design. Considering how quickly tastes changed, professional players were thus likely to have state of the art equipment,[8] regardless of its country of origin. As for playing style, the 'French' way of playing had been the model from the beginning, with French players teaching the instrument; it was simply the normal way to play the hautboy, and gradually came to be seen as the international standard.

Considering the number of eighteenth-century makers and players still known today, there must once have been a great many hautboys, certainly many times the number of instruments that survive at present (of hautboys probably made before 1760, fewer than 400 are now known). Since designs changed so quickly and most hautboys were probably played for no more than a generation, obsolete models were not old enough to be valuable as antiques; with no monetary value and no use, most of them were probably thrown away.

In distinguishing the different models of hautboy that existed before about 1800, the easiest aspects to compare are the differences in outer profiles, such as the placement and number of beads (or rings) in the turning, or the way the keys are fashioned. These characteristics, which were originally inspired by architectural mouldings, are shown in ills 14 to 17. There are certain features like the tenon-socket

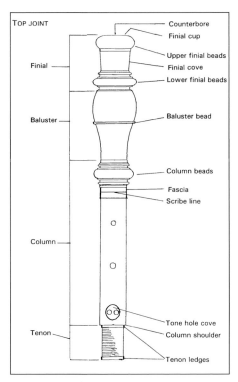

14. Diagram of top joint.

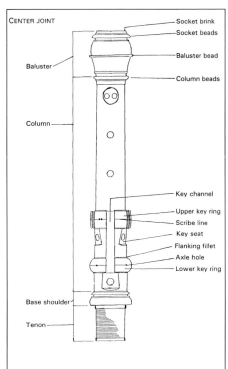

15. Diagram of centre joint.

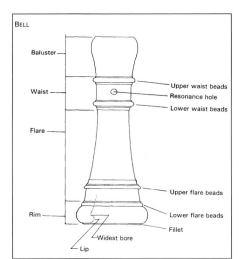

16. Diagram of bell.

17. Diagram of keys.

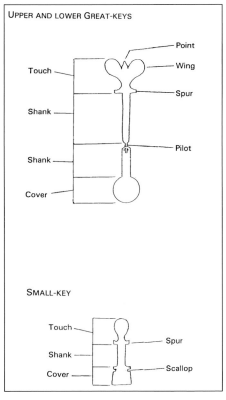

connections between the joints, the columns (the straight sections along which the tone-holes are bored), and the rings for mounting the keys that most or all models have in common. On the hautboy shown in ills 14 to 17 (as on most antique instruments) there is also a certain design unity achieved through the use of balusters of similar shape at the top of each joint, and the larger beads that give the top and bottom of the instrument a sense of conclusion.[9]

In ills 14 to 17, only one particular type of turning style is shown. While each individual maker had his own idiosyncrasies that could change over time, there were more general patterns of design, and when these patterns were shared by more than one maker, they can be regarded as *types*. Surviving hautboys made between the end of the seventeenth century and the beginning of the nineteenth were made in many different styles, but for the sake of comprehension they can be divided into nine general types.[10] Examples of these types are shown in ill. 18. Let us consider them briefly now.

Type A1 hautboys were made before the form was completely standardized, like the one in ill. 12. As might be expected of these earliest hautboys, few survive. Jan Bouterse (1999) has suggested that it might be possible to discover common roots by comparing the traits that the earliest makers have in common, especially those that do not occur later (like the *fascie* below the top column beads).[11] Hautboys of Type A1 do not seem to have been made after about the end of the seventeenth century. The last evidence of their existence is a work of art dated 1704.[12]

We know of some fifteen hautboy makers active in France in the last decades of the seventeenth century who could have made the Type A1.[13] Three of the more interesting were Jean-Jacques Rippert, Pierre Naust and Nicolas (Colin) Hotteterre. Rippert, who is survived by two hautboys (both magnificent specimens), was described by a contemporary as one of the best woodwind makers in Paris.[14] He had been working 'a long time' by 1696. Naust took over Fremont's workshop in about 1692.[15] I own Naust's one intact surviving hautboy, which is an excellent instrument, and plays very much like the single surviving hautboy by Colin Hotteterre (now in Brussels).[16] Colin Hotteterre was called a 'master' player as well as instrument maker in 1692; besides running a large atelier, Hotteterre was the solo hautboist at the Opéra from some time before 1704, and his instruments were played by the hautboists of Handel's opera orchestra in London (the bassoons were made by Rippert).[17]

Although these makers could well have made Type A1 hautboys, the instruments that survive them are the more standard Type A2, as represented by ill. 18b. This is the profile generally thought of as typically Baroque, and was relatively standardized until about 1730. Type A2 oboes were soon being copied in other countries. There were several excellent makers of hautboys in England before 1700. Peter Bressan (1663–1731, originally Pierre Jaillard) had moved to London from France in 1688.[18] Bressan was an hautboist, and became one of the leading recorder makers of his day. None of his hautboys is extant, but James Talbot measured one in some detail in the 1690s, and his notes on it survive. Shortly after Bressan's arrival, two English hautboy makers set up shop: Joseph Bradbury (p.1689) and Thomas Stanesby (1691). Both are survived by superb hautboys, and both had been apprenticed in the 1680s to Thomas

a) type A1   b) type A2   c) type A3   d) type B   e) type C   f) type E

g) type D1   h) type D2   j) type D3   18. The nine general hautboy types.

Garrett (who may himself have been a maker of French-type woodwinds).[19] Bressan and Stanesby made instruments until the early 1730s, and Stanesby's son Thomas Jr established his workshop in about 1713. In Italy in the period before about 1730, the only maker presently known is Giovanni Maria Anciuti of Milan (fl. c.1709–p.1740), who may have learned the trade from a French hautboist resident in Milan, Aléxis Saint-Martin.

By far the greatest number of the earliest surviving hautboys – more than two-thirds – were made in the city of Nuremberg. Nuremberg had traditionally been a centre of wind instrument making, famous all over Europe. In 1696, two of its better-known craftsmen, Christoph Denner and Johann Schell, requested permission from the city to make and sell new models of 'French musical instruments'.[20] Denner's hautboys resemble the one shown in Mignard's painting of 1691 (ill. 19). Many early Nuremberg hautboys, including about half of Denner's as well as those of his colleague Benedikt Gahn, were apparently pitched at A + 1 (which was a holdover of the old traditional instrumental pitch described by Praetorius in 1618, and was still common on most church organs in Germany in the eighteenth century). A substantial fraction of Denner's surviving recorders are also at this high pitch. Two of Denner's sons became woodwind makers; his elder son Jacob (born before 1681), who was a contemporary of Sebastian Bach and Telemann, became one of the best-known hautboists in Germany in his day. Jacob Denner also made instruments that are prized by players today; he may have supplied hautboys to a number of other important players in his own time.[21] He died prematurely in 1735, but his younger brother David worked until the middle of the century. There were several other important Nuremberg makers in this period, including Wilhelm Oberlender Sr and Jr, whose instruments resemble those of the Denners and Gahn.[22]

The other important centre of German woodwind making in this period was Leipzig.[23] The dean of Leipzig's woodwind makers was probably Andreas Bauer (b.1636), who worked until 1717. Given his age, he may have been the teacher of some or all the later Baroque makers of the city, including Johann Poerschman, Heinrich Eichentopf, Cornelius Sattler, and his son Gottfried. It is among these

19. Pierre Mignard, 1691: detail from 'Sainte Cécile jouant de la harpe' (oil on canvas, 74 x 56 cm).

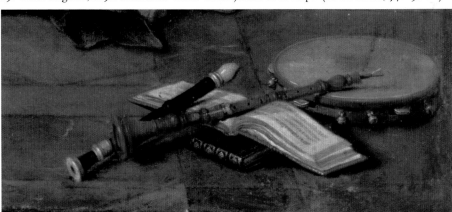

makers that the inventors of the hautbois d'amour and oboe da caccia are to be found (see below). It is a reasonable assumption that they also supplied the instruments for which Bach wrote his miraculous obbligatos when he arrived in Leipzig in the 1720s.

By the late seventeenth century there was a thriving woodwind-making industry in the Dutch Republic, based mostly in Amsterdam. Richard Haka, a Dutchman with English antecedents, founded a school of makers that included Coenraad Rijkel, Jan Steenbergen and Abraham van Aardenberg, all of whom are survived by a number of instruments. There were at least ten other makers, and the number of surviving Dutch hautboys from this period is quite out of proportion to the small size of the country. Considering the relatively few players who seem to have been active in the Republic, it seems that some German, English and even French hautboists must have played Dutch hautboys.

The other hautboy type that was current before the turn of the century was the A3, associated with some Dutch makers (see ill. 18c). Its attributes are a short bell and unusually sharp flares at the finial and bell. Type A3 is a Dutch development, but Dutch makers also made Type A2 hautboys.[24] Only a few of the Type A3s are first-class musical instruments, although many, like those of the Richters, are elaborately finished with rich materials (ebony, ivory and silver) and elaborate decorations. Type A3 was made from the late seventeenth century until possibly as late as the 1760s.

The workshop of J. H. Rottenburgh, who worked from about 1700, was in Brussels. Rottenburgh's instruments are excellent, and his hautboys have a similar acoustic profile to those of Rippert and Naust;[25] they are wide-bored and the tone-holes are relatively small. Rottenburgh worked until about 1735, and his workshop was continued by his three sons.

Among the acoustical properties that give an hautboy its characteristic feel in playing are the 'choke' diameter, the bore length, and the aggregate tone-hole size. The *choke* (or *minimum bore*) is a short cylindrical segment at the top of the hautboy's bore, roughly at the height of the baluster. The bore of the hautboy's top section is reamed not only from the bottom but from the top as well. The relatively short top taper (into which the reed fits) is known as the *counterbore*, since it gets narrower as it descends, unlike the rest of the hautboy's bore, which expands. On surviving originals, the choke ranges in diameter from 4.4 to 7.15 mm; the average is 5.95 mm. Although it is far from the only factor, sounding length, or SL, is an indication of the pitch of an hautboy; the SL is the distance from the top of the instrument to the middle of hole 8 (the hole under the Great-key).[26] Hautboys can also be compared by their aggregate tone-hole size, which is the total of the diameters of the open tone-holes 1, 2, 5 and 6 (these are the holes that are not twinned). The contrast in playing qualities between hautboys with smaller or larger tone-holes is quite noticeable; a small-holed instrument will have a more defined pitch level, crisper intonation and sharper differentiation of notes, whereas larger tone-holes produce a more fluid intonation and a higher pitch. Tone-hole size is independent of minimum bore size; there are original hautboys with small bores and large tone-holes, and vice-versa. Holes were generally undercut (that is, the end of the tone-hole that enters the bore was wider than the external hole), which affected intonation, response, and tone quality. All these features influence the playing characteristics of hautboys.

Because pitch generally went up in the course of the eighteenth century, it is possible that tone-holes on antique examples were enlarged at some point to raise the instrument's pitch. When an hautboy is raised in pitch, the lowest notes tend to remain flat, so in order to have played an instrument higher than it was originally intended, holes 7 and 8 (the ones closed by keys) would have had to be enlarged. Hole 8 averages 7.5 mm in diameter on antique hautboys, although Talbot in c.1692 (normally a reliable source) gave 5.3 for the Bressan he measured.

On an hautboy, as on any oboe, the reed is the most important component in the production of sound (e.g., tone, response, flexibility, pitch, tuning, and so on). A player using the same reed on different hautboys would therefore find many of the same playing characteristics. This means that the provenance and date of an hautboy are less important to how it performs than those of a harpsichord, violin or traverso. If only the body of an hautboy survives, effectively less than half of the functional 'system' of the instrument is preserved.

Original reeds and information about them are therefore of prime importance to an understanding of the hautboy, and it is thus unfortunate that neither of these survive from before about 1770, when Baroque hautboys were no longer current.[27] Reeds are delicate, and their importance is not obvious to the layman. It is rare to find old ones that still work (and even if they do, they must first be soaked in water). There is also very little written evidence on how reeds were made, partly because it is a difficult subject to put down on paper, and partly because tutors were addressed to amateurs who would have bought their reeds. In any case, the processes were often regarded as part of instrument making, and as such were both ignored by players and protected as trade secrets.

The closest we can come are staples (the brass part of the reed) that have been found with hautboys by Anciuti (dated 1718) and Stanesby Jr. Their dimensions are as follows:

	Total L	Top ID	Bottom ID	Taper
Anciuti[28]	43.7 mm	1.2/2.7	about 5.13	.073
Stanesby Jr [29]	43	about 1.5/3.5	5.0	.058

There is no way to be certain that these staples were actually used on the instruments at the time.

Talbot's manuscript of c.1692 also gives sufficiently detailed dimensions to allow a reconstruction of a late seventeenth-century hautboy reed (see Haynes 2000b). Otherwise, the closest to substantive information on reeds that survives comes from the graphic arts, which give an idea not only of proportions and shapes of reeds, but of real dimensions that can be deduced by comparing the instruments in the pictures with similar surviving instruments.[30] Appendix 1 lists dimensions for ten reeds from works of art dating from 1691 to c.1767. The dimensions vary widely; tip width goes from 7.2 to 16.7, for instance. It seems clear from a number of indirect indications that reed-making techniques in this period were at least as divergent as they remain today (cf. the remarkable variety of reed types for the French Conservatoire oboe described in Ledet 1981). Techniques for making recorder windways, labia and blocks (an art analogous and related to reedmaking) also varied considerably from maker to maker.

The first step in making an hautboy reed is to *gouge* the cane, that is, to scrape from the inside longitudinally with the grain, removing all but the outermost layers of the cane. Since the early nineteenth century, gouges have been of uniform thickness from one end of the piece of cane to the other, but it is possible that early hautboy reeds were made with a tapered gouge, which would have been easy when cane was gouged by hand. With a tapered gouge, the cane is thinner in the area that becomes the tip. There is no documentation of tapered gouging on hautboy reeds, but it is described in several bassoon tutors from the late eighteenth and early nineteenth centuries.[31] The end result of tapered gouging is that the hardest outer layers of the cane form the tip, whereas with even gouging the tip is made up of softer strata from the inner layers. A harder tip produces a reed with a brighter tone. These variables would have been influenced, of course, by the general hardness of the cane that was used; a generally harder cane might not have needed a tapered gouge.

It is partly because no original reeds survive that it is difficult to know for certain at which pitches original hautboys played. This ambiguity is compounded by the fact that notes on the same hautboy can quite plausibly be 'bent' to accommodate pitch levels as much as 40 cents apart (almost a quarter tone). Not only do different players produce different pitches, but the same player and instrument can produce different pitches by using reeds of different dimensions. There is in fact no objective method of being certain of the historical pitch of an hautboy, although estimates can be made by taking into account:

- known historical pitch standards of the time and place where the instrument was made and/or played
- instruments by the same maker that give more reliable pitches, such as recorders, traversos, and clarinets
- comparisons of bore lengths of different hautboys by the same maker.[32]

Alternative top joints for altering pitch became common in the later eighteenth century, although they can already be documented from the 1720s; an instrument dated 1722 by the Milanese maker G. M. Anciuti has two top joints. Giuseppe Sammartini, a well-known hautboy virtuoso from Milan, probably played such an instrument. Sir John Hawkins, in his *History*, told the following story about him:

> About the year 1735 an advertisement appeared [in London] in the public papers, offering a reward of ten guineas for a hautboy-reed that had been lost. It was conjectured to be Martini's, and favoured the opinion that he had some secret in preparing or meliorating the reeds of his instrument, though none could account for the offer of a reward so greatly disproportionable to the utmost conceivable value of the thing lost. It seems that the reed was found, and brought to the owner, but in such a condition as rendered it useless.[33]

Since Sammartini could probably have made another reed, the size of this reward seems out of proportion to the object lost. Could the missing article have been something more than a reed? As it turns out, this question was answered by Redmond Simpson, a well-known London hautboist of the next generation, who added in the margin of his copy of Hawkins (now at the Public Library in Minneapolis):

> In the note which says a reward of 10 Guineas was offered for a Hautboy reed that had been lost, it was the upper joint of his Hautboy, for which he was inconsolable 'till he got one that suited him. The lat[t]er was purchased at his sale by the late D. of Ancaster for 20 Guineas who gave it to me. It is still in my possession.

Sammartini may well have needed to use an alternative top joint to offset the pitch difference between Milan and London.[34]

A new kind of hautboy with a shorter bore and higher pitch (A−1, or about A−415) appeared in Germany and Italy at the beginning of the century and by about 1715 all over Europe. Aside from the change of pitch and general character, these shorter hautboys used a different fingering for c3.[35] Thus, even though the outward turning patterns did not change (Type A2 in both cases), we are probably justified in speaking of a new design of instrument.

Playing the hautboy

The self-help instruction books for hautboy that began appearing in the 1680s were aimed at amateurs, since professional musicians usually got their training from older family members or through an apprenticeship. Most of these tutors are quite elementary and general, but they are among the few bits of evidence on early technique that have come down to us. By far the most complete and insightful written information on playing the hautboy was in Joachim Quantz's *Essai d'une méthode pour apprendre à jouer de la Flûte Traversière*, which appeared in 1752 in both French and German. Despite its title, the *Essai* is much more than a flute tutor; only five of the eighteen chapters deal specifically with flute technique, the rest being on more general musical subjects. Quantz himself played hautboy in his early career, and recommended his book to hautboists. Although, like every other book of the period, it speaks little about specific techniques for playing the hautboy, it is full of eminently practical advice for making music, reflecting the ideas of a gifted and thoughtful woodwind player of the 1730s, 40s and 50s.[36]

Tutors mention posture and bearing. Hotteterre le Romain's advice on traverso playing was probably applicable to hautboy as well: 'If you play standing, stand firm, with ye left foot a little advanc'd, and rest the weight of your Body on the right leg, and all without any constraint.'[37] An example of the stance that was considered correct can be seen in ills 20 and 21. The hautboy was normally held fairly high. Hotteterre (1707:44) suggested that 'You should hold the hautboy more or less like the recorder, but with the difference that it should be held even higher. This will make your head level, and you will place your hands high.' Quantz (1752:VI/

20. Johann Christoph Weigel, c.1720: plate from *Musicalisches Theatrum*.

21. Anonymous, c.1746: front plate
for *The Compleat tutor for the hautboy.*

Suppl./§6) was concerned with the effect of the angle on sound: 'In an orchestra, the
hautboy player should hold his instrument up as much as he can. If he sticks it below
the stand, the notes lose their force.' It was at Dresden that Quantz played the
hautboy. An hautboist is depicted (ill. 22) in the Dresden Hofcapelle (possibly
Christian Richter) playing in the pit for a performance of Lotti's opera *Teofane* in
1719; interestingly, he is indeed holding his instrument above the stand.

With the lighter reed that is necessary to produce clear cross-fingerings, and
less breath pressure, an hautboy embouchure required less muscle power than the
Conservatoire oboe. This meant that embouchures could be set and released both
quickly and frequently, and as a result, hautboy players may have given the
impression of being under less strain than modern players of the Conservatoire
oboe. Many early depictions of embouchures show relatively little tension (see ill.
23).

As for the relative force of the hautboy's sound, Banister remarked in 1695 (ii),
'With a good Reed [the hautboy] goes as easie and as soft as the *Flute*' (meaning, of
course, the recorder).[38] He added that at the same time it was 'Majestical and Stately,
and not much Inferiour to the Trumpet'. In orchestras, where violins and hautboys
frequently played the same line, the ratio of violins to hautboys ranged from 2:1 to as
much as 11:1. One would therefore assume that hautboys were louder than violins, or

at least that their sound carried better in large spaces. But much of the hautboy's most important repertoire combined it with a single voice (in arias) or other instruments (in chamber works), indicating that hautboys were – or could be – similar in volume to other instruments.

Mutes were sometimes called for in hautboy music, most of it German.[39] A mute consisted of a wad of paper (Baroque paper being rather thick and made of rag), a dampened sponge, or cotton or wool, placed in the bell below the resonance holes. Mutes were used for the musical effect they gave: they were often associated with death and mourning; they also had practical uses, as they not only softened the volume of the hautboy but changed the tone quality.

Eight fingering charts survive from the period prior to the emergence of the Classical hautboy. They date from 1688 to c.1758,[40] and some of them were recycled many times. They are collated in Appendix 2.

The normal range of the hautboy was c1 to d3. The c1 is documented from the 1660s, and Bismantova gave a fingering for d3 in 1688. At the beginning of the eighteenth century, Hotteterre implied that the hautboy occasionally played higher.[41] Bach, who was one of the more demanding composers for the hautboy, was unwilling to go beyond d3 for hautboy (see music ex. 3.1), although he did call for higher notes on the hautbois d'amour (this was perhaps to compensate for the fact that the

22. C. H. J. Fehling. Detail of the orchestra, left, from *Elévation du grand théatre roial, pris de face.* The Dresden opera house is shown 'am Zwinger' during a performance of Lotti's *Teofane* in 1719.

23. Antoine Watteau, c.1714. Head of hautboist in *Huit études de têtes* (chalk and pencil drawing, 26.7 x 39.7 cm).

instrument sounded a minor third lower than the treble hautboy – its fingered d3 was thus only a sounding b2).[42]

Higher notes began to be more frequently requested with the development of the new smaller-bore instruments, which produced them more readily. Higher notes started appearing in about the middle of the eighteenth century, first in Italy. The first known f3 occurs in Matteo Bissoli's sonata, probably written about 1750; the piece also contains several e3s. In his surviving portrait (see ill. 33), Bissoli holds a Type C hautboy.[43] A higher range and tessitura had become normal by about 1770, when most hautboys were narrow-bored.

On a woodwind instrument, the scale that uses its natural fingerings (as opposed to cross-fingerings and half-holing) is called the primary scale. On the hautboy, the scale that uses all natural fingerings is D major, beginning on the six-fingered note, d1. From the point of view of fingering combinations, D major is by far the simplest and easiest scale on the hautboy; to play it is simply a matter of starting on the d1 and lifting one finger after the other. As tonalities get further away from D major, adding accidentals to this primary scale, they begin using more cross-fingerings and half-holes, thus making them more complicated to play.

The most awkward and uncertain fingering on the hautboy is probably the one that produced G sharp/A flat (123). As Vandenbroek observed in 1793, '[The tonalities

Ex. 3.1 Bach, BWV 35/1, bar 108. The upper staff is the hautboy part, the lower is the first violin.

of] E flat and A major are overly difficult as a result of the A flat or G sharp in both octaves'.[44]

Cross-fingerings and half-holes were not the only fingering issues. When the hautboy ventured into four sharps and four flats, the player began using the sequence d♭2–e♭2 (or c♯2–d♯2). Each of these notes was normally played with one of the two keys, and moving the little finger between the two keys without inadvertently sounding the note in between, d2, was nearly impossible. The usual solution was to play c♯/d♭2 with the alternative fingering 'all open', but it was flat as a d♭, and had an unsavoury sound.

The easiest tonalities were thus the ones with the fewest cross-fingerings and half-holes, and those that demanded neither 123 or the sequence d♭2–e♭2. The keys that tended to avoid these problems were D, G, C, F and B flat major. In other words, the keys on either side of C major with up to two sharps or flats were the most effective. It was thus at the appearance of three to four sharps or flats that fingering problems began to be noticeable.[45] The hautboy's surviving repertoire in its totality centres on F major/D minor.[46]

It is interesting that the hautboy shared an almost identical fingering with the traverso, and yet in the many eighteenth-century pieces that survive in versions for the two instruments, the hautboy version is normally written a step lower than the one for traverso[47] (the best-known example is probably the Mozart concerto, in C for hautboy and D for traverso[48]). It seems that composers wrote for traverso systematically a tone higher than for hautboy. This is presumably because both instruments projected better that way, since the low register of the traverso is introverted, whereas that of the hautboy tends to be too strong. Also, dropping the hautboy tonality a step had the effect of giving it two more cross-fingerings than the traverso (as there are none in D major, one in G, two in C, three in F, and so on).[49] The hautboy was thus more often cast in the darker, covered sound of cross-fingered tonalities. This may have been to balance its brasher, brighter tone. The reverse was true of the traverso: the clearer, more open sound of tonalities that used simple fingerings helped it project.

Because it sold better, the hautboy's solo literature was often published in collections for 'traverso, violin or hautboy'; this was true even of music written by well-known hautboists. Hautboy players had thus to choose what worked best on their instrument, and (considering its relation to the traverso) one possibility was to transpose down a step. This was occasionally useful not only because the traverso and violin preferred sharper tonalities than the hautboy (the violin's open strings were G, D, A, E, all favouring sharp keys) but because they both went easily up to e3, one note higher than the hautboy's top note. The hautboy, on the other hand, could play a note lower than the traverso (whose lowest note was d1). Thus much of this music existed in keys more suited to traverso and violin, but sounded better on hautboy a tone lower, thereby producing a more appropriate range and moving the key signature flatwards.

Most charts either fail to offer a distinct fingering for low c♯1/d♭1 or suggest half-closing the Great-key (which is idealistic at best). Still, we have to assume that some hautboists were able to produce the note; it was regularly requested in exposed situations,[50] and at this time compositions were normally written with specific players in mind. The fingering 123 456 8 is tuned on many original hautboys so it sounds between c♯1 and c1, thus potentially offering both notes to players adept at lipping (that is, correcting pitch with the embouchure).[51]

Woodwinds often used special fingerings for trills and other ornaments. These 'false trill' fingerings (Hotteterre called them 'borrowed' fingerings) served two purposes: not only were ornaments easier to play, they had a clearer sound. Some trills are blurry and muffled using the normal fingerings, as for instance A–B flat, and difficult for the fingers (moving between the fingerings 12 and 1 3). False trills used one basic principle: they involved moving only a single finger. For A–B flat, as an example, Hotteterre suggested beginning with the normal fingering for the B flat appoggiatura (1 3) and then playing the trill as for A to B natural, beating hole 2. False trills produce an interval larger than the regular notes; if this is then corrected with the embouchure,[52] it produces a clearer interval than the normal fingerings.

Something the hautboy can do better than any other instrument is to make extreme and sudden changes of dynamics, covering a range from barely audible to very loud; Banister's comment quoted above reckoned the hautboy's sound to be as soft as the recorder and 'not much Inferiour to the Trumpet'. These nuances were useful for the music of the period. Composers in the eighteenth century were not in the habit of marking dynamics in parts, nor were musicians in need of being told; that was a custom that came in with what is now called 'prescriptive notation'. As a kind of exercise, Quantz (with some apparent reluctance) did write out an example of the dynamics he considered appropriate for an adagio. There were twenty-two changes in the first two bars alone.[53] This was highly unusual at the time, comparable to writing out music in detail for a jazz musician now. But Quantz's example is interesting to us now, as it gives an idea of the subtleties of dynamic practice in the early to mid-eighteenth century.

The use of unequal, paired tonguing already had a long history on woodwind instruments by the time the hautboy was developed.[54] Many wind tutors described articulation syllables and unequal tonguing. Although the practice is often thought of nowadays as particularly French, the historical evidence does not associate it with any national style or specific language; in all probability Bach and Vivaldi would have known unequal tonguing as well as did Hotteterre and Montéclair.[55] These articulations were still being described by woodwind tutors from various countries into the early nineteenth century.[56]

Paired tonguings consisted of alternating two contrasting tongue movements, often *tu* and *ru* (the latter syllable was pronounced with a dental *r* as in modern Spanish, so the tonguing pair effectively consisted of *tu* and *du*). Combining contrasting tongue movements like *tu* and *ru* gave a woodwind player two technical possibilities that were difficult with the single tongue: speed and contrasted accents. The rebounded tongue motion helped sustain extended passages in quick tempos, and it created strong and weak stress in slower movements.

Paired tonguing was related to the common practice of playing *notes inégales* (playing equally-written subdivisions of the beat unequally, like a shuffle rhythm in jazz).[57] Most players today use the term *notes inégales* to mean the iambic lilt represented by a word like 'below' (music ex. 3.2a), but in the eighteenth century the concept of *notes inégales* was broader. It included not only the *pointed* inequality of the slower iambic kind (as in the words 'Baroque' or 'enough') but also *lombardic* inequality (the 'Scotch snap', which put the accent on the first syllable as in the words 'money' or 'forest' – see music ex. 3.2b). Thus the two basic kinds of paired tonguing were lombardic and pointed. In lombardic tonguing the *tu* was played on the beat (*tú-ru*); it was used for quick tempos and was primarily meant as a technical aid. In pointed tonguing (*tu-rú*) it was the *ru* that came on the beat with a pickup *tu*, and its main use was as an expressive device in slower movements. On the cornett, recorder and traverso (for which most tonguing instructions were written), the *tu* and *ru* were performed very much like they were spoken. On the hautboy, however, the reed prevented the tongue from touching the teeth or roof of the mouth in the way described in the instruction books, so (although the principles remained the same) it was the reed that the tongue touched.[58]

Ex. 3.2 Examples of the two basic kinds of paired tonguing: (a) pointed tonguing; (b) lombardic tonguing.

Eighteenth-century vibrato is distinguished from modern practice in two ways: it was used intermittently, as an ornament; and (except for special effects) it was not produced with the breath. Although the kind of breath vibrato used at the end of the twentieth century started to appear as early as the 1910s, recordings show that continuous vibrato did not become widely used until the 1940s.[59] None of the early wind tutors speak of an uninterrupted vibrato, since it would not have made sense to apply an ornament continuously.[60]

The kind of vibrato used on the hautboy was operated by the fingers, and was called the *flattement* or 'lesser trill'. In England it was known as the 'softening', which captures its effect of briefly unfocusing a note's tone quality. It was produced much like trills, but involved half-closing holes or shaking a finger over a hole (notes like D and E flat that involved closing all the finger-holes were 'softened' by shaking the entire instrument). Vibrato as it was used at this time demanded degrees of intensity; as a note became louder, a flattement became faster or wider, or both, and as the dynamic decreased, the vibrato became less intense. Control of both speed and amplitude in vibrato is needed in seventeenth- and eighteenth-century music because it involves many quick turns of direction, accompanied by complex dynamic shading. With practice, it is a lot easier to control changes in intensity with fingers than (as in modern vibrato) with the diaphragm or throat. In its role as a species of mild trill, the flattement was frequently performed on longer notes with the *messa di voce*, or swell, and was also used on last notes of phrases to suggest continuation (as for repeats). Flattements were rarely marked; when they were, they were wavy horizontal lines above notes.[61]

The flattement is documented in the second half of the seventeenth century and was in use into the mid-nineteenth century. Like *notes inégales*, it was not limited to France (as is sometimes supposed) but was common all over Europe, and there is every reason to think that Telemann, Handel and Albinoni heard it regularly.

The other more specialized forms of vibrato on the hautboy were the *tremolo* and *glissando*. The tremolo was a group of repeated notes of the same pitch under a slur; it amounted to a breath vibrato, but the defining characteristic of the tremolo was that it beat in the rhythm of the piece in which it was used (usually eighth-notes). Bach used the tremolo regularly for hautboy; examples include the oboe da caccia solo 'Zerfließe, mein Herze' in the St John Passion, and the remarkable recitative 'So geht denn hin', BWV 248/18, with two hautbois d'amour and two oboes da caccia playing piano tremolos.[62] The glissando was a special form of the tremolo: it used the same marking, a wavy horizontal line, but instead of remaining on the same note it went up or down by half-steps; it, too, is often found in Bach's scores.

The hautboy did not escape criticism by contemporaries for its technical limitations. To 'split' a note, as sometimes happened because of accidentally playing in two registers at once (or in the one not intended), was known in France as *canarder* (literally, 'to duck', as in the cry of a duck). Francoeur wrote of the hautboy in 1772 (13): 'This instrument is not perfect in all its notes. Some [hautboys] exist that no performer can manage to play perfectly in tune. . . .' Vivaldi was evidently aware of the hautboy's limitations in playing passages with quick and large leaps, because when he adapted some of his bassoon concertos for hautboy, he simplified such passages. Scheibe may have been thinking of similar problems when he wrote: 'In a solo for the violin, a composer can be as extravagant as nature will allow, in order to show off the instrument. But a solo for the hautboy must be more singing, because this instrument is very similar to the voice.'[63]

The music and its players

The surviving solo and chamber repertoire for hautboy – up until the shift to the keyed oboe around 1800 – includes something over 10,000 pieces.[64] These are works officially for hautboy – works that mention the instrument, for instance, on the title page. But hautboists probably adapted other pieces to their use as well. Obviously, there isn't room to survey all this literature here.

The dearth of records in the hautboy's earliest years affects our understanding of its first repertoire; at present the first music known to have been written for the hautboy are pieces in Lully's *Trios de la chambre* (LWV 35), an anthology of fifty-four movements.[65] These nine 'Trios' (single movements) were written for the Mousquetaires in 1667 for performance in the open air at Fontainebleau Palace;[66] they may have been designed to demonstrate the qualities of the new hautboy. They were followed by the trios in *Le Bourgeois gentilhomme* of 1670 mentioned above, the first time Lully had asked for hautboys since May 1664. These were probably played by the court ensemble known as the Hautbois et Musettes de Poitou. In the years that followed, Lully regularly included hautboys in his operas. The military début of the new model may have occurred in the same year, 1670, with a new march and drum roll by Lully preserved in the Philidor Manuscript (Sandman 10/M1, LWV 44). This march was written by order of the King, and played by the hautboy band of the newly-created Régiment du Roy.

For this brand-new instrument, printed music was rare, and players often resorted to instrumental arrangements of well-known operas; a number of manuscripts of this type survive, for one to three generic treble instruments and a bass. One of the earliest collections, apparently performed originally at court, is entitled *Livre de Triôts appartenants à [Nicolas] Dieupart Fluste et Cromôrne ordin.^{re} de la Chambre du Roy. 1680.*[67] It consists of six collections of movements from Lully's *tragédies* and *ballets*, some pieces by Louis Grabu, two *Trios* by Nicolas Lebègue, and other miscellaneous pieces.

Woodwind players may also have adapted vocal chamber music of the day, such as the *Airs sérieux* by Michel Lambert (see chapter 2).[68] Hotteterre le Romain, for instance, wrote *Airs sérieux* in a collection that appeared in 1701;[69] his later *Airs et brunettes* were for two or three traversos without bass, and were arranged from seventeenth-century pieces by Lambert, Lully, Boësset and others that had originally included a bass part. When they first began playing in the 1680s, Hotteterre and other players who were later to become important performers and composers of woodwind music might have used this material, with or without the bass. These exquisite songs have much to offer the enterprising player. They apparently served as models for some of the movements of the early woodwind solo collections by Philidor, Hotteterre and La Barre (it was La Barre who considered the breakthrough to 'perfection' in music to have been realized by seventeenth-century writers of chamber airs). The slow movements in a number of Hotteterre's suites resemble such airs.[70]

Among the finest surviving examples of pieces for treble instrument and continuo in classic Lullian style are those of Robert de Visée, guitar instructor to King Louis XIV. Visée's pieces, mostly written by the 1680s, were originally for guitar, but he later set them for 'Dessus et Baße'. Between 1694 and 1705, Visée performed frequently at court, and two of his colleagues were René Descoteaux[71] and Philippe Philbert,[72] members of the Hautbois et Musettes de Poitou, and the first musicians to hold positions as traverso players at court. Both played hautboy and recorder in the Chambre, so they might well have performed Visée's *Pièces* at court on all these instruments.

An early collection for 'toutes sortes d'instruments' were Hendrik Anders's *Trioos*, op. 1, published in Amsterdam in 1687. The 'trioos' are in the form of dances and short 'Sonatinas', and there are some airs by Lully at the end. As noted above, Lully's operas were regularly staged in Amsterdam in the 1680s, and were probably performed by French players.

In London, a *Collection of several simphonies and airs in three parts*, probably composed by Louis Grabu for two violins, flutes, or 'Hoe-boys' and continuo, was published by Nott in 1688.[73] It consists of eight trios in suite form; the music is of some interest, and resembles Purcell.

History by decade

THE 1690S

At the French court, the atmosphere changed noticeably in the 1690s. Lully had died in 1687. Grand pieces were no longer needed to promote the King's reputation, nor apparently was he any longer interested in them. Chamber concerts became the norm at court, often written by the players themselves. The first solos specially composed for the traverso and violin appeared in 1702 and 1704, but a repertoire specifically for hautboy never developed in France. What the hautboy played were the magnificent pieces for unspecified treble instruments that began to be published in the 1690s. The instrumentation of these pieces was usually left ambiguous, presumably on purpose. If instruments were named at all in chamber music, the usual formula was the one in Anders's and Grabu's collections: 'violins, flutes and hautboys'. This generic approach, known as *en symphonie* instrumentation, was parallel to the familiar choices of various bass instruments to play the continuo; the hautboy would be one of the possible treble instruments. A number of important works in the hautboy's repertoire are written *en symphonie*.[74]

There are numerous good French *symphonie* trios. The best collection is that of the famous gambist Marin Marais. Evidently written over the course of the last decades of the seventeenth century, Marais's six large trio-suites appeared in print in 1692. For musical content and scope of expression, no collection ever equalled Marais's, though Rebel's *Recueil de 12 sonates* (written in the 1690s) and Couperin's *Nations* (also partly from the same decade) came close.[75] The hautboy was not mentioned in Marais's earliest print, though almost everything in the trios is playable on the instrument, and hautboy is specified in later editions of the works; the original title page includes four hautboys, together with other instruments. Marais's trios can be telescoped, like most *symphonies*, all the way from a small ensemble of one to a part up to a large orchestra.

German music for hautboy from this decade consists of solo obbligatos with voice. As mentioned in the previous chapter, this was the earliest music to explore the unique sound and character of the solo hautboy. Arias using an hautboy in dialogue and imitation with a solo singer were novelties in the 1690s, not only because of the new hautboy, but because the singers for the first time were women.[76] Arias began to be composed regularly in this decade, the soprano and hautboy relating to each other much like the two treble parts of a trio sonata.

As early as the year of Lully's death, 1687, Steffani produced an aria with hautboy obbligato, 'Care soglie a voi mi porto'. It was written for the court at Munich, which had sent four of its young and promising musicians to Paris to study with one of the Hotteterres. 'Care soglie', which is in the opera *Alarico*, was no doubt written on their return. Its date qualifies it as the earliest hautboy solo at present known. Steffani wrote similar solos (usually for two hautboys with voice) for Hanover in 1689, 1692 and 1694, and for Hamburg in 1695. These not only represent the earliest true solo parts that feature the hautboy, but they are beautiful pieces as well.

There must have been accomplished players at a number of courts in Germany by the late 1680s, as Steffani's solos for hautboy suggest. Typical music played by instrumental ensembles and small orchestras in German courts in the 1690s was in the Lullian style, often consisting of pieces brought back from trips to France – orchestral suites, French dance movements, instrumental concertos, cantatas, and opera arias. Musical life in Hamburg was particularly lively and cosmopolitan in the 1690s. An opera house had been established some years before, and in about 1695 the Opera established permanent posts for hautboy players. The names of the players are not known, but they must have been good, because many excellent hautboy obbligatos were written for opera performances during the next few years (by Graupner, Steffani, Kusser, Handel, Mattheson and especially Keiser). Reinhard Keiser began producing his much-loved operas at Hamburg in 1694. Only 17 of his 60 to 65 operas survive; many of them contain superb and expressive solos for hautboy, in subtle interaction with singers. Johann Mattheson wrote of Keiser, 'In his treatment of instruments, especially the *Hautbois*, he was quite pleasing. . . .'[77] Sebastian Bach's approach to instrumental arias may well have been influenced by his visits to Hamburg in the first years of the eighteenth century, where he probably heard performances at the Hamburg Opera.

Braunschweig also had an opera. Its first known hautboy solo, by Kusser (who had studied the Lullian style in Paris), was performed in 1692.[78] A large number of obbligatos for hautboy survive from Braunschweig by von Wilderer, Österreich and Schürmann, so it is clear there were good players there.

Friedrich August I became Elector of Saxony in 1694, and in 1698 the Dresden court Capelle was reorganized, making the switch to French instruments. The two hautboists were Charles and Jean-Baptiste Henrion.[79] In 1699, Dresden secured the services of François La Riche (1662–c.1733).[80] La Riche is one of the extraordinary hautboy players of this period, and by chance we know more about him than most hautboists, thanks to the Talbot Manuscript, which noted the fingerings he used (in two different charts) and possibly his reed and instrument. Born in 1662 in Tournay (then part of France), by the age of twenty-three he was in England, where he began by playing for James II. He went on to have an active career in England, but (perhaps because of religious intolerance) eventually moved to the Catholic court of Dresden. At Dresden, La Riche was not only Hautbois de la Chambre but acted as an agent for the Elector in purchasing luxury goods from abroad, such as jewellery and horses; his salary (3200 Thaler per year) was two and a half times that of the Capellmeister, Heinichen.[81] La Riche was responsible for teaching several young players at Dresden who were later to become important hautboists; we know he taught Christian Richter, probably taught Michael Böhm, and possibly Caspar Gleditsch (Bach's solo hautboist at Leipzig).[82]

By the early 1690s, solo hautboy arias were also being heard in Venice, where hautboys were used in operas by Pollarolo and Perti.[83] Venice had been famous for its cornett makers, so it is symbolic that in this decade the hautboy took over the cornett's functions in the Capella of San Marco.[84] The hautboist at San Marco was Onofrio Penati (c.1662–1752),[85] who had made his Venetian debut, together with his younger violinist colleague, Antonio Vivaldi, on Christmas Day 1696.[86] The earliest regular player in Venice, Penati was the only hautboist permanently employed by San Marco during the early years of the eighteenth century, and his salary was by far the largest of any of its members.[87] Evidently there were other hautboy players in the city, and, by 1700, the ospedali were training foundling and orphan girls to be hautboists; several of them became teachers at their institutions, and Vivaldi was later to write a number of solos for them.

In London by the 1690s, musical performances to a paying public had become established and popular. Concerts were usually financed by subscription, and often took place in taverns. 'Music Rooms' were also used, such as Hickford's and the room in York Buildings, each of which held about 200 people. Hautboys were frequently heard in these concerts, 'to which for the reputation of the musick', as Roger North wrote, 'numbers of people of good fashion and quallity repaired'.[88] After 1689, musical posts at court were closed for religious reasons to many French wind players resident in London, so the public concerts were probably important to them as a means of livelihood.

In the early 1690s the United Company employed two hautboists to play Henry Purcell's operas and other large works; a complete hautboy band appeared in Purcell's *Dioclesian* in 1690. It is quite possible that La Riche served as Purcell's hautboy soloist, since he had no employment at court and was clearly an extraordinary player. The Purcell Society published the obbligato to 'O let me weep' (or 'The Plaint') from *The Fairy Queen* (1692) for violin, but it is now thought that this exquisite part was originally for hautboy.[89] The piece has traits in common with other hautboy obbligatos in *Come, ye sons of art, away* (1694) and *The Indian Queen* (1695). Purcell's odes also contain a number of hautboy solos.

In Holland, the Stadholder William III, having become king of England, returned for a visit in 1691. He brought with him a remarkable hautboy band that included La Riche, Bressan and Michel Granville[90] (formerly one of the Douze Grands Hautbois). In Amsterdam, Hendrik Anders founded a Collegium Musicum in 1698 that included Carl Rosier, who in 1697 had published an unusual collection of fourteen sonatas for trumpet or hautboy and strings 'ou tous hautbois' ('or all hautboys').

1700–1710

The eighteenth century was clearly the oboe's Golden Age of repertoire (I use the word 'oboe' deliberately here). Literally thousands of good chamber pieces and solos survive. This surely reflects the roles and reputation of the instrument at the time.

Between 1700 and 1710, two interesting collections of French solo suites and trios with continuo were published. Michel de La Barre's *Pièces*, op. 4, printed in 1702 and modelled on Marais's superb gamba solos, were the first solos to be published for traverso. In the last edition of these pieces (1710), the title page expands the instrumentation to include the violin and 'autres instrumens', which we take to include the hautboy (an instrument that La Barre played). These were among the best solos to appear in the early eighteenth century. And shortly afterwards, in 1708, Hotteterre le Romain published his *Premier livre de Pièces*. Hotteterre had played these pieces for Louis XIV, to whom he dedicated them. Although the *Pièces* were advertised for traverso, Hotteterre noted that they were suitable for any treble instrument. And indeed they all go well on the hautboy (the third and fifth suites work better down a step). Modelling their solos on vocal lines, woodwind players fashioned solos that were simple, graceful and dignified. 'A [French] singer's virtuosity was demonstrated by smoothness of style, sweetness of tone, elegance of phrasing and clarity of diction, rather than by vocal pyrotechnics', as Raynor put it.[91] Translated onto woodwind instruments, these same qualities demanded clarity of articulation, and precision and control of the fingers in executing ornaments. French music tends therefore to require a good technique, although it does not necessarily sound like it. As Quantz remarked, 'the small [French] ornaments require an even greater [finger-]speed than passagework'.[92] The 'speaking' style of French music contrasted in many ways with the more 'singing' quality typical of pieces in the Italian style.

Among the good *symphonie* collections of trios and quartets from this decade were those of La Barre and Charles Desmazures. La Barre published three books of *Pièces en trio* (1694, 1700, 1707), and these exist also in an interesting manuscript copy at Paris bound with Hotteterre's trios.[93] The manuscript is noteworthy because it has many more marked ornaments (such as the flattement) than the published versions. Desmazures's *Pièces de simphonie*, published in Marseilles in 1702, are also excellent. Being 'en symphonie' (see above), they can be performed by a band of hautboys, a quartet of different instruments, or an entire orchestra.

The hautboists in the orchestra of the Opéra were Colin Hotteterre (principal from before 1704 to 1727),[94] Julien Bernier (second and traverso from before 1704 to after 1719),[95] and Jean Rousselet (third from before 1704 to 1711).[96] From 1709, at the precocious age of thirteen, Esprit-Philippe Chédeville joined the Opéra orchestra. He played there until 1736; as well as playing hautboy, he was well known as a musette player and composer.[97]

The hautboy was by now well established in Italy. In 1709 a German hautboist named Ludwig ('Lodovico') Erdmann (fl. early 1690s–1759) entered the service of Prince Ferdinando de' Medici (b.1663), son and heir of the Grand Duke of Tuscany in Florence, and an active patron of music.[98] Erdmann had been in Italy for some time. He had played in Bologna at the turn of the century, and by 1706 was appointed to teach hautboy at the Pietà in Venice, where Vivaldi taught violin. The Pietà was one of several ospedali, Venetian institutions for girls of unknown parentage. The ospedali trained their residents to very high standards, and their musical performances were one of the attractions of the city. Vivaldi's earliest dated piece that includes the hautboy, RV 779, is a sonata written in about 1707 for violin, hautboy and organ, on the score of which the name of the hautboist, Pelegrina 'dall'Oboè', is written.[99] This piece was probably written during the time Erdmann was teaching at the Pietà, or just afterwards (when Pelegrina herself became the hautboy teacher there). Erdmann married a student at the Mendicanti, one of the other ospedali[100] (her name is not known, but it might have been Barbara, who taught hautboy there).

At Florence, Erdmann played operas by Perti in 1709 and 1710[101] and was no doubt featured in the hautboy solos of Scarlatti's *Pirro e Demetrio*, which was produced there in 1712. Erdmann may have played on instruments by Christoph Denner when he was at Florence, and possibly before. There is a good chance that he and Denner worked together in the 1690s, when Denner in Nuremberg began copying French woodwinds and Erdmann was employed at nearby Ansbach. Prince Ferdinando received a delivery of hautboys from Denner in 1707, who had finished making them just three days before he died. Erdmann may have been the one who recommended Denner's instruments to Ferdinando (Denner is known to have made woodwinds at the higher pitches that were common in Italy).

Handel was in Florence each autumn between 1706 and 1709, and since his *Sonata pour l'Hautbois* (!) *Solo* in B flat, HWV 357, was written in Italy, c.1707/09, it is conceivable he wrote it for Erdmann on Ferdinando's commission. Alternatively, it could have been written in Rome for one of the hautboy players working for the Marquis of Ruspoli at the time; Handel was a composer-in-residence at Ruspoli's Palazzo Bonelli in Rome during most of 1707–8. Of Ruspoli's hautboists, 'Ignatio' (probably Ignazio Rion) was principal,[102] but (considering the quasi-French title of the Sonata) it could have been written for 'Monsù Martino', probably Aléxis Saint-Martin, a French hautboist resident in Milan who was in Rome in 1707 and 1709.[103]

The most important event in the German hautboy world in this decade was probably La Riche's move from London to an official post at the Dresden court in 1699. La Riche actually spent 1700–2 in Berlin, where he is known to have played with the lutenist Laurent de Saint-Luc.[104] In 1707/08, Saint-Luc published an exceptional collection of solo pieces in the style of Lully, the *Suittes pour le luth avec un dessus et une basse ad libitum*. Walther mentioned these pieces in his *Lexicon* (page 372), and according to him, the 'dessus' (treble) part was for traverso or hautboy.[105] Many pieces in this collection do suit the hautboy, and they may have been played by La Riche and the composer when they were together in Berlin.

At the Queen's Theatre in London, the hautboists from 1708 or before were the Fleming John Loeillet[106] and the Frenchman Pierre La Tour.[107] 1708 was the year Scarlatti's *Pyrrhus and Demetrius*, which contained a number of hautboy solos, was produced at the Queen's; the aria 'Thus in a solitary Grove' was sung by the famous Mrs Tofts, and the hautboist was presumably Loeillet.[108] The London Opera band, and specifically Loeillet, were highly praised in 1709.[109]

Hautboists were appointed to the court Capelle in Vienna for the first time in 1701.[110] In that same year, Johann Joseph Fux, beginning a long and successful career at the court, published his 'Nürnberger Partita', a witty little trio that featured a contrast between French and Italian composing styles. The piece is for hautboy, 'flauto' (recorder) and continuo. The third movement has the flauto playing an 'Aria Italiana' in 6/8, while the hautboy plays simultaneously an 'Aire françoise' in common time, and in the style of a dotted *ouverture*. The two distinct styles are ingeniously combined to make a convincing movement. The trio's title might well have been a reference to Christoph Denner (or one of his fellow Nurembergers) as the maker of the woodwind instruments for which it was written (there is documentation of Nuremberg woodwinds ordered from Austria in the 1690s).

THE 1710S

This decade was an active one for the hautboy. Many new pieces were premiered, and the instrument had an important presence in virtually every kind of music being made in Europe.

Hotteterre le Romain's splendid second book of *Pièces*, his op. 5, came out in 1715. It consisted mostly of suites, shorter than those in the first book. But the third and fourth pieces were called 'Sonates' and adopted a number of Corelli-like effects.[111] All four pieces in this collection can be played on the hautboy in their written keys except the fourth, a suite in B minor, which is better down a step in A. Hotteterre also wrote some intriguing duets for various treble instruments; two suites appeared in 1712 and 1717, his op. 4 and op. 6.

Couperin described in the preface to his *Goûts-réünis ou nouveaux concerts* how he performed these 'New Concertos, or Tastes United' in 1714 and 1715 'at the small chamber concerts that Louis XIV had me come play almost every Sunday of the year'. Louis died in 1715, so these must have been among the last pieces he heard. The collection was not published until 1724. Most of it can be played on a single hautboy with bass, although a few pieces have two treble lines, suggesting they were conceived for a group of instruments playing together and in alternation.[112] The *Concerts* that succeed best on hautboy are numbers 6, 7, 11 (which is the most intricate, demanding and fascinating) and 14. This collection is a continuation of the four *Concerts royaux* published in 1722. Like the *Goûts-réünis*, the *Concerts royaux* are excellent on hautboy, either as solos or in combination with other treble instruments. Couperin listed the performers who played for the King in these *Concerts royaux* as 'Messieurs Duval, Philidor, Alarius, et Dubois'; he himself played the harpsichord. Duval was a violinist, 'Alarius' (Hilaire Verloge) a bass gambist. 'Dubois' may have been Pierre Dubois, a bassoonist. The 'Philidor' in question is less clear, as three Philidors were close to the King; it could have been André Philidor l'aîné,[113] André's eldest son Anne,[114] or André's nephew Pierre.[115]

André Danican dit Philidor l'aîné (c.1647–1730) was a player of cromorne as well as the compiler of the famous multi-volume Philidor Collection. This vast anthology contains most of the surviving music of 'l'école classique française'. In his position as Garde de la Bibliothèque de la Musique, Philidor was responsible for supplying all the musical material used at court; he employed numerous copyists in the 'ateliers Philidor'. Anne Philidor was André's son, and Pierre Philidor was the son of his brother Jacques. Both Anne and Pierre had distinguished and remarkably parallel careers. They were born in the same house within months of each other in 1681, and were brought up together. Both of them were appointed to the Chapelle as 'dessus de hautbois' in 1704, and both had the special distinction of being appointed to the Chambre in 1712. Anne Philidor later founded the famous concert series known as the *Concert Spirituel*: he is survived by two books of solos with continuo, published in the 1710s.

Pierre Philidor held four important positions at court; in addition to the Chapelle, he was both hautboist and gambist in the Chambre, and was a member of the Douze Grands Hautbois. A colleague of Couperin, Marais and Forqueray, he was honoured by Louis XIV in 1714 with a special gratuity for the 'satisfaction His Majesty has of his services'.[116] Pierre Philidor's collection of remarkable *Suittes* appeared in 1717–18. These pieces are more difficult both musically and technically than those of La Barre and Hotteterre. The fourth suite contains an 'Air en Musette' that ranks with the best of Couperin's character movements. Philidor's *Suittes* are unusually thorough in marking ornaments and dynamics; Suitte 9 is especially detailed; the first movement, which is only 14 bars long, contains 13 flattements, 6 battements and 18 trills.[117]

François Chauvon's excellent collection of solos, called *Tibiades*, was published in 1717. Chauvon was a pupil of Couperin, and apparently an hautboist.[118]

More than a dozen concertos for hautboy and orchestra are known from before 1710, the best-known probably being Handel's in g minor. Vivaldi wrote his first hautboy concertos around 1709–12. The first concertos to appear in print were Tomaso Albinoni's *Concerti a cinque*, op. 7 (1715), which were immediately successful and have remained popular. Albinoni worked in Venice, where the hautboists active in the years prior to 1715 were Penati and Ignaz Sieber;[119] Giuseppe Sammartini may have been in Venice by this time as well. A collection was published by Roger a year after Albinoni's group, and included hautboy concertos by Sammartini, Rampini and the famous Marcello concerto. Despite the amount it is played, the Marcello remains fresh and likeable. Bach transcribed this concerto for harpsichord (BWV 974), adding elaborate written-out ornaments to the slow movement.

It is in this decade that the Besozzi family began to be well known. The Duke of Parma had created an hautboy band called the Guardia Irlandese in 1702.[120] Cristoforo Besozzi, progenitor of many celebrated hautboists,[121] and his eldest son Giuseppe were members of this band in 1711;[122] his other two sons, Alessandro and Paolo Girolamo (who were later to be famous in Turin on hautboy and bassoon), were appointed in 1714, at the ages of twelve and ten. The Guardia was active until 1731. When he was in Parma in 1726, Quantz heard an opera in which one of the Besozzis played with Farinelli and Carestini. Quantz called him 'sehr geschickt' ('very capable').[123] In 1727, Giuseppe's son Antonio (who would later be a notable soloist at Dresden) also joined the band.

The court orchestra at Berlin was very active in the first years of the century. It included four hautboists: Peter Glösch (principal),[124] Friedrich Schüler (assistant principal),[125] Carl Ludewig (*sic*) Fleischer (later principal at Braunschweig),[126] and Johann Ludwig Rose (later principal for Bach at Cöthen). They formed part of a court orchestra that included ten violins, two violas, five cellos, four bassoons, and harpsichord. Glösch had been appointed to the Capelle in 1706, and may have taken part in performances for Queen Sophie Charlotte in the years before that (when, presumably, he had been directly influenced by La Riche). He had the highest salary in the Capelle in 1713.

It was in that year that the Prussian 'Barracks King', Friedrich Wilhelm I, came to power. He immediately abolished the Capelle, firing all the musicians; the money he saved went for armaments. Several members of the disbanded Berlin orchestra were hired by Prince Leopold of Anhalt-Cöthen, who was in the process of building an orchestra that would soon be led by Sebastian Bach (who arrived in 1717). Among the musicians Leopold hired from Berlin was Johann Ludwig Rose, who became his principal hautboy player. (As he came from Berlin with all its Huguenots, playing hautboy, being also a fencing expert, and having a name like Rose, one wonders if his given names were not 'Jean-Louis'.)[127]

The Prussians began building up their army in the late seventeenth century, and continued through the eighteenth. By 1713 there were some 1266 musicians attached to the infantry, cavalry and dragoons, many of whom would have played the hautboy.[128] What has happened to all the hautboys played in this vast army is now a mystery; few seem to have survived. Friedrich Wilhelm continued to enlarge the army, and he had also a private twelve-member hautboy band made up of black players who had been brought to Potsdam as children.[129]

As for Dresden, because of Vivaldi's ties with musicians there, some of his manuscripts found their way to Dresden and are still in its library, including three sonatas for hautboy and continuo and an hautboy concerto.[130] These pieces may date from the visit to Venice in 1716 of the Crown Prince of Dresden, together with an entourage that included court musicians. One of those musicians was Christian Richter, who had been trained by La Riche and was soon to become the principal hautboist of the Dresden court.[131] Vivaldi's well-known c minor hautboy sonata, RV 53, has themes similar to one of his operas, *L'incoronazione di Dario*, produced in Venice in 1717; since the sole source of this sonata is preserved at Dresden, it may have been written for Richter.[132] Vivaldi's interesting oratorio *Juditha triumphans*, RV 644, was also written in 1716 and may have involved Richter, as there is a solo bass aria (Holofernes's 'Noli o cara te adorantis') with obbligato hautboy and organ.

Martin Blockwitz played second hautboy in the Dresden Capelle from c.1717 to 1733, doubling on traverso.[133] Blockwitz is survived by an extraordinary 'well-tempered' collection of fifteen suites (*60 Arien*) in every practicable key, for continuo with either a traverso, a violin, or an hautboy.

In February 1711, two well-known musicians from Saxony, Georg Pisendel and Michael Böhm, were invited to Darmstadt to perform in the production of Graupner's opera *Telemach*. Pisendel was later to become the concertmaster of Dresden's Capelle. Walther (1732:99) called Böhm 'a fine [vortrefflicher] hautboist'; he was also a recorder virtuoso. Böhm was trained in Dresden, presumably by La Riche, and had played (with Pisendel) in the Collegium Musicum at Leipzig directed by Telemann.[134] At Darmstadt, both musicians were offered positions; Pisendel declined, but (perhaps because Richter had just been appointed to the important principal hautboy post at Dresden) Böhm accepted the engagement, which came with the title of *Concertmeister*.[135]

It was soon after Böhm's appointment at Darmstadt that Telemann settled in Frankfurt, which is nearby. Böhm often played for him there. The two men later became brothers-in-law,[136] and Böhm was one of the four hautboy players (with Richter, Glösch and La Riche) to whom Telemann dedicated his *Kleine Cammer-Music* or *Petite Musique de chambre* in 1716. These six partitas (TWV 41) are a particularly effective collection for solo treble instrument (violin, traverso, harpsichord, but 'especially hautboy'[137]). Published in September 1716, this is the first known collection of solos with continuo written principally for the hautboy.

The library at Darmstadt is today one of the richer sources of hautboy and recorder music, especially pieces by Telemann. Most of that music was probably written for Böhm, and is a monument to his talent. Among the remarkable chamber pieces by Telemann at Darmstadt is a trio for hautboy and violin, TWV 42:F4, II, conceived, like many of his chamber pieces, 'auf Concertenart' (in the manner of a concerto).[138] It may originally have been played by Böhm and the violinist Johann

Kreß. There is also an interesting group of trios for treble viol and hautboy, probably written for Böhm and the gambist Ernst Hesse, known as the 'German Forqueray'.

Telemann's well-known hautboy concerto in e minor is also at the Darmstadt library, as is his excellent trio in c minor from *Essercizii musici* for recorder, hautboy and continuo. Telemann published the *Essercizii* in Hamburg after 1740, but parts of it may have been written much earlier; Böhm may have used this manuscript when he was at Darmstadt. The A minor trio with recorder by Telemann, another good piece, is also at Darmstadt. One wonders whether Böhm played the recorder or hautboy part, and who played the other (Carl Fleischer was briefly at Darmstadt in 1719; he had been principal second hautboy to Glösch at Berlin). There were other woodwind players at the Darmstadt court in this period (Johann Corseneck and Johann Kayser[139]), and to judge from the surviving music, they would have been put to good use (playing, for instance, the wonderful concerto in B flat by Telemann for three hautboys, three violins, and continuo).

There was also regular church music at Darmstadt, much of it by the court composer Christoph Graupner, whose cantata *Wie wunderbar ist Gottes Güt* (1717) is probably for hautbois d'amour, making it the earliest known piece for that instrument. Many of Graupner's cantatas are of high quality (he was considered after Telemann but before Bach for the Leipzig job, but Duke Ernst Ludwig, his employer, raised his salary and refused to let him go). A compelling aria with beautiful obbligato work is 'Seufzt und weint ihr matten Augen' for soprano, 'hautbois' solo and strings in Graupner's cantata *Ach Gott und Herr*, performed in June 1711, when Böhm had been four months at the court.

Starting in 1717, during Telemann's time in Frankfurt, another exceptional hautboist was making regular visits there. This was Jacob Denner, performing at the Pfeifergericht, an ancient ceremony held each year in Frankfurt.[140] The music for this event was traditionally provided by three musicians from Nuremberg.[141] It would have been difficult for Denner and Böhm not to have met during this time, and perhaps played together; at any rate, Böhm would probably have known Denner's hautboys and recorders, and might possibly have played them himself.

Although Jacob Denner's instruments are among the finest-playing that survive, in his own day he was better known as a 'world-famous musician . . . particularly on the hautboy'.[142] Born in 1681, Denner first studied with his illustrious father Christoph (who was discussed above), and later with his godfather, Jacob Lang, Principal Musician of Nuremberg, a title Denner himself acquired in 1727. By 1708, Denner was already well-known as a performer; he became a Stadtpfeifer in 1706 and a Stadtmusicus in 1717.[143] He was said to have played with 'radiant grace and sensitivity' in the courts of Ansbach, Bayreuth, Sulzbach, Hildburghausen, and elsewhere.

In London, the Queen's Theatre orchestra was crystallizing into a regular, institutionalized entity consisting of some twenty-five players just when Handel settled in London (Handel produced his first opera, *Rinaldo*, in February 1711). There are no orchestra lists for 1711 to 1717,[144] so it is unclear who was playing hautboy in most of Handel's early London operas. It seems Loeillet had temporarily retired in 1710, and it is likely that his place as hautboy soloist was taken by Ernst Galliard.[145]

There is documentation that Galliard was the hautboist in Handel's *Teseo*, produced at the Queen's in 1712; the opera includes six (!) hautboy solos with soprano. Galliard lived in London from 1706; he had studied the hautboy at Celle, and composition at Hanover. He was a notable and prolific composer, and his translation of Tosi's *Observations on the florid song* is well known. Galliard's masque, *Pan and Syrinx*, included important hautboy work; written in the same year as Handel's *Acis and Galatea*, it is in much the same style. Galliard wrote several hautboy solos that are now lost. Because of his proximity to Handel at the time, and the common backgrounds of the two men, Galliard is the likely recipient of Handel's solo sonatas in C minor, HWV 366, and HWV 363a in F, written in London c.1712/16.

Between 1717 and 1720, Handel worked for James Brydges, Duke of Chandos, at his residence known as Cannons. Handel produced a number of exquisite hautboy solos and chamber pieces for Cannons: a sonata for hautboy, two violins and continuo (HWV 404), the Chandos Anthems, which include three obbligatos for hautboy, *Esther* (with only one hautboy), and *Acis and Galatea* (1718) with its prominent and delicate hautboy parts. *Acis* was for two hautboys doubling on recorders. The identity of the principal hautboy is unknown, but it could well have been Jean Christian Kytch, who is documented at Cannons from 1719, when he was the highest-paid instrumentalist there.[146]

Kytch had played bassoon in the London Opera orchestra from about 1708, and Handel had written an obbligato bassoon part for him in *Rinaldo*.[147] He took over the second hautboy desk at the Opera in about 1712.[148] Kytch later became solo hautboy at the Opera. From 1719, he was active as a recitalist at public concerts, mostly at Hickford's Room. He may have played the Babell solos, which were published and available by about 1725, and Handel's solo sonatas, which Walsh brought out soon afterwards. For a concert in April 1729, he played arrangements of arias from operas by Handel and Bononcini 'on hautboy, also little flute and bassoon'.[149] Kytch probably played his own arrangements, combining the solo lines and tuttis, in the manner of Prelleur's attractive set of Handel opera excerpts in his *Instructions upon the Hautboy*, 1730.

It is noteworthy that until the third decade of the century, none of the Opera hautboy players was a native Englishman: Galliard was German (of French extraction), Kytch possibly Dutch, Loeillet from the Spanish Netherlands, and La Tour from France. William Smith had been considered for second hautboy at the Queen's Theatre in 1707 but not hired. Richard Neale was apparently the first native son to join the section in 1720 as fourth hautboy.[150]

THE 1720S

The 1720s saw great stylistic changes in music everywhere in Europe. In France, soon after Louis XV was crowned in 1722, there was a clear shift to a newer, lighter style of chamber music, in which suites gave way to 'Italian' sonatas. Meanwhile the last great culmination of the Louis XIV style appeared in the decade of the 1720s. We have already spoken above of Couperin's *Concerts royaux* (1722) and *Goûts-réünis ou nouveaux concerts* (1724), the epitome of this style.

Few pieces in the hautboy's literature can match the nobility and depth of feeling of Couperin's four *Nations*, published in 1726 for two treble lines and continuo: La Françoise, L'Espagnole, L'Impériale and La Piémontoise. Each 'Nation' consists in fact of two pieces: a 'Sonade' in Italian style and a French suite of dances. Of the 'Sonades', three were actually composed in the 1690s. The music is difficult on any of the standard *symphonie* instruments, but almost all the movements are playable on hautboy, sometimes with minor adjustments.

Another important solo collection in this style is Montéclair's *Concerts* (1724–5), for traverso with movements appropriate 'au Violon, Haubois, ou à la Flute à bec'. The fourth Concert, for an unspecified treble instrument and continuo, is especially interesting; it is in unusual keys: both B minor and B flat major (it works better for hautboy in A minor and B flat, with a selection of movements). We shall discuss the newer French 'Louis Quinze' style, represented by composers like Boismortier and the Chédevilles, below (p. 82).

In Italy, Vivaldi produced an important group of hautboy concertos (nearly two dozen in all). Few of them are dated; the earliest were written between 1709 and 1712,[151] perhaps for students at the Pietà, and a later group was written in the 1720s.[152] These too may have been for the Pietà, although the most difficult of them (RV 449, RV 451, RV 460, RV 461 and RV 463) could also have been conceived for professionals who were in Venice at the time, like Sammartini or Giovanni Platti.

In 1722, Roger published a second set of *Concerti a cinque* by Albinoni, this time his wonderful op. 9. These concertos became well known all over Europe and inspired many a fine adagio; Handel's glorious slow movement in the Concerto Grosso, op. 3/2 (1734), for instance, seems inspired by the Adagio of Albinoni's second concerto. Albinoni's twelfth and last concerto, for strings and two hautboys, is the gem of the set. Opus 9 was dedicated to Maximilian Emanuel of Bavaria, and Albinoni visited his court in Munich in 1722, the year of the dedication. The solo hautboy concertos were no doubt performed then by the court's 'vornembste Instrumental-Virtuos' ('most distinguished instrumental virtuoso'), Jacob Loeillet (younger brother of John Loeillet of the London Opera orchestra, and the musician with by far the highest salary of any at the Munich court).[153] (After Max Emanuel's death, Loeillet was hired away from the Munich court by the Queen at Versailles, to become Hautbois de la Chambre du Roi and official Compositeur de la Chambre to the French court. He held those posts until his return to his home town of Ghent in 1746.) The double concertos in Albinoni's collection would have added the other chamber hautboist at the court, Franz Schuechbauer, who was also a maker of woodwind instruments (most of those that survive are pitched high at A + 1 [A–464]).[154]

An unusually good Italian collection of six solos was written by the hautboist Domenico Dreyer. It survives in a beautifully copied manuscript at Paris, and was probably written by 1727. Dreyer, whose father was German, seems to have grown up in Florence (where he may have studied with Erdmann).[155] Dreyer is known to have played a concert in Lucca in 1726, and in 1731–4 he was engaged as a musician at the court of St Petersburg. Of this manuscript collection, the fifth and sixth are the best sonatas.

In 1721, Telemann moved from Frankfurt to Hamburg, and in the 1720s and 30s produced some of his best hautboy pieces there. Telemann was himself an hautboist, and from his compositions it is clear he had a particular fondness for the instrument.[156] He wrote more than a thousand cantatas, many involving hautboy. Among those that have been published are two sets called *Der Harmonische Gottesdienst* (1725–6 and 1731), one for single voice, treble instrument and continuo, the other (the *Fortsetzung*) adding a second treble instrument. The first set contains fifteen cantatas with hautboy, the second twenty-two.[157] Over 100 small chamber works for hautboy survive by Telemann, including duets, solo sonatas, trios and quartets.[158] Many of his forty-three trios that involve hautboy are worthy of mention, such as the one from *Musique de Table* II/4 with traverso (with its Minuet in E major), the 'Trio I' for recorder and oboe with continuo from *Essercizii musici*, the 'Trio XII' from the same collection for hautboy and obbligato harpsichord (one of the few pieces for this combination that succeeds), and the many trios for violin with hautboy (or hautbois d'amour) and continuo. Many of this last category of trios survive in manuscript copies in more than one library, an indication that they were frequently played.[159]

A composer close to Telemann (both personally and in style) was Friedrich Fasch, who is survived by many interesting pieces involving hautboy. His solo concerto in G minor (K 12, FWV L:g1) is an excellent piece of music, as are his numerous quartets for two hautboys, obbligato bassoon, and continuo.

In England, William Babell published his twenty-four solos 'for a violin, hoboy or German flute' with 'proper Graces adapted to each Adagio by ye Author', in about 1725. This format was probably inspired by the Corelli solo sonatas that appeared at about the same time, and that claimed to reproduce the ornaments as the composer himself played them on the violin. In the mid-1720s, a first-rate collection of solo sonatas compiled by Pietro Chaboud was published; they were by various composers. The best of the collection is an Italian-style sonata by Pietro Castrucci, concertmaster of the Opera orchestra in London. Handel's famous collection of trios, op. 2, was published about 1730; only the first, third and fifth trios, all apparently written about 1718 (the year of *Acis and Galatea*), call for hautboy.

At the court in Vienna the chief player in this period seems to have been Ludwig Schön, who had a court appointment from 1711 to 1740.[160] Schön had come to Vienna in 1700 as a member of the band of students La Buissière had brought from Berlin. Archduke Joseph, heir apparent to the throne, sponsored this band from 1701, and when he was crowned Emperor in 1705, employed four of the hautboists at the court. Schön's original name had been Joli, and he had grown up in Berlin, probably in a Huguenot family. He was involved in the sumptuous production of Fux's opera *Costanza et Fortezza* in Prague in 1723 (as were Quantz, Richter and other Dresden court musicians).[161]

Standard continuo instruments for the hautboy

Which instruments played the basso continuo line in chamber music was often left to the players and depended on who was available. But certain bass instruments were associated with certain trebles. Boismortier indicated the standard associations in his well-known op. 37 sonatas of 1732. The title page of this collection suggests the use of cello with violin, gamba with traverso, or bassoon with hautboy. Interestingly, there was a final quintet for all these instruments (traverso, violin, hautboy and bassoon obbligato, with gamba and harpsichord as continuo), implying that the complete opus would make an interesting concert programme.

Many pieces for hautboy specifically called for bassoon on the bass line, normally with harpsichord. Sometimes the bass, like the treble lines, is marked 'Hautbois', as if the bassoon was the bass member of the hautbois family. Mattheson wrote that 'der *stolze* Basson' ('the proud bassoon') was 'the normal bass and the continuo or accompaniment for the hautboy'.[162]

In practical experience, however, the bassoon is less flexible as a bass instrument than the cello and especially the gamba. The sonorities of the gamba, harpsichord and hautboy blend uniquely well together, and are ideal in French music.

'Bach's wood': music by Bach for hautboy

LEIPZIG AND GLEDITSCH

Bach wrote well over twice as many solos for hautboy as for any other instrument, bar none. His most fertile period was the mid-1720s, when he was producing as many as eight new cantata arias a month for his hautboy soloists, Gleditsch and Kornagel (who, like himself, were employed by the city of Leipzig).[163] Through their playing, these two musicians inspired Bach to write close to 200 hautboy solos at Leipzig (he had written some three dozen before then).

In the course of his life, Bach ended up writing more solos for Caspar Gleditsch, his first hautboist, than for any other musician except himself, and this vivid repertoire is still prized by every oboist; it can be looked on as the greatest single testimonial to the genius of an oboe player in the history of the instrument. Bach and Gleditsch were close contemporaries, and both were at the peak of their careers in the 1720s when Bach wrote most of his hautboy solos and Gleditsch played them. As a Stadtpfeifer, Gleditsch would have been able to play many types of woodwinds when Bach needed them, including recorder, traverso and bassoon,[164] so it is quite possible that he played the solos for these instruments in the cantatas as well. Gleditsch was close to several Leipzig woodwind makers, and was at the forefront of the experiments in new instruments being made in Leipzig in the 1710s that produced the new hautbois d'amour and oboe da caccia. Like Bach, Gleditsch may have occasionally performed concerts or tours outside Leipzig (it is possible he was away on extended trips of several months at the end of 1725, in early 1726, and early 1727, when there are conspicuous gaps in the hautboy solos in cantata performances).

Gottfried Kornagel, Bach's second player, never attained the status of Stadtpfeifer, remaining a Kunstgeiger all his life, although he had to work nearly as hard as Gleditsch. In many of Bach's pieces, Kornagel's parts are equal in difficulty to Gleditsch's, and he too was expected to play all sizes of hautboy as well as other instruments. Bach made some disparaging comments about the qualities of his municipal musicians in 1730,[165] but, considering his realistic approach to composition and the large number of solos he wrote for two hautboys, he must surely have considered his two principal hautboists exceptions to the norm. Players today can be glad Leipzig's violinists did not inspire more solo writing, or there would probably be fewer superb solos for the hautboy from Bach's pen.

When Bach arrived in Leipzig in 1723, he found himself in one of the principal German centres of woodwind makers and dealers. Because there was no instrument-maker's guild in Leipzig (as there was in most cities, like Nuremberg), there were none of the usual restrictions on setting up a workshop, limitations on materials one was allowed to use, period of apprenticeship, and so on.[166] Thus many exceptional players and instrument builders were attracted to the city. And it was probably in Leipzig that the two larger sizes of hautboy Bach regularly used, the hautbois d'amour and oboe da caccia, were first invented and played.

Like his contemporaries Richard Haka in Amsterdam and Christoph Denner in Nuremberg, Andreas Bauer (mentioned above, p. 46) began by making 'Renaissance' woodwinds and later adopted the new French models. He worked until 1717. The earliest known surviving hautbois d'amour, dated 1719, was made by his son Gottfried Bauer, and two oboes da caccia dated 1724 survive by Gottfried's son Gottlob.

Among the larger sizes of hautboy below the treble in C were various kinds of hautboy in A (called generically 'hautecontre de hautbois' and alto hautboys) and instruments in F (called 'taille de hautbois' or tenor hautboys; these will be discussed in a moment). The best-known form of alto hautboy today is the hautbois d'amour, which appeared in Germany in the mid-1710s (see ill. 24). While 'oboe d'amore' is the popular name nowadays, the instrument was commonly called the 'hautbois d'amour' at the time (by Bach, for instance). Most of the instrument's earliest music was written by composers either from Leipzig or closely associated with it, and the majority of surviving instruments were made there. The hautbois d'amour's repertoire comes almost exclusively from Germany. The most obvious trait of the hautbois d'amour is its bulb-bell, which is not in fact as acoustically important as the position of its tone-holes (which are placed, on a similar bore, considerably lower than on the treble hautboy) and the missing resonance holes normally found in the bells of treble hautboys.

The hautbois d'amour, like the oboe da caccia described below, was a true child of the Baroque. Its vogue lasted about forty years, and its most active period was the dozen years after its first appearance. The instrument would scarcely be known today had Bach not written so many beautiful solos for it in his cantatas (he wrote almost exactly the same number of solos for hautbois d'amour as for treble hautboy). Bach

24. Hautbois d'amour. Gottfried Bauer, Leipzig, 1719.

even altered his audition piece for the post at Leipzig (BWV 23) in order to feature the instrument, probably as a gesture to the city where it was invented, and he included hautbois d'amour in his inaugural cantata at Leipzig (BWV 75) as well as eight other cantatas before the end of his first year there. Two of his concertos for hautbois d'amour, BWV 1053 in D and BWV 1055 in A, survive only in arrangements he later made of them for harpsichord. Bach's compositions account for some forty per cent of the hautbois d'amour's surviving solos and chamber music. In its heyday, however, the composer who actually made the instrument famous was Telemann (by far the most popular composer in Germany at the time). Forty-two of Telemann's d'amour pieces are known; they include chamber music, concertos, and obbligatos with voice.[167]

One reason for the interest shown in the hautbois d'amour by Baroque composers was its unusual key, A major. Bach was particularly fond of F sharp and B minor, for instance, and many of his hautbois d'amour obbligatos were written in these keys. He rarely required them of the treble hautboy, but on hautbois d'amour, sounding F sharp and B minor were the relatively straightforward fingered tonalities of A and D minor.

The tenor hautboy, in F a fifth below the treble, was a fairly well-known instrument at the time, used in the hautboy band along with the treble hautboy and the bassoon. Talbot wrote in c.1692–5: 'The Tenor Hautbois differs not from Treble in shape, only in size & bore of holes which being at greater distance are bored more slantingly downwards that the tops may be covered with the Fingers.' The tenor was also commonly called the 'taille de hautbois', but the name has caused confusion, as 'taille de violon' or just 'taille' means viola. (Some libraries have a special category of music in their catalogues of early pieces for two hautboys, 'viola' and bassoon that are actually pieces for double-reed band.)

To judge from surviving music, the straight tenor hautboy was not considered a solo instrument. Solos for F-hautboy are normally for a specialized form of tenor called the oboe da caccia (or some variant of this name). This instrument too would be virtually unknown today if Bach had not written about two dozen important solos for it (practically the whole of its surviving solo literature, all of which was written at Leipzig).

The oboe da caccia was built in imitation of the hunting horn in a nearly circular curve with a widely flaring bell (in brass or wood). The wooden body was covered in leather and had a faceted octagonal cross-section similar to the cornett (see ill. 25). The oboe da caccia evidently had a soft sound, since Bach often scored it with boy sopranos and traversos or recorders.[168] The leather covering (which disguised and sealed the saw-cuts used to achieve its curve) tended to dampen its sound. Incongruously (considering its name and image as the 'hunting oboe'), Bach usually used the sound of the oboe da caccia in arias whose texts expressed grief, tragedy, sin or sorrow;[169] it has a somewhat melancholy sound.

It was a typical Baroque conceit that caused the oboe da caccia to have two different names depending on its function. When it was a tutti instrument, Bach called it a 'taille', and when it played solos it became an 'oboe da caccia'. The third hautboy part in Bach's orchestra, when it existed, shared the tuttis with the string viola.[170] There are no obbligato parts for taille, but some of Bach's cantatas call for both taille and oboe da caccia. In these cases, the da caccia parts, which are solos, are not copied into the taille part, but appear in the first hautboist's part.[171] It seems the

25. Oboe da caccia. Eichentopf, Leipzig, 1724.

apprentice hautboist who was playing a 'taille de hautbois' that doubled the viola passed the warmed-up instrument over to his teacher, Maestro Gleditsch, who proceeded to play a solo on it as an 'oboe da caccia'.[172] Bach began writing for the oboe da caccia within a month of his arrival in Leipzig. Gleditsch played the first solo aria (BWV 167/3) on 24 June. Further solos appeared throughout Bach's most active period of composition for hautboys, 1724 to 1727, as well as in the Passions.

SPECIAL PROBLEMS INVOLVING PITCH IN BACH'S MUSIC

Bach's cantatas reach us still mostly through the vehicle of reprints of the standard old Bach-Gesellschaft (BG) edition. True, there is a new Bach complete works (the *NBA*), but it is not finished yet and is more expensive and difficult to access. We are therefore basically working with editorial decisions made at the end of the nineteenth century. To scholars of that time, one of the mysteries of Bach's original manuscripts was that he had sometimes notated the parts to the same piece in different keys. We have since discovered the reason for this: that in his earlier works written for Mühlhausen and Weimar, Bach had thought of the woodwinds as transposing instruments, much like the so-called 'B flat clarinet' today (the clarinet's parts are always notated a tone higher than those of most other instruments in the orchestra because it sounds a tone lower).

The pitch difference in Bach's time was the result of the old seventeenth-century European tradition of tuning strings high (about a semitone above modern pitch, or A + 1, which in Bach's day was called *Chorton*), while the new woodwinds imported from France were generally a tone or tone-and-a-half lower (at A − 1 or A − 2, which Bach called *Cammerton*). During his career, Bach worked with hautboys at both A − 1 (Mühlhausen, Weimar, Leipzig most of the time) and A − 2 (Weimar, Cöthen, Leipzig in the early years). The question of how to notate the pitch discrepancy between *Chorton* and *Cammerton* was worked out on an ad hoc basis, and during his career Bach used different strategies for handling this problem. His solution at Leipzig was to tune the strings at *Cammerton*, like the woodwinds, so they could be written in the same key (although in Leipzig the organ was still at *Chorton*, so its parts had to be transposed down a step).

By the time the BG was publishing its performing edition of the cantatas (between 1851 and 1900), the editors were assuming that all the instruments would be at the same pitch level, so they had to transpose some of Bach's original parts. Their policy seems to have been to adopt the key of the majority of the parts; at the time, this must have seemed reasonable. In practice, however, it meant that the hautboy parts sometimes got transposed down a step from their original keys. As long as Conservatoire oboes were used, most of the cantatas were still playable in these altered keys, and the anomaly was (if not unnoticed) at least accepted.

The problem came to a head when original instruments began to be used for the cantatas, and it was soon clear that certain pieces were virtually unplayable on the hautboy in the keys to which the BG editors had transposed them. An example is Cantata 131, which is virtually an hautboy obbligato from beginning to end. Bach had originally written the 'Obboe' and 'Fagotto' parts in A minor and the other parts in G. The parts in a minor fit exactly the range of the hautboy (c_1 to d_3). But in the BG edition, with the wind parts transposed down to G minor, the hautboy went a whole tone below its range, and had to play low $c\sharp_1$ (a note that composers avoided, because it is virtually impossible to play on the hautboy).

Bach's earlier works thus got 'untransposed' in the BG edition. The pieces that were problematic were BWV numbers 12, 18, 21, 31, 54, 63, 70a, 71, 80a, 106, 131, 132, 147a, 150, 152, 155, 161, 162, 172, 182, 185, 186a, 199 and 208. The editors of new Bach edition (the *NBA*) are aware of the problem, and have usually (although not always) provided enough material to make it possible to play in Bach's original keys.[173]

LOST HAUTBOY REPERTOIRE BY BACH

While in his vocal works Bach gave the hautboy literally hundreds of solo obbligatos, the instrument is conspicuous for its absence in his surviving chamber music. This anomaly must have to do with the transmission of Bach's works after his death. A mere handful of chamber pieces of any kind survive, and of these, only a single movement (BWV 1040) is for hautboy. Yet we know that when he died, Bach left behind 'eine Menge . . . Instrumentalsachen, von allerley Art, und für allerley Instrumente' ('a mass of instrumental works of all kinds, and for various instruments').[174] Most of the manuscripts of 'Instrumentalsachen' went to Bach's oldest son, Wilhelm Friedemann, who was frequently in financial difficulties and presumably sold off or lost much of his musical inheritance.[175]

Bach was a great arranger, and it is quite possible that lost chamber works originally conceived for hautboy still exist in the form of later arrangements. If we are ever to recover any of these pieces, the obvious place to look is among Bach's keyboard music, because we can assume he would regularly have adapted his own pieces when he needed solos to play. The best-known examples of this process are the harpsichord concertos, which are Bach's arrangements of concertos he had originally written for other instruments.

The most effective method of discovering pieces that might originally have been for hautboy is to play them in every reasonable key, considering each movement separately. Applying criteria discussed in Haynes 2001, two of the harpsichord concertos were probably for hautbois d'amour (BWV 1053 in D and 1055 in A) and one was for hautboy alone or hautboy and harpsichord (BWV 1059 in d). There are two other concertos with missing movements (BWV 1056/2 and 3 in G/g and 1060/1 and 3 in c).[176] Although the evidence that all these pieces were initially for hautboy is indirect, it is historically quite plausible.

There are other less obvious survivors among the keyboard works and existing chamber music that (using the same criteria) might originally have been for hautboy. They include suites in F (BWV 817), A minor (BWV 823), and G minor (BWV 997) for hautboy and continuo, and trios with gamba or violin and continuo (BWV 1015, 1027, 1030, and 1032), plus many separate movements.

Hautboy bands

Most hautboists did not play in orchestras in the Baroque period; their more customary environment was bands. The hautboy band was a continuation of the Renaissance tradition of similar instruments playing together in consorts. Bands provided 'ambience' like live music at a party or a wedding nowadays, and their music was not intended to be listened to with complete attention. Bands were often made up of players with the least accomplishments; some were beginners hoping later for a more rewarding position either at a court or a city, some were failures unable to find a better job. And not all hautboy bands were of mediocre quality; Mattheson described a group in Hanover that he heard in 1706 as a 'most exquisite band of wind players'.[177]

Hautboy bands were first used in armies, but were soon adopted in civilian settings. They were sponsored by regimental officers, city governments, and virtually any aristocrat who maintained a court. Court bands provided all the daily music other than the actual concerts played by the Capelle: Tafelmusik, ceremonies, processions, weddings, dances and so on. Like court chamber musicians, bandsmen were sometimes expected to travel with their employers.[178] Throughout the eighteenth century, many financially strapped courts made do with a small wind group that doubled on strings and was relatively inexpensive to maintain, since (though they were better paid than military Hautboisten) the players did not have the status of court musicians. An hautboy band playing at court could also serve as a source of wind and string players to add to chamber music when needed. Mattheson wrote disdainfully of every miniature 'Grand-Seigneur' and 'Dorff-Herrscher' who wanted to have his band of 'Kunst-Pfeiffer' kept at lackey's accommodation and pay, instead of professionally trained musicians.[179]

Bands varied in size from three to about eight members. In the second half of the seventeenth century, the usual number of hautboys in French regiments was three to four.[180] In Germany, the standard formation of Regimentsoboisten consisted of six players: two trebles, two tenors, and two bassoons. Given the standard four-part texture, the most practical division of forces would have been to double the top and bottom voices.

Hautboy bands played marches, dance suites, processions, funeral music, calls and fanfares for the hunt, and so on. Music of this kind was often played by heart and little of it was written down, so what remains on paper is therefore probably a fraction of what was once played. Despite this, over 500 band pieces are known to survive, about a third of them written between 1670 and c.1710, and most of the rest between c.1710 and c.1740.[181] Among the better-known composers who contributed to this repertoire are Fasch, Finger, Förster, Handel, Lully, Pierre Philidor and Telemann. Surviving music includes the Philidor Manuscript (mentioned in chapter 2), Krieger's *Lustige Feld-Musik* (1704), the Sonsfeld collection of fifty-two multi-movement pieces for two to three hautboys, one tenor hautboy, and two bassoons,[182] Fischer's *Tafelmusik* (1702), and his *Musicalische Fürsten-Lust* (1706). André Philidor's remarkable miniature opera-farce of 1688, *Le Mariage de la Grosse Cathos*, was actually built around an hautboy band, whose nine members provided all the instrumental music.[183]

Very few pieces for bands of double-reeds appeared after about 1740, reflecting the changing fashions in the instrumentation of wind bands during the eighteenth century.

The transformations of the 1730s and beyond

NEW INSTRUMENT TYPES

By the 1680s, the hautboy had pretty well settled into the generic form (Type A2) that it would retain until about 1730. There were many minor variations, of course. But the parameters and proportions of its design (the outer profile, for instance, the inner bore, and tone-hole size and placement) were quite consistent. This stability of design began to fragment in about 1730, and several new types appeared. The general unifying concept of an archetypal 'French hautboy', personified by Type A2, broke up into several distinct models. By the 1730s the Italians had developed the straight-top Type C (ill. 18e) and, probably somewhat later, the Type D1 (ill. 18g). Type C became popular in England, along with Type B (ill. 18d). The French developed the new Type E (ill. 18f). Given our sketchy ability to date hautboys, it is not possible to be specific about chronology, but the indications are that Type A2 was abandoned by all but the more conservative makers and players, and that the music of the period 1730–60 was mostly played on these new models: Types B, C, D1 and E.

The hautboy of the period before 1730 represented, like the harpsichord, the end of a relatively long and stable era, the culmination of years of development, while the designs that appeared after that were innovative and experimental, like early pianos. The outward turning styles were strikingly different, and were of course an indication of the change, but it was the acoustical tendency towards a narrower bore, smaller tone-holes and higher pitch that changed the instrument fundamentally. These were the developments that affected the hautboy's character and response, leading it in the direction of the smaller and finer-featured instrument of the Classical period (to be discussed in the next chapter).

Types B and C represent two general trends of the period. Beading was simplified or completely absent in Type B (ill. 18d), although bulges remained at the points that had formerly been balusters. Instead of key-rings, Types B and C (ills 18d and 18e) often had *bosses*, in which only the part of the encircling ring necessary to hold the key axles was present, the rest being cut away. Compared with Type A, the side walls of the top column (the straight section) of Type B were often thicker, whereas those of Type C could be thinner. Type B instruments are comparatively rare; examples survive by Stanesby Jr, Van de Knikker, Thomas and Martin Lot, and Schuchart, among others.

Type C is commonly known as the 'straight-top', because the top joint was turned without finial, baluster or beads (except, rarely, one at the top); the side walls expanded slightly towards the bell. The centre joint and bell retained their balusters, which were normally reinforced with ivory or metal. The straight-top appears to have been developed in Italy by Anciuti, and was popularized in England by Sammartini, who probably used it. Type C instruments, which are not uncommon, are seen in Italian and English works of art; examples survive by Anciuti, Cosins, Palanca, Stanesby Jr, Gedney, Milhouse, Goulding and others.

Chronologically, the next stage is represented by Type D, which first appears in iconography in about the middle of the eighteenth century. This type has several variants. Type D1 (ill. 18g) used elements of the old Baroque Type A2, but was somewhat simpler, lighter, and more elegant. Its beading was thin and fine, and there was less of it (the lower waist bead had disappeared from the bell, for instance). This model was developed earlier than Type D2 (ill. 18h), the form generally thought of as the 'Classical' hautboy. The bell of Type D1 forms a single simple flare from the baluster to the rim, and the rim expands slightly but blends into the flare. This is different from Type D2, where the bell flare progresses only to the flare beads, after which the bottom third of the bell profile is almost vertical, with a strikingly prominent rim. The centre baluster of Type D1 is more rounded than in Type A, while on Type D2 the widest point is raised to be closer to the top of the baluster, creating a shape like a question mark. On the top joint of the Type D2 the thickest point of the baluster is extremely wide ('bold', as it is called by turners) compared with that of A2 models of the early eighteenth century (such as Jacob Denner's or Paulhahn's). Makers of Type D1 included Palanca, Crone, Grenser, Sattler, Baur, Schlegel, Delusse, Goulding and others. We shall discuss Type D2 further in chapter 4.

Finally, Type E (ill. 18f) appeared in the decades before 1750 and continued to be made until the end of the century. It seems to have been popular in French-speaking areas (including France, the Austrian Netherlands and Switzerland). Compared with other models, Type E looks as if it has been stretched, and the many extant originals are among the longest hautboys that survive; the swellings at the balusters and bell flare are very gradual and 'streamlined'; although beads are present, they are minimal. A good example of Type E is being held by the hautboist in ill. 26. Makers of Type E included Charles Bizey, Thomas Lot, Martin Lot, Gilles Lot, the Rottenburgh sons G. A., Petrus and J. H. J., the Schlegels, and 'Prudent'. The association of Type E with France was probably due to its low pitch. Within France, however, there was also a countering tendency in this period. While the Opéra remained rigidly traditionalist, French instrumental music was being strongly influenced by Italy. It may be because these two trends could not easily be reconciled that there arose a dichotomy, a 'French' Type E hautboy and an 'Italian' Type D1, probably used for different types of music.[184]

26. Anonymous (?c.1750). Portrait of an hautboist (?French). Oil.

All the Rococo models soon lost ground, however, to the Classical hautboy, Type D2, that came to be the most popular design everywhere after 1770. Examples of Type B have barely survived to the present, suggesting its history was relatively short-lived. Type E has yet to be studied and understood. Type C, the straight-top, enjoyed great popularity in England until the end of the century, but even there was overshadowed by Type D2.

PLAYERS

That two of these new models should come out of northern Italy is not surprising. These new designs were first heard in the hands of Italian virtuosos, who quite convincingly demonstrated their qualities. That they were immediately adopted by the rest of Europe indicates what sort of an impression they made. Much of the music played by Italian hautboists featured virtuosic display and extended the limits of technique; it was therefore logical for experimental instruments to be made by Italians.

The period after 1730 was in fact dominated by great Italian virtuosos of the instrument. In every important musical centre, Italians were playing solos. In Paris, the success of the Besozzi brothers at the Concert Spirituel was extraordinary. In Germany, Italians like Platti, Antonio and Carlo Besozzi, the Ferrandinis, Schiavonetti, Stazzi, Secchi, Ciceri and Colombazzi[185] transformed the hautboy's image. Italian hautboists in England included Barsanti, Mancinelli, Giustinelli, and of course Sammartini, who left a lasting impression on audiences and other players. The dominance of Italians was far from complete, but it is a fact that in this period, no other country was represented by so many remarkable players of the hautboy.

To take several examples, the famous Besozzi brothers, Alessandro and Paolo Girolamo, played duets on hautboy and bassoon in Paris at the Concert Spirituel in 1735.[186] Their approach (and no doubt their skill and sensitivity) were a revelation to audiences there. They enjoyed a spectacular success, played repeated command performances, and were rewarded by the Académie Royale with 100 gold Louis each.[187] By the time they left for home, they had probably altered the course of French woodwind playing. One contemporary remarked, 'the two Bezzuzzi [*sic*], one an hautboist and the other bassoonist, . . . held little musical conversations together that make one almost swoon with enjoyment; I cannot express the raptures into which one is thrown. I have never in my life experienced anything more enchanting. . . .'[188]

The nephew of these Besozzis, Antonio, was probably the most influential hautboist in Germany in his time.[189] He had been in the opera orchestra in Naples in 1732 when Hasse was conducting there. Soon afterwards, Hasse was appointed maestro di cappella at Dresden, and Besozzi was brought in (at the age of twenty-four) as solo hautboy. Besozzi held the post with great success until 1764, and was much admired. He was the teacher of his son Carlo, who also became famous, and of other players of the next generation, including (probably) J. C. Fischer. Antonio Besozzi's playing of one of Hasse's arias was so 'heavenly' that it inspired a verse in a local journal:

Der Mann mit
Hautbois er woll' die Leute zeigen
Wie mit sein Athem
er kann biß in Wolken steigen.[190]

That man with the
Hautbois wanted to show
How on his breath he
could ascend to the clouds.

The aria, marked Andante, was the lovely, bittersweet 'Già sereno il disperai' in the opera *Solimano* of 1753, and was sung by the tenor Angelo Amorevoli. The audience, according to Fürstenau, was in raptures.

Another remarkable hautboist was Giuseppe Sammartini.[191] Hawkins grew up hearing Sammartini play concerts in London, and wrote of him: 'As a performer on the hautboy, Martini was undoubtedly the greatest that the world had ever known.'[192] Sammartini deeply affected his audiences and (in an age when musical fashions changed quickly) his playing was fondly remembered well into the next century. He performed at the Opera, gave public concerts, and from 1736 was music master of the family of the Prince of Wales. Sammartini was never a regular member of the Opera orchestra, but was featured as an invited soloist, like the star singers. He appeared with Farinelli in February 1735 in the aria 'Lusingato dalla speme' in *Polifemo*, which Porpora had written for the two of them. In 1737, Handel featured Sammartini in three virtuoso arias in different operas at Covent Garden.[193] These arias showed off Sammartini's technique in many exposed passages, and even offered him long solo cadenzas.

NEW MUSICAL CURRENTS, 1730–1760

More solo and chamber music for hautboy survives from between 1730 and 1760 than from any other thirty-year period. And this music was changing: in a lighter, simpler, 'galant' style, it avoided counterpoint and independent movement. Short-limbed melodies, rhythmic squareness and slow harmonic rhythm are typical of music in this period written for hautboy.

In France, music underwent a sudden and dramatic change. From the profundity and sincerity of the music of Couperin and Philidor to that of Corrette and Naudot, composition spurted a 'trifling, frothy Music'[194] like champagne, too long bottled up in the oppressive uniformity of the end of Louis XIV's reign. Composers of hautboy music like Boismortier, the Chédevilles, Guillemain, Lavaux, Lavigne and Mondonville, writing in the new 'Louis Quinze' style, combined buoyancy, nonchalance and frivolity with graciousness. The character of this period seems epitomized by one of Lavigne's sonatas, *La D'Agut*, two of the five movements of which are marked 'Gracieusement' (another movement is 'Légerement'). Vivaldi became popular in Paris in this period. Even Rameau's operas, still reflecting the conservatism of the Opéra (which had become an untouchable national icon), included obbligatos for one or two hautboys with voice that were exceptionally short in comparison with those of either Bach or the opera seria.

Germany produced a significant repertoire for hautboy in this period. Fasch's hautboy compositions from after 1730, for instance, are very engaging, continuing the style of writing for woodwinds that Telemann had pioneered but neglected towards the end of his life. Fasch's sonata in g minor for two hautboys and continuo (FWV N:g2) is particularly good. It survives in two manuscript copies (Berlin and Brussels, the latter with added ornaments), an indication of its popularity. This piece is obviously written by someone with an appreciation of the playing qualities of the hautboy, and it contains many interesting musical ideas. It has a curious similarity to Emanuel Bach's solo sonata, also in g minor, in its form and character.

Emanuel Bach's benchmark sonata (H 549) is one of the masterpieces of the hautboy literature. It was probably composed in the first half of the 1730s, when he was in his late teens and still in Leipzig.[195] It might well have been performed at one of his father's Collegium sessions by any of a number of good players (Böhm is known to have visited Saxony – probably Leipzig – in the 1730s, for instance, and Richter and Antonio Besozzi, based in Dresden, could easily have played in Leipzig as well).

Because the Berlin style ossified, several pieces published as late as the 1770s are still very convincingly in the *galant* rather than the Classical style. Kirnberger's wonderful Sonata 'für die Oboe' from *Vermischte Musikalien* (Berlin, 1769) is an example. The piece is not unlike Emanuel Bach's sonata composed a generation earlier. In his *Musikalisches Vielerley* (1770), Emanuel Bach also published two remarkable 'Sonate[n] für die Hautbois' by the hautboist Carl Ludwig Matthes.[196] The style is similar to Bach's own. Among the more interesting chamber pieces from this period are the twenty-two trios and quartets by J. G. Janitsch, written in Berlin in the 1750s and 60s.

Another delightful *galant* hautboy solo is the *Sonata a due* in C minor by the Catalan hautboy virtuoso Joan Baptista Pla, probably written while he was at Stuttgart.[197] Pla cleverly chose technical effects that 'play themselves' on the hautboy but sound 'difficult' to the ear.[198]

Alessandro Besozzi published several good hautboy pieces, although only one of his 'little conversations' for hautboy and bassoon is known to survive. His *Six solos with continuo* were published in London in 1759; they are all good, especially the second and sixth. They were advertised for 'German Flute, Hautboy, or Violin', but were no doubt conceived for hautboy. Besozzi is also survived by sonatas for two hautboys and continuo as well as several hautboy concertos.

Matteo Bissoli's excellent hautboy sonata in g minor, probably written about 1750, is a virtuoso display piece full of unusual harmonies, and the earliest known composition to use f3. Bissoli, a close colleague of Tartini and Vallotti at Padua's Sant'Antonio cathedral, was a celebrated player whom Burney praised in his diary when he stopped at Padua in the 1770s.[199]

In England in 1748, Sammartini's pupil Thomas Vincent Jr published a charming set of *Six Solos*, op. 1, for 'Hautboy, German Flute, Violin, or Harpsichord' that fit the hautboy well. Vincent would probably have been using a Type C hautboy like his teacher.[200]

André Philidor's youngest son, François-André Philidor (born when his father was 79), was notable in Paris as an opera composer. Philidor is generally acknowledged to have been the best chess player of his generation and probably the next as well; his opening defence (he usually played black) is still well known.[201] He lived in England in the years preceding the publication of his *Art de la modulation* (1755), which consists of six quartets for hautboy, two violins and continuo, and is of considerable interest musically. The use of the names 'oboe' on the part and 'haut-boy' in the title suggests that it was written for an English player.[202] Despite the date, the melodies and harmonies of *L'Art de la modulation* are already very much in a Classical idiom, and the pieces resemble later hautboy quartets.

Parallel with the rise of the string quartet and inspired by the same aesthetic, quartets for violin, viola, cello and hautboy began appearing in the 1750s. In these hautboy quartets, the cello part no longer functions like a continuo bass and is not figured; it is simply the lowest melodic part. The genre was especially popular after about 1770, and virtually replaced the solo sonata as the hautboy's main chamber music solo medium. Early examples are F. L. Gassmann's *Sei Quartetti*, op. 1 (H 481–6). In contrast to later hautboy quartets, Gassmann's *Quartetti* do not cast the hautboy consistently as the soloist but rather as an equal member of the ensemble, and the hautboy parts are not designed for virtuoso display.

Chapter 4

From Classical hautboy to keyed oboe, 1760–1825

The common [traditional two-keyed] hautboy ('le Hautbois ordinaire') is a defective wind instrument; it uses irrational fingerings, uneven tones, and cannot be played in all the keys.[1]

The compleat hautboy: consolidation (1760–1790)

Symbolically at least, historians put the beginning of the Industrial Revolution at 1765, the year the steam engine was invented. Music, however, moves at its own rhythm, and the hautboy was far from becoming industrialized in the late eighteenth century. The many forms that had been developed since about 1730 gradually coalesced at about this time into one principal type, known now as the 'Classical hautboy'. The new model was a response to the innovations in the music of this period: an interest in sharper tonalities, for instance, and an extended upper range, a tendency to remain longer in the higher register, as well as a certain delicacy and precision in expressing musical ideas. The standard model, Type D, answered these new demands; it was the oboe for which composers like Josef and Michael Haydn, Pleyel, Mozart, Stamitz, Boccherini, Cambini, Dittersdorf, Rosetti and Beethoven conceived their music.

To us, this new Type D appears as part of a continuum leading from the Baroque instruments to the Conservatoire oboe – a segment of a larger picture, as it were. But at the time it would of course have seemed different. To hautboists born around 1730 or shortly after, raised and trained on the numerous experimental types of the previous generation, this new model must have seemed 'state of the art' and (for the time) as perfect a model as could be desired to meet the musical demands of the period. Considering the recurrent changes and variations of the previous generation, Type D remained standard for a remarkably long stretch of time. Although by the end of the century there were experiments with added keys, the basic dimensions of the instrument (the bore, layout of the tone-holes, and acoustic length) remained stable for about two generations.

The typical profile of the Type D is shown in ills 18g–j. The earliest form, the Type D1, was developed somewhat before the 1760s. Instruments from the later eighteenth century were often left in the natural golden colour of boxwood, in contrast to earlier models, which were usually stained darker. Type D2, the 'classic' form of the Classical hautboy, is found in works of art from about 1770 to 1828. In outward form, it had abandoned the experiments of the previous generation (represented by Types B, C and E) and reverted to a more complex profile similar to the Baroque A2 design. The external shape, though easy to see, was not the real issue, however. Internally, Type D2 was fundamentally different from hautboys of the early eighteenth century, representing a culmination of tendencies that had begun with previous models as early as 1730. Narrow bores and diminutive tone-holes were the most typical traits of hautboys of the Classical period, and their effect was as revolutionary as the basic alterations that produced the new fortepiano out of the harpsichord. Indeed, the fortepiano came into its own at about the same time as the Type D2 hautboy; both instruments had had earlier prototypes.

Type D, like Type A, was popular during a period of stability. Both types served as archetypal models recognized as consistent standards. The proportions of Type D, however, contrasted with Type A. Late eighteenth-century hautboy balusters followed much more strictly the principles of Classical geometric proportion, quite literally reproducing the antique Greek shapes that inspired moulding design.[2] By contrast, the balusters of earlier eighteenth-century hautboys were freer and less exact in following Classical principles (cf. ills 18a and 18b). It is as if the Type D profile was a self-conscious attempt to improve on the Type A by being more 'correct'; this may reflect the general respect for formalism in the late eighteenth century. The shape of Classical balusters, which to most modern eyes seems exaggerated, was quite stylized and consistent.

Acoustically speaking, an overall narrower bore makes an hautboy brighter and softer in timbre, and this is an accurate description of Type D2. Its flexible, gentle qualities answered to the taste of the period. It was generally at a higher pitch, which also had an effect on its sound and character; Type D2 was a 'lite' hautboy compared with its earlier Baroque counterpart. It was a smaller vessel into which to pour the player's energy, and the Classical hautboy's special gift was its ability to etch details finely, and to express subtle, *empfindsam* moods or affects.[3] Although with its narrower bore and tone-holes it was a less robust instrument than the Baroque hautboy, and had a smaller dynamic range, its sharper and more focused tone blended less than earlier hautboys had done, and helped it to be heard through the strings of an orchestra. With its smaller dimensions, it also reacted more quickly to tuning corrections. The Classical hautboy could be characterized as the greyhound or racehorse of the oboe group, and (like the music it played) its character was quick and evanescent.

Type D was not the only model in use in the Classical period; the straight-top, which had existed from the 1730s, continued to have a minority presence in both Italy and England into the nineteenth century, and in France the Type E still seems to have had some currency.

PLAYERS

There were a great many successful players in this period, and first-class hautboy soloists were in high demand. In 1772, for instance, when Kraft Ernst was putting together a new orchestra at his court in Wallerstein (later to become known as one of the finest in central Europe), his musical adviser, Ignaz von Beecke, wrote to him that 'The oboes and the horns are the soul of the orchestra, and we will have difficulty [finding] good oboes'.[4]

Beecke eventually located two excellent players, the then-young Joseph Fiala (twenty-three years old) and Xaver Fürall, both of whom were later to play in the Hofkapelle at Vienna (a number of beautiful pieces for the hautboy by Fiala survive).[5] Neither player stayed at Wallerstein for long, however; Fiala had moved on to Munich by 1777 and Fürall left in 1779. Fiala was replaced by a friend of the Mozarts from Salzburg, Marx Berwein.[6] On his famous trip to Mannheim in 1777, Wolfgang Mozart, then twenty-one, stopped off at Wallerstein to visit Berwein and gave him a copy of the hautboy concerto he had just written (now known as KV 271k).

The two best-known hautboy soloists in Europe in the 1770s were probably Johann Christian Fischer (1733–1800) and Carlo Besozzi (1738–p.1798).[7] Both players were associated with Dresden, but while Besozzi had returned there in the mid-1760s after the Prussian occupation, Fischer seems to have been on an extended leave of absence. When he was considering a move back from London to Dresden, J. G. Naumann, director of music at Dresden, commented on this possibility: 'It would bestow a singular lustre on the electoral orchestra if not only Besozzi but Fischer (who are at present the two most celebrated virtuosos on their instrument) were to be appointed to it.'[8]

Comparing these two players, Burney recalled of his recent visit to Dresden:

After this, Signor [Carlo] Besozzi played an extremely difficult concerto on the hautbois, in a very pleasing and masterly manner; yet I must own that the less one thinks of Fischer, the more one likes this performer . . . whether from being in less constant practice, or from the greater difficulty of the passages, I know not, [his reed] more frequently fails Besozzi in rapid divisions, than [that of] Fischer. . . .[9]

Besozzi was highly esteemed as a teacher and his *Études* are still studied today on the Conservatoire oboe. Burney went on to say of him:

Signor Bezozzi performed, after this, a new concerto on the hautbois, which was very graceful and ingenious. The *Allegro* was more rapid, and of a still more difficult execution, than that in his preceding piece. He exerted himself very much in this performance, which ended with a pleasing rondeau, and left the company in great good humour. He afterwards was prevailed on, though not without difficulty, to play, by way of *bonne bouche*, Fischer's well-known rondeau minuet, which he had performed here so frequently, and with such applause, that I had been assured he made more of it than the author himself; but I cannot say that his present performance of it convinced me of the truth of this assertion. However, after being accustomed to the exquisite manner in which Mr. Fischer has played it in England, it is no small praise to say, that I heard Signor Bezozzi perform it with great pleasure.

What Burney called 'Fischer's well-known rondeau minuet' was probably the 'famous Rondo', the last movement of Fischer's first Concerto in C (published c.1768), a movement that inspired several later variations, including those of Wolfgang Mozart (KV 179). Gainsborough painted a fine portrait of Fischer, who married his daughter Mary in 1780.

As a boy of nine, Mozart had met Fischer in the Hague, when both musicians were on tour. They did not meet again until many years later, on the occasion of Fischer's visit to Vienna in 1787 (together with Ramm). On that occasion Mozart went to hear Fischer play some of his concertos, but was less than enthusiastic, as he wrote to his father:

> [4 April 1787] If [Fischer] when we knew him in Holland [in 1765] played no better than he does now, he certainly does not deserve the reputation he enjoys. . . . In those days I was not competent to form an opinion. All that I remember is that I liked his playing immensely, as indeed everyone did. This is quite understandable, of course, on the assumption that taste can undergo remarkable changes. Possibly he plays in some old-fashioned style? Not at all! The long and short of it is that he plays like a bad beginner. Young André, who took some lessons from Fiala, plays a thousand times better. . . . Each ritornello lasts a quarter of an hour; and then our hero comes in, lifts up one leaden foot after the other and stamps on the floor with each in turn. His tone is entirely nasal, and his held notes like the tremulant on the organ.[10]

Carlo Besozzi was a member of one of the most phenomenal hautboy families in history. As we saw in the last chapter, the previous generations had already produced notable players, including Giuseppe Besozzi, whose career was cut short by blindness. Giuseppe was probably the teacher of three of the most important Besozzis of the generation just before Carlo's: Giuseppe's younger brother Alessandro (at Turin), and his own two sons Antonio and Gaetano. In the case of Alessandro and his brother, the bassoonist Paolo Girolamo, whose brilliant success was described in the last chapter, we have another memorable description by Burney, who heard them in 1770:

> The compositions of these excellent musicians generally consist of select and detached passages, yet so elaborately finished, that, like select thoughts or maxims in literature, each is not a fragment, but a whole; these pieces are in a peculiar manner adapted to display the powers of the performers; but it is difficult to describe their style of playing. Their compositions when printed, give but an imperfect idea of it. So much expression! such delicacy! such a perfect acquiescence and agreement together, that many of the passages seem heart-felt sighs, breathed through the same reed. No brilliancy of execution is aimed at, all are notes of meaning. The imitations are exact; the melody is pretty equally distributed between the two instruments; each *forte, piano, crescendo, diminuendo,* and *appoggiatura,* is observed with a minute exactness, which could be attained only by such a long residence and study together.

27. Coloured pencil drawing by Wilhelm von Kobell. Friedrich Ramm (middle figure, holding pipe) with the actor F. A. Zuccarini (left) and von Schlösser (right) playing cards.

The eldest brother has lost his under front teeth, and complained of age; and it is natural to suppose that the performance of each has been better; however, to me, who heard them now for the first time, it was charming. If there is any defect in so exquisite a performance, it arises from the *equal perfection* of the *two parts*, which distracts the attention, and renders it impossible to listen to both, when both have dissimilar melodies equally pleasing.

As we have seen, Antonio Besozzi, nephew of these players and Carlo's father, very successfully occupied the position of hautboy soloist at the Dresden court from the late 1730s, probably the most important hautboy post in Germany at the time. Antonio's brother Gaetano (who had begun his career in the Naples Opera at the age of nine) moved to Paris in 1765 and became the leading hautboist in France; he later moved to London.[11] These two brothers, Antonio and Gaetano, like their uncle Alessandro, probably started their impressive careers on hautboys made by Carlo Palanca, but the young Carlo Besozzi, like Fischer, may well have used instruments made in his native Dresden by the two makers there, Grenser and Grundmann (to be described in more detail below).

Among the hautboists with whom Mozart collaborated were Gioseffo Secchi, Giuseppe Ferlendis and Joseph Fiala.[12] Secchi was first hautboy of the Cappella Reale in Turin by 1755, then Kammervirtuos for the Elector of Bavaria (with a corresponding high salary) and from 1776 played again in Turin at the Teatro Regio, replacing the aging Alessandro Besozzi. Mozart knew the other two players, Ferlendis and Fiala, in Salzburg, where they had been in the service of Archbishop Colloredo in 1777 and 1778, and had become family friends. But the only player who was able to inspire a number of hautboy solos from Mozart's pen was Friedrich Ramm (c.1741–1813; see ill. 27).[13] Ramm was one of the soloists in the famous orchestra at Mannheim. Mozart met him there in 1777 and was immediately impressed. Ramm, for his part, enthusiastically adopted the hautboy concerto Mozart had just written (and just given to Berwein as well). In the ensuing years, Mozart wrote a number of solos for Ramm, of which the best-known is the hautboy quartet (KV 370).

Of necessity, hautboists worked for musical establishments, as in the case of Sallantin (the Opéra and Conservatoire) and Gaetano Besozzi (the Chapelle Royale/Chambre du Roi respectively) in France, Richard and Thomas Vincent in England (His Majesty's Band and the Queen's Band), and Franz Joseph Czerwenka in Vienna (the Kaiserliche Hof-Musikkappelle). Some players, however, spent much of their time on the road, travelling as exhibitionist celebrities and often performing music they had written for themselves. Besides Ramm, Fischer and Besozzi, the best-known of these itinerant virtuosos were Ludwig August Lebrun, Ferlendis and Fiala. Space does not permit full biographies of the many well-known virtuosos of this period, so we shall briefly review the careers of a few representative players.[14]

Among orchestral hautboists, those at Mannheim deserve mention. In 1778 this orchestra moved to Munich with the Elector Carl Theodor. The Elector suddenly found himself possessed of two fine orchestras, which he proceeded to amalgamate. Secchi had been at the Munich court until 1776 (when he left for Turin), at which point Fiala took over the first chair (playing clandestinely at Salzburg at the same time). The hautboists who arrived from Mannheim were Ramm, Lebrun and J. W. Hieber. Fiala left Munich when the Mannheim players arrived, Hieber died in 1787, and Lebrun in 1790 (Lebrun, one of the best-known virtuosos of his day, was almost constantly on tour, performing with his wife, the famous singer Francisca Danzi; he was only thirty-eight when he died).[15] Mozart worked with the Munich orchestra in 1780–1, when he produced his new opera *Idomeneo*, and it was in the same months that he wrote the quartet for Ramm.

In Paris, Antoine Sallantin (or Sallentin) was probably the best-known hautboist of the Classical period.[16] He was an active performer at the Concert Spirituel, playing both flute and hautboy solos (his debut was in 1768 at the age of twelve).[17] Sallantin was the first flutist at the Opéra from 1770, later playing principal hautboy, a post he held until 1813. In the early 1790s, just after the Revolution, Sallantin went to London to study with Fischer, whom he had heard play at the Concert Spirituel. On his return in 1792 he was appointed head hautboy professor at the newly-instituted Conservatoire (where, among others, he taught the player who would succeed him in 1816, Gustave Vogt). Sallantin was a friend of the composers François Devienne (the six sonates of 1793 were dedicated to him) and Karl Bochsa (who dedicated his *Trois quatuors concertans* to him in c.1800). Sallantin played with Devienne (on flute and bassoon), the bassoonist Étienne Ozi, and other leading musicians of the day.

Richard and Thomas Vincent, hautboy-playing brothers, were active in London into the early 1780s. The frequent historical references to 'Mr Vincent' are ambiguous because of the parallel careers of the two players. Richard Vincent was the elder and was first hautboy at Covent Garden and Vauxhall Gardens, as well as a member of His Majesty's Band and the Queen's Band.[18] He was a composer of songs. His brother, Thomas Vincent Jr, played in the King's/Queen's Band from 1735 to at least 1778 and was Music Director of the King's Theatre, 1765–9. Thomas Vincent studied with Sammartini and was performing with him by 1744. His playing was praised by Burney and others. His Six Solos (mentioned in chapter 3) are fine pieces. He was the solo hautboy at the Handel Commemoration Festival in 1784.

Franz Joseph Czerwenka worked under Haydn at Esterhazy and moved to Vienna in 1794.[19] He played in numerous ensembles including the orchestras of the Kärntnertor Theatre (1794–1829) and the Hofkapelle (from c.1801). Czerwenka was praised for his 'soft and cultured [gebildet und zart]' hautboy playing,[20] and Salieri called him 'the solo hautboist in Vienna who can truly be called "buonissimo"'. In 1797, Czerwenka played the first part in the première of Beethoven's trio for two hautboys and English horn, and Beethoven's variations on 'Là ci darem la mano' for this same combination was written for him (as was Franz Krommer's Concerto in F, op. 37, 1803). He may have played in the premières of Beethoven's last three symphonies at the Kärntnertor Theatre.[21]

REPERTOIRE

Some of the music written for the Classical Type D2 hautboy is still played today, but the majority of this rich and brilliant repertoire (about half of which was written by hautboists for their own use) remains as yet unknown and untried. Part of the reason for this is that – compared with the late eighteenth century, when this music was written – there are now relatively few opportunities for oboists to perform as soloists with orchestras or in chamber situations. Also, modern musical culture is not especially curious about the music of composers who are not 'great', and comparatively little solo and chamber music for hautboy survives from the pens of Josef Haydn (whose hautboy concerto is now ascribed to Ignaz Malzat[22]), Mozart and Beethoven (including a concerto written in Bonn c.1793, possibly for Georg Libisch (1751–1829), but either left incomplete or lost[23]). Thus the Classical hautboy possesses a sizeable 'buried treasure' of manuscripts in libraries, mostly from Germany and the Habsburg lands, that are as yet unexplored.[24]

By the 1770s, many of the solo and chamber genres that had provided showplaces for the hautboy in earlier times had fallen out of favour. Duets without bass and solo concertos continued to be popular, but the trio and solo sonata had virtually disappeared. They were replaced by the hautboy quartet (sometimes quintet), mentioned at the end of the previous chapter. Mozart's quartet is the most famous of this genre, but a hundred or so hautboy quartets survive, many of them excellent.[25]

Another new form was the wind octet, which was cultivated especially in Vienna along with other small wind ensembles collectively known as Harmonie-Musik. Ensembles of this type attracted a number of composers. Mozart was obliged to make quick arrangements of each of his operas for wind octet, for instance, for fear that some other enterprising musician would beat him to it (such arrangements – by others – still survive and some have been published in modern editions). Mozart also wrote two excellent original wind octets (KV 375 and 388) as well as his superb thirteen-part 'Gran Partita' for octet with added basset horns, horns and contrabass (KV 361).

The instrumentation of the late eighteenth-century wind octet was the logical result of the evolution of the wind band concept. As we have seen, the preferred formation at the beginning of the eighteenth century was exclusively double-reeds (usually a combination of treble hautboys, tenor hautboys and bassoons). As time went on, the tenor hautboys were often replaced with horns. About mid-century, clarinets began to replace hautboys, making a band of pairs of hautboys or clarinets, horns, and one to two bassoons. The wind octet in Vienna built on this basis, using pairs of hautboys, English horns, horns and bassoons. From the early 1770s, with the presence in Vienna of good clarinettists like the Stadler brothers, the clarinet began to take over the English horn parts, making an ensemble of paired hautboys, clarinets, horns and bassoons.

Wind chamber music was very popular in Vienna in this period. Some 400 band musicians were in the service of the Viennese nobility in the 1780s – enough to staff fifty standing octets.[26] David Whitwell has drawn attention to the élitist status of this 'incredible Vienna octet school'. These ensembles had no function beyond providing concerts for the city's privileged classes, and in fact performed only rarely in public.[27]

INSTRUMENTS AND REEDS

The custom of dating instruments became more common among hautboy makers in this period. Some forty dated hautboys survive by one of the best-known Dresden makers, Jacob Grundmann. He worked from 1753 to 1800, and his earliest surviving dated instruments are from 1768.[28] The existence of dated hautboys by a single maker of reputation like Grundmann allows us to trace the changing designs of good, representative instruments between 1768 and 1800 almost to the year.[29]

By this period, Dresden had become the most important centre of woodwind making in Europe; its reputation even gave rise to a number of counterfeit instruments that bore its name. The workshops of Grundmann and his assistant Friedrich Floth, together with those of Augustin Grenser and his nephew Heinrich Grenser, dominated the hautboy market in most countries during the last quarter of the eighteenth century. Instruments by these makers represent nearly a fifth of surviving hautboys from all periods.[30] Augustin Grenser moved from Leipzig to Dresden a year after Antonio Besozzi was appointed principal hautboy there, and Grundmann followed him in the early 1750s. It is likely these two makers moved to Dresden to work with Besozzi and to learn more of his Italian instruments, which they then developed further together. The earliest surviving hautboys by Grenser and Grundmann closely resemble the instruments of Carlo Palanca of Turin, who probably supplied instruments to the Besozzis. It may have been with the active collaboration of the important players at Dresden, Antonio Besozzi, his son Carlo, and Fischer, that Grenser and Grundmann developed the Type D2, an outgrowth of Palanca's design and a model that eventually became the prototypical European Classical hautboy.[31]

Few of the instruments Grenser and Grundmann made prior to 1770 are known. This is probably due to the disastrous Seven Years War of 1756–63, during which Dresden was bombarded and occupied by the Prussians, who destroyed the opera house and caused the break-up of the Capelle. By the 1770s, when the war was finished, these makers were using the D2 profile.

Woodwinds by the Dresden makers were known in most of Europe, and they had a certain following in the Habsburg lands. In 1776, for instance, Leopold Mozart ordered pairs of hautboys and English horns from Grenser for the Salzburg court.[32] But they did not have the market to themselves. In 1766, when Josef Haydn needed new hautboys, he had to look no further than Vienna and the maker Rockobaur,[33] who in his opinion was 'the most skilful in such things'. There were other active workshops in Germany besides the ones at Dresden (for instance, Sattler and Crone in Leipzig, Engelhard in Nuremberg, and Freyer and Kirst in Potsdam).[34]

In Paris, Thomas Lot, perhaps the most successful Parisian maker from the 1730s onwards, worked until the late 1780s, evidently concentrating on the low-pitched Type E hautboy, a French speciality. From the 1780s we first hear of the instruments of Christophe Delusse, which resemble Italian hautboys of the previous generation. Many instruments by Delusse have survived, and they were adopted by the professors

28. Delusse hautboy.

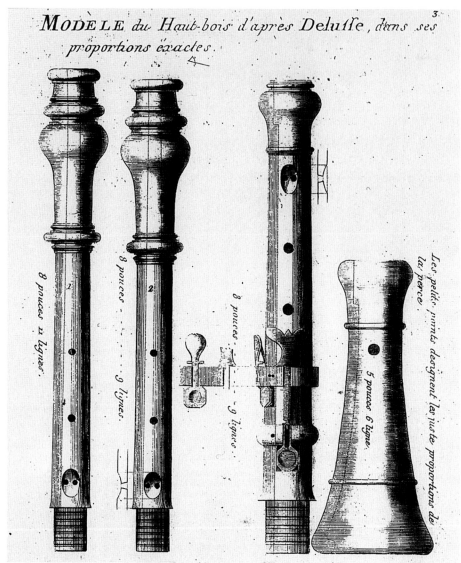

MODÈLE du Haut-bois d'après Delusse, dans ses proportions exactes.

29. Scale drawing of a Delusse hautboy in François-Joseph Garnier, *Méthode raisonnée pour le haut-bois* (Paris, 1802).

of the Conservatoire at the end of the century; Garnier in his *Méthode* of 1802 shows one, and both Sallantin and Vogt are known to have used them (see ills 28 and 29). Delusse's hautboys were played into the 1820s, and extra keys were added to a number of surviving instruments. Delusse used a distinctive top baluster profile that was even wider than those of German makers (see ills 28 and 29 and the Lesti and Fornari instruments in fig. 36 in Adkins 2001).

English hautboys of this period seem to have been strongly under the influence of the Dresden makers, reinforced by the phenomenal popularity of Fischer (who moved to London in 1768). Delusse-type balusters are also sometimes seen on hautboys by London makers, including Kusder, and Goulding & Wood.

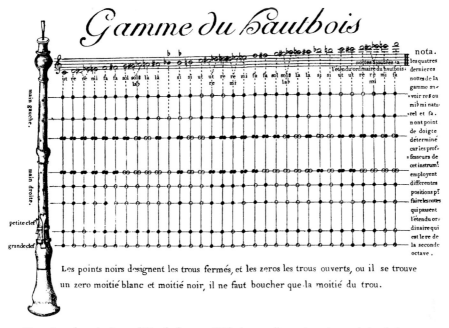

Les points noirs désignent les trous fermés, et les zeros les trous ouverts, ou il se trouve un zero moitié blanc et moitié noir, il ne faut boucher que la moitié du trou.

30. Fingering chart in Amand Vanderhagen, *Méthode nouvelle et raisonnée pour le hautbois*, c.1790.

The most fundamental difference between the hautboys of this generation and earlier ones lies in the diameter of their bores. The bore chokes of hautboys before 1730 averaged close to 6.0 mm; between 1730 and 1760 the average was 5.6, and between 1760 and 1790 it was 4.5. Bores after 1790 went up to 5.0, which was still considerably smaller than the dimensions before 1730. Thus the hautboy of this period (1730–1820) is often characterized as 'narrow-bored'. Furthermore, the tone-

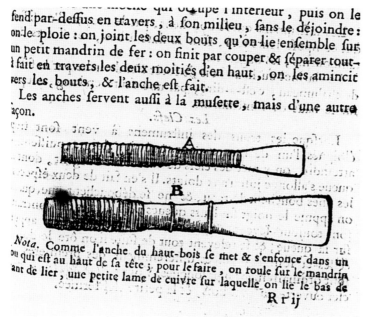

31. Garsault, *Notionaire*, 1761. Hautboy and bassoon reeds.

32. Anonymous, 1767. Portrait of Sante Aguilar (oil?).

33. Joseph Tirabosco (second half of eighteenth century), portrait of Matthoei Bissoli Brixiensis.

holes of the Classical hautboy were minuscule compared with models of any period before (or since).[35]

Pitch, which is one of the basic variables that influence the character and sound of an oboe, also differed. By 1770, as if in reaction to the bewildering variety of standards in the mid-century, most of Europe had settled into a relatively unanimous level. The principal woodwind pitch between 1770 and 1800 all over Europe was in the mid-430s, with woodwinds in Vienna (the centre of the most interesting musical developments of the period) at A–438.[36] This standard needed to be fairly common, since musicians travelled more than ever in this period. As pitch became more or less standardized and the differences that existed became less extreme, discrepancies could be resolved by using alternative top joints,[37] which were probably spaced at intervals of about a comma (roughly 5–6 Hz at A–440). In his *Méthode raisonnée pour le hautbois* of 1802, Garnier showed an hautboy by Delusse with two *corps de rechange* (ill. 29). He wrote: '[The hautboy] has two similar top joints, which are numbered. Number 2 gives the standard pitch; with number 1 the instrument is made longer by two [*lignes*[38] (= 4.5 mm)], and is thus lower [in pitch].'

Alternative top joints survive from many of the best-known makers of the late eighteenth century, and by the turn of the century H. C. Koch mentioned that it was common for hautboys to have three.[39] At the beginning of the nineteenth century, Sallantin and Vogt used hautboys with alternative *corps*. Players who had no need to change pitch between different venues probably used only one joint and adjusted

34. Johann Joseph Zoffany (?), *The oboe player*, c.1770. Oil painting.

35. Anonymous, portrait of a man holding an oboe. Oil, late eighteenth century; ?English.

their reeds to match the pitch they needed. Koch remarked: 'One has the advantage with [the hautboy] . . . that for small variations of pitch the tuning can be corrected with the help of somewhat shorter or longer staples [*Stiefel des Rohres*].' *Corps de rechange* may have eventually been adopted because of the reduction in the size of both bore and reed width in the later eighteenth century. These changes tended to make the pitch more specific and thus more difficult to adjust by means of the reed.

There were other devices for fine adjustments to pitch. Weber describes an hautboy with interchangeable top columns (the straight part of the top joint below the column beads). Tuning slides also appeared. Some were made of wood only, and functioned like sockets and tenons.[40] The flutes and hautboys by Stephan Koch (1772–1828) in Vienna had a thin metal sleeve at the top of the bore that could telescope upwards to increase the bore length. This device, which is shown in Sellner's method, was applied first to the traverso and was discussed by Quantz in the 1750s.[41]

The first mention we have found of the peculiar habit of taking 'the A' from the oboe comes from the early years of the nineteenth century. Sallantin mentioned having to go to the Opéra early to give the pitch to the first violinist.[42] Why the oboe should be regarded as a reliable carrier of pitch (compared with a warmed-up clarinet, or even a flute) is a mystery.

For an idea of what reeds looked like at the time, ills 30 to 36 and 55 show examples from the 1760s to the 1810s. This is the earliest period from which original oboe reeds have survived,[43] and they have the following general dimensions (in millimetres):

36. Drawing of an hautboy with fingering chart in Gustave Vogt, *Méthode de hautbois* (c.1816–25).

	Maximum	Minimum	Average
Tip width	11.5	8.0	
Cane length	27.25	12.5	21.18
Total length	69.2	53.5	
Staple bottom diameter	5.5	4.0	4.71

Since the sample is fairly large (at least twenty-six reeds) and corresponds reasonably well with the iconography of the period (the reed shown in ill. 35 is about 8.9 wide and 22.3 long[44]), these averages are probably representative. But it should be noted that most surviving reeds are English, and reeds in England were influenced by the German hautboists who were active there in the late eighteenth and early nineteenth centuries.[45] Bainbridge wrote in 1823 (17–18): 'On the size of the cane, for making Oboe Reeds, there are different opinions. The French Oboe players use a small sized cane. . . . In England the Reeds are generally made, for professors, of a larger sized cane. The English professors have certainly the fullest tone, and it is accounted for by their Reeds being larger than the French Reeds. . . .' The French hautboist François-Joseph Garnier seems to confirm this with his comment in 1802: 'A reed that is too broad alters the tone quality of the instrument and resembles that of the bassoon.' The reed Garnier shows on his plate (ill. 55a) is about 9.5 mm wide. Interestingly, on Garnier's fingering charts on pages 12 and 16 (ill. 40), this reed is shown inserted very deeply into the counterbore; only a small amount of thread is visible. Sellner in Vienna also wrote in 1824 (7) about over-wide reeds: 'When finished, the reed should not be too wide; otherwise the quality of tone is affected and approaches that of the English horn.'

Not all professionals in the eighteenth century made their reeds themselves; some got them from instrument makers. Haydn made regular orders of hautboy and English horn reeds (by the dozen) from the maker who provided his hautboys, Rockobaur.[46] And Vanderhagen (c.1790:5) commented on his Parisian colleagues: 'There are few professional players [*proffesseurs*] who do not know how to make [reeds]; it would be much easier if every player made them, stronger or weaker according to their embouchures.' That reed-making was often considered a part of instrument making rather than playing is suggested by a passage in Étienne Ozi (1803:142): 'Although reed-making would seem to belong more in the province of the making of Bassoons, and for this reason, perhaps, it may be surprising to find instructions on the subject here, the success of players who have had the patience to work on them has moved us to place at the end of this bassoon method some suggestions on the way to make reeds.'

Two kinds of larger-sized hautboys achieved prominence in the Classical period, both pitched in F. They were probably better known, in fact, than the larger models of previous generations had been (the hautbois d'amour and oboe da caccia, which by the late eighteenth century were moribund). The vox humana or voce umana was a straight tenor in F in two parts (the centre joint and bell were unseparated), with a straight profile.[47] Vox humanas were made as early as the 1730s (by Stanesby Jr) and used in England primarily to accompany church choirs. They existed in Naples and Rome in the 1760s and were used there as solo instruments in opera orchestras; the surviving Italian instruments are all made by Giovanni Panormo, and are provided with ivory rosettes at the bell opening. A vox humana described as in 'cornett' (i.e., probably at cornet-ton, A + 1, a pitch still used at the time in churches) was offered for sale by Friedrich Lempp in 1789.[48]

The vox humana was quickly supplanted in Italy by the new English horn, which became the principal tenor oboe at the end of the century. The eighteenth-century English horn (like the earlier oboe da caccia) was usually curved and covered in leather, although an angular model emerged in the 1790s. It was first used by the composers of Italian opera in Vienna, especially Gluck, starting in the 1750s. The instrument was one of Josef Haydn's favourite woodwinds, and he began using it in the 1760s. His brother Michael in Salzburg also wrote for the English horn, and it was frequently heard in Vienna during the last decades of the century. Michael Finkelman has drawn attention to the Viennese virtuoso Philipp Teimer, around whom a Singspiel similar to Mozart's *Die Zauberflöte* was written by Mederitsch and von Winter in 1797; the work, *Babylons Pyramiden*, featured a Romantic lead singer who played English horn instead of flute (keeping the reed both safe and wet enough to play must have been a challenge: Finkelman 1999 (Tibia 4/99): 19–20). Teimer and his brothers Johann and Franz performed a trio for two hautboys and English horn by Johann Went at the Vienna Tonkünstler Sozietät in 1793 that may have inspired Beethoven to write his trios for the same combination. The English horn's popularity in Vienna may have had its roots in Italy; the instrument was in use in Naples by the 1750s and in Venice by the 70s. From there it may have spread to other courts that emulated the taste of Vienna, such as Schwerin, Wallerstein and Donaueschingen. The surviving music for the instrument from this period is often virtuosic. Among the best-known players of the English horn was Giuseppe Ferlendis, whose fame led him later to be credited with having invented it; Ferlendis played on the excellent instruments of the Venetian maker Andrea Fornari.[49]

It seems the English horn was not cultivated in Paris during the eighteenth century; Gluck had to substitute clarinets for the English horn parts in his Parisian version of *Orfée* (although the first known method for English horn was published by a Frenchman, Frédéric Chalon, in c.1802). The instrument was not available at the Opéra until 1808, when it was first played by Gustave Vogt, who later became famous for his English horn solos.

THE UPPER REGISTER

In the playing technique of the Type D hautboy, the most basic technical issue was that range and tessitura were both going up. The mean range of Mozart's hautboy quartet, for instance, is about a major third higher than Bach's hautboy solos.[50] To meet this demand, players resorted to the use of 'long' fingerings (also called 'harmonic' fingerings) for b♭2, b2, and c3. A speaker key, the so-called 'F-Klappe', also made its first appearance towards the end of the century (see below). Both these expedients helped players obtain security in the high register and response in wide upward slurs (though they were bought at the price of complicated finger combinations, an added register break above a2, and a tone quality different from the notes below).

The long fingerings varied but were often b♭2 = 12 456 7, b2 = 1 3 456 7, and c3 = 23 45 7. These fingerings could even be produced by slurring from below the next register break (that is, from notes below c2). Long fingerings had been known since at least the beginning of the eighteenth century, though they were not included in fingering charts prior to about 1770. Fischer may have been experimenting with the possibilities of the long high-note fingerings with his 'octave shake', described by Mrs Papendiek: '[In London in 1785, Ramm] played a duet concerto with Fischer, who introduced the octave shake in his cadence [cadenza]. The effect drew down applause scarcely ever equalled, and Fischer was extremely gay to have succeeded in this new trickery.'[51] Rapid changes of octave would have been more dependable with the long fingerings.

The usual range of the hautboy throughout the eighteenth century was from low C (c1) to high D (d3). But already at the beginning of the century Hotteterre (1707:45) implied that the hautboy occasionally played higher. As late as 1779, Mozart took Ramm's solo part to the opera scena *Popoli di Tessaglia* (KV 316) no higher than d3, though the virtuosic voice part soars to high g3. Just two years later, however, Mozart wrote the hautboy quartet for Ramm with its high f3s.

Mozart wrote the quartet in 1781; by then the f3 was no longer a novelty for some players. Matteo Bissoli had included it in a sonata written about 1750 (this is the earliest known appearance of the note for hautboy). It is also found in a concerto by Fiala dated possibly as early as 1775. In the 1780s both La Borde and Schubart had given a range up to f3.[52] By the middle eighties the composer William Shield was writing high e3s for W. T. Parke and sometimes f3. In the 1790s Parke performed a concerto 'in which I introduced some of my newly discovered high notes, (up to G in alto [g3],) particularly a shake on the upper D, which was greatly applauded'.[53] On surviving fingering charts, f3 is first included in Vanderhagen (c.1790); Wragg included g3 in his book that appeared in 1792. A sestetto in C by F. Sozzi (c.1800) has a g3. As an author named 'I.P.' noted (1830:192), Fischer's concertos seldom went above c3, but the written-out cadenzas that are bound with the manuscript collection of his concertos at the British Library (in an unidentified hand, possibly Fischer's own) include f3s. It is clear that Lebrun (who died in 1790) considered f3 the top limit of the hautboy; one of his concertos goes to f3 but backs off the g3, even when the sequence demands it.[54]

Solos were naturally more ambitious than orchestral writing, which was restricted to a more conservative range even in the 1790s and into the early nineteenth century. Haydn wrote occasional notes above d3, but as late as 1836 an important French authority on orchestration, Kastner, gave the upper range of the oboe as e3 or possibly f3.[55]

It could be argued that the regular use of long fingerings encouraged composers to write higher for the hautboy, but it was more likely the reverse: a change in taste that fancied the sound of a higher tessitura on the hautboy (and on instruments in general) forced players to find a technical solution, which was the introduction of long fingerings. Long fingerings were probably an effect rather than a cause, since they had been known since the beginning of the century, but were not apparently in common use until about 1770. The trill fingering Hotteterre gave for the combination c3–b♭2 was 12 456 7.[56] This was in fact the long b♭2. But for a normal untrilled b♭2, Hotteterre did not give that fingering, suggesting the short 1 3 instead. Given the choice between long and short fingerings, short fingerings seem to have been preferred. And indeed, short fingerings continued to appear in fingering charts; the short b♭2 and b2 persisted until 1816,[57] the c3 until 1789.[58] The first chart to use long fingerings for all three notes was not published until 1810.[59] Long fingerings seem, then, to have been a stopgap response rather than an aesthetic preference. With the development of the Barret/Triébert oboe in the 1860s, long fingerings were again generally discarded.[60]

THE CLARINET

The notion that a musician specialized on a single instrument was much less common in the seventeenth and eighteenth centuries than it is now, especially among wind players. In Germany as late as 1755, Quantz wrote that the Kunst-pfeifer's instruments were the violin, hautboy, trumpet, cornett, sackbut, horn, recorder, bassoon, 'deutsche Baßgeige', cello, gamba and so on.[61] Many-handed wind players were the norm in other countries as well. It was common for recorder and traverso players to have originally been hautboists. Likewise when the clarinet was developed, it was at first regarded as a kind of speciality hautboy and was played by hautboists. Even so, the clarinet was soon found to have certain advantages over the hautboy in wind ensembles, and players began increasingly to concentrate on it. In 1778, 'Half a dozen lads of the militia were sent up to London to be taught various instruments to form a military band. The German master Baumgarten put into their hands a new instrument called a "clarinet" which, with its fiery tone, was better adapted to lead armies into the field of battle than the meek and feeble oboe.'[62] This opinion spread in the latter part of the eighteenth century, and hautboys were used less and less in bands. In France, Louis XV's minister of war signed an ordinance in 1756 that effectively banned the hautboy from the infantry: 'The ensembles allowed in infantry regiments . . . will henceforth be composed of horns, clarinets and bassoons.'[63]

The clarinet's growing popularity was often at the expense of the hautboy. Mozart seldom used the two instruments together, and several times replaced (or virtually replaced) hautboys with clarinets, as in the later version of the g minor Symphony no. 40, KV 550, and his arrangement of Handel's *Acis and Galatea*. Mozart developed a special affinity for the clarinet in Vienna in the 1780s.[64] Had the recipient of several of his pieces, Anton Stadler, not been the superb clarinettist he apparently was (and perhaps had he not also been a Freemason), we might now have a later Mozart hautboy quintet, or another hautboy concerto. The shift of favour from hautboy to clarinet was not consistent, however; while Mozart performed his Quintet for piano and winds KV 452 with Stadler, he allotted at least as important a part to the hautboy as to the clarinet. The same cannot be said of Beethoven's op. 16 for the same combination, written twelve years later in 1796; Beethoven demoted the hautboy to a more auxiliary role and gave the clarinet centre stage.

The shift from early to modern technique (1790–1825)

If from the 1760s the spirit had been one of consolidating the experiments of the previous generation and standardizing the instrument and the music it played, from the 1790s innovation was again in the air. In the most basic sense, the principles of the Conservatoire oboe and the technique of playing it were first formulated during the period 1790 to 1825, while at the same time those on which hautboy technique had been founded (i.e., cross-fingerings and flexible embouchure) came to be seriously questioned.

Because this process was gradual, its full implications were not spelt out in any single source. A number of documented developments, however, make it clear that a basic transformation was taking place. One was the shift in the player's relation to his instrument in terms of tuning, which came to be limited to minor corrections of intonation (the developing ideal was that corrections should not be necessary at all, though this has never been achieved). Another was the decline of the tuning system known as meantone temperament and with it the switch from low to high leading-tones. A third was the rise of the ideal of 'omnitonic' woodwinds and brass, not limited to keys that were practical because of the way the instruments were constructed. Fourth, probably the most visible evidence of a new conception of oboe playing was the addition of keys, whose purpose was to replace the time-honoured techniques of cross-fingering and half-holing. The new keys removed the traditional responsibilities of embouchure not only in correcting intonation but also in overblowing to higher registers and in correcting 'false trills', and involved new fingerings. Finally, the elimination of the dynamic 'shaping' of individual notes, and the complex small-scale phrasing that had been part of hautboy technique, encouraged a more fixed embouchure used in the context of longer phrasing that involved fewer stops and starts.

These factors will be discussed below. The transition was gradual, and the polarity implied here between oboes played before and after 1800 is purposely overstated. Keyed fingerings were used alongside cross-fingerings well after 1825, but the mechanization of the oboe was part of a general trend. Embouchure still today plays a part in correcting intonation, notes are still sometimes shaped (though leaving their players open to possible accusations of so-called 'bulging'), major thirds are still often played lower than in equal temperament when time permits, and F still needs to be played as a cross-fingering in certain combinations. All the same, compared with the embouchure flexibility required in playing the hautboy, these traits subsist on the Conservatoire oboe to a relatively minor degree. Although it was not until the beginning of the twentieth century that modern technique came into general use, the period that saw these two different approaches to the oboe go their separate ways was the first quarter of the nineteenth century. In fact, what unites the hautboy and the Conservatoire oboe is more important than what divides them. Contrast, however, is often an effective tool for understanding the attributes of things, and that is how I hope to use it here, to shed light on the basic natures of both these forms of oboe.

THE REJECTION OF THE PRINCIPLE OF TUNING CORRECTION/SELECTION

One of the reasons for adding keys to woodwinds – probably the most obvious – was to produce notes that were 'in tune' (by the standards of the early nineteenth century) without needing to be corrected by embouchure adjustments. This principle continues to be axiomatic in modern woodwind playing, and minimal embouchure correction is a primary criterion for the quality of an instrument nowadays. One of the first criticisms of those who began playing Baroque woodwinds in the 1960s was that they demanded extreme tuning corrections, or so they seemed at the time.[65]

It has since become clear that intonation on seventeenth- and eighteenth-century woodwinds required the active participation of the player to an extent that is difficult for players of modern woodwinds to imagine. The reason for this was that (unlike in equal temperament) notes were not always the same in Baroque tuning, but changed according to context. Of course, melody instruments like the hautboy do not actually play consistently in any one tuning system. But the general intonation model in the seventeenth and eighteenth centuries, meantone, was built on the idea that sharps were lower than their equivalent flats (*sic*). Burney commented on how well Carlo Besozzi brought out these differences on the hautboy: 'His taste and ear are exceeding delicate and refined; and he seems to possess a happy and peculiar faculty of tempering a continued tone to different bases, according to their several relations. . . .'[66] An example of what Burney means was given by Quantz in his book. On music ex. 4.1 he advised violinists: 'You should move your finger back a little for the sharp following the flat; otherwise the major third will be too high against the fundamental note.' What Quantz had in mind was that although the notes seemed to be the same (an A flat and a G sharp), their harmonic function required them to be tuned differently: at least a comma apart.

Ex. 4.1 Example of A flat turning into G sharp, from Quantz's *Essai*, Tab. xxiii.

The same fingering had thus to be capable of being inflected higher or lower, depending on whether one wanted a flat or the corresponding sharp; D sharp was produced by the same fingering as E flat, for instance, but these two notes could vary from about 21 to 41 cents (approaching a quarter-tone), depending on the degree of meantone being used.[67] On an hautboy it often happened that two quite different notes were played through the same fingering, and this meant that embouchures had to be adept at discriminating between flats and sharps. In other words, tuning 'correction' – and 'selection' – was built into the system.

The head movements a traverso player has to make to correct intonation are easy to see, but similar modifications, though less obvious, are required on all the early woodwinds. The light, wide reed used on the hautboy (which was necessary to get the cross-fingerings to speak and sound reasonably) made pitch adjustment easier than it is on most modern oboe reeds.

Distinguishing sharps and flats was not the only reason why the embouchure had to be flexible. The fingering 123 456 8 offered the player a choice of low c1 or c♯1, as the uncorrected pitch is usually somewhere between them. And the cross-fingerings of each hand (b♭1 fingered 1 3, and f1 fingered 123 4 6) were both too high if not lipped down. The right-hand one, tuned from hole 5, had an added upward incentive because hole 5 also decided the pitch of f♯1. Using the fingerings given in most fingering charts (123 4 6 and 123 4 7 respectively), f1 and f♯1 sound too close together; if f♯1 is high enough, f is very high. In the spirit of most woodwind tuning (which is always essentially compromise), this usually meant that the F was tuned slightly high and the F sharp was a little low and needed favouring.[68]

It is easy to assume that these anomalies were unintentional, and that they represented the shortcomings of a less technologically advanced period. Since, however, they exist on all the woodwinds of the period, and the option of added keys existed, we are obliged to regard them as deliberate. The reason for their existence was probably that in a system like meantone that demands a distinction between flats and their corresponding sharps, woodwinds with key systems are not practical; they are tuned too specifically, producing a single pitch between each natural fingering. The implication of this is that when key systems began to be common on woodwinds, not only did the tuning system lose some of its refinements, but less was expected of the embouchure: it ceased to be expected to make deliberate tuning selections, and was limited to minor corrections of unintentional tuning faults.

Nor should the existence of instruments that require active pitch selection be considered an indication that tuning was less precise in the past. On the contrary, players had to have good ears when they were required regularly to make distinctions that today are unrecognized, such as the difference between G sharp and A flat. Writers like Hotteterre, Loulié and Quantz all mention tuning corrections for false trills.[69] And Jaubert's remarks (1773:182) suggest that woodwind players then were concerned with a level of good intonation akin to that of their present-day colleagues:

> The six holes . . . [that] are opened and closed with the fingers, as well as the D sharp key, must be properly placed and bored not only according to the principles of art, but also by reference to an accurate ear, so that each tone, in the lower as well as the upper octave, is located at its true point. But to achieve this is so difficult that the most famous players of the flute acknowledge that they have never found an instrument perfectly in tune on all its notes: they are obliged to compensate for this by using more or less wind.

The use of cross-fingered woodwinds is predicated on flexible embouchure, and intentional tuning adjustments on these instruments are assumed and expected. These adjustments added an expressive dimension that disappeared with the adoption of equal temperament. The difference between playing with or without keys is a bit like the difference between automatic and manual gear-change on cars; 'doing it yourself' takes more effort but offers more control to those who master the technique. On the other hand, sharp flats and flat sharps would be a liability in the Romantic repertoire, as they were not in use in that period.

FROM LOW TO HIGH LEADING-TONES

We can explore this idea further by considering leading-tones, and how their role was transformed. This too was a manifestation of a change in ideals of tuning that generally occurred towards the end of the eighteenth century. In Baroque and Classical music, the leading-tone was normally a 'large semitone' below the tonic. In 1/6-comma meantone (which, as we have seen, was a typical woodwind tuning model of the period), the distance from leading-tones to resolutions was 109 cents compared with an equal-tempered semitone of 100 cents (cf. the values for C sharp to D, F sharp to G or B to C in the charts on p. 36). By 1810–11, Fröhlich was talking about a leading-tone as being raised: 'That is why the leading-tones (as for instance C sharp to D, F sharp to G, and in general all notes *that one wishes to raise a little*) should be tempered less strongly and taken in a gentler fashion.'[70]

Vogt's method, written in the 1810s, is between two worlds. He gives detailed instructions on how to finger all notes according to their harmonic context, and while he clearly wanted high leading-tones, in tonic triads he expected major thirds to be close to pure.

Because of this change in the status of leading-notes, by the beginning of the nineteenth century hautboists had a major problem with the low f♯1. In the heyday of meantone, when F and F sharp were tuned closer than a semitone of 100 cents (F was 13 cents high and F sharp 11 cents low), the fact that on most woodwinds these two notes sounded closer together than the average semitone worked well. By the early nineteenth century, however, when F sharp was normally expected to be sharp, something had to be done. The original solution was to add a key to raise the f♯1. A commentator in the *Allgemeine musikalische Zeitung* of 29 January 1812 wrote with some hyperbole: 'The low F sharp key, on the other hand, can be recommended to every oboe player, especially those who play second, since this note is a quarter step too low on every [unkeyed] oboe.' In 1824, Sellner commented: 'A key is also provided for the f♯1 or g♭1, which by the nature of the instrument is too low to serve as a leading-tone and can therefore never be used. It is controlled by the little finger of the right hand. . . .' It will be noticed that besides assuming a high leading-note here, Sellner made no distinction between F sharp and G flat; the difference seemed no longer important to him. There was thus no obvious reason to cultivate an embouchure or a reed that was supple enough to produce any difference between them.

Another solution to the F sharp problem (that is still used on the Conservatoire oboe) was to provide a new, separate hole for the F, closed by a key. The fifth hole was therefore no longer responsible for the F, and could be opened enough to raise the F sharp.

Neither Grundmann (d.1800), Grenser (fl. until p.1798) nor Floth (d.1807) seems to have provided keys to help raise the F sharp on any of their surviving hautboys.[71] Sallantin adapted such a key on his Delusse hautboy,[72] but just when he did so is unknown (he retired in 1812). Koch in 1802 (1082) spoke of the F sharp key for raising F sharp as if it were normal; as we have seen, the key was also recommended in Germany in 1812. In the 1820s, Brod and Sellner both showed an F sharp key. But none of this indicates that hautboists of Mozart's or Haydn's time would have had any help raising their F sharps (had they wanted to).

Other tuning characteristics that came to be seen as problems, like the somewhat sharp cross-fingerings for b♭1 and f1 (both of which had been tuned high in meantone) and the ambiguous c1 (which could also serve as a lowish c♯1), were altered to the newer needs of the nineteenth century by the addition of keys.

FROM GOOD TONALITIES TO ALL TONALITIES

Historically, woodwinds have not always been designed to play in many different tonalities. In fact, the fewer tonalities a woodwind plays, the better in tune it can be. Renaissance woodwind players were very specific, normally playing in three keys, and in some cases only one. Because they were specialists in those few keys, they played them extremely well in tune in a very satisfying tuning scheme, pure meantone (quarter-comma). Of course, they were hopeless in other tonalities, which they never used.

One of the reasons why the new 'Baroque' models of woodwind were developed in the seventeenth century was to increase the number of tonalities available, which meant adopting more accidentals for regular use. To achieve this, musicians chose to use cross-fingerings and half-holing rather than keys (though a key was adopted for E flat, since no other solution was practical). As we have seen, in the cross-fingered system finger technique was challenged with the appearance of G sharp/A flat, which had to be produced with half-3, an awkward fingering. G sharp or A flat marks the presence of three sharps or three flats in the keys of A major and E flat major. Finger technique was pretty straightforward in tonalities with fewer accidentals. Effectively, then, the number of tonalities available on cross-fingered hautboys was up to two flats and sharps, major and minor, going into 4 or 5 if necessary. In 1793, Vandenbroek considered that 'the best tonalities [on the hautboy] are C, D, F, G and B flat'. The fact that woodwinds functioned well in only a limited number of tonalities was not perceived as a disadvantage, since it meant that a tuning system could be employed that used the reasonably pure thirds of various forms of meantone.

Commentators in the early nineteenth century still advocated limiting the number of tonalities in which the hautboy could successfully play. In 1823 Wilhelm Braun was still pointing out the importance of choosing appropriate tonalities on the hautboy: 'Also in the choice of keys, caution is to be recommended: if one goes beyond signatures with two sharps or three flats, one will quickly learn more exactly the nature of the instrument. The easiest tonalities for the hautboy are, without doubt, C, F, d and G.'[73] And 'I.P.' wrote in 1830 (192): 'The best keys for the Oboe are – C, F, B flat, G, D and A; but music, judiciously written, may be smoothly performed as far as four sharps or four flats; though not presto passages in c sharp minor, such as was the case in a MS sinfonia tried by the Philharmonic band this season.' But inexorably the music of the early nineteenth century was moving beyond the reasonable tonal limits implied by the cross-fingered system. Four and five accidentals were no longer exceptions used for special effects. This, and the fact that meantone was out of fashion, brought into question the natural bounds of seventeenth- and eighteenth-century woodwind design.

Beethoven is often blamed for pushing orchestral instruments to the limit of their technical capabilities. In his early orchestral works, Beethoven's approach to the hautboy was largely pragmatic. He generally kept within the conservative range of c1–d3, did not go beyond comfortable keys, and usually avoided difficult note-combinations like c♯2–d♯2 as well as awkward slurs and trills. The most significant exceptions to his cautious treatment of the hautboy are the obbligato in act II of *Fidelio*, which includes numerous f3s (the section featuring obbligato oboe was added in 1814), and the writing in the Ninth Symphony. Did Beethoven learn about high F from Ramm when he played in a performance of Beethoven's Quintet for Piano and Winds in December of 1804 at Prince Lobkowitz's residence?[74] In any case, with the harmonic imperatives of Beethoven's later style, woodwind players were in trouble. By the time he wrote the Ninth Symphony in 1824, Beethoven expected the woodwinds to be fluent in a greater range of tonalities than previously. He avoided notes above d3, but the second oboe touched on low c sharp and, compared with earlier works, the Ninth Symphony included more difficult slurs over wide intervals.

The achievement of omnitonic woodwinds playing in equal temperament was not really possible until they were provided with separate tone-holes for every note. That meant that there were more notes (= tone-holes) than there were fingers to close them. Close-standing keys were the answer; they were used for the notes that fell in between the natural seven-hole scale.

Using keys rather than cross-fingerings to produce the accidentals gave a crisper, more specific tuning to these notes, and obscured the difference between enharmonic pairs like G sharp/A flat, which (as on the piano) came to be regarded as a single undifferentiated pitch. The new keys altered the characteristic sound of the hautboy; the duller quality of notes like F, G sharp and B flat was brightened, and the differences in tone colour between various tonalities tended to disappear. The first oboes with a key for every chromatic pitch, like the Sellner oboe, still allowed for cross-fingerings, but they were used as backups for fingering convenience and were otherwise avoided because of their intonation and idiosyncratic tone colour. All twelve notes of the octave were as close as possible to equal, and both the tuning and sound of the accidentals were as much like the natural scale as could be achieved (in practice, there was still some discrepancy in tone quality between them).

Players at the time were naturally concerned with these issues, and the basic trade-off of key character and more subtly tempered intonation for the sake of equality of sound and facility in more keys was the subject of heated debates. The most forthright champion of the new aesthetic was Joseph Sellner. A noted soloist whose 'sureness and purity of tone and technical brilliance ... raised him to the rank of the finest of oboists',[75] Sellner succeeded Czerwenka at the Vienna Hofkapelle and was oboe professor at the Conservatory of the Gesellschaft der Musikfreunde from 1821 to 1838.[76] From the early 1820s Sellner also collaborated with the Viennese wind instrument maker Stephan Koch to develop a new thirteen-keyed oboe. This oboe, not so much a radical departure as a logical culmination of Koch's experiments in oboe design since the beginning of the century, represented the arrival of the Industrial Revolution in oboe playing.[77] In his *Theoretisch praktische Oboe Schule*, the most progressive oboe method of the period, Sellner expected his students to be able to play scales 'in all twenty-four tonalities, ascending and descending, slurred and tongued'.[78]

The new challenges presented to oboists in the Ninth Symphony suggest that Beethoven was aware of new developments in oboe design. And as one of the leading oboists in Vienna in the 1820s, it is likely that Sellner was involved in performances of Beethoven's works. On 2 September 1825, Beethoven and Sellner spent time in the company of the Danish flute virtuoso Friedrich Kuhlau. The discussion turned to wind instruments, but from the snippets preserved in Beethoven's conversation book, it is hard to tell whether Sellner described his new oboe to Beethoven. Of course, even if the deaf composer understood the description, he could only have imagined what it sounded like. And while he may have had the capabilities of the Viennese oboists foremost in mind when he created his symphonies, these works were soon performed by musicians across Europe on oboes quite different from those used by Sellner and other Viennese players.

ADDED KEYS

Extra keys began to be added to the flute as early as the 1750s,[79] and to the clarinet by about 1770.[80] The first fingering charts to describe an hautboy with more than two keys date from 1816–25 (Vogt) and 1824 (Sellner); in the half-century that preceded those works, every known hautboy chart published anywhere in Europe (seventeen in number) still showed an hautboy with only two keys.[81] Despite the charts, keys are known to have been added in Germany and France from just before the turn of the century. The first original key built on an hautboy by Grundmann of which we are sure dates from 1800; with the exception of several doubtful cases, the other fifty or so surviving Grundmanns were originally made without additional keys.[82] Of the thirteen surviving oboes by Grenser, one, made in 1791, has original additional keys (for c♯1 and the octave). By 1799, Friedrich Hammig of Vienna implied in an advertisement that he was making hautboys with keys for F, G sharp and B flat, as well as low B and C sharp.[83] From the turn of the century, the mutation towards an oboe with holes for every semitone as well as speaker and trill keys had begun.[84]

The idea of adding keys was in diametric opposition to the spirit of woodwind making in the previous century, as so eloquently encapsulated by the flute and hautboy maker Heinrich Grenser in 1800: 'To improve this or that note by adding a key is neither difficult nor clever. The keys are, after all, nothing new. . . . The real art . . . consists in making flutes on which everything can be achieved without keys. We must remove the deficiencies that still afflict such flutes in a way that is just as effective as a key.'

Keys had been used on Renaissance woodwinds as extensions to the reach of the fingers, and in a limited way this principle was carried over and incorporated in Baroque woodwinds; an example is the Great-key on the hautboy. As outlined in chapter 2, however, the makers who developed the new Baroque woodwinds in the second half of the seventeenth century had rejected keys, opting instead for half-holing and cross-fingering as a way to obtain notes that were not part of the natural six-hole scale. The one exception was E flat, which (as discussed in chapter 2) was not feasible using a half-hole.[85] The eventual solution for E flat was a close-standing key known as the 'Small-key', on the lines of the many side-keys of the musette. The Small-key remained closed except when an E flat was needed, whereupon the player fingered a D and opened the key, which raised the D a semitone to E flat. This was precisely the principle that was behind many of the new keys that began appearing in the nineteenth century. The new keys for f1, g♯1 and b♭1 raised respectively the e1, g1 and a1.[86]

This change was revolutionary not only in itself, but for what it represented. 'After all', as Grenser had written, keys were 'nothing new'; they had been used for centuries, and a relatively sophisticated key technology existed as early as the seventeenth century. Musettes de cour, being bagpipes using a closed-finger technique, could not play semitones without the keys. Borjon in his tutor (1672:26) showed a musette with thirteen keys as standard equipment (ill. 37). The real issue was aesthetic, not scientific: keys did not require a new technology, but rather acceptance by musicians. For the first time, woodwind makers and players systematically rejected the Baroque principle of cross-fingered accidentals and used an alternative method of obtaining them, close-standing keys. Such a basic change affected all the important elements of playing technique: fingering, embouchure, tone quality and reeds. The effect on embouchure was fundamental, as we have discussed above. And the sound of accidentals produced from separate holes was more direct,

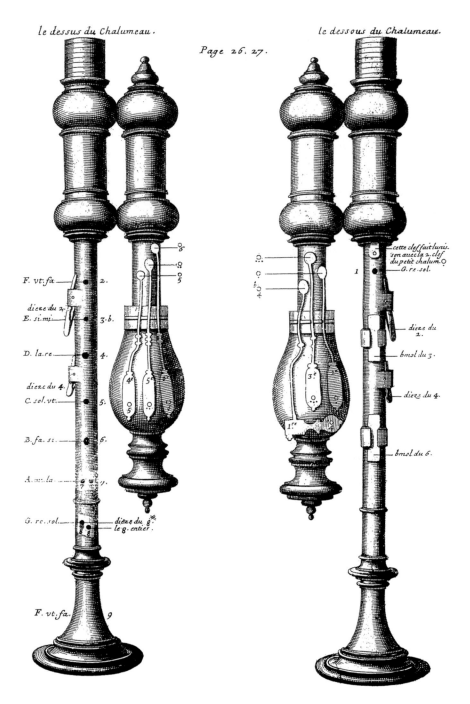

37. Illustration of a musette with thirteen keys in [?]Pierre Borjon de Scellery, *Traité de la musette* (Lyon, 1672).

so that players would have begun to compensate by adjusting their reeds to produce a generally more covered sound. Both a covered sound and a less flexible embouchure point to harder, narrower reeds.

By our definition, instruments with added keys for the accidentals were in principle no longer hautboys (i.e., cross-fingered oboes), though there was no single definitive date when cross-fingerings ceased to be the principal method of obtaining accidentals on the hautboy. Two-keyed hautboys continued to be played into later decades. Even so, the paradigm of the hautboy (that is, the cross-fingered oboe as the ideal design) can be said to have been in decline from the time keys began to be added in order to replace cross-fingerings.

Conservative hautboists like Vogt and Braun (see below) considered the woodwinds of the time as improved extensions of the designs of the late eighteenth century, retaining their original measurements and essential character. These musicians were simply adding a few keys to hautboys that had changed relatively little since the 1770s, either in outward turning style or acoustic dimensions. There are many surviving hautboys from this time with later additions of keys, exemplifying this philosophy. Vogt wrote of the hautboy: 'It may be argued that, since we have added two more [keys], it would be easy to increase further the number in order to facilitate execution on the instrument. I would answer that the two [keys] added in France were indispensable for good intonation and will not cause any harm, for reasons I have mentioned above. . . .'[87]

But the realization that if a few keys were useful, the instrument could be redesigned to incorporate as many keys as it needed must have provoked some basic re-thinking. It was a case of 'one, two, many'. Those of more radical bent began to believe that the woodwinds could be fundamentally re-invented. Louis-Auguste Vény, a pupil of Vogt, quoted at the beginning of this chapter, evoked the ideal of a 'rational' or 'logical' oboe in c.1828. The instrument to which this reasoning was leading was of course the Boehm-system oboe developed in the 1840s. (The history of this radical departure from traditional oboe design is treated in the next chapter.)

Already in 1799, Hammig was arguing that the keys F, G sharp and B flat that he added to his hautboys 'much improved . . . notes, that are otherwise often dull in sound'.[88] By 1824, Sellner summed up the philosophy that had been driving this development over the previous generation in a chapter of his *Oboe Schule* called 'Von der Gleichheit des Tones' (On the equality of notes). This text reads like a manifesto, and unmistakably distanced him from the ideals of the past:

> Although the oboe is generally credited with being superior to the other wind instruments for its equality of tone, it nevertheless possesses certain notes that can never be produced with perfect evenness, despite the most assiduous practice. . . . An example is the b♭1, which in respect of its tone quality as well as its volume is unrelated to the other notes. The two F's are not much better.

These examples are, of course, the standard cross-fingerings of the two-keyed hautboy. He went on:

These three notes, when produced with cross-fingerings as formerly, demand a different pressure and position of the lips, no matter where or in what context they appear. They give the impression of being merely tolerated, compared with the other notes. It is for this reason that, even in the playing of exceptional oboists, many passages can often be played but imperfectly.

Sellner argued that with the new keys 'one has the ability to play many things that, without these keys, would be impossible to perform in tune and with a truly even sound'.

Vény, as we saw, could speak of 'the common [2-keyed] hautboy' as defective and irrational. Aggressive language like this suggests how strongly these ideas were resisted at the time. The conservative position was articulated by an anonymous 'Componist und Virtuose auf der Hoboe' (composer and hautboy virtuoso) in the *Allgemeine musikalische Zeitung* (*AMZ*) of 29 January 1812.[89] Lamenting the deaths of Grundmann and Floth (whom he considered the best makers of hautboys), he wrote:

> The general trend nowadays is to equate perfection on the hautboy, as on the flute, with many keys. In my opinion, however, they are hardly thus improved. Aside from the ease with which keys can get out of adjustment, even during playing, so that one is unable to make a sound on the instrument, the evenness of the scale is also affected. The B flat key [for b♭1], for instance, produces such a sharp tone, that it sounds (compared with the other notes) quite unlike something produced by an instrument. At least, I have found this with most hautboy players who use this key.

As if to balance the views of this writer with one more sympathetic to added keys, the *AMZ* included commentaries by another oboist (also anonymous), who replied: 'Anyone who uses the B flat key and takes the trouble to try to make it similar to the others will eventually succeed, and will certainly notice the manifold advantages that it brings.'

In France, Vogt, who became professeur titulaire at the Conservatoire in 1816, was playing a modified two-keyed Delusse probably made in the 1780s (like the one pictured on the fingering chart of his *Méthode* – see ill. 36).[90] It had two extra keys whose purpose was to correct intonation (a long key to lower the bottom c1, and a key to raise the f♯1 when played with the traditional fingering). These two added keys had been designed by Vogt's teacher Sallantin.[91] The instrument used the standard cross-fingerings and half-holes except for f♯1, so by our definition it was still clearly an hautboy. Vogt played this instrument until about 1824, when he began using another instrument also by Delusse, also possibly made in the 1780s, which had added keys for c♯1, a b♭1, and a c2 trill key.[92] He used this instrument until his retirement as a performer sometime after 1840.[93] Thus Vogt continued throughout his life to produce f1, g♯1, c2, f2, and g♯2 by cross-fingerings or half-holes.

Vogt's career bridged the divide between the two systems, at least as they developed in France. Oboe professor at the Paris Conservatoire during much of the first half of the nineteenth century (he taught there until 1853), Vogt was responsible for founding the modern French school of oboe playing.[94] From early on, Vogt's conservatism must have been quite clear to his contemporaries. In his *Méthode pour hautbois* (dated 1816–24), he commented:

> This is the place to say a word about the hautboys used now in Germany, which have more keys than ours. There is one that has as many as nine. It is claimed that the keys make passagework easier in tonalities with numerous accidentals, such as E flat . . . , A flat, f minor, c minor, D flat, and so on. But these advantages are strongly counterbalanced by the inconvenience that results when the keys do not hermetically seal the holes over which they are placed, an inconvenience that occurs all too often even on hautboys that have only four keys, and that gives us good reason to wonder about those with eight or nine.[95]

Into the 1840s Vogt continued to resist innovations, such as a second octave key and brille for F sharp. His caution was matched by his colleague Tulou, who rejected the Boehm flute in his method of c.1835. Their stand is especially remarkable because France seems to have been the centre of new developments on other woodwinds, including new keys. By 1807, Paris was known for its five-keyed Potter-type flutes.[96] Müller's thirteen-keyed clarinet was officially adopted by the Conservatoire in 1814; in 1815 Reicha composed a concerto 'pour la clarinette perfectionée par Müller'.[97]

The German position remained opposed to keys well into the 1820s and 30s. In 1826 the best-known German hautboist of his day, Wilhelm Braun (1796–1867), was advocating the use of only four keys (C, C sharp, E flat and the F-Klappe). Taking issue with Sellner's efforts to equalize tone production, he commented:

> Keys are of little use for any of the other notes. Too many keys clearly detract from tone quality, and lead to another disadvantage: when they are not accurately made, first one, then another seals incorrectly. All the other keys are quite expendable, and their utility is not great enough to outweigh the problems they bring with them. A few trills or passages made better in tune, that are not appropriate for the hautboy in the first place, are scarcely adequate reason to compromise the entire instrument.[98]

When Braun was asked to review Sellner's method, he reacted conservatively. Since he had no personal knowledge of the Sellner-Koch oboe, and Sellner's advice was often contrary to his own experience, Braun regarded much of it as ill-founded. His main objection was that, despite its claim to being 'theoretical and practical', Sellner's method, as it was written specifically for a new oboe design, was not of general application. Braun's attitude makes it apparent that (because there was a conservative element opposed to his innovations) Sellner was in fact ahead of his time; over the course of the next decades the resistance gradually abated and Sellner's text became the most influential and widely disseminated method of the nineteenth century. Its impact was strongest in Austria and areas like Czechoslovakia and northern Italy that fell directly under the Habsburg political and cultural dominion.

In Vienna the Sellner oboe was used up to the emergence of the Wiener Oboe in the 1880s. Koch's oboes were copied with slight modifications by the Viennese workshops run by Wolfgang Küss (1779–1834) and the Uhlmann and Ziegler families (est. 1810 and 1821 respectively).

In France, Vogt's pupils were less conservative than their teacher. Henri Brod showed an oboe with eight keys in the first part of his *Méthode* of c.1826 (c2, bb1, F♯, F, c1, C♯, Eb and C-tuner[99]). The instrument, significantly, still had no speaker key; it did not fully eliminate cross-fingerings and half-holing, which were retained for g♯/ab1, gb/f♯2, b2 and c3 and used as alternatives for f1, c2, f2, f♯/gb2, g♯/ab2, and bb2. The *Méthode* (c.1828) by Vény, Brod's colleague at the Paris Opéra, showed a similar eight-keyed oboe that retained cross-fingerings and half-holing for g♯/ab1 (despite the presence of dedicated key), f2, f♯/gb2, g♯/ab2, b2 and c3.[100] The Sellner-Koch oboe had keys to replace all the cross-fingerings and half-holes except f♯/gb2 and c2 (Sellner's fingering chart gives cross- and half-hole fingerings as alternatives for F and Ab/G♯ in both octaves, bb/a♯1, and cross-fingerings as principal fingerings for a♯/bb2, b2 and c3).[101]

The new G sharp key, which first started appearing on hautboys in Germany c.1800,[102] replaced a perennially awkward fingering, the half-hole on 3. The twinned third hole had been used on the earliest protomorphic hautboys of the 1650s,[103] and was still used on simple system oboes in the early twentieth century.[104] Although it was a positive technical help, the G sharp key produced a thin, tinny sound. This may have been the reason why it was rejected by some players. The anonymous author in the *AMZ* of 29 January 1812 commented: 'The G sharp key, however, can certainly be counted among the most dispensable [keys], considering the small advantage it offers.' But a half-generation later, Sellner could no longer imagine doing without it: 'Another key that is absolutely necessary is the G sharp (A flat) for the little finger of the left hand, with which, besides providing one specific trill, the so-called "half-hole" operated by the third finger of the left hand is avoided, and much that was formerly impossible is made possible. . . .'

Besides keys to replace cross-fingerings and half-holes, the first key to be regularly added to German hautboys, and in fact the one most commonly added, was the 'Schleif Klappe' (slur-key), also called the 'hohe F-Klappe' (high F key).[105] This key was used as an 'octave-key' or *speaker* (that is, a key that helped the response of overblown notes by minimizing the first mode of the frequency in favour of the second). Of course, the f3 was being played long before the key came into use; as discussed above, the note was used as early as the 1750s and sporadically thereafter. And the f3 is now being produced regularly without keys by a number of modern players of the Classical hautboy.[106] But several sources indicate that this 'hohe F-Klappe' had other uses besides helping the response of f3. The F-Klappe was first described by H. C. Koch in 1802: 'Many oboists have a so-called F-Klappe on this upper joint, controlled by the thumb, specifically intended to help the slurring of the octaves e1-e2, f1-f2 and g1-g2, and partly also to allow the notes e2 f2 f♯2 and g2 to be attacked smoothly and very softly when playing piano.'[107] Koch mentions here only the notes of the second octave, e2, f2, and g2, and not the third.

Ten years later, in 1812, the anonymous 'Componist und Virtuose auf der Hoboe' wrote more about this key in the *AMZ*:

> Even the so-called F-Klappe for the higher notes is dispensable, since these notes can be played without it; although it certainly makes the upper register singularly easy, and also has the advantage that with it notes can be slurred together that are otherwise either impossible to slur, or else very difficult, such as [e1–e2, f1–f2, g1–g2]. This passage is quite easy to do by opening the high F-Klappe on the upper joint with the left thumb on [e2, f2, g2]. This same passage can be done less satisfactorily when these notes are played with the uppermost hole of the left hand half opened.[108]

A dissenting footnote added to the above reads

> Note: The high F-Klappe on the upper joint is in no way dispensable, but on the contrary most useful, even necessary. It creates in the first place complete security on all the high notes that could not be produced before its invention, when one was dependent only on the reed.

In any case, in Germany in 1812, the F-Klappe is mentioned in connection with two different sets of notes: those of second octave (e2, f2, g2), and those of the 'upper register' that were difficult or impossible 'before its invention'. The 'upper register' thus probably meant the third octave. In 1823 Wilhelm Braun counted the F-Klappe along with the C, C sharp and E flat keys as among the 'four most essential' keys.[109] Braun's opinion is confirmed by surviving German hautboys, where these four keys are the most common. In 1824 Sellner gave further information on the F-Klappe. In his fingering chart it was open only on the highest notes: e3, f3, f♯3, g3, and g♯3.[110] Sellner used the F-Klappe for the notes of the second octave as well, but in a different way. He explained that it was 'virtually indispensable [*fast unentbehrlich*]' for the notes e2 to a2, either for slurring up from lower notes or to help on long notes when the lips became tired. Sellner commented: 'If you touch [the F-Klappe] lightly each time on the second, higher note, you need have no fear that the note will drop to the lower octave, nor will it be necessary to blow much harder.' Interestingly, however, Sellner added that the F-Klappe should not be held open permanently for long notes, as it affected intonation and tone quality. This indicates that for these second-octave notes, the F-Klappe was not kept open constantly like the octave key on the Conservatoire oboe, but rather used like the 'flick key' on the modern bassoon.[111]

The F-Klappe, acting as a speaker key, offered a smoother technique. It also took over the role of the embouchure in making octaves, so that the embouchure could remain more stationary. A remarkable and particularly compelling example of the kind of playing that the introduction of octave keys ultimately produced is John de Lancie's recording in 1966 of Françaix's *L'Horloge de flore* (see Discography). This recording shows how on the Conservatoire oboe the octaves can give the impression of being interchangeable because sound quality, breath pressure and embouchure adjustments are so similar between the registers. This consistency of technique is not possible without octave keys; on an hautboy, by contrast, each of the registers requires special attention in terms of embouchure and breath pressure, thereby investing each register with its own unique sound and character.

It was some time before a speaker key was adapted to French instruments. Around 1812–1815, Frédéric Chalon gave a table of alternative fingerings to overcome the problem of slurring octaves (*octavier*) without a speaker key in the second edition of his *Méthode pour le Cor Anglais,* and Vogt's solution for difficult intervals was to tongue the upper note lightly. Brod did not mention a speaker key in either part of his *Méthode*, although his last oboe (now owned by Han de Vries) has one. Speaker keys may have been introduced later in France because of the smaller reeds that were used there; such reeds probably responded more readily in the higher registers without extra help. As for the question of the unreliability of keys, in 1808 an anonymous writer in the *AMZ* noted with apparent surprise that his new nine-keyed clarinet (by Koch?) 'had been played daily for nine months without needing a single repair'.[112] This issue faded away in the 1810s as the keywork of makers like Koch and Tobias Uhlmann, responding to criticisms like Vogt's and Braun's, took on an astonishing sophistication (their keywork has, in fact, probably never been equalled for its precision and beauty).

As the compositions of the nineteenth century gradually moved into more extreme tonalities and modulations became commonplace, homogeneity of sound was a necessity. Schubert's orchestral writing is representative. In general, Schubert was less sensitive to the technical limitations of the oboe than Beethoven, and he disregarded Braun's advice to adhere to a small range of tonalities. In the Fourth Symphony of 1816, for example, he expected the oboists to be equally fluent in keys as disparate as E flat, A and D flat major. Both the Fourth Symphony in C minor and the Fifth in B flat (both 1816) contain exposed c♯1s, and legato playing over the interval d♭2–e♭2 is demanded on a regular basis. The second movement of the Unfinished Symphony (1822), which is in E major and takes the oboe into D flat major, includes some of the most extreme tonal mixes required in pre-Wagnerian music. The Great C major Symphony, no. 9, written the same year as the release of Sellner's oboe method, is actually more conservative in its technical demands than the earlier symphonies because of its more limited range of tonalities, but the extensive solo passages are still particularly taxing.

Curiously, the first generation of players of keyed winds did not associate the new keys with finger facility. Keys were seen as a brake on speed, and they certainly do have this effect in simple tonalities like C major. To quote Tromlitz (1791), 'That [extra keys] are very useful, particularly for playing trills in tune,[113] . . . is undeniable. In the Adagio and in movements of moderate quickness they are of sterling service; but in fast and very fast movements they are difficult to use.'[114] Sellner noted that 'the [new] keys in no way supplant the old fingerings, with which many passages are easier to play than they are with the keys . . .'.[115] The Mozart hautboy concerto, for instance, is actually easier to play on a keyless recorder or a two-keyed hautboy than on the Conservatoire oboe, and Rossini's hautboy solos, which are still today among the instrument's technical touchstones, were apparently written for a two-keyed hautboy.[116]

One of the ironies of the Conservatoire oboe is that because keys were super-imposed on the original Baroque fingering system, they grew onto it by a process of accretion, and remain without ever having been replaced by a more consistent system like Boehm's that was applied to the flute and clarinet, or the revolutionary oboe design of Maino and Orsi (see chapter 6). The result is a fingering scheme that is not without its illogicalities to the user, as it sometimes raises notes by adding fingers and lowers notes by removing fingers. To *go up* to an F after playing an E (123 45), one has to *put down* a finger to open the F key. To *go down* to a G after playing an A flat, one has to *raise* the left-hand little finger. To call these accessories a fingering 'system' with a unified logic, and the resulting instrument 'rational' (as in Vény's vision), was a goal that has unfortunately never been achieved.

FROM THE NUANCED PHRASE TO THE LONG LINE

The eighteenth-century hautboy reed, relatively wide and scraped to be soft in order to accommodate cross- and half-hole fingerings, made it easy to start and stop quickly and change dynamic levels both extremely and instantaneously. The reeds used in the first decades of the nineteenth century must not have changed dramatically (since cross- and half-hole fingerings continued to be used in a limited way), but the flexibility implicit in a lighter, broader reed was becoming less needed and less valued as the concept of the Romantic 'long-line' phrase emerged. As extra keys were added to the hautboy, they tended to equalize tone quality, intonation and blowing technique, so the player could more easily develop a smoothly-arched phrase without needing to trouble with the minutiae of tuning and response on individual notes.

There are no real stops or silences in the long-line phrase – indeed, players of the Conservatoire oboe with its relatively heavy reed tend to be reluctant to interrupt the air flow or disturb their embouchures by stopping, even when there are brief rests written in the music (see the discussion of performances of the Strauss concerto in chapter 6). The long-line phrase also approaches the thousands of small, constantly changing musical gestures (called figures) in a way that differed from that of the eighteenth century. The wide, soft reed and wide bore of the eighteenth-century hautboy favoured the kind of playing of which Quantz wrote: 'Each note, whether it is a quarter-note, eighth-note, or sixteenth, should have its own Piano and Forte, to the extent that time permits.'[117] In the long-line phrase, by contrast, a note cannot 'have its own Piano and Forte', because it is a segment of a larger shape, and goes essentially in a single direction (towards, or away from, the climax note).

In a tongue-in-cheek passage called 'How not to always play beautifully', Anner Bijlsma describes the player he calls 'Mr. Authentic', who he says 'looks for the best, most telling notes, and the others he glosses over a bit. He likes the "good" notes to stand out.'[118] Bijlsma considers this approach as the converse of that of musicians who play 'all notes equally perfect and equally loud. . . .' 'It might very well be', he suggests, 'that here we find the basic difference between the so-called "modern" playing (a relic of the 1940s?) and the so-called "authentic" (which never can be true) playing.' It is certainly true that on the radio the first and most obvious give-away that one is listening to a Baroque piece played by a traditional 'modern' orchestra is the emphasis given to unimportant notes like passing sixteenths.

The kind of playing that uses detailed dynamic nuance based on smaller musical units than the phrase was no more popular with Henri Brod in the 1820s than it is nowadays in traditional conservatories. In the first part of his *Méthode* Brod spoke of 'papillotage' ('fluttering', as of a butterfly). He compared this older style using dynamic nuance with the simpler long-line phrase, and commented on the passage in Example 4.2: 'Generally speaking, a player should make broad nuances (that is, no more than one crescendo or decrescendo in a phrase consisting of three or four measures) rather than many small nuances, one after the other, which is not only harmful to the smaller sections but also destroys the effect of the music, and becomes what is called "papillotage".'[119] 'Papillotage' has been unfashionable in the last generations.[120] Under 'Bad habits' in her book *Oboe Technique* written in the 1950s, Evelyn Rothwell lists 'Bulging':

> Beware always of the very common bad habit of making a 'bulge', i.e. a little <>, on each note, or over every few notes. It is a monotonous, niggling form of expression, which is unmusical, and maddening to the listener. Unfortunately, it seems fatally easy for oboe players to acquire this bad habit. . . .[121]

Ex. 4.2 Two ways of phrasing in Brod 1825:10.

In transcribing vocalises by Crescentini for hautboy, Vogt 'ironed out' the small-scale dynamic nuances on individual notes (the 'papillotage') in favour of phrase units of about four bars. Interestingly, Vogt's own earliest compositions still contain dynamic nuance similar to Crescentini's, suggesting that taste in phrasing was in a process of change during Vogt's lifetime.[122]

Note-shaping and complex dynamic nuance was evidently on the way out as early as 1770, when Burney met Quantz; Burney specifically commented that Quantz did not play in 'the modern manner . . . of gradually enforcing and diminishing whole passages, as well as single notes'.[123] This is evident in Quantz's Adagio example in his *Essai* (reproduced with dynamic markings in Haynes 2001:226–7), which contained twenty-two dynamic changes in the first two bars, and continued in the same manner.[124]

Related to note shaping was the *messa di voce* or 'fine swell'. By the late eighteenth century, writers were encouraging the use of the messa di voce on every long note, including fermatas and the beginnings of cadenzas. Several authors commented on the hautboy's ability to make this ornament. Wragg (1792:13) observed: 'A Swell . . . is executed by touching the Note, over which it is placed, at the first gently, and by degrees increasing the tone till it arrives at its full pitch; then diminishing it almost imperceptibly, till it falls off to its first softness. This I cannot recommend too much, having one of the finest effects on the ear which the Instrument is capable of producing.' Burney remarked (1773:II:45–7) that '[Carlo] Bezzozi's messa di voce, or swell, is prodigious; indeed, he continues to augment the force of a tone so much, and so long, that it is hardly possible not to fear for his lungs.' Leopold Mozart wrote in 1778 to his wife and son of a concert he had heard by Carlo Besozzi:

> In short, he has everything! Words fail me to describe his precision and the extremely pure tone he preserves in the most rapid runs and jumps. What is particularly remarkable is his ability to sustain his notes and his power to increase and decrease their volume, without introducing even the slightest quiver into his very pure tone. But this *messa di voce* was too frequent for my taste and has the same melancholy effect on me as the tones of the glass harmonica, for it produces almost the same kind of sound.[125]

By the time the keyed oboe was established, however, the messa di voce had passed into the realm of a technical exercise. It was being used that way by the singing teacher Domenico Corri (1810), and Sellner in his *Oboe Schule* (1824:4). The messa di voce is now known as 'long-tones', the model for the dynamic shape of a long-line phrase.

Given the eighteenth-century conception of music, the use of dynamics and articulation to bring out the hierarchy of beats, dissonances and figures was only logical. But seen from the viewpoint of early nineteenth-century hautboists like Sellner, Vogt and Brod who were developing the concept of the long-line phrase, every aspect of seventeenth- and eighteenth-century music seemed to combine to distract and break up the long line into points of greater and lesser emphasis.

In phrasing, as in the other ways discussed above, the early nineteenth century appears as a watershed, looking back on past ideas and ahead to new ones. As we have seen, the steps the keyed oboe took away from the hautboy included a reduction of tuning adjustments, the elimination of the distinction between sharps and flats (often played with the same fingering), the new idea that the oboe should be capable of playing in all tonalities, the replacement of cross-fingering and half-holing with separate tone-holes for every note of the range (opened by keys), and the use of a speaker-key to get the upper register to respond rather than depending solely on breath support and embouchure. Added to this was the developing Romantic concept of broad phrasing, which had a fundamental effect on embouchure, breath technique, and reeds. Each of these steps contributed to the process that produced the oboes of the Romantic period, and the changes in technique that went with them. They eventually culminated in the modern Conservatoire oboe and a way of playing that contrasts sharply with that of the eighteenth-century hautboy.

Folk hautboys: the continuing hautboy tradition in the nineteenth and twentieth centuries

While in the 'art music' world the hautboy gradually mutated into the keyed oboe, the hautboy remained extremely popular in what is now called 'folk music' or 'traditional music'. The separation of music into categories like 'classical' and 'popular' had its roots in France in the seventeenth century and was symbolized by two institutions, the ancient Guild (officially known as the Confrérie de Saint-Julien-des-Ménétriers and documented as far back as 1321) and the Académie de Musique created by Louis XIV. These two institutions fought legal battles with each other from the moment the Académie was founded in the 1670s.[126] The issue had social overtones; the Guild was very like the modern musicians' union in North America, and court musicians and composers resented having to take tests administered by the Guild, many of whose members played in popular orchestras without written music. Guild members were accused of playing 'mechanically' and being mere craftsmen, while the newly-composed music of the Académie was called 'libérale' and 'scientifique'.[127] In the course of the late seventeenth and early eighteenth centuries the musicians of the Guild were steadily marginalized and excluded from formal concert life. Eventually they came to be seen as 'street fiddlers', ridiculed and caricatured, left to play mostly dances and lower-class entertainments.

The hautboy, played in both these contexts, took two different directions. Whereas today popular music changes constantly while music performed by symphony orchestras in concert halls is relatively static, the roles were reversed at the end of the eighteenth century. 'Art music' was in constant flux, and as taste changed, so did instruments. Thus, as we have seen, the hautboy (that is, the cross-fingered oboe with ornamental turnery) gradually disappeared from the art music world in the course of the nineteenth century, to be replaced by various forms of keyed oboe. But the instruments of members of the Guild became associated with a music that emphasized an oral 'tradition'; they evidently changed more slowly, since many traditional instruments generally recognizable as hautboys survived well into the twentieth century.

In France today, folk oboes take many forms, and not all of them derive from the hautboy that was used at the French court. The recent appearance of the first overview of these instruments (a book called *Les hautbois populaires*, edited by Luc Charles-Dominique and Pierre Laurence) makes it possible to include this report here. Traditional oboes that resemble most closely the hautboy are the *aubòi* of Languedoc (whose players are called *auboissaires*) and the *aboès* of the Couserans in the Pyrenees (ill. 38). Both these instruments, which are seen as symbols of separatist national cultures, are now in a process of revival parallel to that of the hautboy. The difference is that the traditional instruments were still being played within living memory.

The *aubòi* of Languedoc was played in urban settings until just after the end of World War II. Some of its best-known players, who travelled widely in Languedoc and were well paid for their playing, are still remembered.[128] The *aubòi* was played together with a small drum. As it is known today, the instrument is carefully made,

38. Five *aubòi* of Languedoc.

a  b

39. Two reeds for the *aubòi*.

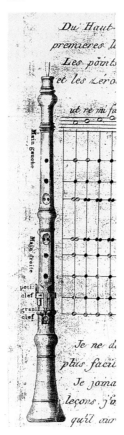
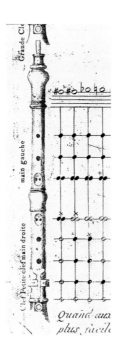

40. Detail of fingering charts, pp. 12 and 16 in François-Joseph Garnier, *Méthode raisonnée pour le hautbois* (Paris, 1802).

has a consistent design, is similar in outer turning to hautboys of the early eighteenth century, and is usually made of boxwood, often with ivory, horn or metal tips. The *aubòi* includes a seventh hole that produces D, the same hole that is closed by the Great-key on the hautboy. Curiously, although the two standard key rings are usually present on the *aubòi*, keys are not provided, and there is no key channel. The key rings thus have no function other than ornamentation, and are probably a vestige of the original hautboy design from which the *aubòi* appears to have developed.[129]

The oldest surviving examples of the *aubòi* are pitched below A–440.[130] They average 49 cm in length (which matches the length of historical hautboys that play at about A + 1; hautboys at about A − 1 average 57 to 58 cm in length). The tone-holes are relatively large. Balusters are present on the top of each joint as well as a finial on the top joint and a bell rim at the bottom. Beading is less complex than on the hautboy. None of the holes are twinned. The bell has two resonance holes (called 'trous de clarté').

The *aboès* of the Couserans are 47 to 53 cm long and are made in three joints, with the same tone-holes as on the hautboy, except that hole 7 (E flat on the hautboy) is missing,[131] as is the key needed to close hole 8 (the Great-key on the hautboy). The *aboès* has the same finial-baluster forms as the hautboy, and like the *aubòi* of

Languedoc has a key ring below hole 6 despite the lack of keys. The form, mouldings, and occasional tips in bone are similar to the hautboy. The instrument was played very loudly, like a shawm; according to one witness, 'If they played the *aboès* in [the village of] Astein, people heard it as far away as [the village of] Loutrein'. The range was from c1 to f2.[132] The instrument was played absolutely horizontally, and players probably used circular breathing. Normally played alone, it was used at dances, carnivals and weddings, and players were able to play for four or five hours without stopping.[133]

The histories of the *aubòi* and *aboès* are mostly oral, and are now obscure. The *aubòi*, which on certain special occasions is still played today, is documented as far back as 1679.[134] There are records of the existence of the *aboès* at least as far back as the seventeenth century and it was played until about 1950.

An instrument that preserves elements of the Baroque *Schalmey* of the late seventeenth century (often called the *deutsche Schalmey*) is the *graile* of the Tarn and Aveyron in France; it has a finial in the form of a pirouette and a thicker section at the top of the bell that resembles a fontanelle.[135] The *graile* was the same length as the *aboès* of the Couserans, 47 to 53 cm long. It was played, according to spoken accounts, quite alone, without drum or other instruments. Players could play for hours, and there are accounts of contests between players as to who could play longest; one famous player had to stop when 'blood started coming out of his ears',[136] and players sometimes 'conversed' back and forth between villages. The best music was slow and uncomplicated. *Grailaires* also played for wedding processions and dances; their style involved many ornaments. They could play in several tonalities and had a range of an octave and a half.[137] Certain players seem to have played with the reed entirely free within the mouth.[138] Reeds were often made by the fireplace during the winter, and they 'lasted a long time'. The instrument stopped being played just after the World War I.

If, as the evidence seems to suggest, these instruments are descendants of the seventeenth- and eighteenth-century hautboy and related instruments, they may preserve traces of Baroque techniques. Among the practices on the *aubòi* are rubbing garlic on one's lips to increase endurance, cleaning reeds after use with a feather, and avoiding the eating of salad before playing because of the oil. The resonance holes of one surviving instrument are closed with cork plugs. Joseph Albert, a famous *grailaire*, soaked his reeds in vinegar the day before playing, and others did the same, to make the cane pliant.[139] Players also soaked their reeds in wine or *pastis*.

The dominant type of reed for the *aubòi* was 75 to 88 mm long and was mounted on a metal staple.[140] The reed was tied with cobbler's thread covered in pitch (see ill. 39). The cane was the usual type, often picked by the player or obtained from fishing poles; dense cane was preferred. Cane length for finished reeds varied but averaged 22 to 26 mm. The shape was slightly triangular, like modern bassoon reeds, and rather wide at the tip (one example was 15 mm). The scrape seems apparently to have been a V or U without heart.

A second type of *aubòi* reed, less commonly used in the modern revival, was carved out of a whole tube of cane first hollowed (drilled?) and then formed with a heated mandrel. The staple was thus replaced with cane. The shape of these reeds was distinctive: the reed was wide, short and squat with perfectly parallel sides narrowing suddenly at the base to form a circular tube. The scrape was a deep U; it could be described as 'all tip' (see ill. 39b). Reeds of this kind were commonly used on the *aboès* and, it seems, exclusively on the *graile*. Modern players of these instruments find that this type of reed lasts less long than stapled reeds and does not play as high, but its tone is preferable, being rounder and richer.

Chapter 5

From keyed oboe to the Conservatoire oboe, 1825–1880

The tone of the oboe is like those delicate tints that are easily changed even by the light of day; the slightest change to the bore or to the instrument's length results in a loss of its touching and sweetly melancholic sound, so highly prized in the orchestral palette.

Lavoix, *Histoire d'instrumentation*, 110

The oboe in the industrial age

As much as the nineteenth century was for the Western world a period of political ferment and social revolution, for the oboe it was a period of instability and change. The adoption of Triébert's système 6 by the Paris Conservatoire in 1881 marks the beginning of the stabilization of the physical form of the instrument, but is better understood as an isolated event in a continuum of change and amidst considerable regional variation. Increasingly complex mechanisms, streamlined external profile, narrower reeds and to a lesser extent modifications to the bore all affected not only the oboe's appearance and technique, but its tonal character and ultimately its expressive potential and extra-musical associations.

Until recently it was assumed that there was virtually no nineteenth-century music written for oboe outside the orchestra; histories have consequently focused on the oboe's physical development, and in particular on mechanization. But while works for solo oboe by the most significant composers of this period are indeed rare, the corpus of Romantic oboe music is not negligible. A comprehensive account of the oboe in the nineteenth century should entail a discussion of the sequence of added keys and model numbers, as well as a consideration of interconnections between the prime agents in the instrument's development – its players, makers, composers. This and the next chapter discuss the instrument's physical development, its principal makers and players; chapter 7 deals with its symbolic associations in orchestral music, operatic scores and cultural texts.

For Philip Bate the nineteenth century was a period of the oboe's 'improvement and refinement', when 'empirical growth gave place to organized development at the hands of skilled craftsmen and distinguished artists in the service of an ever more exacting music'.[1] However, the array of different models and key systems in use throughout the period challenges the first assumption, as does the limited success of the only radically novel oboe design, the Boehm oboe. Nineteenth-century oboe builders were just as open to experimentation as their eighteenth-century predecessors, and today the notion that nineteenth-century music was increasingly more 'exacting' seems condescending to the demands of earlier musical styles.

The first quarter century had seen the provision of separate holes for all chromatic notes of the instrument; the next decades saw the introduction of *interactive* key mechanisms that facilitated the use of these added keys. Once stabilized in the 1830s, bore dimensions, hole size and placement remained largely the same, but the number and arrangement of keys varied considerably not only from country to country but within each national school. This abundance of different key systems means that, instead of taking external profile as the main criterion for categorizing oboes as we do with eighteenth-century instruments, the date and provenance of nineteenth-century oboes is better gauged from the organization of their keywork.

In earlier periods oboe design was distributed internationally, but by the middle of the century France had become the most highly industrialized nation in Europe, with the most progressive oboe builders of the period concentrated in Paris. This chapter could have been called 'The Triébert Era' as it covers the period corresponding almost exactly to the activities of the pre-eminent dynasty of French oboe makers. Even so, this would not have taken into account the diversity of oboes in use outside France. Previous historians focused on the French oboe tradition precisely because it was the most progressive and had the most decisive influence on today's oboe. They did this, however, at the expense of oboes and playing styles associated with what we now consider the core of the Romantic repertoire – the German symphonic tradition and Italian bel canto opera.

Industrialization provided for the rapidly growing urban populations and also affected the arts. Developments in publishing made art music available to a wider public and in turn fostered domestic music making. The result was that, instead of being the prerogative of the aristocracy, art music became increasingly accessible to a broader population. It was particularly the members of the bourgeoisie who appropriated music for their own and elevated it to the élitist status that it continues to hold today.

Mass-production techniques made it possible to make larger numbers of instruments with increasingly complex keywork. Even so, the oboe never gained popularity as an amateur instrument, largely because of its purported difficulties and reputedly temperamental nature. Non-professional players often bore the brunt of criticism in print and visual representations (see ills 41 and 42). Consequently, unlike brass instruments, flutes, saxophones and clarinets, oboes were never mass produced, and production remained in the hands of small-scale specialist ateliers.

Oboe makers nevertheless took advantage of certain innovations. One of the most important was the invention of silver electroplating in 1844. Most often applied to a base of nickel (or German) silver (an alloy of copper, nickel and zinc discovered around 1825) and used initially in the manufacture of cutlery, nickel silver was soon adopted by woodwind makers as a strong and economical alternative to the brass or solid silver formerly used for keywork.

41. Karl Muller (1813–72), portrait of an unknown oboist.

The oboe and virtuosity

At the heart of Romantic aesthetics lies a paradox. On the one hand music was extolled as the most profound embodiment of the Romantic spirit – in the words of Carl Maria von Weber, 'the purest, most ethereal language of the emotions'[2] – while on the other it was unashamedly exhibitionist. The virtuoso who flourished in the late eighteenth century continued to be a fixture in the Romantic concert scene. And, as Alexander Ringer has written, 'In a society in which wealth was rarely the lot of those who produced it, much attention focussed on the expert performer, the appealingly re-creative rather than uniquely creative individual.'[3]

As in the eighteenth century, pot-pourri concerts continued to be popular in the Romantic period. Invariably concertos, virtuosic fantasies, variations on well-known themes and concert arias were interspersed among overtures, symphonies, vocal ensembles and so forth, providing occasions for solo artists to showcase their talents. Artists like Paganini and Liszt dazzled audiences across Europe, and in the process accumulated small fortunes. While there were no oboe virtuosi of comparable charisma or wealth, a number of oboists were celebrated in the concert halls of Europe and some, like Centroni and Pasculli, even earned the accolade 'the Paganini of the oboe'.

Professional musicians came mostly from middle and lower classes, and when they did not, in all cases but for the most highly valued virtuosi their occupation relegated them to a subservient position. This was no more true than with wind and brass players. Many musicians continued to depend, like their eighteenth-century predecessors, on court positions, but even in countries where revolution had emancipated musicians from aristocratic servitude, their livelihood still depended on the patronage of the privileged few.

The oboe virtuoso of previous times held his own against other instrumentalists, but as the nineteenth century progressed, the oboe was increasingly under-represented as a solo instrument and increasingly ignored by major composers. In general, much more chamber and solo music was composed in the nineteenth century for strings and piano than for wind instruments, and of the wind instruments the oboe was far from the Romantics' favourite. It lost ground to the flute and, to an even greater extent, the clarinet, with its rounded tone, expansive compass (in both pitch and dynamics) and superficially more facile technique was better suited to the new Romantic long-lined cantabile style.[4] Indeed, alongside the clarinet the oboe was something of an ugly duckling. Its incisive sound was not so attuned to the Romantic sound ideal. Deemed too delicate for military music, too difficult for the amateur player and too brash for the domestic salon, the oboe ceased to have a prominent solo existence and, with the waning popularity of the woodwind concerto, the travelling virtuoso oboist became all but extinct. Hardly any writer failed to point out its inherent difficulties. The oboe entry in Pierre Larousse's widely-consulted *Grand Dictionnaire universel* left the reader with no doubt that it should be undertaken by none but the most diligent:

> The study of the oboe is full of traps for the student, and he must deploy great perseverance in order to arrive at a clean execution and attain a certain facility. As much as the tone of the oboe can be soft and velvety (albeit a little nasal) when in the hands of a skilled virtuoso, it can be sour and screeching when the player is inexperienced or lacks the taste of a true artist.[5]

At least two inventors proposed alternative instruments that replicated the oboe's tone without the associated effort. In 1837 a Monsieur Paris patented the harmoniphon, 'a sort of accordion which is sounded by blowing through a flexible tube, with a keyboard like a piano which issues forth sounds like those produced by an oboe, with the advantage that it is much easier to play'.[6] Around the same time in

42. 'Suite et progrès de l'enseignement mutuel de Musique'.

Edinburgh D. Hamilton invented a similar instrument 'in the shape of a small box' with a 'quality of tone . . . as perfect as the instrument it represents', [7] and some years later yet another such invention was exhibited in performance in New York.[8]

The paucity of Romantic oboe music has led to the belief that there was simply no solo repertoire at all. Leon Goossens called this an 'unforgivable oversight . . . , a badge of historical injustice that oboists must wear'.[9] Even Heinz Holliger, who has done much to uncover abandoned nineteenth-century music, has declared that 'there was no tradition of oboe playing during the nineteenth century. There was very little solo playing and the instrument nearly disappeared.'[10] At the very least, this is an overstatement. While there may not be works for oboe with as enduring qualities as some works for clarinet – Weber's three concerti, Brahms's trio and quintet, Schubert's *Shepherd on the Rock*, or the haunting clarinet melodies in Tchaikovsky's Pathétique Symphony – a considerable quantity of nineteenth-century oboe music was produced and stands as evidence for the existence of several lively traditions.[11]

The majority of nineteenth-century solo oboe music was written by lesser composers, or oboist-composers for their own use, and so is variable in quality. Also, as much of it is cast in a style that has since fallen out of fashion, the life of the nineteenth-century oboe outside the orchestra has gone virtually unexplored. This, however, is starting to change. A number of virtuosic fantasies, *morceaux de salon* and the like have re-entered the repertoire, notably works by Kalliwoda, Molique and Pasculli, but much music still remains to be unearthed.[12]

From about the middle of the eighteenth century the oboe sonata waned in popularity, and this continued to be the case through the Romantic period. A number of works were published with accompaniment for either piano or harp. Transcriptions of songs were also popular, particularly among players of more modest ability.[13] Up to the 1820s the combination of oboe with string trio or quartet was popular, but from that time the genre disappeared almost entirely. Trios for two oboes and cor anglais[14] in imitation of works by Beethoven were written by the French school into the 1840s. There are a few works for oboe, bassoon and piano by Vogt and Brod, and Carl Reinecke's trio is the best-known of a small number of works for oboe, horn and piano.[15] Perhaps the most important nineteenth-century contribution to wind ensemble repertoire was the wind quintet. Early examples were published by Cambini around 1800, but it was some twenty years later with the premières of Anton Reicha's quintets (opp. 88, 91, 99 and 100) that the genre attracted attention. Gustave Vogt, the oboist in these performances, received high praise for his technique and musicality.[16] Around the same time Franz Danzi and Henri Brod published quintets for flute, oboe, horn and bassoon; but apart from three works by Georges Onslow (1852), few wind quintets were written until the establishment of Paul Taffanel's Société de Musique de Chambre pour Instruments à Vent in 1879 (Taffanel himself wrote a quintet for the group). Renewed interest came in the 1920s with works by Carl Nielsen (1922), Hindemith (*Kleine Kammermusik*, 1922) and Schoenberg (1924).[17] There are also a number of chamber works for larger ensembles with prominent oboe parts. These outgrowths of the eighteenth-century wind serenade often mixed wind and string instruments and piano: the Septet by Hummel (c.1816), Nonet by Spohr (1813) and Serenade by Dvořák (1878).[18]

The orchestral arena

> It is much to be regretted that, because of its peculiarities, the oboe is much neglected at present and good oboists are also much rarer even in orchestras than clarinettists and flautists.
>
> F. A. Wendt, 1822

Even if the oboe was not a central player in nineteenth-century chamber and solo music and good players were rare, a special role was reserved for it in orchestral music. A growing interest in instrumental music gave rise to the burgeoning concert series across Europe; few towns were without their own orchestra, chamber-music and choral societies. The 1820s saw the foundation of co-operative-based orchestras in London (Philharmonic Society) and Paris (Société des Concerts du Conservatoire), and orchestras and opera houses on the American continent were also founded around this time. In Paris alone there were over fifty venues used regularly for concerts and theatrical performances, each with its own orchestral ensemble.[19] The oboe's place in art music has largely been guaranteed by the continuing status of the Romantic orchestral repertoire. If there were opportunities for only a handful of oboe soloists, there was plenty of work for oboists in the increasing number of orchestras in both concert halls and theatres.

Early in the nineteenth century, composers continued to score for pairs of oboes (the first player doubling on cor anglais where required), but oboe sections were gradually expanded to balance the other sections of the orchestra. In an effort to create a more colourful orchestral palette, Romantic composers scored for an increasingly diverse array of instruments, and this inevitably resulted in an overall increase in volume. The introduction of valved brass instruments around the middle of the century was also decisive because it both provided more even and sustained tone production and allowed the brass section now to participate more continuously and in a more melodic capacity. Berlioz was one of the first composers to realize the potential of valved brass, but Wagner's *Lohengrin* (1850) and Schumann's *Konzertstück* (1849) were the first works to require all valved horns rather than the mixture of natural and valved instruments common in scores of the preceding decades.[20]

The other sections of the orchestra were obliged to match the dynamic level set by the brass. For the strings, the main solution was to increase the number of players, but this was dependent on financial availability. In 1825 the string section of the Paris Opéra orchestra was one of the largest at about fifty; but around the same time the section in the Weimar under Liszt's direction numbered only eighteen.[21]

A similar strategy was often adopted to bolster the woodwind section. To avoid being swamped, in larger orchestras woodwind parts were often doubled. Even before the increased threat posed by valved brass, Beethoven doubled the wind parts in his Seventh and Eighth Symphonies in 'festive' performances in 1813 and 1814. By the middle of the century a pair of oboes plus another player specializing in cor anglais were required in many scores, and this was further expanded in Wagner's mature works to a total of four oboists – three playing oboe, and a fourth occupied for the most part with English horn. Instrument design also played a part, although in the case of the oboe the results were limited. Colin Lawson has argued that the eight-keyed oboes that became prevalent in Beethoven's lifetime 'could better provide the sheer volume now demanded'.[22] While it is true, however, that keys helped to equalize tone, their effect on overall volume was relatively insignificant compared with the influence of player and reed. Nor could it be taken for granted that all oboists owned instruments with all the latest keywork. Most orchestration manuals were cautious, advising composers to base their expectations on the capabilities of instruments with the least rather than the most keywork.[23]

THE RISE OF NATIONALISM

Despite improved transportation, music's status as a universal language, and the presence of travelling virtuosi, Romantic music developed along distinct and strongly defended national lines. Political, economic and ideological attitudes reinforced cultural boundaries drawn by language and history. Among oboists, the type of instrument used, the approach to tone production, reed-making and musical style were all governed by national style. The preferences of one particular school were rarely appreciated elsewhere. For instance, British audiences who heard Continental players like Centroni, Vogt, Barret and Lavigne complained of their nasal sound, although they acknowledged that it was the oboe's 'true' tone.

Distinctive national styles of performance were nurtured by the conservatories that began to appear at the turn of the century. The founding of the Paris Conservatoire, the first of a new order of institutions specializing in music education, coincided chronologically and ideologically with the French Revolution. It grew out of the École de la Garde Nationale, which had been set up to train musicians for the grandiose populist Fêtes Nationales. The Conservatoire's charter provided for six oboe professors with a minimum of twenty-four students at any one time, but these figures were never realized. As Revolution progressed to Consulate and Empire to Restoration, the Conservatoire's goals shifted and a single professor became sufficient to train oboists for orchestral careers in Paris and the provinces. Conservatories on the Parisian model were established across Europe – Milan (1807), Naples (1808), Prague (1811), Vienna (Gesellschaft der Musikfreunde, 1817), London (Royal Academy of Music, 1822), Brussels (1832) and Leipzig (1843).

The Conservatory marks a distinct break in tradition. Instead of entrusting musical education, as in the past, to religious institutions or to apprenticeship and dynastic traditions, the new institution was an efficient way of training technically proficient instrumentalists and singers in a consistent style. The conservatory-trained musician (as distinct from the autonomous virtuoso) was closer to functionary than artist: more a faithful reproducer of a composer's text than a creative interpreter. The type of pedagogical material used by these institutions illustrates this point. Given in large part to exercises rather than explanatory texts, nineteenth-century instrumental treatises are, above all, technical manuals organized systematically and progressively, and are less concerned with providing guidance on matters of interpretation than the treatises of the previous century.

While it remained permissible for virtuosi to display their ability to embellish well-known tunes and operatic arias in their variations and fantasias, composers became increasingly intolerant of orchestral musicians who exercised their creativity in improvised embellishments. Wagner believed that performers should neither add nor take anything from the composer's score, and Berlioz, equally renowned for his disdain of presumptuous musicians who elaborated his scores, chastised at least one oboist for adding free ornamentation. In Dresden he noted that

> the first oboe has a fine tone, but an old-fashioned style, and an irritating mania for inserting trills and grace-notes which outraged my deepest convictions. He indulged in some particularly disgusting embellishments at the beginning of the 'Scène aux champs' [in the *Symphonie fantastique*]. I expressed myself on the subject in vigorous terms at the second rehearsal. The sly dog refrained at the two subsequent rehearsals, but it was a feint. At the concert, knowing that I would not stop the orchestra and arraign him personally in the presence of the court, he treacherously resumed his little tricks, eyeing me with a quizzical air the while. I nearly collapsed with indignation.[24]

Amongst schools of oboe playing, the Parisian had already by the 1830s developed into the strongest and most influential. It owed its pre-eminence as much to the centralized cultural position of Paris as to the talents of its distinguished line of professors who collaborated closely with the Triébert workshop. Numerous foreigners enlisted in Vogt's class and many of his students earned international reputations.

Austria likewise had a continuous playing tradition based in Vienna. Up to 1871 the rest of German-speaking Europe still comprised a collection of principalities nor was it as technologically advanced as France. Consequently, no single centralized school of oboe playing developed in Germany. It nevertheless makes sense to refer to a German oboe school – characterized as much by its lack of uniformity as its separateness from other schools. Other geographic regions – Italy, England, Spain, the Bohemian lands, Scandinavia, Russia and the New World – were each in their own way influenced by and connected with either the French, German or Austrian school.

France

In 1823, when he took up residency in Paris, Rossini encountered a phenomenal oboe section at the Paris Opéra comprising Gustave Vogt (ill. 43) and his two pupils Henri Brod and Auguste Vény. Rossini would have occasion to call on their talents in works written or adapted for Paris. When reworking *Maometto II* (1820) as *Le Siège de Corinthe* (1826), he redistributed the prominent clarinet obbligato at the beginning of act III between oboe and clarinet, and three years later he wrote the delicious cor anglais solo in the overture to *Guillaume Tell* for Gustave Vogt.

Around this time the Paris players had additional keys fitted to their Delusse oboes. Up to this point the mechanization of the oboe in France remained behind Germany. This was certainly a consequence of the almost constant social turmoil unleashed by the Revolution. In addition, French oboists seem not to have viewed mechanization as so necessary as their German contemporaries. In his *Méthode de hautbois* (written 1816–25, but never published) Vogt adamantly defended his four-keyed Delusse oboe and was critical of the keys added to German oboes, observing that 'orchestral parts are never difficult enough to necessitate resorting to these mechanical excesses', an apt reflection of the conservatism of orchestral writing in France at that time. (See a drawing of his oboe, ill. 37)

Vogt apparently had consummate technique, but as some reviewers noted, was apt to be reserved in his style of performance: a disciplined artisan rather than a true genius: 'With respect to technique, his performance is so perfect and coupled with such wise circumspection and experience that this artist gains in wise and worthy sobriety [*verdienstvoller Nüchternheit*] what he lacks in genius.'[25] Nevertheless, Vogt apparently felt the need to change his instrument when composers like Rossini and Donizetti began placing greater demands on wind instruments by, among other things, writing in more difficult tonalities. By 1824 he was playing another Delusse instrument equipped with a total of seven keys.

We can discover much about Vogt's musical character and technique from the large corpus of music that he left for his instrument. Certainly the most prolific composer for the oboe of the century, Vogt wrote virtuoso showpieces for his own use, *morceaux de concours* for his pupils at the Conservatoire, chamber music and incidental pieces connected with his official positions at the Opéra, Chapelle and various chamber music societies.[26]

Even if today Vogt's technical prowess and copious musical output are forgotten, his reputation as founder of the French oboe school is well established. During the thirty-five years of his professorship at the Conservatoire he trained a veritable phalanx of oboists who went on to take prominent positions around Europe.

43. Romagnesi, medallion showing Gustave Vogt (1822).

Amongst more than eighty pupils, Vogt seems to have identified Henri Brod (1799–1839) as his heir-apparent (ill. 44).[27] Brod took over the first chair at the Opéra and enjoyed a considerable reputation as soloist, appearing more frequently than his teacher at the Société des Concerts du Conservatoire. He also made concert tours through France, sharing the stage at times with Chopin and Liszt and the French violinist Pierre Baillot, but died prematurely before he was able to succeed Vogt as Conservatoire professor and even before completing the requisite period of service at the Opéra for his widow and children to benefit from a pension.

44. Silhouette of Henri Brod, after Jean-Pierre Dantan.

Like his teacher, Brod composed extensively for his instrument (with fifty-eight opus numbers), and mostly performed his own music. He wrote salon music, songs and chamber music that included wind quintets (op. 2), a trio for oboe, violin and piano (op. 15), oboe duets and numerous sets of variations on Swiss, Austrian and Spanish tunes, and on operatic themes by Donizetti, Rossini and Bellini.[28] Brod seems to have made a special study of *piano* and *cantabile* control. He built oboes of cedar designed to play softly in chamber music,[29] and was known for his sweet and somewhat small tone. Decades after his death, one writer compared his playing with his teacher's: 'Vogt distinguished himself by a most remarkable technical prowess, although his tone was a little raw and hard [*les sons un peu crus et durs*]. Brod, Vogt's pupil, established a well-merited reputation by avoiding his teacher's principal fault; he played with lightness, delicacy and perfect taste.'[30] Brod's small tone seems not to have been appreciated by all. It was rumoured that when Cherubini learnt of Brod's death, he had nothing more to say than 'So what? Ugh! Meagre tone [*petit son*]!'[31]

As well as being a fine player, Brod was a key figure in the development of the French oboe (ill. 45). His earliest oboes closely resemble those of Delusse, whose instrument-making tools he had acquired. It is likely that Brod collaborated with the Triébert firm, although the exact relationship is difficult to ascertain because contemporary documents and attributions of specific inventions give a confused picture.[32] His oboes are the work of a superb musician and craftsman: they are easy to play, excellently tuned and show great ingenuity. He almost certainly had a hand in inventing the half-hole plate for hole 1; he added a 'see-saw' key connecting the E♭ and C keys to allow legato connection between c1–e♭1 and c♯2–e♭2 (this was before duplicate left-hand keys were adopted by French makers; see ill. 46d). He extended the range of the oboe to low b♭ with the aim of improving the tone of the instrument; he attached tiny wheels to the springs to guarantee the smooth operation of the keys; and he threaded the key rods so that instead of screwing into the posts they screwed into the keys themselves (see ill. 46e).[33]

In the second part of his oboe method published in 1830 Brod presented his *cor anglais moderne*, the first straight-bodied tenor oboe to be constructed in the nineteenth century (see ills 54a and 71). Designed to be played with a long crook, this instrument substituted for the traditional curved design. About twenty years later most other French makers had abandoned the curved cor anglais in favour of the straight form, but these were longer-bodied instruments that behaved acoustically quite differently from Brod's. Most likely Brod and Vény would have played *cors anglais modernes* at the Opéra in the duet accompanied by two cors anglais in act IV of Halévy's *La Juive* (1835), the famous cor anglais solos in Meyerbeer's *Les Huguenots* (1836) and Berlioz's *Symphonie fantastique*.[34]

Brod also made small *hautbois barytons* pitched in C an octave below the oboe, with a boot joint and long curved bocal, and small *hautbois pastoraux*. These designs were replicated by Triébert. Brod's reed-shaper and gouging machine mechanized the process of reed-making and form the basis of the machines still used by oboists and bassoonists.[35] Brod did not direct his ingenuity only to the oboe; he also invented a system for tuning timpani which, despite high praise from Berlioz, had only limited success.[36]

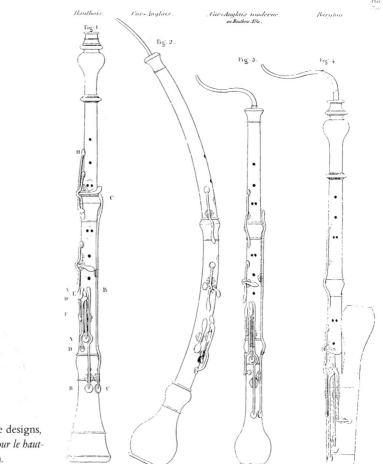

45. Brod's oboe designs, from *Méthode pour le hautbois*, pt II (1830).

The French were proud of the new level of technique set by Vogt and his school. In 1845 Berlioz was particularly appalled at the poor oboe playing at the Beethoven Festival in Bonn and commented ironically: 'What a great tragedy if, in place of the bad oboist, for example, whose playing of the solos in the symphonies was so mediocre, one had brought Vény or Verroust from Paris, Barret from London, Evrat from Lyon, or any other player of sure talent and excellent style!'[37] Each oboist named was a pupil of Gustave Vogt.

The advanced industrialization of France in the middle of the century is reflected in the organization of French woodwind production. While the Saxon workforce was slightly larger than the French, it was more dispersed, distributed amongst ten times the number of workshops. Pontécoulant reports that the forty master woodwind makers registered in France in 1861 employed around 600 workers, with a total annual production of some 5000 clarinets, 4000 flageolets, 3000 flutes, 900 bassoons, 800 fifes, 350 serpents, but just 200 oboes. By comparison, the total number of workers employed in wind instrument manufacture in Saxony just ten years prior was 712, spread amongst 380 registered makers.[38]

The oboe workshop founded in Paris by Guillaume Triébert received the highest awards of any oboe manufacturer at the international trade fairs, and also had the most decisive impact on the development of the French oboe.[39] Other French makers such as Adler, Martin frères, Godefroy, Buffet, Leroux and Tulou were generally neither as progressive nor as consistent as Triébert; indeed these makers often simply imitated Triébert's designs. Triébert's reputation was promoted considerably by his being named the official provider of oboes to the Conservatoire.

TRIÉBERT'S *SYSTÈMES*

Guillaume Triébert (1770–1848) was born Ludwig Wilhelm Triebert in Storndorf bei Alsfeld, Hesse, and journeyed to Paris on foot in 1804. Once there, he worked as a cabinet maker, and trained with the woodwind maker Viennen. In 1810 he earned the title *maître facteur*, enabling him to set up his own workshop. His sons, Louis-Charles (1810–67) and Frédéric (1813–78), studied with Vogt and were involved in the family business. Charles worked in the orchestras at the Opéra Comique, Paris Opéra and Théâtre Italien, and the Société des Concerts du Conservatoire from 1853. For the last four years of his life he taught at the Conservatoire, taking over from Stanislas Verroust, Vogt's immediate successor. At the chamber music gatherings such as those of the professional music club known as the Société Académique des Enfants d'Apollon, Charles Triébert played works by Vogt and Brod as well as his own waltzes, fantasies on operatic themes and songs, including the nostalgic 'Les bergers d'autrefois' with oboe accompaniment.[40] Although more a performer than an oboe builder, Charles Triébert nevertheless had a hand in oboe design. Little is known of Frédéric's life other than that he also studied with Vogt, devoted most of his energies to oboe manufacture and took over the workshop from his father around the middle of the century.

Regarding Triébert's oboes Fétis remarked: 'Since 1855, M. Triébert has, while retaining the advantages of new construction, succeeded with exacting care to rediscover the delicate tone [*joli son*] of the French oboe, much preferred over the fat sound of the German instrument.'[41] A principal contributing factor to the *joli son* of Triébert oboes was their narrow bore and slender body. The choke dimensions of French instruments stayed where they had been at the end of the eighteenth century (no wider than 4.5 mm), whereas nineteenth-century German, Austrian and English oboes tended to be slightly larger at around 5 mm.[42] By 1840 Triébert had reduced much of the ornamental turning. The baluster was eliminated, finial minimized and, with the exception of the external bell rim, turning elsewhere vanished altogether. Ivory mounts also became a thing of the past, often replaced with metal sleeves to protect the ends of the joints. Triébert replaced the wooden key mounts and metal saddle key supports used by Brod with axles and posts derived from Boehm (ill. 46). This mechanism drew on another recent invention, the needle spring, which very soon made redundant the flat springs found on earlier wind instruments. The simplification of the oboe's external profile was not only aesthetic: it had practical and acoustic implications. It freed the surface of the instrument for the placement of keys, and meant that the instrument was able to vibrate more freely and evenly along its length than with the disruptions caused by the mounts.

The keywork on French oboes from the 1840s was often incredibly delicate, again designed to disturb the resonance of the instrument as little as possible. To guarantee the surer sealing of the keys, the holes were countersunk. This technique was first used from 1811 on clarinets by Iwan Müller and meant that, instead of meeting the curved or potentially uneven surface of the instrument, the pad came into contact with the clean edge of the hole. The pads themselves were also redesigned. In place of the flat keys with soft leather overlay on eighteenth-century oboes, another invention of Müller was adopted. 'Salt-spoon' keys had cavities to hold a padded leather bag (the pad). Later, pads were mounted on a card backing and the concave cup keys were replaced with a flatter design.

Developments benefited from mass-production techniques. The emergence of specialist workshops that provided pre-formed components allowed oboe builders to assemble them as required. Such a distribution of labour made the addition of keywork increasingly more feasible, although mechanically intricate oboes were still labour intensive. They were designed largely for the professional market and understandably came with the highest price tag.

It was in the 1840s that Triébert dispensed with the inside rim in the bell and the sudden steps in the bore from the end of one joint to the beginning of the next. This resulted in a bore with a gradual and uninterrupted expansion, and with no points of resistance to the airstream. Triébert also redesigned the 'reed well'. In place of a counterbore merging into the choke and bore of the instrument found on earlier oboes, Triébert's new reed well had parallel walls with a step at its base. This arrangement behaves differently from the counter-bore of hautboys. The step is usually narrower than the bottom of the staple and provides some resistance to the airstream.[43]

The series of oboe designs brought out by Triébert in the 1840s addressed specific technical problems through the application of *interactive* keywork.[44] The simplest such mechanism is the ring (or *Brille*), patented in 1808 by the Revd Frederick Nolan, although it is Boehm who is credited with realizing its full potential.[45] Triébert first added rings to holes 5 and 6 on his système 3 (c.1840) to facilitate the fingering for ♯1. The rings are connected by means of a rotating rod to a key over the ♯ hole. Unlike the ♯ holes on earlier oboes, here the key stands open and is closed only when either or both of holes 5 and 6 are closed. This mechanism was of primary use for ♯1; many players continued to use the fork fingering in the second octave (see Collation of fingering charts, Appendix 2).[46]

Système 3 was also the first French oboe designed with a speaker key (*clef d'octavier*).[47] While the *Schleif-Klappe* had been one of the earliest keys added to German oboes, a comparable addition to the French oboe came relatively late. The earliest known instruments with this key were made by Brod between 1835 and 1839, and the first French oboe method mentioning a speaker key, Miller's *Méthode de hautbois*, dates from 1843.[48] With the exception of Boehm oboes, speaker keys on all other oboes continued for some time to function more like flick keys than the octave keys on the Conservatoire oboe.[49] Buffet's Boehm design (1844) was the earliest oboe with two 'octave keys' in the fullest sense of the term: that is, a necessary adjunct to overblowing the second octave and held open for the duration of notes. These keys

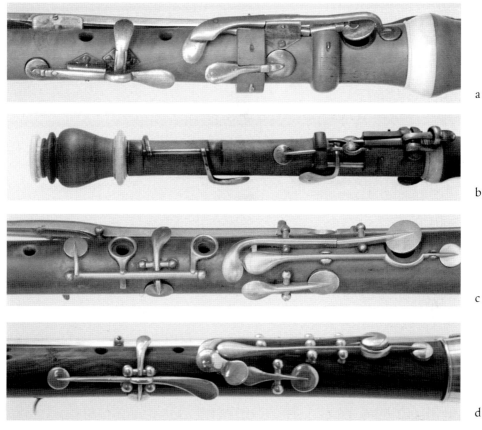

a

b

c

d

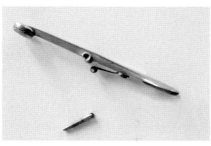

e

46. Keys and key supports: a) wooden mounts and metal saddles screwed into plates, including a piggy-back C sharp key on a Triébert oboe; b) an unusual rod supported by wooden mounts on an anonymous German oboe; c) rods and posts and brille on the lower joint of a Triébert oboe; d) Brod's see-saw key; e) a key from a Brod oboe showing wheel on spring and thread on screw.

allowed the same fingerings to be used for both first and second octaves. This system was later adopted by Barret on his 1862 model, and Triébert on système 6 (1875).

On système 4 (1843) Triébert added a second speaker key,[50] replaced the long levers for the little finger of the left hand with a double-action rod for the low b and alternative e flat, and improved the c2 with the addition of an extra hole operated by a ring mechanism. This model was used by Charles Triébert and consequently earned the epithet Système Charles Triébert (ill. 47).

Système 5 (c.1849) was the first design Frédéric released after his father's death. It became the most popular design for the remainder of the century in France and, along with système 4, was emulated by makers across Europe. The most important development on this oboe was the simplification of the fingerings for b♭1 and c2. Up

a   b

47. Mechanisms on a) Triébert's
système 4 and b) système 5.

to this time these notes were produced either with fork fingerings or with side keys operated by the index finger of the right hand – neither of which was practical in rapid passagework. From the early part of the century Austrian and German makers had added a second touch to the b flat key operated by the left thumb (ill. 48), but this solution was never applied to French oboes. On système 5 the c2 and b♭1 keys are held closed by light springs that could be overridden by a heavier spring on touches for the left thumb or right index finger (approximately where the old b♭1 key was situated). This mechanism, patented by Triébert in 1849, was one of the first to take advantage of the new invention of opposing springs.

Triébert's final model, système 6, was patented in 1872 and appropriated important features of Barret's design of the previous decade (discussed below). Here all holes had rings (not yet the pierced pads or *plateaux* that were added to the design in 1905); in place of the long harmonic fingerings formerly used for b♭2–c3, short fingerings were standardized on this model, and the range was extended down to low b♭. Like Brod's earlier experiments with lengthening the bell, the addition of the low b♭ was intended to improve the instrument's overall tone and the response of notes in the range d3–f3 at least as much as to extend the playable range downwards an additional semitone.[51] Système 6 had two semi-automatic keys, and the b♭1 and c2 keys were opened by the ring over hole 4. It is often said that the b♭1–c2 mechanism on système

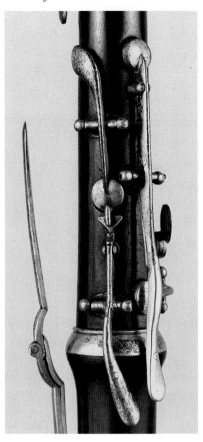

48. Double touch on an oboe by Stephan Koch; the long b♭ key is visible at the rear of the instrument with its folding mechanism.

6 was devised for oboists who were uncomfortable with operating these keys with the left thumb as on système 5 and the Barret model.

All of Triébert's models up to and including système 5 are illustrated in a detailed catalogue probably prepared for the 1862 London Exhibition (ill. 49).[52] This catalogue has become a familiar reference point for identifying nineteenth-century oboes, including non-French instruments, even though it was never intended as anything more than the price list for one maker. Perhaps the most important point to be gleaned from this catalogue is that the newer models did not automatically render previous designs redundant: all models from the most simple to the most complex were available at the time of printing. Triébert took pains to describe the main functions of each design. Many players – even gifted virtuosi like Pasculli – were satisfied with less than the most sophisticated key systems. In some cases models were depicted in a way that made them appear to differ from their original conception, and the differences between all except the Barret and Boehm models concerned the amount and organization of keywork much more than bore and hole size and placement. As the catalogue was not prepared as a historical record, but illustrated what was currently available for sale, it did not show how the earlier models were first conceived, but how they could be ordered in the 1860s. Thus pre-1840 oboes are shown with speaker keys, although they were originally made without. Customers

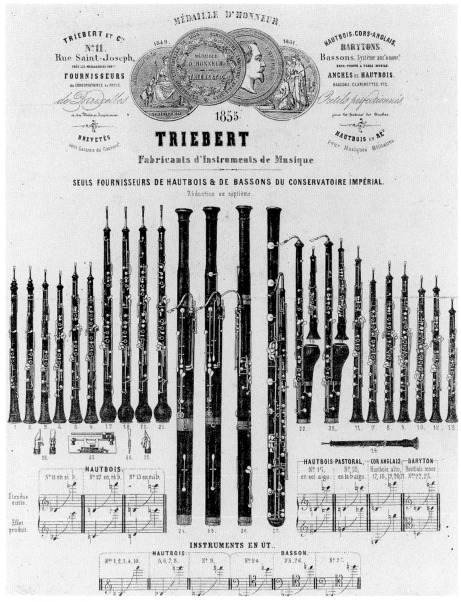

49. Triébert catalogue.

could also order customized instruments and the practice of adding keywork after manufacture continued, so many Triébert oboes survive with mechanisms that do not exactly match any of the numbered systèmes.

The increasingly complex keywork placed the body of the instrument under extra strain. *Buxus sempervirens* (commonly known as boxwood), the hardest woodwind timber endemic to Europe, was long admired for its excellent acoustic properties, but as it tends to warp with climatic changes that can easily throw the mechanisms out of alignment, makers turned to more stable exotic hardwoods. The most important of these woods were various species in the extensive *Dalbergia* genus, including *Dalbergia nigra* (Brazilian rosewood or palisander), *D. stevensonii* (Honduras rosewood), *D. variabilis* (Brazilian tulipwood, 'bois de rose'), *D. ceanrensis* (Brazilian violetwood or kingwood) and *D. melanoxylon* (mpingo, African blackwood, grenadilla, or in French 'ébène de Mozambique'), and *Brya ebenus* (West Indian cocus/cocoswood, one of the most popular in woodwind manufacture because of its stability), as well as *Diospyros melanoxylon* (ebony), which had already been known and used in instrument manufacture for some time.[53]

In 1828 Vény praised the 'brilliant and mellow [*brillant et moëlleux*]' qualities of boxwood over the 'bright and nasal [*clair et nazillard*]' tone of ebony and grenadilla.[54] But because the increased keywork could suppress the instrument's natural vibration, the brighter tone produced by the hardwoods was gradually sensed as an advantage. Barret insisted on the superiority of violetwood (*Dalbergia ceanrensis*), which he found combined the acoustic properties of boxwood with the stability of the other hardwoods. By the 1860s Triébert was recommending box only for oboes with simple keywork and otherwise preferred palisander or grenadilla. Nevertheless, boxwood was not abandoned entirely. In its first years the Lorée firm filled more orders for oboes in boxwood than any other timber.[55] The fact that it was the cheapest material certainly contributed to its popularity, but surviving specimens are, surprisingly, still in stable condition.[56] Later, when Gillet came to revise Brod's oboe method in 1890, he suppressed all reference to boxwood, mentioning in its place palisander, ebony and grenadilla. A few builders also experimented with metal bodies (primarily for military use). Metal bodies have to be made much thinner in order to emulate the resonance of wood, with the holes built up to provide comparable internal bore volume. Although sturdier than wooden instruments, metal oboes were generally considered inferior in tone (ill. 50).[57]

Apart from the standard oboe in C, the Triébert firm also made oboes in a range of different sizes and pitches. Most surviving cors anglais are curved in form. In 1810 Guillaume Triébert made one of his earliest two-keyed cors anglais for Vogt, whose performance of the mad scene in Dalayrac's *Nina* on this instrument made a strong impression on Berlioz in his first year in Paris (1821).[58] Triébert also made an eight-keyed *hautbois baryton* for Vogt that was awarded a gold medal at the 1827 Paris Exposition. Its intended function, however, is unclear as no music appears to have been composed for it. Lavoix later suggested that it had been designed as the tenor voice in a double-reed choir,[59] but even the adventurous Berlioz made no mention of it in his orchestration treatise and never scored for it. The 1862 Triébert catalogue also shows oboes pitched in D flat, E flat and B flat suitable for use in military ensembles alongside clarinets and brass instruments pitched in flat keys. These oboes were available with any of the key systems except système 6 and Barret's design, which were reserved for orchestral and solo use.

If Triébert's innovations transformed the oboe's appearance, they had an equally significant effect on the instrument's tonal characteristics. The harder exotic woods made for a brighter tone, the streamlined body also favoured a lighter sound, but, particularly with the narrower reeds used by French players, the volume could not be pushed beyond a fairly modest ambitus. Ever given to hyperbole, Berlioz described

50. Metal oboe by Eugène Thibouville.

the Romantic French oboe as a fragile being, out of place – even ridiculous – in its traditional place in military music. What he wrote in his influential orchestration treatise (1841) seems today an unjust accusation against composers of the previous generation, notably Mozart, for their inappropriate scoring:

> Candour, artless grace, soft joy, or the grief of a fragile being, suits the hautboy's accents; it expresses them admirably in its cantabile. A certain degree of agitation is also within its powers of expression; but care should be taken not to urge it into utterances of passion – the rash outburst of anger, threat or heroism; for then its small acid-sweet voice becomes ineffectual, and absolutely grotesque. Some great masters – Mozart amongst them – have not escaped this error. In their scores passages are to be found, the impassioned meaning and martial accent of which contrast strangely with the sound of the hautboy that executes them; and thence result, not only effects missed, but startling disparities between stage and orchestra, melody and instrumentation. The theme of a march, however manly, grand, or noble, loses its manliness, its grandeur, and its nobility, if hautboys deliver it; it has a chance of preserving something of its character if given to flutes, and loses scarcely anything by being assigned to clarinets.[60]

Inasmuch as his image of the oboe was indebted to Gluck and Beethoven, Berlioz was clearly unaware of the transformation the instrument had undergone since the late eighteenth century. He took a keen interest in developments in instrument design and would certainly have been familiar with the later Triébert models. Nevertheless, the detailed listing of difficult and impossible note combinations in his treatise is not au courant with the improvements of even Triébert's système 3 and was never updated in revisions of the treatise.[61] Perhaps he intentionally avoided describing the technically most advanced oboes because they were still not widely used.

At the same time, Berlioz's orchestral writing stretched the oboe's range more than any other mid-nineteenth-century composer did. From the 1830s on, he frequently wrote e3s and f3s, notes that only a couple of decades before Vogt described as 'extremely risky [*scabreuses*]' and 'without effect in the midst of the orchestra'.[62] Berlioz did this in an effort to create more brilliant orchestration than Gluck, whom he criticized for constantly keeping the treble instruments in their middle register.[63] Berlioz reserved the oboe's low register for special effects: 'The low notes of the oboe, ungracious when they are revealed, can be useful in certain strange and lamentable harmonies, combined with the low notes of the clarinet, flute and cor anglais.'[64] The same register of the cor anglais was, in Berlioz's words, 'particularly well suited to casting a menacing colour upon musical ideas in which fear and anguish predominate'.[65]

England

From the late seventeenth century until well into the nineteenth, English musical culture depended in no small measure on the importation of foreign musical styles and musicians. So in spite of – and perhaps as much because of – the presence of foreign instrumentalists, nineteenth-century English oboists did not always stay abreast of developments on the Continent. Both teachers and talented students were in short supply, and English oboes from the period by makers such as John Dunkin Goodlad (1826–38) and Joseph Wallis (p.1848) were mechanically less advanced than Continental instruments.[66]

Johann Friedrich Alexander Griesbach (?–1823) was, like J. C. Fischer, a German immigrant who established a fine reputation in London (ill. 51). He arrived some time before 1794 when he was admitted to the Royal Society of Musicians. Already in 1809 he had been first oboist at the King's Theatre for several years, and in 1813 was a founding member of the Philharmonic Society.[67] Griesbach's death in 1823 left a gap that no local player could fill, and his playing became a point of comparison for any pretenders, both foreign and local.

At first, the brothers William and Thomas Ling promised to be worthy successors,[68] but neither was apparently up to fulfilling the responsibilities of principal oboist at either the King's Theatre or the Philharmonic Society.[69] Another highly regarded British oboist was William Thomas Parke (1762–1847). Described as having a 'remarkably sweet tone, rapid and articulate execution, brilliant shakes' and 'varied and fanciful cadenzas',[70] Parke had been principal oboist at Covent Garden from 1784 to 1824, succeeded Fischer in 1800 as oboe soloist at Vauxhall Gardens, but retired in

51. Anonymous portrait,
possibly of J. F. A. Griesbach,
from the Royal Philharmonic
Society's oboe 1 part of the
overture to Spohr's *Jessonda.*

the year of Griesbach's death.[71] Neither Griesbach nor Parke produced any worthy successors. Parke did have students, including an African servant who had been 'acquired' by General O'Hara in America, and whose character and musical abilities impressed Parke.[72]

These circumstances forced London entrepreneurs to look abroad for oboists. In 1824 the Italian virtuoso Baldassare Centroni was invited to play at the King's Theatre. Rossini, at the time acting director of the theatre and also a personal friend of Centroni, was probably responsible for the appointment, 'the great melodist being unwilling to entrust his elaborate oboe parts to any English pretender'.[73] The following year Gustave Vogt played as principal oboist at the Royal Philharmonic Society and was invited back in 1828 by the King's Theatre. However, neither of these players fully satisfied British expectations. The English admired Vogt's technique, but his tone disappointed, particularly for those still with Griesbach's playing in their ears.

> His tone we did not like at first; we had been accustomed in our youthful days, to the elder Parke, and F. Griesbach, whose instruments, partaking of the nature of the clarionet, were remarkably full, rich and less reedy than Vogt's. But his is the true tone of the oboe, we admit, and, by use, loses what to many is its objectionable quality.[74]

After Vogt's second visit one writer, decrying the dearth of English oboists, did remember 'a Mr. Vogt, or some such name; but 'Ods' ducks and ducklings . . . defend us from him!'[75] Parke was equally incensed by the 'importation of lots of Frenchmen from Paris',[76] and when it came to foreign oboists, his memoirs, which on other subjects are remarkably candid, particularly when there was opportunity to discredit a rival, are conspicuously silent and contain no references to either Vogt or Centroni.

The future of oboe playing in Britain seemed to rest on the shoulders of the Royal Academy of Music's most promising oboe pupil, Henry Angelo Michael (known as Grattan) Cooke (1808–89), the son of the Dublin-born vocalist and composer Thomas Simpson Cooke. Could it have been the twenty-year-old Grattan Cooke, who is mentioned in the review of the Philharmonic Society's first concert of the 1828 season: 'Poor fellow! Instead of going to the opera at 8 o'clock he had much better be thinking of some other operation, of retiring to his natural rest'?[77] In 1830 one reviewer believed that his 'execution fully warrants us in placing Cooke, young as he is, at the head of living English oboeists [*sic*]',[78] and some years later, although not considered an equal to Griesbach 'in power and richness of tone', he left nothing to be desired 'in brilliancy of finger, in delicacy and expression, and in the precision and effect of his orchestral performance'.[79]

Cooke was appointed first oboist in the Philharmonic Society and King's Theatre, and he also taught at the Royal Academy of Music. Despite his talents, his career was not without difficulties. In 1841 he was said to be 'filling up some of the bars rest in his oboe engagements by practising singing under the instruction of Signor Crivelli', and some were concerned that England's finest oboist would abandon his instrument altogether in favour of singing. However, his appearances as vocalist were few.[80] Cooke finally came to grief over an incident with the Philharmonic Orchestra. In 1848 he was held responsible for a mistimed entry in the passage for solo flute and oboe in the finale of Mendelssohn's 'Scottish' Symphony (music ex. 5.1). This triggered a flurry of accusations culminating in Cooke's public disgrace. He tried to exonerate himself by putting blame on the flautist Ribas, but his falsification was divulged.[81] Soon after, Cooke resigned from the orchestra and was bandmaster of the Second Life Guards from 1849 to 1856.[82]

Clearly the British oboe scene was in need of rescue. When Fétis visited London in 1829, he had nothing positive to say about the first oboist of the Philharmonic

Ex. 5.1 Mendelssohn, Scottish Symphony, Finale, *Allegro vivacissimo*: flute and oboe parts.

52. Anonymous etching of Apollon-Marie-Rose Barret.

Society.[83] He recommended that the Society replace him with a French player. Shortly after, Barret was appointed to the King's Theatre, and from that time on, the British preference for German oboists shifted in favour of French players.

After studies at the Paris Conservatoire with Vogt culminating in a premier prix in 1824, Apollon-Marie-Rose Barret (1804–79) gained experience in the Odéon Théâtre (1824–7) and Opéra Comique in Paris (ill. 52). On his arrival in England he seems to have played second to Cooke,[84] and was promoted to first by 1839. In 1847 Costa invited Barret to be first oboe at the restructured Italian Opera (Covent Garden), and by 1853 Barret was also playing with the Philharmonic Society (a letter of recommendation from Berlioz helped to convince the Society of his qualities).

Barret's playing was described as 'charming' in tone and execution, but 'inferior, however, in quality, to old Griesbach'.[85] Barret's arrival in London still proved decisive for the history of the oboe in England. He taught a new generation of British oboists,[86] and developed an oboe that is the direct predecessor of the instrument still used by British players. In 1850 he published the first edition of his important oboe method. The following extract from a review gives a sense of the esteem in which it was held:

> What M. Barret has to say about the Oboe cannot fail to interest every amateur and admirer of the instrument. An accomplished master himself, he is anxious to impart some of the secrets of his skill to others. Hence the present work, which is not unreasonably styled a 'complete method,' since it leaves nothing untouched that has any bearing on the subject.[87]

Largely because of the quality and variety of its musical elements – scales, études, duets, sonatas and other pieces, all designed with specific pedagogical functions – this method has proved one of the most popular and adaptable. Since first appearing in print it has been available in both French and English versions almost continuously and to the present day is used by oboe students throughout the world.

The 1865 revision of Barret's *Complete Method* was even more significant as it described a new oboe design that Barret had developed with Triébert (ill. 53). This new oboe introduced three important innovations that would later find their way onto Triébert's own système 6: extension of the range to low B♭, short fingerings in the second octave, and additional interactive mechanisms added to facilitate certain note combinations and trills. Like Brod, Barret claimed that the overall tone of the instrument improved with the lengthening of the bell to produce low B♭. Barret found that the long harmonic fingerings for b♭2–c3 impeded technical fluency, and so by modifying the bore and the placement of speaker keys, he provided a means for the fingerings of the first octave to serve for the second just by adding a speaker key. Short fingerings had been available on earlier French models, but were used mainly as alternatives. Most players probably continued to prefer the security and tone of the harmonic fingerings. On Barret's oboe they now served as the principal fingerings. Indeed, an elaborate automatic octave-key system obliged players to use them in place of the harmonic fingerings. The technical advantage of the short fingerings was offset by a sacrifice in tone quality, and these notes remain the most impoverished on the modern French oboe.

The most important mechanical difference between Barret's model and the système 6 involves the mechanism for b♭1 and c2 – the so-called 'thumb-plate', which was adapted from Triébert's système 5. Instead of the somewhat illogical system on the Conservatoire oboe by which the b♭ and c keys are *opened* by *closing*

53. Barret-model oboe.

hole 4, on Barret's oboe they are opened by releasing the thumb-plate. It was no doubt because of Barret's influence in England that many British oboists still prefer the thumb-plate to the Conservatoire system. The most important British oboe maker of the nineteenth century, Alfred Morton (1827–98), also made oboes with this mechanism.

Another significant difference between the Barret and Conservatoire models was their pitches. Barret's oboe was designed to play at high pitch (A–453), while système 6 was designed to comply with *diapason normal* (A–435), set as the standard pitch level by a French commission of 1858.[88]

Germany

Unlike in England, where French oboe makers exercised considerable influence, French innovations had relatively little impact on oboe manufacture in German-speaking countries until later in the century. The most important German maker was Carl Theodor Golde (1803–73) in Dresden. Golde probably trained with Carl Gottlob Bormann (1770–1839, an apprentice of Floth, who had in turn been apprenticed to Jakob Friedrich Grundmann). His boxwood instruments had between eleven and thirteen keys, supported on wooden mounts, were quite conservative in design, and were praised for their excellent intonation.[89] Most descend to low b, with the key operated as on the French oboes with the little finger of the left hand, rather than a key for the left thumb as on Austrian oboes. The high regard in which Golde's oboes were held can be seen in the numerous imitations by other German makers, notably Johann Wendelinus Weisse (1780–1864) of Berlin.[90]

Golde probably built his oboes to play close to A–440, the pitch at the Dresden opera house. At the same time, the Kapelle played in the Catholische Hofkirche with the celebrated 1754 organ by Silbermann and Hildebrandt that was maintained at about A–415. The wind instruments were apparently never able to play quite so low, as the chapel orchestra averaged A–424. This difference of 15 Hz must have forced oboists to play instruments of different pitches according to where they worked.

The simultaneous existence in Dresden of multiple pitches of such difference was almost unique at that time. By the middle of the century most other cities had adopted a single pitch. Even Paris, where earlier in the century every theatre had its own slightly different pitch standard, had settled for the *diapason normal* A–435 by 1859. Earlier in the century, pitch varied considerably from place to place and the coexistence of different pitches within the same city was not unusual. More than anyone, this affected the travelling virtuoso. A number of reports indicate that oboe soloists performing in foreign cities were not able to tune to the local pitch. In 1819, a writer in the *AMZ* commented on a performance given in Frankfurt by Wilhelm Theodor Johann Braun (1796–1867), who was on a visit from Schwerin, that 'it was only regretful that the lower pitch of his instrument, compared with the local orchestra, was only too apparent'.[91]

The oboists Friedrich Wilhelm Rose (1783–1845) and his son Eduard (1817–76) are likely to have played instruments like those by Golde. In 1827 Friedrich performed in Kassel a programme that included a concerto by Maurer and one of the best-known concerted works for oboe of the nineteenth century – the Introduction, Theme and Variations, op. 102 (1824), by Johann Nepomuk Hummel.[92] This arrangement of a work originally for two pianos was widely performed from the 1820s and soon became a cornerstone of the oboist's repertoire.[93] Its technical demands are not great, although the F minor Introduction contains some rapid legato connections between d♭2 and e♭2, and the enharmonic modulation from F minor through the Neapolitan G flat major to A major requires a firm sense of intonation.

Golde's oboes continued to serve oboists up to the middle of the century. Rudolf Theodor Hiebendahl (c.1818–90), oboist and English horn player with the Königliche Sächsische Kapelle (Royal Saxon Court Orchestra) during Wagner's directorship (1842–8), probably played his oboes,[94] and when Robert Schumann's orchestral music was first played in Dresden it was probably oboes by Golde that were used. Schumann's Second, Third and Fourth Symphonies (composed 1846–51) include occasional c♯1s and b♮s, and combinations of c♯–d♯ and d♭2–e♭2 occur frequently. The duplicate E♭ keys standard to Golde's oboe helped here. Other makers fixed rollers that allowed the right-hand little finger to move across the keys.[95] Special oboe moments in Schumann's orchestral music are rare, but when they occur, they take full advantage of the instrument's lyrical qualities, the melody at the beginning of the Piano Concerto and the Romanze in the Fourth Symphony being the most memorable.

Schumann's *Drei Romanzen* (op. 94) are amongst the few solo compositions for oboe by a major nineteenth-century composer, but are unlikely to have been originally conceived for the instrument. They were composed in 1849 as a Christmas present for his wife, who probably played them with the violinists Franz Schubert (concertmaster of the Dresden Kapelle) and Josef von Wasielewski.[96] Almost a year later, Schumann seems to have rehearsed the Romances with the Düsseldorf oboist Friedrich Rougier, and this experience may have resulted in the wording of the title for the first edition as *Drei Romanzen für HOBOE, ad libitum Violine oder Clarinette mit Begleitung des Pianoforte* (Simrock, 1851) – that is, with oboe as first choice, and violin or clarinet as alternatives. The first documented public performances of the Romances on oboe date from the next decade when they began to find their way into recital programmes by Christian Schiemann and Emil Lund in Stockholm, Uschmann in Leipzig and A. L. de Ribas in Boston.[97] In England they were better known in performances given on the alternative instruments.[98]

The Schumann Romances use the full chromatic range from c1 to d3 (the oboe version avoids an e3 for violin). While the actual note-combinations would have presented few difficulties on a mid-nineteenth-century German oboe (only the slurred c1–c♯1 in no. 2 would have been tricky), the 'breathless' style of Schumann's cantilene has caused many an oboist to come to grief, and others to avoid the pieces altogether. In 1897 Prout reported that the 'very eminent' Belgian oboist Eugène Dubrucq, then resident in England, 'always refused to introduce the second [of Schumann's Romances] into concerts, as it was quite impossible to play'.[99]

Next to Golde, the most important German mid-nineteenth-century manufacturer of oboes and bassoons was Heckel of Biebrich. Johann Adam Heckel (1812–77) had trained with Schott in Mainz, and would have been familiar with the Schott oboe so similar to the Sellner design. Heckel had been in partnership with the bassoonist Carl Almenräder and made bassoons from 1831, but began developing oboes only from 1850. Like Golde's instruments, early Heckel oboes are in boxwood, retain traditional turning and have simple key systems. Heckel soon introduced rods and posts; his ingenious key construction was more robust than the delicate work on French oboes. Heckel's later instruments, with their right-hand mechanism, resemble Triébert's système 5 with rings over holes 5 and 6, but retain the side keys for b♭1 and c2, and the octave keys are not coupled. The Heckel firm gained fame through its connection with Richard Wagner, who was familiar with the workshop from the time of his residency in Biebrich and later made specific recommendations, including the Heckelphone developed by Johann Adam's grandson Wilhelm (discussed in chapter 6, pp. 185–7).

The oboe builder Johann Simon Stengel (1805–1902) also established a connection with Wagner. Benefiting from his location in Bayreuth, which from 1876 Wagner's Festspiel transformed each summer into a national musical pilgrimage site, Stengel not only came into contact with professional musicians from around Germany but was called on by Wagner to provide instruments for his music-dramas, notably the Altoboe (see chapter 6, p. 185).

As well as Hummel's Introduction, Theme and Variations, another two of the best-known nineteenth-century concerted works for oboe were written for German oboists. It is likely that Bernhard Molique wrote his Concertino for Friedrich Ruthardt (1800–62). The first performance of this delightful concerto took place in 1829 in Stuttgart, where Molique was music director. The dedicatee of Johann Wenzel Kalliwoda's Concertino op. 110 was Reuther, oboist at the grand-ducal chapel in Karlsruhe during the period when Kalliwoda was also in the duke's employ. Kalliwoda's *Morceau de salon* and Divertimento were also likely to have been written for Reuther.[100]

Austria and Italy

Meanwhile, in the Austrian Empire (until 1860 this included northern Italy) the Sellner-Koch model enjoyed enduring popularity, and formed the basis of oboe designs by Wolfgang Küss, Martin Schemel and the Uhlmann family in Vienna, Ludwig & Martinka in Prague (fl.1857–86) and Pietro Piana (fl.1811–42) in Milan. Sellner's oboe method (1825) was also one of the most widely disseminated of the nineteenth century. French and Italian translations appeared shortly after the German edition, and signs of its direct influence can be found in three other Italian methods.[101] Despite a French translation of Sellner's treatise, the Sellner-Koch oboe does not appear to have been played in France, and interest was also slow to develop in Saxony.[102]

Before Italy's nationhood in 1860 oboe playing developed along regional lines. In the north, Carlo Yvon (1798–1854) was active in Milan during the first half of the century. He had enrolled at the Milan Conservatory in 1808, just a year after its establishment by Napoleon, studying with the bassoonist Giuseppe Buccinelli. At the age of twenty Yvon was appointed principal oboe at La Scala, a post he held for more than thirty-five years until his death; in 1828 he became the first oboe professor at the Milan Conservatory. In 1839 his fellow-student Giovanni Daelli (?–1860) joined the oboe section at La Scala. Yvon also played cor anglais in premières of works such as Bellini's *Il pirata* (1827)[103] and in 1840 he published the only known nineteenth-century sonata for English horn and piano (the publication gives viola as alternative). His three *Capricii* for three oboes and duets for two oboes were pedagogical in function.[104] Daelli, too, left a small quantity of music for oboe. His virtuosic variations on *Rigoletto*, like so much music written by oboist-composers, coincide with his employment at the opera.

Another flourishing school grew up in Bologna under the influence of Baldassare Centroni (1784–1860). Undoubtedly one of the most famous Italian oboists of the first part of the century, Centroni played concurrently with the Accademia Filarmonica, the Teatro Comunale and other theatres as well as at San Petronio (up to the age of seventy-five), and made occasional journeys to nearby Modena, Rimini, Pesaro and Bergamo. From 1810 to 1855 he taught at the Liceo Musicale. When he was living in Bologna Rossini met Centroni, certainly knew of the oboist's ability, and probably took it as his model when writing his demanding oboe solos.

As was typical of Italian oboists of his day, Centroni played an oboe with few keys. His instrument, which was built by Heinrich Grenser in about 1806, originally had only two keys, but an F key, register key and a second e flat key were added to it some time later.[105] Few keys are required for even the most demanding oboe parts in Rossini's early operas. Indeed, in rapid passages such as the solos in *La scala di seta* (1812, see music ex. 5.2) and *L'italiana in Algeri* (1813), keywork can be more a hindrance than a help. Although Rossini certainly wrote these solos with the talents of a virtuoso such as his friend Centroni in mind, both operas were premièred in Venice, and so Centroni could not have been involved. From the little we know about oboists in Venice at that time, it is possible that Giovanni Battista Delai (c.1765–p.1805) played these premières, perhaps with an oboe by the Venetian maker Andrea Fornari (1753–1841).[106]

Centroni was perhaps the first oboist to earn the epithet 'Paganini of the oboe'. If the account of Ricordano De Stefani, an Italian oboist of the next generation, is reliable, it was probably Centroni's appearance – 'with swollen cheeks and neck and eyes about to pop out of his head'[107] – that inspired comparison with the Mephistophelian violinist. It may also have arisen from Centroni's musical inventiveness. In London in 1823–4 Centroni not only played a solo of his own composition (in clear breach of the Philharmonic Society's guidelines), but made himself conspicuous by his predilection for adding ornaments. 'Signor Centroni's best quality may also be said to be in a degree his worst, for the facility of execution which he possesses is apt to seduce him into the practice of more ornament than sound taste would dictate in performing the compositions of the great masters.'[108]

Ex. 5.2 Rossini,*La scala di seta*, Overture.

None of Centroni's own compositions survives, but several works dedicated to him, including sets of *Capricci per oboe* by his pupils Giuseppe Berti and Raffaele Parma, and a trio for oboe, violin and cello by Nicola Petrini-Zamboni, have. Another of Centroni's fifty-five students was Giovanni Cattolfi, for whom his fellow-student Gaetano Donizetti wrote his Concertino for cor anglais (premièred 1817), a rare work for tenor oboe pitched in G instead of the more usual F.[109]

In Naples Carlo Paessler (1774–1865) studied and worked at the Cappella di Corte and later succeeded a member of the Ferlendis family at the Teatro Grande and Cappella Civica in Trieste. Other important Italian oboists include Egisto Mosel (1787–1825), whose activities centred on the grand-ducal chapel in Florence, and Giovanni Paggi, one of the most widely travelled musicians of his day (his career is discussed below, p. 169).

Even more than Centroni, Antonino Pasculli (1842–1924) was deserving of the title 'Paganini of the oboe'. A native of Sicily, Pasculli began his career as an itinerant soloist in 1856 at the age of fourteen. In 1860 he was appointed professor of oboe and English horn in Palermo, but in 1884 he was forced to stop playing suddenly because of deteriorating vision that was believed to be caused by his playing (a case of the proverbial excessive air pressure on the optic nerves?). Earlier in 1877 he had become director of the Municipal Musical Corps of Palermo. This band was one of a number of such ensembles that performed music written specially for wind and brass instruments as well as transcriptions of 'Classical' symphonic repertoire, including symphonies by Haydn and Beethoven, and contemporary works by Debussy, Grieg, Sibelius and Wagner.

Around the middle of the century the supremacy of Austrian and German oboes in Italy began to be challenged by the arrival of French instruments. In 1848 Vito Hinterland included drawings of an early Triébert-model oboe and cor anglais in his manuscript *Nuovo trattato generale*, and Giuseppe Cappelli's *Metodo teoretico-pratico* (c.1853) is written for Triébert's système 5. Around 1855 Pasculli acquired a Triébert système 3 oboe. Even by then, this model had been twice superseded, but Pasculli used this instrument for the balance of his career. His cor anglais was slightly more modern – a straight-bodied Triébert système 4.[110]

Pasculli's numerous oboe compositions give a vivid impression of his talent. There are nine fantasias or grandi concerti, most based on themes from operas by Donizetti, Verdi and Rossini – each loaded with passagework of staggering virtuosity (composing and writing out these works is just as likely to have caused Pasculli's blindness as any effects from his playing). As well as being in general technically more demanding than music by contemporary French oboe-composers, Pasculli's music uses a noticeably wider range of tonalities and greater chromaticism. One of his favourite tricks was to give the illusion of double stopping by setting a slow-

Ex. 5.3 Pasculli, cadenza from the Concerto on Themes from Donizetti's *La Favorita*.

a   b   c

54. a) Henri Brod: oboe and *cor anglais moderne*; b) oboe by Stephan Koch; c) detail of scallop-shell keys on Koch oboe.

moving melody against constant florid motion, reminiscent of Paganini's études (see music ex. 5.3). In addition to his concerted works, Pasculli wrote original studies on scales, the notorious study *Le Api*, transcriptions of Rode's violin études, all undoubtedly intended for his and his students' technical regimes.

Although in places dizzyingly difficult, Pasculli's writing took full advantage of the technical potential of his oboe. He generally avoided difficult note combinations (including a♭–b♭) and exploited the colouration of those cross-fingerings he still used. Even though his oboe did not have an F♯–G♯ coupler, he was still unreserved in his use of this note-combination. Judging from the prevalence of rapid passages around a2–c3, it is likely that Pasculli used short fingerings at least where technically advantageous. Some passages are actually easier with cross-fingerings than with keys. For example, the passage (beginning at the *fff*) from the Concerto on Themes from Donizetti's *La Favorita* given in music ex. 5.3 is virtually impossible to play at speed with a b♭1 key on either the Conservatoire or thumb-plate system, but presents no difficulties with the cross-fingered b♭ (1 3). Pasculli's concerted works languished unplayed for some time until they were rediscovered in the 1970s, but perhaps the favourite nineteenth-century Italian concerto has been the much earlier work by Bellini. Much surrounding its creation remains obscure. Who was the oboist Bellini had in mind when he wrote this work at the tender age of fifteen before he had left Catania for study in Naples (c.1819)?[111]

Just how marked differences between national schools of oboe playing were is, of course, impossible to say. The French and Austro-German schools are usually considered the most antithetical. However, Henri Brod and Joseph Sellner, prime exponents of each and almost exact contemporaries who are likely to have known of each other's reputation, were both known for their sweet, supple tone and technical precision. Even so, as no direct comparisons of their playing exist, the closest we can come to know how they sounded is to make educated guesses from their oboes and music. Brod, who made his own oboes, and Koch, who supplied Sellner's oboes, made them from both boxwood and exotic hardwoods (ill. 54). Koch's oboes retained traditional turning, wooden mounts, slightly wider bore and larger tone-holes, while Brod's were more delicate, with smaller tone-holes and slimmer profiles. From this we might conclude that Koch's oboes might have had a heavier, somewhat more direct and projecting tone than Brod's, which might have been more responsive and perhaps lighter in tone. This picture remains incomplete, however, because of how little we know about their reeds.

Reeds

Detailed instructions on reed-making start to appear in the nineteenth century, but most information remains sketchy, suggesting that many important techniques were still passed on orally. Both Braun and Sellner felt that as the process of reed-making was so widely known, it was not necessary to write about it.[112] Perhaps they thought that students were better advised to learn directly from demonstration than from a book, but if only they had said *something* we would have a clearer picture of their oboe playing and the tonal qualities of nineteenth-century oboes.

The paucity of written documents is partially offset by a reasonable number of surviving reeds.[113] Like the instruments for which they were fashioned, reeds varied considerably from school to school. The most detailed information is found in French oboe methods; sources from other traditions are less uniform. Oboe methods by Garnier (c.1800), Brod (1830), Barret (1850), Fahrbach (1843), Salviani (1848) and Cappelli (c.1853) include illustrations of the tools used in reed-making and reeds at various stages of manufacture. In accord with the maxim that a picture is worth a thousand words, these illustrations can speak for themselves and restrict my commentary to general observations (ill. 55).

It is likely that, as in earlier periods, not all nineteenth-century oboists made their own reeds. William Bainbridge maintained that 'those who play the oboe ought to have some idea of finishing their reed', implying that it was by no means common practice, or else that players normally acquired partially made reeds.[114] Instruments may have been supplied with several finished reeds and there were a number of professional reed-makers (like Thomas Ling in London) who met the needs of both amateurs and professionals. In his revised version of Brod's method published in 1895, Gillet completely excised the chapter on reed-making, presumably because he deemed it of no value to his students at the Paris Conservatoire.[115]

In the nineteenth century there was still a good deal of variation in the size of oboe reeds (ill. 56). In the most general terms, it can be said that over time they

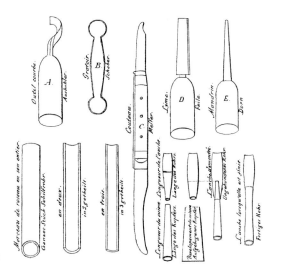

Modèle du Roseau et des Outils nécessaires a la facture de l'anche dans leurs proportions exactes.

MODELL des SCHILFROHRS und der NÖTHIGEN WERKZEUGE nach ihrem genauen Maaße, um Haut-bois-Rohre zu machen.

a

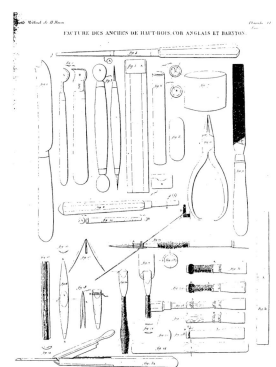

b

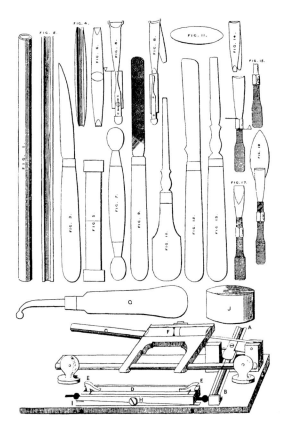

c

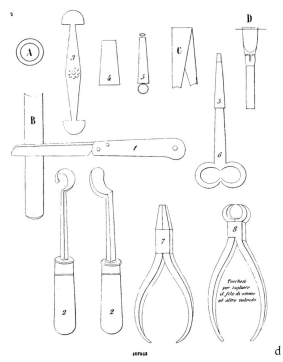

d

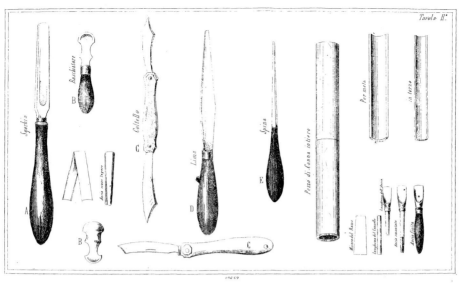

e

55. (*facing page and above*) Illustrations of reed-making equipment and reeds from nineteenth-century oboe method books: a) François-Joseph Garnier, *Méthode raisonnée pour le hautbois* (1802); b) Henri Brod, *Méthode pour le hautbois*, pt II (1830); c) Apollon-Marie-Rose Barret, *A Complete Method for the Oboe* (2nd ed., 1862); d) Clemente Salviani, *Metodo completo per oboe* (1848); e) Giuseppe Cappelli, *Metodo teoretico-pratico* (c.1853).

became narrower, were made from cane tubes of smaller diameter, gouged thinner and tied onto narrower staples. Many of these changes occurred in the early part of the century and can be attributed to the rise in standard pitch. Smaller bore volume required smaller reeds to set the air in vibration. As French instruments had the narrowest bores, it is not surprising that French reeds were also the narrowest. Most surviving examples are 7–8 mm wide (that is, about the same as used for the Conservatoire oboe today).

German and English oboists used wider and more resistant reeds, and this contributed to differences in tone colour. Brod observed in 1825:

> Reed-making is not at all the same in each country where the oboe is played; Italians, Germans and practically all foreigners make them harder than us. They also have a hard and muffled tone [*un son dur et sourd*] which denatures the instrument, and makes their playing laborious and fatiguing as much to the audience as the player. The tone that French oboists manage to draw from their instrument is without question the best, and brings the instrument closest to the violin.[116]

Italian oboists likewise used broad, sometimes exceptionally wide reeds. Italian oboe methods by Giovanni Battista Belpasso (c.1840–61), Giuseppe Cappelli (1853) and Salviani (1848) all show very wide reeds. It is difficult, however, to get an accurate idea of exact measurements from these sources, as the different parts of the reed and stages of manufacture were not always drawn to scale.

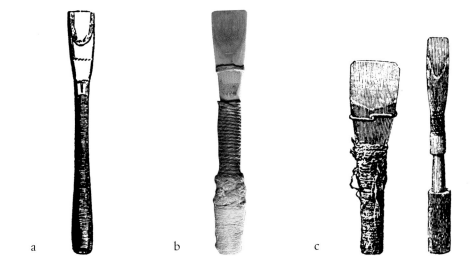

56. Nineteenth-century oboe reeds: a) illustration from Giuseppe Fahrbach, *Novissimo metodo per oboe* (1843); b) oboe reed by Thomas Ling; c) French reed and reed from Centroni from *Gr1*; d) single-reed mouthpieces for oboe and cor anglais

The article on the oboe in *Gr1* includes scale drawings of reeds from Centroni and Triébert (ill. 56c). These represent the extremes of nineteenth-century oboe reeds. Centroni's reed is supported with a wire and is more than twice the width of Triébert's. On Centroni's Grenser hautboy, a wider reed would have been beneficial for the response of the forked fingerings, whereas the narrower bore of Triébert's oboes, and particularly the elimination of forked fingerings as principal fingerings on the later models, meant that narrower reeds were more suitable. Even so, Centroni's reed seems disproportionately wide, and may actually be for English horn.

The technique of scraping the reed also differed markedly from that used for modern-style reeds (ill. 57). Reeds by the highly-esteemed English maker Thomas Ling do not have a 'spine' like most modern reeds, and in some cases are thicker at the edges than at the centre.[117] How typical this was of reeds of the time is hard to say. There was undoubtedly a great deal of variation in the way reeds were finished: perhaps just as much as was the case with clarinet reeds. In 1803 Heinrich Backhofen noted that clarinettists' preferences differed to the extent that some made reeds with a convex surface, while others scraped them concave.[118]

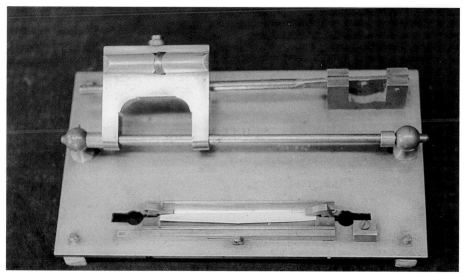

57. Gouging machine by Triébert.

Some oboe reeds were wired. Fahrbach considered wired reeds old-fashioned, but observed that their advantage was that the aperture of the reed could be controlled better than with the newer unwired reeds.

Henri Brod's gouging machine provided greater accuracy and evenness for gouging the inner surface of the cane than had been available from the hand chisels, gougers and scrapers used up to that time.[119] But the machine tended to be less flexible when it came to producing a tapered gouge, or varying the gouge to suit the quality and diameter of the cane. Barret seems to have combined both machine and hand scraper, while for Cappelli the machine was a substitute for hand gouging. Gouging machines were standard in France, but until the twentieth century they were not as widely used elsewhere. Fahrbach 1843 reports that the Viennese builder Uhlmann used one, but no mention is found in late nineteenth-century methods by the German oboists Georg Pietzsch (c.1885) and Richard Rosenthal (1901).

The mechanization of the oboe also affected reed design. With the introduction of the octave key, reeds no longer needed to be as responsive to changes in breath pressure for overblowing. This in turn meant that the exact dimensions of reed and staple were not as critical because the octave key allowed the intonation of the upper octave to be adjusted without risk of the note 'dropping'. The increased use of notes above d3 also required slightly harder reeds and this could affect the overall tone of the instrument.[120] But for as long as cross-fingerings were in use, reeds needed a certain degree of lightness and flexibility to aid their response.

The only written documentation concerning cor anglais reeds is found in Brod's *Méthode*, which shows staple-less reeds designed to fit directly onto the bocal. In the second part of the century most English horn reeds were tied onto staples, although isolated players continued to use staple-less set-ups.[121] Single reeds were occasionally used on oboes and cor anglais. A small number of special mouthpieces survive (see ill. 56d).[122]

An experimental digression: the Boehm oboe

Boehm's revolutionary flute design of 1832 provoked as much enthusiasm as controversy. Its devotees hailed it as a truly logical solution and awaited the invention of an oboe that would incorporate Boehm's principles.[123] To Comettant, 'despite the improvements to the oboe made in recent times . . . this instrument does not lend itself to the performance of rapid or brilliant passage-work; its technique remains cumbersome. Without doubt, these faults will disappear when an oboe is built according to the excellent Boehm system.'[124] Comettant was apparently unaware that there had already been at least three attempts to create a Boehm oboe. Brod was said to have worked on one, but this model never saw the light of day,[125] and the French virtuoso Antoine-Joseph Lavigne was involved in at least two other projects.

After studying with Vogt (premier prix, 1838) and a period working at the Théâtre Italien, Lavigne (1816–86) seems to have had no fixed appointment. He travelled extensively in the 1830s and later moved to England. From 1861 to 1881 he played in the Hallé Orchestra in Manchester, where he died in poverty. Reports indicate that he was a remarkable soloist, but less sensitive as an ensemble player and, particularly later in his career, was known for his a harsh tone. In 1839 a Parisian critic commented that his tone lacked volume ('manque d'ampleur dans le son')[126] and four years later in a recital in Vienna when he played an 'Adagio and Rondo', a medley of Alpine tunes and a fantasy on themes from Bellini's *Sonnambula*, he was praised for his beautiful *piano*, portamento and astounding trills.[127] But shortly after, in Dresden, he was criticized for harshness of tone, which the critic attributed to his otherwise commendable use of a Boehm oboe.[128] In the 1840s and 50s Lavigne was on tour in the US with Louis Jullien, playing in the orchestra and featured as soloist alongside flautist Reichardt and the Italian double-bass virtuoso Giovanni Bottesini. The oboe was still a rarity in the New World, and Lavigne's playing captivated audiences but, as in the case of the English reaction to Vogt and Barret, his reedy tone displeased.[129]

> His tone is thinner and finer than that of some of our best oboeists [*sic*]; but it is a purely reed tone, more sharply contrasted with the clarinet tone than theirs, and never harsh. His execution is most smooth and flexible; he plays it *con amore* and with exquisite expression, looking like a Pan with half-closed eyes, and reeling jolly figure, half-drunk with the delight of his own music. Verily he was born with a reed in his mouth. In him you have the whole individuality of his instrument embodied.[130]

In the early part of his career, Lavigne played a Boehm oboe that he had developed in collaboration with the maker August Buffet jeune (1789–1885?) and Lavigne's fellow Vogt pupil Pedro Soler (1810–50). In addition to developing a Boehm oboe, Buffet also collaborated with the flautist Victor Coche on an improved Boehm flute. The oboes (patented in 1838) are finely crafted, but their hole sizes and bore dimensions do not depart as radically from traditional models as Boehm oboes by other makers. The most significant difference involves the fingerings for F and F sharp (1234 and 123 6). During his short career as first oboe at the Théâtre Italien in

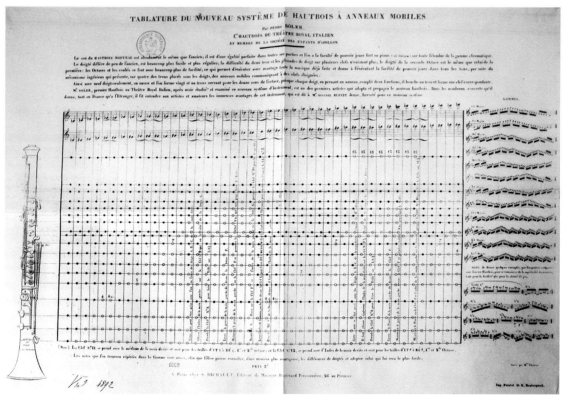

58. Fingering chart for the Buffet Boehm oboe from Soler's *Tablature du nouveau système de hautbois à anneaux mobiles* (1850).

Paris, Soler was one of the few to adopt the Boehm oboe in a professional orchestra. Soler also published a fingering chart (see ill. 58) and was probably responsible for the dissemination of the Boehm oboe in Spain. Later, in 1870, a Spanish method for Triéberts Boehm oboe was written by Enrico Marzo.

Lavigne also visited Boehm in Munich in 1850 and together they worked on an oboe design. This came shortly after a period of intensive experimentation, during which Boehm had developed a cylindrical flute and learnt much about tone-hole placement and the effects of different materials on the sound of the flute. He developed a mathematical scheme for woodwind design (ill. 59), and his calculations for the oboe are followed most closely in a unique instrument by Rudall, Rose & Carte, whom Boehm licensed to make his flutes in England (see ill. 60). With Lavigne, Boehm expanded on this work and aimed to create an oboe that was uniform in both tone and intonation. He rejected cross-fingerings, and constructed a bore of uniform conicity and based hole placement on strict acoustic principles for an equal-tempered scale, with the keywork organized to produce a chromatic scale by successively uncovering each hole. The model he arrived at was exhibited in London in 1851. It descended to low a, had no fewer than three speaker keys and, like most Boehm oboes, was bored in one piece down to the bell in order to minimize interference with correct hole placement.[131] Boehm seems to have bored instruments to which Triébert adapted keywork.[132] Two oboe bodies with holes but no keys, and two instruments with unique and exceptionally complicated key-systems (known

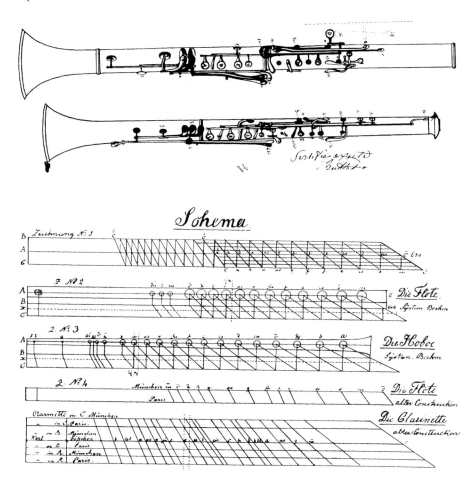

59. Boehm's drawings and calculations for woodwinds.

affectionately as 'old spider-keys'), now in the Bate Collection (Oxford), were probably the fruit of Lavigne's continued experimentation.

Lavigne was undoubtedly the person referred to in the Triébert catalogue as the 'fervent partisan of the Boehm oboe, an exceptionally competent artist and experienced inventor', whose 'obsequious interventions' enabled Frédéric Triébert to complete his own Boehm oboe in the 1850s. Notwithstanding Triébert's own dissatisfaction with the sound quality of this design, it was awarded a gold medal at the London Exhibition in 1862. Ernst Pauer was particularly impressed, commenting that 'the tone has become fuller and rounder, resembling much more that of the clarinet, however with greater precision and reliability. The oboe's future as a solo instrument is indebted to the new system, and this invention is of even greater significance to the oboe's potential as an orchestral instrument.'[133]

As with the Boehm flute, the reception of the Boehm oboe was decidedly mixed, particularly when in the hands of its principal advocate Lavigne. Of his participation in a performance of Hummel's Septet in 1883 in Birmingham, one writer remarked:

a   b

60. Experimental Boehm designs: a) body without keys, probably by Triébert based on Boehm's design; b) 'spider keys', probably an experimental key design by Lavigne.

'In one or two passages the full, powerful tone of M. Lavigne was almost too much for the maintenance of the *ensemble*';[134] Christopher Welch described Lavigne's playing as 'reedy' and 'piffero-like', and observed that in the orchestra Lavigne 'did not always refrain from using the extra power he had at his command and so caused the oboe to unduly predominate'.[135]

Boehm oboes, along with the Barret and Conservatoire models, are the only oboes with a 'logical' fingering system that virtually eradicates cross-fingerings and half-holes, and standardizes short fingerings in the second octave. But, whether on account of its inherently non-traditional tonal character,[136] the elimination of the tonal differences from note to note characteristic of more traditional designs, or Lavigne's brash playing, the Boehm oboe, the only radical redesign of the oboe attempted since the seventeenth century was destined to be no more than a digression. Despite meeting with considerable opposition,[137] the Boehm flute, and particularly Boehm's cylindrical design, was nevertheless a key stage in the creation of the modern flute. By contrast, the Boehm oboe had less direct impact on today's model. Moreover, apart from a small number of works by Lavigne and Soler, there appears to have been virtually no music written with the specific capabilities of the Boehm oboe in mind.

Production of Boehm oboes did continue into the twentieth century. A good number of instruments survive from both highly regarded workshops, including Lorée, Triébert, Lafleur and Millereau,[138] and larger mass-production businesses such

a   b   c   d

61. Boehm oboes: a) Rudall, Rose & Carte; b) Triébert; c) Buffet;
d) Sharpe.

as Kohlert (Graslitz, Czechoslovakia) and Boosey and Hawkes (London). Most of those made in the twentieth century were destined for military ensembles where simpler fingerings and stronger tone were advantageous, but some Boehm oboes – presumably for special orders – were made for mainstream Classical players (ill. 61).[139] But despite the endeavours of some of the most talented oboe makers, the Boehm oboe failed to become the dominant design and is no longer in production.

Despite its ultimate demise, the Boehm experiment did serve to affirm the desired attributes of the traditional design. Western art music demanded an oboe that could accommodate the acoustic shortcomings of the traditional design rather than a revolutionary design that set out to correct them afresh.

Expanding horizons

Throughout the nineteenth century, oboe manufacture and playing in areas beyond the principal European powers remained peripheral and conservative, and in most cases emulated activities in France, Germany, Italy, England and Austria.

In Scandinavia and Russia the predominant influence was German. Russia, hungry to satisfy its desire to keep abreast of Europe's social and cultural development but lacking trained musicians, welcomed itinerant virtuosi. The paucity of Russian-made oboes and oboe methods up to the very end of the century suggests that local players were few.[140] Oboists from Italy, France and Germany found ready employment in Russian cities. Angelo Ferlendis, a member of an illustrious Venetian family of oboists, resided in St Petersburg for some time and participated in the upsurge of cultural activity under Czar Alexander I from 1801 up to 1823.[141] Relatives of the famous Viennese oboist F. J. Czerwenka were employed at the Russian Imperial court from the 1790s into the 1820s, and from 1839 to 1860 Johann Heinrich Luft (1813–77), who had studied oboe in Magdeburg, played solo oboe at the imperial chapel in St Petersburg. Among Luft's concerted works for oboe is a *Fantaisie sur des thèmes russes nationaux* (op. 12), which probably pleased the marketing instincts of Luft's European publishers, although there is little in the music to identify it as exotic. Other Europeans who worked in St Petersburg were Henri Brod's brother Jean-Godefoy (1801–?), who played in the Russian Theatre from 1836, and in the 1850s the Dutch oboist Eduard Auguste Schmitt.[142]

THE OBOE IN THE NEW WORLD

The incredible exodus from Europe during the nineteenth century took the European oboe to colonies in new worlds around the globe. Opportunities for European-style music making were most favourable in North America, but for some time the lack of competent wind players made it hard for fledgling orchestras to fulfil their aspirations. The flute had taken root in most American cities from the middle of the eighteenth century,[143] but there was a pressing shortage of good oboists. Fingering charts published in the early nineteenth century suggest a growing interest in the oboe, but as one of them states, the oboe is 'a very imperfect instrument, except in the hands of a great player, and therefore is seldom used in this country'.[144] A report on the state of music in North America published in an English music publication of 1831 decried the lack of competent wind players:

> There are seldom two clarinets, and generally no bassoon. . . . Oboes are almost unknown in this country; in the whole of North America there is only one player, who lives at Baltimore. Notwithstanding the imperfection of their orchestras, they play the sinfonias of Haydn; and although the want of instruments often brings them to a stand-still, they treat the silence as if it were a pause, and play on.[145]

Few of the oboists who journeyed to the New World were significant enough figures for their biographies to have come down to us, but one who stands out is Gottlieb Graupner (1767–1836), who is remembered less as an oboist than as the 'father of the American symphony orchestra'. Possibly a distant relative of the Darmstadt composer Christoph Graupner (b.1683), Gottlieb came from a family of regimental *Hautboisten* in Hannover. After a sojourn in London, when he may have played in Salomon's orchestra under Haydn in 1791–2, he emigrated to America.

62. Oboes by Berteling and Lauter.

From 1795 to 1797 he played in the orchestra at the City Theatre in Charlestown, occasionally performing concerti by Fischer and Lebrun and duets with Catherine Hillier, a well-known British soprano and actress whom he was later to marry. In 1797 the couple moved to Boston, where they continued their activities in musical theatre.[146]

Graupner did much to enrich the musical life of nineteenth-century Boston. He established a music business and school, and was instrumental in setting up the Philo-Harmonic Society, the nation's first 'meagre combination which could be called in any sense an orchestra'.[147] Initially comprising some fifteen musicians, this orchestra was the first to be independent of any theatre or choral society and its concerts featured the latest European music – movements excerpted from works by Haydn, Kreutzer and Beethoven, as well as concertos and works for smaller combinations. The Society also collaborated in performances of choral works such as Handel's *Messiah* and Haydn's *Creation* with the Handel and Haydn Society, which Graupner also had a hand in founding.

A copy of Peter von Winter's Concerto in F (1814) survives in Graupner's hand,[148] but whether he ever had a chance to perform this piece is unclear, as practical considerations forced him to put his oboe aside after the 1810s. During his later years

Graupner devoted more energy to his music business and teaching than to playing the oboe. Nor is it likely that anyone came to his music school for oboe lessons. His clientele comprised mostly young ladies eager to acquire the skills requisite for a genteel life – pianoforte playing and singing. Indeed there was little call for oboists in colonial Boston, and Graupner himself turned to playing either double bass or piano, or to conducting.

By 1833 New York audiences had developed sufficient appetite for the establishment of an Italian opera company under the artistic direction of Lorenzo Da Ponte. To mount their productions, famous singers and key instrumentalists needed to be imported from Europe. With the invitation of Giovanni Paggi (1806–87) in 1832, the company gained not only a principal oboist but a fine tenor.[149] Paggi remained in the States for a decade during which he exercised his diverse musical talents in New York, Philadelphia and Boston. He was a fine oboist, 'eminent master in Vocal Music', and was also praised as a 'highly scientific teacher on the piano forte'.[150] On his return to Europe, Paggi continued to appear in major centres as oboist and tenor into his seventies. His virtuosic works for oboe are closely related to the operatic stage, while his vocal music was tailored to the salon.[151]

The Philharmonic Symphony Society of New York was founded in 1842, following the lead of the Philharmonic Society in London and the Société des Concerts du Conservatoire in Paris. The personnel of the new group were predominantly German and Bohemian, reflecting the provenance of the majority of the immigrants arriving in New York at that time. For its second season the oboists were Stark and Weise.[152] Another oboist active on the New York scene at the time was Señor de Ribas. Spanish by birth, de Ribas was a prominent soloist in salon concerts, and also earned a reputation for playing what was then a curiosity in the colonies, the 'cornet anglaise'.[153]

By the middle of the century at least three oboe makers had set up workshops in New York. Oboes by German immigrants Theodore Berteling (1821–90) and Franz Lauter (fl. New York, 1845–85) followed the German tradition with concessions to French key design (ill. 62). The quality of their workmanship gives every indication of catering to the needs of professionals. Despite the dominance of German influence, there was apparently still room for French-style oboes. An oboe bearing the name of Edward Baack (1802–p.1871), who also operated out of New York, is strongly reminiscent of Brod's later instruments.[154]

Chapter 6

From Romanticism to Modernism: the adoption and dissemination of the Conservatoire oboe, 1880 to 1950

> The nature of this melodic instrument par excellence, being poorly suited to virtuosity, gives rise fatally to monotony; this is a pitfall that not all composers are able to avoid.
>
>

L'Art musical, 19/48 (1880): 338

Introduction

The adoption of Triébert's système 6 oboe design as the official instrument of the Paris Conservatoire in 1881 and the death two years later of Richard Wagner coincide with the end of the Romantic era, but like all stylistic shifts, the transition from Romanticism to Modernism[1] was by no means as clear-cut as these events might imply. As much as fin-de-siècle Modernism was a new departure, it took Romanticism as its foundation, and it was only by World War I that it can be said that composers began to forge a new style. The generation after Wagner faced the challenge of responding to the new characteristics he had developed in his late works – notably the chromaticism of *Tristan* and the sophisticated timbral mixes of *Parsifal*. The efflorescence of Wagner's musical language led to the dominance of the German compositional style from the 1860s. Still, in spite of the German hegemony, oboe playing retained distinct national styles. Moreover, it was not the German oboe, but the French model that was the most widely used instrument in the Modernist period – and still is up to the present. It is a happenstance of history that, since the early twentieth century, three out of the four orchestral wind-instrument families – oboe, flute and clarinet – have been dominated by French playing style as well as instrument design. In the case of the bassoon the outcome has been the reverse, with the French bassoon now virtually obliterated by the German instrument.

For many, the endorsement of système 6 by the Paris Conservatoire marks the arrival of the oboe in the modern age. It would take some decades, however, for this model to gain international acceptance. Its dissemination was largely through the appointment of Georges Gillet's pupils beyond France – notably in the US. For the oboe, therefore, the Modernist period was still one of transition and diversity.

The orchestra remained the oboe's principal arena of activity. The availability and stability of orchestral appointments tended to draw musicians away from pursuing solo careers; this was particularly the case with the oboists. The general prosperity enjoyed in fin-de-siècle Western society led to an increase in both the number and size of orchestras. The Romantic predilection for the grandiose became an obsession. By 1900 a normal string section consisted of about sixteen first violins, sixteen second, twelve violas, twelve celli and eight basses, with wind and brass sections standing typically at around twelve to fifteen each. While numerically no stronger than the winds, the brass had a definite advantage in volume. A section of three oboists, the third doubling on cor anglais, was now standard and many works called for more. Wagner's late scores require three oboes plus cor anglais, and this was exceeded in exceptional works such as Schoenberg's *Gurrelieder* (1901), Mahler's Eighth Symphony (1906) and Stravinsky's *Sacre du printemps* (1913), which all call for a total of five oboists with either one or two playing English horn. And even then, some feared that the oboes could not be heard in a *fortissimo* tutti. When Mahler felt the oboists would not be heard he asked them to play *Schalltrichter in die Höhe* (bells in the air).

The adoption of the Conservatoire oboe

INITIAL RECEPTION

In 1939 Adam Carse wrote that 'when the Conservatoire model was complete, the last word in French oboes had been spoken'.[2] While it is true that since that time the Conservatoire oboe has remained virtually unchanged and now enjoys an international monopoly, much has changed with regard to its technique and the expectations that players and composers place on it. Most developments of the oboe have taken the form of refinements to the same basic design. It is easy to claim (as has often been done) that because it has withstood the test of time, the Conservatoire oboe is the most 'perfect' oboe design. But rather than invoking perfection in instrument design, it seems more meaningful to speak of 'a shifting of interest that enriches one element and impoverishes another, gain in one area compensating for loss in another'.[3]

The Conservatoire oboe did not immediately meet with unanimous approval. In the same way that valved brass instruments were initially treated with circumspection even by progressive-minded composers like Berlioz, and the Boehm flute was met with both enthusiastic approval and derision, the last of Triébert's models had its share of detractors.[4] Lavoix complained that 'in gaining better intonation, the oboe, cor anglais and bassoon have lost something of their characteristic timbres', and that by searching for new effects 'they no longer have the same sonority that they had fifty years ago'.[5] The design leaves a number of acoustic problems solved only provisionally – the G$\sharp$ hole is not ideally placed, the octaves of the long-fingered notes c$\sharp$1–e1 are often faulty, the c2–d2 trill is deficient in sound, and the complexity of the keywork makes for a heavy instrument. The Conservatoire oboe's endurance for more than 125 years certainly attests to its adequacy in a wide range of music. But as much as a sign of its versatility, this can be seen as a product of the blandness of mainstream twentieth-century musical tradition that reduces three centuries of music to the uniform tonal palette of the available.

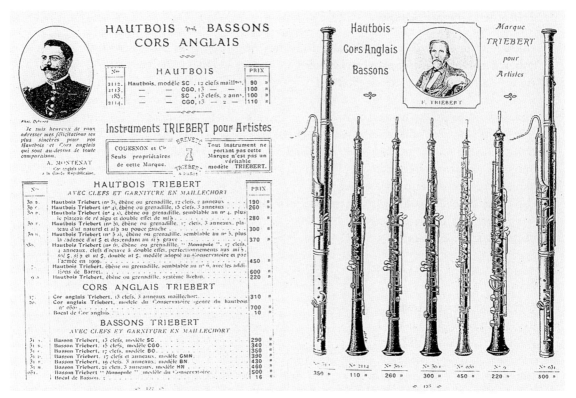

63. Couesnon: catalogue c.1910 showing Triébert systèmes 3, 4, 5, 6 and Boehm-system oboes.

The Triébert atelier did not last to see système 6 named the Conservatoire oboe. After Frédéric Triébert's sudden death in 1878, the firm was directed for a few weeks by Mme C. Dehais, before being bought out by one of the former keymakers, Félix Paris. Not long after, the company declared bankruptcy, and in 1881 the foreman François Lorée (1835–1902) jumped ship to start his own business. Although Triébert's subsequent proprietors, Gautrot aîné and Couesnon et Cie (ill. 63), continued to advertise oboes with the authentic Triébert bore as late as 1934, it was effectively Lorée who carried on the Triébert tradition.[6] The new firm's standing was guaranteed by Georges Gillet's endorsement of their système 6 as the official instrument of the Conservatoire. Between 1881 and 1900 Lorée made 1500 oboes. The most popular model was système 5 (over 500, including variants), followed by système 6 (just over 400), some 275 cors anglais, only 9 oboes d'amore and 3 musettes. There was a surprising number of special orders, and at least 49 Barret-system instruments, but only 11 Boehm instruments and similar numbers of systèmes 3 and 4 were made. Many of Lorée's instruments went to French professionals, conservatories and music academies, as well as to dealers outside France like Rudall Carte in London (who usually ordered instruments at Old Philharmonic pitch); the records also list a few German customers.[7] In the first years boxwood was the most commonly used timber, then palisander, ebony and, from the 1890s, grenadilla.

Non-French oboes were quite different from the Conservatoire model. They descended only to b♮, using cross-fingerings and second-octave harmonic fingerings. Even at the Brussels Conservatoire, which in other respects mimicked the Parisian institution, the oboe professor Guillaume Guidé (1859–1917; professor from 1885) favoured système 5 instruments by the Belgian company Mahillon. Indeed, until the early decades of the twentieth century, the Conservatoire oboe remained something of an exception. At first it was used only by soloists and professional orchestral musicians. In 1909 was it adopted by the French army, but decades later French and British builders were still making oboes with less complicated keywork for military and educational use.[8] Standard reference works from the turn of the century rarely show the Conservatoire model: in its place it is usual to find système 5,[9] and most orchestration manuals cautioned composers to avoid b♭o, an indication that the Conservatoire oboe could by no means be taken for granted.[10]

GERMANY AND BOHEMIA

With the founding of the German nation in 1871, German productivity began to outstrip that of other countries, but the production of musical instruments and particularly oboe manufacture in Germany continued to be decentralized and conservative in relation to the concentration of progressive builders in Paris. An internal bell rim was still common on many German oboes and harmonic fingerings for b flat 2–c3 were standard, and only some of the French mechanical innovations made their way onto German oboes. The *Schule für Oboe* (c.1890) by Georg Pietzsch, who was a chamber musician in the Royal Saxon Capelle (see ill. 64), describes a

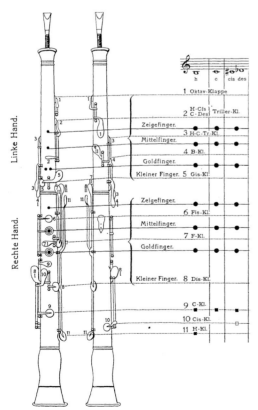

64. German oboe illustrated in Pietzsch's *Schule für Oboe.*

65. Two oboes by Otto Mönnig (1907–10).

a   b

typical German oboe. The name of the oboe builder is not given, but Pietzsch's illustration resembles oboes by Pinder, who supplied woodwind instruments to the Saxon court from 1895. While from the perspective of the Conservatoire oboe, late nineteenth-century German instruments might seem clumsy, there is no reason to doubt their efficiency. German-style oboes continued to be used in orchestras throughout Germany, Denmark, Norway, Sweden, Bohemia, Poland, the Netherlands and Russia. Important German makers included Heinrich Franz Eduard Pinder (1857–1913), Heinrich Friedrich Meyer of Hanover (1848–early twentieth century) and Otto Mönnig (1862–1943) of Markneukirchen and later Leipzig, the last of whom was largely responsible for the continued existence of the German oboe into the twentieth century (ill. 65).[11] In the same tradition, the Kohlert factory in Graslitz (now Kraslice in the Czech Republic) was one of the largest producers of woodwinds of any time in a city renowned for its unprecedented concentration of wood- and brass-wind instrument manufacturers.

Around the same time as the adoption of the Conservatoire oboe, Christian Schiemann (1824–1913) collaborated with Heckel of Biebrich on a new oboe designed to meet the technical requirements of the younger generation of German and Scandinavian oboists.[12] Schiemann was trained in the school established by Christian Samuel Barth and Philipp Barth in Copenhagen, where he was also a

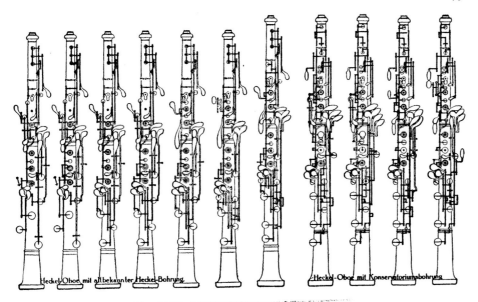

Fig. 13 Heckel oboes from catalogue, *c.* 1935

66. Table of models available from Heckel, c.1935.

member of the royal court music from 1845. His design may have been the first oboe model released by the Heckel company, which had already established a considerable reputation for its bassoons, but advertised oboes only from 1886. In 1900 the firm patented a new oboe design with automatic octave keys, but still with side keys for b♭ and c (ill. 66).

It is generally considered that German oboists preferred a fuller, darker tone to the brighter and more flexible sound concept cultivated in France. Nevertheless, French influence began to filter through to Germany in the first years of the twentieth century. Fritz Flemming (1873–1947) is known as the first oboist to play a French instrument in a German orchestra. After studying in Paris, Flemming went on to play first oboe in the Berlin Philharmonic, and from 1907 taught at the Berlin Hochschule. Richard Strauss would have been familiar with his playing from his time as Kapellmeister in Berlin from 1898, and it was probably his high regard for Flemming's playing that influenced his disposition towards the French oboe: 'The French instruments are of finer workmanship, their registers are more even, they respond more easily in the treble and allow a softer *pp* on low tones. Correspondingly, the style of playing and the tone of French oboists is by far preferable to that of the German players. Some German methods try to produce a tone as thick and trumpet-like as possible, which does not blend in at all with the flutes and clarinets and is often unpleasantly prominent.'[13] It is ironic that this great orchestrator in the post-Wagnerian German tradition and director of the Vienna Staatsoper should have preferred the French oboe to German and Viennese models. Strauss's stamp of approval of the Conservatoire oboe reinforced its status, much as his preference for the Boehm flute was decisive in establishing its privileged status.

By 1920, practically all German oboists had followed Flemming's lead and were playing French-style oboes. To satisfy this market, Georg Urban of Hamburg (fl.1920–30) created a hybrid design combining French keywork with German bore, and by 1925 Heckel was offering clients the choice of oboes with either the German bore with scale to b♮ or French bore with b♭o, both with numerous options for key layouts based on French and German designs (see ill. 66b).[14] Since then virtually all German firms have provided only French-style oboes with only slight variations, including slightly wider bores and thicker walls. Hans Kreul in Tübingen (est. 1919) was the most important producer of oboes in the Germany and continued making Conservatoire-system oboes in isolation from French manufacturers. Karl Steins (1919–), professor at the Berlin Hochschule from 1959 and principal oboe with the Berlin Philharmonic 1949–81 under Furtwängler, Klemperer and Karajan, was another early advocate of the French oboe in Germany and was responsible for its eventual ascendancy over German instruments.

Russia, and St Petersburg in particular, maintained strong cultural links with Germany; most oboists were trained by German players and continued to use German-system oboes even after they had been supplanted by French instruments in Germany. A. V. Petrow (1913–85) was responsible for introducing the Conservatoire oboe to Russia and from World War II up to the dissolution of the USSR most Russian oboists were obliged to play oboes of East German manufacture.

AUSTRIA: THE WIENER OBOE

In addition to the adoption of the Conservatoire oboe and Schiemann's collaboration with Heckel, the 1880s saw the birth of another oboe in Vienna. This oboe, the only distinctive oboe design to withstand the international monopoly of the Conservatoire oboe, was a hybrid of Austrian and German models and came about in response to the needs of a specific player. When Richard Baumgärtel (1858–1941) moved from Dresden to join the Wiener Hofkapelle in 1880, he discovered that his Golde oboe would not function at A–435 Hz, the pitch set in 1862 by Austrian imperial decree in compliance with the French *diapason normal*.[15] Baumgärtel preferred his oboe by Golde to the Koch-system instruments used by Viennese oboists at the time.[16] But as Golde had died in 1873, Baumgärtel asked Josef Hajek (1849–1926) to make a modified copy of his Golde oboe that would play at the lower pitch. The result was the so-called *lange Modell Wiener Oboe*. Hajek retained the baluster and finial, the steps in the bore between the joints and the internal lip in the bell, but elsewhere simplified the external turning. He used keys on rods supported by posts, and added rings on holes 3, 4 and 5, perforated plates for 1 and 2; b♭1 and c2 were operated by side keys and the instrument was equipped with two octave keys as well as a *hohe-F Klappe*. Hermann Zuleger (1885–1949), who copied Hajek's model, became the principal supplier of Wiener oboes in the twentieth century (ill. 67).[17]

The Viennese oboe retains more of the hautboy's characteristics than the Conservatoire oboe. Likewise, modern Viennese players preserve techniques which have been associated with the hautboy. The notes from b♭2 to c2 are produced with harmonic fingerings, *Stützfinger* technique is used extensively to stabilize intonation

67. Wiener oboe by Zuleger.

by closing holes low down the bore (see, for instance, fingerings for c_1 in ill. 68),[18] and the F♯ hole stands closed, opened by the ring on hole 4, and closed again by a ring on hole 5. Acoustic tests have shown that the harmonic fingerings are richer in overtones and thus more effective in projecting through the orchestra.[19] Although these fingerings complicate certain passages, this is a sacrifice that Viennese players are willing to make.

A special bell to produce low B♭ was designed in 1906 by Hajek and Stecher, but it did not gain popularity because of the detrimental effect it had on tone and intonation. In 1949 Zuleger produced the *kurze Wiener Oboe* at the higher pitch of A–447 Hz, but still without a low B♭. Up to the present, Viennese oboists have been obliged to exchange bells to play the additional semitone. Mahler, who wrote much of his orchestral music for Vienna, generally marked b♭o as optional in his scores, and provided alternatives.

As the English horn has not undergone the same technical development as the oboe in Vienna, there is at present a pressing need to bring this instrument up to date; and very few Viennese-style oboes d'amore have been made.

Baumgärtel remained in Vienna for the balance of his career. He played at the Burgtheater and was professor at the Staatsakademie für Musik from 1885 to 1919. His pupils Alexander Wunderer (1877–1955; first oboe in the Vienna Opera from 1914

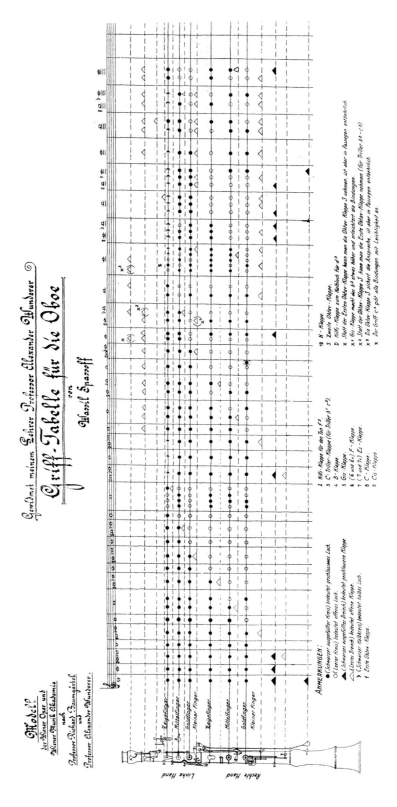

68. Spassoff, *Griff-Tabelle für die Oboe, Modell der Wiener Oper und Wiener Musik Akademie* (p.1935).

and professor at the Staatsakademie from 1919) and Hans Kamesch (1901–75; professor from 1935) were his heirs. Hans Hadamowsky (1906–86), from 1936 principal oboe and English horn at the Staatsoper, defended the Viennese tradition against foreign influence and wrote an extensive *Oboeschule.*[20] An important aspect of traditional Viennese oboe technique is the absence of vibrato,[21] but this is beginning to change with the continued internationalization of playing styles.

The creation of the Wiener oboe coincided with Brahms's activity in Vienna. His approach to orchestration, like that of his contemporary Bruckner, was traditional. Both scored for paired winds and never used supplementary instruments such as the cor anglais. The oboe solos in the symphonies and violin concerto notwithstanding, on the whole Brahms treated the winds as a homogenous choir with an emphasis on blend, rather than on colourful soloistic writing such as practised by Wagner and Mahler. Brahms's writing for the oboe is technically more demanding than that of earlier German and Viennese composers. While he never wrote above d3, the second player is occasionally required to play low C♯ and B. More challenging, however, are the tonalities and note combinations. Legato 'black-note' passages demand an instrument with reliable intonation, duplicate keys for E flat and F, and a speaker key to assure stability in the second octave. These would have been amongst Baumgärtel's and Hajek's principal concerns when designing the Wiener oboe.

Since World War I, Vienna has self-consciously – even obstinately – preserved its musical heritage in the face of growing odds. More than in any other major city in Europe, musical style in Vienna might seem to have stood still. Along with the Vienna horn, the Viennese oboe contributes to the idiosyncratic 'Vienna sound'. However, contrary to popular belief, neither of these instruments is older than its counterparts used elsewhere, nor is it true that musical performance in Vienna is totally stultified. Comparisons between early twentieth-century and more recent performances reveal that performance style in Vienna has been far from static.

With the death of Hermann Zuleger in 1949, the Viennese oboe faced imminent extinction. Were the twenty-five or so orchestral positions sufficient to sustain this unique instrument? Who would take over the production of new instruments? A few European makers, notably Rudolf Tutz of Innsbruck and Guntram Wolf in Kronach,[22] have made copies of the Zuleger's oboes, but it is mainly thanks to the Japanese firm of Yamaha that the Wiener oboe is still in production. Yamaha made its first Viennese oboes in 1980 and since then has maintained a high level of workmanship for this small market. The firm's substantial capital base, generated by its popular- and band-instrument departments, has enabled it to underwrite the preservation of the Viennese oboe. It may seem curious that a Japanese firm should support a dying European tradition, but Yamaha's initiative is understandable, given the élite status that Vienna has in Japanese culture and the seminal role played by the Viennese musician Jürg Schaeftlein in introducing the oboe to Japan in 1954.[23]

ITALY

At the turn of the twentieth century many Italian oboists remained conservative in their choice of instruments (ill. 69). Cesare Confalonieri (1831–1902), soloist at La

69. Italian oboe design from the turn of the twentieth
century: Maino and Orsi model, with low B♭ key.

Scala in the last quarter of the nineteenth century and professor at Milan
Conservatory from 1862, continued to play a Sellner-system oboe by the Viennese
maker Wolfgang Küss (1779–1834).[24] Ricordano De Stefani (1839–1904), professor of
oboe at Parma Conservatory, was also noted for his conservatism and, like
Confalonieri, remained faithful to a Koch oboe into the 1880s which he played with
exceptionally wide reeds. Largely passed over by history, De Stefani's substantial
musical output is still awaiting full investigation. As well as compositions including a
Fantasia on *Il Trovatore*, a Divertimento for oboe and piano on Verdi's *Attila*, Songs
without Words, variations and other pieces for oboe and piano, De Stefani produced
a monumental three-volume *Gran Metodo pratico per Oboè e corno inglese* and a further
sixteen volumes of unpublished studies.[25]

Perhaps in reaction to the conservatism of these oboists, some of the most radical
experiments in oboe design of the early twentieth century came out of Italian
workshops. The Milanese team of Paolo Maino and Romeo Orsi (ill. 70), known for
its experimental woodwind designs, produced an oboe incorporating elements from
the Viennese and French key systems (with low b and b♭ keys on the rear of the
instrument), and what appear to be split keys operating additional holes, possibly for
enharmonic notes. This particular design, created for the Roman oboist Ricardo
Scozzi (1878–1955), ultimately had little impact on oboe design.[26] Scozzi was one of

a   b   c

70. Radical oboe designs by Maino and Orsi: a) Schaffner and Giorgi model; b) detail of keywork of (a); c) composite Italian-French design built for Ricardo Scozzi.

the most renowned Italian oboists of the early part of the century, praised for the beauty of his sound and musicality (Debussy noted that he did not play in the French way, but simply superbly), [27] and took particular interest in designing an Italian oboe.

Maino and Orsi were also responsible for producing oboes based on an even more revolutionary concept (ills 70a and 70b). The dental surgeon H. L. Schaffner (fl.1888–99) and woodwind inventor C. T. Giorgi (1856–1953) came up with a completely new type of oboe that took Boehm's acoustic priorities to an extreme. Their aim was to create an acoustically perfect instrument with 'logical' fingering system that shifted the burden of effort from the player to the mechanism. A small number of these oboes built by Maino and Orsi survive, but it is unclear to what extent they progressed beyond experiments. These instruments are made in one piece from vulcanite, with seventeen large square holes operated by a complex system of levers and keys connected to square finger pads and swivel keys.

ENGLAND

Given the presence of Barret and other French-trained oboists from the middle of the nineteenth century, it is not surprising that England was the first country to adopt French oboes. Even so, the most mechanically complex models did not gain the support of all British musicians. William Stone (1830–91), the renowned physician, bassoonist and clarinettist who contributed to the first edition of Grove's music dictionary, remarked of the Barret and Conservatoire designs:

> Hardly any new wind instrument, except the flute, has been so altered and modified . . . in its mechanism as the oboe. . . . It has thus become by far the most elaborate and complicated of reed instruments, and it is a question whether a return to an older and simpler pattern, by lessening the weight of the machine, and the number of holes breaking the continuity of the bore, and by increasing the vibratory powers of the wooden tube, would not conduce to an improved quality of tone.[28]

In addition to importing woodwind instruments from France and Belgium, a burgeoning local industry gave British players a choice of oboes. The needs of professional players were met by Alfred Morton (1827–98), who was one of the few successful independent English makers of oboes and bassoons. After apprenticing with Uhlmann in Vienna, Morton returned to London around 1870 where he made oboes based on Triébert's designs with slight differences in bore and keywork. Around the time of Morton's death, George Howarth (1860–1933) started producing oboes. As a worker at Boosey from around 1880, Howarth established a workshop specializing in oboes in 1894 that has subsequently become England's leading producer of professional-quality oboes. Between the World Wars another small company, the Louis Musical Instrument Company (1923–40), produced oboes of high quality based on Lorée's design. These oboes were favoured by Goossens and his pupils, but the company was not able to see out two decades. A number of companies specialized in making oboes for the military and amateur markets. In 1879 Boosey & Sons added reed instruments to their inventory, and in 1902 acquired Morton's tools in order to continue making his oboe designs. From the 1880s Boosey's principal competitor, Hawkes & Co. (est. 1860) had been making a full range of French oboes, from the equivalent of Triébert's système 3 to the full Barret, Conservatoire and Boehm models.[29] The two companies merged in the 1930s and directed their attention to mass production.[30]

An important difference between Britain and the Continent in the late nineteenth century was pitch. 'Old Philharmonic pitch' (officially A–452.4 Hz, although, as with any pitch standard, there was fluctuation) was maintained in Britain after the adoption of the lower standard of *diapason normal* in France and other parts of Europe. Morton was one of the few makers to provide high-pitched oboes for professional British oboists. Oboes could also be ordered at the higher pitch from French companies. The pitch was lowered at Covent Garden in 1879, Queen's Hall Orchestra in 1895 and a year later at the Philharmonic Society. The wind players at the Queen's Hall were supplied with new instruments by Mahillon at what was then considered a compromise pitch of A–440 Hz.[31] Even in 1908, when Leon Goossens's parents bought him his first oboe, the question of pitch was not entirely settled. Charles Reynolds advised purchasing a high-pitched instrument because, as only the most distinguished orchestras had adopted 440 Hz, it would be some time before the young Leon could benefit from a low-pitched oboe. Instruments at 'Old Philharmonic pitch' could still be found in 1952, when Evelyn Rothwell cautioned students to verify the pitch of second-hand instruments.[32]

The extended oboe family

Next to the treble in C, the most common oboe has always been the tenor instrument in F – the cor anglais or English horn[33] – but the last decades of the nineteenth century saw the creation of new sizes both larger and smaller, as well as the revival of earlier forms including the oboe d'amore and musette.

COR ANGLAIS – ENGLISH HORN

Frédéric Triébert began making straight-bodied cors anglais in the 1850s,[34] probably shortly after the appearance of the portrait of Barthélemy (ill. 71). Outside France curved (ill. 72) or angled forms continued to be used for some time. Oboists at the Milan Conservatory were still playing curved instruments up to 1889,[35] although straight instruments were available from Riva of Ferrara. Maino and Orsi remained the last firm to make curved leather-bound cors anglais, as late as 1908.[36] Straight joints were certainly less complicated to make, could be fitted with keywork more easily, and were also less cumbersome for the player. Still, De Stefani for one complained that the straight and angled instruments did not possess the poignant melancholic tone of the curved cor anglais.[37] One factor contributing to tonal

BERTHÉLEMY
Lauréat du Concours in 1849.
ÉLÈVE DE M. VOGT, PROFESSEUR AU CONSERVATOIRE.

71. A. Colette: engraving of Félix-Charles Berthélemy, a recent graduate of the Conservatoire, with a curved cor anglais.

72. Nineteenth-century cors anglais:
a) Triébert; b) Brod *cor anglais moderne*;
c) Koch; d) Triébert.

a   b   c   d

difference was certainly the harder woods (predominantly rosewood and palisander) used in place of the maple that had been the timber of choice for curved instruments.

Low B♭ has never been applied systematically to the English horn, even full Conservatoire models. Probably with an interest both to keep the instrument manageable and to avoid redesigning the acoustically complex bulb bell, makers have shunned adding this note and today it still remains unavailable on all but a small number of instruments.[38] Mahler, whose penchant was to explore the extremities of all instruments, occasionally scored the note but always provided alternatives. In the first movement of *Das Lied von der Erde*, the cor anglais plays a fanfare motif beginning on low B♭. Here Mahler's alternative recommendation is B♮, which gives a peculiar inflection to the triadic motif.[39]

Ex. 6.1 Mahler, *Das Lied von der Erde*, 'Das Trinklied vom Jammer der Erde', bars 28off.

In the nineteenth century, at least three different notations were used for cor anglais:

1) In France it was most common to write parts at sounding pitch in mezzo soprano clef (C_2). The advantage with this notation was that all the player had to do to transpose the part was to substitute a treble clef (the key signature is given in treble-clef configuration – see music ex. 6.2).

2) Italian composers generally notated cor anglais parts in bass clef an octave lower than sounding pitch. This may have been a convenience for bassoonists who played the part either on cor anglais or, when no instrument was available, on bassoon. By substituting a tenor clef, the part is already transposed for cor anglais. Rossini used this notation in the score of *Guillaume Tell* (see music ex. 7.2, p. 220), but the separate oboe part was notated according to the French convention.

3) From the 1840s, notation in treble clef a fifth above sounding pitch became increasingly standard. Berlioz gave this as the norm in his orchestration manual (1843), and since then it has met with universal acceptance (see music ex. 7.3, p. 222).

Ex. 6.2 Vogt, *Variations on Nina* for cor anglais, notated in C$_2$ clef.

Wagner was concerned that the lower end of the oboe family lacked strength. In the first editions of the scores of *Siegfried* (1875) and *Götterdämmerung* (1876), he expressed his dissatisfaction with the weak (*schwache*) cor anglais, and recommended that it be replaced by the Altoboe in all of his scores. From this it is clear that, for Wagner, 'Altoboe' was not simply another name for *Englisch Horn*, but a special instrument. It referred to an F-oboe with flaring bell that he commissioned from Stengel of Bayreuth. Friedrich Feyertag (a member of the Bayerische Hoforchester in Munich) played such an instrument at the Bayreuth Festival from 1882 to 1894, but shortly afterwards the instrument seems to have totally disappeared.[40]

HECKELPHONE AND BASS OBOE

A communication with Heckel from 1879 records that Wagner sought an instrument combining 'something of the character of the oboe with the mellow but powerful sound of the Alphorn' sounding an octave below the treble instrument.[41] Oboes in this register had been made in small numbers by French makers since the eighteenth century. At the 1827 Exposition, for instance, Triébert exhibited an *hautbois baryton*, which the judges recommended for orchestral and military use, but for which no composers seem to have scored.

Heckel undertook to realize Wagner's request, but the resulting instrument, the Heckelphone, was not ready until some time after Wagner's death. The Heckelphone (released in 1904) was developed by Wilhelm Heckel and his two sons Wilhelm Hermann and August,[42] and their firm remains the exclusive provider.[43] The basis of the design is the *basse de musette*, a wide-bored shawm with large holes unique to Protestant western Switzerland.[44] This accounts for the Heckelphone's extremely wide bore. The Heckelphone also has a perforated spheroid bell, descends to b♭ or A, and was originally designed to be played with German fingerings by either oboists or bassoonists. Two approaches to reed-making – oboe-style with staple, and bassoon-style without – still exist. These idiosyncrasies place it on the perimeter of the oboe family.

Important parts for the Heckelphone appear in Strauss's *Salome* (premièred in 1905, a year after the instrument was first available), *Elektra* (1909) and *Alpine Symphony* (1915, in which the composer often exceeds the downwards range of the instrument). Strauss rarely wrote exposed passages for the Heckelphone; rather, he used it to strengthen the lower end of the oboe section, to extend phrases that went beyond the range of the cor anglais, or to add colour to other tenor-register instruments. A fitting example of its use to strengthen the oboe section is the first statement of the 'Fate' motive in *Salome* intoned by the pungent sound of the complete oboe family in unison octaves.

Ex. 6.3 Strauss, *Salome*, Fate motif, sc. 3.

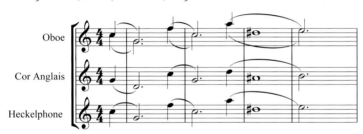

The Heckelphone makes occasional appearances in later scores such as Edgar Varèse's *Amériques* and *Arcana* (1921 and 1927) and more recently in works by Hans-Werner Henze (*Das Floß der Medusa*, 1968), and in a sonata by the Viennese composer Raimund Weissensteiner. There is a better-known Trio with viola and piano by Hindemith (1928).[45]

Before the Heckelphone was available, Lorée had already released a new *hautbois baryton* in 1889. Referred to in English as either baritone or bass oboe, this instrument resembles a large cor anglais with slender straight body and bulb bell, with a range of B1–g2, which is exactly an octave below the oboe.[46] A favourite amongst English composers of the early twentieth century, the bass oboe features in many large-scale orchestral scores. One of the most beautiful and earliest passages is the trio with oboe and cor anglais in Delius's *Mass of Life* (1905); the *Dance Rhapsody No. 1* (1908), also by Delius, begins with a duet for English horn and 'oboe basso' in which the two instruments circle around each other. Percy Grainger's 'imaginary ballet' *The Warriors* (1913–16) includes an important solo, marked in the composer's inimitable style simultaneously 'nasal, snarling *and* languishing'. The most demanding obbligato written for bass oboe is found in Tippett's Triple Concerto for violin, viola and cello (1979). Still, the instrument is certainly most frequently heard in Holst's *The Planets* (1918), where, however, its part is barely audible in the midst of the orchestral

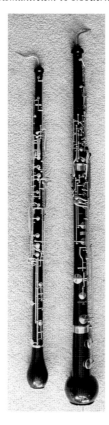

73. *Hautbois baryton* (left) and Heckelphone.

texture.[47] Bass oboes are available from the three principal French makers, Lorée, Rigoutat and Marigaux, but production remains very small. Rigoutat, for instance, has produced a total of only ten.

Heckelphone and bass oboe are often considered interchangeable, but in reality they are separate entities. The Swiss group Les Roseaux Chantants, directed by Alain Girard, has performed a number of new compositions for extended oboe family, including Nicolas Rihs's *A4* (1963), which calls for both Heckelphone and bass oboe.[48] Apart from this work, opportunities to compare bass oboe and Heckelphone are rare. Few orchestras have access to both, so it is common for one to be substituted for the other. Alfred Blatter described the bass oboe as 'potentially valuable, but its tone is very thin and stuffy, especially in the lowest register', while he noted that the Heckelphone 'has a full, reedy and rich tone quality that provides both an excellent bass to the oboes and a pungent treble to the bassoons. It is an agile instrument with good clear tonguing capabilities.'[49] However, with so few instruments and players of either instrument, it is difficult to hold to such comparisons. While it might seem surer to distinguish the two along national lines, this too is complicated by the fact that, from 1926, Heckel also produced bass oboes, although the patent held by Heckel prevents French makes from reciprocating (ill. 73).

SMALLER SIZES

Small oboes, either *hautbois pastoraux* or musettes, were made by French builders throughout the nineteenth century (ill. 74). The 1862 Triébert catalogue shows a range of small one-piece oboes with minimal keywork, made in either high G for orchestra or A flat for use in military bands. Verroust, who taught at the Gymnase Musical Militaire before becoming professor at the Conservatoire in 1853, published a *Petite Méthode pour le hautbois* with music written specifically for these small oboes. Some makers also produced musettes distinguished from *hautbois pastoraux* by the presence of a left-hand thumb hole (see ill. 74).

Louis-Jean-Baptiste Bas (1863–1940; premier prix, 1885), principal oboist at the Paris Opéra, was associated with the firm of Thibouville-Cabart who made a fully-Conservatoire 'musette' in E flat in the 1890s. Since then, similar instruments in F have been made by Marigaux and Lorée. One of the first works to use this instrument was *La Burgonde* (1898) by Paul Vidal. The high florid oboe part in 'Ound'onorèn gorda?' from Canteloube's *Chants d'Auvergne* (1923) is often played on musette, an appropriate substitution given its pastoral theme.

Wilhelm Heckel also created a piccolo Heckelphone with wide bore and spheroid bell, intended to strengthen the upper register of the wind section (see ill. 81 on p. 232). It does not seem ever to have been scored for, although it was tried out as a substitute

74. a) Oboe in E flat (système 4) by Triébert; b) and c) *hautbois pastoraux* by Triébert; d) musette in F, prototype by Rigoutat (1970s).

a   b   c   d

for the oboe in the solo in act II of *Fidelio*, and used around 1909 by Richard Strauss in place of the clarino trumpet in Bach's Second Brandenburg Concerto.[50] Today the piccolo Heckelphone is no more than a historical curiosity. Its wide bore made for unstable tuning, and this may have been the cause of its disappearance.

OBOE D'AMORE

While the Heckelphone, baritone oboe and musette were constructed to fit specific needs in modern music, the motivation behind creating an oboe d'amore in the nineteenth century was to recapture the 'authentic' timbre of the Baroque orchestra, and only later was it adopted by modern composers fascinated by its hybrid timbre, 'less incisive than the oboe, less cavernous than the cor anglais'.[51]

Mendelssohn's 1829 Leipzig performance of the *St Matthew Passion* initiated a renewal of interest in the music of J. S. Bach. While Mendelssohn made every effort to use appropriate instruments, the Cantor's music presented a number of specific problems, notably the realization of the oboes d'amore and oboes da caccia parts. Mendelssohn used clarinets in place of oboes da caccia,[52] and even into the 1940s some continued to believe that the modern cor anglais, particularly when played 'with all the refinements of French technique', was not a substitute for Bach's 'rough and virile oboe da caccia'.[53] In the nineteenth and twentieth centuries Bach's

75. Oboe d'amore by Mahillon.

oboe d'amore parts were played on either modern oboe or cor anglais, according to the range of the part.[54]

Around 1874 the director of the Brussels Conservatoire, François Auguste Gevaert, ordered oboes d'amore for Bach performances from Victor-Charles Mahillon (1841–1924).[55] Although pitched in A like eighteenth-century hautbois d'amour, Mahillon's 'reconstruction' was equipped with modern keywork and did not have the bulb bell that gave the Baroque d'amore its unique tonal character (ill. 75). Mahillon's instrument was awarded a gold medal at the Paris exposition of 1878 and was heard for some time around Europe.[56] Some were made with a thumb-plate mechanism, possibly for the British market, although there was competition from Morton when he began making oboes d'amore with bulb bells in the 1880s. The first Conservatoire-system oboe d'amore was released by Lorée in 1889.[57]

Heard mostly in performances of Bach's music, the oboe d'amore's distinctive tone often elicited special comment. When the Berlin oboist Paul Wieprecht played it in Bach's B minor Mass in Eisenach in 1884, a British critic spoke of the instrument's 'peculiar pathos, quite distinct from that of the simple hautboy'.[58] A half-century later the British musicologist Sir Donald Tovey proposed to Goossens a reconstruction of Bach's A major harpsichord concerto (BWV 1055) for oboe d'amore, giving the revived instrument its first concerto.

The oboe d'amore appears occasionally in orchestral scores from the late nineteenth and early twentieth centuries. For Richard Strauss, the composer who put it to greatest use, it combined the 'dreamy' character of the cor anglais with the more 'playful' and 'gay' nature of the oboe.[59] In the *Sinfonia domestica* (1897–1903) he used the oboe d'amore to represent Bubi, his own baby son. There are passages in the same work where it is used to provide harmonic filler, strengthening the viola part, to play in unison with the bassoons, or where it is itself reinforced by the English horn.

Ex. 6.4 Strauss, *Sinfonia domestica*, Bubi's theme played by oboe d'amore.

In France the oboe d'amore was invested with exotic qualities. Debussy used it in his vaguely oriental evocation of the Baroque in 'Gigues' (*Images* for orchestra, 1909–13); it forms part of the exotic paraphernalia in Ravel's *Boléro* (1928); and Charles Koechlin explored the subtle gradation between cor anglais, oboe d'amore and oboe in his opera *La Divine Vesprée* (1918) and symphonic poem *La Course de printemps* (1927).

Of the few composers who have written solo or chamber music for oboe d'amore, Charles Koechlin contributed a number of pieces;[60] in 1954 Mary Chandler wrote the first modern concerto for oboe d'amore (dedicated to Goossens), and Jennifer Paull has been responsible for a number of new compositions, including another concerto by John McCabe (1972), a significant obbligato in McCabe's Violin Concerto (1979), as well as solo works by Edwin Carr (1965) and *Cantiga Mozarabe* by Leonard Salzedo (1970).[61]

Despite this repertoire, the oboe d'amore remains a rarity in orchestral and chamber music. With the availability of a wide range of tonalities provided by the oboe's mechanization,[61] an important function of the eighteenth-cenutry *hautbois d'amour* – to extend the oboe's workable range of tonalities into sharp keys – is no longer relevant. Some feel that the oboe d'amore is not different enough in tone colour from the other members of the oboe family to warrant extensive use. But perhaps the most important reason why the oboe d'amore has not featured more in modern music is practical. Those early twentieth-century oboists who were drawn to this instrument invariably complained of how hard it was to play. Apparently makers did not give the same degree of attention to their oboes d'amore as their oboes, and few players were willing to risk their reputation on out-of-tune and temperamental instruments.[62]

'The orchestra is where oboists are valued'

The last decades of the nineteenth century saw the decline of the itinerant oboe virtuoso. Barret had died in 1879, followed two years later by the virtuoso-composer and Paris Conservatoire professor Charles Colin, Lavigne's career had ended by 1880, and Pasculli retired in 1884. Younger players such as Christian Schiemann, his pupil Emil Lund (1830–93), and the French players Casimir-Théophile Lalliet (1837–92, author of some thirty virtuoso *fantaisies* and *morceaux de salon*) and Auguste Bruyant (1827–1900) occasionally appeared as soloists, but there seem to have been few players of the calibre of the finest of the previous generation.

The shortage of outstanding players resulted in both a drop in the oboe's reputation and a reduction in the quantity of solo oboe music. As early as 1929, the German composer G. Christophe predicted that, as the oboe was hardly ever heard in a solo capacity, new compositions for it would probably never be performed.[63] After that time, woodwind concertos were less in vogue and there was also less chamber music written involving oboe. In the 1880s, Gevaert, apparently oblivious of the wealth of virtuoso oboe music from the past decades, stated that 'grand *solos de concert* are not written for the oboe, and it does not often play in chamber music'.[64] Saint-Saëns was the only composer of international stature to write a work for solo oboe in this period. (Debussy died before composing two projected chamber works involving oboes – one for violin, cor anglais and piano, the other for oboe, horn and harpsichord.) Schlesinger blamed the situation on the oboe's 'want of variety in tone and colour',[65] while others spoke disparagingly of the oboe's dogged low register.[66]

Few oboists were able to eke out a living as soloists; most took refuge in the more fertile ground provided by orchestras. At the end of the nineteenth century Hanslick, recognizing that 'the times are past when crowds of these wandering musicians came to give recitals on their boring little pipes', considered the orchestra 'the proper place for us to appreciate clarinettists, flautists, oboists and bassoonists'.[67]

By the end of the nineteenth century the symphony orchestra was the premier cultural institution in American cities. The cultural 'authenticity' of these orchestras was guaranteed by a considerable foreign contingent, and the Conservatoire oboe owes its survival more to the proliferation of the symphony orchestra than anything else. Even though much of the symphonic orchestra's repertoire had been written for quite different types of oboes, the Conservatoire oboe was pressed into service for all music – whether Baroque arrangement, Classical symphony or Modernist tone poem. The fact that the core of the modern symphony orchestra's repertoire has departed little from the canon institutionalized at the turn of the twentieth century is an important factor in the preservation of most instruments in the form they had reached a century ago.

There was also an effort to reinstate the oboe into wind band ensembles. Gabriel Parès (1860–1934), director of music of the Garde Républicaine from 1893, repudiated certain 'eminent artists' who claimed that 'oboes and bassoons have no place in military bands [*les musiques d'harmonies*]' because their 'small, frail [*grêle*], almost childlike voices' were not able to make themselves heard above 'the massive volume of modern brass instruments'. In his treatise on military music, Parès argued that the oboe was, on the contrary, indispensable to any 'large military band wishing to excel in the performance of Classical and modern musical works',[68] supporting his case with examples of oboe solos taken from fin-de-siècle French works, mostly in his own transcriptions. The cor anglais also had a place in Parès's *harmonie* as a substitute for solo cello in arrangements of orchestral works.[69] Rimsky-Korsakov, who belonged to one of Russia's great military-naval families and was an inspector of naval bands (1873–84), composed a curiosity – the Variations on a Theme of Mikhail Glinka for oboe and band (1878).[70] In the early twentieth century, when the English military band tradition was at its height, Holst gave the oboe a solo based on the folksong 'I'll Love my Love' in the second movement of his Second Suite for Military Band (op. 28/2, 1911) and Vaughan Williams also used the oboe to introduce the tune 'My Bonny Boy' in his *English Folk Song Suite for Military Band* (1923).

Georges Gillet and the modern French oboe school

Of the few outstanding oboists of the modernist period, Georges-Vital-Victor Gillet (1854–1920) stands out. At the age of eighteen, and three years after receiving his premier prix, Gillet was playing at the Théâtre Italien. Six years later he was with the orchestra of the Opéra Comique, and in 1895 he was appointed to the orchestra of the Paris Opéra, where he remained until he retired in 1904, aged fifty. Gillet was also a founding member of the Concerts Colonne (1872–6) and Paul Taffanel's Société des Instruments à Vent, and was principal oboist in the prestigious Société des Concerts du Conservatoire from 1876 to 1899.

According to his pupil and successor Louis Bleuzet (1874–1941, and Conservatoire professor 1919–41), Gillet was responsible for establishing the character of the modern French oboe. Bleuzet called Gillet 'undoubtedly the most extraordinary oboe virtuoso ever' and described his tone quality as 'ravishing [*délicieuse*], with finesse and subtlety without excluding the *forte*, coupled with a perfect technique and prodigious articulation'.[71] A review of a performance given by Gillet in 1880 praised him for clothing 'the somewhat shrill tone of the oboe with the velvety quality of the flute or the more veiled tone of the clarinet'.[72] Tone production became a central concern of the French oboe school. As with the new style of flute playing introduced by Gillet's contemporary Paul Taffanel, this may have been an attempt to refocus musical taste away from what had become viewed as the vacuousness of Romantic virtuosity. More than anything, it was Gillet's attention to sound production that he passed on to the next generation of French oboists.

Gillet was one of the first oboists to make recordings. The technology of musical reproduction had become available in the 1880s, and commercial recordings constitute one of the most valuable sources documenting twentieth-century performance practice. However, recordings featuring oboe from the early part of the century are exceptionally rare. As the oboe did not have sufficient popular appeal to warrant commercial recordings, few oboists had opportunities to record until the 1950s; also, the poor sonic quality of acoustic and early electric recordings preserves but a pale impression of the players' qualities.[73] Still, what we can hear of Gillet's playing in extracts from *Guillaume Tell* he recorded in 1905 with Léopold Lafleurance (1865–1951, Gillet's flautist colleague from the Paris Opéra) is 'impeccable' articulation and 'fluidity of line and smooth, round tone' which Laila Storch takes as confirmation of 'the legendary elegance of [Gillet's] style'.[74]

As Conservatoire professor (1881–1919), Gillet broke with tradition on two counts: he had not learnt directly from Vogt, but from one of his pupils, Stanislas Verroust (1814–63, professor 1853–63), and he was not a prolific composer. Instead of being celebrated as a performer of his own music, Gillet was known for his interpretations of the music of others – either contemporary compositions or, what was more unusual for his time, eighteenth-century works including sonatas and concertos by Handel, transcriptions of Bach sonatas, and the Oboe Quartet by Mozart. Gillet and his colleague the flautist Paul Taffanel were among the first wind players to revive the chamber music of Bach. Concurrently with the founding of a Bach society in Paris (1905), they published modern editions of Baroque music. Two works became Gillet's (and later his pupils') signature pieces: Handel's Concerto in G minor, and the charming D minor Concerto by the Vicomtesse de Grandval. One critic remarked that by complying with the oboe's inherently melodic character this work was consequently not able to avoid a certain degree of monotony.[75]

Gillet did, however, compose some music for pedagogical use. He adapted Brod's *Méthode* for the Conservatoire oboe, and his own *Études pour l'enseignement supérieur du hautbois*[76] set new standards in technical accomplishment on the oboe.[77] Instead of composing music for his pupils' exams, Gillet adopted three strategies to generate the annual *pièces de concours*. First he recycled former *concours* pieces, including works by Charles Colin and Gustave Vogt and contemporary works such as the Grandval Concerto. Secondly, like Paul Taffanel, he prescribed Baroque sonatas. Thirdly, he commissioned new compositions, some of which have enjoyed enduring success. Among the better-known are Émile Paladilhe's *Solo* (1898), Henri Busser's *Pièce en si bémol* (op. 22, 1901) and *Eglogue* (1916), and others by Charles Lefebvre, Louis Diémer, Adolphe Deslandres and Guy Ropartz.[78] Owing to the conservative taste of the French oboe school, much of this music continued to be available in print well into the twentieth century.

Gillet exemplified the distance that grew between composer and performer in this period. Into the twentieth century, composers took increasingly detached positions as social critics, even prophets. This led to the identification of the composer (typically male) as the creative artist, while the re-creative performer (in all but exceptional cases also male) was credited with the more mundane role of artisan or functionary. The Conservatoire, where education was based on technical proficiency, trained musicians to reproduce faithfully the work of the composer, who prescribed his intentions in scores of increasing detail. The virtuoso-composer became virtually extinct, and throughout the twentieth century the finest-crafted and most idiomatic instrumental works resulted from collaborations that bridged the gap between composer and performer.

Two important solo works from the period were closely associated with the Gillet school. The more significant, and the only one to have found a place in the oboe's standard repertoire, is Saint-Saëns's Oboe Sonata (1920). One of the composer's last works, it is dedicated to Gillet's pupil Louis-Jean-Baptiste Bas. Its simple lyricism – particularly the lilting Siciliana rhythm of the second movement with its framing arabesque incantations – has endeared the piece to oboists worldwide. The other work is the Sonata by Charles Koechlin (op. 58, 1915–16), premièred by Louis Bleuzet in 1922, but widely known only after its publication in the 1950s.[79]

Perhaps more than anything, Gillet is remembered for his collaboration with Lorée. Refinements to the Conservatoire design derived from his personal experiences. Lorée's most significant modification to Triébert's système 6 was the addition of pierced key-pads above all six finger-holes. This constitutes the only change incorporated in système 6bis of 1906 (also dubbed the Conservatoire model *à plateaux*, or Gillet model). As well as giving a somewhat more covered sound and allowing the last of the remaining tricky trills and tremoli to be negotiated by moving just one finger, the finger-pads have a significant effect on the 'feel' and response of the instrument. Around the same time the forked F resonance hole was added. This hole between hole 6 and the E♭ hole which improves the response and intonation of this cross-fingering had been applied to larger oboes before 1900. Gillet's struggles with a hitherto impossible passage in Lalo's opera *Le Roi d'Ys* (1888) resulted in the invention of another key, the so-called 'Gillet' or 'banana' key beside hole 6, which makes a trill between c1 and d♭1 possible.

The Conservatoire oboe also bears traces of its antecedent the hautboy. Not all fork fingerings are eliminated. Even with the left-hand long F key, forked F is still required in certain note-combinations, and b♭1, c2, b♭2 and c3 are also forked fingerings in the strict sense, as they involve closing holes below open holes. (These notes are fully open on the English thumb-plate system.) No oboe is, or ever can be, impeccably tuned, nor is absolute tonal equality possible on all notes, so some degree of flexibility of embouchure and breath is still required to master the oboe, though the flexibility is far less than that required for the hautboy. Even so, the Conservatoire oboe, as developed by Lorée and its principal competitors Rigoutat and Marigaux, has greatly reduced the degree to which flexibility is an essential part of oboe technique.

The school formed by Gillet earned international fame. Paris-trained oboists took up appointments around the world, notably in the United States. German oboists had formerly been in the majority in American wind sections, but from the last years of the nineteenth century the top orchestras sought out French players. Wherever their appointments took them, Gillet's pupils took their master's exacting technical demands, sense of sonority, and their Conservatoire oboes. At least fifteen Gillet pupils took orchestral appointments in the United States from the 1890s to 1930. Those who exercised the most lasting influence were Georges Longy (Boston SO, 1898–1925), Alfred Barthel (Chicago SO, 1903–29), Fernand Gillet (Boston SO, 1925–46) and Marcel Tabuteau (Philadelphia O, 1915–54).[80]

Georges Longy (1868–1930) was the first French oboist to move to the US.[81] He had already followed a distinguished career in France as oboist, playing successively with the Concerts Lamoureux and Colonne (from 1888), Folies Bergères and at the Opéra Comique. In 1881 he purchased the seventh oboe from the Lorée factory – a système 6 model in stained boxwood.[82] In 1895, together with the flautist Prosper Mimart, he reconstituted the Société de Musique de Chambre pour Instruments à Vent and the same year was named Officier d'Académie. When he began in the Boston SO (founded 1881) in 1898, Longy took over from oboists of German extraction. Over the period 1909–13 he made five solo appearances.[83] Throughout his appointment, Longy was celebrated for the beauty of his playing. When Fritz Kreisler played the Brahms Violin Concerto with the orchestra in 1915, he was 'captivated by the perfection of Mr Longy's great art, [and] became so absorbed that he missed his entrance'.[84] Longy composed a few pieces, including arrangements of French folk songs; Charles-Martin Loeffler's *Deux Rhapsodies* for oboe, viola and piano (1905) were written for him. In 1925 Longy took early retirement. His decision may have been triggered by an uncomfortable relationship with Sergei Koussevitsky, who had taken over as principal conductor the previous season. Longy returned to France and, despite his entrepreneurial engagement with Boston culture, never again visited America.

Like Gottlieb Graupner almost a century before, Longy was celebrated as a key figure in the musical life of Boston. In 1899, with the support of philanthropist and saxophonist Mrs Richard J. Hall, he founded the Boston Orchestral Club, where he conducted the first Boston performances of new music including Debussy's *Prélude à L'Après-midi d'un faune,* Enesco's *Poème roumain* (1897), Moussorgsky's *Night on the Bare Mountain* and Chausson's *Hymne védique* as well as Rameau's *Les Indes galantes* (recently edited by Paul Dukas under the supervision of Saint-Saëns) – programming that would have presented a serious challenge to the Boston Symphony Orchestra. In 1913 Longy founded the New York Chamber Music Association, was involved with the Cecilia Society in 1916, and conducted the MacDowell Club Orchestra for the decade from 1915.

The new century saw the founding of the Georges Longy Club, modelled on the Paris Société de Musique de Chambre pour Instruments à Vent, and set up to introduce eighteenth-century as well as contemporary wind music to Boston audiences. Foreigners were in the majority amongst the group's founding members. The flautist André Maquarre and second oboist Clément Lenom were Belgian, two

Frenchmen Georges Grisez and Paul Mimart played clarinet, the horn-players Franz Hain and Heinrich Lorbeer were German/Bohemian, and the bassoonists Peter Sadomy and John Helleberg were German and Danish respectively. The only American-born performer was the pianist Alfred de Voto. Longy also worked to raise the standard of music education in Boston and shortly before he returned to France he established a French-style conservatory, the Longy School of Music, which his daughter, the pianist Renée Longy, helped to run. The school is still in operation although it no longer holds to the French model (see Dovergne 2003).

The vacancy Longy left in the Boston SO allowed for Gillet's nephew and pupil, Fernand Gillet (1882–1980), to be appointed to the principal chair in 1925 (retired in 1946). A year after Gillet's appointment, his compatriot Jean Devergie, who had substituted as first oboe at the Paris Opéra, arrived to play second. Already before they had joined, another Frenchman who was a Gillet pupil, Louis-Marius Speyer (1890–1976), was playing solo English horn (1919–65).

A similar sequence of events took place in the oboe section of the Chicago SO (founded 1891). Here, too, the first oboists had been German, and this tradition was broken by the appointment of another Gillet pupil, Alfred Barthel (1871–1957), who played principal oboe there from 1903 to 1928. A loyal Gillet disciple (premier prix, 1891), Barthel played a concerto by Guilhaud in his first season with the orchestra, and in subsequent seasons another two warhorses of the French oboe school – Handel's G minor concerto (1904) and the Grandval concerto (1907–8). Like Longy in Boston, Barthel was an active chamber musician and also established a music school. He was a founding member of the Chicago Wood-Wind Choir and of the Rameau Trio, which specialized in French Baroque repertoire. In his day Barthel was the most highly respected oboe teacher in the Mid West, and after he retired in 1928 he set up a Conservatory. This venture was, however, not as successful as Longy's, and foundered just two years after it opened.[85]

A ray of hope: Goossens and Tabuteau

Even though Gillet was the most famous oboist of the late nineteenth century, he was still little-known outside France, but with the next generation the oboe regained status as a viable solo instrument, and this made it possible for at least one artist to develop an international career. That artist, Leon Goossens (1897–1988; ill. 76), was responsible almost single-handedly for putting the oboe back on the map as a solo instrument. The unprecedented number of concertos and sonatas that were dedicated to him has been exceeded only in the case of Heinz Holliger.[86]

Goossens came from a distinguished musical family of Belgian origin. His grandfather Eugène was a gifted violinist who had moved to London towards the end of the nineteenth century and by 1889 had become the principal conductor of the Carl Rosa travelling opera company. Leon's father and older brother (Eugène and Eugene) were also conductors, while his two sisters Marie and Sidonie had significant careers as harpists. Leon began his oboe studies in 1908 with Charles Reynolds (1843–1916), who had been a pupil of Lavigne. In 1915, benefiting from the war-time

76. Leon Goossens.

shortage of players and a sudden vacancy created by Henri de Busscher's departure for the US,[87] Leon was appointed to the Queen's Hall Orchestra at the age of seventeen. His audition must have impressed with a flashy *pièce de concours* by Charles Colin. At the invitation of Sir Thomas Beecham, Goossens moved from the Queen's Hall Orchestra to the principal chair of the new London Philharmonic Orchestra. He remained with the LPO until World War II, when he devoted more time to solo performance. Throughout his career Goossens played a 1907 Lorée ring-model with single-action octave keys and thumb-plate. His choice had a decisive impact on the British oboe scene; the Conservatoire *plateaux* model has become popular in England only relatively recently.

For many, Goossens's playing was a ray of hope for the oboe's future that metamorphosed 'the ill wind that no one blows good' into the 'delicate silver thread in the midst of the orchestral wind section'.[88] Countless writers remarked how Goossens 'transformed the oboe from a necessary, but often unpleasant, bleating noise into the instrument capable of producing unimagined refinement and beauty of tone'.[89] Evelyn Rothwell summarized her teacher's achievement as the creation of 'a new style of playing and a new tone', that was 'warm, singing and vibrant, far from the dead, reedy and rather ugly sound which was generally accepted before his time'.[90] One of the principal elements in this new style was the introduction of breath vibrato as an essential ingredient in the tone production (discussed in detail in chapter 8).

That Goossens introduced a new style of oboe playing is undeniable, but how far the references of his predecessors' 'unpleasant, bleating noise' can be believed is more difficult to establish. Was it really true, as Goossens reported, that his own teacher Charles Reynolds had to dampen his strident sound with a handkerchief when playing Wagner in the pit?[91] How much of these stories was apocryphal, exaggerated to enhance Goossens's reputation? What of Eugène Dubrucq, who played from the 1890s in Manchester and also at Covent Garden and was praised for his 'simply heavenly' tone and impeccable technique?[92] With so little evidence from recordings, it is difficult to arrive at an objective conclusion. In addition, the comparisons were confined to a British perspective. This situation probably arose as much from the political tensions between England and the Continent (France in particular) and musical nationalism as from Goossens's own desire to affirm his role as founder of a new British school of oboe playing. At that time, British players appear to have had little contact with the Paris school. Later in life, Goossens did mention Henri de Busscher as an inspirational figure: an interesting admission, given their shared Belgian heritage.[93]

Goossens's début as soloist took place at the Goossens Orchestral Concerts in 1921 in the Queen's Hall, London, when he played a Bach suite for organ, oboe and strings arranged by Sir Henry Wood. Shortly after, he premièred works by Holst, Bax and Bliss, and in 1929 the concerto by his brother Eugène. Solo appearances, premières of concertos, sonatas and chamber music continued into the 1960s. In 1950 Goossens was awarded the CBE. Goossens's reputation was due in no small part to the considerable number of recordings he made for radio and commercial release. Up to the middle of the century, the only recordings featuring oboe available in most parts of the world were by Goossens. His first recording was made in 1923, and over the years he recorded the standards of the oboe repertoire (in 1947 he was the first oboist to record the oboe concerto by Richard Strauss) as well as arrangements of Classical favourites, renditions of folk songs and popular tunes.[94]

At the age of sixty-five, Goossens was involved in a car accident that seriously damaged his jaw and embouchure. Any other oboist would have taken this as a sign to retire gracefully, but Goossens went through the painful experience of re-forming his technique. Just four years after the accident he returned to the stage as concert soloist. Those able to compare his playing before and after report that, although not lacking in control or beauty of tone, his sound was perhaps smaller than before. Goossens's energies seemed inexhaustible and even in his seventieth year he premièred a new concerto by Wilfred Josephs (op. 58, 1967), and at seventy-eight recorded Edward Elgar's *Soliloquy* for oboe and orchestra.

Soliloquy is a fragment of a projected three-movement suite for oboe and orchestra that Elgar was writing for Goossens, but left incomplete at his death in 1934. The autograph was bequeathed to Goossens and the work lay unplayed, and unknown, until 1967, when Goossens commissioned Gordon Jacob to complete the orchestration. Goossens held exclusive performance rights for the rest of his life; this remarkable tone poem has recently become available in published form.[95]

The same year that Goossens was appointed to the Queen's Hall Orchestra, the equally influential and perhaps even more legendary Marcel Tabuteau (1887–1966)

77. Marcel Tabuteau.

was appointed to the Philadelphia Orchestra. Of all oboists active in America in the twentieth century, Tabuteau has been the most venerated (ill. 77). While Tabuteau did not have the same opportunities as Goossens to develop a solo career, made nowhere near the same number of solo recordings, composed or inspired no new solo works, and was not even particularly well-known outside the United States, his reputation rests on his role in the formation of the American oboe style.

Tabuteau received his premier prix in 1904 after just two years of study with Georges Gillet.[96] The following year he went to the US to play English horn in the New York SO, and from 1908 to 1914 he played first oboe at the Metropolitan Opera, New York. The war had brought about a shortage of woodwind players in New York, and the orchestra imported five Paris-trained musicians into its predominantly German population at the same time. Although still young and relatively inexperienced, Tabuteau acquitted himself admirably in one of the house's most exciting periods under the direction of Arturo Toscanini. In 1915 Tabuteau was appointed first oboist in the Philadelphia Orchestra, where he remained until 1954, and was responsible for playing solo oboe parts through the Stokowski era. Tabuteau's playing is preserved on many recordings of standard orchestral repertoire, but only a small number of solo recordings, including performances of J. S. Bach's Double Concerto for oboe and violin with Isaac Stern, and Mozart's Sinfonia Concertante and Oboe Quartet.[97]

It is ironic that the US school of oboe playing should count as its founder and principal inspiration a Frenchman who, throughout his life, never discarded a thick foreign accent. In a sense Tabuteau represented the French style of playing frozen in time, and his teaching preserved the Gillet heritage more than contemporary French oboists. At the same time that French oboists were developing the instrument's virtuosic potential and placing increasing demand on digital agility, Tabuteau focused on beauty of sound and refinement of phrasing. His concept of tone production was based on a *dolce* sound. Even if he extended the oboe's range to c4 and sought as wide a scale of shadings as possible, he never strayed beyond the boundaries of scrupulous good taste. He preferred gentle tongue strokes (to use his expression, 'articulation on the wind') to crisp staccato, his tonal palette excluded the brightness favoured by many of his European contemporaries, and his vibrato was subtle. Tabuteau always played brand new oboes from the Lorée factory but, ironically, he refused certain innovations including the forked F vent hole, opting instead for the stuffy sound of the uncorrected fork fingering. Tabuteau's keen sense of sonority led him to convince Stokowski to maintain the pitch of the Philadelphia Orchestra at A–438 for the sake of the wind players, even after other orchestras in the country had settled on A–440 as their official standard, or were playing appreciably higher.

Tabuteau's most individual musical contribution, and the one best known to his pupils and those who came into contact with him in chamber music coaching, is what is generally referred to as the 'number system'.[98] This involved grading tonal intensity and colours on a scale from 1 to 9. The opening of the oboe solo in the second movement of *Sheherazade*, for example, he rendered as follows:

Ex. 6.5 Rimsky-Korsakov, *Sheherazade*, second movement, Andantino, bars 26ff.

Such a system that translates musical expression into numbers might seem highly analytical, but Tabuteau did not see it as 'music by numbers'. The way he formulated and used his system in teaching and in his own practice was highly intuitive and revealed a close affinity with the harmonic structure of the music.[99] It is important to realize that, for Tabuteau, the essence of tonal shading that he tried to encapsulate in the number system involved not only changes of volume but vibrato, speed of air and tonal intensity.

As they were almost exact contemporaries, it is informative to compare the playing of Goossens and Tabuteau. Goossens, being above all a soloist, cultivated great panache and bravura in his style. Tabuteau, more firmly rooted in the orchestral tradition, had less motivation to develop such an extrovert musical personality. These differences are apparent in many of their recordings, but no less so than in their interpretations of the Mozart Oboe Quartet, made almost twenty years apart of each other: Goossens's dates from 1933, while Tabuteau made his in 1951. It is of course questionable to base any conclusions of how oboists of the past sounded on individual recordings, but these two performances seem to characterize the two players' approaches and are readily available on CD.[100] Both are mono-aural, and on each the oboe is sonically somewhat disadvantaged. The limitations of the available recording technology are naturally more evident in the earlier recording, but even in Tabuteau's interpretation the oboe seems to have lost some of its lustre in comparison with Isaac Stern's violin.

Differences in tempo between the recordings are minimal. Tabuteau adheres more strictly than Goossens to a regular tempo throughout each of the three movements. This is most noticeable in the finale, where Goossens fluctuates in order to accommodate the figuration of the oboe part. Goossens's tone is generally light, his articulations crisp, particularly on semiquaver (sixteenth-note) passages which he often plays (not always impeccably) with a two slurred, two tongued articulation pattern. On the whole, Goossens observes Mozart's phrasing indications, and gracefully releases the final notes under slurs. Tabuteau's tone is well poised and his vibrato is less apparent. Compared with Goossens, his articulation is more 'on the breath' – that is, less crisp and with more length given to individual notes, to match the accompanying string players' 'on the string' bowing. Indeed, Tabuteau joins whatever notes he can. He does not lighten the ends of phrases as Goossens does, and takes more opportunities to slur passage work. Where he does detach notes, his articulation creates minimal interruptions. Even the leap from low D up an octave and a half to a♭2 in the slow movement, Tabuteau plays legato (Goossens 'places' the a♭). Tabuteau gives an even and well-rounded rendition of the outer movements, while Goossens's perky articulation imbues them with jovial vivacity. In the slow movement Goossens adds a short cadenza – a scale leading down to the cadential trill;[101] Tabuteau is content to leave Mozart unadorned.

One oboe, a world of styles

This comparison of performances by the two leaders of the first generation of twentieth-century oboists leads inevitably to a discussion of the regional styles of oboe playing that continue to be central to the history of the instrument in the twentieth century. Just as Goossens's incisive articulation and present vibrato have become prominent markers of English oboe playing, so have Tabuteau's round tone, subdued tonguing and modest use of vibrato become hallmarks of the American style.

The spread of the Conservatoire oboe did not result in a universal consistency of style. Regional differences became, if anything, more pronounced in the early twentieth century. With virtually all schools using the same basic equipment, it became easier to make direct comparisons of playing styles. So whereas in earlier periods instrument choice was an important factor in distinguishing regional styles of oboe playing, since the international adoption of the Conservatoire oboe, reed-making, interpretation and technique have become principal defining characteristics.[102]

By a school of playing, I mean a group of players who have had the same musical education, whose technique and instrumental equipment are more or less standardized, who share similar ideals of tone production and musicality, and apply these principles to a circumscribed repertoire. The most distinctive schools of oboe playing that emerged in the twentieth century comprised Gillet's pupils in Paris, Goossens's in London, Tabuteau's in the US, Wunderer's in Vienna and Flemming's in Berlin, but there were also unified styles in other countries, notably Italy, Czechoslovakia, Russia and the Netherlands.

Undoubtedly the most delicate topic when talking about different schools of any instrument is tone quality. The terminology used not only is a rhetorical issue but can be highly subjective and controversial. Think of the adjectives in use at present (in no particular order) – 'dark', 'bright', 'pure', 'warm', 'rich', 'thin', 'reedy', 'silvery', 'delicate', 'coarse' – each as distinctive in its emotional qualities as it is polarized as either complimentary or critical assessment. Some are best avoided altogether (warm, pure, rich). Others have developed an inverted value connotation: at present most traditions value a 'dark' above a 'bright' tone. I nevertheless find these last two terms the most useful when applied neutrally. For me, 'dark' refers to sound production which de-emphasizes the upper partials (particularly the fifth harmonic, which is largely responsible for the oboe's nasal character),[103] and a 'bright' sound is one in which these higher partials are more present. It is, of course, practically impossible to analyse tone in isolation. Other factors exercise an effect on the perception of musical sound. Articulation, for instance, has an important influence. Incisive attacks tend to release upper partials during the transient phase and can give the illusion of a brighter sound.

FRANCE

Gillet and his students constituted a distinctive approach to oboe playing that, because of the pre-eminence of the Conservatoire oboe, has had perhaps the widest influence of any modern style. The poised ringing tone and clean articulation of Gillet's playing continued to be characteristic of the next two generations of French players. This is borne out in recordings of those who succeeded Gillet as professor at the Conservatoire – Louis Bleuzet (professor 1919–41), Pierre Bajeux (1941–61) and Étienne Baudo (1961–73) – and also those who held the most important orchestral appointments in France – Louis Bas (Gillet's successor as first oboe at the Paris Opéra and the Société des Concerts), Roland Lamorlette (solo oboe at the Opéra Comique and Société des Concerts) and Albert Debondue (first oboe at the Opéra Comique and Concerts Pasdeloup).

Since the 1950s the French school has moved away from the Gillet tradition, Pierre Pierlot (1921–, professor 1973–87) being perhaps the most forthright in effecting this change.[104] Pierlot was soloist with Lamoureux's concerts and at the Paris Opéra, and premièred works by leading contemporary French composers. With his light reeds and dazzling technique Pierlot once again redefined the sound and technique of the modern French oboe, to the extent of obscuring its former traits. Today Pierlot's bright tone and constant fast vibrato are taken as the hallmarks of the French style of oboe playing. From the 1950s he was one of the most recorded oboists of the twentieth century. His legacy includes copious recordings of Baroque concerti with the Jean-François Paillard Chamber Orchestra and I Solisti Veneti, chamber music recordings with Jean-Pierre Rampal (with whom he founded the Ensemble Baroque de Paris) and the 'Pierre Pierlot Collection', a library of new and standard works for oboe published in Paris by Billaudot.

The French school stood apart from others also because of the Conservatoire training. With *études* at the centre of its practice routine and the *morceaux de concours* its showpieces, the French oboe school developed as an institution of technical virtuosity and was sometimes criticized for privileging digital proficiency over beauty of tone and interpretation. Pupils and composers associated with the Conservatoire built on the example of Gillet's *L'Enseignement supérieur* with sets of *études* of ever increasing technical difficulty. More studies were written by and for the oboists of the Paris Conservatoire than any other.[105]

ITALY

In terms of both technique and sound, the Italian school is close to the French. Pierlot's work with I Solisti Veneti encouraged cross fertilization between Italian and French oboists. Giuseppe Prestini (1875–1955) was probably the most influential Italian player of the twentieth century. For much of his career a professor in Florence and one of the first Italians to use the Lorée model, Prestini also developed an important modification to the Conservatoire oboe, basing it on the Koch model with the low b key at the rear of the instrument operated by the left thumb. Prestini wrote at least one concerto for oboe, and several volumes of studies.[106] Other prominent players include Omar Zoboli, whose diverse interests include resuscitating the music of Pasculli.

ENGLAND

From 1924 Goossens taught at the Royal Academy of Music. Amongst the most prominent of his pupils were Evelyn Rothwell (1911–), Sidney Sutcliffe, Peter Graeme and Joy Boughton. In England the oboe enjoyed a flourishing existence as a solo instrument. Perhaps more than in any other country, newly composed and classical oboe concertos featured regularly in concerts and radio broadcasts in the twentieth century. Characterized by oboes either French-made or -inspired and light, responsive reeds, British oboe playing is usually identified as closer to the French than to the German school. The thumb-plate mechanism, which derives from Barret's design, is used hardly anywhere outside Britain. It operates the keys for $b\flat 1$ and $c2$ and the corresponding notes in the next octave and, as well as facilitating the technique of certain note combinations such as the rapid slurred passages in 'Bacchus' from Britten's *Metamorphoses*, provides a way of producing these notes with straight fingerings rather than the fork fingerings of the Conservatoire oboe. Even though the thumb-plate directly affects only two notes, it still influences the general tone of the instrument, as players blend neighbouring notes to match the b♭ and c.

As in any school, the individual players have their own musical personality. Baines mentioned Alec Whittaker and Sidney Sutcliffe (1918–2001, principal oboe of the

Philharmonia Orchestra) as two important players who used reeds 'of the thick-gouged, far scraped-back kind' in order to produce 'a more flexible tone, capable of greater variation in dynamics and colour' than those more firmly in the Goossens tradition.[107] Terence MacDonagh (1908–86) was responsible for another stream in British oboe playing with a more direct French influence. The son of a distinguished cor anglais player, MacDonagh studied in Paris with the Gillet pupil Myrtile Morel before joining the Scottish Orchestra in 1926. After World War II he was principal oboist in Beecham's Royal Philharmonic Orchestra and a member of the London Wind Soloists, and can be heard on a highly praised recording of the Quintets for piano and winds by Mozart and Beethoven with Vladimir Ashkenazy.[108] Gordon Jacob wrote his *Rhapsody* (1950) for cor anglais and strings for him. Since MacDonagh's time, it has become more common for British players to train in Paris. Malcolm Messiter (1949–), for instance, famous for his virtuoso performances of Pasculli, is a pupil of Pierlot.

GERMANY

In the twentieth century, German oboe playing has stood apart from the French and English schools. Donington outlined what he believed were the fundamental differences:

> There has been a remarkable French tradition favouring all that is most poetical and exquisite in the oboe's potentialities. Expressiveness is at a premium; robustness has a little suffered; the sound itself could be called relatively pinched or nasal. The German and above all the Viennese tradition has remained more faithful to the original qualities: warmer, less cutting, even a little veiled by comparison with the silvery French sounds.[109]

Already in the 1920s Sir Henry Wood found German double reeds quite different from the more 'cultivated' sound of British oboes and bassoons: 'In England and France the oboes and bassoons, with their beautiful scales of even quality, have almost lost their "bite". . . . Hence, when we go to Germany, the first thing which strikes us is the 'bite' of the oboes and bassoons, even while we dislike their throaty quality.'[110] Ebenezer Prout also found the tone of German oboists coarse and blamed this on their wider reeds, which he took to be a carry-over from earlier traditions.[111]

Since the time of these writings, German oboe playing has become renowned for its dark tone, minimal vibrato and overall more 'solid' tone than the flexible approach to tone production in French and British playing. This has been carried perhaps the furthest by players of the Berlin school – Lothar Koch (1927–) and the current principal oboists with the Berlin Philharmonic, Hansjörg Schellenberger (1948–) and Albrecht Mayer (1965–). Other significant figures are Burkhard Glaetzner (1943–), the most important oboe soloist of the former East Germany, at present teaching in Berlin, and Ingo Goritzky (1933–), who has also recorded extensively.

The French school has not been completely ostracized from German musical culture. Paris-trained oboist André Lardrot (1932–), for instance, worked exclusively in Germany, Austria and Switzerland throughout his career, which began in the 1950s.

THE NETHERLANDS

Tonally, the Dutch style lies between the French and German styles and is the product of the distinctive reed-making and playing style of Jaap Stotijn (1891–1970), principal oboist in the Residentie Orkest, The Hague (1919–46), and teacher at the Koninklijk Conservatorium up to 1959.[112] Stotijn and his followers make reeds from wide cane tied on to short staples and take relatively little of the reed into the mouth. The Dutch style is also characterized by the use of French oboes with a special automatic octave-key mechanism with manual override. Stotijn's most important pupils were his son Haakon (1915–64), principal oboe in the Concertgebouw Orchestra from 1935 until his premature death at forty-nine, and Haakon's successor Werner Herbers. Among works inspired by the Stotijns are the 'Dutch Neo-Baroque' concertos by Alexander Voormolen (1933 and 1938) used in a series for Dutch television based on Louis Couperus's *De boeken der Kleine Zielenand*.[113] Today the school's principal exponents are Han de Vries (1941–) and his pupil Bart Schneemann, since 1987 the principal oboist and artistic director of the Netherlands Wind Ensemble, a position that was formerly held by Edo de Waart and Werner Herbers, both of whom have turned from oboe playing to conducting.[114]

SWITZERLAND

A distinctive school has emerged in Switzerland only with the rise of Heinz Holliger. Even so, to speak of a Swiss oboe school is problematic, because Holliger himself was trained in Paris, has taught for many years in Freiburg in South Germany, and has exercised an immense influence on oboe playing throughout the world. Within Switzerland itself, oboists have been influenced by neighbouring France and Germany. If anything, this school is characterized by hybridity.

AUSTRIA *see Wiener oboe, p. 176*

THE USA AND CANADA

Of all schools, arguably, the existence of a homogenous American style is the hardest to justify. The differences separating the playing of John de Lancie (1921–2002; Philadelphia Orchestra, 1946–77), Ray Still (1920–; Chicago Symphony Orchestra, 1953–92) and his successor Alex Klein (1964–, Chicago SO 1992) – to mention just three of the best-known figures of the American school past and present – seem to outweigh the similarities. Nevertheless, all three are bound by an allegiance to the American oboe school. Indeed, it is perhaps precisely because of its considerable internal variation that the American school has been ideologically the strongest. It was the first to establish a national organization – the International Double Reed Society – which through its publications has documented the history of the oboe in the USA.

The edifice of the American school is far less unified than its rhetoric would imply. The Tabuteau tradition remains strongest in Philadelphia, where Tabuteau's pupil John de Lancie took over after Tabuteau's retirement in 1954 and continued up to 1985, and where de Lancie's pupil Richard Woodhams now continues the tradition. Distinctive sub-traditions have grown up at the Eastman School of Music in Rochester, NY, where the second-generation Tabuteau pupil Robert Sprenkle (1914–88) taught from 1937 to 1982, in New York City with Josef Marx (1913–78) and in Los Angeles under the Belgian-born Henri de Busscher. These alternative approaches, although often overlooked as not compliant with the standard model, certainly add to the varied richness of oboe playing in the USA.

Despite its origins in the Gillet pupils who moved to the States and particularly the influence of Marcel Tabuteau, the American school has developed largely in isolation, and on many counts stands apart from the other schools discussed so far. This is due not only to its geographic isolation from Europe, but to its resistance towards influence. When asked to characterize their national preference in oboe playing, American oboists use epithets such as 'dark, warm controlled, stable tone' in contrast to the 'reedy, wild and uncontrolled' playing of Europeans.[115]

Almost forty years after his death, Marcel Tabuteau still holds the place of highest esteem among US American oboists. His almost revered status stems from his inspiring teaching at the Curtis Institute in Philadelphia, where his ideas reached a wide number of musicians, not only oboists but other performers who encountered him as a chamber-music coach.[116] Tabuteau's fascination with sonority has become a national obsession – sometimes at the expense of other aspects of performance, and his attachment to Lorée's oboes led to the virtual exclusion of any other model from the American professional scene, although today one encounters more variety. Some American players believe that authentic equipment can guarantee the closest approximation to their master's sound. Strict Tabuteau disciples even refuse models with innovations that were not sanctioned by the master, such as the fork F vent or 3rd octave key. In the 1980s Lorée provided a special oboe to satisfy this particular fixation. Their 'AK' model purportedly replicates the bore of oboes from around 1940, when Tabuteau was at the peak of his career.[117] These energies, however, are largely misdirected, as they overlook Tabuteau's own disposition for constant experimentation to the extent that he rarely played one instrument for more than a few months.

Among the oboists in Tabuteau's class were many who would become foremost players in the next generation. I list the most important in alphabetical order: Rhadames Angelucci (Minnesota Orchestra), Robert Bloom (Philadelphia Orchestra, Bach Aria Group), John de Lancie (Philadelphia Orchestra), Alfred Genovese (Cleveland Orchestra, Boston Symphony Orchestra), Harold and Ralph Gomberg (New York Philharmonic and Boston Symphony Orchestra), Marc Lifschey (Cleveland Orchestra, Metropolitan Opera Orchestra, San Francisco Symphony), John Mack (Cleveland Orchestra), Wayne Rapier (Boston Symphony Orchestra), Joseph Robinson (New York Philharmonic), Louis Rosenblatt (Philadelphia Orchestra), Harry Shulman (American Symphony Orchestra, Brooklyn Philharmonic, etc.), Dan

Stolper (professor at University of Michigan, Lansing) and Laila Storch (Houston Symphony Orchestra, later Washington State University).

The principal technical elements that distinguish the Tabuteau school from others relate to reed and breath. In general, American oboe reeds are scraped longer than those used by players elsewhere. While French and German reeds taper fairly consistently from the bark to the tip, American reeds will often have bulges and 'windows' to balance response and tone.[118] This set-up is designed to work with lower breath pressure and lower playing angles than those common among European players.

The oboe in the public eye: the oboe concerto in the twentieth century

The re-emergence of the oboe soloist could not have come about without remedying the dearth of solo oboe music from the immediate past. At first, oboists living in the shadow of a lost Beethoven oboe concerto, unfashionable Romantic salon music and aborted chamber music by Debussy turned to works by eighteenth-century composers. Handel's oboe concertos had been performed regularly in the latter part of the nineteenth century. Chrysander's edition appeared in 1862, and in the ensuing years J. Schuberth and Emil Lund performed them in Leipzig, and Gillet featured them in concerts in the 1880s in Paris.[119] These works, however, were viewed largely as historical curiosities. When Lavigne played one of Handel's concertos with the Philharmonic Society in London, the reviewer indicated that the work could 'only excite curiosity with musical antiquarians'.[120] Nevertheless, Handel concertos continued to be played by the new generation of twentieth-century oboe soloists. Louis Bas prepared an edition of three Handel concertos in 1913,[121] and Goossens and Tabuteau both recorded their own versions. Most early performances respected Handel's text to the letter. One of the first recordings of a Handel oboe concerto with added ornamentation was made in 1941 by Florian Mueller (1904–83).

The reconstruction of hypothetical lost oboe concertos by J. S. Bach came some time later. The assignment of the solo parts in the Double Harpsichord Concerto (BWV1060) to oboe and violin was first proposed in the 1920s,[122] Goossens first performed the oboe d'amore concerto based on a surviving harpsichord concerto (BWV1055) in 1937,[123] and in 1955 Hermann Töttcher first proposed Bach's harpsichord concerto in E major (BWV1053) in a version for oboe (transposed into F major).[124] Being conceived with the modern oboe in mind, often these arrangements pose problems of range and tonality when played on hautboy, casting suspicion on their credibility as historical reconstructions.

Other eighteenth-century works have become essential to the oboist's repertoire. Beginning in the late 1950s, André Lardrot recorded four volumes of concertos by Baroque and Classical composers. The immense popularity of these albums stimulated others to follow suit – notably Pierre Pierlot, Heinz Holliger and Burkhard Glaetzner (1943–), who all recorded copious amounts of Albinoni, Vivaldi and Classical concertos. More Baroque works appeared in editions by Bas, Rothwell, Richard Lauschmann (1889–?) and Hermann Töttcher. Later, in the 1960s and 70s, Helmut

Winschermann (1920–, German oboist and conductor of the Deutsche Bach Solisten and oboe professor in Detmold) and the flautist and musicologist Raymond Meylan (1924–)[125] greatly expanded the available repertoire from the German Baroque in editions of neglected chamber and solo works by composers such as Fasch, Telemann, Stöltzel, Hasse, Hertel, Janitisch, Platti and Bach.

Classical concertos were also revived by the new oboe virtuosi. The C major Concerto attributed to Joseph Haydn has been played ever since it was first edited by the Viennese oboist Alexander Wunderer in 1926;[126] the popular Boosey and Hawkes edition with piano reduction and cadenzas by Evelyn Barbirolli appeared in 1964.[127] The oboe concerto by Mozart has had a shorter revival history. Bernhard Paumgartner discovered the manuscript parts in the library of the Salzburg Mozarteum only in 1950, but despite its late arrival on the scene, this work became immediately popular and has been recorded countless times.[128]

Concurrently with the revival of eighteenth-century works, many new twentieth-century compositions for oboe also made reference to earlier styles. In some cases new works were created from eighteenth-century material. Sir John Barbirolli made 'free transcriptions' of movements and attributions by Giovanni Pergolesi (1935) and Arcangelo Corelli (1945) for his wife Evelyn Rothwell. Following his example, Arthur Benjamin composed an equally delectable pastiche of movements of keyboard sonatas by Domenico Cimarosa (1939), and Gordon Bryan did the same with keyboard sonatas of Domenico Scarlatti (1946).

The practice of arranging early music for these concertos partook of the same Neo-Classical fervour that seized European art culture in the 1910s to 40s. It was undoubtedly Gillet's rediscovery of the oboe as a protagonist of Baroque music that influenced Ravel to give it star billing in the orchestration of *Le Tombeau de Couperin*.[129] Likewise, the oboe occupies a central place in Stravinsky's Neo-Classical soundscape. If, for Stravinsky, Bach's music gave the listener the sensation of being able to 'smell the resin in his violin parts, taste the reeds in the oboes',[130] how much more intense these sensations become in Stravinsky's own Bachian emulations. In addition to the poignant lyricism in the 'Serenata' and 'Gavotta' from *Pulcinella*, there are the grating dissonances of colliding oboes in *Orpheus* (1948), and in the *Symphony of Psalms* the awkward leaping dialogue between solo oboe and bassoon in the first movement, the lone oboe outlining the fugal subject in the second movement and the penetrating sound of five oboes playing the simple oscillating theme in triple octaves in the third movement. But whereas Stravinsky took delight in playing with the tension between original material and twentieth-century compositional and instrumental techniques, there is little irony in either Barbirolli's or Benjamin's arrangements to disrupt the illusion that they are anything but genuine eighteenth-century works.

Other composers drew less direct inspiration from the Baroque and Classical periods. Walter Piston's Suite for Oboe and Piano (1931), for instance, is organized as a Baroque dance suite (Prelude, Sarabande, Minuetto, Nocturne, Gigue). Saint-Saëns, who was one of the editors of the Rameau collected edition, wrote a Siciliana as the second movement of his Oboe Sonata, and Gabriel Grovlez's *Sarabande et Allegro* (1929) is another familiar example of this type of stylistic retrospection.

In the US, Robert Bloom (1908–94) was particularly noted as a Baroque interpreter. Bloom, the son of the cantor of a Pittsburgh synagogue, developed a close affinity to the Lutheran church music of Bach through his work with the Bach Aria Group from 1946 to 1980.[131] Like the group's philanthropist William Scheide, Bloom believed in the healing gift of Bach's music. Bloom's interpretation of Baroque music differed considerably from the Bach and Handel of the previous generation, and particularly that of his teacher Tabuteau. While Tabuteau's Handel verges on the monumental, Bloom brought to his Baroque performances greater flexibility, light and shade, and above all, lyricism. Like Tabuteau, he ardently steered away from the crisp staccato style that was so prominent in Baroque performances by European exponents. Bloom's habit of successively lengthening repeated notes with crescendo became a trademark of his playing, but owes less to historical awareness than to personal preference.[132] Bloom was not afraid to embellish the music he was playing, but eschewed the spontaneity of improvisation. Like a diligent composer assigned the task of completing an original masterpiece, he fashioned ornamented versions of slow movements (which he preferred to call 'elaborations') with consummate care in advance of the performance.[133]

Goossens, who was interested in having modern companion pieces to play with the Mozart Oboe Quartet KV370, led a revival of the genre. Britten's 'Phantasy' Quartet (1932) has become the most widely known and served as a model for later works from British composers, including a quintet by Sir Arthur Bliss (c.1928), Sir Arnold Bax's Quintet inspired by Irish folk songs (c.1925), Gerald Finzi's *Interlude* (1936), E. J. Moeran's 'Fantasy' Quartet (1946) and Gordon Jacob's Quartet (1938).[134] The tight motivic intertwinings and symmetrical arch form Britten borrowed from the sixteenth-century English instrumental fantasy in his 'Phantasy' Quartet recur in Lennox Berkeley's Quartet (1967, written for Janet Craxton) and Finzi's *Interlude*. *Diversions* (1977), by Britten's composition student Malcolm Hawkins, takes his teacher's quartet as a starting point.[135]

Thanks to Goossens's charismatic personality and exquisite playing, the oboe enjoyed a heyday in England. The new works written for him and his pupils did much to bolster the reputation of the oboe in general, but this was still a peculiarly British phenomenon. Nowhere else was there anything like the same upsurge of interest. Gustav Holst had written a double concerto for flute, oboe and strings in 1923 premièred by Goossens, but the first true oboe concerto of the twentieth century was composed by Goossens's brother Eugene. This work explored new technical dimensions. The family joked that the cadenza mimicked Leon's warm-up exercises, but in reality it was as technically challenging for him as for any oboist.

The stream of new works continued. In the 1930s there were concertos by Gordon Jacob[136] and Rutland Boughton,[137] and in 1944 by Ralph Vaughan Williams. Other composers to write for Goossens include Arnold Cooke (Oboe Quartet, 1956, and Oboe Sonata, 1965), Cyril Scott (Concerto, 1949),[138] Malcolm Arnold (Concerto, 1957), Gordon Jacob (Oboe Quartet, 1938, and the Second Oboe Concerto, 1956), Herbert Howells (Oboe Sonata, 1943),[139] Walter Stanton, Sir George Henschel, John Addison, Dame Ethel Smyth, Franz Reizenstein, Alec Templeton, and the list goes on.

Although the renewal of interest in composing for the oboe soloist was nowhere more evident than in Britain, there is a small number of significant pre-World War II works from outside Britain. In 1927, an 'Oboistenbund' was formed in Germanic countries. This collective, which included amongst its membership such prominent figures as Fritz Flemming (Berlin), J. E. Konig (Dresden), P. Ch. Felumb (Copenhagen), K. Mille (Munich), L. Bechler (Weimar) and A. Wunderer (Vienna), aimed to encourage interest in the oboe, foster the composition of new oboe music, encourage further research into its history and supervise design improvements. The alliance's publication, *Die Oboe*, was printed by the music publisher Merseburger of Leipzig, who hoped that it would promote sales of their editions of new and obscure works for oboe. However, few significant works appear to have emerged from the initiative, and the venture struck difficulties just four years after it was founded.[140]

Important works from the second quarter of the twentieth century that have become established in the oboist's repertoire are Paul Hindemith's Sonatas for Oboe (1938) and Cor anglais (1941), and Henri Dutilleux's *Sonate* (1947, written for Pierre Bajeux), but these pale alongside Richard Strauss's Oboe Concerto (1945–7) and Benjamin Britten's *Six Metamorphoses after Ovid* (1951). These two works – produced for neither Tabuteau nor Goossens, but for pupils of each – have, over the past half century, acquired status as the most important oboe compositions of the twentieth century.

THE STRAUSS CONCERTO

Although it dates from 1945, the Oboe Concerto by Richard Strauss is stylistically a relic of fin-de-siècle Modernism.[141] With its luxuriant harmonies, its allusions to the Neo-Classical decadence of *Rosenkavalier* and the playfulness of *Till Eulenspiegel*, it represents Strauss's attempt to escape from the devastation of World War II into the autumnal warmth of the 'lush, perhaps rather over-ripe world of the 1890s'.[142] Ever since its composition, it has been a staple in oboists' repertoire. Indeed, as practically every oboist of note has recorded it, its discography serves as a veritable catalogue of oboe players and playing styles of the second half of the twentieth century.[143]

The creation of the greatest 'Romantic' oboe concerto ever written resulted from a happenstance that brought the composer into contact with an oboist. At the end of World War II John de Lancie was stationed in Germany near Garmisch, where at the time Richard Strauss was living. De Lancie knew Strauss's rich and inventive orchestral writing for the oboe from working under Fritz Reiner in the Pittsburgh Symphony Orchestra. He casually asked the composer if he had ever thought of writing an oboe concerto. Strauss' answer was a curt 'No'. But apparently de Lancie's association with Reiner, a personal friend of Strauss and an eminent interpreter of his music, impressed the composer and shortly after he began work on a concerto. De Lancie heard no more until 1946, when he was invited to attend the première of the new concerto played by Marcel Saillet, the principal oboist of the Zurich Tonhalle Orchestra, conducted by Volkmar Andreae, who had been instrumental in securing political asylum for Strauss in Switzerland.

Strauss had granted the right to the US première to de Lancie, who in the meantime had transferred to the Philadelphia Orchestra and was playing under his former teacher Tabuteau. Not surprisingly, Tabuteau took this news as a personal insult. The idea that one of his pupils had inspired one of the greatest living composers to write an oboe concerto was enough, but that this pupil would perform it with the Philadelphia Orchestra was out of the question. So, to avoid further conflict, de Lancie turned the US première over to Mitchell Miller of the CBS Symphony. De Lancie played the concerto only once with the Philadelphia Orchestra, under Eugene Ormandy in the late 1960s, and eventually recorded it at the age of sixty-six in 1987. Why didn't de Lancie programme the concerto more often? The main reason was that, at the time, oboists in the USA did not have the same opportunities to play concerti as other instrumentalists – particularly violinists, pianists and cellists. But it is also possible that although he had planted the seed in Strauss's imagination, de Lancie, like many oboists in the 1950s, found the work overly challenging – almost unplayable. In 1995 he wrote that 'from the first moment I saw the *Concerto*, I had concerns about the many inordinately long passages in the first, second and third movements – passages more suitable for violin than for oboe'.[144] When de Lancie did come to record the work in 1987, he sought the approval of Strauss's heirs to modify sections in the first two movements which gave the oboe more breathing space, and he also reinstated the original 1945 ending, saving an additional eight bars.[145]

Despite being the son of a horn player, Strauss took an almost perverse delight in ignoring the need for wind players to take breath. The *Alpine Symphony* (1915) includes exceptionally long sustained notes for all the wind instruments. In this case he knew that what he was demanding was impossible, and so directed the players to use the *Aerophor*, an invention of the Dutch flautist Bernhard Samuels, comprising an air pump with a tube to take air to the player's mouth.[146] Strauss must not have known how impractical this invention would prove, or how limited its acceptance would be. The organ-like sustained notes are simply unplayable as written. This experience notwithstanding, Strauss continued to compose seemingly never-ending phrases for wind instruments throughout his career, and this predilection is nowhere more apparent than in the first pages of the Oboe Concerto where the elision of phrase beginnings and endings not only suppresses any opportunity to take breath but protracts closure. This constant avoidance of any respite in the musical outpouring also operates on a larger scale, as the three movements of the concerto flow uninterrupted one into the next.

If Strauss's phrasing is observed accurately, the performer is forced to use special breathing techniques; otherwise the composer's intentions can be tactfully modified. Goossens, the first to record the Concerto, opted for the latter approach, believing that 'oboe playing sounds unnatural and artificial if phrasing-through-breathing is absent from a performance'.[147] He takes the first movement at a fairly vigorous tempo with considerable rubato in the semiquaver (sixteenth-note) passages, breaks the tied notes and breathes quickly through the nose, all of which help to alleviate the difficulty of sustaining the phrases. While Goossens's reading is by no means technically the cleanest, its panache and fluidity convey a naïve optimism rarely encountered in later performances that take the movement slower and consequently exacerbate the need for breath. Bert Lucarelli and Gordon Hunt both make a point out of the need to breathe. They time their breaths to give a sense of the larger phrase structure, thus directing the listener's attention to points where the music takes new turns.

Another difficult passage from the point of view of breathing is the cadenza leading into the third movement. De Lancie, like many other oboists, broke the slurs at the points marked 1 in music ex. 6.6. Goossens, Hanták, Pierlot and Koch all opted for this solution.

An alternative is to breathe 'on the ties' before the demisemiquaver groupings (marked 2). This is how Erich Ertel recorded the passage. Holliger, Black, Indermühle, Hunt, Still, Woodhams and Klein all observe Strauss's phrasing more strictly. Holliger uses circular breathing and even draws attention to this effect by making a crescendo on the tied notes.

Ex. 6.6 Strauss, Oboe Concerto, cadenza leading into last movement.

In other instances where Strauss clearly indicated shorter phrase units, some oboists perversely ignore the opportunity for musical and constitutional breaths (listen to Nicholas Daniel at the beginning of the second movement, for example, where he connects the one-bar phrases).

Despite its overtly fin-de-siècle Viennese style, Strauss did not conceive his concerto for the Viennese oboe and until recently it has been shunned by Viennese players. The work was recorded for the first time on Wiener oboe in 1997 by Martin Gabriel. This performance affords a fine opportunity to compare the qualities of the French and Viennese instruments. The differences are most marked in the middle register, which is reedier and more pungent, and the upper register, which is richer in harmonics on the Viennese oboe. There is a hardly perceptible loss of fluency in the passage-work in the high register because of the long fingerings. (Gabriel does not adhere strictly to the Hadamowsky tradition and *does* use vibrato.)

BRITTEN'S *SIX METAMORPHOSES AFTER OVID*

As much as Strauss's Oboe Concerto looks backwards to the 'golden age' of pre-war Europe, Britten's *Six Metamorphoses after Ovid*[148] set a precedent for future musical styles. These six miniatures are perhaps the best-known and most influential pieces for unaccompanied oboe. They were written for Joy Boughton to play at the 1951 outdoor concert given by the Cambridge University Madrigal Society on the Thorpeness Meare, a couple of miles from Britten's home in Aldeburgh. Britten wanted them to be played on a raft, but Boughton felt insecure, and she played them from an island. Joy Boughton (1913–63), a former Goossens pupil and the daughter of the composer Rutland Boughton, was well known to Britten. She was a member of the London Harpsichord Ensemble[149] and had contracted the orchestra for the 1948 Aldeburgh Festival.

Britten was no stranger to writing for the oboe. Twenty years earlier he had written three chamber works: the 'Phantasy' Quartet (1932) and two works for oboe and piano, *Temporal Variations* (1932) and *Two Insect Pieces* (1935). The last two pieces (both written for female oboists)[150] used the oboe in interesting and novel ways, but remained virtually unknown and only gained the recognition that would normally be accorded works for oboe by a major composer once they were published posthumously in 1995 and 1980 respectively.[151]

The *Metamorphoses* continues to be a favourite among oboists around the world, more than anything because each piece showcases a different aspect of the oboe's character within a fascinating compositional metamorphosis. What stimulated Britten's choice of the particular episodes from Ovid is not known, or whether he had a specific programme in mind for each piece.[152] It is likely that the rustic setting of the first performance and the instrumentation were key factors to his selection. The image of Pan improvising on his reed-pipe syrinx is an obvious subject for solo oboe music intended for outdoor performance. The galloping horses drawing the chariot commandeered by Phaeton are represented well by the oboe's staccato, and Niobe's weeping is captured equally well by its lyrical qualities. 'Bacchus' touches on the more raucous aspects of the instrument – the hubbub of the orgy, the babble of women's tongues and excited shrieks. With 'Narcissus', Britten introduced the theme of the oboe dialoguing with its own echo, a theme that recurs in later solo oboe music. The set comes to an end with the fluid arpeggios and spurting trills representing the bubbling fountain 'Arethusa'.

Chapter 7

The oboe in Romantic and Modernist music: cultural themes and implications

> Now come with me beside the sedgy brook,
> Far in the fields, away from crowded street;
> Into the flowing water let us look,
> While o'er our heads the whispering elm-trees meet.
> There will we listen to a simple tale
> Of fireside pleasures and of shepherds' loves.
> A reedy voice, sweet as the nightingale,
> As tender as the cooing of the doves,
> Shall sing of Corydon and Amaryllis;
> The grasshopper shall chirp, the bee shall hum,
> The stream shall murmur to the waterlilies,
> And all the sounds of summer-noon shall come,
> And, mingling in the Oboe's pastoral tone,
> Make thee forget that man did ever sigh and moan.
>
> *Dwight's Journal of Music* 3/21 (1853):164

This chapter considers the uses to which the oboe was put and its cultural associations in music from the end of the eighteenth century up to World War II, with some glances forward to the end of the twentieth century.[1] Such an investigation of the oboe's *extra*-musical 'persona' inevitably entails exploring its *inner* life in scores and literary texts. Opera and programme music are particularly suited to this task: their literary texts explicate the music as much as the music amplifies their texts.

Tracing the cultural use of the oboe during this period reveals how topics were transformed over time and how the changes to the instrument's physical form and musical abilities affected its cultural identity. Although much changed over the broad sweep of almost two centuries encompassed by the Romantic and Modernist periods, there are also a number of threads that remain intact.

Romantic music and art constructed a markedly different world from that of the Classicism of the previous century. Although the production and consumption of art was situated in the Romantic age's new urban spaces, its artistic realm was broader, encompassing the virgin pastures within Europe, the idealized spaces of the antique past, and the exotic climes brought to Europe's awareness through colonization. And in these three domains the oboe occupied a central role.[2] The oboe was the quintessential pastoral instrument; it contributed to the Romantics' image of antiquity by arousing nostalgia for an idealized past; and it was also conventionally associated with the exotic. Regardless of its context, the oboe was haunted by the ambiguity of its gender assignment.[3] We shall trace how, over the course of the nineteenth century, this instrument, so obviously phallic in design and always in the hands of a masculine performer, came to be associated with femininity.

Painting the oboe's tones

In Romantic music, instrumental timbre took on particular symbolic significance and the extra-musical connections of specific timbres were codified and theorized. Alongside scores in which composers were increasingly adventurous in their use of instrumental timbre, the science of orchestration was charted in a series of theoretical texts. Berlioz's *Traité d'orchestration et d'instrumentation* exercised the most enduring influence, with an important revision by the equally eminent authority, Richard Strauss, appearing in 1904.

Numerous Romantic composers, notably Berlioz, believed that musical timbre had hardly been explored prior to their time. This was of course an exaggerated claim. While Baroque composers had often left the choice of instruments to the performer, Classical composers were in general more precise in their instrumental designations, and the idiomatic treatment and poetic associations that accrued to instruments over the course of the eighteenth century served as the basis of the Romantic instrumentarium. Still, it is true that in the Classical period tonal colour rarely supplanted the structural significance of other musical ingredients, and Berlioz's insistence that instrumentation be given equal consideration alongside melody, harmony and rhythm is typical of a Romantic approach to the expressive potential of musical timbre.

At the same time that the importance of instrumental timbre over other musical aspects was occupying musical discourses, in the graphic arts a parallel debate arose centring on the relative importance of colour and form. Berlioz was one of many musicians who recognized the parallel and asserted that 'instrumentation is to music precisely what colour is to painting',[4] an analogy still alive in expressions like 'tone colour'. The type of synaesthesia by which sounds are seen and colour heard became central to Romantic imagery. E. T. A. Hoffmann's *Kreisleriana*, one of the earliest and most influential references to instrumental timbre as colour, developed an analogy between the formal aspects of composition (the counterpoint) and a painter's sketch which then needs to be 'painted' with instrumental colours: 'The rules of counterpoint naturally relate only to the harmonic structure, and any piece correctly worked out in accordance with them is only a painter's sketch correctly laid out according to the fixed rules of proportion. But when it comes to colour, the composer is left to his own devices, for orchestration is nothing other than that.'[5]

The poet Charles Baudelaire, who was largely responsible for introducing German Romanticism to French artistic circles, transformed Hoffmann's musings into a sophisticated theory. In the *Salon de 1846*, he quoted from *Kreisleriana* and included the following passage mentioning the congruity of colours, sounds and fragrances, 'all produced by beams of light in the same mysterious manner, and . . . combined into an extraordinary concert'.[6] But the Romantics did not only cultivate instrumental timbre for its own sake. As Alexander Ringer has pointed out, 'musical colour, like that of the english horn . . . took on powers of characterization which, especially in association with particular keys, permitted composers to convey more or less definite meanings, at least for the benefit of adequately informed listeners'.[7]

In the Romantic imaginary, the oboe had a very specific, albeit delicate, colour. Lavoix wrote in 1878: 'The oboe's sonority is like those delicate tints that are altered even by daylight; the least change in the bore or in the length of the instrument robs it of its touching and sweetly melancholic tone so essential to the composer's palette [*le coloris instrumental*].'[8] If any one colour was identified with the oboe, it was a pastoral green. Baudelaire expressed this in the following couplet from *Correspondances*, where images of youthful innocence, green pastures and the sweet oboe intermingle in synaesthetic fusion.

Il est des parfums frais comme des chairs d'enfants,
Doux comme les hautbois, verts comme les prairies.

There are some fragrances cool as the flesh of children,
sweet as oboes, green as the meadows.[9]

Echoes of the pastoral

As the nineteenth-century urban metropolises encroached on rural lands and industrialization impinged on agrarian life, the Alps seemed to be the only wholly 'natural' and 'untamed' terrain left in Continental Europe, and it was consequently the Alps more than any other landscape that came to be identified with the pastoral.[10] The oboe and cor anglais have an ongoing association with the pastoral. For Ernst, the oboe 'easily stirs pastoral or bucolic feelings'[11] and, according to one late nineteenth-century writer, it 'has never lost the pastoral character inherited from its ancient prototype, and it is, therefore of the greatest use in portraying rural effects'.[12] Though Gustave Vogt was eager to expand the oboe's range of expression, he was never able to extricate it entirely from its bucolic associations. According to an unnamed commentator, one was transported on a journey through the Alpine pastures of Switzerland 'just by closing one's eyes and listening to Vogt's oboe'.[13]

The pastoral theme permeates both solo and orchestral music for oboe. From the countless solo works in this genre I shall list a short but representative sample: *La Savoyarde* by Henri Brod (1825); *Souvenirs de la Suisse* by Édouard Sabon; *Le Pâtre du Tyrol* for oboe and voice, by Bérat (c.1839); Rudolf Tillmetz's *Notturno Alpenreigen und Rondoletto pastorale*; F. Theodor Fröhlich's *Pastorale und Rondo*; Bernhard Eduard Miller's *Abendempfindung im Gebirge* for cor anglais and piano, op. 12; and Théodor Lalliet's *I Pifferi, Fantaisie Calabraise*, op. 3.[14] The title page of Gustave Goublier's *pastoral* for oboe or violin and piano entitled *Dans la montagne* (1891) illustrates the central elements of the genre. A shepherd with his flocks sits playing his

78. Gustave Goublier, *Dans la montagne.*

shawm/oboe on the rocky mountains, high above the civilized world represented by a village barely visible in the valley below (see ills 78 and 79).

In the symphonic realm, Beethoven's Pastoral Symphony exercised a decisive influence on the pastoral of the Romantics. In addition to imitating bird calls in the second movement, the oboe plays a merry peasant tune accompanied by bassoon that reminded Berlioz of 'a young girl dressed in her Sunday best, accompanied by the old bassoonist who knows how to blow only two notes'.[15] In the theatre, the oboe was equally prominent in operas on Alpine themes, a genre which enjoyed great popularity from the end of the eighteenth century. Cherubini's *Elisa* (Paris, 1794) includes the aria 'Je vais revoir tout ce que j'aime' in which the heroine, yearning to be reunited with her lover, is supported by a virtuosic oboe part ascending to high F (music ex. 7.1a).[16] And then of course there is the apparition of Leonora in the form of a soaring oboe obbligato in Beethoven's *Fidelio* (discussed below, music ex. 7.1b).

Another protagonist of the Romantic Alpine-pastoral was the cor anglais. Although it shared many of the poetic associations of the oboe and gave a credible imitation of the alphorn, most writers, when describing its tone, believed that it was less suited to expressing convivial and joyous than melancholic and lugubrious emotions. Around 1785 C. F. D. Schubart commented that 'for the expression of despondency and profound melancholy, the English horn is exquisitely suited. . . . With such a horn, accompanied by a glass harmonica, suicide is appropriate.'[17] Similarly, Rimsky-Korsakov mentioned the cor anglais's 'restless, dreamy quality'.[18]

a   b

79. *Pifferi*: a) modern
Italian *piffero*; b)
Viktor Barvitius:
Shepherd with Shawm.

And, in relation to the cor anglais solo in his *Symphonie fantastique*, Berlioz noted that 'the feelings of absence, of forgetfulness, of sorrowful loneliness, which arise in the bosoms of the audience on hearing this forsaken melody would have only a quarter of their power if played by any other instrument than the English horn'.[19] The shadow of nostalgic longing cast by the cor anglais was not at all antithetical to the pastoral. As I hope the following musical examples will bear out, nostalgia for an idealized past was central to the representation of the pastoral in the nineteenth century. In the words of the anonymous poet quoted at the head of this chapter, the pastoral recalled a time before 'man did ever sigh and moan'.

Rossini and Berlioz provided telling examples of the pastoral use of the cor anglais. In the overture to Rossini's *Guillaume Tell* (1829), the dreamy introduction is interrupted by a musical depiction of a storm, from which a cor anglais emerges unscathed playing a delicious tune resplendent with post-storm freshness (music ex. 7.2). This *ranz des vaches*, with its triplet figures and arpeggiated loops reminiscent of yodelling, paints the Alpine scene of the ensuing opera. A flute answers the cor anglais's phrases, initially copying the *ranz des vaches* and later adding its own elaborate filigree – a maiden responding to the shepherd's call, or the twittering of birds?

The term *ranz des vaches* referred to the tunes used by Swiss herdsmen to muster their flocks and, ever since Jean-Jacques Rousseau's report of their virtually miraculous properties, has symbolized melancholia. Rousseau claimed that when Swiss estranged from their homeland heard a *ranz des vaches*, they would break into spontaneous weeping or, in extreme cases, die. The power of these tunes, Rousseau explained, was not to be found in the notes themselves but came from 'the habits, the recollections of a thousand circumstances which, touched on by this tune, remind

Ex. 7.1a Cherubini, *Elisa*, act II, sc. 2, oboe introduction to 'Je vais revoir tout ce que j'aime'.

Ex. 7.1b Beethoven, Pastoral Symphony, third movement, 'Lustiges Zusammensein der Landleute'.

Ex. 7.2 Rossini, *Guillaume Tell*, Overture, facsimile of published score (Paris, 1829). Note the use of bass clef for cor anglais (see ch. 6, p. 185).

those who hear it of their homeland, their former pleasures, their youth, indeed their entire way of life, and excite in them a bitter sadness to have lost all this'.[20] While Rousseau avowed that the effect was lost on foreigners, the Romantic tradition expanded the effect of the *ranz des vaches* to become one of the most potent musical symbols of memory, nostalgia and loss. For Sénancour, for instance, the *ranz des vaches* epitomized music's power to express the sublime,[21] and it took little for others to implicate the oboe and cor anglais in such primitive and moving music. Comettant remarked that 'of all instruments, only the oboe has the sufficient charm to sound the primitive Alpine melodies, so poetically sad, so touching and so chaste in their naïve simplicity. . . . The soul becomes sick from that mysterious illness, that mix of happiness, sadness, regret, hope and love that is called nostalgia.'[22]

An equally famous evocation of the *ranz des vaches* occurs in the duet for oboe and cor anglais that frames the 'Scène aux champs' in Berlioz's *Symphonie fantastique*, composed one year after the première of *Guillaume Tell* (music ex. 7.3). Berlioz's programme explains how the artist-narrator witnesses a dialogue between two shepherds – one playing the cor anglais, the other answering from a distance with an oboe. As in so much Romantic poetry and music, this music operates on two planes: the experienced reality of the present surroundings and the recollected past. The musical entities of cor anglais and oboe merge into protagonist/composer and his lover. This 'interior' aspect is explicit from Berlioz's programme. Even in the distant meadows the protagonist cannot escape from the haunting vision of a woman: 'But what if she had deceived him! – This mingling of hope and fear, these ideas of happiness disturbed by dark premonitions form the subject of the Adagio.'[23] The protagonist's anxiety is confirmed at the end of the movement where the cor anglais plays the *ranz des vaches* again. But this time there is no answer from the oboe; in its place there is only the distant sound of thunder. While Rossini's piping shepherd withstands the imminent storm and is answered by his companion represented by the flute, the figure in Berlioz's landscape is abandoned; the object of his desire is silenced by the storm. This image of the oboe's small voice lost in a storm was to be revisited in countless nineteenth-century works both musical and literary.

The autobiographical aspects of the *Symphonie fantastique* are well known. The work was composed while Berlioz was infatuated with the English actress Harriet Smithson. Shortly after the symphony's première, Berlioz was awarded the *prix de Rome* and left Paris for Italy. This was still before any intimate encounter had taken place between composer and actress, but if his memoirs are to believed, Smithson was rarely absent from his thoughts. In Italy Berlioz had little contact with contemporary composers, but was drawn instead to what he believed to be the vestiges of an ancient music: performances by shepherd-pipers who came down from the mountains above Rome. In his own words:

There still exists in the Roman States a musical custom which I am strongly inclined to believe is a tradition of ancient standing: I am speaking of the pifferari, which is the name given to the itinerant musicians who, just before Christmas, come down from the mountains in groups of four or five armed with musettes and pifferi (a type of shawm) to give pious performances before Madonnas. Normally they are robed in great coats of brown cloth, wearing the pointed hats of brigands, and their whole demeanour is stamped with a certain mysterious savagery full of authenticity. I passed whole hours contemplating them at Rome, their head slightly tilted towards their shoulder, their bright eyes of living faith, their fixed gaze of pious love on the blessed Madonna, almost as immobile as the effigy they worshipped. The musette, supported by a large piffero playing the bass, produces a harmony of one or two notes, over which a

Ex. 7.3 Berlioz, *Symphonie fantastique*, 'Scène aux champs', opening.

double piffero of medium length performs the melody; then above all this two very short little pifferi tootle runs and trills, inundating the rustic tune with a flood of ornaments. After jubilant refrains which are repeated many times over, a slow prayer, of patriarchal veneration, full of the most humble expression, the naive symphony comes respectfully to a close. Close up, the sound is so loud that it can hardly be tolerated, but at a certain distance this strange orchestra produces a delightful effect, touching, poetic, to which even the least sensitive cannot fail to be moved.

For Berlioz, these modern-day shepherds playing their oboe-like *pifferi* symbolized the simple life of the Arcadian shepherd, their primitive innocence recognizable in their dress and religious sincerity.[24]

Later, Berlioz visited the Abruzzi mountains where these shepherd-musicians dwelled. The awe-inspiring landscape gave him cause to contemplate his own lovesick desires, and even the very origins of civilization:

> Much later I heard the pifferari in their native climes. If I had found them remarkable in Rome, how much greater was my emotional response in the wild mountains of the Abruzzi where my Wanderlust had taken me. Those volcanic rocks, those black pine forests, sanctuary of bandits, formed the natural decoration, and complement to this primitive music. When this is joined with the façade of one of those mysterious monuments from another age, known by the name of the Walls of Cyclops, and several shepherds clothed in raw sheepskin, with the whole fleece behind (as is the custom amongst the shepherds of the Sabine), I could believe that I was with the ancients, in the midst of whom the Arcadian Evander had formerly brought his hearth. Virgil was no doubt referring to the pifferari in these verses:
>
> . . . Ite per alta
> Dindyma, ubi assuetis biforem dat tibia cantum
> Go to the heights of
> Dindyma, where you are accustomed to hearing the tibia [*flûte à double son*][25]

These events in Italy, Berlioz's love and their artistic expression in music and prose form an unbreakable bond. If the composition of the *Symphonie fantastique* had not pre-dated his Italian sojourn, these experiences could have served as the inspiration for the 'Scène aux champs'. The inspiration of Berlioz's Alpine excursion is also clear in the third movement of *Harold en Italie*, in which the 'Sérénade d'un Montagnard des Abbruzes à sa maîtresse' is again intoned on the orchestral alphorn, the cor anglais. This concerto-symphonic poem has another connection with the pastoral-alpine. Its *idée fixe* was originally conceived for cor anglais in his *Rob Roy* overture, descriptive of the wilds of Scotland, an equally favourite Romantic landscape. The double temporality and intertwining of internal and external realities in both travelogue and symphony represents the quintessentially Romantic view that the world can be fully known only through the power that creative imagination exercises over physical experience. Could Berlioz have read Sénancourt's theories that identified the *ranz des vaches* as the strongest of musical expressions because of its ability to communicate through 'a strange interior language'?[26] Whether the case or not, it could have been no accident that in a movement called 'Tristesse' (*Roméo et Juliette*, part II) Berlioz again chose the cor anglais to represent Romeo's loneliness as he awaited his Juliet, the role in which Harriet Smithson had so affected Berlioz.[27]

O still small voice of calm

> Breathe through the heats of our desire
> Thy coolness and thy balm;
> Let sense be dumb, let flesh retire;
> Speak through the earthquake, wind and fire,
> O still small voice of calm.

J. G. Whittier (1807–92)

Berlioz's image of the oboe had been strongly indebted to the contributions of Gluck and Beethoven, those twin 'boughs under which [the French Romantics] dreamt'.[28] Gluck had already established a connection between women and loss, prompting

Ex. 7.4 Agamemnon's air from Gluck, *Iphigénie en Aulide*, bars 16–31: 'J'entends retentir dans mon sein le cri plaintif de la nature [In my breast I hear the echo of nature's plaintive cry]'.

Berlioz to eulogize: 'these complaints of an innocent voice, these continued supplications ever more and more appealing – what instrument could they suit so well as an hautboy?'[29] Berlioz was referring to passages like the off-stage oboe in *Orphée*, the echo of Euridice's voice rising from the Underworld, Iphigénie's lament 'O malheureuse Iphigénie' (*Iphigénie en Tauride*, II, 6), act I, scene 3 of *Alceste* where Alceste remembers her children, the grating dissonances played by the two oboes in act III of *Armide* where the eponymous heroine sings 'Sauvez-moi de l'amour', and Agamemnon's aria 'Peuvent-ils ordonner' (*Iphigénie en Aulide*, I, 3) where an oboe's simple ascending sequence of appoggiaturas represents the anguished cries of Iphigénie rising in her father's imagination (*le cri plaintif de la nature*) as he reflects on his obligation to deliver her for sacrifice (see music ex. 7.4).[30]

Oboe solos such as these by Gluck or the Funeral March of Beethoven's Eroica Symphony continued to occupy the thoughts of those who dreamt under their boughs. F. A. Gevaert used the line 'le cri plaintif de la nature' from Agamemnon's aria to epitomize the very 'soul' of the oboe,[31] and the association between the oboe and female characters pervades Wagner's music dramas.

In *Lohengrin* (1850), when Elsa is brought before the people and king, her leitmotiv is played in unison by oboe and cor anglais (act I, scene 2, music ex. 7.5). The king asks her 'Bist du es, Elsa von Brabant?' but Elsa is speechless. She can only nod as the oboe and cor anglais intone the first phrase of her leitmotiv. When she finally finds words – 'Mein armer Bruder! [My unfortunate brother!]' – she sings them to the falling line of her leitmotiv in unison with the oboe: unspeakable loss is given verbal form.

Later in the scene when Elsa narrates her dream of the knight in shining armour, her voice is fused with the tone of the oboe: 'Herr! Nun meinem Ritter sage, dass er mir helf' in meiner Noth! [Lord! Now say to my that he should help me!]'. Here Elsa's fantasized desire, first represented by the disembodied sound of the oboe, becomes manifest in the person of Lohengrin. Just as her voice is amplified by the oboe, Elsa is herself fulfilled and transcended in the person of Lohengrin. Appropriately, Wagner re-introduces the oboe when Lohengrin appears and Elsa exults, 'O fänd ich Jubelweisen, deinem Ruhme gleich, dich würdig zu preisen, an höchstem Lobe reich!

Ex. 7.5 Wagner, *Lohengrin*, act I, sc. 2, Elsa's leitmotiv.

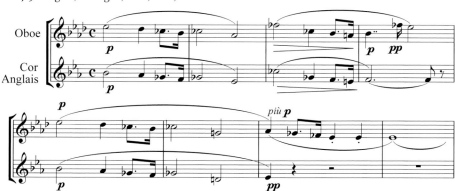

[Oh, if I could only find tones of jubilation full of the highest honours to match your fame!]'. But as much as Lohengrin comes to Elsa's rescue, he is equally dependent on her. She summons him from her own imagination, and must promise never to ask his name to guarantee his presence in the real world.

Was Alfred Guichon thinking of passages like these in *Lohengrin* when he compared the oboe to a timid girl who, without calling upon all the tricks of rhetoric, is still capable of captivating an audience by uttering a few simple words?

> . . . but whose voice has such grace, such feminine softness, such secret charms that everyone seems to hang on her every word, and when the young girl retires, her heart still palpitating, no one dreams of applauding, because all remain under the charm of a celestial spell. . . . You have heard the oboe![32]

The modest volume of the nineteenth-century oboe was often commented on, and this also fed into its feminine association. Still, despite its small volume, the oboe could penetrate through the orchestra. Grétry's epigram 'the oboe . . . provides a ray of hope in the midst of torments'[33] became a commonplace. Quoted by Gevaert in his *Nouveau traité d'instrumentation*[34] and paraphrased by Sellner as 'the oboe emerges victorious from the cacophony of the other instruments',[35] the metaphor gained perhaps its most picturesque elaboration from Victor Hugo in his veritable symphony in verse, *Les Rayons et les ombres*:

> Ciel! violà le clairon qui sonne. A cette voix,
> Tout s'éveille en sursaut, tout bondit à la fois.
> La caisse aux mille échos, battant ses flancs énormes,
> Fait hurler le troupeau des instruments difformes,
> Et l'air s'emplit d'accords furieux et sifflants
> Que les serpents de cuivre ont tordus dans leurs flancs.
> Vaste tumulte où passe un hautbois qui soupire!

> Heavens! That's the clarion call. At its voice
> everyone wakes with a start, all at once everyone jumps.
> The drum with a thousand echoes, hitting its enormous belly,
> makes the company of mis-shapen instruments shriek,
> and the air fills with wild and hissing chords
> distorted by the brass serpents in their bowels.
> Vast tumult through which passes a sighing oboe![36]

One is reminded of the oboe cadenza emerging from the tumultuous reiterations of the 'fate' motif in the first movement of Beethoven's Fifth Symphony (music ex. 7.6). Wagner admonished oboists to hold the voice of the soprano Wilhelmine Schröder-Devrient (1804–60) in mind when playing this solo.[37] This recommendation takes on particular significance when it is remembered that Schröder-Devrient was noted particularly for her portrayal of Leonora, the saviour-heroine of *Fidelio*. Act II of Beethoven's opera begins with the desperate Florestan alone in his cell. As his

Ex. 7.6 Beethoven, oboe cadenza in Fifth Symphony, first movement.

Ex. 7.7 Beethoven, *Fidelio*, act II, sc. 1, 'Und spür' ich nicht linde'.

thoughts turn from desolation to hope, a vision of his wife Leonora appears to him. The A flat major *Adagio cantabile* 'In des Lebens Frühlingstagen', with a clarinet taking the principal melodic part, gives way to a luminous F major *Poco Allegro* in which an oboe, representing the radiant apparition of the heroine, soars over the orchestral texture, reaching f3 on the word 'Freiheit' (music ex. 7.7).[38]

Here, as much as a signal of loss, the oboe brings the promise of hope as the tears shed by the lamenting instrument become the redeeming tears of a self-sacrificing woman. The small voice of the oboe in the midst of torments not only was symbolic of loss, but was also the thread on which men could depend for salvation: the Leonora who rescues Florestan, Isolde who cures Tristan, or the Elsa whose inspiration brings Lohengrin to life.

If the oboe represented the essence of femininity, the woman's glance – that telling moment when the man's desire is reflected back to him – also lay within the oboe's powers of representation. In the glance (*le rayon d'espoir*) the fear of rejection dissolves.

The exchange of glances, the desire to be seen, and to see one's desire reflected back, has been developed in myriad forms in Western art, but again it is Wagner's music dramas that provide the most cogent examples involving the oboe. In the final scene of *Das Rheingold*, Fasolt accepts the gold in place of Freia only if it is sufficient to shield him from her gaze. Appropriately, the oboe continues to sing forth her leitmotiv until she is completely hidden from view. Again, in *Die Walküre*, Wagner depicted the exchange of glances between Siegmund and Sieglinde in a dialogue between the oboe and the cellos and basses (see music ex. 7.8). When Brünnhilde refers to the sibling lovers at the end of act III, it is again the oboe that plays their leitmotiv. Finally, in *Götterdämmerung* II, 4, when Siegfried asks what dulls Brünnhilde's sight ('Was müht Brünnhildes Blick?'), an oboe is heard. Was it that the oboe's small but penetrating tone was thought an apt analogue to the power of the gaze?

In his settings of Rückert's poems on the death of children, *Kindertotenlieder* (1904), Mahler drew on several of these symbolic references, subjecting them to fresh interpretations. Throughout the song cycle, which is an emotional response to the

Ex. 7.8 Wagner, *Die Walküre*, act I, sc. 1, exchange of glances between Siegmund and Sieglinde.

death of children, the sound of oboe and cor anglais is present. In the first song the oboe sets the tone of lamentation, in the third it depicts innocent child and consoling mother, in the last song oboe and cor anglais are joined in unison by clarinet to represent the voice lost in the storm, while in the second the oboe symbolizes the child's gaze, the ray of hope obscured by the clouds of destiny that are metamorphosed in the mourning parents' phantasms into glistening stars.

In the course of the nineteenth century, as I have already pointed out, even more than the oboe, it was its larger brother the cor anglais that was associated with the nostalgic aspects of the pastoral, and melancholic and lugubrious subjects in general. This theme is prominent in theatrical works by French, Italian and German composers. Recalling the *cri plaintif de la nature* in Gluck's *Iphigénie*, Halévy's *La Juive* (1835), the plot of which revolves around female sacrifice, makes poignant use of the cor anglais. Eléazar realizes that by standing firm to his Jewish faith he sentences both himself and his foster-daughter Rachel to execution. In act IV he recalls the moment when he had first vowed to care for Rachel and imagines her voice still calling for his succour. Halévy represented the tragic pair with the unique sound of duetting cors anglais.[39]

If Berlioz nurtured the cor anglais as a distinctive solo voice and intensified the connection between treble double reeds and the pastoral, it was Wagner who affirmed these associations. As Pierre Boulez reminds us, '[Berlioz], and he alone, formed the "spectacular" link connecting the symphonic composer and the essentially "theatre" composer. In the *scène aux champs* the cor anglais looks back to the Pastoral Symphony and on to *Tristan*.'[40] Wagner had become familiar with Berlioz's writing for cor anglais during a visit to Paris in 1839, and *The Flying Dutchman*, which he drafted while still living there, was the first of his scores to include the instrument. The opera was premièred in Dresden, where the presence of the cor anglais expert Rudolf Hiebendahl (c.1818–1890) no doubt gave Wagner incentive to add a short solo in the overture and to explore further the instrument's potential in his next opera, *Tannhäuser*. Hiebendahl played the cor anglais parts in the performances of *La Juive*, *Robert le Diable* and *Les Huguenots* that Wagner conducted in Dresden, and when Berlioz visited in 1843 he praised Hiebendahl's playing in his *Symphonie fantastique*.[41]

Wagner used a cor anglais in I, 3 of *Tannhäuser* (1845) to realize the sounds of a shepherd playing 'auf der Schalmei', a reminiscence of Berlioz's *Symphonie fantastique* and Wagner's own ramblings in the wildernesses of Bohemia where he had sketched the opera's scenario (music ex. 7.9).[42] From this time on, the cor anglais is the most consistent marker of the pastoral in Wagner's music dramas, including the amusing moment in *Siegfried* (1876) when the hero's frustrating attempts to imitate the woodbird's song on a reed pipe are played from backstage by a cor anglais. Schumann, who heard the première of *Tannhäuser*, probably took up the idea of using a solo cor anglais to express the 'natural music of the mountain reed' in his 'Manfred' Symphony (1849), and Liszt also followed Wagner's lead in a number of works written for Weimar in the 1850s and 60s.[43]

Still, it is the great solo in *Tristan* (1865) that stands out as the most significant solo for treble double reed in Wagner's operas: indeed, it is the most extensive solo Wagner wrote for any instrument. A piping shepherd keeps watch for the ship bearing Isolde,

Ex. 7.9 Wagner, *Tannhäuser*, act I, sc. 3, 'Der Hirt spielt auf der Schalmei'.

the only person able to restore health to the mortally wounded Tristan. The oscillating triplet figures suggest a *ranz des vaches*, but the tune's chromatic distortions lend it a more anguished tone (music ex. 7.10). After being played unaccompanied on stage, the tune infiltrates the orchestral texture and fragments are passed between the instruments. On its journey between stage and pit, the tune seems to take on an existence between reality and illusion as Tristan struggles with the memories that it stirs in his unconscious. Like other instances in Romantic opera, here the sound of the cor anglais re-awakens welcome memories of youth but at the same time is pregnant with tragic foreboding. The 'alte ernste Weise' reminds Tristan of the tune that had announced the passing of his parents and now, as he listens from his own deathbed, it foretells the loss of his own life:

> Muss ich dich so verstehn, du alte ernste Weise,
> mit deiner Klage Klang?
> Durch Abendwehen drang sie bang,
> als einst dem Kind des Vaters Tod verkündet.
> Durch Morgengrauen bang und bänger,
> als der Sohn der Mutter Los vernahm.
> Da er mich zeugt' und starb, sie sterbend mich gebar.
> Die alte Weise sehnsuchtbang
> zu ihnen wohl auch klagend drang,
> die einst mich frug und jetzt mich frägt:
> zu welchem Los erkoren, ich damals wohl geboren?
> Zu welchem Los?

Is that the meaning of this old sad tune with its plaintive sound? On the evening breeze it sent its lament when once to a child it announced his father's death: through morning's grey, more fearful yet, when the son learnt of his mother's fate. When he begot me and died she, dying, gave me birth. To them too must have wailed the old tune's mournful plaint that once asked me, and asks me now, to what fate was I destined when I was born? To what fate?

When Isolde's ship finally appears, the shepherd changes his tune, and for this Wagner sought a fresh timbre. To signal Tristan's sudden elation, he envisaged the more vibrant tone of a specially-built 'powerful natural instrument [eines sehr

Ex. 7.10 Wagner, *Tristan and Isolde*, act III, sc. 1, the shepherd's sad tune (sounding a fifth lower).

kräftigen *Naturinstrument*]' made of wood 'in the style of the Swiss Alphorns'.[44] But, until such an instrument was realized, he recommended that a cor anglais be used, reinforced if necessary with oboes and clarinets. The tessitura of this joyous tune is higher than the sad one, and dwells on the least resonant register of the cor anglais, already considered by Wagner to be a weak instrument (music ex. 7.11).

A new instrument was in fact ready for the 1865 première. Designed by Wilhelm Heckel, the 'Tristan Schalmei' is sounded with a double reed, has a sharply conical bore with a bell rim and six finger holes with no keys apart from a half-hole pad over the first hole (ill. 80). Another invention from the same workshop, the Heckel-Klarina, was used for this passage in the 1890s (ill. 81). This instrument resembles a wooden saxophone (or tárogató), was played with a single reed, used oboe fingerings

Ex. 7.11 Wagner, *Tristan and Isolde*, act III, sc. 1, the joyful tune (sounding a fifth lower).

80. Tristan Schalmei by Heckel.

HECKEL-   PIKKOLO-
KLARINA   HECKEL-
             PHON

81. Heckel-Klarina (left) and piccolo Heckelphone.

and came in two sizes (soprano in B flat and sopranino in E flat). Still, it is yet another instrument that probably comes closest to Wagner's ideal Alphorn. The Holztrompete consisted of a wooden body with either cylindrical or conical bore, had a bulb-bell from a cor anglais, and was played with a trumpet mouthpiece. This seems more like an ad hoc experiment than a legitimate invention.[45]

In addition to the Berlioz connection, the melancholy shepherd's tune in *Tristan* drew on a tradition already established in Italian opera, where either an oboe or cor anglais complements the psychological estrangement of female characters as they recall happier times. The pastoral themes are pervasive as are simple strophic settings. In 'Al dolce guidami' in act II of *Anna Bolena* (1830), Donizetti uses a cor anglais to introduce and to add poignant interjections in Anna's slow aria in which she recalls 'the green plane trees, and the quiet river that still murmurs our sighs' around the castle where she was born.

From the loss of bright dreams, shattered childhood memories, it is not far to devastated landscapes, insanity and ultimately death, realms in which the undone operatic heroine is conventionally accompanied by a cor anglais. In Bellini's *Il pirata* (1827) a cor anglais signals the lovesick distraction of the heroine Imogene (music ex. 7.12). The *cantabile* introduction, written for the famous Milanese oboist Carlo Yvon, accompanies a pantomime in a way reminiscent of the oboe solo (played by Vogt) in *Nina* that had so impressed Berlioz. In the sleepwalking scene in *Macbeth* (1847) Verdi has a cor anglais obstinately repeat a two-note motif of a minor sixth degree falling to the fifth, a melodic figure that has been described as 'the internal cries of the conscience'[46] and seems to evoke Lady Macbeth's anxious obsession ('Out, damned spot!'). Act II of Verdi's *Ballo in maschera* (1859) opens on a deserted field with gibbets where Amelia searches for a herb to cure her lovesickness. To represent this desolate landscape and Amelia's desperation ('Che ti resta, perduto l'amor . . . [What remains after love is lost?]'), Verdi wrote a plaintive tune for cor anglais.[47] Verdi again introduced a cor anglais in Desdemona's 'Willow Song' in *Otello* (1887), which, like other instances, is redolent of foreboding of the character's imminent fate.[48]

With few exceptions, the characters who mourn their loss are women.[49] In these contexts, the oboe or cor anglais provides symbolic poignancy by acting as an instrumental corollary to the women's voices, representing the essence of the expression of their loss; it stands for desire that gains its psychic force from being configured as lost, absent, dead or otherwise irretrievable.

How might we account for the identification of the oboe with women and loss? Nineteenth-century writers portrayed the oboe as temperamental. Treated with

Ex. 7.12 Bellini, *Il pirata*, act II, sc. 10, *mélodrame* with cor anglais accompaniment.

gentle but persuasive control, it was capable of producing a timbre of voluptuous beauty, but if unrestrained it was likely to emit extraneous squawks and cracked notes. In its technical makeup, therefore, the oboe resembled the highly stigmatized nineteenth-century image of womankind as being always on the verge of hysteria. The changes that the oboe underwent over the course of the century sought to increase its technical capacity but above all to attenuate its waywardness. But despite these modifications, the oboe still had to be brought under subjugation through the concentrated energies of a skilled performer who until the twentieth century was, without exception, male. Whereas all wind and brass instruments (apart from the flute) were never played professionally by women, feminine rhetoric is particularly prominent in writings about the oboe. Furthermore, the oboe was not cast in the role of virtuoso – as much because of its technical limitations as of the notion that it was thought improper for a 'feminine' instrument to engage in virtuosity, which was viewed as a predominantly masculine form of exhibitionism.[50]

Another aspect of the oboe's appropriateness as a symbol for lost desire is its ability to represent human presence along with the instrument's ultimate failure to replace it satisfactorily. For long the oboe has been used as a substitute for the human voice, and as its range and tone colour best match the soprano voice, it has been used as a stand-in for the female voice. As Joseph Sellner remarked, 'in a word, a beautiful [oboe] tone should resemble a well-modulated soprano voice which is plaintive, round and sonorous in the expression of sorrow, piquant and bright in joy and gaiety'.[51] While the oboe's clean articulation emulates a singer's voice, it can never replace language. But the oboe's very inability to convey linguistic meaning is what also allows it to transcend words and communicate more directly through emotion. Resembling a disembodied voice, the oboe is not unlike the 'cry' of a singer's ecstatic high note where text dissolves into pure sound (*le cri plaintif de la nature*) – voice without language, cry without body, desire without object, 'an unattainable but always desired vocal object, hidden somewhere behind and beyond the signifying voice'.[52] A telling illustration of this concept occurs in Mahler's setting of the poem 'Urlicht' (*Des Knaben Wunderhorn*; reused in the Second Symphony), where the soprano's voice finishes at the words 'Je lieber möcht' ich im Himmel sein! [The sooner I am in Heaven, the better!]', but where the musical line is carried on seamlessly by the oboe (music ex. 7.13). The music performs the yearning expressed in the poem, transcending the words as voice dissolves into 'pure' instrumental sound.

This survey of Romantic operatic and symphonic solos for oboe and cor anglais might appear unbalanced, dwelling as it does on lyrical, melancholic and lugubrious passages. What of the *Scherzo* from Beethoven's Pastoral Symphony, or the vivacious solos in Rossini's overtures to *La gazza ladra* and *L'italiana in Algeri*? While some, like Castil-Blaze, described the oboe as 'always pleasing', whether heard in 'martial or pastoral, joyous or melancholic' contexts,[53] most writers drew attention to the *cantabile* potential of the oboe, and more particularly to the lugubrious quality of the cor anglais. So while merry tunes are certainly present in the repertoire, perhaps in slightly smaller numbers than sad ones, they were not seen as representative of the

Ex. 7.13 Mahler, 'Urlicht' from Second Symphony, bars 23ff.

oboe's character. Brod registered this when he noted that 'the great composers used the oboe only as a solo instrument in melodic passages [*des chants mélodieux*] and most often in slow tempi',[54] and in the 1880s Gevaert wrote that the core of the oboe's character resided less in the expression of rustic gaiety than in 'the direct expression of emotions – and above all, feminine emotions'.[55]

A veil for Salome: the oboe in orientalist contexts

Helpless abandoned virgins and chaste redeemers are not the only women represented by the oboe in musical dramas of the nineteenth century. There are also the seductresses and exotic women who sing and dance to the lyrical charms of an oboe. The oboe introduction to Delilah's bacchanale in Saint-Saëns's *Samson and Delilah* (1877) comes to mind, as do the sinuous lines woven by an oboe around Aida as she sings of her estrangement from her native Ethiopia ('O patria mia, mai più ti rivedró! [O beloved homeland, I will never see you again!]': music ex. 7.14), the accompaniment to the young Babylonian woman's song 'Que ce philtre amoureux dissipe ton ennui [May this love potion relieve your boredom]' in act II of Massenet's *Hérodiade* (1881), the Arabian dance in Tchaikovsky's *Nutcracker* (1892), the Persian dances from Moussorgsky's *Khovanshchina* (1872–80), the cor anglais solo in Engelbert Humperdinck's *Maurische Rhapsodie* (1898–9) and the extended arabesques in Delibes's *Lakmé* (1883, ex. 7.15). The craze for arabesques and oriental bacchanales reached its culmination in the 'Dance of the Seven Veils' from Strauss's *Salome* (1905, ex. 7.16),[56] in which the oboe injects frenzied energy from its first impassioned utterance.

Ex. 7.14 Verdi, *Aida*, act III, Aida: 'O patria mia'.

Ex. 7.15 Delibes, *Lakmé*, act II, Persian Dance.

Ex. 7.16 Strauss, *Salome*, 'Dance of the Seven Veils'.

As defined in nineteenth-century Europe, the 'Orient' had a very different meaning from the one it has today. At the beginning of the century it already embraced a vast agglomerate of geographic regions, radiating outwards from the Middle East, including Jewish, Turkish, Greek, Persian and Arabic cultures along with their incursions into Africa and southern Europe. In addition, for the rest of Europe, the folklore and music of Spain, with its conjunction of Arab and European influences, was as much part of the Orient as were lands that lay further to the east. Later in the century, as European expansion and commerce pushed eastwards, the Slavic lands, India and the Far East were added to the Oriental catalogue.

The Treaty of Passarowitz in 1718 had brought an end to the threat of invasion from the Ottoman Empire and opened the way for Europe to cultivate increasing political dominance over the Orient.[57] During the eighteenth century the Turkish janissary band formed the principal agent of musical exchange between Europe and the East. Its characteristic mix of wind instruments (predominantly shawms and trumpets) and jangly percussion instruments was imitated in countless Classical compositions.[58] The *alla turca* style was marked as masculine and, in operas, typically accompanied barbaric male despots. During the nineteenth century, however, the janissary band no longer occupied the centre stage in European depictions of the Orient. In its place is found the sensual and above all sexually available Oriental woman. With this shift, the Orient and the feminine become inextricably intertwined.[59] The sensuality and apparent moral wantonness of the stereotyped Oriental woman stimulated European curiosity and voyeurism. The harem became a popular subject: famous canvases by Jean-Auguste-Dominique Ingres and Eugène Delacroix are but the earliest in a tradition that reached into the twentieth century.

Europeans saw the Orient as a mirror of western civilization at a more primitive stage. Those Europeans who undertook journeys to the east tended to find what they predicted: their travels reified pre-existent fantasies. While in Egypt in 1849, Gustave Flaubert openly admitted what was true for many, that the Orient awakened long-forgotten memories and desires:

> Anyone who is a little attentive *re*discovers here much more than he discovers. The seeds of a thousand notions that one carried within oneself grow and become more definite, like so many refreshed memories. . . . I have found, clearly delineated, everything that was hazy in my mind . . . as though I were suddenly coming upon old forgotten dreams.[60]

A parallel in the nostalgic longing stirred by the *ranz des vaches* is immediately evident.

When considering nineteenth-century Orientalism, what is striking is not so much the 'authenticity' of the references to other cultures, but how superficial the veneer of exoticism could become without losing the ability to signify otherness. The diversity of cultures encompassed by the 'Orient' was conflated into a virtually non-differentiated amalgam. Western musical emulation reduced the diverse spectrum of authentic oriental musical idioms to a select set of tropes: modal writing (ancient Greek modes, pentatonic scales, and so on), drones, imitations of folk instruments (notably colourful Turkish percussion or the ululations of folk shawms), but above all the arabesque, which became one of the most unmistakable markers of Orientalism. This elaborate, sinuously decorative melodic gesture, usually involving modal writing, the augmented second-semitone configuration and chromaticism, drew its inspiration from a blend of Muslim chant and Middle-Eastern shawm playing and was pressed into service more or less indiscriminately to provide local colour to evoke practically any culture from the Near East, India, Russia, Egypt or Spain.

Likewise, the oboe became one of the most characteristic oriental sonorities. In addition to its purported origins amongst the same cultures that the West labelled Oriental, its feminine associations made the oboe doubly appropriate to these contexts. Glenn Watkins has gone as far as to assert that the oboe became the oriental colour par excellence,[61] and the coupling of oboe and arabesque took on such widespread currency that Ralph Locke, thinking no doubt of solos such as those mentioned above, has spoken of the 'nearly obligatory florid-oboe slow movement'.[62] Thus the oboe that had formerly led Western emulations of the janissary band now summoned forth Salome from her magic bottle to dance for the voyeuristic pleasure of Western (male-dominated) audiences.

Characteristic of the way the oboe was handled in orientalist scores are the solos in *Le Désert* (1844) by Félicien-César David. Although today virtually forgotten, this 'symphonic ode' earned instantaneous international success, and its depiction of the East became the touchstone of Romantic French Orientalism.[63] Unlike other Romantic composers, David based his music on first-hand experience of oriental music cultures during field trips in Turkey and Egypt from 1833, in addition to Egyptian material collected by Villoteau for the *Description de l'Égypte*. In the 'Marche de la caravane' the oboe plays an arabesque, imitating the improvisation of an Arab *zurna* player sitting atop a camel, and in the 'Danse des almées' its sinuous lines represent the seductive oriental female dancer (music ex. 7.17).

Ex. 7.17 David, *Le Désert*, 'Marche de la caravane' and 'Danse des almées'.

Marche de la caravane

Danse des almées

The versatility of the oboe arabesque fitted almost indiscriminately a range of cultural settings. This is illustrated by Bizet's *Les Pêcheurs de perles* (1863), originally set in pre-Columbian Mexico and later transposed to Ceylon. At the beginning of act III the oboe introduces Nadir's offstage song 'De mon amie fleur endormie'. The Phrygian-mode melody set above A minor harmonies gives a generic flavour of Mexico or Ceylon, or simply 'out there somewhere',[64] and is also strongly reminiscent of the more elaborate arabesque at the beginning of the Adagio in Bizet's Symphony (in this case shared by the two oboes), but which has no specific exotic connection.

Ex. 7.18a Bizet, *Les Pêcheurs de perles*, act II, oboe solo introducing Nadir's *chanson* 'De mon amie fleur endormie'.

Ex. 7.18b Bizet, Symphony, second movement, Adagio, bars 9ff.

The western image of Spanish music, like that of other oriental cultures, was not created by indigenous composers. French composers like Verroust, Garimond, Sabon and Brod all wrote fantasies for oboe solo on Spanish themes (according to Berlioz, Brod performed his with castanet accompaniment),[65] cor anglais solos are featured in Ravel's *Rhapsodie espagnole* (1908), and in the Spanish composer Rodrigo's *Concierto de Aranjuez* (1939) the cor anglais takes a particularly vocal role, accompanied by the guitar.

In addition to these Iberian examples, the cor anglais had its fair share of exotic incantations. These are generally more heartfelt in sentiment than the oboe's erotic snake-charming. The solos in Borodin's *In the Steppes of Central Asia* (1880; music ex. 7.19a) and the second movement of Dvořák's New World Symphony (1893; music ex. 7.19b) are cast in this vein. Dvořák's melody, with its predictable phrasing and smooth melodic profile, is remarkable for its sense of groundedness. Purportedly derived from an authentic native American tune, this solo stands apart from conventional Romantic representations of the musically exotic and is closer to the melancholic piping shepherds of Berlioz or Wagner.

Ex. 7.19a Borodin, *In the Steppes of Central Asia*, cor anglais solo.

Ex. 7.19b Dvořák, New World Symphony, slow movement, opening theme played by cor anglais.

In both the European Alps and the Arabian desert, the oboe maintained a feminine connection, but the female inhabitants of each were radically different. On the one hand there was the 'domesticated' woman – the virtuous heroines such as Elsa, Leonora and Berlioz's distant beloved, and demure, virginal Alpine maidens like Elisa – who embraced all that Victorian morals sought to uphold. On the other there was the erotic temptress of Orientalist fantasies. While the former often represented her honest qualities in simple tonal tunes, the music of her counterpart was more serpentine in its melodic meanderings, and often laced with chromaticism, characteristics suggestive of both decadence and sensuality. That the oboe bridged these antithetical images of femininity can be taken as tacit acknowledgement that real women actually integrated features of both. As Richard Leppert has described so eloquently, 'bourgeois patriarchy, which defined women by principles governing domesticity, constructed two contradictory categories of women: the privatized angel of the house, not subject to the pleasured gaze, and her radical public opposite, the prostitute. . . . General suspicion that she was both fed both fear and loathing and was also the fantasy and the guarantee of her transfixing look.'[66] This duality might also apply to the oboe itself. Didn't the suave and expressive Romantic oboe also have another side – the rustic folk shawm that threatened to surface if not brought under subjugation by a skilled player?

Looking ahead, glancing back

As the oboe has remained largely unchanged since the 1870s, its representational trinity of pastoral, melancholia and orientalism has continued to permeate oboe music to the present day. At the turn of the twentieth century, the pastoral was still central to the oboe's persona. The second movement (entitled 'Was mir die Blumen auf der

Wiese erzählen [What the wayside flowers tell me]') of Mahler's Third Symphony (1896; music ex. 7.20) begins with a simple pastoral melody intoned by the oboe; Frederick Delius used a trio of oboe, cor anglais and bass oboe to represent the meadows at noontime in *A Mass of Life* (1909); Vaughan Williams's *In the Fen Country* (premièred the same year) opens with a solo for cor anglais; Richard Strauss chose an oboe to depict the point of arrival at the summit of the mountain 'Auf dem Gipfel' in his *Alpine Symphony* (1915; music ex. 7.21), and in his Don Quixote (1897) a cor anglais intones the familiar *ranz des vaches*.

Ex. 7.20 Mahler, Third Symphony, second movement, 'Was mir die Blumen auf der Wiese erzählen', opening oboe solo.

Ex. 7.21 Strauss, *Alpine Symphony*, 'Auf dem Gipfel'.

With Berlioz not far behind, Percy Grainger wrote his two *Hill-Songs* (1901–7, orchestrated 1923) in response to the 'hard-toned rustic oboes' he had heard in Italy and the 'extremely nasal Egyptian double-reeds' he had encountered at a Paris exposition. The score instructs the oboes and bassoons to 'produce a wild, nasal, "bagpipe" quality of tone'. Double reeds also dominate the scoring of Respighi's Christmas pastorale *Lauda per la natività del Signore* (1928–30), with Mary's meditation being accompanied by solo cor anglais.

The theme of the piping oboist continued in twentieth-century literature. A fascinating passage from Schmid's *Assoziationen um das Orchester* written towards the middle of the twentieth century reawakens associations already familiar from Romantic musical iconography: the shepherd, the tragic lover, the fragile being at odds with a brazen world (lusting after innocent flutes, but thwarted by impertinent clarinets), and the idealization of the Classical past (recalling the Golden Age of the eighteenth century?) when the oboe could be its authentic self.

THE OBOE:

When the shepherd sees the lambs gathered around him, he reflects on his dear love in the valley, he looks up into the blue, which sings of the meadows; then, brother broad-muzzle clarinet [*Bruder Breitmaul, Klarinett*], speak! But if one lamb is missing from the flock, may he be tortured with jealousy knowing that it is alone — Then I speak!

Do I speak? — Doesn't the tone from my knotted-up throat wither? — Doesn't my forced smile devour any word, no matter how beautiful? Others can chat, laugh and console themselves; my strength remains in solitude [*meine Güte bleibt unendlich einsam*]. I am called unsociable, whereas in fact it is only the upsurge of belated love that flickers in me.

On those nights when the moon shows but a quarter, I stand on my rickety balcony, and cut the darkness with my absurd longings, the envy for young flutes seething within me (if only it were a lie!) after the comfortable self-righteousness of the chubby-cheeked clarinets (if it were stupidity!), I long to go beyond myself — oh, I am sickly! Blessed be my ancestors who didn't know themselves and, not knowing, were allowed to wander through the crowds!

Blessed classical period! [*Selige Klassik!*][67]

In response to the nostalgia for the rural life after the devastation of two world wars, the pastoral style was cultivated with particular fondness in Britain. Vaughan Williams's Oboe Concerto, written in the midst of World War II, is characteristic. Its second movement ('Muzette') is the most obvious invocation of the pastoral, but the serene folk-like tune that emerges from the maelstrom of prestidigitation at the end of the last movement seems to represent the sense of comfort that the British people desperately sought in nature. Other English composers who wrote oboe concertos with equally strong pastoral connections include Eugene Goossens (1929), Rutland Boughton (1937), William Alwyn (1945, and *Autumn Legend* for cor anglais and strings, 1954) and Cyril Scott (1949).

Orientalism far from disappeared from twentieth-century western music culture and the arabesque pervades oboe writing also. Recall the poignant oboe solo dripping with oriental fragrance in the Lullaby from Stravinsky's *Firebird* (1910), Eugene Goossens's concerto, with its melodic contours and 'Oriental' use of percussion in the cadenza,[68] and the slow movement of Saint-Saëns's Oboe Sonata which begins with an imitation of oriental incantation. Two pieces by Jacques Ibert speak for France's ongoing investment with oriental imperialism in the twentieth century. 'La Mosqué de Paris', the third movement of his symphonic suite *Paris* (1932), begins with an oboe arabesque, and Ibert admitted that the principal melody in the second movement of his *Escales* (1922) was taken directly from Moorish chant remembered from a trip to Tunisia. Arabesques also surface in works where they are least expected. Varèse's experimental orchestral work *Octandre* (1923) begins with an arabesque (hinted at more through the suppleness of the rhythms than its melodic contours); the oboe part in the 'Dances of the Ancient Earth', the second movement of George Crumb's *Ancient Voices of Children* (1970), does not fail to reference the overused augmented second; Xenakis's evocation of ancient Greek Dionysian revels in *Dmaathen* (1976) opens with the tell-tale semitone-augmented-second melodic formula and the Oboe Concerto (1996) by Australian Carl Vine (1954–) explores what the composer labelled the 'inordinately idiomatic' oboe arabesque.

At the beginning of the twenty-first century, when the customs of the most distant provinces are brought via television, radio and internet into our homes on a daily basis, composers have increasingly responded to the global-village paradigm by drawing on an expanding range of exotic musical idioms. New musical horizons have opened up to Western composers – notably the Caribbean, Brazil, African-America, Japan, India, Indonesia and Bali. But because it is not as directly associated with these musics as with the traditional oriental cultures, the oboe no longer has the same prominence as a marker of the exotic. Indeed, if anything it has become more strongly associated with the Classical European tradition.

In the last movement of his Oboe Concerto (1975), John Corigliano casts a backwards glance at the Orientalism of former generations. 'Rheita dance' refers to the sounds of Marrakesh shawms and plays out a competition between the oboe's traditional-Classical and exotic personae. This exotic frolic is meant as a parody, but its underlying intention remains unclear. In the first section, the soloist is called upon to renounce classical technique and play 'Oriental fashion' with the reed entirely in the mouth while the orchestra accompanies in the European pseudo-Orientalist style of Rimsky-Korsakov or Ibert. The dance is interrupted by the orchestral oboist playing a solo which initiates what the composer originally described as 'a minor competition between a rebellious orchestral oboe and the soloist',[69] but later rephrased as a fully-fledged clash of cultures:

> Formally it is a rondo with two subsections. In the first, the music suddenly changes from the rough sound of the Marrakech oboe to a kind of refined, perfumed Stravinskian *orientale*, almost a satire on Orientalisms-via-Paris. Then the wild dance returns, leading by way of a frenzied climax to a second interruption, where suddenly the orchestral oboe is heard playing a long-lined melody in the pure and beautiful Western tradition. This is interrupted by the solo's contrasting 'ugly' sound, and eventually the two oboes play in duet, then join in the conclusion of the dance, as the concerto ends exuberantly.[70]

Corigliano's work is unmistakably a Western Orientalist fantasy. On the one hand the solo oboe is meant to sound like a genuine *rheita*, but on the other it remains an imitation. The piece is a Western fabrication of what we 'should' think of Moroccan shawm playing – 'rough' and 'ugly' – and no matter how exuberantly the concerto ends, any hope for the Orient to assert its 'own' voice is quashed as the *rheita* is subsumed into the refined technique of the Western oboe soloist.

From the Abruzzi to Auschwitz

The association of treble double-reed instruments with melancholia, dejection and alienation continues through the Modernist period. In particular, the role of cor anglais as harbinger of melancholia and death has persisted. Sibelius's choice of cor anglais to intone the swansong of death itself in *The Swan of Tuonela* (1895) stands in the tradition of the *Tristan* solo. This tone poem is all that Sibelius salvaged from an

82. Gallen-Kallela, *Lemminkäinen's Mother*.

opera based on the Finnish *Kalevala* saga (begun in the 1890s). In 1896 he used *Swan* as one of the *Four Legends* based on episodes in the *Kalevala*, but in 1900 he finally published it as an autonomous tone poem. Lemminkäinen, the hero of the *Kalevala*, falls in love, but before his love can be consummated, his beloved's father demands that he perform three tasks, one of which is to kill the swan of the River Tuonela and pass into the realm of death.[71] Transfixed by the beauty of the swan's singing, Lemminkäinen cannot bring himself to kill it, and so, like Orpheus in Greek legend, is torn apart. Lemminkäinen's mother senses what has happened and is able to bring him back to life by reassembling his body (the moment captured by the Finnish artist Gallen-Kallela; see ill. 83). Sibelius's tone poem does not actually describe this narrative: it was originally written as an instrumental prologue for the opera and simply paints the scene haunted by the swan's transfixing song.

Aaron Copland discovered the desolation and emptiness that the Romantics had identified with the Alpine landscape in the urban spaces of the US. *Quiet City* (1939), for cor anglais, trumpet and strings, was based on themes Copland had used for incidental music to a stage play of the same name by Irwin Shaw which, in the words of the composer, evoked 'the nostalgia and inner distress of a society profoundly aware of its own insecurity'.[72] The incidental music was written for a small jazz ensemble of saxophone, clarinet, piano and trumpet, but when Copland recast it for orchestra, he chose a cor anglais to take a leading part.

Following in the tradition of *Un ballo in maschera* and *The Swan of Tuonela*, the cor anglais became expressive of those most desolate of landscapes: the battlefield and the concentration camp. Respighi scored for solo cor anglais in the last movement 'Pines of the Appian Way' in *The Pines of Rome* (1923), which paints a ghostly image of Roman legions returning with the weight of warfare and death on their shoulders. Shostakovich gave it substantial solos in his Fifth and Eighth Symphonies (1937 and 1943). Written at a time when Russia had cause to celebrate the Nazi retreat, the Eighth Symphony is considered one of the composer's most uncompromising anti-war statements, and shortly after its première it was singled out by Soviet authorities for its 'unhealthy individualism and pessimism' and withdrawn from Soviet concert programmes. Shostakovich did not provide a programmatic explanation of his intentions, but the cor anglais recitation is usually read as the composer's own views on the futility of war. The cor anglais emerges from a series of violent climaxes. Its first phrases are in recitative style, wrought with anxiety and set above subdued string tremoli, but gradually the solo takes on lyrical fluidity and concludes peacefully. However, the cor anglais's lone voice is powerless to resist the driving force behind the symphony and the only response to its lonely pleas are relentless fanfares.

An even more distressing depiction of war is provided in Britten's *Nocturne* (1958). The sixth song in this cycle for tenor and orchestra treating various nocturnal themes is a setting of 'The Kind Ghosts' by Wilfred Owen and features an obbligato for cor anglais. Known for his pacifist sentiments, Britten was drawn to the grim prophecies in Owen's war poems, others of which he used four years later in the *War Requiem*. Who is it who 'sleeps on soft, last breaths', who never asks herself 'why her roses never fall/Nor what red mouths were to make their blooms' but Death herself? The strings pace her ominous stride in pizzicato chords as cor anglais and tenor waft above. What more horrifying depiction of the devastation of war than the spine-chilling effect of the stifled gasps that Britten draws from the cor anglais?

In the last decades of the twentieth century the *déploration* of war has been voiced more urgently in two major concerted works for cor anglais. *The World's Ransoming* by James MacMillan was commissioned by Christine Pendrill and the London Symphony Orchestra, who premièred the work in July 1997. Described as 'a concertante work for cor anglais and orchestra', it calls for a large orchestra with expanded percussion section, and uses musical material from the hymns 'Pange lingua' and 'Ubi caritas' from the Maundy Thursday liturgy as well as the Bach chorale 'Ach wie nichtig'.

The theme of lamentation is even more clearly etched in Aaron Jay Kernis's *Colored Field* (1994). Like *The World's Ransoming*, this is a concertante work for cor anglais and orchestra, and also like MacMillan's work, is permeated with traditional religious chant – in this case medieval Christian and Jewish cantillation. In *Colored Field* Kernis recollects the emotional impact of visits to the Nazi camps at Auschwitz and Birkenau. Of a section in the first movement where the spectre of the Holocaust is clearly present, Kernis has written: 'it's like first seeing a drawing of a green field from straight on, but then you see it from the side, and you see more, something dark and troubling'.[73]

Colored Field is one of the most effective works for cor anglais of the past century, but not because it is a brilliant showpiece for the instrument.[74] It exploits the dramatic effect of pitting the cor anglais's inconsolable voice against the vast, almost overwhelming orchestral mass surrounding her. And yes, my choice of pronoun is intentional. This work was also composed for a female soloist – in this case Julie Ann Giacobassi of the San Francisco Symphony Ochestra. Composer and dedicatee agreed that the cor anglais should be placed as usual in the wind section so that, rather than standing apart from the orchestra, it is enshrouded by it. Like the cor anglais in Shostakovich's symphonies, the soloist in *Colored Field* is a passer-by who cannot help being drawn into and commenting on the orchestral maelstrom. In each of the movements, the cor anglais is the voice of commentary, expressing by turns curiosity, anxiety and desperation. And like the obsessive fanfares in the Shostakovich that engulf the voice of the cor anglais, the optimism of the only major-key harmonies near the end of Kernis's work are obliterated by a cloud of unresolved dissonance.[75]

'the expression of emotions . . . and, above all, feminine emotions'

In the twentieth century the oboe continued to be identified with femininity: it plays the role of female protagonist in Richard Strauss's tone poems *Don Quixote* and *Don Juan*; literature is likewise scattered with references to the oboe as the 'lady amongst the wind instruments'. In 1941 Nicholas Bessaraboff described the modern oboe as 'an ultra-refined, almost effeminate descendant and the sole survivor of what at one time promised to be a complete family of oboes'.[76]

As we have seen, this engendering was not conditional on the gender of the player, but today the oboe can no longer be thought of as a fragile being dominated by a masculine artist. Professional oboe playing, formerly an exclusively male prerogative, was opened up to women in the early twentieth century, and this has influenced the persona of the oboe. In 1917 the first woman oboist was admitted to the Paris Conservatoire. Odette Rey, daughter of an oboist, was the only woman admitted by Georges Gillet at the Paris Conservatoire. The shortage of musicians due to World War I provided her with opportunities to play on with the Paris Opéra, but after a short career in light music she gave up the oboe shortly after the war.[77] Goossens welcomed female pupils more openly. He believed that 'the oboe was very much the lady of the orchestra',[78] and similar rhetoric often appeared in the reviews of his playing: 'We think of the oboe among instruments as the "Lass with the Delicate Air". She did not step out of her character, to be sure – she could not be other than herself – yet there was a scope of performance in the hands or at the lips of Léon Goossens which presented a new vista of tonal possibilities.'[79] And so it seems natural that it should have been Goossens 'who showed the way to making the instrument (previously considered "too strenuous") into one suitable for young ladies'.[80] Evelyn Rothwell, Janet Craxton and Joy Boughton were but the best-known of Goossens's female students who went on to have distinguished careers as soloists and to inspire new works. In an interview with Nora Post, Goossens confessed that the presence of the female oboist did present complications for his understanding of the instrument.

Nora Post. One of the most fascinating things you've said is that you feel the oboe is a lady.

Leon Goossens. Yes.

NP. And I feel that it's definitely a man!

LG. Well, I suppose it depends upon your inclination. . . . You notice the oboe is used on TV and on the radio whenever it's something that is very romantic.

NP. Well, why does romanticism have to be something with women?

LG. Well, from the man's point of view, of course it is.

NP. So you think the oboe is a woman because you're a man, and I think it's a man because I'm a woman! . . . That's the only answer.

Evelyn Rothwell. Do you think that it can take on the characteristics of both?

LG. An androgynous oboe? I don't know![81]

'Young ladies' might have been able to show their worth on the oboe, but in the orchestras they still had a battle to fight. It was alleged that they were unsuited to the strain of long rehearsals and strenuous performances and that they distracted their male co-workers.[82] The following statement attributed to Sir Thomas Beecham is as chauvinistic as it is pompous:

> I do not like, and never will, the association of men and women in orchestras and other instrumental combinations. . . . My spirit is torn all the time between a natural inclination to let myself go and the depressing thought that I must behave like a gentleman. I have been unable to avoid noticing that the presence of a half-dozen good-looking women in the orchestra is a distinctly distracting factor. As a member of the orchestra once said to me, 'If she is attractive, I can't play with her; if she is not, then I won't.'[83]

Women first gained access to orchestras in Britain and the States. Evelyn Rothwell was appointed to the post of first oboist at Glyndebourne in the early 1930s by music director Fritz Busch, who appreciated her tone over that of any of the (male) players from the London Symphony Orchestra who had traditionally performed at the Festival. Her success at Glyndebourne gave her access to the renowned Busch Chamber Orchestra, where she played for several seasons. Rothwell also became famous as a soloist, appearing frequently in concerts conducted by her husband, Sir John Barbirolli.

In the US Lois Wann (1912–99) was one of the first female oboists to gain a professional appointment. After studying with Bruno Labate in New York, Wann played in the New York Women's Symphony, and in the mid-1930s was first oboist with the San Diego and Pittsburgh Orchestras. Later she returned to New York to teach at the Juilliard, Manhattan and Mannes Music Schools and trained several prominent oboists, including Ronald Roseman, Henry Schuman and Steven Taylor. Darius Milhaud dedicated his *Sonatine* (1955) to her. June Wollwage (1921–) was another pioneering woman oboist. A pupil of Florian Mueller, Wollwage had her first break in 1943, when she was invited to replace a member of the oboe section of the Chicago Symphony called to military service. Laila Storch, one of the few women to be admitted to Tabuteau's class (1943–6), went on to become solo oboist with the Houston Symphony (1948–55), and to work with her teacher at the Casals Festivals in Prades and Perpignan, and later taught at Washington State University, Seattle. These women blazed trails for later female oboists who have taken top positions, such as Julie Ann Giacobassi, solo cor anglais with the San Francisco Symphony, Cynthia Koledo DeAlmeda who at present holds the principal oboe chair in the Pittsburgh Symphony, and Elaine Douvas of New York's Metropolitan Opera.

In a recent survey, out of a total of 152 positions in 46 major US orchestras, 57 are held by women; only 9 are principal positions, but a higher percentage of cor anglais specialists are women while the rest are section players. These figures are higher than in Continental Europe, where women are conspicuously absent from oboe sections in the major orchestras of France, Italy, Germany and Austria (the Vienna Philharmonic continues to refuse admission to women).[84] The British and American example was adopted in British colonies, particularly Australia and New Zealand. Claire Fox, a laureate of the Paris Conservatoire, played in the Sydney Symphony Orchestra from the 1950s into the 1980s, and at present the principal player is the Swiss-trained Australian Diana Doherty, who dazzled audiences with a sensational new concerto written for her by Ross Edwards (2002).

If throughout the nineteenth and twentieth centuries the oboe had been invested with feminine attributes, then why could it not be played by women? This was not possible in the nineteenth century as it would have contradicted the established ideology by relinquishing the symbolic male control. With the burgeoning women's liberation movements in the early twentieth century the masculine hegemony began to crumble. Still, the female oboist signals more than women proving their equality with men. As the oboe was traditionally aligned with 'the expression of emotions . . . and, above all, feminine emotions', the rise of the female oboist also takes on meaning as the re-appropriation of the voice of femininity by women, as the wresting of masculine control over what had originally belonged to women.

Chapter 8

Diversifying streams since World War II: the traditional stream

The oboe is a narrow channel through which one must push a flood of expression. It takes control and restraint. When I play, I feel all this emotion, expression, concentrated – like continual knife stabbing at your heart – but never going into – never damaging.

Robert Bloom[1]

Introduction

During the second half of its active lifetime, the Conservatoire oboe has become increasingly distanced from the technical demands of the most progressive musical styles. Although originally designed for late nineteenth-century tonal and chromatic music, the Conservatoire model is now required to negotiate a variety of 'extended' techniques such as microtones, multiphonics and extreme high notes. Change, however, has not been forthcoming and no new design has challenged its dominance. Perhaps the primary concern has been the fear of compromising the oboe's traditional personality for the sake of technical gains. Nora Post states the problem succinctly:

> Which aspects could – and should – be further developed? Which changes would be possible without sacrificing the oboe's 'personality'? Could the performer have, at last, an instrument whose design takes into account the technical difficulties of the twentieth-century repertoire, while simultaneously improving the instrument's ability to execute the traditional repertoire? And what kind of instrument might have the inherent flexibility necessary to adapt to the unforeseen demands of the future?[2]

Alternatives to the Conservatoire design were explored by exceptionally few twentieth-century oboists and it is fair to say that today 'sameness is triumphant'.[3] As long as the western Classical musical tradition remains in place, there is little chance that the very symbols of that tradition – the instruments of the symphony orchestra – will change significantly.

With any thought of redesign put aside, oboe manufacturers have focused instead on refining the existing model. Today the Conservatoire oboe has a virtual monopoly (with the exception of Vienna), and the international market is largely in the hands of three French companies – Lorée, Strasser-Marigaux and Rigoutat – each with an annual production of close to one thousand oboes. Differences in the oboes made by these companies are minimal, but sufficient to generate debate in the market place. Lorée and Rigoutat give buyers the choice of three different bore profiles to favour different musical situations (orchestral, recital, and so on). Similarly, oboes made outside France differ only subtly from the basic French design. Howarth is the principal provider of thumb-plate instruments for the English market, likewise the German firms of Heckel (Biebrich), Josef Püchner (Nauheim) and Hans Kreul (Tübingen) supply the German market, and the Patricola brothers are the most important of Italian makers. A small portion of the market is dedicated to the more personalized workmanship provided by virtually one-man operations. Alfred and Paul Laubin of Scarsdale, NY, Paul Covey, of Atlanta, GA, and Dupin in Zurich have, between them, a small but discerning international clientele. At the other end of the spectrum, large numbers of mass-produced instruments are built mostly for student use. Often with less complicated keywork and more economic materials such as plastic bodies and lower-grade metal for the keys, such oboes are produced both by the high-end suppliers and by companies that specialize in mass production like Selmer, Yamaha and Fox.

One of the most significant refinements in oboe design over the twentieth century was the progressive thickening of walls of the top joint. This is immediately noticeable when comparing older and newer oboes and has been developed further by the firm Josef. As well as supporting the general preference towards a darker sound, this modification also has the practical benefit of helping to prevent cracks in the instrument's most vulnerable area. A number of manufacturers have also experimented with different substances to address this problem. Buffet's Greenline series is built from a material reconstituted from grenadilla dust and carbon, while other makers line the bore of the top joint with compressed rubber.[4]

Makers have been forced to provide models suited to players from schools outside their own national market. Lorée makes a model for the German market (DM) and their AK series, released in the mid-1980s, purports to replicate the bore of instruments from the Tabuteau era sought after by many American oboists. Likewise, in addition to producing thumb-plate models for the domestic British market, Howarth was the first British company to make full Gillet-system oboes and now also makes narrower-bored instruments for American oboists.

While in the first part of the twentieth century the different schools of oboe playing proliferated and grew in diversity, the general trend over the past three or four decades has been the reverse. There is now a noticeable increase in homogeneity of sound concept and technique across national boundaries. Oboe playing is no longer the sure indicator of an orchestra's national identity that it was up to the 1970s. Not all British oboists remain faithful to the thumb-plate design; it is increasingly common to hear Viennese oboists use vibrato; and there is a world-wide trend towards a darker sound ideal (an influence coming largely from Germany). Within the French school the German influence was already apparent in Maurice Bourgue's playing in the 1970s and 80s, and today is further cultivated in the playing of oboists like Michel Benet (Orchestre de Paris) and François Leleux.

Some non-European countries remain strongly identified with specific European or US American traditions. Oboe playing in Japan, for instance, has been influenced by German and US American schools;[5] in Canada there is a good deal of exchange with the USA, with European influences more in evidence in Quebec. Playing styles elsewhere are often more 'polyglot'. In Argentina, for instance, although most oboists active today are second-generation students of Edmond Gaspart (a pupil of Guidé in Brussels and up to 1966 first oboe at the Teatro Colón, Buenos Aires), it is difficult to identify a unified national school. Gaspart encouraged his pupils to develop their own musical personalities rather than insisting on a single approach, and so his pupils have been drawn to different styles. In Australia, too, it is common for oboists with British, Czech, German, Dutch and Australian training to play alongside each other in the same orchestra.

Sound recordings constitute the single most important source documenting oboe playing in the twentieth century. They record the work not only of famous soloists, but of orchestral oboists playing symphonic repertoire. The substantial enhancement to reproduction quality that came with the invention of the long-playing record (1948) and stereo sound (1958) meant that artists' finesse could be reproduced with greater accuracy. As a result of international marketing, foreign music styles are now only as distant as the closest record store. The homogeneity in oboe playing in the last decades is largely the result of the way in which the recording industry has promulgated an internationally accepted recorded oboe tone.

If the oboe changed little in physical form over the course of the twentieth century, its technique and application expanded enormously. This development has not only attested to the versatility of the Conservatoire design but challenged the consistency of the oboe's identity. It no longer has one clearly defined persona, nor is it confined to a set of closely interconnected musical styles as tended to be the case in earlier periods. The oboe's newly found diversity condensed in two distinct streams. The first nurtured the oboe's traditional functions, by continuing to value the oboe's unique tone quality as featured soloist in orchestral and chamber music. The second grew out of the search for new possibilities, and itself divides into two parallel channels: the avant-garde and the Early Music movement. These might at first seem antithetical in their aesthetic aims, but the radically modern outlook and the revival of historical instruments and techniques share the same fundamental quest of expanding the horizons of Western music – one by looking forward, the other back.

Following the traditional stream

The second half of the twentieth century has seen a continuing stream of works in the traditional mould. Composers and oboist-composers of nearly all nationalities have written for the instrument in traditional genres. As well as the revived oboe concerto and sonata, the oboe has made a return to chamber music. The wind quintet enjoyed a resurgence with important works written by Ibert, Françaix, Milhaud, Barber and Arnold, and in more modern idioms by Stockhausen, Ligeti, Holliger and Arvo Pärt. Poulenc's Oboe Sonata (1962) has become a particular favourite, and Jean

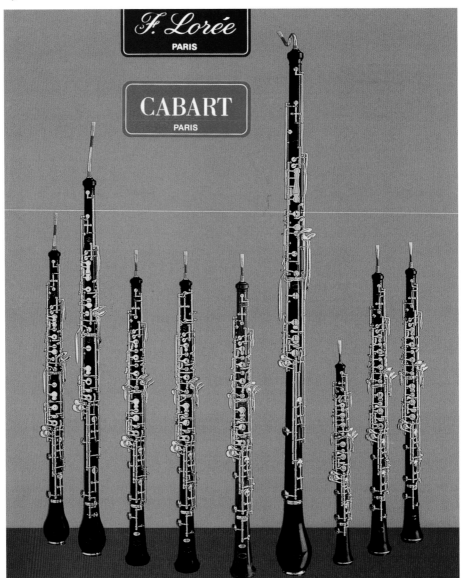

83. Full range of oboes produced by Lorée (*left to right*): oboe d'amore, cor anglais, three Royale model oboes, *hautbois baryton*, musette in F, Conservatoire model, Cabart student oboes.

Françaix's *L'Horloge de flore* (1963, commissioned by John de Lancie) and *Trio pour hautbois, basson et piano* (1994, commissioned by the IDRS) wittily fuse Classical and jazz idioms. British composer Alan Richardson wrote numerous works for his wife Janet Craxton; likewise Richard Rodney Bennett, Gordon Jacob and Lennox Berkeley have contributed significant concertos and sonatas. In the US Robert Bloom made good the lack of Romantic compositions for oboe by writing his own works in that style (including *Requiem*, 1951, and *Narrative*, 1963). Like Elgar, Samuel Barber started to write a concerted work for oboe which he, too, left incomplete. Within a year of the composer's death in 1981, Harold Gomberg (1916–85) performed the *Canzonetta* with the New York Philharmonic.[6] There is a substantial repertoire of oboe music from composers in Scandinavia and the Netherlands;[7] František Hanták (1910–90) was responsible for commissioning new Czech works by Jan Novák and Jaroslav Kvapil among others; the Russian oboist Ivan Poushechnikov has also composed a great deal for his instrument;[8] in Australia Franz Holford and Margaret Sutherland (1897–1984) wrote sonatas for oboe and cor anglais, Graham Powning has written many works, including six trios for two oboes and cor anglais,[9] Bohuslav Martinů wrote his Oboe Concerto (1955) for the Czech-born Jiří Tancibudek who emigrated to Australia in 1950, [10] and Carl Vine's thrilling Oboe Concerto (1996) received its première recording by David Nuttall.

Gradually a standard repertoire has been established for the oboe. The requirements of international oboe competitions provide a good indication of what this comprises. Among regular inclusions are the concertos by Mozart, Haydn (attrib.), Strauss, Poulenc's Sonata, Britten's *Metamorphoses* and rediscovered nineteenth-century showpieces by Pasculli and Kalliwoda, alongside more recent works such as Bernd Alois Zimmermann's Concerto and Luciano Berio's *Sequenza VII*. The annual concours at the Conservatoire National Supérieur de Musique, Paris, continues to be a significant source of new oboe music. Belonging largely to the mainstream tradition, several of these pieces have found their way into recital programmes around the world: *Fantaisie pastorale* by Eugène Bozza (1939), Jolivet's *Sérénade* (concours of 1945) and Shinohara's *Obsession* (1960). Since the 1980s, in place of newly commissioned works, students have been required to prepare standard works such as the oboe concertos of Strauss (prescribed 1982 and 1985), Martinů (1986) and Vivaldi (1986), Berio's *Sequenza VII* (1996) and Antál Dorati's 1983 *Duo Concertant* (1989).

ASPECTS OF OBOE TECHNIQUE USED IN TRADITIONAL REPERTOIRE

This section treats techniques associated with the oboe's traditional repertoire, leaving the discussion of 'extended' techniques for the next chapter. This separation, however, is arbitrary and so some overlap is inevitable. Many of the new techniques have been applied to both streams, while others such as circular breathing and double- and triple-tonguing started out as unorthodox and have subsequently been incorporated into traditional performance practice.

Breathing

One does not 'blow' the oboe, one sets the air in vibration.

Stevens Hewitt

Much of the oboist's command over an audience comes from the management of the breath. While breath is the concern of every wind player, the demands placed on the oboist are unique. The oboe requires the lowest air-flow rate of any wind instrument: between three and five litres per minute. (The clarinet uses about three times as much and the average for the tuba is forty to sixty litres per minute.[11]) At the same time that the oboe requires very little air, the air must be forced through the reed at relatively high pressure. In this regard, the breath technique of the oboe is close to that of the Baroque clarino trumpet and cornetto. Different sizes and types of oboes require a different balance of breath pressure and air flow. The larger-bored English horn, for instance, requires a greater volume of air, while the hautboy operates best at lower breath pressures.

The breath technique used by most modern woodwind players is usually thought of as centring on the diaphragm. During exhalation, however, the diaphragm is in a relaxed state; in reality it is the abdominal muscles that control the airstream. The concept of 'diaphragmatic breathing' is nevertheless advantageous, as it trains the player to use the full capacity of the lungs and to keep breath support low in the body. Diaphragmatic breathing seems to be a relatively modern concept. In earlier periods the mechanics of breathing were described quite differently. The eighteenth-century flautist Quantz, for instance, recommended wind players to prepare particularly long phrases by 'enlarging the throat and expanding the chest fully, drawing up the shoulders'.[12] This suggests that Quantz used the upper part of the lungs more actively than in diaphragmatic breathing. Few modern oboists are likely to heed this advice because of the tensions that such a technique can produce in the upper torso. Fundamental differences between the hautboy and oboe account for other differences in breathing techniques. The hautboy actually requires more sophisticated breath support than the Conservatoire oboe, because without octave keys, the player must use the breath to overblow and adjust intonation and tone.

Although it is easier to play long phrases on the oboe than on any other wind instrument, maintaining air pressure and embouchure support for long stretches is taxing, and the apparent strain of holding the breath while playing is largely responsible for the oboe's reputation for being a difficult instrument. Extreme pressure exercised by the breath on the brain is a popular explanation for the reputed insanity of oboe players.[13]

Because the oboe requires very little air, stale air accumulates in the lungs and must be expelled before inhaling. Oboists have at their disposal three techniques to deal with this problem. The first, and most usual, is the two-part breath comprising the rapid expulsion of residual air, followed by inhalation. The second involves alternately inhaling and exhaling between phrases and is used particularly where there is insufficient time for the two-part breath. This technique works because after exhaling there is always sufficient air in the lungs to continue playing for a short time. Thirdly, oboists can circular breathe. This is a way of breathing without stopping the sound and involves taking in air through the nose while air held in the mouth is forced into the instrument with the cheek muscles.[14] The ability to sustain long phrases on the oboe is a virtue easy to abuse. Great oboe playing can be literally breath-taking – for the audience as much as the player – but care must be taken for the music-making to be exhilarating without exhausting. This means that the oboist must not only overcome the instrument's difficulties but convince the audience that his or her breathing requirements are natural.

While most nineteenth- and twentieth-century composers took care not to overtax oboists, in some instances they gave oboists occasion to show off their breath control. The oboe concertos by Corigliano and Richard Rodney Bennett include notes that the oboist must sustain for as long as possible while the orchestra continues. But other composers have been less sympathetic. I have already mentioned the difficulties presented in the Strauss concerto, but problems occasionally arise in orchestral repertoire. Passages such as the oboe solos in Schubert's Unfinished Symphony or the second movement of Tchaikovsky's Fourth Symphony provided strong motivation for oboists to learn circular breathing, and situations such as those recounted by American composer Stephen D. Burton are familiar to every oboist: 'Anyone who has noticed the oboist at the end of a long solo passage at a concert will recall the uncomfortable feeling that the oboist was about to pass out as his face turned a deeper shade of red at each succeeding phrase.'[15]

There is a long-standing connection between circular breathing and non-western instruments,[16] and up to the middle of the twentieth century this technique was used only sporadically by European wind players. Berlioz encountered an Indian *shahnái* player who held a drone for hours, presumably by means of circular breathing.[17] Another account by a German traveller dating from 1875 describes the use of circular breathing by a folk clarinettist from the Caucasus and makes it clear that the practice was not generally known in Europe at the time.[18] Perhaps under the inspiration of players from other cultures, the technique began to be practised by a small number of European oboists. J. C. Fischer may have used this technique, as there are extended passages in his concertos that must be performed without breaks. Lavigne is reported to have been able to sustain a single note, 'now swelling, now diminishing', for a full minute and ten seconds – beyond the natural capabilities of most oboists without recourse to circular breathing, [19] and Charles Reynolds (1843–1916) was famous for performing the English horn solo from *Tristan* 'with no apparent break for breath'. Goossens later surmised that his teacher had 'perfected the form of nose-breathing' used by oboists of other cultures.[20]

Of all the orchestral wind instruments, the oboe is perhaps best suited to circular breathing because the reed provides sufficient back pressure to form a stable reservoir of air in the mouth and sustain the sound while the player inhales. For some, however, circular breathing is antithetical to good musicianship. Baines dismissed it as a 'stunt' learnt from glassblowers and of no musical value.[21] It can go counter to the true sense of *cantabile*, as it suppresses the breathing points that would come naturally to a singer, thereby transforming the lyrical oboe into a breathless machine.

Still, with judicious use, circular breathing can be a powerful musical asset. Today circular breathing is used by oboists on a more regular basis, particularly in avant-garde music. Some twentieth-century oboe compositions, including Globokar's *Atemstudie* (Breathing study, 1971), Berio's *Sequenza VII* and Holliger's *Studie über Mehrklänge* (1971), are unplayable without circular breathing. Since about the time these pieces appeared, oboists have used the technique when playing earlier music, particularly to negotiate the long lines in Baroque music that seem to take little account of the physical needs of the player. Prout reported that 'older composers were sometimes very thoughtless in the matter. Bach, especially, has written in some of his works solo passages for the oboe which are so long as to be almost impracticable.' He also referred to the 'very eminent player' Dubrucq, who refused to perform the second of Schumann's *Romances*, 'as it was quite impossible to play'.[22] In my experience Bach's breathless phrases are easier on the hautboy than Conservatoire oboe. This is in part due to the lower air pressure required by the hautboy, but also because the articulations and dynamic nuances that are implicit in the Baroque style and come naturally to the hautboy allow more space for catching breath than the seamless continuity characteristic of Baroque performances of Prout's day.

Embouchure and instrument angle

Embouchure, from the French *emboucher*, 'to put in or to the mouth', most basically refers to the way the mouth, lips and jaw are formed around the reed. The embouchure is responsible not only for sealing around the reed, holding it in place, but manipulating its aperture. It has a direct bearing on the amount of air that passes into the instrument and consequently affects pitch and volume. The embouchure also influences the size and shape of the vocal cavity and this in turn affects resonance. How far the reed protrudes into the mouth also has a direct influence on pitch and tone. The general principle is that the more reed there is inside the mouth, the sharper the pitch. By making the tissue around the mouth firmer or softer, the player can control the degree to which the reed's vibrations are dampened, and this also influences tone.

Being so closely connected, embouchure and reed influence each other directly. As much as the player's embouchure controls the reed's aperture, ease of response, pitch and so forth, personal reed preferences arise from the make-up of each player's embouchure. It takes an oboist years to form a reliable embouchure, but the embouchure must remain flexible, constantly responding to changing needs. As well as tempering the pitch and tone of individual notes, helping with the shaping of dynamics and facilitating the attack and release of notes, most oboists agree that the embouchure should be gradually tightened when ascending and relaxed when descending.

The angle at which the instrument is held is also directly connected with the embouchure. French methods from the nineteenth century onwards recommended holding the instrument at an angle of about thirty degrees from the body (Garnier is higher, about forty-five degrees); Barret preferred an even lower angle, saying that this improved the tone (see ill. 52). Lower angles tend to dampen the reed's vibrations, and having the bell of the instrument pointing down also affects projection. The American school has adopted a lower angle, while in Europe players prefer higher angles (compare illustrations of Goossens and Tabuteau, ills 76 and 77).

Range

It is tempting to assume that the range of the oboe has expanded progressively, but this is not entirely true. Already in 1825 Sellner gave fingerings for notes up to a3 and this was the standard upper limit given in Austrian and Italian methods throughout the nineteenth century. While the Conservatoire oboe expanded the range downwards to b♭0, notes above g3 have traditionally been considered unplayable, and those above d3 avoided by all but experienced players. This avoidance of the extreme high register arose from a number of considerations. Firstly, the notes in the extreme high range do not have the oboe's characteristic pungent tone quality. Secondly, these notes, even with the assistance of a *hohe-F Klappe*, *Hulfsklappe* or third octave key, require expert management of reed, breath and embouchure. Thirdly, the fingerings of the notes in this register, being based on second and third harmonics, are more complicated than those of the lower octaves.

Since the beginning of the twentieth century, composers have demanded increasing facility in the high register. Stravinsky occasionally took the oboe beyond f3, but was careful to give the player time to prepare fingers and embouchure. In the *Symphony of Psalms* (1930) the first oboe plays high Fs and Gs in octaves with the other oboists, and in *Jeu de Cartes* (1937) and *Rake's Progress* (1951) the first oboe part occasionally touches g3. French composers tended to be more demanding. In *Daphnis et Chloë* (1912) Ravel created a spine-chilling effect with an oboe in its highest register piercing through the haze of the orchestral texture. In Ravel's *L'Enfant et les sortilèges* (1925), Dukas's *Sorcerer's Apprentice* (1897) and Milhaud's *La Création du monde* (1923), oboists must negotiate rapid passages involving combinations of the complicated high-note fingerings up to f♯3.

Reeds

The eighteenth-century hautboist who bought finished reeds is often contrasted with the autonomous modern oboist who makes reeds from scratch,[23] but this is in need of qualification. First, some professional hautboists of former times certainly made their own reeds or were able to adjust the reeds they purchased to suit their own needs.[24] Secondly, many of today's professionals also play on bought reeds. Indeed, two of the twentieth century's most important players, Leon Goossens[25] and Heinz Holliger, relied on reeds made by others for much of their careers. Thirdly, relatively few oboists undertake all the stages of the process from tube cane and sheet brass to finished reed; many prefer to buy pre-gouged cane which they tie onto ready-made staples and scrape according to personal taste.[26]

Arundo donax, the material used for oboe reeds, grows in swampy lands across the world. The cane-fields of the Var region of Southern France remain the prime source of cane for the world's oboists, although cane grown in comparable climates in other parts of the world is gaining a foothold in the market. The quest for a more durable and consistent material to replace the ephemeral *Arundo donax* has proven only partially successful.[27] Fibreglass and plastic reeds are used principally by beginners and players in particular situations, such as in marching bands or where the oboe is amplified, where sound quality is less critical than reliability and durability.

With the monopoly of the Conservatoire oboe, staple and reed design might be expected to have become standardized. However, national schools – even individual players – maintain distinctive approaches to reed-making.[28] Players can choose from a wide variety of subtly different staple designs, though the greatest differences are to be noticed in the gouging and scraping of the cane, and here the American school stands farthest apart from others.

There has been much speculation about the origins of the American 'long scrape' reed. It was most likely developed by Tabuteau in his early years in Philadelphia at a time when European and particularly French players were using short scrapes (5–9 mm in length). Typically, America scrapes extend to near the binding, often with a pronounced spine down the middle. The characteristic W scrape frequently incorporates 'windows' from which extra cane is removed. This design is intended to strike a balance between vibration and resistance, by allowing the reed to vibrate freely but at the same time have stability, and so helping the production of the desired 'dark' tone. The 'American' scrape differs markedly from the even gradation from tip to back on the shorter U or V scrapes used virtually everywhere outside North America.

Articulation

Articulation on the oboe is achieved by stopping the vibration of the air column. This is usually done by bringing the tongue into contact with the reed. Articulation requires precise co-ordination of tongue, fingers and breath. The quality of articulation – from sharp and crisp to gentle and round – is achieved largely by varying the length of interruption and the speed of the tongue-stroke. It is also possible to articulate without the tongue, either with the breath alone or in combination with a slight push from the throat. The breath start is particularly useful for *pianissimo* entries.

As described in chapters 2 and 3, seventeenth- and eighteenth-century wind players developed an extensive palette of articulations. In the woodwind methods of the next century these were replaced with one basic tongue-stroke. Garnier's was the first oboe method to assert one basic articulation technique, but this could be varied in quality.[29] Instrumental methods written for the Paris Conservatoire in the first years of the nineteenth century codify three basic styles of articulation that remain basic to modern articulation: detached (*détaché*), *mezzo staccato* or legato-tonguing, and slurred.

Most oboists are able to single tongue at speeds up to about crotchet (quarter note) = 120, but the tongue easily fatigues, and endurance becomes an issue. Three or four detached notes or passages with alternating slurred and staccato patterns at a faster tempo are manageable, but prolonged sequences of uninterrupted tonguing are tiring. In these cases some players resort to double- or triple-tonguing. With these techniques the player punctuates the airstream with alternately the front and back of the tongue as in pronouncing the syllables *ter* and *ker*. Double- and triple-tonguing are more difficult on the oboe than on other wind instruments because the protrusion of the reed into the mouth interferes with the motion of the tongue. Care also has to be taken to equalize the syllables (the back *ker* often sounds weaker than the forward *ter*). Despite these difficulties, over the last decades double- and triple-tonguing have become firmly established in oboe technique.[30]

The paired tonguing used by seventeenth- and eighteenth-century hautboists always required the tongue to touch the reed and the modern (*ter ker*) double-tongue seems never to have been used on the hautboy. Indeed, Quantz and others asserted that double-tonguing was not possible.[31] The reason for this is probably related to the hautboy's low air pressure requirement and wide reed. One of the first references to double-tonguing appears in Auguste Bruyant's transcription of Hugot's *25 Grandes études*.[32] Bruyant recommended using the syllables *te que*, but admitted that although double-tonguing is practical in rapid passages, it is not always pleasant to the ear.

During the twentieth century, opinions have differed on the benefits of double-tonguing. Goossens made much use of it and after his accident relied on it even more. However, his pupil Evelyn Rothwell preferred to develop a fast single-tongue.[33] Goossens's double-tonguing in the overture to Rossini's *La scala di seta* has often been held up as a model, but in the recording of the piece with the London Philharmonic Orchestra under Beecham (1933) he was not able to maintain absolute uniformity. Since that time the technique has been mastered by other players. Lothar Koch, for instance, negotiated the same passage at a faster tempo and with more even control.[34]

The singing reed

Whether Mattheson speaking of the 'gleichsam redende Hautbois', amazed reviews of Gustave Vogt's *cantabile* playing, or Wagner urging oboists to imitate the soprano Wilhelmine Schröder-Devrient, the analogy with the human voice has been one of the most enduring in the oboe's history. The Czech-Australian oboist Jiři Tancibudek has recently scrutinized the subject in his article 'The Oboe and the Human Voice'. Taking as his starting point the observation that 'singing is an instinctive expression of human feeling and must be assumed to go back beyond all record of human kind',[35] Tancibudek accepts the theory that early Baroque singing style heralded the emergence of the hautboy. In addition to pointing out that the oboe is, of all the wind instruments, closest in range to that of the soprano voice, he reinforces the connection by comparing the singer's and the oboist's technique of tone production. He likens the way singers modify the size and shape of the vocal folds to the oboist's manipulation of the reed. But, for Tancibudek, it is above all the similarities in the way that oboist and singer handle the air stream that allows the oboist to attain the integration of instrument and body that is natural to the singer: 'for an oboist it is indeed the uninterrupted, intense and perfectly controlled air stream which closely connects the player with his instrument and integrates both into one unit'.[36]

Because of its persistence, the analogy with the human voice is often taken as a sign of stylistic consistency over time. This assumption, however, overlooks the considerable changes in both taste and technique that singing has undergone over the centuries. The eighteenth-century instrumentalist sought to emulate the rhetorical quality that text gave to vocal music. The emphasis was thus on articulateness and dynamic suppleness rather than on volume and uniformity of sound with the complicit sacrifice to the comprehensibility of the text that are pervasive in opera houses today.

Vibrato[37]

Few aspects of musical performance provoke such emotionally charged debate as vibrato, and this alone makes it a subject worthy of examination in detail. In the most general terms, vibrato can be defined as any form of regular and intentional fluctuation in a steady tone. It can involve oscillations in timbre, intensity and pitch or any combination of these. Whether instrumental or vocal, vibrato is closely associated with human physicality, and this adds to its controversial status. A tremulous voice is taken as a sign of strong emotion, and the purportedly 'natural' vibrato of the singer is the model for instrumental 'imitations'. Even so, despite the connection with the body, the mechanics of vocal and woodwind vibrato production are not well understood, and most explanations remain frustratingly enigmatic. Today most wind players produce vibrato by manipulating the airstream, but in the past other techniques were used.

For some, vibrato is integral to sound production, something that beautifies and enlivens the tone, but to others it is the very opposite, a mannerism superimposed on the tone that disrupts its purity. These divergent opinions arise from different traditions and historical perspectives. Arnold Schoenberg was intrigued by these ambivalent aspects of vibrato. For him vibrato acted as a supplement to a pure musical sound in that it both enhanced and contaminated it. He explained that it was able to transform 'pure, isolated, stiff, clear, and lifeless tones' into 'living, interesting, lively, warm, sounds', but that it achieved this at the expense of purity of tone. He reasoned that 'the basis of what we feel to be a living, beautiful, warm tone is a certain impurity. . . . Now, is it that what is pure, the ultimate discovery, is already so clarified that one has to destroy its purity (by admixture) in order to establish any contact with it; or is it that since the material (even, if one may say it, the material of ideas) is faulty, it calls for touching-up, which throws the true relationships into shadow and makes the defects invisible?'[38] Schoenberg was particularly unforgiving of the vibrato then in fashion, which he described as the 'goat-like bleating used by many instrumentalists to curry favour with the public'.[39]

Already some decades before, at the turn of the twentieth century, vibrato had been stigmatized as a contagion. In the 1880s Chorley felt that vibrato gave the impression of fatigue and premature decay,[40] George Bernard Shaw declared that vibrato was 'sweeping through Europe like the influenza',[41] and the noted American laryngologist Dr Holbrook Curtis saw it as a foreign pollutant.[42] The cultivation of vibrato almost certainly began among singers in the late nineteenth century and was later copied by instrumentalists.[43] Oboist André Lardrot recalls that even in the 1950s, 'vibrato' was never discussed at the Paris Conservatoire, but that the effect was implied in the expression *chanté*.[44] To the present day, an invitation to an oboist to 'sing more' is often taken as an invitation to increase vibrato.

By the 1940s, when Carl Seashore was writing his classic study on the subject, vocal vibrato was a 'natural given', a universal indicator of authentic musical expression that occurred 'automatically whenever [a] person sings with genuine feeling'.[45] After analysing the tone production and vibrato of several famous singers, Seashore reported that the average vibrato of 'the best singers' was about 6.5 cycles per second, with an amplitude of about a semitone above and below the pitch. The vibrato of the violinists he measured had an amplitude approximately half as wide, but this is still wider than what is tolerated by present taste. Seashore was the first to undertake a scientific study of vibrato, but his work lacked historical perspective. He limited his sample to contemporary Classical musicians and consequently disregarded earlier approaches to vibrato and divergent styles in popular and non-Western traditions. Historical documents and early recordings indicate that, far from being the universal constant that Seashore wanted to make it, the use and practice of vibrato in western music has been closely connected with changes of musical style and taste.

Vibrato as an ornament

In the seventeenth and eighteenth centuries, woodwind players used a type of microtonal trill (called *flattement* or *softening*) produced by partially closing the tone-holes (see chapter 3, p. 57). They applied this sparingly to individual notes, often in conjunction with the *messa di voce* and specific musical contexts.[46] Later in the eighteenth century, wind treatises mention a variety of techniques. Around 1760 the French flautist Delusse mentioned *flattement*, along with a type of breath vibrato (which he said was called *tremolo* in Italy) produced by pronouncing the syllables *hou hou*, and the *tremblement flexible* produced by rolling the flute. When these techniques were applied to individual notes, they created specific emotional effects.[47]

In the absence of more concrete evidence, we can only surmise that oboists followed similar principles in the application and production of vibrato. Still, it appears that personal styles have varied considerably. Leopold Mozart praised Carlo Besozzi's remarkable 'ability to sustain his notes and his power to increase and decrease their volume without introducing even the slightest quiver into his very pure tone',[48] implying a total absence of vibrato. But his son's derogatory remarks on J. C. Fischer's playing make it clear that this equally famous player had a pronounced vibrato: 'The long and short of it is that he plays like a bad beginner . . . his vibrato is like the tremulant on the organ.'[49]

Different techniques of vibrato continued to be practised into the nineteenth century. The flautist Anton Bernard Fürstenau discussed both finger vibrato (*Klopfen*) and a breath vibrato produced by the lungs or lips (*Bebung*) that he said was used to imitate the human voice, but advised reserving these ornaments for special effects on single notes.[50] The bassoonists Carl Almenräder and Eugène Jancourt also advocated the selective use of finger vibrato,[51] and the French violinist Charles Bériot stressed the connection between vibrato and singing. These musicians still recognized non-vibrato as the basis of tone production. One of Bériot's vocal models would probably have been his brother-in-law, the famous tenor Manuel García, who described vibrato (which he called *tremolo*) not as a constant element of tone production but as an ornament reserved for sentiments which, 'in real life, are of a poignant character such as anguish . . . or tears extorted by certain acts of anger, revenge, etc.'.[52]

As for the eighteenth century, information specific to how nineteenth-century oboists produced or used vibrato is sparse. Garnier's oboe method from 1800 catalogued an effect produced by shaking the lips (*frémissement de lèvres*) as the subtlest form of articulation. However, as it never appears in any of the music in the method, it is hard to draw conclusions about its application.[53] Gustave Vogt cautioned oboists to maintain a firm embouchure in order to avoid any 'trembling which is harmful to the tone quality',[54] suggesting that he did not appreciate vibrato. Other players do seem to have used vibrato of some sort, particularly in passages that called for greater expressivity. Franz Czerwenka was praised for 'the strength and length of his sustained tones, his *crescendi*, vibrato [*Vibrieren*], and the tender beauty of his sound, as well as the heartfelt expression in his performance of the Adagio'.[55] Later, in 1865, the revised edition of Koch's *Musikalisches Lexikon* indicated that 'on many wind instruments, such as the oboe and flute, vibrato is not only very possible, but also of very good effect'.[56]

The integration of vibrato and tone production

In the last years of the nineteenth century, vibrato became generally more widespread, and was applied to many instruments and voices. In wind playing, finger vibrato was abandoned and from this time any reference to 'vibrato' meant a regular oscillation in the air column. At the same time, vibrato became an issue of considerable controversy. References to its abuse proliferated. In the 1880s, the first edition of Grove's *Dictionary* offered the following advice: 'When the vibrato is really an emotional thrill it can be highly effective . . . but when, as is too often the case, it degenerates into mannerism, its effect is painful, ridiculous, or nauseous, entirely opposed to good taste and common sense, and to be severely reprehended in all students whether of vocal or instrumental music.'[57]

In his excellent study *Early Recordings and Musical Style*, Robert Philip sketches the progression from the 'old-fashioned' use of vibrato as an ornament to its 'modern' function as 'a continuous colour'.[58] This paradigm serves as a working model for considering vibrato in oboe playing of the first half of the twentieth century, but it is difficult to make any hard-and-fast division between 'old-fashioned' and 'modern'; it is equally difficult to locate a number of exceptional oboists into this chronological scheme, and regional preferences often complicate matters further.

Vibrato on woodwind instruments was first used as an adjunct to tone production around the turn of the twentieth century. The first players to cultivate breath vibrato were associated with the Paris Conservatoire. When Richard Strauss compared Austro-German and French playing in 1904, he described the French sound as 'thinner and often vibrant [*dünner und oft vibrierend*]'.[59] This may indicate that he had already heard French oboists using vibrato; alternatively, his inference may rather be that vibrato complemented the inherently vibrant tone of the French oboe.

According to Taffanel's pupil Marcel Moÿse, when breath vibrato was introduced as a regular adjunct to tone production on the flute in Paris around 1905, it was a hotly debated topic. 'Vibrato? It was worse than the plague!'[60] he later recalled, reminiscent of G. B. Shaw's epidemic analogy. Fernand Gillet reported that when he was a student at the Paris Conservatoire in the last years of the nineteenth century, vibrato was officially forbidden, but that his uncle Georges Gillet used it and was imitated by his pupils.[61] One of the few recordings made by Gillet (excerpts from Rossini's *Guillaume Tell*, made in 1904–7), however, reveals a clear, straight tone with no trace of vibrato,[62] and a 1946 recording of the Second Brandenburg Concerto with Fernand Gillet and the Boston Symphony Orchestra under Koussevitsky shows that he was still using much less vibrato than his flute- or violin-playing colleagues.

Leon Goossens seems to have been the first oboist to adopt breath vibrato as a conscious adjunct to tone production. Indeed, vibrato was to become something of a Goossens trademark. Sixty years later he described the atmosphere when he introduced it in around 1915:

The fashionable woodwind sound in the early days of this century was more wooden. *Vibrato* was rarely, if ever used, and certainly not as a fundamental aspect of tone production. Those first days at the Queen's Hall Orchestra represented for me a period of isolation from the prevalent style of sound reproduction. I suffered a great deal of abuse and jibing from other players at this time for persisting with my own concept of a beautiful oboe sound incorporating *vibrato* as an essential aspect of its singing quality[63]

Goossens's tone must have stood out in the wind section at Queen's Hall, since at the time none of the other wind players was using vibrato. Even the flautists resisted 'infection' from across the Channel and continued to play without vibrato on wooden flutes. According to Goossens's own report, Henri de Busscher, his predecessor at Queen's Hall, used some breath vibrato.[64] The earliest surviving recording made by de Busscher dates from the 1940s and shows a fairly slow vibrato on selected notes, so it is still likely that Goossens's faster and more present vibrato was indeed new in the 1910s. Another source of inspiration for Goossens was undoubtedly the playing of Fritz Kreisler. The two can be heard side by side in a recording of the Brahms Violin Concerto with the London Philharmonic. In the oboe solo at the opening of the slow movement, Goossens anticipates the violinist's vibrato. Kreisler had recorded the same work with the Berlin State Opera Orchestra under Leo Blech in 1927, but here the vibrato-less oboe tone contrasts markedly with Kreisler's style.

While vibrato is virtually always present in Goossens's playing, it is far from uniform: sometimes faster, sometimes slower, at others almost imperceptible. He was the master of modulating vibrato to enhance the shape of the music. As he built a phrase, he would increase the intensity of his vibrato; on resolutions and final notes of phrases, his vibrato would melt into a straighter tone, and he would enhance diminuendos on sustained tones with a gradual slowing of his vibrato. As one of the first oboists to record extensively, Goossens influenced the next generation of oboists throughout the world, but his influence is most apparent among his own pupils in Britain. By the 1950s most British oboists had adopted a rather broad vibrato that was not only constant but prominent. 'It is a good axiom', wrote Evelyn Rothwell, 'that you should not have to think about making a vibrato, but about stopping it!'[65] In 1959 Baines complained of the slow 'incessantly-continued tremulant' practised by British oboists and preferred the type of vibrato produced by French players which, 'if heard at all, is typically of the fast "instinctive" kind, introduced to heighten a phrase at its climax. . . . One may feel that one is hearing the oboe for a change, rather than the oboist.'[66]

Baines was probably thinking of oboists of the older French school who stayed relatively close to Gillet's style – Bleuzet, Lamorlette, Bas and Bajeux. The 'ample' vibrato today considered a hallmark of French oboe playing was introduced towards the middle of the century and is associated, more than anyone else, with Pierre Pierlot.[67] And while in many respects Heinz Holliger's playing is the antithesis of Pierlot's, his bright tone, and constant and intense vibrato are not unlike his teacher's.

Holliger's style of vibrato has also remained surprisingly uniform – both over the course of his career and over the enormous range of musical styles that he performs.

Wind players in Germany and Austria in the first part of the century used virtually no vibrato. It was with the widespread adoption of French oboes in Germany in the second quarter of the twentieth century that German oboists began to incorporate 'French' vibrato.

Twentieth-century American oboists generally favoured faster vibrato with smaller amplitude than European players, particularly the French and English schools.[68] This distinction is most apparent when comparing John Mack (principal oboist of the Cleveland Orchestra, 1965–2001) or John de Lancie (Philadelphia Orchestra, 1954–77) with players like Pierlot, Holliger or Gordon Hunt. The American ideal is still Tabuteau, who used vibrato judiciously to enhance his range of expression and to reinforce the intensity of certain notes. In preference to the forward placement adopted by European players like Goossens, Tabuteau's vibrato ranged from a hardly perceptible shimmer behind the sound to a warm resonance. Unlike Goossens in the Queen's Hall Orchestra, therefore, Tabuteau was always more restrained in his use of vibrato than William Kincaid, his flautist-colleague in the Philadelphia Orchestra, who cultivated a pronounced fast and constant vibrato.[69]

The diversity of approaches to vibrato demonstrates that 'modern' vibrato is not, as is often claimed, simply constant and unvaried. Fine players have always modulated their vibrato to suit musical circumstances. If constant vibrato was ever a standard practice, it was in the decades around the middle of the twentieth century, but even then each national school cultivated its own ideals, influenced closely by the flexibility of its reeds. 'No vibrato' was then a disparaging remark,[70] or a technique used to create eerie effects.[71] It is often claimed that constant vibrato resulted from the demand for increased volume in ever larger concert halls, but the relationship between vibrato and volume of sound deserves more investigation. Furthermore, early recordings demonstrate that constant vibrato became a regular feature of woodwind technique well after large concert halls became the norm.

Since the 1980s, there has been a reaction against constant vibrato. Increasingly players are sensing that when constantly present, vibrato is depleted of its emotional significance, and it is no longer seen as an essential element of tone production. Instrumentalists and singers alike have (re)discovered more sophisticated ways of utilizing it. In addition, with the rapprochement between French and German schools, younger French oboists like Michel Benet are cultivating vibrato that is less obtrusive than Pierlot's, just as the contemporary German oboists such as Hansjörg Schellenberger spice their dark German oboe tone with French-style vibrato. The more nuanced application of vibrato has also been influenced by players of the hautboy (discussed in chapter 9, p. 286).

So far, I have intentionally avoided discussing the technique used to produce breath vibrato on the oboe. Some players believe that vibrato is a mysterious grace, a result of 'proper' tonal placement and support. As Allan Vogel wrote of Robert Bloom's teaching on vibrato:

When the wind is of sufficient intensity, and the embouchure holds the reed perfectly, a vibrato comes naturally into the sound, almost as if to reward the player for doing everything so well. This is the column of air vibrating. Vibrato after all is natural: the sound of a gong playing in a large room pulsates. No part of the body has to make the vibrato. It may be generated in the good support of the abdominal muscles and diaphragm, but all parts of the body should be flexible enough to be vibrated by the column of air.[72]

Interestingly enough, in Vogel's recollection, Bloom promoted a 'holistic' approach that did not locate the production of vibrato in any fixed place in the body, but required an integrated approach to tone production to foster its development.

Goossens was equally at a loss to describe the mechanism of vibrato. He mentioned 'mobility of embouchure' and 'abdominal support', but believed that the 'real control rests with the diaphragm'. His general remarks muddy the waters still further: '*Vibrato* is a quality which defies close analysis in any useful sense, nor indeed can it be induced by exercises and explanations. If all the physical conditions of good playing along with freedom from tension are achieved, *vibrato* becomes an expressive inflection of musical personality and sensibility.'[73] He seems to be intentionally evading any physical explanation. At the same time, he does not say that, given the right conditions, vibrato will happen automatically, rather his point is that it should *seem* effortless and authentic.

Vocal vibrato has for long been the instrumentalist's model, at least as a guiding principle, even if oboists resist emulating the exaggerated wobble prevalent among mature operatic stars.[74] But if vibrato is a 'natural' acoustic phenomenon, how is it that singers and instrumentalists can adjust its speed, and turn it on and off? Clearly, modulating vibrato requires a very sophisticated – albeit elusive – technique, and this means that it cannot be entirely natural. At the same time, as Bloom and Goossens observed, the effectiveness of any vibrato rests on the artist giving the impression that it is natural and effortless.

The vagueness of technical discussions of vibrato arises in part from the numerous confusing theories and contradictory practices. Some claim to produce vibrato with the diaphragm, others with the throat, the jaw or even lips.[75] Like many oboists, I was taught 'diaphragmatic vibrato' and experienced the frustration of pulsing with the breath while waiting for something to happen. Eventually a 'shimmering' vibration took over from the slower regular pulses. The shift felt like a gear change. Where the vibrato came from was impossible to tell. It seemed to be involuntary, to have a life of its own.

But just like 'diaphragmatic breathing', 'diaphragmatic vibrato' is a fallacy: it is not the diaphragm but the abdominal muscles that do the work. However, it is physically impossible for the abdomen to move at the speed required for vibrato (5–7 cycles per second).[76] Studies using a fluoroscope have demonstrated that during vibrato production the diaphragm is stationary, but the thorax is in motion.[77] From this it would appear that the abdomen functions primarily as a catalyst to initiate the oscillation of the air column, and that a fully developed vibrato technique calls on other muscle groups as well. It is probably through the integrated use of abdomen, thorax, larynx and lips that wind players are able to modulate the speed and intensity of their vibrato.[78] Consequently, different players have found it beneficial to focus on certain muscle groups, while others prefer to leave the source of vibrato elusive.

Thinking of vibrato as originating with the diaphragm has two important advantages. First, it directs the player's attention away from the throat and lips, and if these are not well supported, they can produce the 'nanny goat' bleating (*chevrotement*) which, although popular in the early years of the twentieth century, shortly afterwards became an object of ridicule. Secondly, it associates the technique with the muscle which, as well as being one of the least discernible,[79] is closely connected with the source of breath that brings life to the music.

Chapter 9

Diversifying streams since World War II: from the avant-garde to Postmodernism

> It would be hard to find another musical epoch in which every aspect of musical technique and aesthetics has been subjected to such radical discussion and dispute as in ours. Even the term 'music' has acquired a wider meaning and in many contemporary instances . . . has a widely different meaning from that recognized by tradition.
>
> Bruno Bartolozzi 1967:1

The two exploratory channels

The postwar era saw not only the flourishing of the oboe in traditional settings but its involvement in two lines of escape from the musical establishment: the avant-garde and the revival of 'period instruments', including the Baroque hautboy.

Ideologically, the avant-garde sought to extricate 'Classical' music from the artistic values of the nineteenth-century bourgeoisie and take it in new directions. Similarly, from its outset the Early Music movement was invested in providing an alternative music culture that both eschewed the formality of Classical concerts and challenged the canonic status of the mainstream repertoire. One of the paradoxes that haunts our postmodern era is that now, almost half a century after their instigation, these movements have become just as institutionalized as the structures that they sought to dismantle. Over time, the aesthetics and techniques of the avant-garde have become incorporated into the mainstream, while the boundaries of Early Music have been stretched in order to reclaim the traditional 'Classical' repertoire from its official custodians. These two movements have both extended the technique and potential uses of the oboe. In fact, there are many points of contact in both compositional and instrumental techniques; in the case of the avant-garde, they have been newly invented, whereas in the case of the hautboy the techniques were based on historical practices. The following sections will focus on extended techniques that transformed the soundscape of the Conservatoire oboe, and comparable techniques used on the hautboy.

THE AVANT-GARDE

Central to the avant-garde agenda was the deconstruction of the formal division between music and noise. Adopting Kandinsky's anti-formalist manifesto 'colour makes a more insidious attack on the emotions than form',[1] sounds formerly considered extraneous to music were incorporated into the new musical soundscape.

Futurists such as George Antheil, Erik Satie and Edgard Varèse were the first to introduce 'noise' into their music, but it was later, in the 1940s, that John Cage articulated the first theory of an all-inclusive music.

The first explorations in 'extended techniques' were applied to the voice. Schoenberg's concept of *Sprechstimme* – used in *Erwartung* (1909), *Pierrot Lunaire* (1912) and *Moses und Aaron* (1932/54) – was an attempt to develop a fluid interchange between song and speech. Henry Cowell's *Aeolian Harp* (1923) and John Cage's compositions for 'prepared piano' from the 1940s were among the first works to exploit unconventional piano techniques, and in the late 1950s a number of musicians began exploring new possibilities on woodwinds. Those disconcerting quacks, clicking of keys and the noise of breathing were legitimized as sonic resources. The earliest instance of a woodwind multiphonic occurs in Berio's *Sequenza I* for flute (1958), but analogous techniques appear in oboe music only somewhat later.

Largely because of its strong identification with conservative musical traditions, the oboe did not play a central role in the avant-garde. Excluded from the most influential new works like Berio's *Chamber Music* (1954), Peter Maxwell-Davies's *Eight Songs for a Mad King* (1969) or Hans-Werner Henze's *El cimarrón* (1970), the oboe eventually made its mark on the avant-garde scene in the 1970s through the exploits of prominent players – Lothar Faber, Han de Vries, Lawrence Singer and, above all, Heinz Holliger.

While composers needed to consult oboists on the new extended techniques, the pushing of the performer beyond the possible became an aesthetic imperative. For the first time in the history of the oboe, there was a disparity between instrument design and use. Composers knowingly expected the impossible and wrote intentionally at the limit of existing technique – and beyond. Avant-garde performance practice, like that of any style, is integrally connected to the instrument for which it was conceived. Most avant-garde compositions were written for full Conservatoire system with plateaux, forked F vent key, alternative F and third octave key, but without automatic octave keys and low b–c coupler. Additional keys can impede the production of certain techniques. For instance, harmonic and double harmonics cannot be produced with automatic octave keys. If a new oboe design were to appear, created specially for this repertoire (perhaps with simplified fingerings in the extreme high register, or with greater possibilities of pitch sliding and multiphonics), it would eliminate some of the tensions that were 'composed into' this music – tensions that arise from performing music on an instrument that was not designed for it.

Aspects of extended oboe technique

This survey is intended neither as a complete catalogue of effects nor as a technical guide for oboists, but rather as a commentary on the most important aspects from both historical and musical perspectives.[2]

MONOPHONICS

RANGE: One of the most obvious ways to extend the technique of the oboe is to use extreme registers. Over one hundred years after it first appeared in Sellner's fingering chart, a3 still caused the first performance of Stefan Wolpe's *Suite im Hexachord* for oboe and clarinet (1936, composed for Josef Marx) to be delayed until the 1950s.[3] Since then, a3 and higher notes have become increasingly common. The solo part in Zimmermann's Oboe Concerto (1952) maintains a generally high tessitura and ascends frequently to a3. By the 1980s a3 was firmly within the range of the virtuoso oboist, as is seen from its frequent appearance in works such as Elliott Carter's Oboe Concerto (1984).[4]

Notes above g3 are easiest when approached chromatically from below in slurred passages, but are difficult to attack. Some players bring the teeth into contact with the reed to help the response of these notes. This technique, which raises the pitch of the instrument about a semitone,[5] requires a complete readjustment of embouchure and can produce a strident tone. The oboe's highest register is almost devoid of the instrument's characteristic pungent tone and lyrical qualities, and some composers have taken advantage of this. Aiming to produce a sterile 'white' quality in *Instruments III* (1977), Morton Feldman confined the oboe to d3–a3. Occasionally notes below the accepted range of the oboe appear. Wilfred Josephs wrote a0 in his *Solo Oboe Piece* (1974), but does not specify how it is to be produced. Modern players and reeds are rarely flexible enough to lip the b♭0 down a full semitone. Barney Child's *Nonet* calls the player to insert a cardboard tube in the bell of the instrument to produce notes below b♭0.[6]

BEYOND CHROMATICISM: MICROTONALITY AND PITCH SLIDES: The earliest experiments using microtones date from the first decades of the twentieth century and were confined to string-instruments where tuning is more flexible than on winds. As the Conservatoire oboe was designed to play chromatic music, special techniques are required to produce smaller intervals. Its narrow reed minimizes the pitch variation available on each fingering, and this is compounded by the pitch stability (even inflexibility) of current oboe design for microtones. For microtonal music, therefore, players need to learn special fingerings that are often complicated and unequal in tone quality, and to develop additional flexibility in embouchure and breath. Composers are generally selective in their use of microtones, in most cases heeding the advice of oboists.[7] Microtonal passages occur in a many avant-garde works for oboe, including the notation of eighth-tones by Xenakis in *Dmaathen* (1976) and quarter-tones in Edison Denisow's *Solo* (1971), to name but two works.

As with microtones, pitch sliding on the Conservatoire oboe is fairly limited. Although integral to vocal and string techniques and widely used in the nineteenth and early twentieth centuries, portamenti and glissandi were rarely used in traditional wind playing. These effects are particularly difficult on instruments with covered finger-holes because these preclude the fingers from being drawn gradually across the holes. Portamenti and glissandi not only require special digital technique involving the gradual uncovering or covering of holes, but subtle manipulation of the lips and breath to disguise the steps and to compensate for the changes in resistance resulting from partially closing the holes.

ALTERNATIVE FINGERINGS: Alternative fingerings on the Conservatoire oboe are used most commonly to facilitate certain note combinations (e.g., left-hand E♭ and F keys,

Ex. 9.1 Berio, *Sequenza VII*, opening line.

right-hand g♯) rather than to produce different colours. In place of alternative fingerings, oboists tend to vary tone colour by adjusting embouchure and breath. Exceptions are the one remaining forked fingering for F, and the 'harmonic' fingerings available for f♯2–c3, produced by overblowing the notes a twelfth below – b0–f1. Georges Gillet introduced these harmonics in his *Etudes pour l'enseignement supérieur* (1909), and although composers rarely specified them prior to the 1960s, oboists have used them for special colouring in appropriate passages.

This is but a small selection of the total number of alternative fingerings available. Berio's *Sequenza VII* provides perhaps the best example of the use of alternative fingerings in an avant-garde composition. The opening *Klangfarbenmelodie* (tone-colour melody) uses five different fingerings and a variety of articulations and dynamics from *fff* to *ppp* on the single pitch b1 (music ex. 9.1) As well as being a tribute to its dedicatee Heinz Holliger (H.H.: in German B♮ is H),[8] Berio undoubtedly chose b1 because there are more alternative fingerings for this pitch than for any other note on the oboe.[9]

The different timbres produced by alternative fingerings for the same note are heard to best advantage when juxtaposed. One commonly used effect involves the rapid alternation between different fingerings for the same pitch and is called variously timbral trill, colour trill, enharmonic trill, unison tremolo, *bariolage* or pedal key. Closely related to this effect is the microtonal trill which is also available on many pitches. (Together these constitute the twentieth-century equivalent of the Baroque *flattement*.) Double trills are also possible on selected pitches. These are produced by the rapid alternation of two fingerings (such as a trill on D using alternately the left and right E flat keys). Music ex. 9.2 shows harmonics, glissandi, timbral and double trills in the second of Ernst Krenek's *Vier Stücke* (1966).

VIBRATO: In response to its increased use in recent decades, composers have harnessed vibrato (i.e., breath vibrato) as a compositional element. Brian Ferneyhough's

Ex. 9.2 Krenek, extract from the oboe part from no. 2 of *Vier Stücke für Oboe und Klavier*.

Coloratura (1970) calls for different levels of vibrato from *non vibrato* to *vibrato molto*, and in *Images* (1986) Isang Yun specifies *non vibrato*, *poco vibrato*, *vibrato* and *vibrato poco a poco crescente*.

Ex. 9.3 Castiglioni, *Alef* (1967).

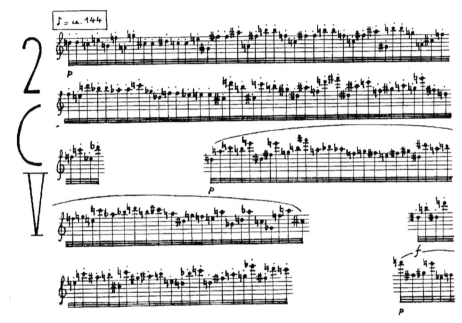

ARTICULATION: Double- and triple-tonguing are virtually mandatory for the avant-garde specialist to negotiate rapidly articulated passages such as music ex. 9.3.

Flutter-tonguing on the oboe is less an articulation than a special effect. It first appeared in scores from the early twentieth century. At the end of Schoenberg's *Erwartung* (1909) flutter-tonguing on the wind and brass instruments dissolves into an upwards chromatic slide; in *Le Sacre* (1913) Stravinsky used it on rapid scales that he presumably thought too fast to tongue; and in his *Alpine Symphony* (1915) Strauss used it in combination with cowbells to imitate the sounds of grazing livestock. The protrusion of the reed into the mouth is an even greater impediment to flutter-tonguing than double- and triple-tonguing, but the technique is nevertheless possible for some oboists. Others substitute a type of ululation in the throat similar to gargling. This usually sounds less like rapid re-articulations than a muffled growl and can distort the pitch of the notes. (The resulting sound is not dissimilar to the overblowing specified by Berio in *Sequenza VII*.) Sensing the difficulty of flutter-tonguing for oboists, Elliott Carter recommended timbral trills as an alternative in his *8 Etudes and a Fantasy* (1955).

Ex. 9.4 Table of extended techniques accompanying *Sequenza VII*.

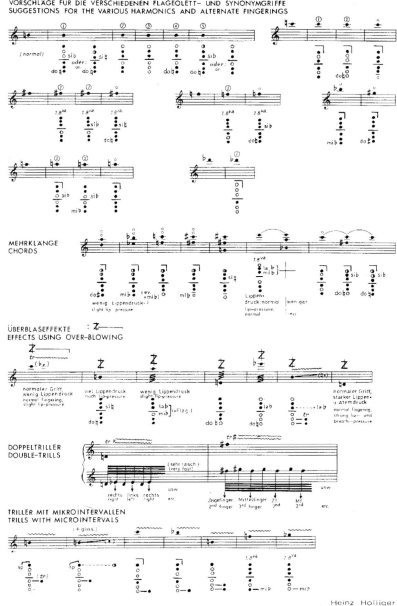

Heinz Holliger

REEDS: The sonic requirements of avant-garde music require different styles of reeds from those that might be appropriate for traditional repertoire. Pitch bending, chords, rapid articulation and the mastering of other special effects call for reeds with both exceptional flexibility and resilience. In general, French and German scrapes have become standard for contemporary music, largely because the performers who have developed the essential techniques come from these traditions. American-style reeds are not always able to produce the same effects.[10] Some compositions call for the reed to be played independently of the instrument. At the end of Globokar's *Discours III* (1969) the five oboists play on their reeds alone and also produce sounds on their oboes without the reeds by buzzing with the lips as on a trumpet.

MULTIPHONICS

Multiphonics (or chords) constitute one of the most important categories of extended oboe techniques. The oboe's complex harmonic spectrum produces a particularly rich selection of multiphonics, many of which attenuate the instrument's natural reedy quality towards strident dissonance. These remarks apply to all oboes: multiphonics are just as accessible on the hautboy (often distressingly so) as on the Conservatoire oboe.

Up to the middle of the twentieth century the objective in woodwind performance was homogeneous monophonic sound production, but this is only a part of the sonic potential of these instruments. From the mid-1960s Bruno Bartolozzi set out to explore the full tonal range of modern woodwind instruments. After working with bassoonist Sergio Penazzi, and later oboist Lawrence Singer,[11] flautist Pierluigi Mencarelli and clarinettist Detalmo Corneti, Bartolozzi presented his findings in *New Sounds for Woodwind* (1967), still the standard reference work on the subject.[12] At the same time, Holliger was conducting his own experiments, and his earliest work to use multiphonics is *Siebengesang*, 1966–7.

Twenty years ago multiphonics caused perplexed astonishment among some listeners. Philip Bate could not disguise his scepticism towards what to him seemed like the tricks at a musical freak-show:

> Some players have, by means of special fingerings and a very sensitive control of the generator (be it reed or air-jet) found a method of reinforcing some partials simultaneously to an abnormal extent. Some are able to sustain one of these frequencies while trilling on another. . . . How far these new sounds may find acceptance is impossible to judge, but certain avant-garde composers are already writing for them.[13]

This picture of an immature musical style with a dubious future was, even when it appeared in print in 1980, badly in need of revision.

One may well ask how it is possible to produce multiple pitches simultaneously on a wind instrument. The explanation is that this happens all the time because, in acoustic terms, every note is made up of multiple pitches. Our ears are trained to perceive the harmonic spectra of traditional musical sounds as monophonics. Thus, even though the fifth harmonic of the low B♭ on the Conservatoire oboe is much stronger than the fundamental,[14] our ears recognize – or perhaps it would be truer to say 'reconstruct' – B♭ as the pitch. Because the harmonics are exact rational proportions of the fundamental, they seem to reinforce it and we consequently perceive the sound as a monophonic. On all wind instruments, however, it is also possible to generate harmonics that are not proportionally related, and because they destabilize the acoustic fundamental, they are perceived as isolated pitches or disruptive patterns. Traditionally these sounds have been relegated to the category of noise because their harmonic structures lie outside tonal harmony.[15]

As Edwin Roxburgh observes, 'the fact that the [oboe] is highly susceptible to the vibration of several frequencies at a time with the single air column is a problem to be overcome in the diatonic/melodic music of the past'.[16] The theory can be illustrated with the effect called 'rolling tone' (*rollender Ton*). This type of multiphonic, produced by distorting the harmonics of a monophonic, is easiest when produced on the lowest notes of the oboe by slightly increasing lip and breath pressure until the note begins to 'roll'. The rolling actually consists of the beats between the partials as they become non-harmonious.[17]

When notating multiphonics, Bartolozzi tried to indicate all of the pitches that made up the chord. However, as the pitches are not always distinguishable to the human ear, he used a spectrometer for accuracy. And as it is too much to expect performers to recreate specific multiphonics from notated pitch clusters, he also gave the fingerings in tabular form along with performance instructions including breath and embouchure control.

The most extensive compilation of multiphonics to date is provided in *The Techniques of Oboe Playing* by Peter Veale and Claus-Steffan Mahnkopf, which

Ex. 9.5 Notations for oboe multiphonics: a) Bartolozzi 1967; b) Veale and Mahnkopf 1995; c) Holliger, *Studie über Mehrklänge* (1971), opening, and d) 1st line, p. 45.

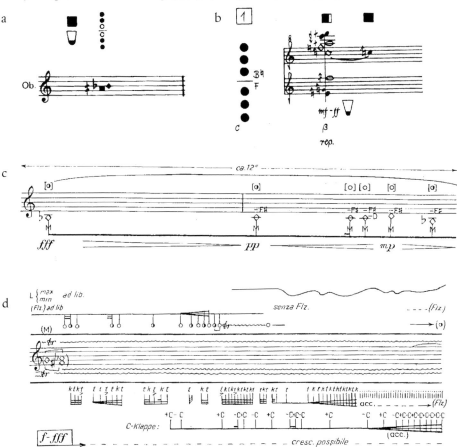

catalogues a staggering 391 distinct fingerings, together with variations resulting from adjustments in breath pressure, embouchure and dynamics. The authors developed a notational system similar to Bartolozzi's by means of computer-assisted analysis of data from a spectrometer, accurate to eighth-tone increments and with indications of the relative volume of the pitches.

A very different notational system was devised by Heinz Holliger. Instead of giving the resulting pitches, his system is like the tablature notations used for lute or guitar (see music exx 9.5c and d). The diamond-headed notes give the basic fingering on which the multiphonic is based, and the holes that must be opened or closed to modify the fingering are given above the note-head. Special instructions are also given for lip position and pressure, breath support and so forth. This is a player's notation conceived by a player.[18]

Holliger used his notation in his *Studie über Mehrklänge* ('Study for Multiphonics', 1971), a work that demonstrates the incredible variety of multiphonics available on the oboe. It opens with sounds generated from the full length of the instrument. The first multiphonic is based on low Bb with the half-hole open, the next is c1 with the right index finger raised and the half-hole open (see music ex. 9.5c). As the piece progresses, the notation becomes increasingly complex: breath, dynamics, articulation and fingering patterns are all shown separately in the spatial-graphic notation. It is as if Holliger envisaged the study to 're-programme' the player's habits by treating these techniques autonomously of each other. This idea had already been used by Berio in *Gesti* for solo recorder (1966).

Notating *Studie über Mehrklänge* in a pitch-specific system like Bartolozzi's or Veale's and Mahnkopf's would not have produced the same piece of music. Instead of prescribing how the piece is to sound, Holliger's tabular notation provides space for each performer's interpretation and technique. There is thus an aleatoric aspect to the piece that arises in the process of negotiating between the distinct tonal events captured in the notation. *Studie über Mehrklänge* also introduces a number of potentially definable multiphonics that do not appear in Veale's and Mahnkopf's catalogue. Of the six multiphonics on the first line of the score, I have found only two in their chart – the third and fifth (nos 249 and 245).

Although Holliger's notation does not specify the exact sonic result, it remains relatively prescriptive. Other composers have used more aleatoric forms of notation, entrusting the choice of multiphonics to the performer. In *Dmaathen*, Xenakis gives only the most prominent note of each chord with the precise fingering above the staff; Globokar's *Discours III* specifies the number of notes in each multiphonic but not the separate pitches; and in the second movement of his Oboe Concerto (1975), John Corigliano uses a simple notation for the three multiphonics, leaving the exact sounds up to the performer, but suggesting fingerings that would produce acceptable effects.

While many multiphonics on the oboe are strongly dissonant, some are tonally more coherent and can give a harmonic dimension to a solo line. Alfred Schnittke uses multiphonics in this way in the solo oboe cadenza in his Concerto for Oboe, Harp and String Orchestra (1971). The oboe part seems to break into prismatic refractions as multiphonics emerge from single notes, and rolling tones close in again on monophonics.[19]

Double harmonics are perhaps the most commonly used multiphonics on the oboe: not because they are the easiest to produce (on the contrary, they require very astute management of lip and breath), but because of their harmonic potential.[20] Roxburgh speaks of their 'hushed ethereal quality. . . . Perhaps the ghosts of Delphic hymns and medieval organum haunt our imaginations in the presence of perfect fifths.'[21] Double harmonics are produced by suppressing the fundamental and isolating the first and second harmonics, and are possible only on certain notes.

A discussion of multiphonics should include vocalizing and playing at the same time, as the two techniques produce comparable harmonic structures. However, because of the difference in their mode of generation, they are usually considered under separate categories. Before it found a place in avant-garde music, the vocal 'growl' was associated with the 'jungle' effects introduced by wind and brass players into jazz in the 1920s.[22] Vinko Globokar uses this effect in *Atemstudie für Oboe* (1971). The piece also explores techniques ranging from changing the shape of the vocal cavity, to singing in either bass or falsetto voice while playing. Simultaneous singing and playing is also called for in Takemitsu's *Distance* (1972), but examples of this technique remain limited because simultaneous vocalizing and playing on the oboe is not particularly effective. This is due to the oboe reed's small aperture which blocks much of the vocal sound and 'rarely emerges as more than a muffled groan'.[23]

OTHER TECHNIQUES

To maximize tonal variety, the modern oboist is often required to switch between different members of the oboe family in the same piece. In the first two of Bruno Maderna's three oboe concertos (1962, 1967 and 1973) the soloist must play oboe, oboe d'amore and cor anglais. Other works leave the choice of instrument to the performer. In *Five Likes* (1971) Theodore Antoniou allows the performer to choose between oboe and oboe d'amore. Modern composers have occasionally revived the eighteenth-century practice of muting. There is no standard form of mute for the Conservatoire oboe, and indications are fairly rare. This may be because mutes tend to change tone colour more than reduce volume and do not affect the entire range of the instrument equally.[24] Some composers have focused on the by-products of sound production. The noise of the player's breath and heartbeat are used as sonic material in Holliger's *Cardiophonie* (1971); key clicks and pad slaps heard on closely-mixed recordings become part of the music in Globokar's *Discours III* and Holliger's *Siebengesang* among numerous other works.

ELECTRONICS

Electronic media can be combined with conventional musical instruments in three ways: 1) They can be used live to manipulate the sounds of conventional instruments. This includes simple amplification and various forms of sonic distortion. 2) Pre-sampled sounds from conventional instruments can be played back in performance either 'straight' or with electronic manipulation. 3) Electronic instruments, such as synthesizers, can be used in performance with conventional instruments.

1) *Amplification and Manipulation*. Several oboists and oboe manufacturers have

explored the possibilities of amplifying the oboe to increase its dynamic range and ability to compete against louder instruments. This is needed nowhere more than in popular music and jazz. From 1993, the French oboist Antoine Lazennec has collaborated with Philippe Rigoutat on an amplification system for the oboe intended primarily for oboists who play oboe in rock and world music groups.[25] Amplification is required in Holliger's *Siebengesang* to make the player's breathing and key clicks audible above the orchestra. Relatively few works call for filters, reverberation, ring modulation and related techniques to manipulate the sound of the oboe electronically. One is Kontonski's Oboe Concerto (1972).

2) Sampling. Most works in this category are for oboe and pre-recorded tape or synthesized accompaniment, and come from a diversity of musical styles. Globokar's *Discours III* can be performed either by five oboists or by one live player with a pre-recorded tape of the other four parts. Thea Musgrave wrote *Niobe* (1977) for solo oboe with a pre-recorded tape of high voices and the tolling of bells. In a completely different style, Kenneth Jacobs's *Sand Castles* (1994) is a mainstream composer's approach to New Age music. The 'accompaniment' resembles a MIDI-generated reduction of an orchestral score, and provides a deliciously 'soft' backing for the live oboist's meanderings.

3) Live Electronics. Music written for the oboe and electronic instruments is also not very common. One of the rare pieces is Martinů's *Fantaisie* for theremin or Ondes Martenot, oboe, piano and string quartet (1973). Here the electronic instrument takes a central melodic part accompanied by various instrumental combinations.

ALEATORY EFFECTS

At the same time that some twentieth-century composers were becoming increasingly more exact in their musical notation, others became aware of the impossibility of controlling every aspect of a performance. Aleatory aspects encompass anything left to chance in performance, the indeterminate space between the music as codified in the notation and the experience of the individual performance. This can take a variety of forms: the chance of what the individual performer brings to Holliger's *Stüdie über Mehrklänge*, free-form pieces such as Globokar's *Atemstudie* and Castiglioni's *Alef* in which it is left up to the oboist to fix the order of the composed fragments, and the graphic notations used by Berio in *Sequenza VII* and the oboe concertos of Bruno Maderna that call for the performer to improvise or otherwise engage in the compositional process. One work that allows great freedom is *A Summoning of Focus*, written by Malcolm Goldstein for oboist Joseph Celli and described by the composer as 'a framework for improvisation, a process of exploring, that is given to the soloist and so relies upon the performing artist's sensitivity to nuance and pacing'.[26]

Heinz Holliger

The 'superstar' of the avant-garde oboe is undoubtedly Heinz Holliger (1939–), a 'Renaissance man' who has not limited his talents to performing as oboist, but has pursued parallel careers as composer, teacher (at the Freiburg Hochschule) and more recently conductor. Holliger began studying the oboe at age eleven with Cassagnaud

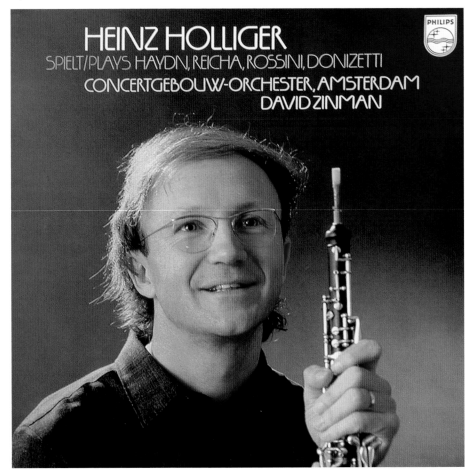

84. Heinz Holliger.

in Switzerland, and after graduating from the Bern Conservatory, studied oboe with Pierre Pierlot and composition with Sándor Veress and Pierre Boulez.[27] At twenty, he was appointed solo oboist with the Basel Orchestra, but stayed only three years before first prizes in the Geneva (1959), Schweizerischer Tonkünstlerverein (1960) and Munich (1961) competitions launched his international career as oboe soloist. Since then he has travelled throughout the world, performing music of all periods and styles. The most recorded oboist of all time, Holliger is proficient across a remarkable breadth of repertoire: from the complete instrumental music of Baroque Czech composer Zelenka, the oboe concertos of Vivaldi and Albinoni, Handel trio sonatas with Maurice Bourgue, a radio recording of the complete sonatas of William Babell, rare Romantic works many of which he himself unearthed, three commercial recordings of the Strauss Concerto to an extensive list of modern works written for him.

Holliger revived the tradition of the oboist-composer, but his compositional activities have not been confined to writing oboe music. His output is remarkably diverse, including chamber music, larger symphonic pieces and theatre works. He has been composer-in-residence with the Orchestre de la Suisse Romande (1993–4) and at the Lucerne Festival (1998). Holliger's compositional training was in rigorous serialism in the tradition of Webern and Boulez, but he gradually moved away from this. Important themes running through his compositions are the reduction of conventional sound production to its noise component, and the questioning of concepts of tonal beauty and even the agency of composer and performer.

As Holliger has been such a dominant influence on the contemporary oboe, even now when younger players are successfully navigating the stream he charted, it is difficult to dissociate his inimitable style from the repertoire. His reedy, somewhat metallic tone coupled with unfailing accuracy gives his performances a steely perfection that seems the perfect match for avant-garde music.[28] Luciano Berio praised Holliger's unique blend of technical mastery, historical insight, intellectualism and experimentalism:

> Today the modern soloist . . . both needs and is able to have an extremely broad angle of vision over historical time. He can interpret the experiences of the past as well as those of the immediate present. In contrast to the virtuoso, he can master extensive historical perspectives, since he uses his instrument not only as a means of pleasure, but of insight (of intellectual analysis). So he is in a position to collaborate in the music and contribute to it, instead of 'serving it' with false humility. By this I simply mean to say that my piece *Sequenza VII* was written with this kind of interpreter – Heinz Holliger – in mind.[29]

Sequenza VII

This insightful virtuosity, which Berio elsewhere described as growing out of a tension 'between the musical idea and the instrument, between concept and musical substance', is the essence of each of the (to date) ten works in the *Sequenza* set.[30] Like the others, *Sequenza VII*[31] was the product of a close collaboration with a performer, and when first composed was out of reach of all but Holliger. But now, thirty years after its composition, *Sequenza VII* is the *cheval de bataille* of advanced oboe study, demanded increasingly at international oboe competitions.[32]

A sustained b1 generated by a separate sound source (either electronic or acoustic) sounds throughout the piece, adding a polyphonic dimension to the piece.[33] During the opening twenty seconds only one pitch – b1 – is heard, varied with kaleidoscopic changes of timbre and intensity, and the rest of the music emerges out of this pitch. It is, as the composer called it, 'a premeditated game [built] on the proposition of twelve notes that have their own definite places'.[34] The twelve-note row is introduced note by note, but not until halfway through the piece are all twelve pitches and their corresponding registers divulged. The resulting pitch class precisely defines the ambitus of the Conservatoire oboe from b♭o to g3.

In *Sequenza VII* Berio uses spatial notation organized on a grid of 13 staves, each divided into 13 'bars' of different lengths calibrated in seconds (3″, 2.7″, 2″, 2″, 2″, 2″, 1.8″, 1.5″, 1.3″, 1.3″, 1″, 1″, 1′). Although this notation seems very precise, it is very difficult to adhere exactly to the timings. Even Holliger deviates by as much as 1′ 50″ over the whole piece.[35] There are extended sections of the piece without space for breath, thus requiring circular breathing. The two pauses of five seconds each (across which the sustained b₁ sounds from an external source) occur well into the work.

Sequenza VII is a veritable catalogue of extended oboe techniques. The performance instructions prepared by Holliger describe most techniques found in the repertoire (see music ex. 9.4). The importance placed on timbral effects calls to mind Berio's fascination with language explored in his vocal works written for soprano Cathy Berberian (*Sequenza III* of 1965–6 and *Recital I*, 1972). Still, Berio does not call on these techniques just for 'effect': there is always a compositional rationale to where and how they are used. The score calls for a small number of multiphonics chosen (no doubt with Holliger's assistance) to fit the piece's tonal organization. Another three techniques represent momentary resistance to the otherwise rigorous control of the pitch material: snatches of sounds beyond the strict serial procedure of the composition. Flutter-tonguing, which as I have already noted is often indeterminate in pitch, is first heard on line 5; 'overblowing' (notated as Ⱦ and intended as an aleatory pitch manipulation) is introduced on line 2; and pitches between the notes of the twelve-tone row occur in the form of microtonal trills from line 3.

Berio indicated that *Sequenza VII* was 'linked to the memory of the English horn in the third act of *Tristan*' and that there are 'hidden fragments of this beautiful melody'.[36] Specific musical references, however, are difficult to identify. Was Berio implying a similarity between the undulating figures in the shepherd's tune and these oscillating triplets towards the end of the piece?

Ex. 9.6 Oscillating triplets in *Sequenza VII*.

Sequenza VII has close connections with two other works by Berio. The first, *Study for Sequenza VII* (1969), is a published draft of the work at a stage before Berio had conceived the grid of thirteen staves, spatial notation, and timings.[37] This draft is in triple metre throughout, with a tempo indication of crotchet (quarter note) = 62. The distribution of pitches is only slightly different from the final version, most involving differences of register. The idea of the five fingerings for b₁ is already in place, but this version calls for a slightly different array of extended techniques. The piece is an excellent preparatory study for oboists learning *Sequenza VII*.

The second related work, *Chemins IV* (1975), belongs to another of Berio's ongoing series that takes existing compositions along new paths (*chemins*). This authoritative 're-write' of *Sequenza VII* provides insights into its compositional procedure and interpretation. To the solo oboe piece, *Chemins IV* adds eleven string parts reminiscent of Penderecki's *Capriccio for oboe and 11 strings* (1965) and in place of the spatial notation of *Sequenza*, shifting time signatures are used to facilitate co-ordination with the ensemble. In general the 3′ measures of the original are transcribed as $\frac{3}{4}$, the 2.7′ ones as $\frac{5}{8}$, 2′ as $\frac{4}{8}$, 1.8′ as $\frac{7}{16}$, 1.5′ as $\frac{3}{8}$, 1.3′ as $\frac{5}{16}$ and 1′ as $\frac{2}{8}$. There are occasional inconsistencies and the pauses in the original are stretched to make space for string

Ex. 9.7 Berio, *Studie zu Sequenza VII* (reproduced from Holliger 1972).

interludes. Although *Chemins IV* is, on appearance, rhythmically more precise than *Sequenza VII*, it gives a more flexible tempo range (quaver or eighth note = 110–20). The pedal B is present throughout *Chemins IV*, often embedded in the string texture and constantly changing in tone colour as it is passed between different string instruments. The string parts provide not only an accompaniment for the oboe part, but a commentary on it. They follow the progressive tonal process in the oboe part, but during the interludes they are tonally autonomous and often introduce pitches that have not yet been sounded by the oboe.

Many oboists of the present generation have followed Holliger's lead and have not only incorporated the necessary technique, but expanded the horizons of contemporary oboe repertoire by commissioning new works. Han de Vries and Pauline Oostenrijk in Holland have inspired works by Louis Andriessen, and new and imaginative solo works have been written for Holliger's pupil Helen Jahren by compatriot Swedish composers Daniel Börtz, Lars Ekström and Göran Gamstorp.

Possibly because of the more conservative musical climate in the USA, fewer American oboists have participated in the exploration of extended oboe techniques to the same extent as their European counterparts. There are, however, a small number of players who have made significant contributions in the contemporary scene. In the 1970s, New York oboist Nora Post was a noted champion of new music and gave numerous US premières including Xenakis's *Dmaathen*, which was dedicated to her.[38] Harry Sargous, former principal oboe with the Toronto Symphony and now teacher at the Music Academy of the West, is one of the most prominent American oboists to have embraced extended techniques, and Joseph Celli has won acclaim for his compelling performances of works with a strong improvisatory component.

'EARLIER THAN THOU': THE HAUTBOY IN THE TWENTIETH AND TWENTY-FIRST
CENTURIES (BRUCE HAYNES)

Right through the nineteenth century there were early music movements and societies
of music 'd'autrefois', but it was not until the second half of the twentieth century
that anyone thought seriously about playing earlier forms of the oboe. Apart from the
organ, the earliest instruments to be revived were those for which no modern
counterparts existed, like the harpsichord, viola da gamba and recorder, which were
already being played in concerts at the end of the nineteenth century. It was quite a
different thing to begin exploring the possibilities of earlier versions of instruments
of the orchestra like the violin and oboe; after all, they were already there (in their
traditional Romantic forms). By the 1960s, however, 'early instruments' had become
a logical step in what seemed an inevitable process, and the first players of the
'retroboe' or hautboy issued their first recordings. The most influential players, and
the ones who continued to be active in the field, were Michel Piguet at the Schola
Cantorum in Basel and Jürg Schaeftlein of the Concentus Musicus in Vienna.[39]

Recording companies promoted the early music ensembles that sprang up, and the
public were presented with a new musical world to discover that consisted of both
'new wine in old bottles' (that is, works already known but played in a new and
supposedly authentic style on original instruments) and recordings that explored the
vast unknown repertoire. One of the first recordings of an hautboy, made by Michel
Piguet in 1964,[40] features the following remark on the cover: 'Ce disque enregistré
avec des instruments anciens, doit être écouté à un niveau plus bas qu'une écoute
habituelle' ('This disc, recorded with early instruments, should be listened to at a
lower level than normal'). Whether this refers to volume or quality is left unclear.

The reasoning behind the 1960s revival was articulated by Nikolaus Harnoncourt,
leader of the Concentus Musicus, in the notes to the milestone Telefunken recording
of the *St John Passion* made in 1965:

> We have today reached the stage where we accept the *music* just as it was written;
> fidelity to the work is a recognized demand (fifty years ago people still believed
> old music could only be presented in re-arranged versions). The sound-producing
> components cannot be excluded indefinitely from these endeavours. The usual
> reason for not using original instruments is the belief that one cannot expect the
> listener to accustom himself to a new (the old) sound-picture, to another dynamic
> scale. . . . One day we shall have to recognize the fact that the wish to hear old
> music in an unedited form, as close to the original as possible, sets off a chain
> reaction (tempi – numbers of performers – acoustics of halls – sound and sound-
> blending of instruments) which cannot be halted, and at the end of which stands
> a performance corresponding to the circumstances at the time of composition in
> every respect.

Harnoncourt's fervour was an inspiration, and was typical of the period. Musicians
who took up the period oboe and violin for the first time had their hands full with
the technical challenges of the new instruments, and few could afford pretensions to

virtuosity. But they were conscious of a mission to discover something new and different in the music they played, in reaction to 'established' performing style. It made no sense, after all, to devote time and energy to learning to play period instruments only to produce music in the same style as on traditional ones.

There was also an unspoken metaphorical link to the 1960s spirit that gave currency to 'natural' foods and handmade sandals, and beyond that to earlier European anti-art and youth movements of the 20s and 30s. The period instruments were 'organic' and 'healthy', and if they were sometimes 'funky' or odd, that was the human touch that put them in another dimension from the self-conscious greatness of the modern concert stage. The early music movement 'back in the 60s' had strong elements of protest and represented an alternative life-style; performances in the formality of dress suits and evening dresses were rare.

For a time, early music's 'purist' image caused it to be thought of as dry and inexpressive. There was undoubtedly an aspect of the movement that was reacting to the 'Romantic' ethos everyone had grown up with, and consequently performed music in a deadpan way. But it was obvious that musicians in the eighteenth century had not thought of their music that way, and desiccated, bland, 'Urtext' performance did not long inspire the musicians who started playing original instruments in the 60s. Urtext is, after all, only a preliminary step. The original manuscripts and prints that the Urtext tried to reproduce were only shorthand 'lead-sheets', giving an outline of the music, to which the musicians who had originally used them added a wealth of unwritten nuance. The notion that being expressive is being Romantic was thus in need of refinement, and has eventually led to a better understanding of just what Romantic music was, by comparing its particular way of moving listeners to that of earlier styles.

Baroque music, whichever instruments it used or forms it took, originated in opera and was invented to express the emotional content of texts. It brought the meaning of words alive by 'speaking' the text. What else is a Handel hautboy sonata, to take an obvious example, but a series of arias set for an instrument? To 'sing' on the hautboy is to play as if one were a singer, and it is a strategy that has its effect on an audience. Baroque musicians often compared music to rhetoric, the art of persuasion, of changing an audience's emotional state. And although they rarely talk of it, I suspect many 'early' musicians today keep in the back of their minds Quantz's conviction that if a musician 'is not himself moved by what he plays, he cannot hope for any profit from his efforts, and he will never move others through his playing, which should be his real aim'.[41]

The idealism and sense of vocation that were typical of this period were encouraged by a sense of discovering an entirely new approach to playing and listening. To a limited degree, the early music movement has managed the remarkable achievement of stepping outside of its time and reinventing musical performance, using the inspiration of the past. It has rejected the received Classical tradition and replaced it with historical practices (again, to a limited degree). And while this project of discovery is far from completed (indeed, may never be completed), times have changed, and moods as well. In the early 1970s the 'Baroque oboe' was a curiosity that had first to be explained to an audience before the playing began. Nowadays, though, the use of period instruments has become commonplace, and students can choose to learn the hautboy in the bosom of any but the most cast-iron conservatories in the world. Thus players who began after about 1980 are less likely to perceive their work as a movement of protest or reaction to a conventional status quo.

It can even be wondered whether the early music movement at the beginning of the twenty-first century is still driven by the assumption that it is restoring a style of performance from the past. There is a striking parallel to the rise of *seconda prattica* in Florence around the beginning of the seventeenth century. Caccini called it *Le nuove musiche*, the new music; it was a reaction to established style, putting the meaning of texts above purely musical elements like counterpoint and rhythm, and it too got its ideas from the past (from the writings of Plato and Aristotle). *Seconda prattica*, which eventually became the dominant aesthetic of the seventeenth century, was the first great stylistic change in European music inspired by a new historical awareness. It was not originally intended to invent something new, but to recreate something old.

The early music movement is not the exact equivalent of the *seconda prattica*, but one wonders what effects, now unforeseeable, it will have on the twenty-first century. Already, it is one of the most viable and vital currents in the modern art-music scene. As Richard Taruskin wrote twenty years ago,

> I hold that 'historical' performance today is not really historical; that a specious veneer of historicism clothes a performance style that is completely of our time, and is in fact the most modern style around; and that the historical hardware [i.e., 'original' instruments] has won its wide acceptance and above all its commercial viability precisely by virtue of its novelty, not its antiquity. . . . It is an authenticity born of its unquestionable relevance to our sense of ourselves at this moment, and to the culture we have invented.[42]

If musical instruments are a kind of physical representation of creative currents in our society, the hautboy, once an artefact of our past, now finds itself transformed into a contemporary form of oboe (which is why – apart from convention – the names 'Baroque oboe' and 'early oboe' are no longer accurate or appropriate). The hautboy can thus be seen as an outlet for musical currents that are not accommodated in traditional Classical settings. The movement that began in the 60s was concerned with practical problems like finding usable instruments, reeds, and music to play. It is ironic that in the end it is not the physical instrument itself that has been important. Early pieces can sound perfectly convincing on the Conservatoire oboe. The instrument has opened new possibilities in our minds, and has become a tool for discovering new ways of playing – 'new', at least, to us. It is not the characteristics of the instrument itself so much as the perspective it gives, by offering a viable alternative option and a sense of new possibilities in performing style, that is the real contribution of the hautboy.

An aspect of the performance of early music that has still to be developed is composing new music in the style of the time. This happens regularly in other musical fields with honoured pasts, like blues or Indian music, where players perform both older repertoire and contribute new pieces. Composing in a bygone style also seems to be something of an aesthetic taboo, probably because of our inherited Romantic attitudes towards 'originality'. The activities of composing and playing music were not as separated in the past as they have become since the nineteenth century. The line between improvisation and composition is thin, and perhaps because most traditional Classical players are not trained in improvisation, very little new music has appeared. If more players were composers, as was the case in earlier times, performances would contain more improvisation. Only when we are able to create from our imaginations new pieces that seem to us to be in historical styles will we be approaching music in the way most historical players did. When pieces composed in earlier styles – not 'modern' styles – start regularly appearing, the early music movement will have escaped from the dusty shelves of libraries and come of age as a living practice.

The historical material offers many possibilities that have not yet been exploited. Many aspects of performing style have yet to be explored and mastered, like improvisation, figural phrasing, rhythmic alterations, other kinds of instruments and instruments at other pitches, and technical issues such as vibrato and fingerings. Some historical procedures have modern counterparts, and it is interesting to compare them with the modern 'extended techniques' like those of avant-garde music that go beyond the familiar performing customs of the Conservatoire oboe. Some of them, like the flattement and muting, can be adapted to the Conservatoire oboe, either to create new effects or to play repertoire written before 1800.[43] It might be interesting to examine some of them.

Tuning

In much the same way that avant-garde composers extend chromaticism into microtonality, the hautboy demands a familiarity with the microtonal adjustments of meantone temperament. Indeed, perhaps the most basic contrast in the techniques of the Conservatoire oboe and the hautboy can be seen in the way the player tunes the instrument. The biggest differences between the two general tuning models of Conservatoire oboes and hautboys, equal temperament and meantone, lie not in the notes of the natural D major scale but in the accidentals between the scale notes. Even in quarter-comma meantone (meantone with completely pure thirds), the natural notes never vary further than 22 cents (i.e., no more than an eighth of a tone) from equal temperament, and on average no more than 10 cents (cf. the charts in chapter 2). The accidentals, on the other hand, can be as far away from equal-tempered ones as 43 cents (nearly a quarter-tone), and their average distance is 30 cents. Not only are the flats and sharps quite distant from equal-tempered accidentals, but the difference between flats and their equivalent sharps is more than a quarter-tone (A♯, for instance, is 65 cents below B♭ (*sic*), and D♯ is 59 cents below E♭). The effect of using meantone instead of equal temperament is audible even to untutored listeners.

On the Conservatoire oboe most of the notes that are not part of the natural scale – i.e., the accidentals – are played by opening dedicated holes that produce no other notes; and since each of these holes is tuned for a single note (and its octave), the accidentals can be placed at the point they need to be for equal temperament. But this precision makes it difficult to play in any other temperament on the keyed Conservatoire oboe. The only way round this is to use alternative fingerings, although long notes and final notes can be adjusted with the embouchure (to make thirds closer to pure, for instance).

Vibrato

Historically, vibrato on the hautboy was not continuous, but was used as an ornament to draw attention to important notes. Up to the latter part of the eighteenth century there is no evidence that it involved the breath or 'diaphragm'; vibrato was produced with the fingers, and was called *flattement*. The flattement, made by closing some part of the holes beyond the fingering for the note, can be thought of as a type of microtonal trill (or more exactly a timbral trill), and indeed in the eighteenth century it was sometimes called a *tremblement mineur* ('lesser shake').

As a former user of constant vibrato, I think that using it in early music gives an effect like a patina over an oil painting, a film that covers and obscures not only accurate intonation but even differences in tone colour between the notes. It also has the interesting effect of conveying a subliminal message that the musician using it is (not always consciously) retaining an attribute of traditional Classical performance. Breath vibrato, which has no known historical precedent, is not uncommon among modern players of the hautboy (who often use the technique as an occasional ornament), and is nearly universal among singers. So we can report that, as of 2003, this aspect of period style has yet to be generally explored.

Alternative fingerings

Used rarely in traditional Conservatoire oboe technique, alternative fingerings are essential to keyless wind instruments. Some are useful for technical reasons. The a2 (12) is surer of attack and can be played very softly with an added right hand (12 456 8). When c♯2 is played in succession with d♯2 (123 456 7), it is often easier to play it 'all open' rather than 123 456 8. G♯2 (and, at a pinch, g♯1) can be played either 123 or 12 4, depending on the context. The notes above a2 (b♭2, b♮ and c3) can be played with either short or long fingerings (that is, either natural scale fingerings or harmonics).

Seventeenth- and eighteenth-century players regularly distinguished enharmonic pairs like A sharp/B♭ with different fingerings, and may well have also used them as in contemporary oboe music, to increase the variety of tone colour (there is no documentation on the subject). Alternating the two fingerings for f1 (with 7 and without), for instance, can help distinguish important and unimportant f1s, as the sound is different (bright and dark respectively). Recorder players regularly rely on alternative fingerings to produce a combination of varying tone colours and dynamics, which they need far more than hautboists, who tend to produce the same effects with the embouchure. Compared with the Conservatoire oboe, variations in tone colour made with the embouchure are relatively easy to produce on the hautboy because of its wide, soft reed and its lower pitch that involves less tension.

Vocalizing while playing

As in avant-garde pieces by Globokar and Takemitsu, simultaneous playing and vocalizing was evidently practised in the eighteenth century. Jacob Loeillet, one of the leading hautboy players of the period, played a remarkable solo concert for the king and queen of France in 1727 in which (playing alone) he somehow contrived to play

> the bassoon, the violin, the traverso, the recorder, and the voice-flute, each playing with the hautboy. After which he went behind a screen and sang a four-part motet, accompanied by a violin and two flutes. Next, Master Loeillet sounded two flutes while simultaneously singing their bass line, which was followed by a large chorus. This seemed to be interrupted by a brawl and a scuffle, and one had the impression of hearing the cries of women and children, the sounds made by men with swords in their hands, and the uproar that a crowd of forty persons might have made. Finally, there were cries for help to the watchmen, and the sounds of the watch arriving on foot and on horse.[44]

Doubling

In a practice comparable to that in Bruno Maderna's concertos, hautboists are also sometimes required to switch instruments in the same piece. Several eighteenth-century composers (Bach, Graupner,[45] Roman,[46] Stölzel, and Telemann[47]) requested players to use both treble hautboy and hautbois d'amour in the same piece.

Muting

As mentioned in chapter 3, a number of pieces written for the hautboy (most of them German) call for mutes. Mutes are put into the bell and consist of wads of paper, dampened sponge, cotton or wool. The mute softens the sound of the hautboy both in volume and in tone quality.

Articulation

Like the traditional oboist playing avant-garde repertoire, hautboists of the past regularly used a wider range of articulations than the three basic forms endorsed in Conservatoire training. The most common way of playing notes in a series, for instance, was using paired tonguing, with the allied use of *notes inégales* (the uneven rendition of evenly written note values, as described in chapter 3).

Special trills and tremoli

Trills and tremoli over intervals larger than a second were used occasionally in the eighteenth century. Quantz noted that 'trills in thirds', using the third above the principal note rather than the adjacent second, 'were used in the past, and are still the mode nowadays among some Italian violinists and hautboy players, but they should not be used in either singing or on instruments (except, perhaps, on the musette)'.[48] 'False trills' and other ornaments are a special case on the hautboy, where unusual fingerings are used to achieve a clearer sound; uncorrected, these fingerings would actually produce intervals larger than those of the diatonic scale.

Sounds produced with unconventional organization of the instrument

Since there is no fingering or key for low c sharp 1 on the hautboy, one way to obtain
the note is to turn the bell upside down and wedge the centre-joint tenon into it,
using the low c1 fingering, 123 456 8. It works better on some instruments than
others. This arrangement (for which no historical evidence is known) effectively
displaces the resonance holes longitudinally, raising their position on the bore, thus
raising the pitch of the c1 to c♯. The range of the hautboy can also be extended
downwards by blocking the holes on the bell with the knees. The b♭ below low C
was sometimes intentionally written for an undoubled hautboy.[49]

Aleatoric techniques and improvisation

Another trait that avant-garde and Baroque repertoire have in common is a tendency
to leave parameters of performance open that were carefully fixed and defined in
Romantic music. Just as late twentieth-century pieces like those by Holliger,
Corigliano and Globokar leave some elements unspecified, much hautboy repertoire
leaves dynamics, articulation and instrumentation to be decided by the performer.
Music that has survived for hautboy (that is, roughly anything written for oboe
before about 1800) was written to communicate somewhat different information from
that in later scores. The music of the Romantic and Modernist periods was put down
on paper to direct the player in performing the piece.[50] This kind of prescriptive
notation does not make the form and structure of the piece obvious, but indicates the
interpretation very precisely; by contrast, the basic idea with most music written for
hautboy was to describe the music itself, the work, and leave the finer details to be
worked out by the performer. This more descriptive approach was natural in a period
when many performers were composers themselves. To paraphrase Libby (1989),

> The hautboy player's contribution to a piece of music in performance was not
> regarded as post-compositional but as the final stage in the act of composition
> itself. It follows that it was not the composer's score but the performed music that
> embodied the finished work of art, one that was both fluid – varying with each
> realization – and ephemeral, not directly recoverable. The concept of performance
> as work of art can be seen as the central principle of the music played by the
> hautboy.

The result is that the music, like some avant-garde oboe parts, looks casual and
incomplete on the page compared with the highly detailed scores of the nineteenth
and early twentieth century. The extreme version of the prescriptive attitude, in which
performers were explicitly discouraged from contributing to the written page, is
Stravinsky's injunction to musicians to neither add nor subtract anything from his
music. This is the antithesis of the common practice in the Baroque period, when
continuo players were not even given all the notes, and the specific instrumentation
of a piece was often left for the performers to decide (even, in some cases, whether
the piece would be played by a chamber group or an orchestra). What we call
'ornamentation' is in fact a part of the performance left unwritten. The hautboy
composer counted on having his music performed by musicians who had enough

familiarity and experience to use parameters like dynamics, articulation and ornamentation to realize its potential.

The early music movement's most obvious attribute is its use of historical versions of instruments. But because we can now see that a period instrument can be played in a later style[51] and a traditional Classical symphonic instrument can be played in a period style, it is not the instruments themselves that define the early music movement, but rather the performance style that players bring to the instruments. When the players wish, they can thus use the movement as a platform for experiment with performing styles beyond the received style generally taught in conservatories.

For the first twentieth-century oboists attempting to make the hautboy a viable musical instrument, there were a number of obstacles. One obviously had to find a decent instrument, which was not as easy as it is today; serious copies did not begin to appear until the late 1960s.[52] The second challenge was to discover a reed that would work reasonably, and that has been a constant experiment with no end in sight; players were obliged to design and make staples, locate larger-diameter cane and gouge it, and find a usable shape. For these first players, there was also the fundamental and immediate need to develop a technique that produced reasonable results, and to locate the instrument's original repertoire. One remarkable aspect of these challenges was that each player had essentially to solve them on his own, as there was no one to consult for answers, and this resulted in the rise of separate schools led by the most prominent players: Schaeftlein in Vienna; Piguet in Basel; Dhont, Ebbinge, and Haynes in Holland; and Dombrecht in Belgium.

There followed a period in which players got much of their training on the job, often being requested to perform things they were doing for the first time: difficult tonalities, extended range – in short, it was an area where angels might fear to tread, as players with traditional Classical training attempted to play pieces that had originally been conceived for players of the past who had been using 'original' instruments all their lives. As recordings from that period document, the results were not always polished but the spirit of experiment was often refreshing, and the instruments yielded serendipitous effects, producing expressive subtleties previously unimagined by the players themselves.

Practice quickly got ahead of the historical props. Using the assumption expressed in Harnoncourt's manifesto quoted above, the hautboy would surely function best in its proper context. But who knew exactly what that was? Players needed information on historical pitch levels and tuning systems, for instance, as well as knowledge of phrasing, articulation, dynamics and so on that had been used on the instrument. Even if that information existed somewhere (and much of it apparently did not and does not), it had at that time not yet been found. There isn't an hautboist alive who would not be glad to have more knowledge of the historical aspects of the instrument, and every player knows those moments of being obliged to produce musical results while lacking relevant documentation on how some detail was originally dealt with. Our understanding of how the few surviving original instruments actually played is also limited. Unlike strings, few old hautboys are regularly played nowadays. Originals are rare, expensive, fragile, and often in only partially playable condition, and most are now owned by museums that are more interested in preserving them than hearing them (on wind instruments, the two activities can easily conflict). But even when every possible parameter of playing has been researched, the musical decisions that remain for the player are vast. Modern hautboists are thus something like writers of historical novels. Just as a novel must have a form, plot and characters even when some of the historical evidence is missing, a successful performance of a piece of early music must play all the notes and make sense to a modern audience.

At present, the original concern to recreate a performing style that corresponds with historical practice has been largely replaced by one that has grown up over the last generation and that could be called 'postmodern', as it casually borrows and mixes elements from various periods. Few players in Baroque orchestras nowadays have read or studied Quantz, for instance, but they have usually had lessons from an older performer who has interpreted Quantz for them. While these players have no objections to incorporating earlier stylistic traits in their performance, neither do they consider it essential. A new, modern style is thus coalescing that is associated with early music but in fact shares many practices and assumptions with musicians in traditional Classical symphony orchestras (whose performing style is also gradually mutating). Just as there is usually no guarantee that one is really buying 'organic' products at the health-food store, faithfulness to historical practices and performing spirit is an open question in the CD bins, regardless of labels like 'authentic' and 'original'.

As the boundaries of period playing have expanded forward in time, other kinds of historical oboe have begun to be played. Performances of Classical orchestral and chamber music often use so-called 'Classical hautboys' with many added keys (which more accurately resemble the instruments in use in the first half of the nineteenth century). Regardless of the number of non-historical keys, the revival of the Classical hautboy has had as yet mixed results, parallel to the often unsatisfactory copies of the fortepiano in its first generation.

And, in the face of the existing recordings of the lush and formidable sounds of Romantic symphony orchestras and their present-day descendants, orchestras of period instruments have also tackled symphonic repertoire by Beethoven, Berlioz, Mendelssohn, Schubert and even Wagner and Verdi, with mixed results.[53] At the very least, such performances give some idea of what kinds of sonorities these composers worked with, and show the instrumentarium of the symphony orchestra in a new light. Although most investigations of Romantic solo repertoire have been undertaken on the Conservatoire oboe, Paul Dombrecht has recorded Schumann, Pixis and Kalliwoda on a Triébert oboe.

In sum, our conception of 'the oboe' has been expanded with the arrival of historical oboes on the modern concert scene. Not only have plausible alternative forms of the instrument appeared, but their presence allows us new insight into the nature of what used to be simply 'the' oboe, the Conservatoire oboe. Acting as a mirror, they offer a comparison, and by doing so show us what is distinctive about the Conservatoire oboe, what it does especially well, and what it was never really intended to do. It is ironic that these two types of western oboe both share the condition of being simultaneously antiquated and modern, in much the same way our present musical culture creates beautiful contemporary results by looking to the past for inspiration.

WHERE OLD AND NEW INTERSECT (GEOFFREY BURGESS)

In the second half of the twentieth century a number of oboists developed concurrent interests at the opposite ends of the oboe's repertoire. For some, the rediscovery of the hautboy and its music went hand in hand with charting new paths in modern music. One of the first oboists to undertake such diverse activities was Josef Marx (1912–78). Marx emigrated from Berlin to the States with his parents at the end of World War I. He developed into one of the most experimental oboists in America at the time and always stood apart from the Tabuteau school. He played solo English horn at the Metropolitan Opera from 1943 to 1950, and in 1946 he and his first wife Beulah McGinnis founded the publishing house McGinnis and Marx which specialized in little-known wind music from the eighteenth and twentieth centuries. Many of the works printed had been performed by Marx himself with the Josef Marx Ensemble or the Columbia Group for Contemporary Music. Gunther Schuller, the horn player in the Metropolitan Opera Orchestra, was involved in some of the editions and also composed his Trio for Oboe, Viola and Horn, and Sonata for Oboe and Piano (1938–41), for Marx. Other works written for Marx include Stefan Wolpe's *Suite im Hexachord* (1936), Sonata for Oboe and Piano (1937–41) and Quartet for Oboe, Cello, Piano and Percussion (1955), Charles Wuorinen's *Composition* for piano and oboe (1965), Chamber Concerto (1965) and *Bicinium* for two oboes (1966), the version for English horn and piano of Elliott Carter's *Pastorale* (1940), and George Rochberg's *La Bocca della Verità* (1959) as well as works by Ralph Shapey.[54]

In addition to his interest in contemporary music, Marx was passionately interested in the history of his instrument and researched the hautboy before anyone had given it serious thought.[55] His seminal article 'The Tone of the Baroque Oboe' (1951) asserted the artistic value of the hautboy and had a great influence on those who began exploring the instrument in subsequent years.[56]

Other oboists built careers around both modern and early oboes. The Dutch oboist Han de Vries (1941–) is equally well known as an exponent of avant-garde music with works written for him by Louis Andriessen, Bruno Maderna, Morton Feldman and Peter Schat, for his performances of eighteenth- and nineteenth-century oboe concertos, and for assembling one of the world's most impressive collections of hautboys which de Vries has drawn on in his activities as hautboist. Jürg Schaeftlein also combined a full-time position as first oboist in the Wiener Symphoniker with participation in Nikolaus Harnoncourt's early-instrument ensemble Concentus Musicus Wien. Ronald Roseman (1933–2000) followed a particularly varied career. He stepped into Robert Bloom's position in the Bach Aria Group, played in the New York Woodwind Quintet, composed numerous works, and played shawm for over ten years in Noah Greenberg's New York Pro Musica Antiqua.[57] Of a younger generation, the English oboist Paul Goodwin (1956–) began postgraduate studies in contemporary music and composition, but switched to hautboy and studied with

Schaeftlein in Vienna. Goodwin has a substantial discography as hautboist, and has recently turned to conducting. He was responsible for the Academy of Ancient Music's first recording of a work by a living composer, John Tavener's *Eternity's Sunrise* (1999).[58]

The oboe's association with eighteenth-century repertoire has led to a number of modern works written for ensembles specializing in Baroque music including oboe and harpsichord. An early example is the Concerto for Harpsichord, Flute, Oboe, Clarinet, Violin and Cello (1923–6) by Manuel de Falla. The uncompromisingly modern writing of Elliott Carter's Sonata for Flute, Oboe, Cello and Harpsichord (1952) certainly challenged the members of the Harpsichord Quartet of New York who commissioned the work.[59] Another work for the same combination by Henry Cowell dates from 1954; Ned Rorem's *Lovers, A Narrative* (1964) is for harpsichord, oboe, cello and percussion, *Collage über B-A-C-H* (1964) by Arvo Pärt is for oboe, harpsichord, piano and strings, and Vittorio Rieti's *Partita* (1973) is for flute, oboe, string quartet and harpsichord. Works for oboe and harpsichord duo include Klaus Huber's *Noctes intelligibilis lucis* (1961) – a tour de force for both players, William Sydeman's *Variations* for oboe and harpsichord (1969), Gordon Jacob's *Sonatina* (1963) and Elizabeth Maconchy's *Bagatelles* (1972, written for Lady Barbirolli and Valda Aveling).

Jennifer Fowler (*Lament*, 1987), Drake Mabry (*6.15.86 for Baroque oboe*, 1986), Benjamin Thorne (*Segalloc*, 1983) and Marc Mellits (*11 Miniatures*, 1996) are among several to have composed music in contemporary idiom for the hautboy; Thorne and Mabry specify multiphonics; Fowler and Mellits are more conservative in their requirements.

Themes in contemporary oboe music

THE POETIC OBOE

The oboe's 'speaking' quality has inspired several modern composers to write works for it with strong ties to poetic texts. Sometimes, as with Vaughan Williams's *Ten Blake Songs* written originally for the film *The Vision of William Blake* (1958), the oboe is used to accompany a singer.[60] On other occasions the oboe is used to emulate the articulateness of a poetic text. 'Limerick', the fifth of Gordon Jacob's *Bagatelles* for solo oboe (1971), is literally a musical 'transcription' of the rhythm and inflection of a popular Irish poetic form (music ex. 9.8).

Britten's *Six Metamorphoses after Ovid* (1951) is certainly the archetype of solo oboe works with an underlying poetic text. At its première, one listener commented that the oboist Joy Boughton played 'with all the incisive gusto of a good story teller',[61] a fitting compliment for performance of a work that metamorphoses Ovid's poetry into single-line musical character pieces. Britten prefaced each movement by a précis of the myth. The incessant triplet rhythm in the second piece, Phaeton – 'who rode upon the chariot of the sun for one day and was hurled into the river Padus by a thunderbolt' – suggests the galloping of the horses that carry the chariot. The music

Ex. 9.8 Jacob, 'Limerick' from *Bagatelles for Oboe Solo.*

becomes agitated, Phaeton loses his nerve, and as the music crashes down to low B♭ we can imagine horses and chariot hurtling with him towards the earth. The triplet rhythm is metamorphosed by the addition of slurs, suggesting the river receiving Phaeton's body.

Other composers developed less precise connections between poetry and music when writing for the oboe. Based on Rainer Maria Rilke's *Sonette an Orpheus*, Elliott Carter's *Inner Song* for solo oboe (1992) is less a literal transcription of the poem than a musical depiction of the mood represented by the line 'Where words give out into the inexpressible'.[62] Similarly, Holliger expressed the solitary desperation of Georg Trakl's poem *Siebengesang* in his piece for oboe, harp and orchestra of the same name (1966–7). As well as providing the general tone for the work, the poem is sung by a female chorus, but in a radicalized form. The text is rendered virtually incomprehensible through fragmentation and being drawn out over extremely long note values. George Rochberg's *La Bocca della Verità* (1955) has an even less direct literary connection. The title, added after composition, refers loosely to the oboe's eloquent nature. The composer explained: 'paraphrasing Loren Eisely's remark "man is an oracular animal", the oboe has always been, for me, an "oracular" instrument'.[63]

Discours III (1969) by Globokar, for oboe soloist accompanied by another four oboes (live or pre-recorded), is based on Baudelaire's sonnet *Correspondances* with its reference to the sweet pastoral oboe ('Doux comme les hautbois, vert comme les prairies').[64] Perversely, the piece is not at all gentle in nature, but literally deconstructs Baudelaire's text. As the composer has written, 'the character of the piece is, in the main, aggressive, resting on the verge of satiety'.[65] Over the course of the work, the oboists must 'recite' Baudelaire's poem in a variety of forms (*discours* means variously lecture, recitation or discourse). The score bears the instructions:

> When performing *Discours*, faithful adherence to the phonetic structure of the text is of major importance and the latter should be treated as a guide and source of reference throughout. Whilst playing, the soloist should attempt to articulate each individual word: timbre of syllables, vowels, and consonants and appropriate speech rhythm. The overall effect which the player should try to create is not a 'played' performance, but rather a recitation.

Baudelaire's poem is introduced into the music in a number of ways. In addition to requiring the players to have the poem as a 'mind set', at one point the fourth and fifth oboists are directed to use their instruments and/or voices to give 'a phonetic

Ex. 9.9 Globokar, *Discours III* (Peters, 1972).

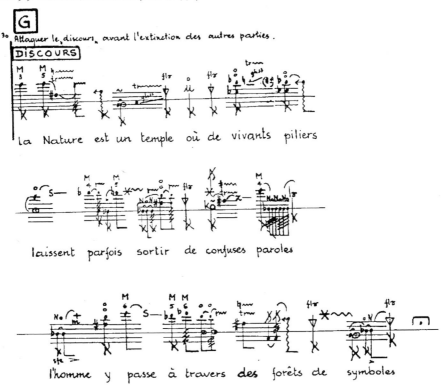

interpretation of the text, reproducing the colour of the syllables, the consonants, vowels articulation, inflections', at another the first player is given an exact musical transcription of the phonetics of the poem (see music ex. 9.9), and later all the players recite the text as fast as possible.

'LIKE A DIAULOS': ECHOES OF NARCISSUS

The fifth of the *Metamorphoses after Ovid* depicts Narcissus gazing into his own reflection in the stream (music ex. 9.10a). Britten devised a counterpoint between Narcissus's melody played *mf* in the oboe's middle and lower registers and his Echo, a *pp* mirror-inversion in a higher tessitura. The two entities gradually become more distinct until suddenly the music is interrupted by a trill which, like a pebble thrown into a still pond, shatters the echoing reflection and leaves Narcissus alone gazing at the spreading ripples.

Britten's two-part writing in 'Narcissus' maximizes the oboe's dynamic range which, while not as extensive as that of other instruments, is shown to best advantage by juxtaposing the extremes of loud and soft. In addition to its aptness for the programme of the piece, the two-part writing in 'Narcissus' echoes the dual personality of the hautboy. As Banister put it, the hautboy 'goes as easy and as soft as the flute . . . and not much inferior to the trumpet', an effect that Bach put to vivid use in the 'Echo' aria in part 4 of the *Christmas Oratorio*, where both the melody and

Ex. 9.10 Two-part writing for solo oboe: a) Britten, 'Narcissus' from *Six Metamorphoses after Ovid*; b) Castiglioni, *Alef*; c) Antoniou, 'Like a diaulos' from *Five Likes*; d) Exton, 'Ostinato'; e) Doráti, 'Fugue à trois voix' from *Cinq pièces pour le hautbois*.

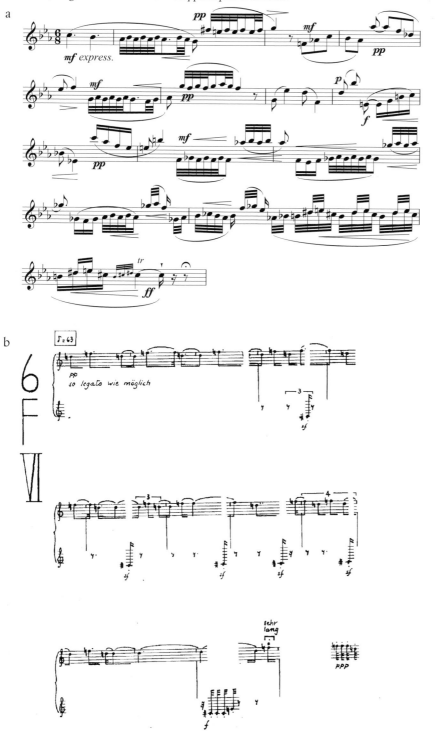

Ex. 9.10 continued

its echo are played by the one instrument (while the vocal echo is supplied by a second soprano).

Since 'Narcissus', two-part writing has become a feature of solo oboe music. In Nicolò Castiglioni's *Alef*, obstinate *ff* low c♯s interrupt a *pp* oscillating figure (music ex. 9.10b). In the third movement of Theodore Antoniou's *Five Likes* (1971), the oboist is directed to play two oboes simultaneously in imitation of the ancient Greek *aulos* (music ex. 9.10c). (The second instrument can be a 'Baroque oboe' with the three top holes blocked, so by operating the right-hand holes the two instruments can be played in counterpoint.) John Exton's *Three Pieces for Solo Oboe* (1972) concludes with an 'Ostinato' where an insidious, climbing chromatic gesture alternates with lyrical phrases and, in the middle section, interrupts a recollection of the theme from the preceding 'Siciliano' (music ex. 9.10e). Wilfred Josephs's *Solo Oboe Piece* (op. 84, 1973) explores different modes of dialogue between two unequal voices. It is written throughout on two staves: the top one marked *fff possibile, quasi martellato*, the lower *ppp possibile* (music ex. 9.10d). Contrapuntal writing for solo oboe is carried a step further in Antál Doráti's *Cinq pièces pour le hautbois* (1980–1), where the third movement is a three-voice fugue.[66]

AULOKITHARA/KITHARAULOS: THE OBOE AND HARP

The *aulos* and *kithara* of ancient Greece represented opposite spirits. The savage, untamed wind instrument was often pitted against the refined lyre. The twentieth century saw a marriage of these opposites in at least two oboe and harp duos: Leon Goossens and his sisters Marie and Sidonie, and more prominently Heinz Holliger and his wife Ursula. The Goossenses played transcriptions of lighter music and inspired a few works,[67] whereas the Holligers brought attention to this instrumental combination by exploring new techniques in numerous works that celebrate their musical union.

Aulokithara and its companion piece *Kitharaulos* (1971)[68] by the Viennese composer Ernst Krenek are but two compositions that combine the inherently incompatible oboe and harp. Others are Holliger's own *Siebengesang* (1966–7) and Trio for Oboe or Cor anglais, Viola and Harp (1971), Double Concertos by Hans Werner Henze (1966), Alfred Schnittke (1971), Witold Lutosławski (1979–80) and Isang Yun (1977), *Trois Danses* (1970) by Frank Martin and *Spiele* (1965) by Hans-Ulrich Lehmann. Because of the disparity in the dynamic levels of the two instruments, the combination can pose balance problems. Most composers retain each instrument's traditional role by writing animated, melodic and occasionally violent parts for the oboe in opposition to more subdued harmonic and accompanimental parts for the harp.

JAZZ — NEW AGE — FUSION

The oboe has never had a strong connection with jazz. Around the 1930s some manufacturers produced oboes with saxophone fingerings to encourage doublers to develop proficiency on oboe, but their efforts did not lead to an increased use of the oboe in popular musics.[69] Apart from its association with élitist music culture, what prevented the oboe from more widespread engagement in jazz is its limited capacity to compete with the volume of the standard jazz instruments, saxophone, trumpet and flugelhorn.

Jazz influence is nevertheless apparent in some oboe works, such as Françaix's *L'Horloge de flore* (1963) with its unabashed references to Rag and Boogie, Alec Wilder's Oboe Concerto (1957) and Sonata (1969),[70] and more recently John Harbison's Oboe Concerto written in 1991–2 for William Bennet of the San Francisco

Symphony. To Bennet's request for an 'apocalyptic swing number', Harbison responded with a work that blends Coplandesque modernism, Stravinskian Neo-Classical harmonies and Gershwinesque jazz. Even though the names of the three movements are reminiscent of Baroque forms, the prominent influences derive from popular musical styles that take the oboe into sonic territories where it has rarely ventured. Harbison discussed the possibilities of jazz techniques on the oboe with Bennet, but left a good deal up to the performer's taste. In his recording, Bennet adds numerous glissandi and a jazzy feel that cannot be captured in notation.

While the oboe has never 'made it' in pure jazz, it has appeared a little more in fusion styles. African-American Yusef Lateef, one of the earliest exponents of jazz fusion – in his case with Middle-Eastern influences – featured oboe on a number of his tracks. Mitch Miller appeared with Roger Mozian around 1950, and imitated an ethnic shawm in 'Desert Dance' (also known as 'Cleopatra Rhumba'). Paul McCandless, whose father and grandfather were oboe-playing doublers and he himself a Robert Bloom pupil, is best known for his performances with the veteran New Age-minimalist-jazz ensemble Oregon (founded 1970). Tracks on the group's recent disc *Oregon in Moscow* (2000) demonstrate McCandless's phenomenal fluency on oboe, English horn, soprano sax and bass clarinet and make one wonder why double reeds were ever strangers to popular music. McCandless extends the oboe's traditional lyrical idiom with pitch slides, timbral modulation, and licks of dazzling virtuosity. In his own composition, *Spanish Stairs*, McCandless takes up the English horn to create a particularly atmospheric quality, and in *Freeform Piece for Orchestra and Improvisors* by Ralph Towner, he incorporates avant-garde techniques as well as more jazz-style improvisation.

POSTMODERNISM AND BEYOND

As we move into the twenty-first century, the postwar avant-garde takes on increasing historical distance. What name (if any) can be given to the present style? The most commonly used label is Postmodernism.[71] Applied to a wide range of arts from architecture to cultural studies, this term carries with it a growing disillusion with the coining of names for any style period. Unlike most previous artistic movements, including the avant-garde of the 1960s, postmodernity does not represent a clean breach from what preceded. Rather than denying its antecedents, it quite unabashedly thematizes its origins, consciously emulating and parodying what came before. Despite its pervasiveness and often reactionary political agendas, much postmodern art retains a self-reflexive and critical stance that brings new awareness to the conventions and styles that it embraces. It is particularly in this alternative sense that I use the term.

In music, Postmodernism is often identified with a return to tonal procedures and the repetitive games of minimalism. Being based in the USA where oboe playing has tended to be conservative, the minimalist movement in music has contributed little to the oboe repertoire. The minimalist aesthetic is also present in the contemplative works of Arvo Pärt, such as the *St John Passion* (1982) scored for SATB plus oboe, bassoon, violin, cello and organ, reminiscent of Stravinsky's *Cantata* which also features an oboe prominently. Other oboe music that fits the postmodern model often involves playful quotation and parody from the Baroque, one of postmodernity's favourite salvage yards.

Anachronie II by Louis Andriessen (1968–9, dedicated to Han de Vries) could be described as the paradigmatic postmodern oboe concerto. The work, which the composer calls *musique d'ameublement* ('wallpaper music'),[72] refers to the anachronistic musical styles that had become the mainstay of the oboe soloist in the 1960s. Although Andriessen abstains from direct quotation in *Anachronie II*, listeners would be forgiven for thinking that he has borrowed from Vivaldi, Albinoni (performed in slick I Musici fashion) or Cimarosa (in Barbirolli's arrangement); other passages sound like Stravinskian reworkings of Pergolesi that didn't make it to *Pulcinella*, the kitsch sentimentality of Michel Legrand or the overwrought melodrama of 1930s soundtracks.

The collage assembled by Andriessen in *Anachronie II* seems to sketch an overview of the oboe's past life. The middle section is a mini concerto almost exclusively within the sound-world of pseudo-Pergolesi-Albinoni-Cimarosa, but this cannot be sustained for long. Its sewing-machine passage work, cadential trills and lyricism give way to dissonant multiphonics, extreme high notes and double trills. The frenetic hysteria of the culminating oboe cadenza fails to rouse any response from the orchestra. The listener is never sure where the music begins and ends, what is intended as quotation and what commentary. Is all of this simply wallpaper? If so, are there no structural walls beneath? The music returns – not to silence but to that quintessential purveyor of sonic wallpaper: the radio. At the piece's beginning and end Andriessen directs a transistor radio tuned randomly to whatever happens to be broadcast at the time of the performance: a reminder of the seminal role recording and radio played in the promotion of Classical music in the twentieth century.

The Oboe Concerto by John Corigliano is another work cast as a historical commentary on its protagonist the oboe. Written in 1975 and premièred the same year by Bert Lucarelli with the American Symphony Orchestra, this work has a shape that could be said to have been inspired by the instrument itself, as its five movements develop different aspects of the oboe's musical persona. The first movement, 'Tuning Game', takes as its theme the pre-performance ritual of the oboe bringing the orchestra together in a unison A. Its meanderings from the tonal centre echo Berio's *Sequenza VII*. The two slow movements (nos 2 and 4) are entitled 'Song' and 'Aria', but despite this indication of shared lyricism, they are not alike. Corigliano has called the former 'less hyper and less concerned with display', dealing in 'non-climactic simplicity'. The sparseness of the orchestral writing, slow pace and loose metrical feel are reminiscent of the tranquil 'music of the open spaces' of Copland and his generation, or the twentieth-century British pastoral style of Vaughan Williams. 'Aria' is cast more in the bravura *bel canto* tradition and climaxes in a dramatic cadenza. The vocabulary of this movement is unashamedly Romantic, and more than anything, is evocative of Strauss's oboe concerto. Framed by these two slow movements is a more animated Scherzo, in which the oboe is accompanied by piano, percussion and harp. The idiom is avant-garde with aleatoric rhythmic elements, although the random appearance of multiphonics and other extended techniques sound like 'effects' and the whole like an imitation of, rather than a committed engagement with, avant-garde aesthetics.

As we enter the twenty-first century, where do these diverse streams lead the oboe? Certainly to territory yet uncharted. To paraphrase what Kurt Birsak has written of the clarinet:

> The idea that each of the widely differing kinds of oboe playing has meaning in its own age and context is an integral part of our thinking. Thus, instead of resigning ourselves to the statement that the history of the oboe in the twentieth century has nothing new to offer us, we should appreciate that we have at last begun to realise the full scope of the instrument.[73]

'Crossover' styles uniting elements of contemporary popular music of the present with other styles, like non-Western musical traditions or western art music of the past, are becoming increasingly prevalent. *Blues for D.D.*, a recent release by Diana Doherty, principal oboist with the Sydney Symphony Orchestra, is a compilation of traditional twentieth-century oboe music and blues by Jeffrey Agrell. Do Hong Quan's *Four Pictures* (*Bon buc tranh,* 2001) for oboe, percussion and piano draw on Vietnamese folk-music idioms. Alfred Schnittke's *Moz-art* (1995) for oboe, harp, harpsichord, violin, cello and bass is a pastiche (de)constructed from music by Mozart. A new Oboe Concerto (2000) written by David Mullikin for Peter Cooper of the Colorado Symphony incorporates Beatles tunes and a theme from Strauss's *Don Juan. Free-form Piece for Orchestra and Improvisors* by Oregon's Ralph Towner draws on the language of the avant-garde oboe. And Brenda Schuman-Post's *Oboe of the World* is a sampling of jam sessions with percussionists from around the globe.

Will there be some oboe of the future that will borrow and unite aspects from several past designs in order to play a music not yet imagined? With what sounds will this oboe, like Gabriel's hautboy-oboe in the celluloid rainforests of *The Mission*, break the silence in a musical terrain still to be colonized?

Appendix 1

Dimensions for ten reeds, 1691–c.1767

Dimensions in mm for reeds, from among the clearest surviving works of art, 1691 to c.1767. For Mignard, see ill. 19; for Stockholm, see ill. 26; for Aguilar, see ill. 32. The other works are reproduced in Haynes 2001.

Date	ID	Tip width	Cane L	EL staple	Type
1691	Mignard	15.1	23.2	25.6	A2
c.1700	Anon.	10.9	19.6	19.7	A2
1704	Bouys	16.7			A2
c.1705	Anon. chalk	9.2	24.2	22.4	A2
c.1720	Anon. Berlin	10.2	23.5	26.1	A2
1722	Delft	14.0	22.5	47.0	A2
1738	Eisel	11.4	22.8	30.6	A2
c.1750	Stockholm		26.5 to 27.6	32.0 to 33.4	E
1752	Lazzari	11.8	18.5	22.8	C
c.1767	S. Aguilar	7.2	24	34	D1

Appendix 2

Collation of fingering charts

This collation includes only charts from the 'Baroque' period; cf. also Haynes (1978). The charts are identified as follows: Bi – Bismantova, 1688; Ba – Banister, 1695; L1 – La Riche (see Talbot, c.1692); L2 – La Richae (see Talbot, c.1692); S – *Second Book of Theatre Music*, 1699; F – Freillon-Poncein, 1700; H – Hotterterre, 1707; E – Eisel, 1738

c1	123 456 8	Bi Ba L1 L2 ('loud'),[1]
		S F H E
c#1	123 456 8	Bi
	123 456 8	Ba L2 ('soft'),[2] F
	123 456 8	L1 ('louder')
d♭1	123 456 8	Bi
	123 456 8	F
d1	123 456	Bi Ba L1 L2 S F H E
d#1	123 456 7	Bi[3] Ba L1 L2 F H E
	123 45 7	S[4]
e♭1	123 456 7	Bi Ba[5] F H
	123 45 7	L1 L2 S[6]
e1	123 45	Bi Ba L1 L2 S F H E
e#1	123 4 6	Bi F
f♭1	123 45	F
f1	123 4 6	Bi Ba[7] F H
	123 4 6 7	L1 L2 S E
f#1	123 4	Bi
	123 4 7	S H
	123 4	L1 L2[8]
	123 4 6	Ba F (H)
	123 5	E (also in upper octave)
g♭1	123 4	Bi
	123 4 6	F H
g1	123	Ba L1 L2 H E
	123 6	Bi S F
g#1	123 4 6	Bi
	123	Ba L1[9] S H
	123 6	F
	12 4	E

a♭1	123	Ba L1 L2 H
	123 6	Bi F
	12 4	S
a1	12	Ba L1 L2 H E
	12 6	Bi S F
a#1	1 3	F
	1 3 6	Bi
	1 3 4 6	L1[10]
	1 3 45	H
b♭1	1 3	Ba F E
	1 3 6	Bi S
	1 3 4 6	L1 L2
	1 3 45	H
b1	1	Ba L1 L2 H E
	1 6	Bi S F
b#1	2 6	F
c♭2	1 6	F
c2	2	Ba L1 L2 H E
	2 6	Bi S F
c#2	123 456 8	Bi[11]
	23 456 8	Ba L1 L2 S H
	+23 456 8	F
	3 7	E
d♭2	123 456 8	Bi
	23 456 8	H
	+23 456 8	F
d2	123 456	Ba (L2) S F E
	+23 456	L1 ('loud')[12]
	23 456	Bi H (as on traverso)

From this point on up the scale, L1, L2
and S require louder blowing

d♯2	123 456 7	Bi[13] Ba L2 S F H E
	₊23 456 7	L1
e♭2	123 456 7	Bi Ba L2 S F H
	₊23 456 7	L1
e2	123 45	Bi Ba L1 L2 S F H E
e♯2	123 4 6	Bi F
f♭2	123 45	F
f2	123 4 6 7	Ba L1 L2 S E
	123 4 6	Bi F H
f♯2	123 4	Bi
	123 4 7	H
	123 56	Ba L1 ('flat') S F H
	123 ₊	L1 ('sharp') L2
	123 5	E
g♭2	123 4	Bi
	123 56	F H L2
g2	123	Ba L1 L2 S H E
	123 6	Bi F
g♯2	12 4 6	Bi
	12₊	Ba L1 L2 S H
	12₊ 6	F
	12 4	E
a♭2	12₊ 6	Bi F
	12 4	Ba L1 L2 S
	12₊	H
a2	12	Ba L1 L2 S H E
	12 6	Bi
	12 6 8	F (possibly to help response)

a♯2	1 3 6 8	Bi
	1 3	F H
b♭2	1 3 6	Bi
	1 3	Ba L1 L2 S F H E
b2	1 6	Bi
	1	Ba H E
	2	L1 L2 S F
b♯2	2	F
c♭3	2	F
c3	2 6	Bi
	-o-	Ba ('all open', 'blow hard') L1 ('all open') L2 ('open all') S F H (H; this is not his traverso fingering)
	456	
	2 7	E
c♯3	6 8	Bi
	23 4 8	E
	23 4 6 8	F
	456	H (= c3, but 'en forcant le vent & serrant l'Anche avec les Levres') Note lack of ₊
d♭3	23 4 6 8	F
	23 456 8	H ('en forcant le vent & serrant l'Anche avec les Levres')
d3	23 8	F (E)
	23 456	Bi H

NOTES

1. The c1 and c♯1 fingerings are evidently reversed.
2. The c1 and c♯1 fingerings are evidently reversed.
3. Bi gives 123 456 8 but this is probably a mistake.
4. Cf. S, L1 and L2 on e♭1.
5. Unlike the d♯1 fingering, 6 is mistakenly left open here.
6. This appears to be a mistake, as it is the fingering for e natural and adding 7 raises it slightly rather than lowering it. It is interesting that the mistake (if it is one) is shared by these three sources.
7. The f1 and f♯1 fingerings are transposed on the chart.
8. Given as 23 4, which appears to be a mistake as it produces c2.
9. L2 gives ₊ 3 ₊ 6, but this is probably a mistake. Cf. L2 on a♭1.
10. Not provided in L2.
11. This produces g2 as a harmonic.
12. L2 gives 123 ₊, which is probably a mistake.
13. Bi gives 123 456 8 but this is probably a mistake.

Appendix 3

The use of keys on nineteenth-century oboes as shown in method books, c.1815–90

KEY TO APPENDIX 3

—	note not included in chart
K	key
f	forked fingering
=	same fingering for enharmonic equivalents (A♭ and G♯)
B	key activated by brille
S	short fingering for notes a2–c3
S/K	a short fingering involving a key
H	harmonic fingering
I, II	indicate first and second octave keys
C	the great key used for c♯2
C♯	C♯ key used for c♯2

parentheses indicate alternative fingerings

fingerings are given in order as they appear in the charts, so '*f*K' indicates that the forked fingering is given as the primary fingering, and the keyed fingering as a secondary or alternative fingering

	Bb0	B0	c1	c#1/db1	d1	d#1/eb1	e1	f1	f#1	g1	g#1	a1	a#1/bb1	b1	c2	c#2/db2	d2	d#2/eb2	e2	f2	f#2	g2	g#2/ab2	a2	a#2/bb2	b2	c3	highest note	register keys
Vogt 1816–25	–	–		–					K																			g3	none
Sellner 1825	–		–	K				Kf	K	=	K3	=	Kf =	Kf	(K) tr	C# =				Kf	f	=	K3 =	(H)	H (K) =	H (S)	H	a3	used for slurring & from e3
Brod 1825	–		–	K				fK	K	=	3	=	K =		f (K)	C =				fK	f	=	3 =		H (K)	H	H	g3	none
Schott c.1825	–		–	K				fK	K		3K	=	fK	fK	fK	C =				fK	f	=	3K =	(H)	H =	H	H	g#3	used as slur key & e3–g#3
Vény 1828	–		–	K				K	K	=	3		K	K	K	C =				f	f	=	3 =		H K =	H	H	g3	none
Brod 1830	–	K	K	K					K							C =								(H)				g3	none shown
Raoulx 1841	–		–	K				fK	K	=	K	=	K =			C =				fK			K =	S	K =	H	H	g3	none
Fahrbach 1843	–		–	K				Kf	K	=	K3	=	Kf	=	f (K)	C =				Kf	Kf	=	K3 =	S	K (H) (H) =	S (H)	H (S/K)	a3	used from e3
Miller 1843	–		–	K				K	K	=	K3	=	K	K	f (K)	C# =				fK	fK	=	K3 =	S	H (K/S) =	S	H (S/K)	g3	as octave key f2–b2 (short fingerings) & f3–g3
Vény 1844–51	–		–	K				Kf B	B	=	K3	=	K	B K C		C# =	C#			fK	fB	=	3K =	(H)	S/K (H) =	S/K (H)	H (S/K)	g3	2: 1st used for slurring and from e3; 2nd for short fingerings a#2–c3

continued on following pages

	Kastner 1844 French	Kastner 1844 11 keys	Belpasso 1850	Le Dhuy 1850	Barret 1850	Cappelli 1853	Verroust 1857	Asioli 1857	Bretonnière 1867
register keys	none	used from eb3	slur key, and eb and e keys used eb3–f#3	none	2: 1st f2–b2 on short fingerings; 2nd c#3–g3	2: 1st f2–a2 & e3–g3; 2nd a#2–c3 (short fingerings only)	used for f2–c3	used for e3–g3	2: 1st used presumably for slurring & e3–g3; 2nd for short fingerings a#2–c3
highest note	g3	g#3	f#3	g3	g3	g3	eb3	g#3	g3
c3	H	H / –II	H	H	H S / –II	H S	K/S	H	H / S/K
b2	H	H S	S H	H	H S / –I	S H	(H)	H	H S
bb2			=	H K		=	=	=	=
a#2	S/K	H S	S H	H	H / S/KI	S H	K/S	H	K/S / H
a2	(H)	(H)	(H)	S	S / (I)	S H	(H)	(H)	(H)
ab2	=	=	=	=	=	=	=	=	=
g#2	K	K3 / ƒ	K	3	K / I	3K	K	3K	K3
g2		=			(I)				
f#2	ƒ	ƒ	ƒ	ƒ			ƒ	ƒ	
f2	ƒK	Kƒ / ƒ	ƒK	fK	Kƒ Kƒ / I I–	ƒK	ƒK	ƒK	ƒK ƒB
e2									
eb2									
d#2									
d2									
db2	=	=	=	=	=	=	=	=	C
c#2	C	C#	C		C#	C#	C	C	C#
c2	ƒK	Kƒ (K tr)		fK	(K)	(K)	(K)	ƒK	ƒK
b1									
bb1	=	=	=	=	=	=	=	=	=
a#1	K	Kƒ	K	K	Kƒ	Kƒ	Kƒ	ƒK	Kƒ
a1									
ab1	=	=	=	=	=	=	=	=	=
g#1	K	K3	K	3	K3	K3	K	3K	K3
g1									
f#1	K	K	K (eb key)	K	B	B	B	no key	B
f1	ƒK	Kƒ	ƒK	f K	Kƒ	Kƒ	ƒK	ƒK	Kƒ
e1									
d#1 /eb1									
d1									
c#1	K	K	K	K	K	K	K	K	K
c1	K	K	K	K	K	K	K	K	K
B0	K	K	K	–	K	K	K	⌐	K
Bb0	–	–	–	–	K	–	–	–	–

V. Chalon 1877																																					
8 keys	–	–		K				*f*K	(K)			3	=		K	=		*f*K	C	=					*f*K	*f*	=		3	=	?	K?		H	H	g3	none
9–10 keys	–	K		K				*f* K	(K)			3 K	=		K	=		*f* K	C?	=					*f* K	K*f*	=		K3	=	?	H S/K		S H	S/K	g3	1 used for short fingerings a♯2–c3, for alt. fingerings c♯3–eb3 & e3–g3
11–15 keys	–	K		K				*f*K	BK	=		3 K	=		K	=		*f*K	C♯	=					*f*K	K*f*	=		K3	=	?	S H		S H	H S/K	g3	1 used optionally e2–e♭3 & e♭3–g3
Wieprecht 1877	–	K		K				K*f*	B	=		K	=		K*f*	=		*f*	C♯	=					K*f*	K	=		K	=	(H)	H K	=	H S	H H	a3	1 used for f2–a♯2, on b2 short fingering and from e3–a3
Kling 1887	–	K		K				K*f*	B			K			K*f*			*f*	C♯						K*f*	B*f*			K		(H)		S/K H	H S	H H	a3	e2–b2 (short fingerings) & e3–a3
Brod rev. Gillet 1890, *système 6*	K	K		K				K*f*	B	=		K	=		K/ B			K/ B*f*	C♮	=					K*f*	B			K	=			K/B	S H	S/K H	g3	1:1st used for e2–g♯2 & e3–g3; 2nd a2–c3, except harmonic fingerings
Pietzsch c.1890																																					
German	–	K		K				K*f*	B	=		K	=		K*f*			*f*	C♯	=					K*f*	B*f*			K	=	S H		H K/S	H S	H (8)	a3	1 used for e2–c3, e3–a3
French	–	K		K				K	B			K			K			K	C♯						K	B			K			K		H	S/K	g3	2:1st used e♭2–g♯2, 2nd a2–c3
Küffner c.1890	–	K		K				K	B			K			K			*f*	C♮	=					K	K			K			H	H S – *8*	H	H	a3	1 used e♭2–a2 & e3–a3

Notes

Introduction

1. Libin 2000:196, where there is an interesting discussion of this subject.
2. Harnoncourt 1988:74.
3. There have been absolute technical 'improvements' in woodwinds, though none that have any major bearing on how instruments were played. Riveting the spring to the key touchpiece rather than attaching it to the instrument body is an example (see Myers 1981:59–60). Another is the commercial distribution of cork, starting in the late eighteenth century, which made it available for tenons in place of the older thread windings.
4. Libin 2000:211.
5. Adlung 1758:590.
6. The term appeared in Barret's method (1850), Corder 1896, in programme notes written by Georges Longy in 1900, and the English translation of Rosenthal's *Oboe Schule* (1901). The editors of the *Musical Times* allowed it into at least the 1880s.
7. Halfpenny used 'hautboy' to refer to seventeenth- and eighteenth-century oboes starting in 1949, and later Philip Bate expressed some misgivings about using the label Baroque oboe (1975:vi).

Chapter 1 The prehistory of the oboe

1. Quoted in Guichon 1874:28. All translations are our own unless otherwise stated.
2. See Olsen and Shechy 1998:II:453.
3. Olsen and Shechy 1998:II:727.
4. Olsen and Shechy 1998:II:576.
5. H. S. Williamson, quoted without citation in Bate 1975:3.
6. These themes will be revisited in chapter 7 in the context of Romantic and Modernist musical traditions.
7. 1998:209.
8. 1981:16.
9. Jung 1986.
10. 1940:38.
11. 1940:72.
12. Chorley 1882:12.
13. David Matthews draws on this myth in his piece for oboe and strings entitled *The Flaying of Marsyas* (for a recording, see Discography).
14. Lemprière, *Classical Dictionary* (orig. pub. 1788), 'Marsyas', 258–9.
15. 1913–27:col.1528.

16. 1976:4.
17. See, e.g., Lemprière 1984 (1788). Filippo Bonanni's *Gabinetto Armonico* (1716) was exceptional for identifying them as antique trumpets (*tromba antica espressa nel Campidoglio*).
18. Longinius, trans. Boileau, *Traité du sublime* (1674) in Boileau-Despreaux 1966:394.
19. Fétis was eager to inform Verdi of his findings on the music of ancient Egypt, but the composer decided to take his own course. See Verdi's letter to Count Arrivabene (quoted in Sachs 1940:99, and Goossens and Roxburgh 1977:7).
20. 1940:138.
21. *Histoire et Théorie de la Musique antique*, quoted in Bleuzet 1913–27:1527.
22. 1940:138.
23. Bate 1969:59.
24. Baines shows drawings based on specimens in the Brussels Conservatoire that have been taken as unambiguous evidence that these instruments were double-reed (1967:193).
25. Marcuse discusses the case of the Pompeiian fresco in the British Museum (1975:655); and the uncanny resemblance between the *tibiae* in a fresco at the Villa Ammendola and the *ciaramella*, an Italian double-reed folk instrument still in use in the vicinity, is questioned by Montagu (1988).
26. Barker 1984:I:188–9.
27. Marcuse 1975:656. See also Jung 1986:6.
28. See Bélis 2001.
29. This is suggested by Plutarch; see Kachermarchik 1994:93.
30. Sachs 1940:72; see also Geiringer 1943:60.
31. 1974:169.
32. 1966:120–9.
33. Many non-Western cylindrical-bored double reeds behave as conical-bored instruments and overblow the octave. See Rimmer 1976:108 and Schneider 1986:88.
34. 1752: art. 'Hautbois'.
35. 1913–27:1530. Bleuzet suggested that, as the cane used for the reeds of these instruments was very spongy and soft, it was incapable of supporting direct pressure from the player's lips. He may have known of Villoteau's report of Egyptian shawms in 1809:940 (discussed below).
36. 1977:9.
37. *Halil* appears in 1 Samuel 10:5, 1 Kings 1:40, Isaiah 5:12; 30:29 and Jeremiah 48:36.
38. The Revised Standard Version (1952) uses 'flute' and 'pipe' inconsistently.
39. For a more detailed account of the characteristics and functions of both *halil* and *hatzotzerot* see J. Braun 2002:13–17.
40. The King James Version gives the former; Coverdale's 1535 translation and the Anglican prayerbook of 1662 give 'shawmes'.
41. From Guichon, 'Le hautbois', 18. The Vulgate uses 'tubis' and 'bucinae'. Other nineteenth-century French translations were more accurate and mentioned only 'trompettes' and 'cornet' or 'cor' (see, for instance, *La Sainte Bible* 1836).
42. Sachs was one of the first writers to present this evidence (1940:288).
43. Kudsi Erguner has undertaken some research to uncover the pre-nineteenth-century tradition of the Janissary band. His recording, *The Janissaries*, provides an overview of the repertoire.
44. 1975:12.
45. 1975:30.
46. Baines and Kirnbauer 2001.
47. 1943:170.
48. Geiringer was comparing the shawm's bore with that of the modern French oboe. Paul Hailperin (1970) has shown that there is actually little difference in the bore profile of shawms and the earliest hautboys.

49. 1943:82.
50. Lip contact with the reed is also part of the technique of some non-Western shawms (Baines and Kirnbauer 2001). It is an essential part of the highly developed *shahnái* technique, and according to Schneider it is used on certain European folk instruments including *piffero, dulzaina* and *bombarde* (1986:99). The players of the *tible* and *tenora* in the Catalan *coblas* require lip control on the reed to produce the extreme high notes (Baines 1952:14–15).
51. Haynes 2001: 12–14, 23.
52. 1967:231.
53. 1975:34; see also Baines 1967:268 and Tobin 1948:46.
54. 1975:11.
55. 1588:23–4.
56. 1920:40, 43; see also Prout 1897:114. Terence MacDonagh also expressed the same opinion (Eaglefield-Hull 1924:356).
57. 1939:132.
58. 1951:16.
59. Jenkins 1983:56.
60. On the different systems of classification, see Kartomi 1990. Typical is Sachs and Hornbostel (1914), widely considered the most comprehensive universal classification, which uses the term 'oboe' to designate all double-reed pipes.
61. 1979:81, 158.
62. 1976:4.
63. 1975:12.
64. For more information on 'forked shawms' see Montagu 2001:16–17.
65. 1809:940.
66. Dick 1984:728.
67. 1956:251.
68. Schneider 1986 includes extensive lists of these categories. Photographs of many of these instruments being played can be found in the entries for the individual instruments and their respective countries in *NG2*.
69. Sachs 1940:288.
70. See Haynes 2001:37ff. and below, pp. 120–4.
71. See Ziegler 1990.
72. On French traditions, see Charles-Dominique and Laurence (2002).
73. For a list of currently available recordings see Discography, 'Cobles'. Important histories of the instruments are Capmany 1948 and Anon. 'Les Instruments de la Cobla' posted at the website of the Association Française du Hautbois (http://assoc.wanadoo.fr/hautbois/accueil.htm).

Chapter 2 *From consort oboe to 'eloquent' oboe, 1610–1680*

1. Alfred North Whitehead, *Science and the Modern World*, New York, 1925, quoted in Grout 1960:269.
2. See Baines and Kirnbauer 2001.
3. Given as 'cacbouc'; probably 'saqueboute'.
4. La Barre 'Mémoire'.
5. These are (respectively) Sebastien Le Camus, Antoine Boësset, Honoré D'Ambruys and Michel Lambert.
6. Le Camus published works in 1678, Boësset in 1617–42, D'Ambruys in 1685, 1696 and 1702, and Lambert in 1660 and 1689.
7. These new developments, initiated by Pierre de Niert, are exemplified in Michel Lambert's *Airs* published in 1660, and codified in a remarkable book by Bénigne de

Bacilly that appared in 1668 entitled *L'Art de bien chanter*.

8. 'Gleichsam redende' (Mattheson 1713:268).

9. There were other changes in design described in Haynes 2001:22–34.

10. Cf. Hailperin 1970. More study is needed to establish the relation between shawm and hautboy bores.

11. These two are based on the same original design (called a *carton*), which is now lost. Copies of it survive in several different media. The tapestry 'L'Air', also called the 'Arazzo Gobelins', was made by the Lefebvre studio in 1666–9 (see Fenaille 1903:II:51–66). It is now at Florence in the Palazzo Pitti and is called there *Allegoria dell'Aria*.

12. Prunières 1931:xxii. As Eppelsheim pointed out in 1961:104, that some form of hautboy took part in *L'Amour malade* was only conjecture by Prunières. But there seems to be no reason to dispute it. Cf. also Harris-Warrick 1990:98.

13. There were numerous members of the Hotteterre family with the same names (there are four prominent 'Jean Hotteterres', for example). In ambiguous cases, I use the genealogical numbers in Giannini 2001:754.

14. On the cromorne, see Haynes 2001:37.

15. Giannini 2001:752.

16. Pure 1668:274.

17. Hautboys were mentioned in nine operas dating from 1672 to 1685. For a detailed list, see Haynes 2001:125.

18. La Gorce 1989:109.

19. This would have been true even if two or three of the hautboists were in costume for on-stage appearances and never played in the pit.

20. North c1710–28:221. Philippe Beaussant (1992:120) speaks of a *son français* in this period, a 'typically French *sound medium*, that of a mass of strings seasoned [*corsée*] by hautboys'.

21. Eppelsheim 1961:117–20.

22. See Haynes 1997 and Haynes 2001:37–45.

23. See Haynes 2001:45.

24. For a more complete explanation of this subject, see Écochard (2001).

25. The Small-key resembled the simple close-standing side keys of the bellows-blown musette de cour, an instrument on which keys had to be used, because its 'closed' finger technique did not allow cross-fingerings.

26. Hotteterre 1737:65.

27. Talbot included a fingering chart for the treble shawm that excluded $c\sharp 1$, $d\sharp/e\flat 1$, $f1$, $g\sharp/a\flat 1$, $c\sharp 2$, $d\sharp/e\flat 2$, $f\sharp 2$, $g\sharp/a\flat 2$, whereas he gave fingerings for an entire chromatic scale for the 'French hautbois'.

28. Herbert W. Myers★. For a discussion of lower-bore resonances, see Smith 1992:29ff.

29. A similar effect was cultivated by Marcel Tabuteau on the modern French oboe by using the forked $f1$ with a disabled forked F vent, and can be heard on his recordings. (I have this from my teacher, Raymond Dusté, who studied with Tabuteau.)

30. The low $c1$ was usually sharp and had to be lipped down as well. The wide reeds seen in illustrations of the time would probably have helped.

31. These sources included authorities like Telemann, Quantz and W. A. Mozart.

32. For more background on non-keyboard tuning systems, see Barbieri 1991 and Haynes 1991.

33. Benoit 1971a:226.

34. The manuscript is described in detail in Sandman 1974.

35. A contemporary description of the job of 'Grand Hautbois' is reproduced in Benoit 1971b:453–4.

36. See Haynes 2001, ch. 1 §C.

37. Ford 1981:60.

38. Banister *Sprightly Companion*, i, ii.

39. Geoffrey and I had the pleasure of playing this opera together in Boston in 2001.
40. Banister *Sprightly Companion*, i, ii. The word 'charm' often appears in connection with the hautboy. Cf. the Prologue to Ben Jonson's play *Volpone; or, The Fox* (produced in 1676), Etherege *Man of Mode* (also 1676), and Fischer c.1780b:i.

Chapter 3 *The sprightly hautboy, 1680–1760*

1. The parallel and equally rapid adoption of the hautboy in the twentieth century, almost exactly 300 years later, is also remarkable.
2. Buttrey 1995.
3. Buttrey 1995:209.
4. See Lasocki 1988:348.
5. Bouquet 1969:13, Wind 1982:16–17, and Bernardini 1985a:3.
6. Kenyon de Pascual 1984:431; cf. also Benoit 1953–4.
7. Biber 1974:134.
8. Modern woodwind players frequently replace their instruments, even though models change much less radically than they did in the eighteenth century.
9. This terminology has been developed together with Cecil Adkins. Adkins suggests two further external comparisons of hautboys: the ratio of the baluster curve (expressed as a fraction of the baluster diameter) and the baluster apex (the height of the widest diameter divided by the length of the baluster). These two characteristics can be further quantified as a 'baluster index number', or BIN, that can be used to indicate baluster configuration. See Adkins 2001.
10. The type categories were first proposed in Halfpenny 1949.
11. Cf. Bouterse 2001:364.
12. *Caecilia de Lisorez (Vide, & Audi)* by André Bouys, reproduced in Haynes 2001.
13. They include Rippert, Jaillard (alias Bressan), Dupuis, Jean Rousselet, Rouge, Pelletier Sr, Fremont, Naust and seven Hotteterres (Jean [3] and [8], Nicolas [4] and [10], Martin, Louis [11], and Colin).
14. Sauveur 1704–16:335.
15. Cf. Giannini 1993:4, 6.
16. Cf. my Couperin recording (ATMA) using the Naust and a copy of the Hotteterre interchangeably.
17. On Colin Hotteterre, see Giannini 1987; Bowers 1980:735; Marx 1951:12; Benoit 1971a; Benoit 1971b; Semmens 1975:71; La Gorce 1989:104; Du Pradel 1692; Waterhouse 1993; La Gorce 1979:178; Dunner 1988:182.
18. Cf. Byrne 1983 and 1984.
19. Waterhouse 1993:42, 128.
20. Nickel 1971:203–6.
21. Including Böhm, Glösch, Fleischer and Rose; see more on these players below.
22. Nickel 1971:289–90.
23. Adkins implies in 2001 a line of influence from Nuremberg to Leipzig, but historical indications are few, and developments may well have been independent.
24. Van Aardenberg, Beukers Sr, Boekhout, Haka, Rÿkel, Steenbergen, and Terton. Rÿkel (who with Haka made in my opinion the best-playing Dutch hautboys) shows hautboys of Type A2 on his trade card, dated 1705.
25. Acoustic profiles will be discussed below.
26. This concept is a more accurate refinement of the unit I used in *The Eloquent Oboe*, which I called the acoustic length or AL. Since hautboy bells can vary in length, SL is a more reliable indicator of pitch than the overall length of an instrument.
27. Cf. Burgess and Hedrick 1989 and 1990.
28. Rome. Museo degli strumenti musicali, 0828 (1368). SL 393.2, minimum bore 5.9,

aggregate tone-hole size 14.4. Bottom badly deformed. Information from Alfredo Bernardini. The dimensions I gave for this staple in *Eloquent Oboe* were mistaken.

29. London. Horniman, 1969.683. SL 415.5, minimum bore 6.3, aggregate tone-hole size 15.9. Brass, lapped in string. Information from Paul Hailperin. According to Geoffrey Burgess, in 1986 the museum could not find this staple.

30. This information is surveyed in Haynes 2001, ch. 2, §E3.

31. Burgess and Hedrick 1989 observed all strata of cane on the lays of the late eighteenth- and early nineteenth-century hautboy reeds they measured; the parenchyma (the softest strata) generally appear on the last 2–5 mm of the tips of these reeds. A tapered gouge would presumably have eliminated the parenchyma, however (although, as Burgess* points out, whether it was eliminated entirely would depend on the relative density of the strata).

32. For a more detailed discussion of this subject, see Haynes 2001, ch. 2, §D2.

33. Hawkins 1776:V:370 n.

34. In Haynes 2002 I speculate that Sammartini played at about A–423 in the three virtuoso opera arias he played for Handel two years later in 1737, rather than at his earlier pitch (about A–415).

35. The new fingering was like the lower octave (2), whereas the older fingering charts (Banister, La Riche, *Second Book of Theatre Music*, Freillon-Poncein, and Hotteterre, dating from around the turn of the century) used the fingering 'all open'. These older charts were intended for the lower-pitched model of hautboy that had served the seventeenth century (and continued to be current in some places into the eighteenth century). Only Bismantova's chart of 1688 (which gives 2 6 for c3) was probably intended for an hautboy pitched higher than A–2 or A–1½.

36. Quantz published his book in 1752. But in 1770, Burney (who had just met him) commented that Quantz's taste was 'that of forty years ago' (= 1730).

37. Hotteterre c.1729:2.

38. There are forty-one surviving trios for hautboy and recorder.

39. For a list, see Appendix 5 in Haynes 2001. Cf. also Page 1993.

40. The last original chart before c.1770 is in Eisel 1738. For a more detailed discussion of hautboy fingerings, see Haynes 2001:201.

41. Hotteterre 1707:45.

42. There was a solo e♭3 in BWV 55/1:20 (premiered November 1726). The secular Cantata 201 included e3s and f3s, the only examples in non-unison or solo passages. Movement 1 had both notes (within a large orchestra) and movement 9 had an e3 in a solo aria, totally exposed and impossible to fake. There are a number of e3s in unison with other instruments in 17/1 (second Hautb.; Sept. 1726), 49/1 (Nov. 1726), 115/2 (Nov. 1724) and 145/3 (April 1729). There are also f3s in unison with other instruments: 120/2 (before 1729), 195/3 (before 1730), and 244/36.

43. On Bissoli, see Burney 1770:70; Burney 1771a:136, 142; Lalande 1769 (1765–6). Gerber 1790; Sartori card catalogue, Milan Conservatory; Guerrini 1934:11–12; Bernardini* 29.iv.87; Nalin 1991; Barbieri 1987:32; Bernardini 1985:22; Bernardini 1987:5, 15–16.

44. Vandenbroek 1793:58.

45. Certain trills were also complex, poorly in tune, or unpleasant in sound in the keys of A, A flat and E major and their relative minors.

46. If numbers are substituted for keys (so that one flat = –1, three flats = –3, two sharps = + 2, etc.) and the total keys are divided by the number of pieces, the average for all oboe solos for the period 1650–1800 is –0.56. Solo sonatas average –0.29, solo concertos –0.64. This is somewhere between no flats and one flat, leaning slightly toward the latter.

47. For lists of examples, see Haynes 1979 and Haynes 2001, ch. 4, §H3.

48. Mozart's hautboy quartet in F, KV 370, also appeared in its first published form as a traverso quartet in G (Vienna: Hoffmeister, 1801. See Vester 1985, M627).

49. These two extra cross-fingerings meant that the same piece was somewhat more difficult to finger on the hautboy than on the traverso, a reason amateurs would have been more likely to take up the traverso.

50. For a list, see Haynes 2001, Appendix 7.

51. In fact, if the c_1 is not tuned a little high, the $d\flat 2$ (which uses the same fingering, often minus hole 1) could not be played high enough. If c_1 is tuned low enough, $d\flat 2$ is 10 to 50 cents flat, depending on the temperament used.

52. Hotteterre, Loulié and Quantz all mentioned correcting the intonation of ornaments. See Haynes 2001, ch. 4, §G4.

53. Quantz 1752:XIV:§41 and Tab. xvii, xviii and xix. For a transcription, see Haynes 2001, ch. 4, §I2a.

54. The first known printed instructions for woodwinds by Ganassi (1535) described several forms.

55. For more on this subject see Haynes 2001, ch. 4, §J.

56. There are 28 sources extending from Ganassi (1535) to Drouet (c.1827); the most relevant are the 15 from Mersenne (1636) to Lorenzoni (1779). Most of the texts are included in the appendices of Castellani and Durante 1987.

57. Cf. Fuller 2001:197.

58. This is explained in Quantz 1752:VI/Suppl/§2.

59. See Philip 1992:139, 109–39, and ch. 5, 'Woodwind vibrato'.

60. Moens-Haenen 1988:143, 272. Some sources from the second half of the eighteenth century rejected continuous vibrato (thereby indicating its existence). There is a reference to 'zitterndem odem' in Agricola 1529, but none in the seventeenth or eighteenth centuries; cf. Dickey, Leonards and Tarr 1978:102 and Moens-Haenen 1988:83.

61. For a more complete discussion of vibrato on the hautboy, see Haynes 2001, ch. 4, §K.

62. There are many other examples in Bach; for a list see Moens-Haenen 1988:242n752.

63. Scheibe *Critische Musicus* (1745), 682–3, quoted and tr. in Swack 1988:9.

64. Cf. Haynes 1992a. This number includes only pieces in which the hautboy is specified; how many pieces hautboists borrowed from other instruments is of course unknowable.

65. Paris (MS Rés. 1397), copied out after Lully's demise by André Philidor. It is published by Heugel as *Trios pour le Coucher du Roy*, ed. by Herbert Schneider. Cf. Anthony 1988.

66. Hugo Reyne*.

67. Now held at Yale University (Filmer MS 33). See Ford 1981.

68. Although Lambert's collection is for treble and bass voices with continuo, the continuo essentially doubles the bass voice line, giving a potential solo treble and continuo texture.

69. House 1991:276ff.

70. Cf. Suite 2 (G) from the *Premier Livre* as well as 'La d'Armagnac' in Suite 1, 'Le Plaintif' in Suite 3, 'Le depart' in Suite 4, and the Sarabande in the second *Livre*, Suite 1.

71. On René Pignon dit Descoteaux, see Langwill 1980:39; Benoit 1971b; Benoit 1971a; Sandman 1974:113; Waterhouse 1993; Brossard 1965:240; La Gorce 1989:104; Powell*; Ecorcheville 1903:633ff., 637ff.; Borjon 1672:38; Huygens clxxiii. Descoteaux played in the premiere of Lully's *Thésée* in 1675.

72. On Philippe Rebillé dit Philbert, see La Barre c.1740; Marx 1951:11, 14; D'Aquin 1752:148; Mattheson 1722:114; Benoit 1971b:77, 140, 151, 200, 224, 225, 286, 298, 383, 413–15; *NGI*; La Gorce 1989:105, 109; Ecorcheville 1903:633ff, 636ff.; Harris-Warrick and Marsh 1994:30–2.

73. See Ford 1981:54–6.

74. They include more than 1500 trios, countless solo sonatas and suites, about 100 quartets, and even many concertos. The *en symphonie* concept is discussed in more detail in Haynes 2001:168.

75. The Rebel *Recueil de douze sonates* has at last been published in a modern edition in four parts (Edition Walhall).

76. Braun 1987:138–9.
77. Mattheson 1740:129.
78. McCredie 1964:159.
79. On the Henrions, see Fürstenau 1861:II:12, 19, 50; Landmann 1982:49; Oleskiewicz 1998:21, 42, 44, 645.
80. On La Riche (Le Riche), see Ashbee 1987:3–6, 18(2), 21, 24, 39–41, 122, 136, 137(2), 139; Becker-Glauch 1951:29; Byrne 1983:16; Engel 1971:48; Eitner 1898–1904; Fürstenau 1861:50, 66, 135; Gerber 1812:853; Jeans 1958a; Jeans 1958b; Kahl 1948:273; Lafontaine 1909:371–2; Lasocki 1983:33, 34 , 128, 957; Lasocki 1988:353; Quantz 1755:239; Rackwitz 1981:301, 362, 385; Sachs 1908:99, 111; Swack 1988:22; Telemann 1716; Telemann 1740/R1981:201, 359; Tilmouth 1961:22, 34; Walther 1732:526.
81. Heinichen was paid 1200 Thaler, and the average in the orchestra was 250–600.
82. La Riche probably taught Glösch in Berlin as well (see above).
83. Wolff 1968:102.
84. Selfridge-Field 1987:118; Bernardini 1988:374.
85. On Penati, see Arnold 1965:76; Arnold 1966:4, 7, 11; Giazotto 1973:322, 369(2x), 370–2; Kolneder 1979:223; Selfridge-Field 1975:19, 43, 183, 305; Selfridge-Field 1971:5; Kirkendale 1966:62; Quantz 1755:232; Bernardini 1987:12; Arnold 1985; Caffi 1855; Bernardini 1985a:3, 18; Talbot 1990:162.
86. Talbot 1980:162.
87. Bernardini 1988:378.
88. North c.1710–28:352.
89. Wood and Pinnock 1993, note 29.
90. Jeans 1958a:185 and 1958b:92.
91. Raynor 1972:231, 227.
92. Quantz 1752:ch.X, §10.
93. 40 Vm.848[1–3].
94. On Colin Hotteterre, see note 17.
95. Montéclair paid a touching tribute to Bernier's musicianship in the preface to his collection of brunettes (1724–5). On Bernier, see Brossard 1965:29; Machard 1971:14.ii.1737; Benoit 1971a:110, 141; Benoit 1971b; La Gorce 1979:178, 184; Giannini 1993:14, 16, 34, 45.
96. On Rousselet, see Lasocki 1988:354; Giannini 1993:4, 6, 44, 45; La Gorce 1989:104; Benoit 1971b:17 etc.; La Gorce 1979:178; Waterhouse 1993.
97. On Chédeville, see Dunner 1988:174–85; Giannini 1993:14, 16, 28, 34, 47; Marx 1951:10; *NG1*; Benoit 1971a; Machard 1971:57, 150–2; Benoit 1971b.
98. On Erdmann, see Enrico 1976:20; Schnoebelen 1969:52; Arnold 1965:77; Giazotto 1973:319, 320, 353, 358; Selfridge-Field 1975:43; Quantz 1755:231; Kahl 1948:267; Talbot 1980:44; Bernardini 1987:14; Schmidt 1956:74; Arnold 1985; Bernardini 1985a:19; Talbot 1990:163; Weaver and Weaver 1978:219; Smither 1977:287; Kirkendale 1993:21, 447–9, 496, 549.
99. On Pelegrina, see Kolneder 1979:46, 151; Vivaldi 04.8 (D-Dlb 2389–Q–14); Giazotto 1973:348, 355; Selfridge-Field 1986:374; Bernardini 1988:374.
100. Kirkendale 1993:449.
101. Schnoebelen 1969:52 and Kirkendale 1993:447, 448, 496.
102. 'Ignatio' was paid the most of Ruspoli's four hautboy players. On Rion, see Bernardini 1987:13; Talbot 1990:163; Kirkendale 1966:355; Bernardini 1988:378; Rodicio 1980:117; Burney 1789:III:553.
103. On Saint-Martin, see *NG1*, 16:457; Kirkendale 1966:62; Lasocki 1983:886; Marx 1983:109, 114.
104. Couvreur and Vendrix (*NG 2*, 22:107) attribute the *Suittes* to Jacques de Saint-Luc. The title-page gives 'Monsieur de St Luc'.
105. The Sarabande 4 goes down to c♯1, and there are low bs, however. As these notes are

virtually unplayable on either instrument, players may have replaced these notes ad hoc.

106. On Loeillet, see Lasocki 1988:353; Lasocki 1983:53, 54, 875; Tilmouth 1961:60, 69, 70; Benoit 1971:277–8; Janzen 1982:2–3; Deutsch 1955:138, 170, 181; Ashbee 1987:91, 102; Milhous and Hume 1983:157ff.; Burrows 1985:355, 357.

107. On La Tour, see Lasocki and Thompson 1979:35, 49, 53, 56, 102, 107, 118, 144, 159–60; Tilmouth 1961:48, 49, 55, 68, 71; Byrne 1983:17; Lasocki 1988:348, 353; Lasocki 1983:870; Ashbee 1987:65, 69, 91, 102; Burrows 1985:355; Kirkpatrick 1953:334.

108. The aria had been performed as 'Tortorella' in 1694 in Naples. As mentioned above, the opera was performed at Florence in 1712.

109. By the English translator of Raguenet's *Paralèle* (who may have been Galliard).

110. Köchel 1869:25. Selfridge-Field 1987:124 makes it 1702.

111. Cf. Bowers 1972 and House 1991:180–2. Hotteterre's compositional style is excellently described in House's ch. VI.

112. They are 'a l'usage de toutes les sortes d'instrumens de musique', but the *Apothéose de Corelli* attached at the end is (appropriately) only playable on violins. Many movements of the *Apothéose de Lully* of 1725 succeed well on hautboy; the work is most effective when played *en symphonie*.

113. On André Danican dit Philidor, see Marx 1951:13, 14; Benoit, see index p. 457; Dufourcq 1963:196; Sandman 1974:32; *NGI*; Thomas 1973:43ff.; Waquet 1980; Brossard 1965:81; LaGorce 1989:105; Benoit 1971b; Ancelet 1757:29.

114. On Anne Danican dit Philidor, see Marx 1951:11, 13; *NGI*; Benoit 1971b; Benoit 1971a; Dufourcq and Benoit 1963:196; *MGG* X:1192; Thoinan 1868:18, 29.

115. On Pierre Danican dit Philidor, see *NGI*; Benoit 1971a; Benoit 1971b; Dufourcq and Benoit 1963:196; *MGG* X:1194; Titon du Tillet 1727:676 (cited in Fleurot 1984:102); Giannini 1993:8, 9, 34; Thoinan 1868:37, 38.

116. Benoit 1971b.

117. The first page of Philidor's 9th Suite is reproduced on page 263 of Haynes 2001.

118. On Chauvon, see *MGG* II:1650; *NGI* 4:185; Bowers 1972:45.

119. On Sieber, see Arnold 1966:7, 11, 17; Giazotto 1973:367(2x), 377; Selfridge-Field 1975:43, 308; Selfridge-Field 1971:41; Talbot 1980:44; Bernardini 1987:14; Arnold 1985; Bernardini 1985a:19; Talbot 1990:163.

120. Bernardini 1985a:17.

121. On Cristoforo Besozzi, see Wind 1982:5; Anon. 1827:468 (called there 'Joseph').

122. On Giuseppe Besozzi, see Wind 1982:5; Petrobelli 1992:78; Pelicelli 1934.

123. Quantz 1752:235.

124. On Glösch, see Baron 1727:85; Bill 1987:199; EQL 281; Gerber 1812:344 (under his son); *NGI* under Carl Wilhelm G.; Haynes 1986a; Hodges 1980:260; Kahl 1948:305, 316; Marpurg 1754:157; *MGG*; Noack 1967:181, 192; Noack 1969:16; Quantz *Solfeggi* 4; Sachs 1908:68, 69, 184–5, 230; Schneider 1852:35, 55; Telemann 1716; Telemann 1718/R1981:103, 169; Walther 1732:285.

125. On Schüler, see Schneider 1852:35, 55; Sachs 1908:186, 230.

126. On Fleischer, see Schneider 1852:35, 55; Nagel 1900:54; Sievers 1941:60; Hildebrand 1975:56 quoting Noack 1967:184; Sachs 1908:184–5, 230.

127. On Rose, see Smend 1951:22, 23, 26, 96, 154; Denton 1977:27; Schneider 1852:35, 55; Sachs 1910:185, 229, 230; Bunge 1905:23, 24, 27, 36–7; Williams 1985:125; König 1959:164.

128. Heyde 1986:49.

129. Panoff 1938:74.

130. RV 34 in B flat, RV 28 in g minor, RV 53 in c minor, and RV 184.

131. Fürstenau 1861:2:135 and Quantz 1752:207. On Richter, see Telemann 1716; Walther 1732:526; Quantz 1755:207; Forkel 1782:107; Gerber 1790:2:Sp.283f. (mistakenly named Friedrich August); Fürstenau 1861:50, 66, 135; Kahl 1948:259; *NGI* under Johann

Christoph R.; Reilly 1966:xiv (quoting Quantz 1755); Burgess 1988:7; Burney 1775:2:186 (paraphrasing same Quantz); Noack 1967:181, 192; Talbot 1980:47; Haynes 1986a; Landmann 1989:22; Burney 1773:II:168; EQL; Landmann 1993:186; Oleskiewicz 1998a:42, 44.

132. Bernardini 1988:376. Richter might also have played in *L'incoronazione di Dario* itself.

133. On Blockwitz, see Mattheson 1740:118; Schering 1926:341; mentioned also by 'Stölzel': see Schering 1926 bibl.; Mennicke 1906:270; Oleskiewicz 1998a:50, 61.

134. On Böhm, see Noack 1969:15; Smithers 1987b:13; Nagel 1900:53, 63; Noack 1967:176, 177, 180f, 188, 190, notes 46, 192, 206, 208, 213, 214; Hildebrand 1975:33; Kross 1969:28–9 citing Telemann 1718; Telemann 1718:96, 165; Walther 1732:99; Gerber 1812:I:446 (not in Gerber 1790); EQL; Sittard 1890b:124; Sittard 1890a:8–10, 58, 69; Biermann/Bill 1987:62; Owens 1995:317(2x); Mattheson 1731:173–4.

135. Noack 1967:176–7, 180. Few concertmasters these days are oboists.

136. See Noack 1967:180.

137. 'Besonders aber vor die Hautbois'. See Haynes 1986.

138. Cf. Swack 1988, esp. 134.

139. On Corseneck, see *Tibia* 4/91:594; Biermann/Bill 1987:62; Noack 1967:174, 188, 213, 218, 225, 228; Hodges 1980:184. On Kayser, see Biermann/Bill 1987:62; Noack 1967:173, 190, 206, 261 (cites Schmidt); Schmidt 1956:74.

140. On Jacob Denner, see Nickel 1971:193, 243–4; von Huene 1980:5:374; Kirnbauer and Thalheimer 1995:83ff.

141. Hofmann 1954:85.

142. Doppelmayr, p.1730, quoted and translated in Kirnbauer and Thalheimer 1995:84–5.

143. Nickel 1971:245.

144. Burrows 1985:361, 349.

145. On Galliard, see Lasocki 1988:349–52; Lasocki 1983:853; Marx 1951:6; Lasocki and Thompson 1979:35, 55, 155–6; Burney 1776:2:686; Drummond 1978:272; Stockigt 1980:29, 32; Dean 1959:103; *NGI* on Marechal (107); Gerber 1812:242; Walther under 'Galliard' (according to Gerber 1790); Newman 1959:4; Deutsch 1955:181; EQL 131–3; North c.1710–28[87]; Bate 1975:192; Page 1988:361.

146. On Kytch, see Ashbee 1987:102; Baines 1957:280 citing Burney in Rees's *Cyclopaedia*.; Baker 1949:126, 132; Burney 1776:II:994, 1001; Burrows 1985:355; Dean 1970:186; Deutsch 1955:84, 111, 127, 163, 457; Drummond 1978:269(2x); I.P. 1830:192; Lasocki 1983:54, 55, 57, 58, 73, 74, 81, 82, 139–43, 864; Lasocki 1988:352; Milhous and Hume 1983:157ff.; Page 1988:361; Tilmouth 1961:73, 93, 97, 104, 105(2x), 106(2x), 107; Williams 1985:7, 10, 12, 17, 80.

147. Lasocki 1983:865.

148. Lasocki 1988.

149. Cf. Lasocki 1988:350 and Haynes 1992a:78. It is possible that the 'little flute' was the same sopranino recorder he used in the premiere of the now well-known aria 'Oh ruddier than the cherry' in *Acis and Galatea*.

150. On Neale, see Burrows 1985:355; Lasocki 1988:353; Lasocki 1983:959; Fiske 1973:187; Milhous and Hume 1983:160.

151. Cf. Bernardini 1988:376. These may include RV 464 and RV 465.

152. It includes RV 449, RV 454, RV 456, RV 460, and possibly RV 455.

153. Nösselt 1980:80. On Jacob Loeillet, see *NGI* 11; *NGI* 12:783; Brenet 1900:171ff.; Benoit 1971a; Machard 1971:50, 87, 95, 98; Janzen 1982:2; Nösselt 1980:72, 80; Benoit 1971b:503, etc.; *MGGI*; Münster 1993:301.

154. See Haynes 2001:306. On Schuechbauer, see Nösselt 1980:68, 80, 234; Waterhouse 1993.

155. On Dreyer, see Mooser 1948:I:86, 90, 100, 377.

156. On Telemann as an hautboist, see Petzoldt 1974:13; Telemann 1740:357; Cahn 1995:3:649.

157. In the first set, the most interesting cantatas are numbers 2, 26, 31, 35 and 55. The second set is consistently equal in quality to the best cantatas in the first.

158. Haynes 1992a:304–10. Good recent studies of this material are Swack 1988 and Zohn 1995.

159. Of Telemann's many good violin-hautboy trios, all the best are in g minor. They are: TWV 42:g12, I. N.25 Trio/Sonata à 3, MS parts, Dresden, 2392–Q–49; MS Herdringen Fü 3597a. Trio III from *Essercizii musici*. Sonata. MS Darmstadt 1042/56. N.2 Trio. Dresden, 2392–Q–51.

160. On Schön, see Walther 1732:555, Gerber 1790:xxxv:630. EQL; Dlabacz 1815:III:58; Selfridge-Field 1987:150; Köchel 1869:71, 79; Seifert 1987:10, 21.

161. Cf. Nettl 1957:5.

162. Mattheson 1713:269. His statement was quoted by Majer 1732:34, Walther 1732:79, and Eisel 1738:100.

163. On Johann Caspar Gleditsch, see Bach 1963:I:65, 148; Dahlquist 1976:127; Denton 1977:30, 69; EQL 277; Gerber 1790 on another Gleditsch; Rubardt 1949; Schering 1921:34, 44(2x), 51, 53; Schering 1926 (generally useful on Stadtpfeifer, esp. 261, 264, 268–72, 285(2x), 296, 341–2; Smithers 1987b: 28, 32–3; Spitta 1884:II:248. On Johann Gottfried Kornagel, see Smithers 1987b:32–3; Denton 1977:30, 69; Spitta 1884:II:248; Schering 1921:44, 51, 53; Schering 1926:267–8; Bach 1963:65.

164. The recorder part to BWV 69a/3, 'Meine Seele, auf! erzähle', was in the second hautboy part (Kornagel's part), and the oboe da caccia part was in the first hautboy part (Gleditsch's).

165. *Bach-Dokumente* I:63 (23.viii.1730).

166. Powell and Lasocki 1995:17.

167. See Haynes 1992:384.

168. In the middle of a vocal passage in BWV 101/6 (bars 31 and 33), the traverso and da caccia are both marked *forte* (the traverso is low and the da caccia high).

169. Denton 1977:175–7.

170. Because the taille normally had no independent line in the score, its part sometimes exceeded its range, and corrections were presumably made ad hoc. Denton (1977:156ff.) discusses technical considerations of Bach's taille writing, including range, tonalities, dynamics, ornaments, phrase-lengths and awkward passages.

171. See Prinz 1979:166–9, 180, 181ff. Most of the distinctions between taille and oboe da caccia outlined here are based on Prinz. A complete table of da caccia and taille parts in Bach's works, with source, date of performance, and other relevant information is located in Prinz.

172. Less likely was that Gleditsch had his own da caccia. Piet Dhont* has pointed out that no straight tenor hautboys are known to exist by any of the numerous Saxon woodwind builders of the time.

173. For a more detailed discussion of this question, see Haynes 1995 and Haynes 2001, ch. 6, §D.

174. From an obituary cited in Wolff 1985:166.

175. Cf. Helm 1980:842.

176. Cf. Haynes 1992d and the recordings in the Discography below.

177. Mattheson 1740:195.

178. Owens 1995:320.

179. Mattheson 1722–5:169.

180. Sandman 1974:88.

181. For titles and locations of these pieces, see Haynes 1992a.

182. Herdringen, Fü 3741a.

183. Cf. Harris-Warrick and Marsh 1994.

184. The presence of these two currents in French hautboy playing is apparent in Corrette's fingering chart (1773), which distinguishes French and Italian fingerings.

185. Vittorino Colombazzi was also known as Colombazzo. See Sittard 1890a:70; Landon 1976:II:289; Edge 1992:73; Marx 1976:41.

186. On Alessandro Besozzi, see Wind 1982; Burney 1789:III:422; Pierre 1975:98, 243–4; Bernardini (Oct 1985):22; Burney 1773:II:179; Burney 1771:65, 69ff.; Da Silva; Anon. 1827:468; Bernardini 1985:5ff.; Petrobelli 1992; L. Mozart letters II:244; Pelicelli 1934; Ancelet 1757:29; Bouquet 1976:351, 170, 281, 324; Bouquet 1969:26, 161.

187. Pierre 1975:98.

188. De Brosses 1739–40, Lettre LVIII:497.

189. On Antonio Besozzi, see Wind 1982:7; Pierre 1975:128, 274; Sittard 1890a:70; Meusel 1778:I:14, II:15; Ongley 1993; Anon. 1827:469; Engländer 1922:50; Hiller 1784:301–2; Fürstenau 1862:II:234, 275; Pelicelli 1934.

190. Fürstenau 1861:II:275.

191. On Sammartini, see *NGı* 457; Tötscher introd. to Sammartini concerto (Sik 243k); Hawkins 1776:369–71; Lasocki and Thompson 1979:57, 58, 148, 150, 151–3; *MGGı* 11:1334; Bate 1975:194; Burney 1776:i:389, 405, 422, ii:997, 1008, 1013; Burney 1775:i:64, ii:192; Marx 1951:17; Drummond 1978:272; Houle 1984; Kirkendale 1966:355, 62; Deutsch 1955:277, 514; Burney 1789:iii:405, 422; Lasocki 1983:885; Burney 1773:ii:186; Burney 1771:79; Daub 1985:266–7; Anon. 1827:466; EQL; Dean 1970:187, 198; Dean 1959:103; Quantz 1755:232, 236; Kahl 1948:268; Gerber 1812:343; Page 1988:361, 369; Matthews 1985:98.

192. Hawkins 1776:894.

193. These were 'Quella fiamma' in *Arminio* (produced in January), 'Quel torrente che s'innalza sulla sponda' in act II of *Giustino* (February), and 'Chi t'intende?' from *Berenice* (May).

194. Robert Price, *Observations on the Works of George Frederic Handel*, 1760, quoted in Hogwood 1984:38.

195. David Schulenberg*.

196. On Matthes, see Meusel 1778:II:130 citing Nicolas: *Beschreib. von Berlin*, vol. 3, ch. iii, pp. 58ff.; Introd. to Sikorsky ed. of Hautb. sonata in C; Forkel 1782:107; Hodges 1980:450.

197. On Pla, see Mainwaring 1760:61; Pierre 1975:(see index 364); Forkel 1782:107; McClymonds 1978:63, 76, 460, 492; Ancelet 1757:29; Deutsch 1955:18; Sittard 1890a:70; Krauss 1908:58; Dolcet 1987:132; Pla entry at GB-Lbl calling José the elder brother; Burney 1773/I:107; see Kenyon de Pascual introd. to published music; Anon. 1827:473; Schubart 1806/R:137; D'Aquin 1752:217; Kenyon de Pascual 1990; Avison 2/1753:120.

198. Another excellent sonata in c minor (Dresden Mus 2782–S–2) that is in much the same style; it is probably by Pla but is attributed there to Giovanni Platti.

199. Burney 1771b:70.

200. On Vincent, see Mortimer 1949:29; *NGı* 19:782; *NGı* 8:323 (on Hawkins); *MGGı* 13:1656; Burney 1776:ii:870, 1008; Drummond 1978:269; Deutsch 1955:459, 751, 752, 800, 804, 806, 832; Page 1988:369; Daub 1985:179; Anon. 1827:467; Burney 1785:14, 23; Matthews 1985:148.

201. See Allen 1858.

202. It might also have been written for Pla, who was in England in the early 1750s.

Chapter 4 from Classical hautboy to keyed oboe, 1760–1825

1. Vény c.1828:30.

2. Cf. Adkins 1999:119ff.

3. *Empfindsam* is untranslatable, but means literally 'sensitive'.

4. Piersol 1972:53.

5. On Fiala, see Piersol 1972:374; Paumgartner 1950:31; Storch 1969; Mozart 1962:40;

Sidorfsky 1977:341; *NG1*; van der Straeten 1915; Meusel 1778:II:40; L. Mozart letters II:470; Nösselt 1980:106, 111, 117. On Fürall, see Piersol 1972:407; Edge, Dexter: Handout, Mozart Conference, Juilliard 1991; Edge 1992:68.

6. On Berwein, see Paumgartner 1950:25; Piersol 1972:120, 329; L. Mozart II:96.

7. On Fischer, see *ABCDario Musico* 1780:21; Anon. 1827:470, 473; Bauer and Deutsch 1963:IV:40–1; Bell (biog. of Gainsborough):X; Braun 1971:155; Broughton 1887:65, 144, 155, 186, 203, 207, 224, 231 (143 describes wager with J. C. Bach); BrTC 9x; Burney 1771/73:I:172 and II:45; Burney 1775:II:60; Burney 1776:I:405, II:943, 961, 1015, 1018, 1022, III:1018(1789); Burney 1785:14, 39, 83; Burney 1789:III:405; Conrey 1986:9; Cudworth in *MGG1* IV:269; Engländer 1922:50; Evans 1963:56; Forkel 1782:107; Fulcher 1856; *Gr5*:144; *NG1*; Halfpenny 1953:25ff.; Haydn 1965:500–1; Humiston 1968; I.P. 1830:192; Jerome 1973:20, 28, 223–8; Landmann 1993:187; Langwill 1949:40; Matthews 1985:52; Meusel 1778:II:42; Mozart 1962–75:40; Ongley 1993; Page 1988:368; Parke 1830:I:33, 86, 334, 335 (+ others); Pierre 1975:149, 293; Reichardt 1782:168–9; Ribock 1783:701, 711, 722, 727; Thibault 1973; Warner 1964:141; Weber 1989:312. On Carlo Besozzi, see Reichardt 1782:169; Wind 1982:8; Pierre 1975:128, 274; Sittard 1890a:70; Meusel 1778:I:14, II:15; Burney 1773:II:27ff, 45–7, 52; Ongley 1993; Anon. 1827:469; Engländer 1922:50; Fürstenau 1862:II:234; Landmann 1993:186–7; Ribock 1783:701.

8. Quoted in Engländer 1922:50.

9. Burney 1773:II:45–7.

10. Mozart 1962–75:1350 [4 April 1787]. Tr. from Anderson 1938:1350.

11. On Gaetano Besozzi, see Wind 1982:10; Pierre 1975:(see index 347); François-Sappey 1988:155; Burney 1771:24–5; Anon. 1827:469; Hodges 1980:417; Morby 1971:48, 75; Meude-Monpas 1787:27.

12. On Secchi, see Burney 1772:II:60, 61; Forkel 1782:108; EQL 126; Bouquet 1976; Gerber 1790:2; letter from G. Ottani to Padre Martini 5 Aug. 1778 (in I-Bc); Pierre 1975; Nösselt 1980:91, 101, 102, 234; Burney 1773:I:172, 174; Meusel 1778:I:135; Eisen 1992:98; Rudhart 1865:159; Bernardini 1985:10ff.; Schubart 1806/R:119; Hodges 1980:606. On Giuseppe Ferlendis, see Bernardini 1987:18–20; Landon (*Haydn in England, 1791–95*); Fétis 1834:7; Paumgartner 1950:24, 25; Mozart 1962:282; Sidorfsky 1977:340; *NG1*; Sartori card catalogue, Milan; Haydn 'London Notebook' 1794; Bernardini 1988:380ff.; Bernardini 1989:55; Arnold 1985; L. Mozart letters II:10, 96, 431, 434–5.

13. On Ramm, see Paumgartner, Introduction to his ed. of Mozart Htb conc. in C; Bate 1975:164–5, 197; Bechler and Rahm 1914:40; Baines 1957:281; Paumgartner 1950:25, 29; Wlach 1927:110, 116; Brenet 1900:331; Fitzpatrick 1971:169; Mozart 1962:40, 101, 162(2x), 280, 282, 259, 261; Sidorfsky 1977:350; Pierre 1975; Nösselt 1980:105, 234; Goossens 1977:135; Meusel 1778:II:171; Zaslaw 1990b:263; Levin 1988:2–3; L. Mozart letters II:470; Eisen 1991:49–50; De Smet 1973:66–7; Broughton 1887:231 (called 'Kamm'); Junker 1787:I:37ff.

14. Among other remarkable players were Giuseppe Caravoglia, François-Joseph Garnier, Sante Aguilar, Giuseppe and Pietro Ferlendis, Christian Samuel Barth, Johann Friedrich Braun, Carl Ludwig Matthes, Giovanni Palestrini, Franz Rosiniach, Vittorino Colombazzi, Georg Druschetzky, Georg Triebensee, Johann Went, Friedrich Griesbach, Sir William F. Herschel, John and W. T. Parke, Charles Suck and Gaspar Barli. Biographies of most of them can be found in the revised *New Grove*.

15. Anton Fladt, a pupil of Ramm, succeeded Lebrun, and became well known in the next generation. On Lebrun, see Pierre 1975; Nösselt 1980:105, 234; Braun 1971:155; Ribock 1783:701, 711; Bate 1975:198; *MGG1* 420; Forkel 1782:107; *Tibia* 1/81:295; Brenet 1900:312, 317, 371; BrTC ix, Suppl XV:39(797); *AMZ* xiv:70; *NG1* 581; Riemann 1915:xviii; *ABCDario Musico* 1780:33–4; Burney 1773:I:92; Meusel 1778:22; L. Mozart letters II:469–70, and just after 11.ii.1785 (cf. Zaslaw 1990:116); Schubart 1806:130; Höft 1992:64ff.; Sittard 1890; Hodges 1980:414.

16. On Sallantin, see Bate 1975:207; *Almanach musical* 1781:139, 145;1782:95, 109, 134; Brenet

1900:244, 271, 292; Devienne opp. 70, 71; Haynes 1992, 'Bochsa'; Machard 1971; *NG1* 422; Conrey 1986:8–9; Pierre 1975:213; Sidorfsky 1977:351; *MGG* (see index); Pierre 1900; Ellis 1880:36 citing Lissajous 1865.

17. Cf. Pierre 1900, Pierre 1975, and Burgess 2001:22:163. The improbability of Sallantin's extreme youth and the idea that he was supposed to have played two different instruments, together with confusion about other musicians with similar names, suggest the possibility that two different individuals are combined under this name.

18. On Richard Vincent, see Mortimer 1949:29; *NG1* 19:782; Deutsch 1955:463, 832; Page 1988:369; Matthews 1985:148; Burrows 1985:353–5.

19. On Czerwenka, see Wlach 1927:114; Sidorfsky 1977:337; Köchel 1869:94, 98; Angermüller 1985:169; Hodges 1980:188–9.

20. *AMZ*, 4/43 (1820) 339–40. See Wlach 1927:114, Sidorfsky 1977:337, Köchel 1869:94, 98, Angermüller 1985:169, and Hodges 1980:188–9.

21. The other players were Reuther and Teimer (the Teimer brothers are mentioned below). On the Beethoven symphony premières, see Albrecht 2002.

22. Haynes 1992a:220. See also Bruce Haynes, 'Haydn, Mozart, Hummel', notes to CD with soloist Ernest Rombout and the Concertgebouw Chamber Orchestra, Decca 440 605–2.

23. This concerto has recently been reconstructed; see Lehrer 1982.

24. These are by (among others) Barth, Carlo Besozzi, Bochsa, Druschetzky, Giuseppe Ferlendis, Fiala, Fischer, Garnier, Gassmann, Hoffmeister, Kleinknecht, Kreutzer, Krommer, Ignaz and Johann Michael Malzat, Matthes, Myslivecek, Thomas Vincent, Eichner, Devienne, Lebrun, Vanhal, Went, Cannabich, and Anton and Paul Wranitzky. All this material is listed in Haynes, *Music for Oboe* (1992).

25. See Haynes 1992a:370, 372.

26. Braun 1983:135.

27. Whitwell 1969:I:31. Listings of music for larger wind ensembles can be found in Whitwell 1983c.

28. A number of dated instruments survive by contemporaries of Grundmann. Cf. Augustin Grenser Y4 (1790), Y11 (1778), Y13 (1791), Collier Y2 (1791), Doleisch Y1 (1781), Doleisch Y2 (1787), Doleisch Y3 (1792), Fornari Y2 (1792), Fornari Y9 (1793), Liebel (1798), Engelhard Y1 (1799), Engelhard Y14 (1799), Otto Y1 (1785), Otto Y2 (1799), etc.

29. See Young 1993:112ff. Each of these 32 years is represented by at least one dated hautboy except 1769, 1770, 1772, 1773, 1775, 1776, 1783 and 1786.

30. 18 per cent, or 103 complete instruments.

31. Cf. Adkins 2001:26, 32ff., where the Italian influence is not discussed.

32. When they arrived two years later he complained about the intonation of the English horns; see his letter of 6 July 1778. Giuseppe Ferlendis (known for his close association with the instrument) was in Salzburg at the time, and was a friend of the Mozarts. Since Leopold was not himself an hautboist, in order to evaluate the instruments he must have consulted someone like Ferlendis whose judgement he trusted.

33. There is confusion about this maker's name, which may have been Matthias Rockobaur or Rocko Baur. Cf. Waterhouse 1993:24.

34. Cf. Waterhouse 1993. Kirst had a lucrative contract supplying the Prussian army with 'Hautboisten-Instrumente' (Heyde 1994:73).

35. Whereas the aggregate size of the single tone-holes 1, 2, 5 and 6 averaged 16.58 mm before 1730, by 1760 it was only 15.43, the smallest of any period in the instrument's history.

36. This is not to say that other pitches did not exist. A level that averages A–413 is observable in some regions, but in none of them does it represent more than a third of the surviving pitch evidence. Flutes and clarinets by both Grensers show a range of 410 to 441; they are most frequently between 430 and 440. For more detail on the subject of pitches in this period, cf. Haynes 2002, ch. 8.

37. Alternative joints on hautboys were called *Muttationen* or *Motazionen* in Austria (Hellyer 1975:54, 55, 57). In France, they had the same name as on the traverso, *corps de rechange*.

38. Although Garnier wrote that the two joints differed by two *pouces*, he apparently meant two *lignes*, i.e. 4.5 mm (and not 54.14 mm), and this is the difference shown in his diagram.

39. Koch 1802:1082.

40. Weber 1992:296 points out that slides on old instruments are often difficult to detect because they are placed at a point where there is ornamental turnery. The grease that was used to lubricate the joint, now hardened, sometimes keeps them from moving.

41. Quantz 1752, I§15. The only known surviving hautboy that has a tuning slide is by Grundmann, who stopped working in 1800 (Y48 in Meiningen).

42. AJ[13].46.II (item 2); see Burgess 2003.

43. See Burgess and Hedrick 1989:59–64, Burgess and Hedrick 1990, and Piguet 1988:91–5. Another reed, rather wide and long, also survives with an Engelhard hautboy dated 1799 (Y1, Leipzig 1323; information kindly supplied by Alfredo Bernardini).

44. These dimensions are based on a comparison of the picture and existing instruments; specifically, of the width of the top of the finial.

45. J. C. Fischer, Johann Christoph Kellner, Charles J. Suck and William Teede (Tiede), for instance, and later Friedrich Griesbach, in London 1794–1824.

46. Haydn 1965:56. Cf. Maunder 1998:172, 181.

47. See Finkelman (2/99:453–6) and (4/99:618–24).

48. Maunder 1998:185.

49. See Bernardini 1986 and 1989.

50. Tessitura is mean range, or the average of the length of time each note in the range is used. Tessitura can be quantitatively analysed by assigning numbers to each note in an instrument's range, multiplying these by the length each one is used, and averaging the result. The mean of ten representative hautboy solos in Bach's cantatas is between $c\sharp2$ and $d2$ (it was necessary to count over 8000 individual notes to conclude this). The quartet's movements are somewhat above $f\sharp2$.

51. Broughton 1887:231. The effect of Fischer's shake, probably consisting of repeated slurred octave shifts, must have resembled Clementi's use of the octave trill on the piano, reported in 1784 (see Williams 1985:62). This procedure (often called a *tremolo* nowadays) is fairly common on the piano.

52. La Borde 1780:266, Schubart 1806:319 (Schubart wrote this book in prison in 1784–5).

53. Parke 1830:I:215.

54. Concerto 2 in g minor, ed. T. Herman Keahey (Classical Winds Press, 1995). See, for instance, III:250, which in a sequence would continue up to g3. Even more striking is I:140, a sequential passage that simply drops an octave when g3 should be played.

55. Most orchestration manuals printed in the first part of the nineteenth century continued to caution composers to avoid these notes. See for instance Kastner 1837:34, Fétis 1837:53.

56. This appears on the traverso chart; Hotteterre gave no hautboy trill chart as such, but merely referred to the traverso charts and mentioned any differences.

57. Whitely 1816.

58. Verschuere-Reynvaan 1789.

59. Fröhlich 1810–11.

60. See ch. 5, 'England'. Long fingerings persisted longer in non-French traditions.

61. Quantz 1755:200.

62. Sadie 1956:109, quoting Gardiner 1838–53:7.

63. Cotte 1979:316.

64. Starting with the 'Kegelstatt Trio', KV 498 (1786), written for Anton Stadler. See Shackleton 1980:4:440.

65. I remember the late Frans Vester demonstrating for me an uncorrected D major scale on the 1-keyed traverso, as he rehearsed in 1966 for the first concert in which he used the instrument.

66. Burney 1773:II:45–7.
67. A *comma* was 21 cents, or 21 hundredths of a semitone. Cf. the charts in ch. 2 and Haynes 2001, ch. 4, L.
68. This is the note that usually causes traverso players to 'do the woodpecker', i.e., make sudden adjustments that involve moving the head. The fingering often used by modern players, 123 ♯ 6, was given by Hotteterre (1707:45) and Garnier (1802) for g♭1.
69. Hotteterre c.1729:13–14, Quantz 1752, ch.9, §9 and 10. See Haynes 2001, ch. 4, §G.4.
70. Fröhlich 1810–11:44. Italics mine.
71. Except possibly Floth Y7 (Bruges, Gruuthuse).
72. Burgess 2003.
73. Braun 1823:171.
74. The hautboists who premiered Beethoven's music may have been among Vienna's more experienced players like Franz Rosenkranz, Ernst Krähmer, Czerwenka, Ulhmann, and later Joseph Sellner (1787–1843).
75. *AMZÖK*, 2/39 (1818):363–4.
76. Sellner usually performed his own compositions such as 'Romanze and Rondo', 'Andante and Variations', at least one oboe concerto, and an 'Introduction et Polonaise brilliante' for clarinet and orchestra which may have originally been for oboe, plus music for guitars and other instruments, but was also heard as soloist in the Concertante for oboe and flute by Ignaz Moscheles with flautist Carl Keller in 1818.
77. Koch supplied a 'neu Invenzionirte' oboe to the Vienna Hoftheater as early as 1808 (see Hellyer 1975).
78. Sellner 1824:8.
79. Powell 1995b.
80. According to Young (1993), clarinets by Grundmann and A. Grenser had 4 keys in the 1770s and 5 by the 1790s. The earliest dated clarinet with 5 keys is by T. Collier (1770).
81. See Haynes 1978. The Small-key was sometimes doubled, of course.
82. Grundmanns that may have original extra keys are listed in Young 1993 (Y numbers 14, 17, 22, 24, 28, 46–8); six of these are dated, the earliest being 1781. All of these were either speaker keys or keys for c♯1.
83. Maunder 1998:183.
84. In 1794, a flute with more than 2 keys was being called an *Inventionsflöte* (Schreiber 1938:163 citing Spazier in the *BMZ* 1794:2), and in 1800 clarinets with added keys were called 'Inventions-Clarinetten' (Maunder 1998:188), both perhaps by analogy with the *Inventionshorn* of the same period. An hautboy with added keys would thus have been called an *Inventionsoboe* (we have not seen this name used in any sources, however).
85. Although its corollary, A flat, governed by the same finger of the other hand, was twinned.
86. Fingering charts show that the new keys were normally used only in the first octave: players were presumably satisfied with the traditional fingerings in the second octave.
87. Vogt 1816–25:16.
88. Maunder 1998:183.
89. This may have been Wilhelm Braun or his father Johann Friedrich Braun.
90. This instrument survives at Paris (C.480, E.387).
91. This model has been dubbed the 'Sallantin' hautboy (Burgess 2003). Until recently the long key on Sallantin's oboe was mistakenly taken to be a low-b key. See Burgess 1994a and 2003.
92. Burgess 2003.
93. This instrument survives at Paris (C.481, E.263).
94. This work was probably envisaged as a method for the Paris Conservatoire, but was never published and survives only in manuscript. Cf. Burgess 2003 for a transcription and translation.
95. Vogt 1816–25:15ff.

96. 'Il flauto di Potter, che ha cinque chiavi, è comune in tutta l'Europa, e particolarmente in Parigi si construiscono a perfezione. . .' Giuseppe Cervelli, quoted in Barbieri 1999:286.
97. Shackleton and Rice 1999:184, 189.
98. *AMZ*, 28/26 (1826): 417–25.
99. The illustration of the instrument shows a G sharp key, but the fingering chart does not.
100. In addition, Vény used cross-fingerings for a number of enharmonic notes only (implying a highly developed sense of meantone): e♯1, a♯1 (b♭1 used a key), b♯1, a♯2 (b♭2 used a key), and c♭3. He also used cross-fingerings extensively on the notes above d3: d♯/e♭3, f3, f♯/g♭3 and g3.
101. In addition, there were duplicate touches for the b flat key (left-hand thumb or right-hand forefinger), and for the F and E flat keys (left-hand little finger). These duplicate keys facilitated playing legato in keys with multiple sharps and flats by allowing the keyed fingering to be used. (See ill. 48, which shows folding low b key and the double touch for B flat.) Schott of Mainz produced a design closely resembling the Sellner-Koch oboe with just one additional key (a trill key for c♯2) and the low b key on the side rather than at the back of the instrument.
102. Cf. Koch, 1802.
103. See Haynes 2001, ch. 1.
104. My own first ('military system') oboe had a twinned third hole.
105. Eleven originals (as opposed to later additions) are known, dating from 1781 to 1813. The next most common key was the c♯1, of which there are at least six surviving originals. See Young 1993.
106. Although the key may have existed by 1781, the year Mozart's hautboy quartet was written (it is present on a surviving Grundmann hautboy dated 1781 – Berlin 635), the theory I once advanced that Friedrich Ramm had such a key to help him play the high f3s in the hautboy quartet is probably untrue, since in a passage in his *Méthode*, Vogt cites Ramm (along with Lebrun and Sallantin) as an example of a virtuoso who was 'not acquainted' with more than two keys.
107. Koch 1802:1082.
108. *AMZ*, 29 January 1812: 73.
109. Braun 1823:168.
110. Sellner c.1825:4–8 pointed out that 'those who are familiar with the new keyed flute will notice that the improvements to the B flat and F-Klappe of the oboe described here originated with the flute'. That the hohe F-Klappe was used for f3 is confirmed in Braun's review of Sellner's method in *Cäcilia,* 4 (1826): 222–5, where the notes discussed are clearly given as e3 etc. A fingering chart for Schott's oboe similar to the Sellner-Koch instrument also shows the F-Klappe open for e3–g♯3.
111. See Williams 1995.
112. Lawson 1994:80.
113. Keys were used to eliminate 'false trills'; see 3–3.
114. Ch. 1, §10. Tr. Powell.
115. Sellner c.1825:6.
116. See Bernardini 1987.
117. Quantz 1752:XIV§11.
118. Bijlsma 1998:131.
119. Brod c.1826:10.
120. Hedrick 1974a:58 points out that in Barret's *Method* (1850) 'most of the dynamics look like this [second] example!'
121. Rothwell 1953:11. This is also mentioned by Goossens and Roxburgh 1977:84–5.
122. Geoffrey Burgess*.
123. Burney 1773:158.
124. Quantz 1752:XIV:§41 and Tab. xvii, xviii and xix.
125. Leopold Mozart, 28 May 1778, trans. based on Anderson 1938:798–9.

126. Charles-Dominique 1994:253ff.
127. Charles-Dominique 1994:265.
128. Charles-Dominique 1994:97ff.
129. A. M. R. Barret mentions the *aubòi* in his well known *Méthode* (1876:15n).
130. Fingered d1 sounded about c♯1 in A–440. Charles-Dominique and Laurence 2002:120, 244. In fact it may have been a quarter-step lower. The pitch that was general for traditional wind instruments up until the 1914 War, generally known as 'le la ancien', was about 404 Hz (Claude Girard*). Cf. the recording *France: cornemuses du centre* played by Jean Blanchard and Eric Montbel. Montbel's *chabrette* attributed to Louis Maury (1842–c.1910) is described as 'en la 415' but is pitched on the recording at 406.
131. One surviving *aboès* has a hole where the hautboy's 7th hole (under the Small-key) is found. Charles-Dominique and Laurence 2002:67.
132. Charles-Dominique and Laurence 2002:69.
133. Charles-Dominique and Laurence 2002:243.
134. Charles-Dominique and Laurence 2002:93–4.
135. Charles-Dominique and Laurence 2002:84. Cf. Haynes 2000c.
136. Charles-Dominique and Laurence 2002:82.
137. Charles-Dominique and Laurence 2002:87. This was from e1 to b♭2 (probably fingered as d1 to a♭2, thus sounding a tone above the standard pitch of the time, A–435).
138. Charles-Dominique and Laurence 2002:243.
139. Charles-Dominique and Laurence 2002:84–5.
140. Charles-Dominique and Laurence 2002:240.

Chapter 5 *From the keyed oboe to the Conservatoire oboe, 1825–1880*

1. 1975:59.
2. *AMZ* 19 (1817): 201-8; trans. in Strunk 1965:V:64.
3. 1990:10.
4. See Gevaert's comparison of the two instruments (1863:62), and for a detailed discussion of the progress of the clarinet to the favourite Romantic wind instrument, Birsak 1994:12–19.
5. Ernst 1865–90.
6. The instrument was given an honourable mention at the 1838 Paris Exposition, but appears to have vanished without trace (G. E. Anders, *RGMdP* 4/28 [1837]: 234–6).
7. *Musical World* 4/9 (1836): 62.
8. Charles van Oeckelen's 'clavier oboe' was heard on 19 March 1861 (see Lawrence 1988–95:III:453.
9. 1977:158.
10. Frederic Palmer 1983:49.
11. A comprehensive list of nineteenth-century oboe music is still to be compiled; Hofmeister's and Whistler's *Handbuch der musikalischen Literatur* (1817–27) and annual supplements and Pazdírek's *Universal-Handbuch* are the most important primary sources for printed material; Christian Schneider's repertoire list in *MGG1* 'Oboe', III: 2, includes the most important works and further repertoire can be found in Bechler and Rahm 1914. Also see Lehrer 1984 and his articles on separate oboist-composers Vogt, Verroust, Brod, Luft and Barret which, while often inaccurate in detail, are admirable for bringing Romantic repertoire to the attention of modern oboists.
12. In addition to Han de Vries's pioneering performances of works by Bellini, Hummel and Kalliwoda (1973) and Holliger's recording of concerti by Donizetti, Reicha and Rossini (1978), rarer repertoire has been recorded by Glaetzner, Hommel and Mayer; Lucarelli,

Bortolato and Indermühle have all recorded operatic transcriptions (see Discography).

13. See for instance the review of the amateur English oboist Mr A. A. Pollock's rendition of Beethoven's 'Adelaïde' at a concert of the Amateur Musical Society in 1854 (*Musical World* 32/13 [1854]: 210).

14. On the interchangeability of the terms 'cor anglais' and English horn, see Introduction.

15. Other nineteenth-century works for this combination are listed in Carr 2001.

16. See Burgess 2003 and Sirker 1968.

17. Schoenberg's Quintet was considered unplayable until 1958, when it was premiered by the Danzi Quintet. For a complete repertoire list see Hosek 1979.

18. Less-known works in this category include a nonet by Bertini, septet by Alexander Fesca, nonets by Louise Farrenc and E. Hartmann and septets by A. Blanc and Fritz Steinbach.

19. A particularly detailed study of the Parisian scene between 1828 and 1871 is given in Cooper 1983.

20. On Wagner's use of brass, see Wills, 'Brass in modern Orchestra', in Herbert and Wallace 1997:167.

21. For a tabulation of nineteenth-century orchestral forces, see Carse 1949:46–63.

22. 1994:85.

23. Kastner 1837, Schneider 1834 and Choron and La Fage 1836–9 included fingering charts for two-keyed oboes, implying that these instruments were still in common use.

24. 1970:305–6.

25. Review of Vogt's playing in the wind quintet that premiered Reicha's wind quintets, *AMZ* 20 (4 March 1818): 191.

26. For a complete worklist, see Burgess 2003. From its foundation in 1825 the Société des Concerts was famous for introducing Beethoven's symphonies to Parisian audiences.

27. For general information on Brod, see Lardrot 2001.

28. A comprehensive list of Brod's musical publications can be found in Lardrot 2001: pt II.

29. Garnier also recommended cedar oboes to beginners for their lightness and ease.

30. 1865–90, art. 'Hautbois'.

31. Berlioz 1951:256.

32. See Lardrot 2001:II:130–3; a small number of oboes are signed 'Brod Frères', suggesting that Henri also worked with his younger brother Jean-Godefoy.

33. Several reports indicate that he also made oboes with a low A, but to my knowledge none survive. The explanation for Brod's extended bell comes from Fétis (*RM*, 11 May 1834; see Lardrot 2001:I:31). Other makers of the time made similar experiments. Ziegler of Vienna is succeeded by instruments extending to ao. The earliest low B flats appear in Brod's Variations on a Theme by Mercadante, op. 51 (1837–8).

34. A Brod cor anglais moderne can be heard on Norrington's recording of the *Symphonie fantastique*.

35. See discussion below on reeds, p. 157.

36. *Journal des débats* 21 July 1835; reprinted in Lardrot 2001:II:35.

37. 1956:331. Ange-Philippe Évrard (1805–81) was professor at Lyon Conservatoire.

38. Pontécoulant 1861:II:581. One can gain a general impression of the geographic spread of wind instrument manufacturers from the Index of Makers' Workplace in Waterhouse 1993.

39. The success of the French makers was certainly abetted by the strong French bias of the adjudication and reportage of these 'Universal Exhibitions'.

40. See Decourcelle 1881.

41. 1868:282.

42. See Gerard 1983–4.

43. See Burgess 1997b:215–16.

44. The evolution of the Triébert oboe is treated in detail in Howe 2001–2.

45. Bate and Voorhees 2001:13:552–6.

46. Fingering charts show that the fork fingering for $\natural$2 (123 56) continued to be used for

some time even on oboes with rings.

47. This design also introduced a key for the trill between c2 and d2 (already in use for some time in Germany).

48. The English seem to have been slightly ahead of the French in this regard. In 1830 a writer mentioned a 'key that . . . has been found of great advantage in producing the upper notes, which it renders comparatively easy to produce as high as G in altissimo' (I.P. 1830:192).

49. Bretonnière 1867 still described using the speaker key as a flick key on Triébert système 4 (see Appendix 3, and 'Added keys' in ch. 4, p. 108).

50. The second speaker key first appears in Vény 1844–51.

51. Reported by Alfred Barthel, *The Étude*, August 1929, quoted in Storch 1977:19.

52. The date of the Triébert catalogue has for long been taken as 1855 because this date appears prominently at the top of the first page. However, this is actually the date of the gold medal depicted immediately below. The document must date from 1860–2 because of the inclusion of the full Barret model and the announcement of the Boehm oboe and bassoon.

53. The common names illustrate how confusing the naming of timbers can be, particularly in translation; e.g., 'rosewood' is not the same as what the French call 'bois de rose'. For this reason I have given the botanical names. For further information see Zadro, *Woods Used* and Record and Hess 1943.

54. 1828:15.

55. Of their first 50 instruments, at least 22 were in box, 13 in palisander, and only 1 in ebony. This was to change dramatically from 1885 when references to boxwood disappear almost entirely. (Information from Storch 1981:41, and Lorée records compiled by J. Brown.)

56. One example is to be found in the Rigoutat Collection.

57. De Stefani compared the tone of a brass oboe by Uhlmann with his ebony oboe by Koch (1888:103–4). In 1845 Louis Krüger is known to have played a metal oboe (information from James Brown).

58. This was Persius's ballet version of Dalayrac's opera, in which Nina's famous *romance* was performed as a pantomime, with the cor anglais taking the vocal melody.

59. 1878:108.

60. 1844a:104.

61. Berlioz first published the text of his treatise in 1841, just one year after système 3 was released. ('Hautbois', *RGMdP* 8/63: 550–1, see Hedrick 1974a).

62. 1816–25: 'Explication de la Gamme'. Most nineteenth-century orchestration manuals maintained that these notes were the terrain only of virtuosi.

63. 1844b:II:286–7.

64. 1844a:104. See for example in act I of *Les Troyens* where unison oboe and clarinet intone c1–b0 as Cassandre sings 'Death already soars through the air, and I have seen the sinister lightning'.

65. 1844a:104. Here he quoted a passage from Raoul's air in act IV of *Les Huguenots* where the cor anglais oscillates between low F, G flat and E flat (sounding a fifth lower) over tremolo strings and low *piano* tones in the clarinets.

66. Representative instruments by these makers are found in the Horniman Museum, nos 14.5.47/179 and 14.5.47/186.

67. See *Harmonicon* 7/26 (1829):271.

68. On the Ling family, see Ennulat 1984. Thomas Ling was a highly regarded reed maker (see Burgess 1997b and the section on reeds below, p. 157).

69. See *Harmonicon* 2/16 (1824):75.

70. Sainsbury 1825:II:264–5; *Biographical Dictionary*, 'Parke'.

71. Numerous composers, including Hook, Shield and Incledon, wrote obbligati for Parke, particularly solo movements in overtures, and accompaniments in vocal airs. It is also

likely that Pleyel wrote his Concertante for violin, bassoon, viola, flute, cello and oboe for him. Parke wrote and performed many of his own compositions – mostly concertos, many of which included variations on popular airs – but none of these appears to have survived.

72. 1830:I:263–4.
73. Stone 1880–90.
74. *Harmonicon* 6 (1828):89.
75. *Harmonicon* 7/4 (1829):91–2.
76. 1830:269.
77. *Harmonicon* 6 (1828):48.
78. *Harmonicon* 8/5 (1830):217.
79. *Musical World* 3/38 (1836):179.
80. *Musical World* 15/253 (new series, 8/156) (1841):61–3.
81. *Musical World* 23/2 (1848):17. Cooke's side of the argument is presented in Cooke 1850.
82. For a general biography of Cooke, see the obituary in *Musical World* 30/560 (1889): 602–3.
83. 'One can imagine nothing worse, and at the same time, that is the best that London has to offer' (Fétis 1830:193). Fétis did not name the oboist, but it was possibly one of the Lings (see below).
84. *Harmonicon* (1832):30, 42.
85. *Musical World* I/8 (6.v.1836):126.
86. One of the best-known of Barret's pupils was Alfred Nicholson (1822–70), who played in the Philharmonic Society and at the Royal Italian Opera.
87. *Musical World* 26/24 (14.vi.1851):374.
88. The pitch difference can be seen in the 1862 Triébert catalogue where the Barret oboe is shown as slightly shorter than the système 6 (ill. 49). Later Lorée accepted orders for Barret oboes at *diapason normal* and also produced Triébert's other models for English players at the higher Old Philharmonic Pitch.
89. Golde left detailed notes on this subject ('On Oboe Making', pub. in trans. Golde 1978).
90. No German makers provided instruments with low B flat. Stone 1880–90 cites the Intermezzo in Mendelssohn's *Midsummer Night's Dream* (premiered in Berlin, 1843) as the first occurrence of this note for the oboe, but this was doubtless an oversight on the part of the composer as no oboes of the period were equipped to play it. Apart from the low B flats that appear in late works by Brod, some of the earliest music where this note was clearly intended comes from the Italian virtuoso Ponchielli ('Piccolo Concertino', 1848).
91. *AMZ* 11 (1819):668. Quoted in Brown 2001.
92. Based on the *Notturno* op. 99 for 2 pianos and optional 2 horns.
93. At least ten performancs of the work are recorded between 1825 and 1851. For some references see Brown 2001.
94. See Finkelman 1998–2000:VI:30.
95. Roller keys had also been common on bassoons from the 1820s.
96. Schumann inscribed a copy of the first edition with a dedication to Wasielewski (now owned by Georg Meerwein, oboist with the Bamburg Symphoniker, to whom I am grateful for sharing this and other information on these pieces).
97. See *AMZ* Neue Folge I/6 (1863):106–7; *Niederrheinische Musik-Zeitung* 15/24 (1867):189; *Nordisk Tidsskrift for Musik* 1/2 (1871):11; the performance in Boston by Spanish oboist De Ribas inspired the description of the pieces as 'quaint and full of individual charm' (*Dwight's Journal of Music* 27/1 [1867]:7).
98. Stone 1880–90. The flexibility of Schumann's scoring in these pieces has been taken by at least two leading modern players as justification to transcribe other music by Schumann for oboe. See Discography, Holliger and Schellenberger.
99. 1897:15. When Benjamin Britten accompanied the Dutch oboist Haakon Stotijn at the Aldeburgh Festival in the 1960s, he took the liberty of taking the instrument part on the

reprise, thus giving the oboist eight bars of respite (*J. Brown). Recently Tobias Picker has orchestrated the *Romances*, clothing them in a new orchestral accompaniment with connecting interludes (recorded by Robert Atherholt, see Discography).

100. Stone 1880–90 and *James Brown 2000.

101. Both translations date from 1827. The French version was revised by Fouquier, first oboe at the Opéra Italien, and sold with a fingering chart for a nine-keyed French oboe as well as the Sellner model. Giuseppe Fahrbach's *Novissimo Metodo per Oboe* (1843) and the *Metodo completo per oboe* (1848) by the Centroni student Clemente Salviani describes oboes almost identical to the Sellner model; Sellner's text was also plagiarized by the compiler of the *Transunto dei principi elementari* (c.1827, attributed to Bonifazio Asioli [1769–1823], director of the Milan Conservatory), although in this case, in place of Sellner's fingering charts, two charts probably prepared by Carlo Yvon for a four-keyed oboe and an eight-keyed 'oboe moderno' were substituted (see Bernardini 1987:19, 21).

102. Wilhelm Schneider included a fingering chart for the Sellner oboe in his *Historisch-technische Beschreibung der musikalischen Instrumente* (Leipzig, 1834), but nevertheless referred to the two-keyed oboe as the 'normal [*gewöhnlichen*] oboe' (1834:20).

103. The cor anglais solo is discussed in ch. 7, p. 221.

104. Albrecht 1985.

105. Now in the Museo Civico d'Arte Medievale, Bologna. A good number of Grenser oboes are to be found in Italy, further evidence of Centroni's recommendations. Also several Italian oboe builders modelled their work on Grenser oboes (see Bernardini 1993).

106. Bernardini 1987:22 and 1989:55.

107. 1888:99; see also Bernardini 1987 (1992):101.

108. *Quarterly Music Magazine* 6/21 (1824):68.

109. In order to retain the tonality of the original (G major), the modern editor of this work, R. Meylan (Frankfurt, London, New York: Litolff/Peters, 1966), transposed the cor anglais part up a tone, which makes it exceptionally high and quite unidiomatic for the instrument of Donizetti's day.

110. Amongst the music he wrote for it was *Omaggio a Bellini* with harp accompaniment, probably to perform with one of the two of his six daughters who played harp. For information and a photograph of Pasculli's oboes see Rosset 1987.

111. Players should be cautioned that Gargiulo's edition (Milan: Ricordi, 1961) deviates considerably from the original. The orchestral wind parts are suppressed and numerous passages re-composed. Bellini's text is followed much closer in Meylan's edition (Munich: Leuckart, 1967). A facsimile of the work is printed in *Composizioni giovanili inedite* (Rome: Reale accademia d'Italia, 1941). Both authentic and corrupt versions have been recorded. De Vries used Gargiulo's text, Holliger and Lardrot use Meylan's.

112. Braun 1823:166; Sellner 1824:art. 7.

113. Discussions of surviving nineteenth-century reeds are found in Burgess and Hedrick 1989, 1997b and Hedrick 1974a.

114. 1823:17.

115. 1890:1.

116. 1830:I:2.

117. See Burgess and Hedrick 1989.

118. *Anweisung zur Klarinette* . . . (Lepizig, 1803, 34) quoted in Birsak 1994:45.

119. Brod referred to the gouging machine as a very new invention in part II of his *Méthode* (1830).

120. In the 1880s De Stefani recommended that composers avoid notes above d3 or e♭3 in orchestral writing for the oboe as the higher notes required harder reeds which he believed had a detrimental effect on the tone of the instrument (1888:100). De Stefani continued to use very wide reeds up to the 1870s.

121. Original stapled reeds are preserved in Han de Vries's Collection, Amsterdam, with instruments by Hanken (Rotterdam, ?1835–72) and C. Gherardi (Ferrara, ?1888–1900).

122. As well as the two shown in Fig. 5/16 c), Nicholas Shackleton acquired one with the Ling reeds.

123. Some writers confused the application of Boehm's rod-and-post key construction and interactive mechanisms with a true Boehm oboe that incorporated Boehm's acoustic principles (see, e.g., V. Chalon 1877, in which Triébert's systèmes 4 and 5 are described as Boehm oboes).

124. 1861:317–19.

125. Coche 1838 and Berlioz concert review, *RGMdP* 1.iv.1838, in 1996–:430.

126. *RGMdP* 6/22 (1839):177.

127. *AWMZ* 7/8 (1847):35.

128. *AWMZ* 7/89 (1847):360.

129. For some impressions, see Lawrence 1988–95:I and II passim.

130. *Dwight's Journal of Music* 4/4 (29.x.1853):29.

131. Ventzke 1969:table I shows a copy of Boehm's original by Heckel. The correct placement of the G♯ hole on the Conservatoire oboe, for example, is located directly at the point where top and middle joints overlap. On German oboes from the early years of the nineteenth century, this hole was often moved to the top of the second joint, but shortly afterwards most makers opted for placing a smaller hole higher on the bore at the lower end of the upper joint.

132. The most complete discussion of the Lavigne-Boehm collaboration, including a summary of their calculations for the bore of the new oboe, is found in Fétis 1856:7. See also Hilkenbach 1982.

133. 1863:I:97.

134. *Musical Times* 24/481 (1883):137–8.

135. 1882:7. Lavigne seems to have made his mark on oboe playing in England. Rudall, Rose & Carte developed a Boehm oboe around 1853, and John Sharpe of Pudsey, near Leeds, developed his own style of Boehm oboe around 1920.

136. This explanation is offered by Mahillon 1883:21.

137. Wagner called it a 'cannon' and admonished flautists to use more traditional designs. See Powell 2002:191.

138. Up to 1899 Lorée made only eleven out of a total production of 1500.

139. Boehm cors anglais and oboes d'amore, although rare, were made, indicating that the design was not restricted to military music. I am grateful to Robert Howe for bringing this point to my attention.

140. A parallel German-Russian edition of the *Leichtfassliche praktische Schule für Oboe* by Henri Kling (1842–1918) appeared in 1888.

141. Bernardini 1988:382.

142. Finkelman 1998–2000:VII:109. For a critique of Jean-Godefoy Brod's playing see *AMZ* 39 (1837):727.

143. See Powell 2002, ch. 6.

144. Goodale, *Instrumental Director* (Boston, 3rd ed., 1829); another chart appeared in Whitely's *Instrumental Preceptor* (Utica, NY, 1816).

145. *Harmonicon* 4/37 (1828):10.

146. The Graupners were not the only oboist-soprano couple. In the 1770s Ludwig Augustus Lebrun and his wife the famous soprano Franziska Dorothea *née* Danzi toured the musical centres of Europe, and William Herschel (who also started life as a *Hoboist* in the Hanoverian Guards) performed duets for oboe and soprano with his sister Caroline in the salons of Bath up to the time William was appointed Astronomer Royal in 1788.

147. On Graupner's biography, see Dwight 1881:416, Johnson 1943 and in Lee, 'Graupner, Gottlieb' in *NG2*.

148. US–NYp.

149. Another Italian, Sebastiano Conti, played second oboe in the 1832–3 season.

150. *Philadelphia Evening Post* 17 Oct. 1834; *Boston Courier*, 1840, quoted in Bernardini 2001:374.

151. See Bernardini 2001.
152. A decade later, a Mr Nedham, 'oboe professor in New York', appeared on the list of subscribers to Barret 1850.
153. De Ribas played cor anglais in the 1844 New York production of Michael Balfe's *The Bohemian Girl* (see Lawrence 1988–95:I:266). Paggi had also given performances on cor anglais, but had returned to Europe shortly before.
154. See Univ. of Michigan Museum, no. 671 (c.1860); and for more information on these three makers see Groce 1991.

Chapter 6 *From Romanticism to Modernism*

1. I use the term 'Modernism' to denote the artistic movement originating in the second half of the nineteenth century and reaching its apex around World War I. For a detailed definition, see Botstein 2001.
2. 1939:140.
3. Boulez 1986:36.
4. For a critical reception of the tonal equality of valved brass see Arnold Myers, 'Design, Technology and Manufacture since 1800', in Herbert and Wallace 1997:115–30, and Simon Wills, 'Brass in the Modern Orchestra', ibid., 157–76; and on the Boehm flute, see Anton Fürstenau n.d. I:20, quoted in Birsak 1994:61.
5. 1878:467.
6. See Pierre 1893 quoted in Storch 1981:31.
7. Leon Goossens's teacher Charles Reynolds ordered sixty-one instruments in the space of fifteen years, including fifty-three oboes and eight cors anglais and one oboe d'amore. He ordered several different models until settling on his own particular design that Lorée then duplicated many times. Surely some of Reynolds's orders were made on behalf of students and colleagues. The information comes from the sales register preserved by Lorée. I owe a huge debt of gratitude to James Brown for undertaking the exhausting task of transcribing and assembling the data in machine-readable form.
8. The term 'military system oboe' is often used to refer to anything with less than the full Conservatoire mechanism, such as Triébert's systèmes 3–5. Such instruments generally have simple keywork with side keys for B flat and C, and doubled hole 3. But oboists outside military establishments also played these instruments. They would have been perfectly adequate – and furthermore less expensive – for amateurs, students and the majority of professional orchestral players.
9. See, for instance, Lavignac 1899:100. Anderson 1929 still mentioned syst`ème 4 but called it an 'older-system'.
10. Gevaert 1885:139; Prout 1897:114.
11. Mönnig placed a number of patents for new key systems up to the 1930s.
12. See anonymous biography of Schiemann in *Musikbladet* 35 (1895):267–8.
13. Berlioz rev. Strauss 1948:183.
14. See J. Singer 1994:144, and Bate 1975:96–7.
15. The decree was confirmed by an international conference on pitch held in Vienna in 1885. See Haynes 2002:352.
16. Some of the Viennese oboes would have been the work of Leopold Uhlmann (1806–78), the son of Tobias Uhlmann; others would have been by Wolfgang Küss.
17. Differences between Zuleger's and Hajek's oboes are only slight and mostly involve mechanical details.
18. Viennese players claim that *Stützfinger* technique was practised by eighteenth-century oboists; in fact it is given in only a small number of fingering charts from the period (see Haynes 1978).
19. Sonneck 1994.

20. 1973, published by the author.
21. See Hadamowsky 1969.
22. Wolf has also introduced models that couple the bore of the Viennese oboe with a key system that allows either French or Viennese fingerings to be used. See Anon. 1998b.
23. Yoshimizu 2002.
24. This instrument is now owned by Alfredo Bernardini, Amsterdam.
25. This method has never been published (manuscript found in the library of the Parma Conservatory, Al IV 46–8). On De Stefani see Bernardini 1987 (1992):101.
26. Bigotti 1974:46.
27. Anecdote related in Bonelli 1982:39.
28. Stone 1880–90:II:487.
29. Langey 1885 includes a price list for Boosey and Hawkes.
30. Information on British oboe manufactures taken from Waterhouse 1993 and Post 1982c.
31. See Haynes 2002:ch. 10, and Bate 1975:88.
32. 1953:23; this point retained in the 1962 ed.
33. On the interchangeability of these terms, see Introduction.
34. In 1850 the recent Conservatoire laureate Félix-Charles Berthélemy was shown playing a curved instrument (Stern 1850), and the 1860–2 Triébert catalogue shows only straight ones.
35. Pierre 1890:272.
36. Waterhouse 1993:250.
37. De Stefani 1888:105.
38. There does not appear to be a national preference for including this note as it is found on scattered instruments not only by Triébert but by Heckel and other German makers.
39. The B flat is heard on Karajan's recording with the Berlin Philharmonic (1975) and Haitink's with the Concertgebouw Orkest from the same year. Bernstein's performance with the Vienna Philharmonic is a fascinating illustration with the B natural played on a Viennese cor anglais.
40. Fischer-Wildhagen 1985 and Finkelman 1998–2000:VI:31–2, VII:110–11. A ten-keyed rosewood instrument with flared bell is in the Kunsthistorisches Museum, Vienna. The Altoboe was mentioned rarely by other composers. Works by Hans Kummer and Karl Mille were published for 'English Horn oder Alt-Oboe' (see Fischer-Wildhagen 1985:96).
41. Bate and Finkelman 2001:305–6.
42. Waterhouse 1993:167–8.
43. To date just over one hundred have been produced.
44. See Finkelman 2001 and Girard's extensive study 'Les Hautbois d'église' (2001).
45. The score gives saxophone as an alternative to the Heckelphone.
46. Blatter 1997:95.
47. See Janice Knight 1996.
48. See IDRS programme from Rotterdam Conference, 1995. Other composers who have written for the ensemble are Jacques Castérède (1926–), Michel Wiblé (1923–).
49. 1997:95.
50. On that occasion it was played by Philipp Wolfram (1854–1919) (*Berliner Börsen-Kurier* 5 Nov. 1909, discussed in Baines 1967:100).
51. Lavignac 1899:102.
52. *AMZ* 7 (1829):98. This was also the case in Vienna in 1862 (Hanslick 1950:97).
53. Bessaraboff 1941:124. Practical research carried out by Harnoncourt and Schaeftlein for the Telefunken Bach Cantata recording series in the 1960s and Dahlqvist 1972 disentangled most of the confusion surrounding these instruments.
54. Orchestral parts of Bach's vocal works still used by modern and period-instrument orchestras have the oboe d'amore parts transposed for either oboe or English horn.

55. See Gevaert 1885:138, where he refers to Bach's writing for oboe d'amore, and William Stone, letter to the editor of *Musical Times* 20/437 (1879):385.

56. Maino and Orsi also made oboes d'amore of this type.

57. Bate 1975:113.

58. *Musical Times* 25/501 (1884):643–5.

59. Berlioz rev. Strauss 1948:183.

60. Koechlin's works for oboe d'amore include a little-known *Sonatine* (op. 194, 1942–3, scored for oboe d'amore or soprano saxophone, 2 flutes, clarinet, 2 violins, 2 violas, 2 cellos, harpsichord), *Le repos de Tityre* (op. 216, 1948, for solo oboe d'amore); the *Suite pour cor anglais seul ou hautbois d'amour ou hautbois baryton*, op. 185, and other smaller pieces in the *14 Pièces pour hautbois, oboe d'amore cor anglais et piano*, op. 179. See Register 1990 and J. Singer 1991a.

61. For a more complete list of works, see Finkelman 1998–2000:II:368.

62. Terence MacDonagh, Robert Bloom and Laila Storch each complained at the poor quality of instruments (MacDonagh, 'Oboe Family', in Eaglefield-Hull 1924:357). Bloom worked closely with Alfred Laubin to improve the intonation of the oboe d'amore (*Sara Lambert Bloom). Storch* reports that in the first part of the twentieth century the Philadelphia Orchestra owned one d'amore, but otherwise Bach performances, including those at the renowned Bach Festival in Bethlehem PA, made do without the instrument because those available at the time from French builders were unreliable.

63. *Die Oboe* Nov. 1929, quoted in J. Singer 1994:145.

64. 1885:141.

65. 1910:12.

66. Widor for instance recommended avoiding the low notes altogether because they are 'so aggressive that they always stick out (*si agressive, «l'écouter» toujours)*' (1904:23, see also Elson 1902:156).

67. *Geschichte des Concertwesens in Wien* (Vienna, 1970) quoted in trans. in Rees-Davies, 'The Development of Clarinet Repertoire', in Lawson 1995:83. Earlier in the century Berlioz had commented that 'solos by wind instruments are generally of little amusement, apart from those played by the oboist Brod'; *RGMdP* (18 Nov. 1838):467–8, Berlioz 1996–:III: 556.

68. 1898:29.

69. Parès mentions his arrangement of Lalo's Ouverture to *Le Roi d'Ys*.

70. A possible antecedent to this work is the Concertino by C. M. v. Weber, arranged in 1811, possibly for Thomas Anton Fladt, for oboe and wind orchestra.

71. 1913–27:1542.

72. *L'Art musical* 19/38 (1880):338, referring to a performance of the Grandval concerto (see below).

73. Over the decade 1904–14, Odeon issued a rare series of recordings of French oboists including Gillet, Louis Gaudard of the Garde Républicaine, Montenat, Rey, and two female players, Mme Bantoux and Rachel de Guy (John Gibbs*, Univ. of Washington).

74. Storch 1977:16.

75. *L'Art musical* 19/38 (1880):338. Marie-Félice-Clémence de Reiset (1830–1907) was a composition student of Flotow and Saint-Saëns. The earliest reference to the work is a review printed in *Le Ménestrel* 2 Feb. 1879. The duchess also dedicated *Deux pièces pour hautbois et piano* 'à mon ami Georges Gillet' (1877). Another work written for Gillet was Saint-Saëns's *Caprice sur des airs danois et russes* (op. 79) for flute, oboe, clarinet and piano, written to be played by the composer with Taffanel, Gillet and Turban whilst on tour to Russia in 1887.

76. Paris: Leduc, 1909.

77. See Storch 1985.

78. See Margelli 1996 and Storch 1983.

79. Bleuzet did not record this piece, but his playing is documented in a performance of another work from the period, the *Sonatine pour hautbois* (op. 13, 1928) by Marcel Mihalovici.

80. Laila Storch gave a more complete listing in a paper read at the 2000 conference of L'Association Française du Hautbois.

81. On Longy's life and activities see Jeskalian 1990, Anon. 1925 and Whitwell 1988.

82. Longy also owned a Conservatoire-system oboe by Alexandre Robert (fl.1895–1925) with some added custom-made keys to facilitate c2 and an extra hole between the g♯ vent and hole 4 (now owned by Robert Howe).

83. Listed in Bruch 1936.

84. *Musical Courier* Dec. 1915. A slightly different version of this story is associated with Heifetz and de Busscher in a performance of the same concerto and the Hollywood Bowl (anecdote related by Philip Memoli in Harris 1975).

85. Biographical information on Barthel comes from Conrey 1983.

86. Much information on Goossens's commissions and recordings is to be found in Rosen 1993.

87. Henri de Busscher (1880–1975), born in Belgium, went on to play in the New York Symphony (1913–20) and the Los Angeles Philharmonic (1920–48).

88. See Tobin 1948:46, and Baines, who described Goossens's playing as 'silvery and violin like in tone' (1967:93).

89. Rosen 1993:125.

90. Obituary, *Daily Telegraph* 15 Feb. 1988.

91. Compare Goossens's disparaging remarks in interview with Gerald N. Moore, 1979, with his more positive commentary on his teacher's abilities in print (1977:52).

92. Bate 1975:206.

93. Moore radio interview, 1979. Belgian musicians were quite prevalent in England in the late part of the nineteenth century.

94. A comprehensive discography can be found in Rosen 1993:479–88.

95. Acuta Music, 1996.

96. A definitive biography of Tabuteau is in progress by his pupil Laila Storch.

97. For recordings see Discography. A compilation of orchestral excerpts is available. Apart from the Handel G minor Concerto he recorded in 1952, the only other concerted work he played with the Philadelphia Orchestra was the Mozart Oboe Quartet in an orchestration by Stokowski.

98. *Marcel Tabuteau Lessons*, recorded 1965, tracks 3, 4.

99. Tabuteau explains the number system along with breathing, inflection distribution and other pedagogical principles on *Marcel Tabuteau Lessons*.

100. A comparison of other works that the two players recorded, such as the Bach Double Concerto, the Handel G minor Oboe Concerto, or works in comparable style like Goossens's rendition of Elgar's *Soliloquy* and Tabuteau's reading of Henry Eichheim's *Japanese Nocturne* (1929), would generate similar comments.

101. Quoted in 1975:138.

102. This point is emphasized in Piguet 1997.

103. Veale 1992.

104. Marcel Tabuteau, who also belonged to this school, did not arrive in the States 'with a quick vibrato and nasal tone' typical of French oboists (Rosenberg 2002): these were characteristics that would develop in France after Tabuteau's appointment to the Philadelphia Orchestra.

105. Louis Bas, *Méthode nouvelle* (1905), and one of the first compilations of orchestral excerpts, *Études de l'Orchestre* (3 vols, Paris: Costallat, 1911); Louis Bleuzet, *Technique du hautbois* (3 parts, Paris: Leduc, 1920–41); Ernest Loyon, *32 Études* (Paris: Costallat, 1925, dedicated to Bleuzet); Albert Debondue, two sets of *études* (Paris: Leduc, 1952, 55); Roland Lamorlette *12 Études* (Paris: Leduc, 1954); and Eugène Bozza's *14 Études sur des*

modes Karnatiques (Paris: Leduc, 1972) expand the oboist's technique with an unfamiliar compositional idiom.

106. Including *Raccolta de studi per oboe utili ad un primo e contemporaneo sviluppo dell'agilità e del canto* (Milan: Ricordi, 1944) and *12 studie di carattere moderno e sul cromatismo armonico per oboe* (Milan: Ricordi, c.1950).

107. 1967:93.

108. See anonymous obituary, London *Daily Telegraph* 18 September 1986, repr. in *DR* 10/1 (1987):41.

109. 1982:138.

110. 'Orchestral Colour and Values', in Eaglefield-Hull 1924:364.

111. 1897:114. See also Elson 1902:156: 'It is worth passing mention that the older oboes possessed broader reeds than the present ones, and gave a fuller and more nasal tone, not unlike that of a musette [i.e. the folk instrument]. Even at present the older form remains in many German orchestras.'

112. See *De kunst van het maken van hoborieten* (1967) and his autobiography *Even uitblazen* (1976).

113. Recorded by the Stotijns 1951 (solo concerto) and 1961 (double concerto).

114. Anon. 1998.

115. See Prodan 1979.

116. Pressure from American musicians' unions in the early 1920s curtailed the importation of foreign musicians, and the Curtis Institute was set up to train American musicians. Ironically, the Institute's faculty was made up largely of foreigners like Tabuteau who were responsible for the establishment of an 'American' style.

117. The mark 'AK' refers to serial numbers of Lorée oboes from the height of Tabuteau's career. My response to this model is informed by conversations with John de Lancie and Laila Storch who, being Tabuteau pupils, were aware of his instrument preferences.

118. These differences are clear from the illustrations in Ledet 1981.

119. *AMZ* 2/47 (1867):378–9; Storch, 1977 (1996 repr. p.20).

120. *Musical Times* 351/15 (1872):466.

121. Paris: Costallat.

122. Two editions appeared in the space of one year. Max Seiffert, who edited the work for Peters (1920), retained the c minor of the harpsichord version, while Max Schneider's edition for Breitkopf und Härtel (1921) proposed d minor. Tovey had also made a transcription of this work; his manuscript is in the Goossens Collection housed in the GB–Lbl, MS Add. 71987.

123. Reconstructed by Tovey. Tovey's manuscript is in the GB–Lbl, MS Add. 71987.

124. For more information on hypothetical reconstructions, see Haynes 2001:387–95 and notes by Joshua Rifkin accompanying Steven Hammer's recording, the first complete cycle of hypothetical reconstructions of Bach oboe concertos performed on hautboy.

125. See Lardrot 1999.

126. Leipzig: Breitkopf und Härtel.

127. London: Oxford Univ. Press. For more on this work, see Fedelleck 1979, and a review of a revised ed. of the work, Folkman 1987.

128. Paumgartner 1950; see also Riordan 1995.

129. Based on piano pieces he had written between 1914 and 1917, the orchestral version was prepared for a ballet staged in 1920.

130. 1959:31.

131. Recordings of Bloom with the Bach Aria Group have been re-released in *The Art of Robert Bloom*.

132. Later in his career Bloom educated himself in Baroque performance practice by reading Thurston Dart, Robert Donington, Charles Sanford Terry, Philipp Spitta and Percy M. Young, but he always relied on his own musical common sense. Bloom had no personal experience with historical instruments, but at least three of his students – John Abberger,

Gonzalo Ruiz and Peter Hedrick – went on to be specialists on hautboy.

133. Some of his 'elaborations' have been published in Bloom 1998.

134. It is not known for whom Holst wrote his *Air and Variations* and *Three Pieces*. Written over the period from 1896 to 1910, they are too early to have been for Goossens.

135. *Diversions* is not published, but has been recorded by Simon Dent (see Discography).

136. Jacob initially envisaged the work for Evelyn Rothwell, but when Goossens heard about it, he promised an auspicious première and so the work was dedicated to him.

137. Premiered in 1937 by the composer's daughter Joy Boughton.

138. Praised by Percy Grainger as the best oboe concerto ever written (Goossens 1977:159).

139. Goossens never performed this work. He recalled having 'serious reservations about the structure of the piece' and returned the manuscript to the composer (Peter Dickinson, preface to the Novello ed., 1987).

140. For more information on the Oboistenbund, see Ventzke 1976.

141. London: Boosey and Hawkes, 1948.

142. Goossens 1977:158.

143. A complete list of commercial recordings is included in the Discography.

144. 1995:61. De Lancie also commissioned works by Françaix and Benjamin Lees.

145. Strauss revised the ending in 1948, and it is this version that was printed in the Boosey and Hawkes edition. Other recordings where this version can be heard are Goossens's made in 1946 and Robin Canter's.

146. Anon. 'Aerophor' in *NG2*, 1:178.

147. 1977:158.

148. London: Boosey and Hawkes, 1951.

149. The other members were the parents of the well-known oboist Sarah Francis, Millicent Silver (harpsichord), and John Francis (flute).

150. The oboists were Montagu Slater and Sylvia Spencer.

151. The *Temporal Variations* have been orchestrated by Colin Matthews (1995).

152. For two differing programmatic interpretations, see Mulder 1992 and Hiramoto 1999.

Chapter 7 The oboe in Romantic and Modernist music

1. I have already presented some of the ideas developed in this chapter in 1997a, where I also explain my use of the term 'persona'.

2. These three realms coincide with Dahlhaus's threefold division of Romantic expression into the folkloric, historical and exotic (1989:16–25).

3. I use the term 'gender' to refer to culturally defined categories of masculinity and femininity in contrast to the relatively straightforward biological distinction of sex.

4. 'De la musique en générale', in 1844b:I:252.

5. Trans. from Charlton 1989:113.

6. Baudelaire 1981:51. Charlton 1989:105.

7. 'The Rise of Urban Life between the Revolutions, 1789–1848', in Ringer 1990:23.

8. 1878:x.

9. 1991 (1857). Baudelaire also quoted a passage from Hoffmann drawing a connection between 'the fragrance of deep red carnations' and the 'deep, profound ones of the oboe [*les sons graves et profonds du hautbois*]' (1981:51). This, however, was an error Baudelaire took from a French translation of Hoffmann. In place of the oboe, the original German refers to the basset horn. (Charlton 1989:105; Baudelaire 1991:265).

10. This is discussed eloquently in Seneci 1998:116–36.

11. Ernst 1865–1890.

12. Anon., 'The material of music, V', *Musical Times*, 29/543 (1888): 272–4.

13. Anon. review, *RGMdP* 6 (1839):565.

14. The last work may have been inspired by Berlioz's reports of the Italian *pifferari* (see below).

15. Berlioz recycled this passage in numerous reviews. It also found its way into his 'Étude critique des symphonies de Beethoven' (1862:37). Trans. from Berlioz 1994:23.

16. The composer later adapted this aria to the text 'Dominus noster' (1820).

17. 1806:321–2; Eng. trans. from DuBois 1996:33. Schubart attributed the connection between cor anglais and glass harmonica to Burney, but the exact reference remains obscure. Although these two instruments were never used together in Romantic music, they participated in strikingly similar dramatic settings by Donizetti and Verdi involving women driven to distraction – the harmonica in the mad scene from *Lucia di Lammermoor* (replaced in the final version of the score by a solo flute) and cor anglais in the sleepwalking scene in *Macbeth*.

18. 1964:20.

19. Berlioz 1855:96.

20. 1768:315 ('Musique').

21. 1912–13:147.

22. Comettant 1861:486.

23. Berlioz 1971:28.

24. The *pifferi* were still played into the twentieth century. See Geller 1954.

25. These two extended extracts conflate three sources: 'Lettre d'un enthousiaste sur l'état actuel de la musique en Italie', *Revue européenne*, 15 March 1832 (Berlioz 1996–:I:69–83); 'Souvenirs d'Italie', *Le Rénovateur*, 13 April 1834 (Berlioz 1996–:I:212) and 'Voyage musical', *L'Italie pittoresque*, July 1834 (Berlioz 1996–:I:324–5). The reference is to Virgil's *Aeneid*, Book IV: 617–18.

26. 1912–13:147.

27. Other examples of 'musique primitive' with oboe and/or cor anglais are found in 'Paysans sous les Tilleuls' from the second of the *Huit scènes de Faust* (1828–9), where 'the shepherds leave their flocks', and in part II of *L'Enfance du Christ* (1850–4), where oboes play rustic drones, recalling Bach's oboe writing in the Sinfonia to part II of the *Christmas Oratorio*. The passage from Bach is quoted in Gevaert's *Nouveau traité* with the following comment, suggesting that he was aware of the connection with Berlioz: 'This recalls the concerts of *pifferari* that the old Florentine painters placed in front of the crèche of the infant Jesus' (1885:153).

28. Victor Hugo 1964, 'Gluck et Beethoven, rameaux sous qui l'on rêve'.

29. 1844a:104; 1855:82.

30. 1844a:106; 1855:82.

31. 1885:142.

32. 1874:26.

33. 1914:I:238 (orig. pub. 1789).

34. With reference to passages from Gounod's *Faust*, Beethoven's Seventh Symphony and Weber's *Freischütz* and *Oberon*.

35. 1824:1.

36. First published 1840, section entitled 'Que la Musique date du sixième siècle', 1964:1099–1100. Similarly, in a passage in Ann Radcliffe's gothic novel *The Mysteries of Udolpho* the sound of an oboe in the midst of the storm distresses one of the female characters (1966:623).

37. 'Über das Dirigieren' (1869), trans. as 'About Conducting', in 1869:298.

38. The entire F major section was added by Beethoven as part of extensive reworking of this scene for the 1814 revision. The oboe obbligato was reworked from 'Da stiegen die Menschen ans Licht' from the Cantata on the Death of Emperor Joseph II (1790).

39. In the première season the cors anglais were most likely played by Brod and Vény. In Meyerbeer's *Les Huguenots* (1836) another pair of social outcasts, the Huguenots Valentine

and Raoul, is represented by a single cor anglais.

40. 1986:222.

41. For more information on Hiebendahl, see Finkelman 1998–2000:VI:30–1.

42. 1983:273.

43. Discussed in Finkelman 1998–2000:VI:31.

44. 1911:558.

45. This description is taken from Sachs 1913. I have failed to find a specimen or even an illustration of this 'instrument'. It is probably such an instrument that can be heard on Karl Böhm's 1966 recording. See also Pap 1994.

46. Abramo Basevi, quoted by Tomlinson 1999:96.

47. Many of these pieces are discussed by Hepokoski (1989:259). See also 'Il mio ben sospiro' in Rossini's *La scala di seta* (1812, one of the earliest), 'Il faut partir' in *La fille du régiment* (1840); 'Orfanella in tetto umile' in Verdi's *Simon Boccanegra* (1857); Violetta's aria in act III of *La Traviata* (1853). Similar expressions of desolation and loss signalled by an oboe or cor anglais are also found in non-Italian operas. See Rimsky-Korsakov's *Czar's Bride* (1899, cited in Rimsky-Korsakov 1964:287), where Marfa singing of 'the days when we were carefree'; from Berlioz, Dido's lament 'Adieu fière cité' in V, 2 of *Les Troyens* and Marguerite's *romance* 'D'amour l'ardente flamme' in *Huit scènes de Faust* (1829) and *La Damnation de Faust* (1845); Isabelle's air 'Robert, toi que j'aime' in Meyerbeer's *Robert le Diable* (1831). César Franck took up the tragic tone of *Tristan* in the cor anglais solo in the second movement of his D minor Symphony (1886–9).

48. On *Nina* see ch. 5, p. 143.

49. There is a small number of men who indulge in such songs of lamentation or loss accompanied by double reeds. Rigoletto's 'Miei signori' is accompanied by cor anglais, as is Carlo's lament 'Quale più fido amico' in *Giovanna d'Arco*. In act III of Thomas's *Hamlet* the cor anglais sounds as Hamlet recalls the words of his father's ghost and of course Tristan's vigil is accompanied by the piping shepherd.

50. As an example of this point one need only think of the difficulties Clara Schumann faced in pursuing a career as concert pianist.

51. '. . . tritt sie siegreich aus dem Gewirre der übrigen Instrumenten' (1824:art.7).

52. Tomlinson 1989:85–6, where the author is discussing Michel Poizat's theory of unmediated voice in *The Angel's Cry* (1992).

53. 1821:I:290–1.

54. 1830:II:1. This view was reiterated by several other authors, including Fétis (1837). See also Vény: 'The oboe is never treated ideally unless the composer uses it in sweet, expressive, and calm or staid music [*douce, expressive et posée*]; melodic phrases [*les phrases de chant*] suit it better, perhaps, than passagework, which so often simply astonishes the listeners, whereas simple and pure melody moves them' (1828:14).

55. 1885:141–2, 'interprète immédiat du sentiment, surtout du sentiment féminin'.

56. Florent Schmitt's *La Tragédie de Salomé* (1907–11) also includes a florid chromatic oboe arabesque.

57. My discussion of Orientalism is indebted to Edward Said's classic study (1979), Hunter 1998 and McClary 1992.

58. Hunter 1998:43.

59. Hunter 1998:55.

60. Letter to Jules Cloquet, 15 Jan. 1850 (1979:81).

61. 1994:27.

62. 1998:121.

63. Ralph Locke draws attention to the importance of this work in 1998:112–16.

64. See Locke 1998:119–20.

65. *RGMdP* 8 May 1836; Berlioz 1996–:II:463.

66. 1993:155.

67. Schmid 1945:15.

68. These elements led to the work being described as 'rhapsodical with a good deal of the arabesque and the colour that we Westerns are accustomed to call oriental' (Ernest Newman quoted in Carole Rosen 1993:132).
69. Corigliano 1978 (preface).
70. Corigliano 1990.
71. Sibelius took the story from the monumental mid-nineteenth-century compilation of Finnish myth, the *Kalevala*, assembled by Elias Lönnot (1802–84).
72. Programme notes from performance given by the Indianapolis Symphony Orchestra (1 Feb. 1957), 269, quoted in McMullen 1994:13.
73. Kernis 1996.
74. The piece has already been reworked by the composer for the cellist Truls Mørk (see Discography).
75. Another work also from the 1990s with an ecological theme is Leonardo Balada's *Music for Oboe and Orchestra: Lament from the Cradle of the Earth* (1993), written for Cynthia Koledo DeAlmeida and the Pittsburgh Symphony Orchestra.
76. 1941:117.
77. Storch 2002.
78. Rosen 1993:140.
79. *Daily Telegraph* review of his New York recital in 1928, quoted in Rosen 1993:130.
80. *The Guardian* 15 Feb. 1988.
81. Post 1982a:46.
82. Anon. *The Musical Courier* 31 July 1895 and 3 Sept. 1925, quoted in Mueller 1951:309.
83. 'The Position of Women' in *Vogue's First Reader*, 1944:420, quoted in Mueller 1951:309.
84. Stolper 2001.

Chapter 8 Diversifying streams since World War II: the traditional stream

1. From Sara Lambert Bloom 1998:4. Notice the similarity to Baines's words regarding the oboe's limited compass into which 'is packed a telling vividness and intensity of character unapproached by any other wind instrument' (1967:91). These comments also have resonance with Fétis's remarks: 'The greatest difficulty that must be overcome when playing the oboe is the need to restrain the breath in order to sweeten the sound and to avoid accidents that are vulgarly called *quacks*' (1834c:212).
2. 1984b:41.
3. This remark by Simon Wills refers to brass instruments, but is equally applicable to the oboe ('Brass in the Modern Orchestra', in Herbert and Wallace 1997:175).
4. For more information on raw materials and recent developments in oboe manufacture see Post 1995.
5. See Yoshimizu 2002.
6. Completed orchestration was supplied by Barber's pupil Charles Turner. *Canzonetta* has since been recorded by Lucarelli; see Discography.
7. Register 1990.
8. Fink 1999.
9. Powning 1980.
10. Tancibudek wanted to have a work by a Czech composer to play as a homage to his homeland. Martinů's less performed *Sinfonia Concertante* for oboe, violin, cello and bassoon with orchestra was written in 1949 shortly before Tancibudek requested the concerto and has close musical connections with the Oboe Concerto, to the extent that the outer movements of the two works are virtually rewrites of each other.
11. See Furlong 1974:304.
12. 1752:88; see also Piguet 1997:4.
13. For an amusing diagnosis of this syndrome, see Marx, 'Ill Wind', in Marx 1983:118–27.

14. For a detailed practice regimen see Kynaston c.1980.

15. Burton 1991:127.

16. Fétis reported that oboists in oriental cultures used circular breathing (*Histoire générale* [Paris: 1868], cited in Brown and Adams 1888:120).

17. See ch. 1, p. 22.

18. 'Ein geschickter Hoboist', *AMZ* 10/1 (1875):14. The account originally appeared in Max von Thielmann, *Streifzüge im Kaukasus* (Leipzig, 1875), 184. The writer argued confidently (if from ignorance) that the instrument must have been an oboe as clarinets were unknown in the orient.

19. Review of a Boston performance in *Dwight's Musical Journal* 4/4 (29 Oct. 1853):29.

20. 1975:169.

21. 1967:92.

22. 1897:15.

23. See, for example, Samantha Owens, who identifies Goossens as the epitome of this modern practice (1995:65).

24. Mattheson wrote that 'The best *Maîtres* usually make [their reeds] themselves to fit their embouchures, as in a good reed is half the playing' (1713:269). This is repeated in Majer 1732:34. Cf. also Vanderhagen c.1790:5.

25. Although he declared that 'all serious oboists make their own reeds' (1977:31), for many years Goossens played on reeds made by Tom Brearley of Liverpool and recommended that all his students do the same.

26. Only in America is personalized gouging widespread.

27. This is only because no one has devoted sufficient energy to experimentation. The Canadian physicist Guy Legere has designed highly successful professional-quality clarinet reeds made from a plastic developed in medical research.

28. This is not the place to give a detailed description of the art of reed-making. David Hogan Smith 1992 contains much information useful to oboists. Although designed primarily for players of Renaissance double reeds, his concepts of 'reed resonance' (crow pitch) and 'equivalent volume' are directly applicable to all types of oboe reeds. Standard technical descriptions of the American-style oboe reeds are in Sprenkle and Ledet 1961 and Weber and Capps 1990; and for British style, in Evelyn Rothwell 1975–7. Ledet 1981 presents an extensive survey of international styles. For additional references see Boums 1988 and Burgess 1997c.

29. 1802:ch.8.

30. Up to the present, many authorities have considered double- and triple-tonguing non-standard techniques, although practised by many players (see, for instance, Blatter 1997:93).

31. See 2001:246–8.

32. *25 Grandes études de Hugot, transcrites pour le hautbois et procédées de gammes, arpèges, notes coulés et trilles* (Paris: Richault, 1859).

33. 1975–7:32.

34. Recording with the Berlin Philharmonic under Karajan, 1970 (the music is given in Ex. 5.2).

35. Oscar Thompson 1952:1728.

36. 1980:8.

37. An earlier version of this section appeared as Burgess 2002.

38. '"Space-Sound", Vibrato, Radio, etc.' (1931), quoted in trans. in Schoenberg 1975:149–50.

39. 'Vibrato' (1940), quoted in Schoenberg 1975:346.

40. Quoted in Potter 1998:57.

41. Quoted in Rushmore 1971:190.

42. According to him 'the vibrato is popular among the Latin races, while the Anglo-Saxons will not tolerate it' (quoted in Rushmore 1971:190).

43. Another source of vibrato in mainstream performance that is often overlooked is jazz.

Ernest Ansermet was one of many Europeans to be fascinated by the unorthodox ways in which jazz musicians handled western musical instruments. In an essay entitled 'Sur un orchestre nègre' (1919) he drew particular attention to vibrato on clarinet and saxophone. It is significant that in this case vibrato is identified with a musical style that at the time was stigmatized as 'primitive'.

44. Singer 1999:7–8.
45. 1947:62.
46. The most thorough history of vibrato in the Baroque period is Moens-Haenen 1988. See also Haynes 2001:250–66.
47. 1760:9. Other writers distinguished the tremolo from vibrato as complying with the rhythm of the music.
48. 28 May 1778, Anderson 1938:540.
49. Letter dated 4 April 1787, Anderson 1938:907.
50. n.d.:81–2. Fürstenau's examples show vibrato used to intensify *sforzati* and *crescendi*, and to add colour to *fermati* (79–83). For further references to the combination of breath and finger vibrato in nineteenth-century wind technique, see Manning 1995:73.
51. Almenräder 1822–3, Jancourt c.1847. Jancourt did not think of finger vibrato as an ornament of taste (*agrément de goût*) but rather as the result of profound emotion, although the accompanying musical examples still show its use only on isolated long notes.
52. 1855:66. In a similar vein, the flautist Wragg had limited the use of vibrato to slow movements 'of much pathos and feeling' (1818:67).
53. 1802:11.
54. 1816–25:art. 3 'On the Embouchure'.
55. Review of Czerwenka's performance of an oboe concerto and *Potpourri on Russian Airs* by Maurer in Berlin, 2 March 1819, *AMZ* 21 (1819):250–1.
56. 'Bebung'. Whether the editor, von Dommer, was referring to finger or breath vibrato here is unclear.
57. Deacon 1880–90:5:268–9.
58. 1992:234.
59. Berlioz rev. Strauss 1904:183.
60. 1974:n.p.
61. Post 1982b:36.
62. Discussed in Storch 1977:16. It should not, however, be ruled out that Gillet modified his playing when performing for the microphone.
63. 1977:87.
64. Goossens 1979.
65. 1953:13.
66. 1967:93.
67. For an account of an English oboist's perspective on French oboe playing in the 1940s, see Dobson's report in the *Philharmonic Post*, 1946.
68. See Philip 1992:122.
69. A second-generation Taffanel pupil, Kincaid was a member of the Philadelphia Orchestra from 1921 to 1960.
70. Goossens described the playing of William Malsch, his teacher at the Royal College of Music, as being 'like a comb and tissue paper with no vibrato' (Post 1982a:42).
71. Poulenc's direction *sans couleur* is often interpreted as 'non vibrato' (Oboe Sonata, 1962).
72. 1976:27.
73. 1977:87.
74. John Potter maintains that the type of vibrato that comes naturally to the voice is one not so much of pitch oscillation but of intensity (1998:57). This concept has been discredited to some extent by the emergence of different vocal traditions in Early Music.
75. See Prodan 1979:Q.24.
76. Goossens (1977:88). This is close to the 6.5 that Seashore found was average among

singers (1947:59).

77. Brown 1976; Weait 1988 and Light 1994:191–6. Gärtner has proposed the term 'abdomen-thorax' (1981:28).

78. See Gärtner 1981:126.

79. This point is made by Sprenkle and Ledet (1961:13).

Chapter 9 Diversifying streams since World War II: from the avant-garde to Postmodernism

1. 1911:ch.4.

2. For more detailed technical information, Roxburgh's contribution to Goossens's book *Oboe* is a useful starting point. Post takes different aspects of extended technique, combining historical background with practical know-how (1980a, 1980b, 1981, 1981–2, 1984a, 1984b, 1985). Read 1993 is unsurpassed as a resource for composers and includes an extensive compilation of examples from the repertoire. A detailed survey of avant-garde techniques specific to reed instruments is to be found in Hoppe 1992, which also includes copious musical examples. Veale and Mahnkopf 1994 is the most comprehensive method integrating traditional and extended techniques, and Holliger 1972 is an important anthology of avant-garde music for solo oboe.

3. See Post 1981–2:145.

4. Written for Holliger and, like Frank Martin's *Trois Pièces*, commissioned by the Swiss conductor Paul Sacher.

5. Veale and Mahnkopf 1994:63. This technique is needed in *Dmaathen* by Xenakis to produce notes up to c4 and the 'whistle tone' f♯5.

6. Around 1995 Lorée produced a small number of oboes extending to low A. This was on the recommendation of Alex Klein, who sought an instrument that would allow oboists to play Schubert's 'Arpeggione' Sonata (see Discography), but as yet it does not appear to have been scored for by any composers.

7. Veale and Mahnkopf 1994 gives fingerings at eighth-tone increments (where possible) across the whole range.

8. See Vecchione 1993:23.

9. According to Lawrence Singer, there are over one hundred different fingerings for this note, although he catalogues only ten (1969:3). The timbral effects in Bartolozzi's *Concertazioni* (1965) for oboe and eleven instruments may have been another point of departure for Berio when writing *Sequenza VII*.

10. See van Cleve 1991 for recommended modifications to the standard American-style reed for playing Berio's *Sequenza VII*.

11. As well as a noted exponent of extended oboe techniques (see Discography), Lawrence Singer has published a *Metodo per oboe* addressing contemporary techniques and a number of works for oboe, including *Musica a due* for oboe and guitar (1976), *Work for oboe* (1977), *Metamorphosis* for oboe, violin and orchestra (1981) and *Sensazione no. 2* (c.1990).

12. Many composers have lifted multiphonics directly from Bartolozzi's book; see Lucas Foss's *The Cave of the Winds* for woodwind quintet (1972).

13. 'Oboe' in *New Grove*, 13:475.

14. As measured by a spectrometer; see Veale and Mahnkopf 1994:64–9.

15. This theory of multiphonic generation remains unproven, but as no more adequate explanation has to date been proposed, it is the most serviceable explanation. See Veale and Mahnkopf 1994:70.

16. Goossens 1977:177.

17. *Rollender Ton* is used at the end of Denisow's *Solo* (Holliger 1972:25). Holliger's *Studie über Mehrklänge* concludes with a related effect where the player isolates progressively higher

harmonics of a low B flat.

18. Compared with the other systems, Holliger's is less serviceable for non-oboists and composers interested in a graphic notation of resultant sounds and for this reason has been used by few composers other than Holliger. Alfred Schnittke used it in the Concerto for Oboe, Harp and String Orchestra that he wrote in 1971 for Holliger, no doubt in consultation with the oboist.

19. Discussed in Post 1981:16.

20. Roxburgh gives some useful practical advise in Goossens and Roxburgh 1977:180, and van Cleeve (1991) indicates that some double harmonics work better on Rigoutat oboes, which Holliger has played throughout his career, than on the Americans' favourite, Lorée.

21. Goossens and Roxburgh 1977:179.

22. See Watkins 1994:188.

23. Post 1984a:25.

24. Rimsky-Korsakov 1964:21 mentions muting and provides some examples from his own scores; Stravinsky called for muted oboes towards the end of *Petrouchka* (1911).

25. See Bryan Rulon report in Fried and Post 1995:35–6.

26. Sleeve notes to Joseph Celli, *Organic Oboe*.

27. Most of the biographical information presented here is taken from Palmer 1997, and Kunkel and Stenzl 2001:11:628–31.

28. For an alternative tonal concept in avant-garde oboe repertoire, listen to Malgoire's *Le hautbois moderne*.

29. Sleeve notes to *The Spectacular Heinz Holliger*.

30. Osmond-Smith 1985:90.

31. London: Universal, 1969.

32. Van Cleeve 1991 is a fine introduction to the complexities of preparing this important work, and Osmond-Smith 1991 includes a clearly-written pitch analysis.

33. Berio mentioned this as one of his compositional challenges (see Osmond-Smith 1985:97).

34. Stoianova, 'Chemins en musique', *RM* (1984) 435, quoted in Vecchione 1993:30.

35. Recordings listed in Discography. The absolute timing of the work as notated is 6'30"; Holliger's timings are 8'22" (1969) and 7'01" (1995).

36. Stoianova, 'Chemins en musique', 433, quoted in Vecchione 1993:50.

37. Published in Holliger 1972.

38. Post never recorded the work, but it can be heard on Glaetzner's *Neue Musik für Oboe*.

39. Horst Schneider and Helmut Winschermann recorded Handel's op. 3 Concerti Grossi in 1959 on instruments made in the mid 50s; Schaeftlein gave his first performances on an original hautboy by Paulhahn in 1962; Piguet's first recording on a historical oboe was made in 1964. Helmut Hucke's first recordings on an hautboy with Collegium Aureum date from 1967.

40. With Hans-Jürg Lange (bassoon) and Lionel Rogg (harpsichord).

41. Quantz 1752, 11/21, 11/1, 10/22.

42. Taruskin 1995:102 and 323.

43. More information on how these techniques were used can be found in ch. 3; they are treated in more detail in Haynes 2001:223–50 and 168–72.

44. 'le basson, le violon, la flûte allemande, la flûte douce, la flûte à voix [*sic*], en faisant deux parties, et le hautbois. Il passa ensuite derrière un paravent, et chanta un motet à quatre parties, accompagné d'un violon et de deux flûtes. Le sieur Loeillet fit entendre, après, les deux flûtes et une voix qui chantoit la basse, à quoi un grand chœur de musique succéda. Il parut interrompu par une querelle et batterie, où l'on croyoit entendre des cris de femmes et d'enfants, le bruit que font des hommes, l'épée à la main, et le tumulte que pourroient faire quarante personnes, qu'on entendroit crier au secours, au guet, et l'arrivée du guet à pied et à cheval.' From an anonymous eyewitness account that

appeared in the *Mercure* in August 1727 (p.1905); quoted in Brenet 1900:172.

45. Aria 'Gott wolle unseren David schützen', nr 5 in Cantata 1717/4, G.

46. Concerto 45 . . . a 4. Parte, D. S-Skma. In the B section of the 1st movement, the hautbois d'amour switches to 'Oboe ordinario'.

47. The instruments change within the soprano aria 'Hamburg ruht in süßem Schlafe' in *Kapitainsmusiken, Einigkeit, 1724/S*13.

48. Quantz 1752:IX§4.

49. Cf. Zelenka's trio sonatas.

50. Cf. Harnoncourt 1988:29.

51. Cf. Harnoncourt 1988:95.

52. From Bernard Schermer in Basel, Paul Hailperin in Vienna, and Bruce Haynes in California (Haynes and Hailperin began producing copies of Schaeftlein's Paulhahn within months of each other).

53. For representative recordings, see Discography.

54. For more detail on Marx's life, see C.D. and N. Lehrer 1988. His family still owns many of the original parts of new works from which Marx played with his markings.

55. His writings are collected in Marx 1983.

56. In 1955 Marx had an opportunity to test his theories when he prepared for a television recording in which he played a late eighteenth-century Viennese oboe from his own collection (see 'Preliminary Report on the Baroque Oboe' [in Marx 1983:109–13]; a surviving copy of the film, the earliest audio-visual record of a hautboist, *Princeton 55: 'The Instruments of Bach's Orchestra'* is housed in the Princeton University Library). Later, in 1962, he borrowed original hautboys from the Museum of Fine Arts, Boston (correspondence held by the museum).

57. Roseman's original compositions include a double quintet for winds and brass (pub. 1982), Renaissance Suite for wind quintet (1980) and a challenging Partita for solo oboe (1997).

58. Other crossover oboists include Jean-Claude Malgoire (1940–), director of the early-music ensemble La Grande Écurie et la Chambre du Roy, who also recorded contemporary works including Holliger's *Mobile* and Jolivet's *Controversia*, two works also recorded by the Belgian oboist Paul Dombrecht, better known as hautboist and director of the early-instrument wind ensemble Octophoros.

59. The earliest recording of the work featuring oboist Josef Marx was made shortly after the work was written.

60. Ultimately only eight of the songs were used for the film ('A Poison Tree' and 'The Piper' were omitted); other music was taken from Vaughan Williams's masque *Job*.

61. London *Times*, quoted in Francis 1994:65.

62. This is a telling sequel to the Romantic concept of the oboe as textless voice of desire that I introduced in ch. 7 in connection with Mahler's setting of 'Urlicht'.

63. Liner notes to the recording by Roseman.

64. This poem is discussed in ch. 7, p. 216.

65. All quotations taken from the Peters score (1969).

66. The performance part is written on one staff, but the edition of the music provides an open-score version where each of the polyphonic voices is given a separate staff.

67. P. Hodson dedicated his *Elégie* for oboe and harp to the Goossenses (unpublished manuscript in the GB-Lbl, MS Add. 71969). Walter Piston's *Fantasy* for cor anglais, harp and strings (1952) is also likely to have been written for them; in 1977 Michael Krein composed a short serenade for oboe and two harps involving the three siblings; Eugene Goossens's *Concert Piece* (1958) was also written for the three plus orchestra.

68. The two works share same parts for the two solo instruments, accompanied by prerecorded tape and chamber orchestra respectively.

69. Instruments with saxophone fingering systems survive from Boosey and Hawkes, Kohlert, and even Lorée. See Howe 2002.

70. This concerto was written for Mitchell Miller of the CBS Symphony, the oboist who premiered the Strauss Concerto in the US and went on to become a popular TV entertainer. It has been recorded by Bert Lucarelli.

71. For a discussion of the uses of the term 'postmodern', see Ulmer 1985 and, for a synopsis of the musical characteristics of Postmodernism, Kramer 2002.

72. *Anachronie II* is written in memory of Erik Satie, who first coined the term *musique d'ameublement.*

73. 1994:140.

Bibliography

All IDRS publications (*JIDRS, DR* and *TWO*) are available to members on line at www.idrs.org

Full documentation for the considerable number of reviews and other announcements, mostly anonymous, from the nineteenth-century press and editions of music are cited in the Notes, but not repeated here.

ABCDario Musico (1780). Bath.

Adkins, Cecil (1999). 'Proportions and architectural motives in the design of the eighteenth-century oboe', *JAMIS* 25:95–132.

—— (2001). 'The German oboe in the eighteenth century', *JAMIS* 27:5–47.

Adlung, Jacob (1758/2 1783). *Anleitung zu der musikalischen Gelehrtheit*. Erfurt: H. J. Moser; *R* Kassel: Bärenreiter, 1953.

Agricola, Martinus (1529). *Musica Instrumentalis Deudsch*. Wittenberg.

Albrecht, Carol Padgham (1985). 'In Search of the Romantic English Horn', *DR* 8/1:18–22.

Albrecht, Theodore (2002). 'Franz Stadler, Stephan Ficher and other oboists at the Theater an der Wien during Beethoven's "Heroic" Period', *DR* 25:93–106.

Allen, George (1858/2 1863). *The Life of Philidor, Musician and Chess-Player*. New York, Philadelphia: P. Miller & Son.

Almanach musical (1775–7, 1781, 1783). Paris.

Almenräder, Carl (1822–3). *Abhandlung über die Verbesserung des Fagotts*. Mainz: Schott

—— (1843). *Fagottschule*.

Altenburg, W. (1900). 'Eine Original-Oboe von Theobald Boehm', *ZfürI* 20; *R* in G. Dullat, *Holz- und Metallblasinstrumente: Zeitschrift für Instrumentenbau, 1881–1945*. Siegburg: Verlag der Instrumentenbau Zeitschrift, 1986, 43–8.

[? Ancelet] (1757). *Observations sur la musique, les musiciens et les instruments*. Amsterdam.

Anderson, Arthur Olaf (1929). *Practical Orchestration*. Boston, New York: C. C. Birchard & Co.

Anderson, E., ed. (1938). *The Letters of Mozart and His Family*. London: Macmillan.

Andraud, Albert. (1976). *Practical and Progressive Oboe Method, Reed Making, Melodious and Technical Studies*. San Antonio: Southern Music Co.

Angermüller, Rudolph (1985). *Antonio Salieri: fatti e documenti*.

Anon. (1699). *The second book of theatre musick*. London: Walsh.

Anon. ['Componist und Virtuose auf der Hoboe'] (1812). 'Ueber die Oboe', *AMZ* 14:69–74.

Anon. (1827). 'The Rise and Progress of the Hautbois', *Quarterly Musical Magazine and Review* 9:464.

—— (1925). 'Georges Longy: His Beneficent Activity as Oboist and Conductor in Boston's Music Life', *Boston Herald* 26 April 1925.

—— (1974). *Wind Instruments of European Art Music, Horniman Museum*. London: Horniman Museum and Library, David M. Boston, Curator.

—— (1981). '150 Jahre Heckel-Instrumente', *Tibia* 2/81:345–50.

—— (1998a). 'Bart Schneemann Grabs the Unexpected', *Scrapes International*, 1998; *R* in *DR* 23/2 (2000):39–41.

——. (1998b). 'Gutram Wolf, Kronach: Instrument Builder with a Particular Vision', *Scrapes International* 1:30–4; repr. in *DR* 23/2 (2000):109–12.

—— (1999). 'Pierre Pierlot: A Living Legend', *Scrapes International* 1:4–7.

—— (2001). 'Aerophor', in *NG2* I:178.

—— (2002). 'Interview with Danièle Glotin', *DR* 25:105–10.

Ansermet, Ernest (1919). 'Sur un orchestre nègre', *La Revue romande* 3/10:10–13.

Anthony, James R. (1988). Review of *Trios pour le coucher du roy by Jean-Baptiste Lully and Marin Marais*, ed. Herbert Schneider, *Music & Letters* 69:437–9.

Aquin de Chateau-Lyon, Pierre Louis d' (1752). *Lettres sur les hommes célèbres . . . sous le règne de Louis XV*. Amsterdam and Paris.

Arbeau, Thionot (1588). *Orchésographie*. R Geneva: Slatkine, 1970 (of Paris: 1888 ed.).

Arnold, Denis (1965). 'Instruments and instrumental teaching in the early Italian Conservatories', *GSJ* 18:72–81.

—— (1966). 'Orchestras in eighteenth-century Venice', *GSJ* 19:3–19.

—— (1985). *Notes on the hautboy in eighteenth-century Venice.

Ashbee, Andrew (1986–93). *Records of English Court Music*. Snodland (Kent): Ashbee.

Asioli, Bonifazio (attrib.) (1827). *Transunto dei Principj Elementari di Musica, ossia breve metodo*. Milan: Ricordi.

Avison, Charles (1752). *An Essay on Musical Expression*. London: C. Davis.

Bach-Dokumente (1963, 1969, 1972). (Supplement to *Neue Bach Ausgabe*), ed. W. Neumann and H.-J. Schulze, Leipzig: Deutsche Verlag für Musik.

Bacilly, Béningne de. (1668). *Remarques curieuses sur l'art de bien chanter*. Paris: the author ; R Geneva: Minkoff, 1972.

Badia y Leyblich (1814). *Voyages d'Ali Bey el Abbassi en Afrique et en Asie pendant des années 1803 à 1807*. Paris: Didot l'aîné.

Bainbridge, William (1823). *Observations on the Cause of Imperfections in Woodwind Instruments, particularly in German Flutes; with remarks on the embouchure . . . also remarks on Oboe, Clarionet and Bassoon Reeds*. London: the author.

Baines, Anthony (1952). 'Shawms of the Sardana Coblas', *GSJ* 5:9–16.

—— (1967). *Woodwind Instruments and Their History*. London: Faber and Faber, 3rd ed. (1st ed., 1957).

—— (1969). *Musical Instruments Through the Ages*. Pelican.

Baines, Anthony, and Martin Kirnbauer (2001). 'Shawm', *NG2* 23:228–37.

Baker, C. H. Collins, and Muriel I. (1949). *The Life and Circumstances of James Brydges, First Duke of Chandos*. Oxford: Clarendon Press.

Banister, John Jr. [attrib.] (1695). *The Sprightly Companion*. London: Playford.

Barbieri, Patrizio (1987). *Acustica, accordatura e temperamento nell'Illuminismo veneto*. Rome: Torre d'Orfeo.

—— (1991). 'Violin intonation: a historical survey', *EM* 19:69–88.

—— (1999). 'G. B. Orazi's enharmonic flute and its music (1797–1815)', *GSJ* 52:281–304.

Barker, Andrew (ed.) (1984). *Greek Musical Writings*. Cambridge Univ. Press.

Baron, Ernst Gottlieb (1727). *Historisch- theoretisch und praktische Untersuchung des Instruments der Lauten*. Nuremberg: Rüdiger.

Barret, Apollon-Marie-Rose (1850). *Complete Method for the Oboe*. London: Jullien; 2nd ed. London: Lafleur, 1862.

—— (1866). *Methode complète de hautbois divisée en 4 parties contenante les tablatures de l'Ancien et du Nouveau Système et un précis de la facture des anches*. Paris, London: Triébert.

Bartolozzi, Bruno (1967). *New Sounds for Woodwind*. Oxford Univ. Press.

Bas, Louis (1905). *Méthode nouvelle de hautbois théorique et pratique contenante des photographies explicatives des nombres exercices*. Paris: Enoch.

Bate, Philip (1954). 'Oboe', *Gr5* 6:143–69.

—— (1956/3 1975). *The Oboe: An Outline of its History and Construction*. New York: Philosophical Library.

—— (1969). *The Flute: A Study of its History, Development and Construction*. London: E. Benn; New York: W. W. Norton.

—— (1980) 'Oboe', *NG1* 13:462–76.

Bate, Philip, and Michael Finkelman (2001). 'Heckelphone', in *NG2* 11:305–6.

Bate, Philip, and Jerry Voorhees, (2001). 'Keywork', in *NG2* 13:552–6.

Baudelaire, Charles (1981). *Art in Paris, 1845–1862: Salons and Other Exhibitions reviewed by Charles Baudelaire*. Ithaca, NY : Cornell Univ. Press ; London: Phaidon.

—— (1991). *Les Fleurs du Mal*. Ed. J. Dupont. Paris: Flammarion.

Bauer and Deutsch. See Mozart, W. A.

Beaussant, Philippe (1992). *Lully ou le musicien du soleil*. Paris: Gallimard.

Bechler, Leo, and Bernhardt Rahm (1914). *Die Oboe und die ihe verwandten Instrumente nebst biographischen Skizzen der bedeutendsten ihrer Meister, Anhang: Musikliteratur für Oboe und Englische Horn*. Leipzig: Carl Merseburger; *R* Wiesbaden: Sändig, 1972.

Becker, Heinz (1961). 'Europäischen Oboeninstrumente', *MGG* 9:1781–1813.

—— (1966). *Zur Entwicklungsgeschichte der antiken und mittelalterlichen Rohrblattinstrumenten*. Hamburg: H. Sikorski.

Becker-Glauch, Irmgard (1951). *Die Bedeutung der Musik für die Dresdener Hoffeste bis in die Zeit Augusts des Starken*. Kassel/Basel: Bärenreiter.

Bélis, Annie (2001). 'Aulos', *NG2* 2:178–85.

Bell, Nancy R. E. (1897). *Thomas Gainsborough: A Record of His Life and Works*. London: G. Bell and Sons.

Belpasso, Giovanni Battista (1840–61). *Metodo per Oboè composite espressamente per Real Collegio di Musica*. Naples: Cottra.

Benoit, Marcelle (1953–4). 'Les musiciens français de Marie-Louise d'Orléans, Reine d'Espagne', *RM* 226:48–60.

Benoit, Marcelle (1971a). *Versailles et les musiciens du Roi, 1661–1733*. Paris: A. J. Picard.

—— (1971b). *Musiques de cour: chapelle, chambre, écurie, 1661–1733*. Paris: A. J. Picard.

Bergeron. See Salivet.

Berlioz, Hector (1841). 'Hautbois', *RGMdP* 8/63:550–1.

—— (1844a). *Traité d'Instrumentation et d'Orchestration, nouvelle édition avec L'Art du Chef d'Orchestre*. Paris: Henry Lemoine et Cie; 2nd ed. Paris: Schonenberger, 1855.

—— (1844b). *Voyage musical en Allemagne et en Italie: Etudes sur Beethoven, Gluck et Weber. Mélanges et nouvelles*. Paris: J. Labitte; *R* Westmead: Gregg, 1970.

—— (1855). *A Treatise on modern instrumentation and orchestration dedicated to Frederick William IV, King of Prussia, to which is appended the Chef d'Orchestre*. London, New York: Novello, trans. M. C. Clarke, ed. J. Bennet.

—— (1862). *A travers chants: Études musicales, adorations boutades et critiques*. Paris: M. Lévy frères; *R* Westmead: Gregg, 1970.

—— (1951). *Les Grotesques de la musique*. Paris: Librairie nouvelle.

—— (1956). *Evenings with the Orchestra (Soirées de l'orchestre)*. Trans. J. Barzun. New York: A. A. Knopf.

—— (1968). *Les soirées de l'orchestre*. Ed. L. Guichard. Paris: Gründ.

—— (1970). *Mémoires*. Trans. D. Cairns. London.

—— (1971). *Symphonie fantastique*. New York: Norton.

—— (1994). *The Art of Music and Other Essays (A travers chants)*. Trans. E. Csicsery-Rónay. Bloomington and Indianapolis: Univ. of Indiana Press.

—— (1996-). *Critique musicale*. Ed. H. R. Cohen and Y. Gérard. Paris: Buchet-Chastel.

Berlioz, Hector, rev. R. Strauss (1948). *Treatise on Instrumentation*. Trans. by T. Front of *Instrumentationslehre* (Berlin, 1904). New York: E. F. Kalmus.

Bernardini, Alfredo (1985). 'Oboe playing in Italy from the origins to 1800'. Typescript.

—— (1986). 'Andrea Fornari (1753–1841) "fabricator di strumenti" a Venezia', *Il Flauto Dolce* 14/15: 31–6.

—— (1987). 'Due chiavi per Rossini? Storia e sviluppo dell'oboe a Bologna prima del 1850',

Il Flauto Dolce 17/18:18–32; trans. as 'Zwei Klappen für Rossini? Zur Geschichte der Oboe in Bologna vor 1850', *Tibia* 2/92 (1992):95–107.

—— (1988). 'Oboe playing in the Venetian Republic, 1692–1797', *EM* 16/3:372–87.

—— (1989). 'Woodwind makers in Venice, 1790–1900', *JAMIS* 15:52–73.

—— (1990). 'Vier Oboistenporträts als Quelle zum Studium der Zwei-Klappen-Oboe', *Oboe, Klarinette, Fagott* 1:30–42.

—— (1993). 'Nachtrag zu meinem Artikel "Zwei Klappen für Rossini? Zur Geschichte der Oboe in Bologna vor 1850" ', *Tibia* 3/93:529–30.

—— (2001). 'Giovanni Paggi (1806-87), ein reisender Sänger auf der Oboe', *Tibia* 1/2001:373–9.

Bessaraboff, Nicholas (1941). *Ancient European Musical Instruments: An Organological study of the Musical Instruments in the Leslie Lindsey Mason Collection at the Museum of Fine Arts*. Boston: Boston, Museum of Fine Arts, by the Harvard Univ. Press.

Biber, Walter (1974). 'Aus der Geschichte der Blasmusik in der Schweiz', *Bericht über die erste internationale Fachtagung zur Erforschung der Blasmusik*, 127–43.

Bigotti, Giovanni (1974). *Storia dell'oboe e sua letteratura*. Padova: Zanibon.

Bijlsma, Anner (1998). *Bach, the Fencing Master*. Amsterdam: the author.

Bill, Oswald, ed. (1987). *Christoph Graupner, Hofkapellmeister in Darmstadt, 1709–1760*. Mainz: Schott.

Birsak, Kurt (1994). *Cultural History of the Clarinet*. Buchloe: Obermayer.

Bismantova, Bartolomeo (1688). 'Regole ... del Oboè' (manuscript version of *Compendio musicale*).

Blatter, Alfred (1997). *Instrumentation and Orchestration*. New York: Schirmer, 2nd ed.

Bleuzet, Louis (1913–27). 'Hautbois', in Albert Lavignac and Lionel de la Laurencie, eds. *Encyclopédie de la Musique et Dictionnaire du Conservatoire*. Paris: C. Delagrave, pt 2, vol. 3:1527–1544.

Bloom, Sara Lambert (1998). *The Robert Bloom Collection, Collected Preface*. Cranberry Isles, Maine: The Robert Bloom Collection.

Boehm, Theobald (1862). 'Schema zur Bestimmung der Löchstellung auf Blasinstrumenten', ed. Karl Ventzke, *Tibia* 1/80 (1980):3–20.

Boileau-Despreaux, Nicolas (1966). *Œuvres complètes*. Paris: Gallimard.

Bonanni, Filippo (1722 [plates 1776]). *Gabinetto armonico pieno d'istromenti sonori indicati e spiegati*.

Bonar, Nancy (1983). 'The Evolution of the Mechanized Oboe and its New Music', *DR* 6:27–42.

Bonelli, Alessandro (1982). 'The Oboe and the Oboists of Italy', *DR* 5:38–57.

Borjon de Scellery, Pierre [?] (1672/2 1678). *Traité de la musette, avec une nouvelle méthode*. Lyon: Girin and Rivière; R Bologna: Arnaldo Forni, 1983.

Botstein, Leon (2001). 'Modernism', *NG2* 16:686–75.

Boulez, Pierre (1986). *Orientations: Collected Writings*. Trans. J.-J. Nattiez. Cambridge, MA: Harvard Univ. Press.

Bouquet, Marie-Thérèse (1969). *Musique et musiciens à Turin de 1648 à 1775*. Turin : Accademia delle scienze.

—— (1976). *Il teatro di corte dalle origini al 1788*. Turin: Cassa di Risparmio di Torino.

Bourns, David (1988). 'OBOEREEDBIB: An annotated bibliography of oboe reed material', *JIDRS* 16:93–7.

Bouterse, Jan (1999). 'The deutsche Schalmeien of Richard Haka', *JAMIS* 25:61–94.

—— (2001). 'Nederlandse Houtblaasinstrumenten en hun bouwers tot circa 1775', PhD. diss., Univ. of Utrecht.

Bowers, Jane M. (1972). 'The French flute school from 1700 to 1760', PhD. diss., Univ. of California, Berkeley.

—— (1980). 'Hotteterre', *NG1*.

Braun, Joachim (2002). *Music in Ancient Israel/Palestine: Archaeological, Written and Comparative Sources*. Trans. D. W. Scott. Grand Rapids and London: W. B. Eerdmans.

Braun, Werner (1983). 'The "Hautboist": an outline of evolving careers and functions', in

Walter Salmen, ed., *The social status of the professional musician from the middle ages to the 19th century*, 123–58. New York: Pendragon. (Trans. of *Der Sozialstatus des Berufmusikers vom 17. bis 19. Jahrhundert.* Kassel, 1971.)

—— (1987). *Vom Remter zum Gänsemarkt: aus der Frühgeschichte der alten Hamburger Oper (1677–1697)*. Saarbrücken: Saarbrücker Druckerei und Verlag.

Braun, Wilhelm (1823). 'Bemerkungen über die richtige Behandlung und Blasart der Oboe', *AMZ* 25:165–72.

Breitkopf (Leipzig, 1760–87). Thematic Catalogues (6 parts, manuscripts from the Breitkopf archives, given to Staatsarchiv Leipzig in 1962). Ed. Barry S. Brook, 1966. New York: Dover.

Brenet, Michel [Marie Bobillier] (1900). *Les concerts en France sous l'Ancien Régime*. Paris: Fischbacher ; R New York: Da Capo, 1970.

Bretonnière, Victor (1867). *Nouvelle méthode de hautbois renfermant la tablature de l'instrument dans les tons les plus usités*, op. 400. Paris: Joly.

Brod, Henri (1825, 1830). *Méthode pour le hautbois*. Pt 1, Paris: Dufaut et Dubois (1825); pts 1 and 2, Paris: Schonenberger (1830).

—— (1890). *Méthode de Hautbois*. Rev. G. Gillet. Paris and Brussels: Lemoine et fils.

Brody, Elaine (1988). *Paris: The Musical Kaleidoscope, 1870–1925*. London: Robson.

Brossard, Yolande de (1965). *Musiciens de Paris, 1535–1792*. Paris: Picard.

Broughton, Augusta Mary Anne, ed. (1887). *Court and private life in the time of Queen Charlotte, being the journals of Mrs Papendiek*. London: Bentley and Son.

Brown, Andrew (1976). 'A Cinefluorographic Pilot Study of the Throat While Vibrato Tones are played on Flute and Oboe', *JIDRS* 4:49–57.

Brown, Howard Mayer, and Stanley Sadie (1989). *Performance Practice: Music after 1600*. The Norton/Grove Handbooks in Music. New York, London: W. W. Norton and Co.

Brown, James (2001). 'Die Musikpresse und der Oboist im 19. Jahrhundert, zu Hause und auf Reisen', *Tibia* 3/01:557–63; Engl. version 'The Musical Press and the Nineteenth-century Oboist, at Home and on Tour', in *Double Reed News: Magazine of the British Double Reed Society* 56 (2001):24–8.

Brown, Mary E., and W. Adams (1888). *Musical Instruments and their homes: 270 illustrations in pen and ink, the whole forming a complete catalogue of the Collection of Musical Instruments now in the possession of Mrs J. Crosby Brown of New York*. New York: Dodd, Mead and Co.

Bruch, Gerome (1936). *Boston Symphony Orchestra: Charcoal Drawings of its Members with Biographical Sketches*. Boston: Boston Symphony Orchestra.

Buchner, Alexander (1956). *Musical Instruments through the Ages*. London: Spring Books.

Bunge, Rudolf. (Leipzig: 1905).'Johann Sebastian Bachs Kapelle zu Cöthen und deren Nachgelassene Instrumente', *Bach Jahrbuch*, 14–47.

Burgess, Geoffrey (1988). 'The trio sonatas of Jan Dismas Zelenka', *JIDRS* 16:6–18.

—— (1994a). 'Gustave Vogt (1781-1870) und Konstruktionsmerkmale fanzösischer Oboen im 1. Viertel des 19. Jahrhunderts', *Tibia* 1/94:14–26.

—— (1994b). 'On Writing a History of the Oboe in the 19th century', *FoMRHI* 76:25–44.

—— (1996). 'Berlioz und die Oboe: Bemerkungen über den Umgang eines meisterhaften Orchestrieres mit Klang', *Tibia* 2/96:81–93; 3/96:161–7.

—— (1997a). 'The Evolving Persona of the French Oboe in the 19th century as seen through literature', in Lasocki, ed., *A Time of Questioning*, 89–117.

—— (1997b). 'Historical Oboe Reeds: Avenues for Further Research or "Now, What do we do with all these Measurements?"', in Lasocki, ed., *A Time of Questioning*, 205–22.

—— (1997c). 'Reed Making for Historical Oboes: A Selective Reading List', *DR* 20/1:36.

—— (2001). 'Sallantin', *NG2* 22:163.

—— (2002). 'Vibrato Awareness', *DR* 24/2:127–35.

—— (2003). *'The Premier Oboist of Europe': A portrait of Gustave Vogt, nineteenth-century oboe virtuoso, teacher and composer*. Lanham, MD: Scarecrow.

Burgess, Geoffrey, Bruce Haynes, and Michael Finkelman (2001). 'Oboe', in *NG2* 18:257–87.

Burgess, Geoffrey, and Peter Hedrick (1989). 'The oldest English reeds? An examination of 19 surviving examples', *GSJ* 42:32–69. Trans., with revisions, of 'Die ältesten englischen Oboenrohre? Eine Untersuchung von 19 noch erhaltenen Exemplaren', *Tibia* 1/90 (1990):81–106.

Burney, Charles (1771a). *The present state of music in France and Italy: or the journal of a tour through those countries.* London: Becket.

—— (1771b). *Journal of Burney's travels in France and Italy* (MS British Library, Add. 35122). Published as *Music, Men and Manners in France and Italy, 1770.* Ed. H. Edmund Poole. London: Folio Society, 1969.

—— (1773). *The Present State of Music in Germany, the Netherlands, and the United Provinces.* London: T. Becket and Co.; *R* New York: Broude, 1969.

—— (1776). *A General History of Music from the Earliest Ages to the Present Period.* London: Burney.

—— (1785). *Nachricht von G. F. Händels Lebensumstanden.* Berlin and Stettin: Nicolai.

Burrows, D. (1985). 'Handel's London Theatre Orchestra', *EM* 13: 349–57.

Burton, Anthony (1991). 'A Growing Legacy'. BBC Radio programme about the Craxton Memorial Concert, British National Sound Archive, B8948/07.

Busch, Charles D. L. (1972). 'A Technical Comparison of an 1807, 1916 and a 1968 oboe and related reed-making and performance problems', DMA diss., Louisiana State Univ.

Buttrey, John (1995). 'New Light on Robert Cambert in London, and his Ballet et Musique', *EM* 23:199–220.

Byrne, Maurice (1983). 'Pierre Jaillard, Peter Bressan', *GSJ* 36:2–28.

—— (1984). 'More on Bressan', *GSJ* 37:102–11.

Caffi, Francesco (1854–5). *Storia della musica sacra nella già cappella ducale di San Marco in Venezia dal 1318 al 1797.* Venice: Antonelli.

Cahn, Peter (1995). 'Frankfurt am Main', *MGG2*, 3:643–64.

Capmany, Aureli (1948). *La Sardana a Catalunya.* Barcelona: Montaner I. Simon.

Cappelli, Giuseppe (1853). *Metodo teoretico-pratico.* Milan: Lucca; Firenze: Canti and Berletti; Bologna: Trebli.

Carr, Cynthia (2001). 'Music for Oboe, Horn and Piano Trio', *The Horn Call: Journal of the International Horn Society* 31/2:33–42.

Carse, Adam (1939). *Musical Wind Instruments.* London: Macmillan and Co.

—— (1949). *The Orchestra from Beethoven to Berlioz: A History of the Orchestra in the first half of the Nineteenth century, and of the development of orchestral baton-conducting.* New York: Broude.

Castellani, Marcello, and Elio Durante (1987). *Del portar della lingua negli instrumenti di fiato.* Florence: Studio per edizioni scelte.

Castil-Blaze, François-Henri-Joseph (1821). *Dictionnaire de Musique Moderne.* Paris: Lyre moderne.

Chalon, Frédéric (1802). *Méthode pour le cor anglais ou hautbois.* Paris: Imbault; 2nd ed. Paris: Frère; *R* in Adrien de Lafage, *Nouveau Manuel de musique ou Encyclopedie musicale.* Paris : Librarie Encyclopedique de Robert, c.1840.

Chalon, Victor (1877). *Méthode de hautbois ordinaire et à système Boehm illustré de vignettes représentant les different parties de l'instrument et la pose de l'executant.* Paris: J. Kelmer frères.

Charles-Dominique, Luc (1994). *Les ménétriers français sous l'ancien régime.* Toulouse: Klincksieck.

Charles-Dominique, Luc, and Pierre Laurence, eds (2002). *Les hautbois populaires.* Saint-Jouin-de-Milly: Éditions Modal.

Charlton, David, ed. (1989). E. T. A. Hofmann's Musical Writings: Kreisleriana, The Poet and the Composer, Music Criticism. Trans. M. Clarke, Cambridge Univ. Press.

Charlton, David (1990). 'Woodwind and Brass', in H. M. Brown and S. Sadie, eds, *Performance Practice, Music after 1600.* The Norton/Grove Handbooks in Music. New York, London: Norton, 409–23.

Chorley, Henry Fothergill (1882). *The National Music of the World.* Ed. H. G. Hewlett. 2nd ed., London: W. Reeves.

Choron, Alexandre Etienne, and J. Adrien de La Fage (1836–9). *Nouveau manuel de Musique ou*

Encyclopédie musicale. Paris: Librairie Encyclopédie de Rore.

Christ, Carol (1977). 'Victorian Masculinity and the Angel in the House', in M. Vicinus, *A Widening Sphere: Changing Roles of Victorian Women*. Bloomington: Indiana Univ. Press, 146–62.

Coche, V. (1838). *Examen critique de la flûte ordinaire comparée à la flûte de Böhm, présenté à MM. les membres de l'Institut (Académie royale des beaux-arts, section de la musique)*. Paris: chez l'auteur.

Colette, Marie-Noëlle, and François Lesure (1983). *La Musique à Paris en 1830–1831*. Paris: Bibliothèque Nationale.

Collingwood, R. G. (1946). *The Idea of History*. Oxford Univ. Press.

Comettant, Oscar (1861). 'Instruments et Instrumentistes', *L'Art musicale* 1/40:317–19.

—— (1862). *Musique et musiciens*. Paris: Pagnerre.

Conrey, George (1983). 'The Story of a Great Oboist: Alfred Charles Barthel (1871–1957)', *DR* 6/4:18–31.

—— (1986). 'The Paris Conservatory: its oboe professors, laureates (1795–1984)', *JIDRS* 14:7–17.

Cooke, Grattan (1850). 'Statement of Facts and Correspondence between the Directors of the Philharmonic Society and Mr Grattan Cooke'. London: the author.

Cooper, Jeffrey (1983). *The Rise of Instrumental Music and Concert Series in Paris: 1828–1871*. Ann Arbor: UMI Research Press.

Corder, F. (1896). *The Orchestra and How to Write for It: A Practical Guide to every branch and detail of modern orchestration*. London: Robert Cocks and Co.

Corigliano, John. (1978). *Oboe Concerto*. New York, London: Schirmer.

—— (1990). Notes to *Oboe Concerto*. American SO, RCA, BMG 60395–2 RG.

Corrette, Michel [?] (c.1740/2 1773). *Méthode pour apprendre aisément à jouër de la Flûtte Traversiere* [*sic*]. Paris: Boivin.

Corri, Domenico (1810). *The Singer's Preceptor*. London: Silvester, Longman, Hurst, Rees and Orme.

Cotte, Roger (1979). 'Blasinstrumente bei freimaurerischen Riten', *Tibia* 2/79:315–16.

Couvreur, Manuel, and Philippe Vendrix (2001). 'Saint-Luc, Jacques de', *NG2* 22:107.

Cudworth, Charles (1949). 'Fischer, Johann Christian', *MGG* 4:269–71.

Curtis, Holbrook (1909). *Voice Building and Tone Placing*. London: D. Appleton and Co.

Dahlhaus, Carl (1989). *19th-Century Music*. Trans. of *Musik des 19. Jahrhunderts* by J. B. Robinson. Berkeley: Univ. of California Press.

Dahlqvist, Reine (1973). 'Taille, oboe da caccia and cor anglais', *GSJ* 26:58–71.

—— (1976). 'Waldhautbois', *GSJ* 29:126–7.

Daub, P. E. (1985). 'Music at the court of George II (r.1727–1760)'. Ph.D. diss., Cornell Univ.

Daubeny, Ulric (1920). *Orchestral Wind Instruments*. London: Reeves.

Day, C. R. (1891). *A Descriptive Catalogue of the Musical Instruments recently exhibited at the Royal Military Exhibition, London, 1890*. London: Eyre and Spottiswoode.

Deacon, H. C. (1880–90). 'Vibrato', in George Grove, *A Dictionary of Music and Musicians (= Gr1)*. 1st ed. London: Macmillan, 5:268–9.

Dean, Winton (1959). *Handel's Dramatic Oratorios and Masques*. London: Oxford Univ. Press.

—— (1970). *Handel and the Opera Seria*. London: Oxford Univ. Press.

De Brosses, Charles (1739–40). *Lettres d'Italie du Président de Brosses*. Ed. F. d'Agay. Paris: Mercure de France, 1986.

Decourcelle, Maurice (1881). *La Société académique des Enfants d'Apollon (1781–1880): programmes des concerts annuels liste des sociétaires, des anciens présidents et des cantatrices qui se sont fait entendre aux concerts annuels: résumé des séances mensuelles*. Paris: Durand Schoenewerk & Co.

De Lancie, John (1995). 'Some Thoughts on the Strauss Concerto', *DR* 18:61–2.

De Lerma, D. R. (1973). 'Toward a Concept of Tabuteau's Phrasing', *The Instrumentalist* 28/8:44–54.

Dellamora, Richard (1990). *Masculine Desire: The Sexual Politics of Victorian Aestheticism*. Chapel Hill: Univ. of North Carolina Press.

Delusse (1760). *L'Art de la Flûte traversière*. R ed. by G. Moens-Haenen. Buren: F. Knuf, 1980.

Denton, John William (1977). 'The use of oboes in church cantatas of Johann Sebastian Bach', DMA diss., Univ. of Rochester.

De Smet, Monique (1973). *La musique à la cour de Guillaume V, Prince d'Orange (1748–1806)*. Utrecht: Oosthoek.

De Stefani, Ricordano (1888). 'Della scuola di oboè in Italia: Memoria inviata dall'accademico onorario M. . . . 1885-8', *Atti dell'Accademia dei Realista* 5:98–106.

Deutsch, Otto Erich (1955). *Handel: A Documentary Biography*. London: Black.

Dick, Alastair (1984). 'The Earlier History of the Shawm in India', *GSJ* 37:80–98.

Dickey, Bruce, Petra Leonards, and Edward H. Tarr (1978). 'The discussion of wind instruments in Bartolomeo Bismantova's Compendio Musicale (1677): translation and commentary', *Basler Jahrbuch für historische Musikpraxis* 2:143–87.

Dlabacz, G. J., ed. (1815). *Allgemeines historisches Künstler-Lexicon für Böhmen*. Prague: G. Haase; R Hildesheim: G. Olms, 1973.

Dobson, Michael (1946). Report, January, *Philharmonic Post*.

Dolcet, J. (1987). 'L'Obra dels germans Pla. Bases per a una catalogació', *Anuario Musical* (Barcelona) 42:131–88.

Donington, Robert (1982). *Music and its Instruments*. London: Methuen.

Dovergne, Guy (2003). 'Georges Longy, 1868–1930', *La Lettre du hautboïste* 12:13–30.

Drouet, Louis (c.1827). *Méthode pour la flûte*. Milan: Ricordi. Trans. as *The Method of Flute Playing*, introd. by R. Rasch and S. Preston. Buren: F. Knuf, 1990).

Drummond, Pippa (1978). 'The Royal Society of Musicians in the eighteenth century', *ML* 59:268–89.

DuBois, Ted (1996). 'C. F. D. Schubart's Comments about Double Reed Instruments and Performers', *JIDRS* 24:31–40.

Du Bos, Abbé Jean-Baptiste (1719). *Reflexions critiques sur la poesie et sur la peinture Ut pictura Poesis*. Paris: J. Mariette.

—— (1978). *Critical Reflections on Poetry, Painting and Music*. Trans. T. Nugent. London, New York: AMS.

Dufourcq, Norbert, and Marcelle Benoit (1963). 'Les musiciens de Versailles à travers les minutes notariales de Lamy versées aux Archives départementales de Seine-et-Oise: 1661–1733', *Recherches* 3:189–206.

Dunner, Béatrice (1988–90). 'Musiciens Parisiens au XVIIIe siècle: quatre inventaires après décès', *Recherches* 26:173.

Du Pradel, Abraham [Nicholas de Blegny] (1692). *Le livre commode des addresses de Paris pour 1692*. Paris: Nion.

Dwight, John S. (1881). 'Music in Boston', in J. Winsor, ed., *Memorial History of Boston including Suffolk County, Mass, 1630–1880*. Boston: Ticknor and Co., vol. IV.

Eaglefield-Hull, A. (1924). *A Dictionary of Modern Music and Musicians*. London and Toronto: J. M. Dent and Sons.

Écochard, Marc (2001). 'Fingering, woodwind instruments with side holes', *NG2* 8:851.

Écorcheville, J. (1903). 'Quelques documents sur la musique de la Grande Écurie du Roi', *Sammelbände der Internationalen Musik-Gesellschaft* 2:608–42.

Edge, Dexter (1991). Handout, Mozart Bicentennial at Lincoln Center.

—— (1992). 'Mozart's Viennese orchestras', *EM* 20/1:64–88.

Eisel, Johann Philipp [?] (1738). *Musicus autodidactus*. Erfurt: M. Funcken.

Eisen, Cliff (1991). *New Mozart Documents: A Supplement to O. E. Deutsch's Documentary Biography*. Stanford: Stanford Univ. Press.

Eitner, Robert (1898–1904/R1947 [EQL]). *Biographisch-bibliographisches Quellen-Lexikon der Musiker und Musikgelehrten*. Leipzig: Breitkopf and Härtel.

Ellis, Alexander J. (1880). 'On the history of musical pitch', *Journal of the Society of Arts* (5 March 1880), 293–336; R Amsterdam: F. Knuf, 1968.

Elson, Arthur (1902). *Orchestral Instruments and Their Use: Giving a Description of Each Instrument Now Employed by the Civilised Nations, a Brief Account of Its History, and Idea of the Technical and*

Acoustical Principles Illustrated by Its Performance, and an Explanation of It. Boston: The Page Co.

Engel, Hans (1971). *Das Instrumentalkonzert, Band I: Von den Anfängen bis gegen 1800.* Wiesbaden: Breitkopf u. Härtel.

Engländer, Richard (1922). *Johann Gottlieb Naumann als Opernkomponist.* Leipzig: Breitkopf u. Härtel; R Farnborough: Gregg, 1970.

Ennulat, E. M. (1984). 'William Ling: A Rediscovered English Mozart?' *Journal of Musicological Research* 5:35.

Enrico, Eugene (1976). *The Orchestra at San Petronio in the Baroque Era.* Washington: Smithsonian.

Eppelsheim, Jürgen (1961). *Das Orchester in den Werken Jean Baptiste Lullys.* Tutzing: H. Schneider.

Ernst, A. (1865–1890). 'Hautbois', in Pierre Larousse, *Grand Dictionnaire universel du XIXe siècle.* Paris: Admin. du Grand Dict. univ.

Evans, Kenneth Gene (1963). 'Instructional materials for the oboe, 1695–c.1800'. Ph.D. diss., Univ. of Iowa.

Fahrbach, Giuseppe (1843). *Novissimo Metodo per Oboe di facile intelligenza e colla vista speciale che servir possa alla istruzione de Principianti senza l'ajuto del maestro,* op. 27. Milan: Ricordi.

Fedelleck, Roger (1979). 'A Music Review of the Concerto in C major attributed to Joseph Haydn', *JIDRS* 7:63–8.

Fenaille, Maurice (1903). *État général des tapisseries de la manufacture des Gobelins.* Paris: Hachette.

Fétis, François Joseph (1830). *Curiosités historiques de la musique.* Paris: Janet and Cotelle.

—— (1834a). 'Exposition des produits de l'industrie', *Gazette musicale de la Belgique* 1/41:1.

—— (1834b). 'Exposition des produits de l'industrie: Instruments à vent', *Revue musicale* 8/19:145–9.

—— (1834c). *La Musique mise à la portée de tout le monde: exposé succinct de tout ce qui est nécessaire pour juger de cet art.* Paris: Paulin.

—— (1834d). 'Variétés: Machine à faire les anches de hautbois et de basson', *RM* 8/28:221.

—— (1834e). 'Hautbois, cor anglais, baryton', *Gazette musicale de la Belgique* 1/41 (15 May 1834).

—— (1837). *Manuel des Compositeurs ou Traité méthodique de l'harmonie des instruments.* Paris: P. Maquet.

—— (1839). 'Instruments à vent', in *Exposition des produits de l'industrie française en 1839.* Paris: L. Bouchard-Huzard, II:367.

—— (1851). 'Exposition Universelle de Londres, 14me lettre', *RGMdP* 18:393–5.

—— (1856). 'Fabrication des Instruments de Musique', *Exposition Universelle de Paris, 1855: Rapports du jury mixte international.* Paris: Imprimerie impériale.

—— (1868). 'Groupe II, classe 10', *Rapports du jury international: Exposition universelle, 1867.* Paris: P. Dupont.

Fink, Michael (1999). 'My Dinner with Ivan: A visit with distinguished Russian oboist Ivan Poushechnikov', *DR* 22/4:31–2.

Finkelman, Michael (1983). 'A Study of the English Horn and Other Lower Oboes in the Classical and Early Romantic Eras', Master's diss., Antioch Institute.

—— (1998-2000). 'Die Oboeninstrumente in tieferer Stimmlage' [in 8 parts], *Tibia* 4/98:274–81; 1/99:364–8; 2/99:451–6; 3/99:537–41; 4/99:618–24; 1/00:25–32; 2/00:106–11; 3/00:204–8.

—— (2001). 'Hautbois d'Eglise', *NG2* 11:151–2.

Fischer, Johann Christian [?] (c.1780b). *New and complete instructions for the oboe or hoboy.* London: Longman and Broderip.

Fischer-Wildhagen, Rita (1985). 'Richard Wagner und die Altoboe', in W. Suppan, ed. *Bläserklang und Blasinstrumente im Schaffen Richards Wagners.* Tutzing: H. Schneider, 89–97.

Fiske, R. (1973). English Theatre Music in the Eighteenth Century. London: Oxford Univ. Press.

Fitzpatrick, Horace (1970–1). *The horn and horn-playing and the Austro-Bohemian tradition, 1680–1830.* London: Oxford Univ. Press.

Flaubert, Gustave (1979). *Flaubert in Egypt: A Sensibility on Tour. A Narrative drawn from Gustave Flaubert's Travel Notes & Letters.* Ed. F. Steegmuller. Chicago: Academy.

Fleurot, François (1984). *Le hautbois dans la musique française, 1650–1800.* Paris: Picard.

Folkman, Benjamin. (1987). 'The So-called Haydn *Oboe Concerto: A Curious Modern Edition*', *JIDRS* 15: 53–6; repr. *DR* 19/3 (1996):167–70.

Ford, Robert (1981). 'Nicolas Dieupart's book of trios', *Recherches* 20:45–75.

Forkel, Johann Nikolaus (1782–4). *Musikalischer Almanach für Deutschland*. Leipzig: Schwickertschen.

Francis, Sarah (1994). 'Joy Boughton: A Portrait', *DR* 17/3:63–6.

Francœur, Louis-Joseph (n.d./2 1772 /3 1813). *Diapason général de tous les instruments à vent*. Paris: Le Marchand.

François-Sappey, Brigitte (1988–90). 'Le Personnel de la Musique Royale de l'avènement de Louis XVI à la chute de la monarchie (1774–1792)', *Recherches* 26:133–72.

Freillon-Poncein, Jean-Pierre (1700). *La véritable manière d'apprendre à jouer en perfection du hautbois, de la flûte et du flageolet*. Paris: J. Collombat; *R* Geneva: Minkoff, c.1972.

Fried, Trevor, and Nora Post (1995). 'Oboe Blow-Out New York in Review', *DR* 18:25–39.

Fröhlich, F. J. (1810). *Hoboeschule*. Bonn: Simrock.

—— (1810–11). *Vollständige theoretisch-pracktische Musikschule*. Bonn: Simrock.

Fulcher, George Williams (1856). *Life of Thomas Gainsborough*. London: Sudbury (ed. by his son E. S. Fulcher).

Fuller, David (2001). 'Notes inégales', *NG2* 18: 90–200.

Furlong, William (1974). *Season with Solti: A Year with the Chicago Symphony Orchestra*. New York: Macmillan Publishing Co.

Fürstenau, Anton B. (n.d.). *Die Kunst des Flötenspiels*, op. 138. Leipzig.

Fürstenau, Moritz (1861–2). *Zur Geschichte der Musik und des Theaters am Hofe zu Dresden*. Dresden: R. Kuntze; *R* Hildesheim, New York: Olms, 1971.

Ganassi dal Fontego, Sylvestro (1535). *Opera intitulata Fontegara*. Venice: Sylvestro; *R* Roma: Società italiana del flauto dolce, 'Hortus Musicus', 1991.

Garcia, Manuel II (1855). *New Treatise on the Art of Singing*. London.

Gardiner, William (1838–53). *Music and friends, or pleasant recollections of a dilettante*. London: Longmans, Orme, Brown and Longman.

Garnier, François-Joseph (1802). *Méthode raisonnée pour le hautbois*. Paris: Pleyel; *R* and trans. P. Hedrick, Columbus, OH: Early Music Facsimiles ; *R* in *Hautbois: Méthodes et Traités, Dictionnaires*, 'Méthodes et Traités', 3, Série I: France 1600–1800. Paris: Fuzeau, 1999.

Garsault, François-Alexandre-Pierre de (1761). *Notionaire ou mémorial raisonné*. Paris: G. Desprez.

Gärtner, Jochen (1981). *The Vibrato with Particular Consideration given to the situation of the Flutist*. Trans. E. W. Anderson. Regensburg: Gustav Bosse.

Gassner, F. S. (1851). *Traité de la Partition ou Guide Servant, sans maître à l'instruction des jeunes compositeurs ou de ceux qui desirent apprendre à arranger, à lire la partition, ou se former directeurs d'Orchestres ou de musiques militaires*. Trans. from German by F. Hofer. Paris: Richault.

Geiringer, Karl (1943). *Musical Instruments: Their History from the Stone Age to the Present Day*. Trans. B. Miall. London: Allen and Unwin.

Geller, H. (1954). *I pifferari: musizierende Hirten in Rom*. Leipzig: Seemann.

Geminiani, F. (1751). *The Art of Playing on the Violin*, op. 9. London, repr. ed. D. D. Boyden, Oxford University Press, [n.d.].

Gerard, Michel (1983–4). 'Du Hautbois à trois clefs au hautbois à treize clefs', thèse de Doctorat, Université des Sciences Humaines de Strasbourg, Institut de Musicologie.

Gerber, Ernst Ludwig (1790–92). *Historisch-biographisches Lexikon der Tonkünstler* (2 vols). Leipzig: Breitkopf.

Gerber, Ernst Ludwig (1812–14). *Neues historisch-biographisches Lexikon der Tonkünstler* (4 vols). Leipzig: Kuhnel.

Gervasoni, Carlo (1800). *La Scuola della Musica*. Piacenza: N. Orcesi.

Gevaert, F. A. (1863). *Traité général d'instrumentation. Exposé méthodique des pricipes de cet art dans leur application à l'orchestre à la musique d'harmonie et de fanfare*. Gand, Liège, Paris: Gevaert, Katto.

—— (1885). *Nouveau traité d'instrumentation*. Paris, Brussels: Lemoine et fils.

Giannini, Tula (1987). 'A letter from Louis Rousselet, 18th-century French oboist at the Royal Opera in England', *AMIS Newsletter* 16/2:10–11.

—— (1993). *Great flute makers of France: The Lot and Godfroy families, 1650–1900*. London: T. Bingham.

—— (2001). 'Hotteterre', *NG2* 11:752–7.

Giazotto, Remo (1973). *Antonio Vivaldi*. Turin: Edizioni Rai.

Girard, Alain (2001). 'Les Hautbois d'église et leur énigme', *Glareana: Nachrichten der Gesellschaft der Freunde alter Musikinstrumente* 50/2:66–129.

Gobineau, Arthur de (1965). *Nouvelles asiatiques*. Paris: Garnier (orig. pub. 1876).

Golde, Carl Theodor (1978). 'On Oboe Making', trans. in Karp, C., 'Woodwind Instrument Bore Measurement', *GSJ* 31:9–23.

Goodale, Ezekiel (1829). *Instrumental Director*. Boston, 3rd ed.

Goossens, Leon (1979). 'Collector's Corner: "The Virtuoso Oboe"', Interview with Gerald N. Moore for BBC radio, 23 June 1979, British National Sound Archive, NP3521W C1.

Goossens, Leon, and Edwin Roxburgh (1977). *Oboe*. London: MacDonald and Janes.

Grenser, Heinrich (1800). [Remarks on the writings of J. G. Tromlitz, 15 March 1800], *Intelligenz-Blatt zur Allgemeine musikalische Zeitung* 11:44.

Grétry, A. E. M. (1914). *Mémoires ou Essais sur la musique*. Liège: Éditions de Wallonia (first published 1789).

Groce, Nancy (1991). *Musical Instrument Makers of New York: A Directory of 18th- and 19th-century Urban Craftsmen*. Stuyvesant, NY: Pendragon.

Grout, Donald Jay (1960). *A History of Western Music*. New York: Norton.

Grove, Sir George (1880-90). *A Dictionary of Music and Musicians (= Gr1)*. 1st ed. London: Macmillan.

Grush, James (1972). 'A Guide to the study of Classical Oboe', DMA diss., Boston Univ.

Guerrini, P. (1934). 'Per la storia della musica a Brescia', *Note d'Archivio per la storia musicale*, 11.

Guichon, Alfred (1874). 'Le Hautbois', *Chronique Musicale* 5:18–30.

Hadamowsky, Hans (1969). 'Der Wiener Bläserstil', *Österreichiche Musikzeitschrift* 24:691–7.

—— (1973). *Oboeschule*. Vienna: the author.

Hailperin, Paul (1970). 'Some technical remarks on the shawm and baroque oboe', submitted for the Diploma of the Schola Cantorum Basiliensis.

Halfpenny, Eric (1949). 'The English 2- and 3-keyed Hautboy', *GSJ* 2:10–26.

—— (1953, 1955). 'The French hautboy: a technical survey', *GSJ* 6:23–34; 8:50–9.

Hanslick, Eduard (1950). *Vienna's Golden Years of Music, 1850–1900*. New York: Simon and Schuster.

Harnoncourt, Nikolaus (1988). *Baroque Music Today: Music as Speech*. Portland, OR: Amadeus (trans. of *Musik als Klangrede*, Salzburg and Vienna, 1982)

Harris, Melvin (1975). 'Henri de Busscher, 1880–1975', *TWO* 3/3:1ff.

Harris-Warrick, Rebecca (1990). 'A Few thoughts on Lully's Hautbois', *EM* 18:97–106.

Harris-Warrick, Rebecca, and Carol G. Marsh (1994). *Musical Theatre at the Court of Louis XIV: le Mariage de la Grosse Cathos*. Cambridge Univ. Press.

Hawkins, D. (1987). 'An Interview with Jürg Schaeftlein', *DR* 10/2:4–6.

Hawkins, Sir John (1776). *A General history of the science and practice of music*. London: T. Payne and Son; *R* New York: Dover, 1963.

Haydn, Joseph (1959). *The Collected Correspondence and London Notebooks of Joseph Haydn*, ed. H. C. Robbins Landon. London: Barrie & Rockcliff.

—— (1965). *Joseph Haydn: Gesammelte Briefe und Aufzeichnungen*, ed. H. C. Robbins Landon and D. Bartha. Kassel: Bärenreiter.

Haynes, Bruce (1978). 'Oboe fingering charts, 1695–1816', *GSJ* 31:68–93.

—— (1979). 'Tonality and the baroque oboe', *EM* 7:355–7.

—— (1984). 'Double Reeds, 1660–1830: A Survey of Surviving Written Evidence', *JIDRS* 12:14–33.

—— (1986). 'Telemann's *Kleine Cammer-music* and the four oboists to whom it was dedicated', *Musick* 7:31–5.

—— (1991). 'Beyond temperament: non-keyboard intonation in the 17th and 18th centuries', *EM* 19:357–81.

—— (1992a). *Music for Oboe, 1650–1800: A Bibliography*. Berkeley, CA: Fallen Leaf, 2nd ed.

—— (1992b). 'Johann Sebastian Bachs Oboenkonzerte', *Bach Jahrbuch*, 23–43.

—— (1995). 'Pitch standards in the baroque and classical periods', Ph.D. diss., Université de Montréal.

—— (1997). 'New light on some French relatives of the hautboy in the 17th and early 18th centuries: the cromorne, hautbois de Poitou and chalumeau simple', *Sine musica nulla vita (Festschrift Hermann Moeck)*, 257–70. Celle: Moeck.

—— (1998). 'The Addition of Keys to the Oboe, 1790–1830', *JIDRS* 22:31–46.

—— (2000a). '"Sweeter than Hautbois": Towards a conception of the Schalmey of the baroque period', *JAMIS* 26:57–82.

—— (2000b). 'A reconstruction of Talbot's hautboy reed', *GSJ* 53:78–86.

—— (2001). *The Eloquent Oboe: A History of the Hautboy, 1640 to 1760 (EO)*. Oxford Univ. Press.

—— (2002). *A History of Performing Pitch: The Story of 'A'*. Lanham: Scarecrow.

Heartz, D. (1973–4). 'Thomas Attwood's lessons in composition with Mozart', *PRMA* 100:175–83.

Hedrick, Peter (1974a). 'Henri Brod's *Méthode* pour le hautbois reconsidered', *The Consort* 30:53–62.

—— (1974b). 'Henri Brod on the making of oboe reeds', *JIDRS* 6:7–12; repr. *DR* 19/3 (1996):105–10.

—— (1989). 'A Ten-Keyed Oboe by Guillaume Triébert', *JIDRS* 17:19–28.

Hellyer, Roger (1975). 'Some documents relating to Viennese wind-instrument purchases, 1779–1837', *GSJ* 28:50–9.

Helm, Eugene (1980). 'Wilhelm Friedemann Bach', *NG1* 1:841–4.

Hepokoski, James A. (1989). 'Genre and content in mid-century Verdi: "Addio, del passato", *La Traviata*, Act III', *Cambridge Opera Journal* 1/3:249–76.

Herbert, Trevor, and John Wallace (1997). *The Cambridge Companion to Brass Instruments*. Cambridge Univ. Press.

Heyde, Herbert (1986). *Musikinstrumentenbau*. Wiesbaden: Breitkopf u. Härtel.

—— (1994). *Musikinstrumentenbau in Preußen*. Tutzing: H. Schneider.

—— (1996). 'Produktionsformen und Gewerbeorganisation im Leipziger Musikinstrumentenbau des 16. bis 18. Jahrhunderts', in D. Krickeberg, ed., *Der Schöne Klang*, Nuremberg: Germanische Nationalmuseum, 217–48.

Hildebrand, Renate (1975). 'Das Oboenensemble in Deutschland von der Anfängen bis ca. 1720', Diplomarbeit, Schola Cantorum, Basel.

Hilkenbach, Dietrich (1982). 'Die Böhm-Oboe: Illusion oder verpaßte Chance?' *Tibia* 1/82:21–30.

Hiller, Johann Adam (1784). *Lebenbeschreibungen berühmter Musikgelehrten und Tonkünstler neuerer Zeit*. Leipzig: Verlage der Dykischen Buchhandlung.

Hiramoto, Stephen (1999). 'An Analysis of Britten's *Six Metamorphoses after Ovid*', *DR* 22: 23–6.

Hodges, Woodrow Joe (1980). 'A Biographical Dictionary of Bassoonists born before 1825' (2 vols), PhD. diss., University of Iowa.

Höft, Brigitte (1992). 'Komponisten, Komponistinnen und Virtuosen', *Die Mannheimer Hofkapelle im Zeitalter Carl Theodors*, ed. Ludwig Finscher, 59–70. Mannheim: Palatium.

Hoffmann, E. T. A. (1906). *Hoffmanns musikalische Schriften*. Ed. E. Istel. Stuttgart: Greiner and Pfeiffer.

—— (1989). *E. T. A. Hoffmann's Musical Writings: Kreisleriana, The Poet and the Composer, Music Criticism*. Ed. D. Charlton, trans. M. Clarke. Cambridge Univ. Press.

Hofmann, Michel (1954). 'Über das "Pfeifergericht" zu Frankfurt a.M.', *Fränkische Blätter* 6:76, 85–7.

Hofmeister, Friedrich (1844). *Jahresverzeichnis der deutschen Musikalein und Musikschriften*. Leipzig: F. Hofmeister.

Hofmeister, Friedrich, and Carl Whistler (1975). *Handbuch der Musikalischen Literatur: A Reprint of the 1817 edition and the ten supplements, 1818–1827*. Ed. Neil Ratliff. New York and London: Garland.

Hogwood, Christopher (1980). 'Vincent, Thomas', *GrVI* 19:782.

—— (1984). *Handel*. London: Thames and Hudson.

Holliger, Heinz (1972). *Pro Musica Nova: Studien zum Neuer Musik*. Cologne: H. Gerig.

Hoppe, G. C. (1992). *Die Instrument Revolution. Entwichlung. Anendung und Ästhetisch neuer Spieltechniken für Rohrblattinstrumente*. Europäische Hochschulschriften, series 36: Musicology, vol. 75. Frankfurt am Main and Berlin: P. Lang.

Hosek, Miroslav (1975, 84). *Oboen-bibliographie*. Wilhelmshaven: Heinrichshofen, 2 vols.

—— (1979). *Das Blaserquintett*. Grunwald: B. Brüchle.

Hotteterre, Jacques-Martin (1707). *Principes de la flûte traversiere ou flûte d'allemagne, de la flûte à bec ou flûte douce et du haut-bois*. Paris: C. Ballard.

—— (c.1729). *The Rudiments or Principles of the German Flute*. Engl. trans. of parts of Hotteterre 1707. London: Walsh and Hare.

—— (1737). *Méthode pour la musette*, op. 10. Paris: C. Ballard. R Geneva: Minkoff, 1977.

Houle, George (1984). 'The oboe sonatas of Giuseppe Sammartini', *Journal of Musicology* 3:90–103.

House, Delpha LeAnn (1991). 'Jacques Hotteterre "le Romain": a study of his life and compositional style', Ph.D. dissertation, Univ. of North Carolina at Chapel Hill.

Howe, Robert (2000–1). 'Historical Oboes', *DR* 24:21–8; 24:59–75; 24:17–30.

—— (2002). 'An Oboe-Sax by Lorée', *DR* 25:75–80.

Huene, Friedrich von (1980). 'Denner', *NG1*, 5:373–4.

Hugo, Victor (1964). *Les Rayons et les Ombres*, in *Œuvres poétiques*. Paris: Gallimard, vol. 1.

Humiston, R. G. (1968). 'A study of the oboe concertos of Alessandro Besozzi and J. Chr. Fischer', Ph.D. dissertation, Univ. of Iowa.

Humperdinck, Engelbert (1981). *Instrumentationslehre*. Ed. H.-J. Irmen. Cologne: Verlag der Arbeitsgemeinschaft für rheinische Musikgeschichte.

Hunter, Mary (1998). 'The Alla Turka Style in the late 18th Century: Race and Gender in the Symphony and the Seraglio', in J. Bellman, ed., *The Exotic in Western Music*. Boston: Northeastern Univ. Press, 43–73.

Huray, Peter le, and James Day, eds (1981). *Music and Aesthetics in the Eighteenth and Early Nineteenth Centuries*. Cambridge Univ. Press.

Huygens, Constantijn (1882). Letters, published in W. J. A. Jonckbloet and J. P. N. Land, eds, *Musique et musiciens au XVIIe siècle*. Leyden: E.J. Brill. And in J. A. Worp, ed., *De briefwisseling van Constantijn Huygens (1608–1687)*. The Hague: M. Nijhof, 1911–17.

IDRS programme from Rotterdam Conference, 1995.

Jancourt, Eugène (1847). *Méthode théoretique et pratique pour le basson*. Paris: Richault.

Janzen, Rose-Marie (1982). 'Die Identität von Jean-Baptiste Leila', *Tibia* 1/82:1–6.

Jaubert, l'Abbé Pierre (1773). *Dictionnaire raisonné universel des arts et métiers*. Paris : P. Fr. Didot le jeune.

Jeans, Susi (1958a). 'Seventeenth-century musicians in the Sackville Papers', *Monthly Musical Record* 88:182–7.

—— (1958b). 'Bressan in 1690', *GSJ* 11:91–2.

Jenkins, Jean (1983). *Man and Music: A Survey of Traditional non-European Musical Instruments*. Edinburgh: Royal Scottish Museum.

Jerome, Wilbert D. (1973). 'The oboe concerto before 1775', Ph.D. diss., Bryn Mawr College.

Jeskalian, Barbara (1990). 'Georges Longy', *DR* 13/2:47–50.

Johnson, H. Earle (1943). *Musical Interludes in Boston, 1795–1830*. New York: Columbia Univ. Press.

Joppig, Gunther (1981). *Oboe & Fagott: Ihre Geschichte, ihre Nebeninstrumente und ihre Musik*. Bern

and Stuttgart: Hallwag, Fr. trans. by J. Mottaz, Lausanne: Payot 1981; Engl. trans. by A.
    Clayton, Portland, OR: Amadeus, 1988.

——— (1986). 'Heckelphone, 80 Years Old', *JIDRS* 14:70–5.

——— (1998). 'Sarrusophone, Rothphone (Saxorusophone) and Reed Contrabass', *JIDRS*
    17:35–66.

Jung, Helge (1986). 'Poised between Elegy and Comedy'. Sleeve notes to Burkhard Glaetzner,
    Neue Musik für Oboe, Contemporary Music for Oboe. Berlin Classics 0011722BC reissue, 1996.

Junker: *see* Meusel.

Kachermarchik, Vladimir (1994). 'Some Mysteries of Ancient Greek Auletes', *JIDRS* 22:93–8.

Kahl, Willi, ed. (1948). *Selbstbiographien deutscher Musiker*. Cologne: Stauffen.

Kandinsky, Wassily (1912). *Über das Geistige in der Kunst*. Munich: R. Piper.

Karp, Cary (1978). 'Woodwind Instrument Bore Measurement', *GSJ* 31:9–23.

Kartomi, Margaret J. (1990). *On Concept and Classifications of Musical Instruments*. Chicago and
    London: Univ. of Chicago Press.

Kastner, Jean-Georges (1837). *Traité général d'instrumentation*. Paris: Philippe et Cie.

——— (1839–42). *Cours d'Instrumentation considéré sous les rapports poëtiques et philosophiques de l'art
    à l'usage des jeunes compositeurs*. Paris: A. Meissonnier et J. L. Heugel.

——— (1844). *Méthode élémentaire pour le hautbois, suivi d'airs et exercises gradés, composée à l'usage des
    Pensions*. Paris: Troupenas and Co.

Kenyon de Pascual, Beryl (1984). 'El primer oboe espanol que formó parte de la real capilla:
    Don Manuel Cavazza', *Revista de Musicología* 7:431–4.

——— (1990). 'Juan Bautista Pla and José Pla – two neglected oboe virtuosi of the 18th
    century', *EM* 18:109–10.

Kernis, Aaron Jay (1996). Sleeve notes to *Colored Field*. San Francisco SO, Neale (Argo,
    448174–2).

Kirkendale, Ursula (1966). *Antonio Caldara*. Graz/Köln: Böhlau.

Kirkendale, Warren (1993). *The Court Musicians in Florence during the Principate of the Medici*.
    Florence: L. S. Olschki.

Kirkpatrick, Ralph (1953). *Domenico Scarlatti*. Princeton and London: Princeton Univ. Press.

Kirnbauer, Martin, and Peter Thalheimer (1995). 'Jacob Denner and the development of the
    flute in Germany', *EM* 23:83–100.

Kling, Henri (1888). *Leichtfassliche Praktische Schule für Oboe mit vielen Übungs- und Vortragsstücken*,
    op. 425. Hanover: Oertel.

Knepper, Noah (1978). 'Hans Hadamowsky and the "Oboeschule"', *JIDRS* 6:1–6.

Knight, Janice (1996). 'My Life with the Bass Oboe', *Double Reed News: Magazine of the British
    Double Reed Society*, R in *DR* 22/4 (1999):55–6.

Koch, H. C. (1802). *Musikalisches Lexikon*. Frankfurt a. Main: A. Hermann dem Jungern;
    R Hildesheim: G. Olms, 1964.

– – (1865). *Musikalisches Lexicon*. Rev. ed.

Köchel, Ludwig von (1869). *Die kaiserliche Hof-Musikkapelle in Wien von 1543–1867*. Vienna;
    R Hildeshem, New York: G. Olms, 1976.

Koechlin, Charles (c.1910–20). *Traité de l'orchestration*. Paris: M. Eschig.

Kolneder, Walter (1979). *Antonio Vivaldi: Dokumente seines Lebens und Schaffens*. Wilhelmshaven:
    Heinrichshofen.

König, Ernst (1959). 'Die Hofkapelle des Fürsten Leopold zu Anhalt-Köthen', *Bach Jahrbuch*
    45:160–7.

Koury, Daniel J. (1986). *Orchestral Performance Practices in the 19th century: Size, Proportions and
    Seating*. Ann Arbor: UMI Research Press.

Kramer, Jonathan D. (2002). 'The Nature and Origins of Musical Postmodernism', in Judy
    Lochhead and Joseph Auner, eds, *Postmodern Music/Postmodern Thought*, New York and
    London: Routledge, 13–26.

Krauss, Rudolph (1908). *Das Stuttgarter Hoftheater von den ältesten Zeiten bis zur Gegenwart*.
    Stuttgart: Metzler.

Kross, S. (1969). *Das Instrumentalkonzert bei Georg Philipp Telemann.* Tutzing: Schneider.

Küffner, Joseph (1890). *Oboe-Schule/Oboe Tutor.* Ed. F. Volbach. London: Schott and Co; Brussels: Schott frères; Milan: B. Schott's Söhne; Paris: P. Schott & Cie.

Kunkel, M., and J. Stenzl (2001). 'Holliger', in *NG2* 11:628–31.

Kynaston, Trent P. (c1980). *Circular Breathing for the Wind Performer.* Lebanon, IN: Studio 224.

La Barre, Michel de (?c.1740). 'Mémoire de M. de la Barre: sur les musettes et hautbois, etc.', ms, Archives Nationales (O'.878).

La Borde, Jean-Benjamin de (1780). *Essai sur la musique ancienne et moderne.* Paris: Ph.-D. Pierres; R New York: AMS Press, 1978.

Lacombe, Jacques (1752). *Dictionaire portatif des beaux-arts.* Paris: La Veuve Estienne et fils.

Lafontaine, H. C. de (1909). *The King's music. A transcript of records relating to music and musicians (1460–1700).* London.

La Gorce, Jérôme de (1979). 'L'Académie royale de musique en 1704, d'après des documents inédits conservés dans les archives notariales', *Revue de musicologie* 65:160–85.

—— (1989). 'Some notes on Lully's orchestra', in J. H. Heyer, ed., *Jean-Baptiste Lully and the music of the French baroque: Essays in Honor of James R. Anthony.* Cambridge Univ. Press, 99–112.

Lalande, Joseph Jérôme Le Français de (1769). *Voyage d'un françois en Italie.* Yverdon.

Landmann, Ortrun (1982). 'Französische Elemente in der Musikpraxis am Dresdener Hof des 18. Jahrhunderts', *Studien zur Aufführungspraxis und Interpretation von Instrumentalmusik des 18. Jahrhunderts* 16:48–56.

—— (1989). 'The Dresden Hofkapelle during the lifetime of Johann Sebastian Bach', *EM* 17:17–30.

—— (1993). 'Die Entwicklung der Dresdener Hofkapelle zum " klassischen" Orchester', *Basler Jahrbuch für historische Musikpraxis* 17:175–90.

Landon, H. C. Robbins (1976-). *Haydn: Chronicles and Works.* Bloomington and London.

Langey, Otto (1885). *The Oboe.* London: Rivière and Hawkes.

Langwill, Lyndesay G. (1949). 'Two rare 18th-century London directories', *Music & Letters* 30:37–43.

—— (1980). *Index of Wind-Instrument Makers,* 6th ed. Edinburgh: Langwill

Lardrot, André (1999). 'Raymond Meylan, flûtiste', *La Lettre du Hautboïste* 3:16.

—— (2001). 'Henri Brod: Hautboïste, luthier, inventeur, compositeur (13 juin 1799–6 avril 1839)', *La Lettre du Hautboïste* 8/2:24–39 ; 9:11–23.

Lasocki, David (1983). 'Professional recorder players in England, 1540–1740', Ph.D. diss., Univ. of Iowa.

—— (1988). 'The French hautboy in England, 1673–1730', *EM* 16:339–57.

——, ed. (1997). *A Time of Questioning: Proceedings of the International Early Double-Reed Symposium, Utrecht, 1994.* Utrecht: STIMU, Foundation for Historical Performance Practice.

Lasocki, David, and Wendy Thompson (1979). 'Professional recorder playing in England during the baroque era'. Privately commissioned, unpublished paper (cf. Lasocki 1983).

Lavignac, Albert (1899). *Music and Musicians.* New York: H. Holt and Co.

Lavoix, H. (1878). *Histoire d'instrumentation depuis le seizième siècle jusqu'à nos jours.* Paris: Librairie de Firmin-Didot.

Lawrence, Vera B. (1988–95). *Strong on Music: The New York Music Scene in the Days of George Templeton Strong, 1836–1875.* Oxford Univ. Press.

Lawson, Colin (1994). 'Beethoven and the Development of Wind Instruments', in R. Stowell, ed., *Performing Beethoven.* Cambridge Univ. Press, 70–88.

——, ed. (1995). *The Cambridge Companion to the Clarinet.* Cambridge Univ. Press.

Ledet, David A. (1981). *Oboe Reed Styles: Theory and Practice.* Bloomington: Indiana Univ. Press.

Le Dhuy, Adolphe (1850). *Petite Encyclopédie instrumentale. Collection de tablatures et gammes ou méthodes abrégées en tableaux synoptiques.* Paris: Schonenberger; Leipzig: Breitkopf und Härtel.

Lee, Douglas A. (2000). 'Graupner, Gottlieb', in *NG2.*

Lehrer, Charles D. (1981). 'The Florian Mueller Story', *DR* 4/2:1–15.

—— (1982). 'Beethoven's 1792 oboe concerto in F major', *DR* 5/2:36–7.

—— (1982). 'Beethoven's 1792 oboe concerto in F major', *DR* 5/2:36–7.

—— (1984). 'Repertoire of the Oboe in the 19th century: the Hidden Structure', *JIDRS* 12:10–13.

—— (1988). 'An Introduction to the 16 Oboe Concertos of Gustave Vogt and a discussion of the nineteenth-century performance practices preserved in them', *JIDRS* 16:19–51.

—— (1989). 'The 19th-century Oboe Concert in Czarist Russia: Works of Johann Heinrich Luft', *JIDRS* 17:75–95.

—— (1990). 'Background on the Oboe Concertos of Stanislas Verroust', *JIDRS* 18:59–87.

—— (1991). 'A List of Henri Brod's Compositions with a Short Discussion of his Oboe Concertos', *JIDRS* 19:5–17.

—— (1994). 'How Barret Accompanied his Forty Progressive Melodies', *JIDRS* 22:77–85.

Lehrer, Charles D., and Nancy Lehrer (1988). 'The Josef Marx Story', *DR* 12:44–60; repr. in *DR* 19/3 (1996):128–44.

Lemprière, John (1984). *Classical Dictionary of Proper Names mentioned in Ancient Authors Writ Large.* London and New York: Routledge and Kegan Paul, 3rd rev. ed., originally pub. 1788.

Leppert, Richard (1993). *The Sight of Sound: Music, Representation and the History of the Body.* Berkeley, Los Angeles, London: Univ. of California Press.

Levin, Robert D. (1988). *Who wrote the Mozart four-wind concertante?* Stuyvesant, New York: Pendragon.

Libby, Dennis (1989). 'Italy: two opera centres', in *The Classical Era*, ed. Neal Zaslaw. Engelwood Cliffs NJ: Prentice-Hall, 15–60.

Libin, Laurence (2000). 'Progress, adaptation, and the evolution of musical instruments', *JAMIS* 26:187–213.

Light, Jay (1994). *Essays for Oboists.* Des Moines: Aldorada.

Lindenberger, Herbert (1998). *Opera in History.* Stanford, CA: Stanford Univ. Press.

Locke, Ralph (1998). 'Cutthroats and Casbah Dancers, Muezzins and Timeless Sands: Musical Images of the Middle East', in J. Bellman, ed., *The Exotic in Western Music.* Boston: Northeastern Univ. Press, 104–36.

Longy, Georges (1900). Programme notes written for the Longy Club in Boston.

Lorenzoni, Antonio (1779). *Saggio per ben sonare il Flauto traverso.* Vicenza: Modena.

McClary, Susan (1992). *Carmen.* Cambridge Univ. Press.

McClymonds, Marita P. (1978/1980). *Niccolo Jommelli: The Last Years, 1769–1774.* Ann Arbor, MI: UMI Research Press.

McCredie, Andrew D. (1964). 'Instrumentarium and instrumentation in the north German baroque opera', Ph.D. diss., Hamburg.

Machard, Roberte (1971). 'Les musiciens en France au temps de Jean-Philippe Rameau d'après les actes du Secrétariat de la Maison du Roi', *Recherches* 11:6–177.

McMullen, William W. (1994). *Soloistic English Horn Literature, 1736–1984.* Juilliard Performance Guides: A Scholarly Series for the Practical Musician, 4. Stuyvesant, NY: Pendragon.

Mahillon, Victor (1880). *Catalogue du Bruxelles conservatoire musée.* Brussels: A. Hoste.

—— (1883). *Documents et rapports des membres du jury publiés par la commission royale de Belgique.* Groupe IV, classe 33, Instruments de musique, Exposition internationale, coloniale et d'exportation générale. Bruxelles: P. Weissenbruch.

Mainwaring, John (1760). *Memoirs of the life of the late George Frederic Handel.* London: Dodsle.

Majer, Joseph Friedrich Bernhard Caspar (1732, /2 1741). *Museum musicum theoretico practicum.* Schwäbisch Hall: G. M. Majer, *R* 1954.

Manning, Dwight (1995). 'Woodwind Vibrato from the eighteenth century to the present', *Performance Practice Review* 8/1:67–72; *R* in *DR* 18/3:73–5.

Marcuse, Sibyl (1975). *A Survey of Musical Instruments.* New York, Evanston, San Francisco, London: Harper and Row.

Margelli, Tad (1996). 'The Paris Conservatoire Concours Oboe Solos: The Gillet Years

(1882–1919)', *JIDRS* 24:41–55.

Mariani, Giuseppe (attrib.) (1900). *Metodo populare per Strumenti a Fiato, Oboe.* Milan: G. Ricordi.

Marpurg, Friedrich Wilhelm (1754–78). *Historisch-kritische Beyträge zur Aufnahme der Musik.* Berlin: Schutzens.

Marx, Josef (1951). 'The Tone of the Baroque Oboe', *GSJ* 4:3–19.

—— (1983). *The Writings of Joseph Marx*, ed. Gloria Ziegler. New York: McGinnis and Marx.

Marx, Karl (1976). 'Über thematische Beziehungen in Haydns Londoner Symphonien', *Haydn-Studien* IV/1: 1.

Marzo, Enrico (1870). *Método de Oboé progressivo y completo con nociones de corno inglés.* Madrid: Unión Musical Española.

Mattheson, Johann (1713). *Das neu-eröffnete Orchestre.* Hamburg: the author; *R* Hildesheim and New York: G. Olms, 1993.

—— (1722-5). *Critica musica.* Hamburg: the author; *R* Amsterdam: Knuf 1964.

—— (1731). *Grosse General-Baß-Schule.* Hamburg: Kissners.

—— (1740). *Grundlage einer Ehren-Pforte.* Hamburg: the author; ed. M. Schneider, Graz: Akademische Druck- u. Verlagsanstalt; Kassel: Bärenreiter, 1994.

—— (1981). *Der vollkommene Capellmeister* (Hamburg, 1739). Trans. E. C. Harriss. Ann Arbor: UMI Research Press.

Matthews, Betty [ed.] (1985). *Royal Society of Musicians – Complete list of members, 1738–1984.* London: The Royal Society of Musicians.

Maunder, Richard (1998). 'Viennese wind-instrument makers, 1700–1800', *GSJ* 52:170–91.

Mendel, Hermann (1890-91). *Musikalisches Conversations-Lexikon: eine Encyclopädie der gesammten musikalischen Wissenschaften für Gebildete aller Stande.* Leipzig: List and Francke.

Menestrier, Claude-François (1681, 1685). *Des Représentations en musique anciennes et modernes.* Paris: Guignard.

Mennicke, C. (1906). *Hasse und die Brüder Graun als Symphoniker.* Leipzig: Breitkopf and Härtel.

Mersenne, Marin (1635). *Harmonicorum instrumentum (libri).* Paris: Ballard; *R* Geneva: Minkoff, 1972.

—— (1636-7). *Harmonie universelle.* Paris: S. Cramoisy ; *R* Paris: CNRS, 1963.

Meude-Monpas, J. J. O. de (1787). *Dictionnaire de musique.* Paris: (s.n.).

Meusel, J. G. (1778 and 1789). *Teutsches Künstlerlexikon* (2 vols). Lemgo: Meyerschen Buchhandlung.

Meusel, J. G., ed. (1787). [Article by Junker in] *Museum für Künstler und für Künstliebhaber*, I: 37ff. Mannheim: Schwan und Götz.

Milhous, J., and R. D. Hume (1983). 'New light on Handel and the Royal Academy of Music in 1720', *Theatre Journal* 35:149–67.

Miller (1843). *Méthode de hautbois contenant les principes de la musique, la tablature du hautbois, des exercices, 15 petits morceaux.* Paris: J. Meissonnier.

Moens-Haenen, Greta (1988). *Das Vibrato in der Musik des Barock.* Graz: Akademische Druck- und Verlagsanstalt.

Montagu, Jeremy (1988). 'Did Shawms exist in antiquity?', in E. Hickmann and D. W. Hughes, eds, *The Archaeology of Early Music Cultures: Third International Meeting of the ICTM Study Group on Music Archaeology.* Bonn: Verlag für systematische Musikwissenschaft, 47–50.

—— (2002). *Reed Instruments: The Montagu Collection: An Annotated Catalogue.* Lanham, MD and London: Scarecrow.

Montagu, Jeremy, and John Burton (1971). 'A proposed new classification system for musical instruments', *Ethnomusicology* 15:49–71.

Mooser, R. Aloys (1948–51). *Annales de la musique et des musiciens en Russie au XVIIIe siècle.* Geneva: Mont-Blanc.

Morby, John E. (1971). 'Musicians at the royal chapel of Versailles, 1683-1792', Ph.D. diss., Univ. of California, Berkeley.

Mortimer (1949). 'Lists from London Universal Directory, 1763', *GSJ* 2: 7–31.

Moÿse, Marcel (1974). *Comment j'ai pu rester en forme*. West Brattleboro, VT: the author.

Mozart, Leopold (1936). *Leopold Mozarts Briefe an seine Tochter*. Ed. O. E. Deutsch and B. Paumgartner. Salzburg, Leipzig: Pustet.

Mozart, W. A. (1962–75). *Mozart: Briefe und Aufzeichnungen*. Ed. W. A. Bauer, O. E. Deutsch and J. H. Eibl. Kassel: Bärenreiter.

Mueller, John H. (1951). *The American Symphony Orchestra: A Social History of Musical Taste*. Bloomington: Indiana Univ. Press.

Mulder, Frank (1992). 'An Introduction and Programmatical Analysis of the *Six Metamorphoses after Ovid*', *JIDRS* 20:67–74.

Münster, Robert (1993). 'Courts and monasteries in Bavaria', in *The Late Baroque Era*, ed. George J. Buelow, 296–323. Engelwood Cliffs, NJ: Prentice Hall.

Myers, Herbert W. (1981). 'The practical acoustics of early woodwinds', DMA diss., Stanford Univ.

Nagel, Wilibald (1900). 'Zur Geschichte der Musik am Hofe von Darmstadt', *Monatshefte für Musikgeschichte* 32:1–95.

Nalin, Giuseppe (1991). '"Il vero indicio che una pivetta sii perfetta è . . ."', *Aulos* 4:83–6.

Nettl, Paul (1957). *Das Prager Quartierbuch des Personals der Krönungsoper 1723*. Mitteilungen der Kommission für Musikforschung 8. Vienna: R. M. Rohrer.

Neumann, Frederick (1987). 'Authenticity and Vocal Vibrato', *American Choral Review* 29/2:13–17.

Newman, William S. (1959). *The Sonata in the Baroque Era*. Chapel Hill: Univ. of North Carolina Press.

Nickel, E. (1971). *Der Holzblasinstrumentenbau in der Freien Reichstadt Nürnberg*. Munich: E. Katzbichler.

Noack, Elizabeth (1967). *Musikgeschichte Darmstadts vom Mittelalter bis zur Goethezeit*. 'Beiträge zur Mittelrheinischen Musikgeschichte', 8. Mainz: B. Schott.

—— (1969). 'G. P. Telemanns Beziehungen zu Darmstädter Musikern', *Konferenzbericht der 3. Magdeburger Telemann-Festtage* (2), 13–17. Magdeburg.

North, Roger (1959). *Roger North on Music*. Including 'Theory of sounds', 'Musical grammarian', etc., mss written c.1710–28. Ed. J. Wilson. London: Novello and Co.

Nösselt, Hans-Joachim (1980). *Ein ältest Orchester, 1530–1980: 450 Jahre Bayerisches Hof- und Staatsorchester*. Munich: Bruckmann.

Oleskiewicz, Mary A. (1998). 'Quantz and the flute at Dresden: his instruments, his repertory and their significance for the Versuch and the Bach circle', Ph.D. diss., Duke Univ.

Olsen, D. A., and D. E. Shechy, eds (1998). *Garland Encyclopedia of World Music*, vol. 2, 'South America, Mexico, Central America and the Caribbean'. New York and London: Garland.

Ongley, Laurie H. (1993). 'The reconstruction of an eighteenth-century Basso group', paper delivered at AMS Conference, Montreal.

Osmond-Smith, David (1991). *Berio*. Oxford Univ. Press.

—— ed. (1985). *Two Interviews/Luciano Berio; with Rossana Dalmonte and Bálint András Varga*. Trans. and ed. D. Osmond-Smith, NewYork: M. Boyars.

Ottani G. (1778). Letter to Padre Martini, 5 Aug. 1778 (in I-Bc).

Owens, Samantha (1995). 'The Württemberg Hof-Musicorum ca.1680–1721', Ph.D. thesis, Victoria Univ., Wellington.

—— (2000). 'An Italian oboist in Germany: double reed making, c.1750', *EM* 28:65–70.

Ozi, Etienne (1803). *Nouvelle méthode de basson*. Paris: L'Imprimérie du Conservatoire.

P., I. (1830). 'On the oboe and bassoon', *Harmonicon* 1 (5 April 1830):192–3.

Page, Janet (1988). 'The hautboy in London musical life, 1730–1770', *EM* 16:348–71.

—— (1993). 'To soften the sound of the hoboy: the muted oboe in the 18th and early 19th centuries', *EM* 21:65–80.

Palmer, Andrew (1997). 'Interview with Heinz Holliger', *DR* 20/2:81–3.

Palmer, Frederic (1983). 'A Conversation with Heinz Holliger', *DR* 6/1:43–50.

Panoff, Peter (1938). *Militärmusik in Geschichte und Gegenwart*. Berlin: K. Siegismund.

Pap, János (1994). 'Hirtenpfeifen: akustische Analyse einer Idee von R. Wagner', *Systematische Musikwissenschaft* 2/2:347–52.

Parès, G. (1898). *Traité d'instrumentation et d'orchestration à l'usage des Musiques Militaires d'Harmonie et de Fanfare.* Paris: H. Lemoine et Cie.

Parke, William Thomas (1830). *Musical Memoirs.* London: H. Colburn and R. Bentley; *R* New York: Da Capo, 1970.

Pauer, Ernst (1863). *Amtlicher Bericht über die Industrie- und Kunst- Ausstellung zu London im Jahre 1862.* Berlin: R. v. Decker.

Paumgartner, Bernhard. (1950). 'Zu Mozarts Oboen-Concerto C-dur, K314 (285d) ', *Mozart-Jahrbuch* 1:24–40.

Pazdírek (1904-10). *Universal-Handbuch des Musikliteratur.* Vienna: Verlag des 'Universal-Handbuch der Musikliteratur'. Pazdírek & Co.; *R* Hilversum: F. Knuf, 1967.

Pelicelli, N. (1934). 'Musicisti in Parma nel sec.XVIII', *Note d'archivio per la storia mus.* 11:250–5.

Petrobelli, Pierluigi (1992). *Tartini, le sue idee e il suo tempo.* Lucca : Libreria musicale italiana.

Petzoldt, Richard (1967). *Georg Philipp Telemann.* Leipzig: Deutscher Verlag für Musik. Eng. trans. H. Fitzpatrick (London, Oxford Univ. Press, 1974).

Philip, Robert (1992). *Early Recordings and Musical Style: Changing tastes in instrumental performance,1900-1950.* Cambridge Univ. Press.

Pierre, Constant (1890). *La Facture instrumentale à l'exposition universelle de 1889: Notes d'un musicien sur les instruments à souffle humain nouveaux & perfectionnés.* Paris: Librairie de l'Art indépendant.

—— (1893). *Les facteurs des Instruments de Musique.* Paris: Sagot.

—— (1900). *Le Conservatoire national de musique et de déclamation: documents historiques et administraitifs.* Paris: Imprimerie nationale.

—— (1975). *Histoire du Concert Spirituel, 1725–1790.* Paris: Société française de musicologie.

Piersol, J. (1972). 'The Oettingen-Wallerstein Hofkapelle and its wind music', 2 vols, Ph.D. diss., Univ. of Iowa.

Pietzsche, Georg (c.1885). *Schule für Oboe mit 50 Etüden.* Leipzig: Friedrich Hofmeister.

Piguet, Michel (1988). 'Die Oboe im 18. Jahrhundert', *Basler Jahrbuch für historische Musikpraxis* 12:81–107 (+ Beiheft).

—— (1997). 'Historical Oboes: Sound and Fingering', in Lasocki, ed., *A Time of Questioning,* 3–7.

Poizat, Michel (1992). *The Angel's Cry.* Trans. by A. Denner of *L'Opéra ou le cri de l'ange: Essai sur la jouissance de l'amateur d'opéra* (Paris, 1986). Ithaca and London: Cornell Univ. Press.

Pontécoulant, Adophe Le Doulet marquis de, (1861). *Organographie: Essai sur la facture instrumentale.* Paris: Castel; *R* Amsterdam: F. Knuf, 1972.

Post, Nora (1980a). 'The Development of Contemporary Oboe Technique', PhD diss., New York Univ.

—— (1980b). 'The Oboe in the Electronic Age', *JIDRS* 8:1–16.

—— (1981). 'Multiphonics for the Oboe', *Interface* 10:113–136; *R* in *JIDRS* 10 (1982): 12–35.

—— (1981-2). 'Varèse, Wolpe and the Oboe', *Perspectives of New Music* 20:135-48.

—— (1982a). 'Interview with Léon Goossens and Edwin Roxburgh, August 1, 1982', *DR* 5/3:39–47.

—— (1982b). 'The Twentieth-Century Oboe in France and England: Makers and Players', *DR* 5/3:2–46.

—— (1982c). 'T. W. Howarth and Co. Ltd. Interview with Nigel Clark, July 30, 1982, London', *DR* 5/3:14–22.

—— (1984a). 'Monophonic Sound Resources for the Oboe', *DR* 7/3:16, 7/2:32.

—— (1984b). 'Schönberg, Berlioz and the Oboe: Redesign for the 20th century?' *Darmstädter Beiträge zur Neuen Musik* 19:41-4.

—— (1995). 'New Designs and Material in Oboe Manufacture: Presented at "Oboe blow out New York"', *DR* 18/3:31–5.

Potter, John (1998). *Vocal Authority: Singing Style and Ideology.* Cambridge Univ. Press.

Powell, Ardal (1991). *The Virtuoso Flute-Player by Johann George Tromlitz* [trans. of Tromlitz 1791]. Cambridge Univ. Press.

—— (1995a). 'An English six-keyed flute, circa 1755', *Traverso* 7/3, 1–3.

—— (1995b). 'Flute, 1100-1800' (draft for the article 'Flute' in *NG2* 9:26).

—— (2002). *The Flute.* New Haven and London: Yale Univ. Press.

Powell, Ardal, with David Lasocki (1995). 'Bach and the flute: the players, the instruments, the music,' *EM* 23:9–29.

Powning, Graham (1980). 'The Six Trios for Two Oboes and English Horn', *DR* 2/4:3–5.

Praetorius, Michael (1618 /2 1619). Part 2, 'De Organographia' (1618, revised 1619), and Part 4, 'Theatrum Instrumentorum seu Sciagraphia' (1620), in *Syntagma musicum.* Wolfenbüttel; *R* Kassel: Bärenreiter, 1958.

Prinz, Ulrich (1979). 'Studien zum Instrumentarium Johann Sebastian Bachs mit besonderer Berücksichtigung der Kantaten', Dissertationsdruck, Universität Tubingen.

Prodan, James (1979). *Oboe Performance Practices and Teaching in the United States and Canada.* Akron, OH: Institute for Woodwind Research.

—— (1990). 'Oboists and Their Teachers: A Historical Representation', *DR* 12/3:37–49.

Prout, Ebenezer (1897). *The Orchestra.* Melville, NY: Belwin Mills.

Prunières, Henry (1931). 'Les Ballets', vol. 1 of J.-B. Lully. *Œuvres complètes.* Paris: Editions de la Revue Musicale.

Pure, Abbé Michel de (1668). *Idées des spéctâcles anciens et nouveaux.* Paris: Brunet.

Quantz, Johann Joachim (1752). *Essai d'une méthode pour apprendre à jouer de la Flûte Traversière/Versuch einer Anweisung die Flöte traversiere zu spielen* [separate versions in French and German]. Berlin: J. F. Voss (trans. by E. R. Reilly as *On Playing the Flute.* London: Faber and Faber, 1971).

—— (1755). 'Herrn Johann Joachim Quantzens Lebenslauf, von ihm selbst entworfen', in F. W. Marpurg, ed., *Historisch-kritische Beyträge zur Aufnahme der Musik.* Berlin: G. A. Lange; *R* Hildesheim and New York: G. Olms, 1970, i:5:197–250.

—— (1978). *Solfeggi pour la Flûte Traversière avec l'enseignement* (ms 1729–41; copied 1775–82 by a Quantz student). Winterthur: Amadeus.

Rackwitz, Werner (1981). *Georg Philipp Telemann: Singen ist das Fundament zur Music in allen Dingen, eine Dokumentensammlung.* Leipzig: Reclam.

Radcliffe, Anne (1966). *The Mysteries of the Udolpho: A Romance interspersed with some pieces of poetry.* London: Oxford Univ. Press.

Raoulx, Maurice de (1841). *Méthode de hautbois.* Paris: Naudot.

Raynor, Henry (1972). *A Social History of Music.* London: Barrie and Jenkins.

Read, Gardner (1993). *Compendium of Modern Instrumental Techniques.* Westport CON: Greenwood.

Record, Samuel J., and Robert W. Hess (1943). *Timbers of the New World.* New Haven: Yale Univ. Press.

Register, Brent (1990). 'A Catalogue of Norwegian Oboe Literature', *JIDRS* 18:25-53.

—— (1995). 'Oboe Music Reviews', *DR* 18/2:75-7.

Reicha, Anton (1818). *Cours de composition musicale.* Paris: Gambaro.

Reichardt, Johann Friedrich (1782). 'Über die musikalische Idylle', *Musikalisches Kunstmagazin* I:167-9.

Reilly 1966: See Quantz.

Ribock, J. J. H. (1783). 'Über Musik, an [*sic*] Flötenliebhaber insonderheit', *Magazin der Musik* 1:686-736.

Riemann, Hugo (1915). 'Verzeichnis der Druckausgaben und thematischer Katalog der Mannheimer Kammermusik des XVIII Jahrhunderts', *Denkmäler der Tonkunst in Bayern* 28:ix–lxiii.

Rimmer, Joan (1976). 'The Instruments called chirimía in Latin America', *Studia instrumentorum musicae popularis* 4:101-10.

Rimsky-Korsakov, Nikolay (1964). *Principles of Orchestration with musical examples drawn from his own works*. Ed. M. Steinberg. Trans. E. Agate. New York: Dover.

Ringer, Alexander, ed. (1990). *Music and Society: The Early Romantic Era: Between Revolutions: 1789 and 1848*. Englewood Cliffs, NJ: Prentice-Hall.

Riordan, George T. (1995). 'The History of the Mozart Concerto K314 Based on Letters of the Mozart Family, a Review of Literature and Some Observations on the Work', *JIDRS* 23:5–18.

Robinson, Joseph (1987). 'Oboists, Exhale before Breathing', *DR* 10:16–9; repr. *DR* 19/3 (1996):93–6.

Rodicio, E. C. (1980). 'La musica en la catedral de Oviedo', Departamento de Arte-Musicologia, Univ. de Oviedo.

Rosen, Carole (1993). *The Goossens: A Musical Century*. London: A. Deutsch.

Rosen, Charles (1995). *The Romantic Generation*. Harvard Univ. Press.

—— (1998). *Romantic Poets, Critics and Other Madmen*. Harvard Univ. Press.

Rosenberg, Donald (2002). 'Oboist Leaves Orchestra after 35 Great Years', *DR* 25:67–8 (*R* from *Cleveland Plain Dealer*).

Rosenthal, Richard (1901). *Theoretisch-praktische Oboe Schule*. London, Mainz, Brussels and Paris: Schott.

Rosset, Lucienne (1987). 'Antonino Pasculli, the "Paganini of the Oboe"', *DR* 10/3:44–5.

Rossini, (1829). *Guillaume Tell*. Paris, E. Troupenas; facsim., ed. P. Gossett, New York and London: Garland, 1980.

Rothwell, Evelyn (1953). *Oboe Technique*. London: Oxford Univ. Press.

—— (1975-7). *The Oboist's Companion*. London: Oxford Univ. Press.

Rousseau, Jean-Jacques (1768). *Dictionnaire de musique*. Paris: Duschene; *R* Hildesheim: G. Olms, 1969.

Rubardt, Paul (1949). 'Pörschmann, Johann', *MGG* 10:1366–7.

Rudhart, F.M. (1865). *Geschichte der Oper am Hofe zu München*. Freising: Datterer.

Rushmore, R. (1971). *The Singing Voice*. London: H. Hamilton.

Sachs, Curt (1908). *Die Musikgeschichte der Stadt Berlin*. Berlin: Paetel.

—— (1910). *Musik und Oper am Kurbrandenburgischen Hof*. Berlin: Bard.

—— (1913). *Real-Lexikon des Musikinstrumente: zugleich ein Polyglossar für das gesamte Instrumentengebiet*. Berlin: J. Bard; *R* Hildesheim: G. Olms, 1962.

—— (1940). *The History of Musical Instruments*. New York: W.W. Norton and Co.

Sachs, Curt, and Erich M. von Hornbostel (1914). 'Systematik der Musikinstrumente', *Zeitschrift für Ethnologie* 46:553–90, trans. A. Baines and K. P. Wachsman as 'Classification of Musical Instruments', in H. Meyers, ed., *Ethnomusicology: An Introduction*. New York and London: W. W. Norton, 1992, 444–61.

Sadie, Stanley (1956). 'The wind music of J. C. Bach', *ML* 37:107-17.

—— ed. (1984). *The New Grove Dictionary of Musical Instruments (GrInstr)*. London: Macmillan.

—— ed. (1980). *The New Grove Dictionary of Music and Musicians (NG1)*. London: Macmillan.

—— ed. (2001) *The Revised New Grove Dictionary of Music and Musicians (NG2)*. London: Macmillan.

Said, Edward (1979). *Orientalism*. New York: Vintage.

Sainsbury, John S. (1825). *A Dictionary of Musicians from the Earliest Times*. London; *R* New York: Da Capo Press, 1966.

Salivet, L. G. I. [alias L.-E. Bergeron and P. Hamelin-Bergeron] (1816). *Manuel du tourneur*. 2nd ed. Paris: the authors.

Salviani, Clemente (1848). *Metodo completo per oboe cotenuto: Nozioni preliminari, modo di construire la Piva (ancia) principi elementari di Musica, Intavolatura, Scale, Salti, Esercizi e Duetti*. Milan: Lucca.

Sandman, Susan (1974). 'Wind band music under Louis XIV: The Philidor Collection, music for the military and the court', Ph.D. diss., Stanford Univ.

Sartori, Claudio. Card catalogue, Milan Conservatory Library.

Sauveur, Joseph (1704–16). Various papers written 1700–13, published in *Mémoires de l'Académie royal des sciences.* Republished in Rudolf Rasch, ed., *Joseph Sauveur: Collected writings on musical acoustics (Paris 1700–1713)*. Utrecht: Diapason, 1984.

Schering, Arnold (1921). 'Die Leipziger Ratsmusik von 1650–1775', *Archiv für Musikwissenschaft* 3:17–53.

—— (1926). *Musikgeschichte Leipzigs II: von 1650 bis 1723*. Leipzig: Kistner and Siegel.

Schlesinger, Kathleen (1910). *The Instruments of the Modern Orchestra and Early Records of the Precursors of the Violin Family with over 300 Illustrations and plates.* London: W. Reeves.

—— (1939). *The Greek Aulos: A Study of its Mechanism and of its Relation to the Modal System of Ancient Greek Music.* London: Methuen; R Groningen: Bouma, 1970.

Schmid, Reinhold (1945). *Assoziationen um das Orchester.* Wien and Wiesbaden: Doblinger.

Schmidt, Günther (1956). *Die Musik am Hofe der Markgrafen von Brandenburg-Ansbach.* Kassel and Basel: Bärenreiter.

Schneider, Christian (1986). 'Oboeninstrumente der Volksmusik', *Tibia* 1/86:7–13; 2/86:88–102.

—— (1993). 'Die Permanentatmung auf der Oboe', *Tibia* 1/93:352–4.

Schneider, L. (1852). *Geschichte der Oper und des kgl. Opernhauses in Berlin.* Berlin: Duncker und Humblot.

Schneider, Wilhelm (1834). *Historisch-technische Beschreibung der Musicalischen Instrumente.* Neisse and Leipzig: T. Hennings.

Schnoebelen, Anne (1969). 'Performance practices at San Petronio in the baroque', *Acta Musicologica* 41:37–55.

Schoenberg, Arnold (1975). *Style and Idea: Selected Writings of Arnold Schoenberg.* London: Faber & Faber.

Schott ed. (c.1825). *Gamme de hautbois*, possibly prepared by Foreith. Mainz: B. Schott.

Schreiber, Ottmar (1938). 'Orchester und Orchesterpraxis in Deutschland zwischen 1780 und 1850', Inaugural Dissertation, Univ. of Berlin.

Schubart, Christian Friedrich Daniel (1806). *Ideen zu einer Ästhetik der Tonkunst.* Vienna: J. V. Degen; R Darmstadt: Wissenschaftliche Buchgesellschaft, 1969.

Schubert, Franz Ludwig (1860). *Praktische Hoboe-Schule*, op. 66. Leipzig: Merseburger.

Schumann-Post, Brenda (2000). 'Bali Dancing', *DR* 23/4:53–5.

Seashore, Carl E. (1947). *In Search of Beauty in Music: A Scientific Approach to Musical Aesthetics.* New York: Ronald Press Co.

Seifert, Herbert (1987). 'Die Bläser der kaiserlichen Hofkapelle zur Zeit von J.J. Fux', Johann Joseph Fux und die barocke Bläsertradition. *Kongressbericht Graz 1985* (*Alta Musica* 9, Tutzing), 9–23.

Selfridge-Field, Eleanor (1971). 'Annotated membership lists of the Venetian instrumentalists guild, 1672–1727', *RMA Research Chronical* 9.

—— (1975). *Venetian Instrumental Music from Gabrieli to Vivaldi.* Oxford: Blackwell.

—— (1986). 'Music at the Pietà before Vivaldi', *EM* 14:373–86.

—— (1987). 'The Viennese court orchestra in the time of Caldara', in Brian W. Pritchard, ed., *Antonio Caldara: Essays on His life and Times.* Aldershot: Scolar Press; Brookfield, VT: Gower Publishing Co., 115–51.

Sellner, Joseph (1824). *Theoretisch praktische Oboe Schule.* Vienna: Sauer und Leidesdorf.

—— (1827a). *Méthode pour le hautbois, traduite de l'allemande par Heller et revue par Fouquier, 1er hautbois du Théâtre Royal de l'Opéra Italien.* Paris: Richault.

—— (1827b). *Metodo teorico-pratico per Oboe.* Mendrisio: Pozzi; R Milan: Ricordi, 1832.

Semmens, Richard T. (1975). 'Woodwind treatment in the early ballets of Jean-Baptiste Lully', Master's thesis, Univ. of British Columbia.

Sénancourt, Étienne-Pivert de (1912–13). *Obermann, Lettres.* Paris: Michaut.

Senici, Emanuele (1998). 'Verdi's Luisa, a Semiserious Alpine Virgin', *19th Century Music* 22:144–68.

Seyfried, Ign. v. (1826). 'Recension: *Theoretisch-practisch Oboe Schule* von Joseph Sellner', *Cäcilia*

4/15:215–24.

Shackleton, Nicholas (1980). 'Clarinet', *NG1* 4:429–42.

Shackleton, Nicholas, and Albert Rice (1999). 'César Janssen and the transmission of Müller's 13-keyed clarinet in France', *GSJ* 52:183–94.

Sidorfsky, Joyce Ann (1977). 'The oboe in the 19th century: a study of the instrument and selected published solo literature', PhD diss., Univ. of Southern Mississippi.

Sievers, Heinrich (1941). *250 Jahre Braunschweiges Staatstheater, 1690–1940*. Braunschweig: Appelhans.

Silva, Pinto da (1773 and 1776). Letters to Piaggio (Genoa), in McClymonds 1978:42.

Singer, Julien (1991a). 'Die Technik des Oboespiels im Laufe der letzten vier Jahrhunderts', *Oboe Klarinette Fagott* 6:171–84.

—— (1991b). 'Die Wiederentdeckung der Werke von Charles Koechlin: Eine kommentierte Zusammenstellung der Kompositiononen für Oboe, Klarinette, Fagott und Saxophon', *Oboe Klarinette Fagott* 6:68–80.

—— (1994). 'Le hautbois moderne a 100 ans! L'évolution de sa technique de la fin du XIXe siècle à nos jours', *Schweizer musikpädagogische Blätter Herausgegeben vom Schweizerischen Musikpädagogischen Verband* 82:143–50.

—— (1999). 'Chantez! Chantez! Interview with André Lardrot', *La Lettre du hautboïste* 3:7-8.

Singer, Lawrence (1969). *Metodo per Oboe*. Milan: Zerboni.

Sirker, Udo (1968). *Die Entwicklung des Blaserquintetts in der ersten Halfte des 19. Jahrhunderts*. Regensburg: Bosse.

—— (1973). 'Methoden der Klangfabenforschung, dargestellt an quasi stationären Klängen von Doppelrohrblattinstrumenten', *Musicae scientiae collectanea: Festschrift Karl Gustav Fellerer*. Cologne: Volk, 561–76.

Sittard, J. (1890a). *Zur Geschichte der Musik und des Theaters am Württemburgischen Hofe*, ii. Stuttgart: Kohlhammer.

—— (1890b). *Geschichte der Musik- und Concertwesens in Hamburg*. Altona und Leipzig: Reher.

Smend, Friedrich (1951). *Bach in Köthen*. Berlin: Christlicher Zeitschriftenverlag.

Smith, David Hogan (1992). *Reed Design for Early Woodwinds*. Bloomington: Univ. of Indiana Press.

Smither, Howard E. (1977). *A History of the Oratorio*. 3 vols, 1977–87. Chapel Hill: Univ. of North Carolina Press.

Smithers, Don L. (1987). [Draft for] 'Gottfried Reiches Ansehen und sein Einfluss auf die Musik Johann Sebastian Bachs', *Bach Jahrbuch*, 113–50.

Soler, P. (1850). *Tablature du nouveau système de hautbois à anneaux mobiles*. Paris: Richault.

Sonneck, Gerald (1994). 'Ergebnis von Klanganalysen Wiener und Französischer Oboen,Wien, Institut für Wiener Klangstil', in *Zur situation des Musiker in Österreich: Referate der Musik-Symposium im Schloáhof, 1989-93*. Vienna: Institut für Wiener Klangstil, 151–68.

Spassoff (p1914). *Griff-Tabelle für die Oboe, Modell der Wiener Oper und Wiener Musik Akademie nach Prof. Richard Baumgärtl und Prof. Alexander Wunderer*. Vienna.

Spitta, Philipp (1884). *Johann Sebastian Bach*. London: Novello.

Sprenkle, Robert, and David Ledet (1961). *The Art of Oboe Playing including Problems and Techniques of Oboe Reedmaking*. Evanston: Summy-Birchard Co.

Stern, Sigismund (1850). *Manuel général de musique*. Paris: Bradus.

Stockigt, Janice B. (1980). 'The problems of editing and performing baroque music with special reference to Telemann's oboe works in *Der Getreue Musikmeister*', Master's diss., Melbourne Univ.

Stolper, Dan (1975). 'The Martinů Oboe Concerto and John de Lancie', *The World's Oboists* 3/1:6–7.

—— (1982). 'Lotoslawski's Double Concerto and Heinz Holliger', *DR* 5/2:58–64.

—— (1994). 'Tom Stacy, Ned Rorem, and a New Concerto', *DR* 17/2:65–7.

—— (2001). 'Double Reed Sections in Major Orchestras', *DR* 24:21–5.

Stone, William H. (1880–90). 'Oboe', in George Grove, *A Dictionary of Music and Muscians* (=*Gr1*),

1st ed. London: Macmillan.

Storch, Laila (1969). 'Joseph Fiala – 18th-century oboist rediscovered', *The Instrumentalist*, 305–6.

—— (1977). 'Georges Gillet – Master Oboist and Teacher', *JIDRS* 5:1–19; repr. in *DR* 19/3 (1996):17–35.

—— (1981). '100 years of F. Lorée', *JIDRS* 9:28–42.

—— (1983). 'The Concours solos of Charles Colin', *DR* 6/3:16–17; repr. *DR* 19/3 (1996):163–4.

—— (1985). 'The Georges Gillet Etudes: A Little Known Early Edition', *DR* 8/2:34–8.

—— (2002). 'My Long Search for Odette Anaïs Rey', *DR* 25:29–46.

Stotijn, Jaap (1967). *De kunst van het maken van hoborieten*. Wormerveer: Molenaar.

—— (1976). *Even uitblazen*. Nieuwkoop: Heuff; The Hague: Albersen & Co.

Straeten, E. van der (1915). *History of the Violoncello*. London: Reeves.

Stravinsky, Igor, and Robert Craft (1959). *Conversations with Igor Stravinsky*. Garden City, NY: Doubleday & Co.

Strunk, Oliver. (1965). *Source Readings in Music History*. New York: W.W. Norton & Co., 5 vols.

Swack, Jeanne Roberta (1988). 'The solo sonatas of Georg Philipp Telemann: a study of the sources and musical style', Ph.D. dissertation, Yale Univ.

Talbot, James (c.1692-95). 'Musica' [often called 'The Talbot Manuscript'; Oxford: Christ Church Music MS 1187]. Transcribed in A. Baines, 'James Talbot's Manuscripts', *GSJ* 1 (1948):13.

Talbot, Michael (1980). *Tomaso Albinoni, Leben und Werk*.

—— (1990). *Tomaso Albinoni: The Venetian Composer and His World*. Oxford: Clarendon Press.

—— (1993). *Vivaldi*. 2nd ed. London: J. M. Dent.

Tancibudek, Jiri (1980). 'Oboe and the Human Voice', *DR* 2/4:6–8.

Taruskin, Richard (1995). *Text and Act*. Oxford Univ. Press.

Telemann, Georg Philipp (1716). Introduction and dedication, *Die kleine Cammer-Music*. Frankfurt/M., 24 Sept. 1716; included in Rackwitz 1981.

—— (1718). 'Lebens-Lauff', in J. Mattheson's *Grosse Generalbassschule* (Hamburg, 1731). Included in Rackwitz 1981.

—— (1740). 'Selbstbiographie (1739)', in J. Mattheson's *Grundlage einer Ehrenpforte* (Hamburg, 1740). Included in Rackwitz 1981.

Thibault, G., Jean Jenkins, and Josiane Bran-Ricci (1973). *Eighteenth-Century Musical Instruments: France and Britain*. London: Victoria and Albert Museum.

Thoinan, Ernest (1867–8). 'Les Philidor', *La France Musicale*, 1867/51:397–9; 52 405–7; and 1868/1:1–3; 2:9–11; 3:17–18; 5:29–31; 6:37–8; 7:45–6.

Thomas, O. E. (1973). 'Music for double-reed ensembles from the 17th and 18th centuries: "Collection Philidor"', DMA diss., Univ. of Rochester.

Thompson, Oscar (1952). *International Cyclopedia of Music and Musicians*. New York: Dodd, Mead & Co.

Thompson, Susan E. (1999). 'Deutsche Schalmei: A question of terminology', *JAMIS* 25:31–60.

—— (2002). 'Smaller than Hautbois: a fresh look at James Talbot's Schalmeye,' *JAMIS* 28:246–60.

Tilmouth, Michael (1961-62). 'A calendar of references to music in newspapers published in London and the provinces (1660–1719)', *RMA Research Chronicle* 1 and 2.

Titon du Tillet, Evrard (1727). *Description du Parnasse françois*. Paris.

Tobin, J. Raymond (1948). *A Seat at the Proms: for Lovers of the Orchestra*. London: Evans Brothers.

Tomlinson, Gary (1999). *Metaphysical Song: An Essay on Opera*. Princeton: Princeton Univ. Press.

Triébert (c.1862). *Nouveau Prix-courant* (catalogue of instruments and accessories). Paris: Triébert.

Tromlitz, J. G. (1791). *Ausführlicher und gründlicher Unterricht die Flöte zu spielen*. Leipzig: A. F. Boehme; *R* Buren: F. Knuf, 1985 (trans. see Powell).

Ulmer, G.L. (1985). 'The Object of Post-Criticism', in Hal Foster, ed., *Postmodern Culture*. London and Sydney: Pluto Press, 83–110.

van Cleeve, Libby (1991). 'Suggestions for the Performance of Berio's *Sequenza VII*', DR 13/3 45–51.

Vandenbroek, Othon Joseph (1793 /R 1973). *Traité général de tous les instrumens à vent*. Paris: Boyer.

Vanderhagen, Amand (c.1790 /2 c.1798). *Méthode nouvelle et raisonnée pour le hautbois*. Paris: Boyer; R Geneva: Minkoff, 1971.

Veale, Peter (1992). Sleeve notes to *Computer Music Currents 10: Music with Computer*. Wergo, WER 2030–2.

Veale, Peter, and Claus-Steffan Mahnkopf (1995). *The Techniques of Oboe Playing*. Kassel: Bärenreiter.

Vecchione, Carrie Marie (1993). '*Sequenza VII* by Luciano Berio: Background, Analysis and Performance Suggestions', DMA diss., Louisana State Univ.

Ventzke, Karl (1969). *Boehm-Oboen und die neueren französischen Oboesysteme*. Frankfurt-am-Main: Verlag das Musikinstrument.

—— (1976). '*Die Oboe*: a German periodical appearing between 1928 and 1931', trans. R. Rosenblatt, *JIDRS* 4 (1976):73–4.

—— (1977). 'Henri Brod (1799–1839): Ein Oboenvirtuose als Oboenbauer', *Tibia* 3/77:347–50.

—— (1982). *Boehm-Instrumenten: Ein Handbuch über Theobald Boehm und über Klappeninstrumente seines Systems*. Fankfurt-am-Main: Verlag das Musikinstrument.

—— (1985). 'Zur Biographie der Oboenbauer Triebert in Paris (1810–1878)', *Tibia* 1/85:293–4.

Vény, Auguste-Louis (1828). *Méthode abrégée pour le hautbois*. Paris: Pleyel et Cie.

—— (1844–51). *Méthode complète pour le hautbois à 8 et à 15 clefs, nouveau édition augmentée de Tablatures des systèmes Boehm et Triébert et suivie de 4 Grands Etudes par V. Bretonnière*. Rev. V. Bretonnière, Paris: Cotelle.

Verroust, Stanislas-Xavier (c.1857). *Méthode pour le hautbois, d'après Joseph Sellner*, op.68. Paris: S. Richault.

Verschuere-Reynvaan, Joos (1789 /2 1795). *Muzijkaal Kunst-Woordenboek*. Amsterdam: W. Brave.

Vester, Frans (1985). *Flute Music of the 18th Century*. Monteux: Musica Rara.

Villoteau, Guillaume (1809). Musical texts in *Description de l'Egypt ou Recueil des observations et des recherches qui ont été faites en Egypt pendant l'epédition de l'armée française, publié par les ordres de Sa Majesté l'Empereur Napoléon Le Grand*. Paris: Imprimerie Impériale, 'État moderne', vol. 1.

Vine, Carl (1997). Programme notes to his Oboe Concerto, *A Garden of Earthly Delights*, Tall Poppies, TP113.

Vogel, Allan (1976). 'French, German and American Oboe Playing – Some Reflections on having Studied with Fernand Gillet, Lothar Koch and Robert Bloom', *JIDRS* 6:19–29.

Vogt, Gustave (1816–25). 'Méthode de hautbois' [ms, F–Pc, , F–Pn Ci.50]. Orig. text and Eng. trans. in Burgess, *The Premier Oboist of Europe*.

Wagner, Richard (1869). 'Über das Dirigiren', trans. as 'About Conducting' by W. A. Ellis in *Richard Wagner's Prose Works*, London: Kegan Paul, Trench, Trübner & Co., 1892–9; R Univ. of Nebraska Press, 1995, vol. 4, 'Art and Politics', 289–364.

—— (1876). *Siegfried*. New York: Kalmus.

—— (1911). *Tristan und Isolde*. Ed. F. Mottl, Leipzig: Peters; R New York: Dover, 1973.

—— (1983). *My Life*. Trans. by A. Gray of *Mein Leben*, ed. Mary Whittall. Cambridge Univ. Press.

—— 'Bericht über eine in München zu errichtende deutsche Musikschule', in *Gesammelte Schriften*, ed. W. Golther, Leipzig: E. W. Fritzsch; R Hildesheim: Olms, 1976, 8:173; trans. by W. A. Ellis in *Richard Wagner's Prose Works*, London: Kegan Paul, Trench, Trübner & Co., 1892–9; R Univ. of Nebraska Press, 1995, vol. 4, 'Art and Politics', 171–224.

Walther, Johann Gottfried (1732 /R 1953). *Musikalisches Lexicon*. Leipzig: F. Ramm; R Kassel: Bärenreiter, 1953.

Waquet, Françoise (1980). '"Philidor l'Aîné, ordinaire de la Musique du Roy . . .": Un essai de biographie d'après des documents inédits', *Revue de Musicologie* 66:203–16.

Warner, Thomas (1962). 'Two Late 18th-century Instructions for Making Double Reeds', *GSJ* 15:25–33.

—— (1964). 'Indications of performance practice in woodwind instruction books of the 17th and 18th centuries'. Ph.D. diss., New York Univ.

—— (1967). *An Annotated Bibliography of Woodwind Instruction Books, 1600-1830*. Detroit: Information Coordinators Inc.

Waterhouse, William (1993). *The New Langwill Index: A Dictionary of Musical Wind-Instrument Makers and Inventors*. London: T. Bingham.

Watkins, Glen (1994). *Pyramids at the Louvre*. Cambridge, MA: Harvard Univ. Press.

Weait, Christopher (1988). 'Vibrato Videotape', *Flutist Quarterly* 13:45.

Weaver, Robert Lamar, and Norma Wright Weaver (1978). *A Chronology of Music in the Florentine Theater, 1590–1750*. Detroit: Information Coordinators.

Weber, Rainer (1992). 'Was sagen die Holzblasinstrumente zu Mozarts Kammerton?,' *Tibia* 4/92:291–8.

Weber, Vendla K., and Ferald B. Capps (1990). The Reed-Maker's Manual: Step-by-step Instructions for Making Oboe and English Horn Reeds. Phoenix: the authors.

Weber, William (1989). 'London: a city of unrivalled riches', *The Classical Era*, ed. N. Zaslaw, 293–326. Engelwood Cliffs, NJ: Prentice-Hall.

Welch, Christopher (1882). *History of the Boehm Flute*. London: Rudall Carte & Co.

Wendt, F.A. (1822). 'Über den Zustand der Musik in Deutschland', *AMZÖK* 7/95,753–6.

Weth, Stephanie (1994). 'Die Französischen und deutschen Oboenschulen des 19. Jahrhunderts', diss., Köln Hochschule für Musik.

White, Paul (1984). 'Early Bassoon Reeds: A Survey of Some Important Examples', *JAMIS* 10:69–96.

Whitely, William (1816). *Instrumental Preceptor*. Utica, NY: Seward & Williams.

Whitwell, David (1969/70). 'The Incredible Vienna octet school', *The Instrumentalist* 24/3-6:31–5, 40–3, 42–5, 38–40.

—— (1983). *Wind Band and Wind Ensemble Literature of the Classic Period*. The History and Literature of the Wind Band and Wind Ensemble, 8. Northridge, CA: Winds.

—— (1988). *The Longy Club: A Professional Wind Ensemble in Boston, 1900–1917*. Northridge, CA: Winds.

Widor, Ch. M. (1904). *Technique de l' Orchestre moderne, faisant suite au Traité de H. Berlioz*. Paris: Lemoine et Cie.

Wieprecht, Paul (1877). *Studienwerk für Oboe unter Zugrundelegung der Oboeschule von Garnier*, op.7. Offenbach: André.

Williams, Peter [ed.] (1985). *Bach, Handel, Scarlatti: Tercentenary Essays*. Cambridge Univ. Press.

Williams, Robert S. (1995). 'Bassoon basics for the flicking bassoonist!' *DR* 18/2:44–5.

Wilson, M. (1986). 'Léon Goossens, Oboist', *DR* 9/3:30–7.

Wind, Thiemo (1982). 'Alessandro Besozzi di Torino (1702–1793), een terreinverkennend onderzoek'. Kandidaatsscriptie, Universiteit Utrecht.

Wlach, Hans (1927). 'Die Oboe bei Beethoven', *Studien zur Musikwissenschaft* 14:107–24.

Wolff, Christoph (1985). 'Bach's Leipzig Chamber Music', *EM* 13:165–75.

Wolff, Hellmuth Christian (1968). *Oper, Szene und Darstellung von 1600 bis 1900. Musikgeschichte in Bildern*. Leipzig: Deutscher Verlag für Musik.

Wood, Bruce, and Andrew Pinnock (1993). 'The Fairy Queen: a fresh look at the issues', *EM* 21:45–62.

Wragg, J. (1792). *The Oboe preceptor or the art of playing the oboe*. London: the author.

Wynne, Barry (1967). *Music in the Wind: The Story of Léon Goossens and his Triumph over a Shattering Accident*. London: Souvenir Press.

Yoshimizu, Hiroshi (2002). 'The History of the American Method of Oboe Playing in Japan and Oboe Player Situations', *DR* 25:93–7.

Young, Philip T., ed. (1988). *Loan Exhibition of Double Reed Instruments, University of Victoria*,

August, 1988, printed for IDRS conference (ISBN 0-921408-01-3).

—— (1993). *4900 historical woodwind instruments*. London: T. Bingham.

Zaslaw, Neal, ed., with William Cowdery (1990). *The Compleat Mozart*. New York: Norton.

Ziegler, Susanne (1990). 'Gender-specific traditional wedding music in South West Turkey', in M. Herndon and S. Ziegler, eds, *Music, Gender, and Culture*. Wilhelmshaven: Noetzel, 85–110.

Zohn, Steven (1995). 'The Ensemble sonatas of Georg Philipp Telemann: studies in style, genre, and chronology', Ph.D diss., Cornell Univ.

Discography
Compiled by Geoffrey Burgess

This discography is designed primarily as a list of the recordings referred to in this book, but it has a secondary function as a representative sample of the work of the most important oboists of the twentieth century. For the large part restricted to commercial releases, this discography consequently does not include radio broadcasts and privately distributed material.

The number of recordings of oboists and oboe music is continuously growing, and any attempt to compile an exhaustive listing is doomed to obsolescence as soon as it appears in print. The large number of out-of-print recordings and the often confusing array of re-releases from older formats make the task all the more challenging. I have therefore limited this list to a sampling of the most important recordings. In choosing representative recordings, I have given precedence to recordings of solo works which highlight the musical qualities of the most important oboists and (where possible) recordings still currently available; I have also tried to provide a balanced selection of each player's career.

The discography is organized in two alphabetical listings: the first by artist, with a second by composer with cross-references to mixed programmes given in the first list. Multiple recordings by the same oboist are numbered chronologically according to date of first issue. To facilitate tracking down recordings, I have provided as much information as possible. In addition to the title of the album, the short titles of oboe works, name of the oboist, and where relevant, the name of orchestra and conductor, the distributors item number and date of release are given.

Two archives that include significant collections deserve special mention. The Melvin Harris Collection, housed at the Music Library, University of Washington, Seattle, WA, USA (mostly uncatalogued), includes a large number of recordings of wind players, notably oboists, on a variety of media. Richard Higgins Lea's extensive collection of recordings of double reeds has gone to the libraries of Mt Allison University, Sackville NB, Canada (some 1000 CDs; catalogue accessible at http://library.mta.ca) and the University of Calgary, Canada (6600 33⅓rpm records; listing available at http://archive.ucalgary.ca:591/music).

Abbreviations: S Symphony; O Orchestra; P Philharmonic

Listing by Oboist

Anderson, John
  1. Strauss, Oboe Concerto, BBC SO, Del Mar (live recording 1981, BBC Radio Classics, 15656 9138–2; re-released 1994)
  2. Strauss, Oboe Concerto, Philharmonia, S. Wright (Nimbus NI5330, 1992)
Atherholt, Robert
  Robert Schumann, *Romances*, Houston SO, orchestrated by Tobias Picker (Virgin Classics, VC7 91162–2, 1991)
Bennet, William
  John Harbison, Oboe Concerto, San Francisco SO, Blomstedt (London 443 376–2, 1994)

Bernardini, Alfredo (hautboy)

1. Albinoni Concerti op.9, with Paolo Grazzi, L'Armonia e l'inventione (ARTS 447132–2, 1994)
2. A. Vivaldi *Concerti pour hautbois, basson et cordes*, L'Armonia e l'inventione (Astrée, E 8537, 1995)
   See also Zelenka 3

Black, Neil

Strauss, Oboe Concerto, English Chamber Orchestra, Barenboim (Columbia CBS MS 7423, Y32889, M35160, 1979; re-released CBS, 1984, and Sony SK 62652, 1996)

Blanchard, Jean (*chabrette*)

France: cornemuses du centre (with Eric Montbel) Unesco Collection (Audvis D 8202, 1989)

Bleuzet, Louis

Marcel Mihalovici, *Sonatine pour hautbois* op. 13 (1928) (Columbia DFX3/4, 1929) Harris Collection.

Bloom, Robert

The Art of Robert Bloom: a diverse range of music from throughout Bloom's career (Boston Records, BR 1032–7, 7 volumes, 2000)
See Sibelius 4

Bortolato, Gianfranco

Parigi, o cara works by de Stefani, Lovreglio, Daelli, Gariboldi and Parma, with Arosio (piano) (Rivo and Alto, CRR 9821, 1998)

Bourgue, Maurice

1. *20th-Century Music for Oboe and Piano* by Poulenc, Britten, Dutilleux and Hindemith (EMI EMSP 553, 1968)
2. Francis Poulenc, *La Musique de chambre*, with Jacques Février (piano) (EMI EMSP553, 1973)
3. G. F. Handel (attrib.), *Trios for Two Oboes*, Holliger and Bourgue, with Jacottet (harpsichord) and Sax (bassoon) (Philips 9500 671, 1979)
4. Vaughan Williams, Oboe Concerto, English String O, Boughton (Nimbus NIM 5019, 1985)
5. Britten *Metamorphoses* (Harmonia Mundi MDC902, 1968)
   See also Zelenka 1

Boyd, Douglas

Strauss, Oboe Concerto, Chamber O of Europe, Berglund (ASV CDCOE808, MHS 1988, 1986)

Brewer, Virginia, see Roseman 4

Brüggen, Frans

1. Telemann, Sonatas and Fantasias (recorded 1963 and 1969–72; re-released in *Frans Brüggen Edition* (Teldec 4509-93688–2, vol.1 1995)
2. J. M. Hotteterre Suite for two recorders with Kees Boeke on *Franz Brüggen III* (Teldec 6.48075 DT, 1975)

Busscher, Henri de

Music Masters, Part 2, Education Series of Instrumental Records; solo excerpts from orchestral repertoire (Radio Recordings Inc., Hollywood, and American Record Co., CA, 1940s), apparently never commercially released, Harris Collection

Canter, Robin

1. Britten, *Metamorphoses, Temporal Variations, Insect Pieces*, Phantasy Quartet (Phoenix DGS1022, 1982)
2. Britten, *Metamorphoses, Temporal Variations, Insect Pieces*, Phantasy Quartet (Carlton Classics 30366 10064, 1998)
3. Strauss, Oboe Concerto, London SO, Judd (IMP 30366 0021–2, 1992)

Carter, Roy

Britten, *Metamorphoses* (EMI Anglo-American Chamber Music Series CDC5 55398–2, 1995)

Celli, Joseph
  Organic Oboe, music by Celli, Stockhausen, Schwartz and Goldstein (O.O. Discs #1 1978 and 1991)
Clement, Manfred
  Strauss, Oboe Concerto, Staatskapelle Dresden, Kempe (HMV SLS5067 1975; re-released EMI CDM7 69661–2, 1992)
Cobles
  1. *Cobles catalanes* (recordings from the 1920s and 30s, Silex Y 225102, 1992)
  2. *Catalogne: Les plus belles sardanes*, performed by Cobla Combo-Gili and Cobla Perpignya (recorded 1967; re-released on Arion 64092, 1992)
Cook, Randall (hautboy)
  Montéclair, Hotteterre, Couperin, Marais, with Le Parlement de Musique (Opus 111, OPS 47–9111, 1991)
Cooper, Peter
  Strauss, Oboe Concerto, Academy of St-Martin's-in-the-Fields, Marriner (Summit DCD320, 2002)
Craxton, Janet
  1. Vaughan Williams, *Ten Blake Songs*, with Ian Partridge (tenor) (EMI HQS 1236, 1971; re-released on EMI CDM7 69170 2, 1988)
  2. Britten *Metamorphoses* (London STS 15439, 1977 and Decca Ace of Diamonds SDD531, 1977)
  3. *The Art of Janet Craxton*, music by Britten, Lutyens, Mozart, Musgrave, Poulenc and Richardson (BBC REN 635X, 1987)
Daniel, Nicholas
  1. *The Virtuoso Oboe*, works by Patterson, Finzi and Howells, with Drake (piano) (Pearl SHE 591, 1986)
  2. Matthews, David, *The Flaying of Marsyas*, with Brindisi String Quartet (Metronome MET CD 1005– 01, 1994)
  3. Strauss, Oboe Concerto City of London Sinfonia, Hickox (Chandos CHAN9286, 1994)
DeAlmeda, Cyntha Koledo
  Leonardo Balada, *Music for Oboe and Orchestra: Lament from the Cradle of the Earth*, Pittsburgh SO, Maazel (New World Records, 80503–2, 1996)
de Lancie, John
  1. Jean Françaix, *L'Horloge de Flore*, Ibert *Symphonia Concertante*, London SO, Previn (RCA, LSB4094, 1967; re-released on RCA Gold Seal BMG 7989–2–RG, 1991)
  2. Strauss, Oboe Concerto, Chamber O, Wilcox (recorded 1987; RCA Gold Seal BMG 7989–2–RG, 1991)
Dent, Simon
  1. Strauss, Oboe Concerto, Polish Chamber O, Rajski (Amati, AMI 9205, 1992)
  2. *Fantasies*, music by Britten, Hawkins, Dent and Schumann (Amati Sonomaster, AMI 9801/1, 1998)
Doherty, Diana
  Blues for D.D., music by Agrell, Schnyder, Jolivet, Edwards and Dorati, with Korevaar (piano) (ABC Classics, 465 782–2, 2000)
Dombrecht, Paul (hautboy, oboe and conductor)
  1. *The Oboe Sonata, 1700-1750*, music by Vincent, Babell, Geminiani, Handel, Bach and Förster, hautboy, with W. Kuijken (gamba) and Kohnen (harpishcord) (Accent, ACC 57804, 1979; re-released as AACC8537D, c.1990)
  2. *Hautbois et harpe*, music by Jolivet, Holliger, A. Weber and W. Carron (Pavane ADW7069, 1981)
  3. *The Virtuoso Romantic Oboe,* music by Schumann, Pixis and Kalliwoda using a Triébert

oboe, with Jos van Immerseel (piano) (Accent, ACC 8330, 1983)
4. *Harmonie und Janitscharemusik,* music by Rosetti, Spohr and Beethoven, Octophoros, Dombrecht (Accent, ACC 8860D, 1989)
    See also Zelenka 2

Ebbinge, Ku (hautboy)
1. C. P. E. Bach, Concertos and Solo (Erato ECD 75560, 1990)
    See also Bach Kantatenwerke, Beethoven Symphonies, 3, Zelenka 2

Erguner, Kudsi (ney)
The Janissaries: Musique martiale de l'empire Ottoman, L'Ensemble de l'Armée de la République Turque, Erguner (Audivis B 6738, 1990)

Ertel, Erich
Strauss, Oboe Concerto, Symphony Orchestra Radio Berlin, Rother (Urania URLP7032, 1952)

Francis, Sarah
1. Britten *Metamorphoses,* Phantasy Quartet (Argo ZRG 842, 1976)
2. Oboe Quintets and Quartets by Bax, Holst, Jacob and Moeran, with English String Quartet (Chandos, CHAN 8392, 1985)
3. Rutland Boughton, Oboe Concerto, Royal PO, Handley (Hyperion, CDA 66343, 1989)
4. Chamber music by Howells, Rubbra, Harty, Boughton, Dickinson (piano), Rasumovsky Quartet (recorded 1985, Hyperion, CDH55008, 1999)
5. Britten, *Metamorphoses, Temporal Variations, Insect Pieces,* Phantasy Quartet (Hyperion CDA66776, 1995)

Gabriel, Martin
Strauss, Oboe Concerto, Vienna Philharmonic O, Previn (DG 453 483–2GH, c.1996/8)

Giacobassi, Julie Ann
Aaron Jay Kernis, *Colored Field,* San Francisco SO, Neale (Argo, 448174–2, 1996)

Gillet, Fernand
1. Brahms. *Violin Concerto,* Jascha Heifetz, Boston SO, Koussevitzky (RCA Victor DM 581, 1939; re-released on Pearl GEMM CDS 9167, 1995)
2. Bach, Brandenburg Concerto II, Boston SO, Koussevitsky (Victor DM1118, 1947)

Gillet, Georges
Rossini, 'Pastorale' and 'O Mathilde' from *Guillaume Tell,* with Léopold Lafleurence (flute) (Odeon 36251/2, 1905)

Glaetzner, Burkhard
1. *Neue Musik für Oboe, Contemporary Music for Oboe* by Xenakis, Schenker, Berio and Lombardi (1986; re-released Berlin Classics 0011722BC, 1996)
2. *Virtuose Oboenkonzerte der Romantik* by Kalliwoda, Molique, Pasculli and Ponchielli (Capriccio 10– 281, 1989)

Gomberg, Harold
1. Britten, Fantasy Quartet (Esoteric Records, ES 504, 1951; re-released as CPTS 5504, 1960)
2. Mozart Quartet and Telemann Sonata in c minor, Partita 5 (Decca DL 9618, 195–)
3. *The Baroque Oboe,* concertos by Telemann and Vivaldi, sonatas by Telemann and Handel, with Columbia Chamber Orchestra, S. Ozawa cond., Igor Kipnis harpsichord (Columbia, ML 6232, 1966)
4. *The Art of Harold Gomberg,* Britten, *Metamorphoses* and Phantasy Quartet, Mozart, Quartet (Vanguard VCS 10064, 1969)

Goodwin, Paul (hautboy, conductor)
1. Oboe Concertos by C. P. E. Bach, Lebrun, Mozart, The English Concert, Pinnock (Archiv, 431821–2, 1991)
2. Vivaldi, Oboe Sonatas (Harmonia Mundi France, HMU 907104, 1993)
3. Oboe Quartets by Mozart, Massoneau, Stamitz and Krommer, with Terzetto (Harmonia Mundi France, HMU 907220, 1997)

4. John Tavener, *Eternity's Sunrise*, The Academy of Ancient Music, Goodwin (Harmonia Mundi USA, HMU 907231, 1999)

Goossens, Leon

1. Rossini, *La scala di seta*, Overture, London Philharmonic O, Beecham (Columbia LX 255, 1933)
2. Mozart, Oboe Quartet, with Léner (violin), Roth (viola) and Hartman (cello) (Columbia LX 256/7, 1933; re-released on Goossens 7)
3. Brahms, Violin Concerto, Kreisler, London Philharmonic, Barbirolli (1936; numerous 78 and LP pressings; re-released on Pearl GEMM CD 9362, 1989)
4. G. F. Handel, Oboe Concerto in B flat major (HMV C 2993, 1937; re-released on Goossens 7)
5. Strauss, Oboe Concerto, Philharmonia O, Galliera (COL DX 1444–6 1947; LP: HMV CLP 1698; WRC SH 243, CD: TEST SBT1009, 1977)
5. Eugene Goossens, Oboe Concerto op. 45, with Philharmonia O, Susskind (Columbia DCS 84/5, 1948; LP: Unicorn RHS 348, CD re-released, see Goossens 7)
6. E. Elgar, *Soliloquy*, Bournemouth Sinfonietta, Del Mar (RCA LRL15133, 1976; re-released on Chandos, CHAN 8371, 7 and 8)
7. *Léon Goossens: A Centenary Tribute* (Pearl GEMM CD 9281, 1997)
8. *The Art of Léon Goossens*, with other members of the Goossens family; various works including Finzi, *Interlude*, Saunders, *Cotswold Pastoral* and Elgar, *Soliloquy* (1976) (Chandos CHAN 7132, 2000)

Goritzki, Ingo

Strauss, Oboe Concerto, Lausanne Chamber O, Aeschbacher (Claves CLA 50–9010, 1990)

Grazzi, Paolo (hautboy)

see Bernardini

Hadady, László

Luciano Berio, *Chemins IV*, Ensemble Intercontemporain, Boulez (Sony, SK 45 862, 1990)

Hadamowsky, Hans

Beethoven, Trio for two oboes and cor anglais, and Octett, with Kautzky (oboe) and Hans Kamesch (cor anglais) (Westminster, MVCW–19006, 1954)

Hammer, Stephen (hautboy)

J. S. Bach, Reconstructions of concertos for hautboy, BWV1053, 1055 and 1059 reconstructed by Rifkin, Bach Ensemble, Rifkin (Pro Arte CDD 153, 1983)

Hanták, Frantisek

Strauss, Oboe Concerto, Brno State Philharmonic O, Turnovsky and Vogel (Supraphon 50 486, 1963)

Hanus, Vitezslav

Britten, *Metamorphoses*, and Phantasy Quartet (Supraphon SUA10960, 1969)

Haynes, Bruce

1. G. F. Handel, Sonatas for Wind Instruments, with Brüggen (Seon ABCL–67005/3, 1974)
2. *Hotteterre: Premier Flûtiste Francais* (Seon RCA Red Seal RL 30425, 1980; Seon SB2K 62942, 1997)
3. *Concerti per oboe, archi e cembalo* by Vivaldi, Marcello and Platti, Brüggen (Seon, RCA Red Seal RL30371, 1979; re-released on RCA RD 71056, 1986)
4. François Couperin, *Concerts royaux*, with Napper (gamba) and Haas (harpsichord) (ATMA ACD 2 2168, 1998)
5. J. S. Bach, *Arias and oboe d'amore, arias and concerti for hautbois d'amour* BWV 1055 and BWV 1053, with Taylor (alto) and ensemble (ATMA 22158, 1999)
    See also Bach, *Kantatenwerk*

Hoff, Brynjar

Britten, *Metamorphoses* (Libra Classics LCD 1004, 1995)

Holliger, Heinz

1. *Virtuose Oboekonzerte*, works by Bellini, Salieri, Cimarosa and Donizetti, Bamberger Symphoniker, Maag (Philips 139 152, 1968)
2. Berio, *Sequenza VII* (Philips 6500 631, 1970; also on Philips 426 662–2, and 412 029–1, 1970)
3. Strauss, Oboe Concerto, New Philharmonia O, de Waart (Philips 6500 174, 1970; re-released 438 733–2PM2, 1994)
4. *The Spectacular Heinz Holliger*, music by Berio, Castiglioni, Holliger, Huber, Krenek and Lehmann (Philips 6500 202, 1971)
5. Holliger, *Siebengesang*, H. and U. Holliger, Zürich Collegium Musicum, Sacher (Deutsche Gramophon DG2530 318, 1971; re-released on 445 251–2, 1993)
6. *Die Neue Domäne für Oboe*, music by Veress, Penderecki, Yun, Denisow and Holliger (Denon, OX–7031–ND, 1973)
7. *Heinz Holliger plays Haydn, Reicha, Rossini and Donizetti*, Concertgebouw-Orchester, Zinman (Philips 9500 564, 1978)
8. T. Albinoni, *Concerti per Oboe*, Carerata Bern (recorded 1979; re-released on Arkiv 427 111–2AGA, 1989)
9. G. F. Handel (attrib.), Trios for Two Oboes, with Bourgue (oboe), Jacottet (harpsichord) and Sax (bassoon) (Philips 9500 671, 1979)
10. Strauss, Oboe Concerto, Cincinnati SO, Gielen (Moss Music, MCD 100006, 1984)
11. Globokar, *Discours III*, recorded 1985 (Koch-Schwann Aulos 3–1063–2, 1992)
12. Vivaldi, Concerti, I Musici (recorded between 1976–80; re-released on Philips 411 480–2PH, 1985)
13. Robert Schumann, *Music for Oboe and Piano*, with Brendel (piano) (Philips 6725 034, 1983, re-released on 446 925–2PM5, 1996)
14. *Heinz Holliger at the Opera*, music by Mozart, Rossini, Chopin, Schubert, Donizetti, Pasculli, Ponchielli and Wagner, with U. Holliger (harp) and G. Burgin (piano) (Philips 426 288 2, 1990)
15. Britten, *Metamorphoses, Temporal Variations, Insect Pieces*, Phantasy Quartet (Philips 434076–2, 1994)
16. Berio, *Sequenza VII* (Ermitage ERM 164–2, 1995)
17. Strauss, Oboe Concerto, Chamber O of Europe (Regis Records, RRC 1034, 2001)

See also Zelenka 1.

Hommel, Christian

Romantische Kompositionen für Oboe und Klavier, music by Kalliwoda, Flotow, Schumann, Schunke, Nielsen, Britten and Koechlin, with Eppendorf (piano) (Ars Musici, AM1272–2, 2000)

Honma, Masashi (oboe and hautboy)

1. Takemitsu, *Dream/Window*; includes *Gémeaux* for Oboe, Trombone, 2 Orchestras and 2 Conductors (Denon CO 78944, 1995)
2. G. F. Handel, *Complete Sonatas for a Wind Instrument and Basso Continuo*, with Arita (organ), Suzuki (cello) and Dohsaka (bassoon) (Archiv F84A 20031/3, 1988)
4. *L'Art du Hautbois Français*, French solos for hautboy and bass, with Nakano (gamba) and Owabuchi (harpsichord) (ALM ALCD–1007, 1992)

Hucke, Helmut (hautboy)

J. S. Bach, Cantata BWV 202, with Ameling, Collegium Aureum (RCA Victrola, VIC 1281, 1967)

Hunt, Gordon

Strauss, Oboe Concerto, Berlin RSO, Ashkenazy (Decca London 436 415–2, 1993; re-released 436 415–2DH, 1994, and 460 296–2DF2, 1999)

Indermühle, Thomas

1. *Four Oboe Concertos*, Strauss, Martinů, Zimmermann, Vaughan Williams, Orchestre de Bretagne, Schnitzler (Camerata, 30 CM–346, 1993)
2. *Italian Opera Fantasy*, music by Lovreglio, Pasculli, Ponchielli, Donizetti, Daelli, with

Genuit (piano) (1994, Camerata, 30CM–403, 1996)

Jahren, Helen

1. Alfred Schnittke, Concerto for oboe, harp and string orchestra, Lier (harp), New Stockholm Chamber O, Markiv (Bis, BIS CD 377, 1987)
2. *Oboe con Forza: Helen Jahren plays Swedish contemporary music* by Börtz, Ekström and Gamstorp, with Helsingborg SO, Volmer and Kammerensemble N, Bartosch (Phono Suecia, PSCD 128, 2000)

Kamesch, Hans

Beethoven, Trio for two oboes and cor anglais, and Octet, with Hans Hadamowsky and Manfred Kautzky (obb.) (Westminster, MVCW–19006, 1954)

Kautzky, Manfred

Beethoven, Trio for two oboes and cor anglais, and Octet, with Hans Hadamowsky (oboe) and Hans Kamesch (cor anglais) (Westminster, MVCW–19006, 1954)

Khan, Bismillah (shanhái)

Iraga Todi, Mishra Thumri (The Gramophone Company of India (Private) Ltd, EMI/Odeon MOAE 120, 1956)

King, Nancy Ambrose

Britten, *Metamorphoses* (Boston Records, BR 1030, 2000)

Klein, Alex

1. Vivaldi, Oboe Concertos, New Brandenburg Collegium, Newman (Musical Heritage Society, 513905X, 1995)
2. *The Greatest Music that Schubert (N)ever Wrote* (Boston Records, BR1039, 2000)
3. Strauss, Oboe Concerto, Chicago SO, Barenboim (Teldec 3984–23913–2, 2001)

Koch, Lothar

1. Strauss, Oboe Concerto, Berlin PO, von Karajan (DG 2350 439 and 423888–2GGA, 1974)
2. Rossini, *The Silken Ladder* Overture, Berlin PO, von Karajan (Deutsche Gramophon, DG2530 144, 1970)

Kosmetski, Khristo

Strauss, Oboe Concerto, Bulgarian National Radio SO, Vladigerov (Balkanton, BCA 10465, 197–)

Labate, Bruno

1. Brahms, Violin Concerto, Heifetz, New York P, Toscanini, radio recording, 1935 (released on Historic Broadcasts, 1923–1987, Special Editions, NYP 9702–11, 1997)
2. C. M. Loeffler, *Rhapsodies* with Boynet (piano), Gordon (viola) (Schirmer, 2036–7, mx2031–3, 2039–40, c.1940)

Lamorlette, Roland

F. Poulenc, Trio for oboe, bassoon and piano, with Dherin (bassoon) and Poulenc (piano) (recorded 1929; re-released on EMI CDC5 55036–2, 1994)

Lardrot, André

1. *The Virtuoso Oboe, vol. 1*, Albinoni, Cimarosa, Haydn, Handel, Albinoni and Mozart, Wiener Staatsoper O, Prohaska (Vanguard VRS 1025 –1060, 1958)
2. *The Virtuoso Oboe, vol. 2*, Mozart, Handel, Albinoni, Wiener Staatsoper O, Prohaska (Vanguard VRS 1060, 1960)
3. *The Virtuoso Oboe, vol. 3*, Vivaldi, Fischer, Leclair, Albinoni (Vanguard, VSD 2138, 1963)
4. *Music for People who Hate Opera*, Salieri, Bellini, Rossini and Donizetti, I Solisti di Zagreb, Janigro (recordings from 1957–66; re-released on Vanguard Classics SVC–84, 1998)

Lateef, Yusef

1. *The Complete Yusef Lateef* (Atlantic, SD 3259, 1998)
2. *Imagination!* (Prestige PRST 7832, 1970)

Le Meuet, André (bombard)

Bombard. Temporal and Sacred Music of Brittany, with Rivière (organ) (Fr. Keltia Musique, KM CD52, 1995)

Leleux, François

Britten, *Metamorphoses, Temporal Variations, Insect Pieces*, Phantasy Quartet, with Strosser
    (piano), Sutre (violin), da Silva (viola) and Coppey (cello) (HMN 911556, 1995)

Lencsés, Lajos
1. Strauss, Oboe Concerto Stuttgart RSO, Marriner (Capriccio 10 231, c.1989)
2. Britten, *Metamorphoses* (Cadenza CAD800 815, 1997)

Longy, Georges
Various orchestral works including Prelude to act IV of *Lohengrin*, Boston SO, Karl Muck
    (RCA Victor, 1917; re-released on *First Recordings of the Boston SO*, BSO Classics,
    171002, 1995)

Lucarelli, Bert
1. John Corigliano, Oboe Concerto, American SO, Akiyama (RCA, BMG 60395–2 RG,
    1990)
2. Britten, *Metamorphoses*, and Phantasy Quartet (Lyrichord LLST7195, 1968)
3. *The Bel Canto Oboe*, works by Barret, Vogt, Garimond, Lalliet, Charles Triébert,
    Berthélemy, with Hrynkiw (piano), Jolles (harp), Wynberg (guitar) and the Manhattan
    String Quartet (Price-Less D21062, 1988)
4 Concerted works by Wolf-Ferrari, Strauss, Vaughan Williams and Barber, Lehigh
    Valley Chamber O, Spieth (Koch, 3–7023–2 and CD 311 133H1, 1991)
5. A. Wilder, *Oboe Concerto*, Brooklyn Philharmonic O, Barrett (Koch 3–7187–2HI, 1994)

McCandless, Paul
Oregon in Moscow (includes Ralph Towner's *Free-Form Piece for Orchestra and Improvisors*), with
    Moscow Tchaikovsky SO (Intuition INT 3303 2, 2000)

MacDonagh, Terence
Mozart and Beethoven, Quintets for Piano and Winds, London Wind Soloists, Ashkenazy
    (piano) (London CS 6494, 1966; re-released CD 3556, 1988)

Mack, John
1. Maurice Ravel, *Tombeau de Couperin*, Cleveland O, George Szell (recorded 1965; re-
    released on *The Cleveland Orchestra 75th Anniversry, 1918–93*, Musical Arts Association,
    TCO93–75, 1993)
2. Britten, *Metamorphoses* (Crystal 5325, 1977; re-released on Telarc 5028, 1985)
3. Hindemith, Poulenc Sonatas and pièces de concours by Murgier, Berghmans, Planel
    and Barraud, with Podis (piano) (Telarc, 5034/Crystal S324, 1978); re-released with
    Schumann, *Romances*, and Saint-Saëns Sonate (Crystal CD324, 1990)

Malgoire, Jean-Claude
Le Hautbois moderne, music by Jolivet, Ton-That Tiêt, Holliger, Castiglioni, Shinohara, with
    Salzer (piano), Pierre (harpsichord) (CBS S 34–61142, 1972)

Marx, Josef
1 *Josef Marx plays the oboe*, music by Schumann, Platti, Telemann and Krebs (Marx
    Concert Series, 1981)
2. Elliott Carter, Sonata for Flute, Oboe, Cello and Harpsichord, with Brieff (flute),
    Bernsohn (cello), Conant (harpsichord) (Columbia ML 5576, 1960)

Mayer, Albrecht
1. *Music for Oboe, Oboe d'amore, Cor Anglais and Piano* by Schumann, Daelli, Nielsen,
    Cossart, Yvon and Koechlin, with Becker (piano) (EMI Debut, 7243 5 73167 2 9, 1999)
2. Strauss, Oboe Concerto, Capella Bydgostiensis, Stabrawa (Cavalli-Records CCD 408,
    2000)

Meyer, François
Britten, *Metamorphoses* (Sonpact SPT94011, 1992)

Miller, Mitchell
1. Sibelius, *The Swan of Tuonela*, Philadelphia O, Stokowsky (RCA Victor 12–0585–A/B,
    1948)
2. 'Desert Dance' or 'Cleopatra Rhumba', with Roger Mozian (Mercury, 1949; re-released
    on *More than mambo: the introduction to Afro-Cuban jazz*, Verve 314 527 903–2, 1995)

3. Concertos by Cimarosa and Vaughan Williams, Saidenberg Little Symphony, Saidenberg (Mercury MG 10003, c.1954)

Montbel, Eric, *chabrette*

France: cornemuses du centre, with Blanchard (Unesco Collection, Audvis D 8202, 1989)

Mueller, Florian

G. F. Handel, Concerto in g minor, with Manuel and Williamson Harpsichord Ensemble (Musicraft, 1149–B, 1941)

Nielsen, B. C.

Strauss, Oboe Concerto, Copenhagen Collegium Musicum, Schönwandt (FMSKP32039, KONT 32039, c.1990)

Nilsson, Alf

Strauss, Oboe Concerto, Stockholm Sinfonietta, Järvi (Bis CD470, 1989)

Nuttall, David

Carl Vine, Oboe Concerto, Australian Youth O, Masson (Tall Poppies, TP113, 1997)

Oostenrjik, Pauline

1. Alexander Voormolen, Double Concerto, with Roerade (oboe) Residentie O, Bamert (Chandos CHAN 9815, 1999)

2. Britten, *Metamorphoses, Temporal Variations, Insect Pieces,* Phantasy Quartet (Canal Grande CG 9326, 1993)

Pecha, Pamela

Strauss, Oboe Concerto, Moskauer P, Freeman (Fono Carl 3036600652; IMP 6600652, 1994)

Paradise, George

Britten, *Metamorphoses* (Jecklin 239, 1984, and Music Heritage Society MHS 7032, 1984)

Perrenoud, Roland

Britten, *Metamorphoses* (Swiss Radio International, 1979)

Pierlot, Pierre

1. Strauss, Oboe Concerto, Bamberg SO, Theodor Guschlbauer (Erato STU 70390, 1967; re-released MHS 975, 1969)

2. *Le Charme du hautbois/ The Magic of the Oboe,* re-releases of recordings made in the 1970s of works by Cimarosa, Zipoli, Marcello and Bellini (Erato/Elektra, 74509921–3022, 1993)

Piguet, Michel

1. J. S. Bach, Cantata BWV 170, with Deller, Leonhardt Consort (Harmonia Mundi, HM 30573, 1954; re-released on Vanguard, 08 5069 71, 1994)

2. *Le Hautbois baroque,* music by C. P. E. Bach, Loeillet, Telemann, Hotteterre, Lavigne, with Lange (bassoon), Rogg (harpsichord) (Harmonia Mundi, HM 589, 1964, with later re-issues)

3. *Sonates italiennes pour hautbois,* music by Sammartini, Besozzi, Castrucci and Geminiani, with Coin (cello), Parker-Zylberajch (harpsichord) (recorded 1983; re-released on Harmonia Mundi France HWA 1901096)

Polmear, Jeremy

Britten, *Metamorphoses* (Unicorn-Kanchana DKP(CD)9121, 1992)

Ponseele, Marcel (hautboy)

Telemann Sonatas, with Kitazato (hautboy) and Lindeke (trumpet), v.d. Meer (cello), Jakobs (theorbo) and Hantaï (harpsichord) (Accent ACC 95110D, 1995)

See also Bach, *Complete Cantatas,* Zelenka 2.

Roseman, Ronald

1. *The Best of the New York Wind Quintet,* music by Milhaud, Ibert, Fine, Wilder, van Victor, Villa-Lobos, Hindemith (recordings from 1958–64; re-released on Boston Skyline, BSD 139, 1996)

2. Music by Hindemith and Schumann, with Kalish (piano) (Desto DC6484, 1970)

3. Rochberg, *La Bocca della verità,* with Kalish (piano) on *Metamorphosis* (Ars Nova Ars

Antiqua Records, AN 1008, 1970)

4. Handel, Solo and Trio Sonatas, with V. Brewer (oboe), MacCourt (bassoon), Eddy (cello) and E. Brewer (harpsichord) (Nonesuch, 1976, 78)

Rosenblatt, Louis
See Sibelius

Sargous, Harry

1. *Première Oboe Works*, music by Bolcom, Lawrence Singer, Cowell and Bassett, with Ward (piano) (Crystal, CD326, 1990)

2. *Architecture and Aria*, music by Bach, Pasculli, Wolpe and Mead, with Conway (piano) (Crystal, CD327, 1994)

Schaeftlein, Jürg (oboe and hautboy)

1. *Original Instruments: Oboe, Oboe d'amore, English horn*, Concentus Musicus Wien, Harnoncourt (Telefunken 6.42110 AP, 1977)

2. Mozart, Oboe Concerto, Mozarteum Orchester, Hager (Teldec 6.42361 AW, 1988; re-released 8.44056 ZS, 1997)

See also Bach, *Das Kantatenwerk* and St John Passion

Schellenberger, Hansjörg

1. Britten, *Metamorphoses* (Deutsche Grammophon 255013, 1974)

2. Vivaldi, Concertos, Franz Liszt Chamber O (Sony, SK 66271, 1995)

3. *Salon Music of the 19th Century*, music for oboe and flute by Genin, Demersseman, Kalliwoda and Demersseman-Berthélemy, with Koenen (piano) (Sony SK 48051, 1992)

4. Clara and Robert Schumann, *Romanzen*, with Koenen (piano) (Campanella C 130014, 1998)

5. Britten, *Metamorphoses, Temporal Variations, Insect Pieces*, Phantasy Quartet (Campanella Musica C130038, 1998)

6. Strauss, Oboe Concerto, Berlin PO, Levine (DG 429 750–2GH, 1991)

Schmalfuss, Gernot

Britten, *Metamorphoses* (Dabringhaus und Grimm MDG 301 0925–2, 2000)

Schneider, Horst (hautboy)

G. F. Handel, Concerti Grossi op.3, Concerto Grosso from *Alexander's Feast*, with Helmut Winschermann (hautboy), Cappella Coloniensis des WDR, Wenzinger (Archiv, SAPM 198 017–018, 1959)

Schumann-Post, Brenda

Oboe of the World, with various percussionists (Hiwood Productions, CA, HP0108, 1995)

Secrist, Phyllis

Kenneth Jacobs, *Sand Castles* (Zyode, DS1014, 1994)

Singer, Lawrence

1. *L'Oboe contemporaeo*, music by Valdambrini, Matsudaira, Singer, Sinopoli, Maderna and Bartolozzi (Italia, ITL 70036, 1978)

2. *Music for Oboe*, music by Rochberg, Seeger, Shapey, Schuller, Julian and Singer (Composers Recordings, 1980)

Still, Ray

1. Tchaikovsky, Symphony no. 4, Chicago SO, Kubelik (Mercury, MGW 14024, recorded 1960–70)

2. Tchaikovsky, Symphony no. 4, Chicago SO, Solti (London 414 192–2, 1985)

3. *Ray Still: A Chicago Legend*, music by Bach, Handel, Telemann and Vivaldi, with Sharrow (bassoon), Conant (harpsichord) (Nimbus, NI 5672, 2001)

4. Strauss, Oboe Concerto, Academy of London, Stamp (Virgin VC7 90813–2, 1990 and Angel 61766, 2000)

Stotijn, Jaap and Haakon

1. *Mozart and Haydn*, Concertos, with Vienna S, Loibner and Netherlands Kamerorkest, Golberg (recordings from 1956 and 1960; re-released on Philips Dutch Masters, vol. 37 462 552–2, 1998)

2. Alexander Voormolen, *Concert voor hobo en Orkest* (1938), *Concert voor 2 hobo's en orkest* (1935), Residentie Orkest, van Otterloo (Basart Records International, INTPS 59038, 1982)

Tabuteau, Marcel

1. Mozart, *Sinfonia Concertante*, with Portnoy (clarinet), Schonbach (bassoon) and Jones (horn), Philadelphia O, Stokowski (Victor, 1940; re-released on 6)
2. J. S. Bach, Double Concerto BWV 1060, with Stern (violin), Casals Festival O (Columbia, ML4566, 1951; re-released on Music and Arts, CD–689, 1991)
3. Mozart, Oboe Quartet, with Stern (violin), Primrose (viola) and Tortelier (cello), recorded at Casals Festival, Perpignan, 1951 (Columbia, ML 4566, 1952; re-released on CD Music and Arts CD–689, 1991)
4. Handel, G. F., Concerto in g minor, Philadelphia O, Ormandy (recorded 1952; released on *First Chair*, Columbia ML4629, c.1975)
5. *Art of the Oboe* (Coronet Recording Co., 1965), portions re-released on *Marcel Tabuteau Lessons* (Boston Records, BR 1017 CD, 1996)
6. *Marcel Tabuteau: Excerpts, with Leopold Stokowski conducting the Philadelphia Orchestra*, recorded 1924–40 (Boston Records, BR 1021 CD, 1998)

See Sibelius 1

Tancibudek, Jiri

Concertos by Martinu, Haydn and Telemann, Adelaide Symphony and Chamber Orchestras, Shapirra and Divall (SAREC ACR 1002, 1980; re-released on ABC Classics ABC 461703–2, 2001)

Veale, Peter

Computer Music Currents 10: Music with Computers, sleeve notes by Peter Veale et al. (Wergo, WER 2030–2, 1992)

Vogel, Allan

Oboe Obsession, Britten, *Metamorphoses*, and music by Poulenc, Schumann, Shinohara, W. F. Bach (Delos, DE 3235, 2000)

Vries, Han de

1. *Romantische Oboekonzerte*, works by Bellini, Hummel and Kalliwoda (Electronla, C 063–24 591, 1973)
2. Louis Andriessen, *Anachronie II*, Nederlands Balletorkest, Williams (Donemus Composer's Voice Highlights, CV54, 1994).

Wätzig, Hans-Werner

Strauss, Oboe Concerto, Berliner Rundfunk SO, Rögner (Ed CCC 127–2, EMI ASD 2320, 1967)

Watkins, Sara

Britten, *Metamorphoses, Insect Pieces* (Meridian CDE84119, 1987)

West, Philip

Britten, *Metamorphoses* (Price-Less PPP 3307, 1985; Temp, Insects)

Whiting, Joan

Ennio Morricone, *The Mission: The Original Soundtrack from the Motion Picture* (Virgin, NUMBER 1986)

Wickens, Derek.

Britten, *Metamorphoses* (Unicorn-Kanchana DKP9020, 1984)

Williams, Robin

Britten, *Metamorphoses* (Factory Classics FACD236, 1990)

Winschermann, Helmut (hautboy and oboe)

1. G. F. Handel, Concerti Grossi op.3, Concerto Grosso from *Alexander's Feast*, with Schneider (hautboy), Cappella Coloniensis des WDR, Wenzinger (Archiv, SAPM 198 017–018, 1959)
2. J. S. Bach, Concerto BWV 1053, Winschermann (oboe), with Deutsche Bach Solisten (Cantate 047701, 1963)

Woodhams, Richard

    Strauss, Oboe Concerto, Philadelphia O, Sawallisch (recorded 1994; EMI CDC5 56149–2 released 1996)

Zoboli, Omar

    Pasculli Le Paganini du hautbois, with Ballista (piano) and Albisetti (harp) (Accord, ACC 140042., 1982, and DP 149042, 1986)

Zubicky, Gregor

    1. Britten, *Metamorphoses*, Phantasy Quartet (Simax Conifer 6–PSC1022, 1987)

    2. Strauss, Oboe Concerto, Scottish Chamber O, Saraste (Sima PSC10642, 1990)

Listing by Composer

Agrell, see Doherty

Albinoni, see Holliger 8, Lardrot 1, 2 and 3, Bernardini 1

Andriessen, Louis, *Anachronie II*, see de Vries 2

Babell, see Dombrecht 1

Bach, C. P. E., see Ebbinge, Goodwin 1, Puget 2

Bach, J. S.

    Brandenburg Concerto no.2, see F. Gillet 2

    Complete Cantatas, Amsterdam Baroque Orchestra, Koopman (Erato, 1995–)

    Das Kantatenwerk, Concentus Musicus Wien, Leonhardt Consort, Harnoncourt and Leonhardt (Telefunken, Das Alte Werke, 1972–; re-released Teldec, 1985)

    St John Passion, Concentus Musicus Wien, Harnoncourt (Telefunken SKH 19, 1965)

    Various, see Bloom, Dombrecht 1, Hammer, Haynes 5, Hucke, see Piguet 1, Sargous 2, Schaeftlein 1, Still 3, Tabuteau 2, Winschermann 2

Bach, W. F., see Vogel

Balada, see DeAlmeida

Barber, see Lucarelli 3

Barraud, see Mack 2

Barret, see Lucarelli 2

Bartolozzi, see Singer 1

Bassett, see Sargous 1

Bax, Arnold.

    1. *Bax, Première Recordings*, including *In Memoriam* and *Concerto for flute, oboe, harp and string quartet*, Academy of St-Martin-in-the-Fields Chamber Ensemble (Chandos, CHAN 9602, 1998); see also Francis 2

Beethoven, Ludwig van, complete cycles of the symphonies with period instruments:

    1. Collegium Aureum (Deutsche Harmonia Mundi, 1c 065–99 629, 1976)

    2. Orchestra of the Eighteenth Century, Brüggen (Philips 442 156–2, 1994)

    3. Academy of Ancient Music, Hogwood (L'Oiseau Lyre, 452 551–2 1997)

    4. London Classical Players, Norrington (EMI 7498541–2, 1989)

Beethoven, Octet, see Dombrecht, Hadamowsky, MacDonagh

Bellini, see Holliger 1, Lardrot 4, Pierlot 2, de Vries 1

Berghmans, see Mack 2

Berio, see Glaetzner, Hadady, Holliger 2, 4 and 15

Berlioz, Hector. *Symphonie fantastique* on period instruments

    1. London Classical Players, Norrington (EMI 7 49541 2, 1989)

    2. Orchestre Révolutionnaire et Romantique, Gardiner (Philips 434 402–2, 1993)

Berthélemy, see Lucarelli 2

Besozzi, see Piguet 3

Bolcom, see Sargous 1

Börtz, see Jahre 2

Boughton, see Francis 3

Brahms, Johannes, Violin Concerto, Kreisler, unidentified oboist, Berlin State Opera O, Blech
     (1929, numerous pressings on 78 and LP; re-released on Pearl GEMM CD 9996, 1993)
     Various, see also F. Gillet 1, Goossens 3, Labate 1

Britten, Benjamin. *Six Metamorphoses After Ovid* (commercial releases given in chronological
     order with Britten couplings: Phantasy = Phantasy Quartet, Insects = Insect Pieces,
     Temp = Temporal Variations)

     Maurice Bourgue (Harmonia Mundi MDC902, 1968)
     Humbert Lucarelli (Lyrichord LLST7195, 1968; Phantasy)
     Vitezslav Hanus (Supraphon SUA ST 50960, 1969; Phantasy)
     Harold Gomberg (Vanguard VCS 10064, 1969; Phantasy)
     Hansjörg Schellenberger (Deutsche Grammophon 2555013, 1974)
     Sarah Francis (Argo ZRG 842, 1976; Phantasy)
     John Mack (Crystal 5325, 1977; re-released on Telarc 5028, 1985 and Crystal 323, 1995)
     Jiri Tancibudek (recorded 1977, ABC Classics, 2001)
     Janet Craxton (Decca Ace of Diamonds SDD531, 1978)
     Roland Perrenoud (Swiss Radio International, 1979)
     Robin Canter (Phoenix DGS1022, 1982; Temp, Insects, Phantasy)
     George Paradise (Jecklin 239, 1984 and Music Heritage Society MHS 7032, 1984)
     Derek Wickens (Unicorn-Kanchana DKP9020, 1984)
     Peter West (Price-Less PPP 3307, 1985; Temp, Insects)
     Sara Watkins (Meridian CDE84119, 1987; Insects)
     Gregor Zubicky (Simax Conifer 6–PSC1022, 1987; Phantasy)
     Robin Williams (Factory Classics FACD236, 1990)
     François Meyer (Sonpact SPT94011, 1992)
     Jeremy Polmear (Unicorn-Kanchana/Disque Sweet Melancholy DKP(CD)9121, 1992)
     Pauline Oostenrijk (Canal Grande CG 9326, 1993; Temp, Insects, Phantasy)
     Heinz Holliger (Philips 434076–2, 1994; Temp, Insects, Phantasy)
     Roy Carter (EMI Anglo-American Chamber Music Series CDC5 55398–2, 1995)
     Sarah Francis (Hyperion CD A66776, 1995; Temp, Insects, Phantasy)
     Brynjar Hoff (Libra Classics LCD 1004, 1995)
     François Leleux (Harmonia Mundi HMN 911556, 1995; Temp, Insects, Phantasy)
     Gordon Hunt (BIS CD 769, 1996)
     Thomas Indemühle (Camerata 30CM449, 1997)
     Lencsés Lajos (Cadenza CAD800 815, 1997)
     Robin Canter (Carlton Classics 30366 10064 , 1998; Temp, Insects, Phantasy)
     Simon Dent (Amati-Sonoma Ster 9801/1, 1998)
     Hansjörg Schellenberger (Campanella Musica C130038, 1998; Temp, Insects, Phantasy)
     Marilyn Zupnik (DLM Records, 1998)
     Gernot Schmalfuss (Dabringhaus und Grimm MDG 301 0925–2, 2000)
     Nancy Ambrose King (Boston Records, BR 1030, 2000)
     Allan Vogel (Delos, DE 3235, 2000)
     Helmut Schaarschmidt (Signum SIG X 82–00)

Carron, W., see Dombrecht 2

Carter, Sonata for Flute, Oboe, Cello and Harpsichord, see Marx 2.

Castiglioni, see Holliger 4, Malgoire

Castrucci, see Piguet 3

Celli, see Celli

Chopin, see Holliger 13

Cimarosa, see Holliger 1, Lardrot 1, Miller 2, Pierlot 2, Rothwell

Corigliano, see Lucarelli 1

Cossart, see Mayer 1

Couperin, see Cooke, Haynes 2
Cowell, see Sargous 1
Daelli, see Bortolato, Indemühle 2, Mayer 1
de Stefani, see Bortolato
Demersseman/Berthélemy, see Schellenberger 2
Denisow, see Holliger 6
Dent, see Dent
Donizetti, see Holliger 1, 7 and 13, Indemühle 2, Lardrot 4
Dorati, see Doherty
Dutilleux, see Bourgue 1
Edwards, see Doherty
Ekström, see Jahren 2
Elgar, see Goossens 6 and 8
Fine, see Roseman 1
Finizi, see Daniels 1
Finzi, see Goossens 8
Fischer, see Lardrot 3
Flotow, see Hommel
Förster, see Dombrecht 1
Françaix, see de Lancie 1
Gamstorp, see Jahrem 2
Gariboldi, see Bortolato
Garimond, see Lucarelli 2
Geminiani, see Dombrecht 1, Piguet 3
Genin, see Schellenberger 2
Globokar, see Holliger 10
Goldstein, see Celli
Goossens, Eugene, see Goossens, Léon 5
Handel, see Dombrecht 1, Gomberg 3, Goossens 4, Haynes 1, Holliger 9, Lardrot 1 and 2,
    Mueller, Roseman 4, Schaeftlein 1, Schneider, Still 3, Tabuteau 4, Winschermann
Harbison, see Bennett
Harty, see Francis 3
Hawkins, see Dent
Haydn, see Holliger 7, Lardrot 1, Stotijn 1, Tancibudek
Hindemith, see Bourgue 1, Mack 2, Roseman 1, 2
Holliger, see Dombrecht 2, Holliger 4, 5 and 6, Malgoire
Holst, see Francis 2
Hotteterre, see Brüggen 2, Cooke, Haynes 2, Piguet 2
Howells, see Daniel 1, Francis 3
Huber, see Holliger 4
Hummel, see de Vries 1
Ibert, see de Lancie 1, Roseman 1
Jacob , see Francis 2
Jacobs, see Secrist
Jolivet, see Doherty, Dombrecht 2, Malgoire
Julian, see Singer 2
Kalliwoda, see Dombrecht 3, Hommel, Schellenberger 2, de Vries 1
Kernis, Aaron Jay, *Colored Field*
    1. Julie Ann Giacobassi (cor anglais), San Francisco SO, Neale (Argo, 1996, 448174–2, 1996)
    2. Mørk (cello) Minneapolis O (Virgin, 7243 5 45464 2 6, 2001)
Koechlin, see Hommel, Mayer 1
Krebs, see Marx 1
Krenek, Ernst, *Aulokithara* and *Kitharaulos*, see Holliger 4

Krommer, see Goodwin 3

Lalliet, see Lucarelli 2

Lavigne, see Piguet 2

Lebrun, see Goodwin 1

Leclair, Lardrot 3

Lehmann, see Holliger 4

Loeffler, *Rhapsodie*, see Labate 2

Loeillet, see Piguet 2

Lombardi, see Glaetzner 1

Lovreglio, see Bortolat, Indemühle

Lutyens, see Craxton

Maderna, see Singer 1

Mahler, Gustav. *Das Lied von der Erde*
  1. Berlin Philharmonic O, von Karajan (Deutsche Grammophon 2707 082, 1975)
  2. Concertgebouw Orkest, Haitink (Philips 6500 831, 1975)
  3. Wienerphilharmoniker, Bernstein (London OS26005, 1966, re-released on CD London 417 783–2. 1989)

Marais, see Cooke

Marcello, see Haynes 2, Pierlot 2

Martinu, see Indemühle 1, Tancibudek

Massoneau, see Goodwin 3

Matsudaira, see Singer 1

  Matthews, David, *The Flaying of Marsyas* for oboe and string quartet, Daniel with Brindisi String Quartet (Metronome MET CD 1005–01, 1994)

Mead, see Sargous 2

  Mendelssohn, Felix, *A Midsummer Night's Dream*, Orchestra of the Eighteenth Century, Brüggen (The Grand Tour/Glossa GCD 921101, 1997)

Mihalovici, see Bleuzet

Milhaud, see Roseman 1

Moeran, see Francis 2

Molique, see Glaetzner 2

Montéclair, see Cooke

Morricone, Enrico. *The Mission: The Original Soundtrack from the Motion Picture* (Virgin, 1986)

Mozart, see Craxton, Gomberg 1 and 4, Goodwin 1 and 3, Goossens 2, Holliger 13, Lardrot 1 and 2, MacDonagh, Schaeftlein 2, Stotijn 1, Tabuteau 1 and 3

Murgier, Mack 2

Musgrave, see Craxton

Nielsen, see Hommel, Mayer 1

Oregon, see McCandless

Parma, see Bortolato

Pasculli, see Glaetzner 2, Holliger 13, Indemühle 2, Sargous 2, Zoboli

Patterson, see Daniels 1

Penderecki, see Holliger 6

Pixis, see Dombrecht 3

Planet, see Mack 2

Platti, see Haynes 2, Marx 1

Ponchielli, see Glaetzner 2, Holliger 13, Indemühle 2

Poulenc, see Bourgue 1, 2, Craxton 2, Lamorlette, Mack 2, Vogel

Ravel, see Mack 1

Reicha, see Holliger 7

Richardson, see Craxton

Rochberg, see Singer 2

Rosetti, see Dombrecht 4

Rossini, see G. Gillet, Holliger 7 and 13, Koch 2, Lardrot 4

Rubbra, see Francis 3

Salieri, Holliger 1, Lardrot 4

Sammartini, see Piguet 3

Saunders, see Goossens 8

Schenker, see Glaetzner 1

Schnittke, see Jahren 1

Schnyder, see Doherty

Schubert, see Holliger 13, Klein 2

Schubert, *Unfinished Symphony*, O of the Age of Enlightenment, Mackerras (Virgin, 7592732, 1992)

Schuller, see Singer 2

Schumann, see Atherholt, Dent, Dombrecht 3, Holliger 12, Hommel, Marx 1, Mayer 1, Roseman 2, Schellenberger 3, Vogel

Schunke, see Hommel

Schwartz, see Celli

Seeger, see Singer 2

Shapey, see Singer 2

Shinohara, see Vogel, Malgoire

Sibelius, Jean, *The Swan of Tuonela*

1. Marcel Tabuteau (cor anglais), Philadelphia O, Stokowski (Victor 14726 and HMV D1997, 1929)

2. John Minsker (cor anglais), Philadelphia O, Ormondy (HMV DB5882, RCA M 750; RCA Victor 17702, 1940)

3. Mitchell Miller (cor anglais), Stokowski and his O (RCA Victor 12–0585–A/B, 1948)

4. Robert Bloom (cor anglais), Stokowski and his O (SP 8385 8399, 1957, re-released on *Stokowski, Landmarks of a Distinguished Career*, EMI Classics 7243 565614 2 7, 1995)

5. Michael Winfield (cor anglais), National PO, Stokowski (Columbia M34548, 1977)

Singer, Lawrence, see Sargous 1, Singer 1

Sinopoli, see Singer 1

Spohr, see Dombrecht 4

Stamitz, see Goodwin 3

Stockhausen, see Celli

Strauss, Richard, Oboe Concerto

Léon Goossens, Philharmonia O, Galliera (78: CAX 10030–3 to CAX 10037–8, 2XEA 2457; COL DX 1444–6 1947; LP: HMV CLP 1698; WRC SH 243, CD: TEST SBT1009, 1977)

Erich Ertel, SO Radio Berlin, Rother (Urania URLP7032, 1952)

Frantisek Hanták, Brno State PO, Vogel (Supraphon 50 486, 1963)

Pierre Pierlot, Bamberg SO, Guschlbauer (Erato STU 70390, 1967; re-released MHS 975, 1969)

Hans-Werner Wätzig, Berliner Rundfunk. SO, Rögner (Ed CCC 127–2, EMI ASD 2320, 196–)

Heinz Holliger, New Philamonia O, de Waart (Philips 6500 174, 1970; re-released 438 733–2PM2, 1994)

Lothar Koch, Berlin Philharmonic O, von Karajan (DG 2350 439 and 423888–2GGA, 1974)

Manfred Clement, Staatskapelle Dresden, Kempe (HMV SLS5067 1975; re-released EMI CDM7 69661–2, 1992)

Neil Black, English Chamber O, Barenboim (Columbia CBS MS 7423, Y32889, M35160, 1979; re-released CBS M, 1984, and Sony SK 62652, 1996)

Khristo Kosmetski, Bulgarian National Radio SO, Vladigerov (Balkanton, BCA 10465, 197–)

John Anderson, BBC SO, Del Mar (live recording 1981, BBC Radio Classics, 15656 9138–2; re-released 1994)

Heinz Holliger, Cincinnati SO, Gielen (Moss Music, MCD 100006, 1984)

Douglas Boyd, Chamber O of Europe, Berglund (ASV CDCOE808, MHS 1988, 1986)

John De Lancie, Chamber O, Wilcox (recorded 1987; RCA Gold Seal BMG 7989–2–RG, 1991)

Lajos Lencsés, Stuttgart RSO, Marriner (Capriccio 10 231, c.1989)

Alf Nilsson, Stockholm Sinfonietta, Järvi (Bis CD470, 1989)

Ray Still, Academy of London, Stamp (Virgin VC7 90813–2, 1990, and Angel 61766, 2000)

B.C. Nielsen, Copenhagen Collegium Musicum, Schönwandt (FMSKP32039, KONT 32039, c.1990)

Bert Lucarelli, Lehigh Valley Chamber O, Spieth (Koch KIC 7023, 1990)

G. Zubicky, Scottish Chamber O, Saraste (Sima PSC10642, 1990)

Hansjorg Schellenberger, Berlin PO, Levine (DG 429 750–2GH, 1991)

Ingo Goritzki, Lausanne Chamber O, Aeschbacher (CLA 50-9010, 1990)

John Anderson, Philharmonia, Wright (Nimbus NI5330, 1992)

Robin Canter, London SO, Judd (IMP 30366 0021–2, 1992)

Simon Dent, Polish Chamber O, Rajski (Amati, AMI 9205, 1992)

Gordon Hunt, Berlin RSO, Ashkenazy (Decca London 436 415–2, 1993, re-released 436 415–2DH, 1994 and 460 296–2DF2, 1999)

Thomas Indermühle, Orchestre de Bretagne, Schnitzler (Camerata 30CM–346, 1993)

Pamela Pecha, Moskauer Phil., Freeman (Fono Carl 3036600652; IMP 6600652, 1994)

Richard Woodhams, Philadelphia O, Sawallisch (recorded 1994; EMI CDC5 56149–2, released 1996)

Nicholas Daniel, City of London Sinfonia, Hickox (Chandos CHAN9286, 1994)

Martin Gabriel, Vienna PO, Previn (DG 453 483–2GH, c.1996/8)

Albrecht Mayer, Capella Bydgostiensis, Stabrawa (Cavalli Records CCD 408, 2000)

Alex Klein, Chicago SO, Baremboim (Teldec 3984–23913–2, 2001)

Heinz Holliger, Chamber O of Europe (Regis Records, RRC 1034, 2001)

Peter Cooper, Academy of St-Martin's-in-the-Fields, Marriner (Summit DCD320, 2002)

Takemitsu, see Honma

Tavener, John, *Eternity's Sunrise*, see Goodwin 4

Tchaikovsky, Symphony no. 4, see Still 1

Telemann, see Brüggen 1, Gomberg 2 and 3, Marx 1, Piguet 2, Ponseele, Still 3, Tancibudek

Ton-That Tiêt, see Malgoire

Towner , see McCandless

Triébert, Ch., see Lucarelli 2

Valdambrini, see Singer 1

Vaughan Williams, see Bourgue 4, Craxton 2, Indermühle 1, Lucarelli 3, Miller 2

Verdi, Giuseppe, *Missa da Requiem*, Orchestre Révolutionnaire et Romantique, Gardiner (Philips 442 142–2, 1995)

Veress, see Holliger 6

Villa-Lobos, see Roseman 1

Vincent, see Dombrecht 1

Vine, see Nuttall

Vivaldi, see Gomberg 3, Goodwin 2, Haynes 3, Holliger 11, Klein 1, Lardrot 3, Schaeftlein 1, Schellenberger 1, Still 3

Vogt, see Lucarelli 3

Voormolen, Alexander, *Concert voor hobo en Orkest*, see Stotijn 2

Voormolen. Alexander, Double Concerto, see Oosterijk, Stotijn 2

Wagner, Richard, *Tristan und Isolde*, Bayreuth Festspiel, Böhm (Deutsche Gramophon GG, 39 224 B, 1966)

Wagner, see Holliger 13

Weber, see Dombrecht 2

Wilder, *Oboe Concerto*, Lucarelli 4, Roseman 1

Wolf-Ferrari, Lucarelli 3

Wolpe, see Sargous 2

Xenakis, see Glaetzner 1

Yun, see Holliger 6

Yvon, see Mayer 1

Zelenka, J. D. Trio Sonatas,

1. Holliger and Bourgue (oboes), Gawriloff (violin), Thunemann (bassoon), Jaccottet (harpishord) and Buccarella (bass) (Archiv 2708 027, 1973; re-released on Arkiv 423 937–2, 1988, and ECM 1671–2, 1999)

2. Ebbinge, Dombrecht and Ponselle (hautboys), with Bond (bassoon), Banchini (violin), v.d. Meer (cello), Kohnen (harpsichord) (Accent, 8848 A/B D, 1989, Musical Heritage Society MHS 522670X, 1990)

3. Bernardini and Grazzi (hautboys), with Ensemble Zefiro (Astrée E 8511 and 8563, 1993/5)

Zimmermann, see Indemühle 1

Zipoli, see Pierlot 2

Index

Oboists' names are indicated by an asterisk; pages of illustrations and musical examples are shown in italics.